Paths to Liberation

Kuroda Institute
Studies in East Asian Buddhism

Studies in Ch'an and Hua-yen
Robert M. Gimello and Peter N. Gregory

Dōgen Studies
William R. LaFleur

The Northern School and the Formation of Early Ch'an Buddhism
John R. McRae

Traditions of Meditation in Chinese Buddhism
Peter N. Gregory

Sudden and Gradual: Approaches to Enlightenment in Chinese Thought
Peter N. Gregory

Buddhist Hermeneutics
Donald S. Lopez, Jr.

Studies in East Asian Buddhism 7

Paths to Liberation

The Mārga and Its Transformations in Buddhist Thought

Edited by
Robert E. Buswell, Jr.
Robert M. Gimello

A Kuroda Institute Book
University of Hawaii Press • Honolulu

Printed in the United States of America

92 93 94 95 96 97 5 4 3 2 1

The Kuroda Institute for the Study of Buddhism and Human Values is a nonprofit, educational corporation founded in 1976. One of its primary objectives is to promote scholarship on the historical, philosophical, and cultural ramifications of Buddhism. In association with the University of Hawaii Press, the Institute also publishes Classics in East Asian Buddhism, a series devoted to the translation of significant texts in the East Asian Buddhist tradition.

Library of Congress Cataloging-in-Publication Data

Paths to liberation : the Mārga and its transformations in Buddhist thought / edited by Robert E. Buswell, Robert M. Gimello.
p. cm. — (Studies in East Asian Buddhism ; 7)
Papers presented at a conference held at the University of California, Los Angeles, June 25–30, 1988.
"A Kuroda Institute book."
Includes bibliographical references and index.
ISBN 0-8248-1253-0 (acid-free paper)
1. Spiritual life (Buddhism)—Congresses. 2. Salvation (Buddhism)—Congresses. 3. Enlightenment (Buddhism)—Congresses. I. Buswell, Robert E. II. Gimello, Robert M., 1942– III. Series: Studies in East Asian Buddhism ; no. 7.
BQ4302.P38 1992 91-29277
294.3'422—dc20 CIP

University of Hawaii Press books are printed on acid-free paper and meet the guidelines for permanence and durability of the Council on Library Resources

Contents

Preface vii
Conventions ix

Introduction 1
Robert E. Buswell, Jr., and Robert M. Gimello

Theravāda Buddhist Soteriology and the Paradox of Desire 37
Grace G. Burford

Attainment through Abandonment:
The Sarvāstivādin Path of Removing Defilements 63
Collett Cox

The Path to Perdition: The Wholesome Roots and
Their Eradication 107
Robert E. Buswell, Jr.

On the Ignorance of the Arhat 135
Padmanabh S. Jaini

Paths Terminable and Interminable 147
Donald S. Lopez, Jr.

The Illusion of Spiritual Progress:
Remarks on Indo-Tibetan Buddhist Soteriology 193
Matthew Kapstein

A Tibetan Perspective on the Nature of Spiritual Experience 225
Jeffrey Hopkins

Mental Concentration and the Unconditioned:
A Buddhist Case for Unmediated Experience 269
Anne C. Klein

The Relation between Chinese Buddhist History and Soteriology 309
Yoshizu Yoshihide, translated and edited by Paul Groner

Encounter Dialogue and the Transformation of the Spiritual Path in Chinese Ch'an 339
John R. McRae

Mārga and Culture: Learning, Letters, and Liberation in Northern Sung Ch'an 371
Robert M. Gimello

Shortening the Path: Early Tendai Interpretations of the Realization of Buddhahood with This Very Body *(Sokushin Jōbutsu)* 439
Paul Groner

No-Mind and Sudden Awakening: Thoughts on the Soteriology of a Kamakura Zen Text 475
Carl Bielefeldt

Index 507
Contributors 523

Preface

This volume resulted from a conference on Buddhist soteriology that was held at the University of California, Los Angeles, from June 25–30, 1988. The initial block of funding for the conference was generously offered by the Joint Committee on Chinese Studies of the American Council of Learned Societies/Social Science Research Council, with funds provided by the Ford Foundation and the National Endowment for the Humanities. A Large Grant award from the University of California Systemwide Program in Pacific Rim Studies allowed us to expand the size of the conference and include foreign scholars among the participants. Additional funding and administrative help was provided by UCLA's Center for Chinese Studies and its director, Philip Huang, and the Center for Pacific Rim Studies and its director, Lucie Cheng. Finally, a major subvention to cover much of the production costs of the volume was graciously arranged through John Hawkins, the director of UCLA's International Studies and Overseas Programs. The support of all these agencies and individuals is gratefully acknowledged.

Several papers that are not included in this volume were also delivered at the conference, including those by Professors George Bond, Peter Gregory, Han Ki Doo, Alan Sponberg, and Daniel Stevenson. All the participants benefited from the lively and provocative comments of our discussants, Professors Bernard Faure and Lee Yearley of Stanford University and Professor Karl Potter of the University of Washington, Seattle. The conference ran as smoothly as it did thanks to the help of Chi-wah Chan, Ding-hwa Hsieh, and Kyoko Tokuno. Susan Sugar and Roger Hart assisted with preparing the volume for production. Finally, Victoria Scott did her usual superlative job of copyediting the manuscript and Barbara E. Cohen prepared an excellent index. We greatly appreciate the contributions all these people made to the conference and the volume.

Conventions

Scriptures appearing in the Pali canon are cited according to their standard Pali Text Society editions. Texts from the Chinese Buddhist canon are cited according to standard numbers in the *Taishō* printed edition (abbreviated *T*): *Taishō shinshū daizōkyō,* edited by Takakusu Junjirō and Watanabe Kaikyoku (Tokyo: Daizōkyōkai, 1924–1935). Full citations from the *Taishō* canon are given in the following fashion: title and fascicle number (where relevant); *T*[*aishō*]; *Taishō* volume number; page, register (a, b, or c), line number(s). E.g., *Ta-fang-kuang fo hua-yen ching* 23, *T* 9.542c27–543a1. Citations from the *Supplement to the Canon* (*Dai-Nihon Zokuzōkyō* [Kyoto: Zōkyō shoin, 1905–1912]) are listed as follows: title and fascicle number; *ZZ;* series; case; volume; page, column (a, b, c, or d), line number(s). E.g., *Shih-men Hung Chüeh-fan lin-chien lu* 1, ZZ 2b, 21, 4, 303d13. Citations from the Chinese reprints of the *Supplement* give the *HTC (Hsü-tsang ching)* volume, page, and column references.

Buddhist terminology that appears in *Webster's Third New International Dictionary* we consider to have entered the English language and leave unitalicized: e.g., sūtra, śāstra, nirvāṇa. For a convenient listing of a hundred such words, see Roger Jackson, "Terms of Sanskrit and Pāli Origin Acceptable as English Words," *Journal of the International Association of Buddhist Studies* 5 (1982): 141–142.

Introduction

Robert E. Buswell, Jr., and Robert M. Gimello

> Just as the ocean has but one taste, the taste of salt, even so this Teaching and Discipline have but one taste, the taste of liberation.
>
> *Cullavagga* IX.14; *Aṅguttaranikāya,* IV.203; etc.

> If you would seek the truth, keep to the way, for the way is also the truth. It is where you go; it is the means by which you go. The goal and the way thither are the same.
>
> St. Augustine, *In Johannis evangelium, tractatus* XIII.4

The Importance of Mārga, Both Within and Beyond Buddhism

The comparative or cross-cultural study of religions has long promised to liberate scholars from culture-bound categories, perspectives, and methods. It offers such a variety of traditions, and in them such an abundance of themes, that students of religion need no longer rely exclusively on Western, usually only Judeo-Christian, traditions in establishing the major features of religion or in determining the general rubrics under which religion can and should be studied. Unfortunately, this promise has seldom been fulfilled. It is still all too common to find non-Western religious traditions like Buddhism, Hinduism, and Taoism treated primarily in terms drawn from the European heritage, such as faith, prayer, myth, ritual, eschatology, deity, and so forth. Certain of these originally Western concepts can be very useful in the study of traditions other than those in which they were generated. Others, although they may first have been noted by scholars familiar with only their Western manifestations, are truly universal. Still others, however, prove often to be quite inappropriate, either because they are so closely tied to substantive Western religious beliefs as to be inextricable therefrom or because, unable to accommodate the full range and particular configuration of themes comprising the non-Western tradition to which they may be applied, they simply leave out or distort too much. The problem is really that of one-sidedness, a failure of mutuality. Where, for example, are the Hindu categories used to illumine Christianity, the Taoist concepts employed in analyzing Judaism, the shamanic themes applied to Islam? No doubt such truly cross-cultural studies of religions have been attempted, but only rarely, and more rarely still in any systematic and sustained way.

The present volume is, among other things, an effort to begin the rectification of this situation. Hoping to address an audience of scholars not only in Buddhist Studies but also in Religious Studies, we have undertaken a manifold investigation of the primary Buddhist concept or category of mārga—"the path." Our purpose is twofold: to clarify the range of the concept's meaning and significance within Buddhism, and to suggest ways in which it might prove useful in the cross-cultural study of religion and in the study of religions other than Buddhism. We suggest not only that mārga is a theme central to the whole of Buddhism, but also that it may have scope and theoretical potential sufficient to allow us eventually to speak—with due caution and proper nuance—of Christian mārga, Jewish mārga, Islamic mārga, and so forth. Perhaps the study of Buddhism may be enlisted to illumine those other traditions in ways in which their own categories alone do not. To this end, we believe a focus on Buddhism is especially appropriate because we think that, as a potentially cross-cultural category for the study of religions, the concept of "the path" has been given in Buddhism an explication more sustained, comprehensive, critical, and sophisticated than that provided by any other single religious tradition. And this we would hold even in comparing Buddhism to other Indian religious traditions that also employ the concept of mārga.[1]

Yet we do not wish to exaggerate this point. The Buddhist or Indian notion of mārga is not completely without parallel in other traditions. For example, a Western concept to which the Buddhist category of "the path" seems at least somewhat analogous is that of "soteriology," meaning the theory of salvation. The equivalence is hardly exact, given the English word's etymological implication of "savior" and the common Christian use of the term to label the study of God's (as distinct from man's) salvific activity.[2] However, no other Western term has suggested itself to us as more analogous, and although we prefer to use the terms "mārga" or "the path," we reserve the right occasionally to use "soteriology" or "soteriological" as we discuss the things that Buddhism has located in the domain of mārga. We claim for this usage the same kind of warrant that Max Weber invoked when he used another originally Christian or theistic term, "theodicy," outside of its native contexts. "Theodicy" originally labeled a branch of theology concerned with "justifying" God over and against such deeply distressing facts as the existence of evil and prevalence of apparently innocent suffering. By judicious expansion of the scope of the term's meaning, Weber made profitable use of it in his study of nontheistic religions, for example, in his analysis of the doctrine of karma in Buddhism and in certain kinds of Hinduism.

"Soteriology" may have a similar measure of pliancy and comparative utility. Thus, in any cases in which a Western term for mārga or the theory of mārga is deemed necessary, we recommend this one.[3] However, just as the term "theodicy" did not replace "karma" even in Weber's own work, so "soteriology" does not replace "mārga." Rather, both Western terms should be used only as fulcrums for initiating certain kinds of comparisons among traditions. In the case of soteriology, we would further urge that once such comparisons have gotten underway, it is preferable to use only the Sanskrit term or its literal English translation as often as possible.

In this volume, what we mean by mārga theory, or by "soteriology" in the Buddhist sense, is, generally speaking, the theory according to which certain methods of practice, certain prescribed patterns of religious behavior, have transformative power and will lead, somehow necessarily, to specific religious goals. While it is certainly true that some form of the transformative power of religious practice—its capacity to alter character, values, or worldviews, and, most important, its capacity to effect the ultimate transformation of salvation—is recognized at least implicitly in all religions, nowhere is this recognition given clearer expression, greater emphasis, or more sustained exposition than in Buddhism.

Throughout the two-and-a-half millennia of its pan-Asian career, Buddhism has been consistently explicit in declaring itself to be, above all else, a soteriology, a method of salvation, rather than, say, a creed. Its unflagging concentration on "the path," whether for the purpose of advocating and charting that path or for the purpose of qualifying and criticizing it, has not only led to the careful and detailed delineation of numerous curricula of religious practice and to the privileging of such delineation over other modes of Buddhist discourse. It has also fostered the adoption, as governing principles of thought and discourse, of just those presuppositions that would best secure the primacy of soteriology or "path theory" over other religious concerns such as gnosiology. An example is Buddhism's relatively consistent adherence to the principle of spiritual pragmatism according to which the truth of a religious proposition consists in its practical utility rather than in its descriptive power. Moreover, Buddhism has been, on the whole, rather less troubled than most theistic religions with such doubts about the efficacy of mārga as might be occasioned by the belief that only God can effect salvation. This is one of the points Buddhism makes in its stress on self-reliance, that is, in its fidelity to Śākyamuni's final injunction to his disciples, as recounted in the early canon, that they "work out their own salvations with diligence."[4] There are, of course, exceptions to this rule, the most notable of which is Pure Land Buddhism. Nevertheless, the theme of self-reliance and the intrinsic efficacy of mārga generally dominates the whole of Buddhism and leads it to privilege mārga in ways that other traditions do not. Thus many of the most characteristic features of Buddhism appear to derive from its emphasis on mārga and soteriology.

Consider the recurrence throughout the tradition of the motif of the Buddha as "physician" or therapist rather than theorist. This imagery is more than accidentally congruous with Buddhism's repeated assertion of the superiority of analytical and critical thought over synthetic or constructive speculation. Hence the Buddha is said to have identified himself as an "analyzer" *(vibhajyavādin)* rather than as a "dogmatist" or someone who makes categorical assertions *(ekāṃśavādin).*[5] This reasoning seems also to justify the characteristically Buddhist invocation of pragmatic criteria for the evaluation of doctrines and practices. Buddhism even goes so far as to formalize its spiritual pragmatism by giving it systematic or meta-theoretical expression as the principle of upāya (expedience). According to this principle, resonant throughout the worlds of Buddhist thought and practice, the chief measure of a teaching's truth or value is its efficacy unto religious ends, rather than any correspondence to the facts. It is not unexpected, therefore, that Buddhists should regularly choose disciplined experience (e.g., meditation) over reason, revelation, and authority as the final arbiter of religious truth or efficacy. All these things and more, we would suggest, flow from the primacy of mārga and soteriology among all the components of Buddhism.

The importance Buddhists assign to systematic discourse about "the path" has general implications that could be valuable in the study of other religions, or of religion generally. A case in point is the longstanding tendency within religious studies to focus interpretive attention on doctrines, i.e., on certain cardinal concepts or model propositions to which adherents of particular traditions are believed to give their intellectual assent. This approach has its uses, but it is also fraught with perils. All too easily can it lead to purely abstract, reified, and fragmented conceptions of religions in which excessive emphasis is given to the élite and disembodied religion of the philosopher or the intellectual. The assumption here seems to be that the identity of any religion can be reduced to its dogmatics, that its doctrines somehow comprise its quintessence. The problem with this approach is that religions are much more than just systems of doctrine, although they do harbor doctrines and often assign them crucially important roles. Religions are also, and perhaps most fundamentally, patterns of action based on axiologies that are as often tacit as they are explicit. As such, religions are embodied in complex ways of life. In some cases these are spelled out in meticulous and explicit detail; in other cases they seem to defy precise and definitive codification; but in no case are they exhausted by the abstract principles or general laws said to underly them.

Moreover, it is such systems of practice and performance, as distinct from systems of concept and idea, which are most immediately and intimately familiar to the ordinary adherents of a religion. The truths of a religion are revealed to most of its followers not so much by its doctrines as by the patterns described in the life stories of its ideal practitioners, or by the structured experiences of its clerical and lay communities. In the case of Buddhism, even the most unsophisticated of monks or nuns (who may be quite innocent of basic doctrinal formulae like the twelve-linked chain of dependent origination, not to mention subtler doctrines like emptiness) know intimately the monastic regimen they follow each day, and that regimen informs their religious self-understanding every bit as profoundly as subtleties of doctrine may inform the lives of Buddhist intellectuals.

Now monastic discipline is a kind, or a component, of mārga. The experiences and convictions it fosters in the lives of particular monastics may not immediately yield, or give clearest voice to, the essential propositions of Buddhist thought. Such experiences do not translate easily into doctrine. Thus it is hard to descry, say, the "dependent origination of all things" in the rules of monastic life. Nevertheless, *pratītyasamutpāda* and the other seeming rarefactions of Buddhist thought do lurk in those rules, at least by way of implication, and what those rules may lack in philosophical articulation they more than compensate for with their greater accessibility and practicality. Consider, for example, how poverty and mendicancy can serve as exercises in selflessness or as performances, rather than mere conceptualizations, of *anātman*. One might argue that when it comes to doctrine one ought to seek explicitness and rigorous precision. Yet clarity and definition are often purchased at the expense of nuance and universal availability, and there may well be aspects of the "dependent origination of all things" that escape even the most deft of the cerebrations by which that doctrine is usually expressed. Just such nuances of meaning may be directly ascertainable in the structured immediacy of monastic life, and there are many more Buddhists capable of the rigors of the Vinaya than of mastering, say, Nāgārjuna's negative dialectic.

What can be said of Vinaya in this regard seems also to apply to other dimensions of mārga, such as meditation. In Buddhism, the practitioner of meditation is usually thought likely to have a purchase on basic Buddhist truths actually superior to that of any expert in doctrine who is not also well practiced in meditation. Likewise, Buddhists are taught to be especially alert to the power of doctrine and reflection to distract from, or even to prevent, liberating experience. In the famous simile of the raft, for example, the Buddha makes the point that, after using the makeshift raft of dharma to ferry himself across to the other shore of nirvāṇa, the adept would certainly not put the raft on top of his head and carry it off; rather, since the raft had now served its purpose, it should be abandoned on the beach. And just as the raft of dharma was to be used for crossing over, and was not to be retained, so should the adept eventually abandon even right mental objects (such as the desire for calm and insight), let alone wrong ones.[6] As several chapters in this volume demonstrate, such warnings are especially characteristic of Zen, but Zen abjurations of doctrine may be seen simply as particularly strong or blunt expressions of a belief held generally throughout Buddhism.

It is this sort of existential or experiential embodiment of Buddhist truth—a dimension of Buddhism often ignored in the pursuit of clearly expressible Buddhist ideas and arguments—that we wish to draw into the center of the study of Buddhism. This is what we have in mind when we propose that mārga, as the living context within which all Buddhist truth is tacitly but perhaps most effectively defined, creates a commonality of ultimate concerns that reticulates all the various strands of its religious endeavor[7]—its moral values, ritual observances, theoretical doctrines, and contemplative exercises—to form a complex but unified network of practices tending to liberation.

Related to this, and also recommending mārga as a valuable focus of study, is the way in which it incorporates, underlies, or presupposes everything else in Buddhism, from the simplest act of charity to the most refined meditative experience and the most rigorous philosophical argument. The study of mārga directs attention not to the isolated effects of specific religious practices but to a general pattern of discipline encompassing both the whole life of the individual adherent and the corporate life of the whole Buddhist community. A specific illustration of mārga's function as the ordering mechanism, tenor, or "deep structure" of the Buddhist religion is appropriate at this point.

Consider one of the earliest and simplest statements of the Buddhist path, the so-called "three trainings" *(trīṇi śikṣāṇi).* In this scheme, the practitioner is instructed to begin pursuit of liberation by cultivating *śīla,* the obedience to basic moral rules (nonviolence, avoidance of false speech, etc.) that comprises the first training. These rules restrict human physical, verbal, and mental activity to actions that are effective for liberation. The rationale for such ethical discipline at the outset and foundation of the path is that morality minimizes present mental anguish, guilt, and uncertainty, thereby engendering the more rudimentary forms of tranquillity, which form the basis of meditation or higher tranquillity *(śamatha).* But according to this rationale, tranquillity is no mere abstraction, nor is it an ideal goal divorced from actual practice (in this case, the fundamental practice of morality). Rather, it is something concrete, a pattern of experience embodied in the practitioner's ethical observances.

The control over responses to external stimuli that the student gains through moral observance, and the measure of tranquillity that morality allows, lead to the development of introspection. This then facilitates control over precisely those mental, psychic, and somatic impulses that initiate action in the first place. Such internal control further allows the practitioner to regulate the subtler activities of the mind, permitting still finer mental focus and greater concentration. In fact, it makes possible the growth of higher levels of concentration *(samādhi),* the second of the three trainings, which in turn liberates the student to investigate the world and the "self" in the exercise of discernment *(vipaśyanā).* The insight *(prajñā)* achieved through such investigation (i.e., the third of the three trainings) reveals the nature of the world to be impermanent *(anitya),* unsatisfactory *(duḥkha),* and insubstantial *(anātman),* thus confirming the fundamental Buddhist doctrine of the "three marks of existence" *(trilakṣaṇa).* Finally, such insight brings to an end the impulses that sustain one's ties to the phenomenal world of suffering and so engenders the radical renunciation that is nirvāṇa.

In this example we see that the program of practice outlined in the three modes of training corroborates the most basic doctrinal teachings of Buddhism by bringing them into the whole pattern of discipline comprising the individual's spiritual career. The path thus weaves all these different facets and stages of Buddhist effort into an organic whole, each single part of which incorporates all the other parts. Morality is shown to be the premonition of both concentration and insight; concentration is shown to be the resonance of morality and the anticipation of insight; and insight itself is shown to be both the consummation of morality and concentration and the initiation into liberation.

Similar programs for the integration of doctrine and experience into coherent patterns of practice are available in other formulations of mārga. Some seem designed actually to be followed by real practitioners; others appear to be merely inspirational in intention, mārgas of myth in which the path is presented as one or another kind of heroic quest. The following are only a few of the best known mārga schemes. They are listed here merely to give a general impression of their scope and complexity; limitations of space prevent our glossing them, much less discussing them in detail.[8]

A. The noble eightfold path *(ārya-aṣṭāṅga-mārga)*
   1. *samyagdṛṣṭi* (right view)
   2. *samyaksaṃkalpa* (right intention)
   3. *samyagvāk* (right speech)
   4. *samyakkarmānta* (right conduct)
   5. *samyagājīva* (right livelihood)
   6. *samyagvyāyāma* (right effort)
   7. *samyaksmṛti* (right mindfulness)
   8. *samyaksamādhi* (right concentration)

B. The four approaches *(catvāraḥ pratipannāḥ)* or four fruits *(catvāri phalāni)*
   1. *śrotāpanna* (stream-winner)
   2. *sakṛdāgāmin* (once-returner)
   3. *anāgāmin* (non-returner)
   4. *arhat* (liberated saint)

C. The thirty-seven factors of awakening *(saptatriṃśad bodhipakṣikā dharmāḥ)*
   1–4. *catvāri-smṛtyupasthānāni* (the four foundations of mindfulness)
   5–8. *catvāri-samyakprahānāni* (the four right exertions)
   9–12. *catvāra-ṛddhipādāḥ* (the four requisites of preternatural power)
   13–17. *pañca-indriyāṇi* (the five faculties)
   18–22. *pañca-balāni* (the five powers)
   23–30. *sapta-bodhyaṅgāni* (the seven limbs of awakening)
   31–37. *ārya-aṣṭāṅga-mārga* (the noble eightfold path)

D. The five paths
   1. *saṃbhāramārga* (path of equipment)
   2. *prayogamārga* (path of preparation)
   3. *darśanamārga* (path of seeing)
   4. *bhāvanāmārga* (path of cultivation)
   5. *niṣṭhāmārga* (path of completion) or *aśaikṣamārga* (path beyond instruction)

E. The six or ten stages or "grounds" *(bhūmi)* of the bodhisattva's career (as listed in the *Daśabhūmika Sūtra;* usually coordinated, in sequence, with the ten perfections listed below)
   1. *pramuditā-bhūmi* (stage of joy)
   2. *vimalā-bhūmi* (stage of immaculacy)
   3. *prabhākarī-bhūmi* (stage of splendor)
   4. *arciṣmatī-bhūmi* (stage of brilliance)
   5. *sudurjāya-bhūmi* (stage of invincibility)
   6. *abhimukhī-bhūmi* (stage of immediacy)
   7. *dūraṅgamā-bhūmi* (stage of transcendence)
   8. *acalā-bhūmi* (stage of immovability)
   9. *sādhumatī-bhūmi* (stage of eminence)
   10. *dharmameghā-bhūmi* (dharma-cloud stage)

F. The six or ten perfections *(pāramitā)*
   1. *dāna-pāramitā* (perfection of giving or charity)
   2. *śīla-pāramitā* (perfection of morality)

3. *kṣānti-pāramitā* (perfection of forebearance or patience)
4. *vīrya-pāramitā* (perfection of energy or vigor)
5. *dhyāna-pāramitā* (perfection of meditation)
6. *prajñā-pāramitā* (perfection of insight)
7. *upāya-pāramitā* (perfection of expedient means)
8. *praṇidhāna-pāramitā* (perfection of resolve or vow)
9. *bala-pāramitā* (perfection of strength)
10. *jñāna-pāramitā* (perfection of knowledge)

G. The bodhisattva path in fifty-three stages according to the Hua-yen tradition
- 1–10. the ten faiths (Ch. *hsin*, J. *shin*)
- 11–20. the ten abodes *(chu, jū)*
- 21–30. the ten practices *(hsing, gyō)*
- 31–40. the ten dedications *(hui-hsiang, ekō)*
- 41–50. the ten stages (*ti, ji*—see "E" above)
- 51. virtual awakening *(teng-chüeh, tōgaku)*
- 52. wondrous awakening *(miao-chüeh, myōkaku)*
- 53. buddhahood *(fo, butsu)*

H. The "five ranks" (Ch. *wu-wei*, J. *goi*) of the Ts'ao-tung (J. Sōtō) tradition of Ch'an or Zen (variously named)
1. attaining the relative within the absolute *(cheng-chung-pien, shōchūhen)*
2. attaining the absolute within the relative *(pien-chung-cheng, henchūshō)*
3. emerging from the absolute *(cheng-chung-lai, shōchūrai)*
4. access at once to both the relative and the absolute *(chien-chung-chih, kenchūshi)*
5. simultaneous integration of the absolute and the relative *(chien-chung-tao, kenchūtō)*

Of course, as this list might lead one to expect, the essays comprising this volume do not exhaust the vast and intricate topic of Buddhist mārga. Nor do they enumerate all of its major dimensions. They do, however, touch on several of its more important implications, while highlighting some of the key tensions and debates that have arisen in the history of Buddhist discourse on the subject. It would be well, then, to note several of those implications and tensions in advance. We do so in the conviction that the purposes of an introduction to a collection so various as this are better served by such thematic discussions, incomplete though they inevitably be, than by a preliminary summary of the chapters to follow.

Mārga and the Ideal Person: The Path as a Design for the Universalization of Individual Experience

The emphasis we find throughout Buddhism on the practical needs of the person engaged in religious training seems to have been one source of the profusion of mārga schemes that characterizes the tradition. The notion of "the path" is a valid model for religious endeavor in Buddhism only insofar as it poses a destination to be reached, and only to the extent that someone actively pursues that destination. The claim that it was by their own personal efforts that the Buddha and his disciples achieved enlightenment is one of the fundamental assumptions from which all Buddhist soteriological speculation derives. And yet, based on that very same assumption, the path is often taken out of the realm of the practical and the immediate and exalted to the status of a dramatization, or mythic recapitulation, of the process by which such ideal persons are said to have achieved enlightenment. In some cases, therefore, mārga discourse seems to function in Buddhism less as a practical guide and more in the way that ritual and sacrament function in other traditions. That is to say, rehearsal of mārga may occasionally verge on ceremonial reenactment, in historical and mundane time, of the primal religious experiences achieved *in illo tempore* by the tradition's inaugural figures. It may even be seen as somehow allowing the actual reconstitution or repossession of that original, timeless, time.

This, in turn, fosters a concern in mārga literature with the ideal figure as the embodiment and proof of mārga, an emphasis counterbalancing the impersonal, "objective" tone of so much of the rest of mārga discourse. Indeed, it is clear in the earliest phases of Buddhist soteriological inquiry, and remains clear throughout the history of the tradition, that for all their tendency toward impersonal discourse (as in the Abhidharma traditions), Buddhists had great difficulty conceiving of "the path" in purely theoretical and generic terms, apart from ideal images of persons who either had traversed it or were thought capable of doing so. This helps account for the meticulous care some Buddhists thinkers have taken in arguing about the qualities of the enlightened beings. The issue of whether arhats are ignorant and only buddhas can be said to be omniscient, discussed expertly by Padmanabh Jaini in his contribution to this volume, is a case in point. Such questions about the nature of ideal beings, though they may seem to us far removed from any conceivable practical concern and so may appear to be mere idle speculation, actually do have a practical relevance insofar as they bear on questions of the sacral efficacy of mārga. They provide reasons either to believe or to doubt the claim that mārga allows the full recapitulation of primal sacred or liberating events.

Likewise, the goal of the path, as much as the path itself, is often defined in terms of differences between the ideal person, who has completed the journey and thus become worthy of emulation, and the less-than-ideal person, who is still in transit. As Grace Burford shows in her chapter, early Buddhists often defined both path and goal explicitly in terms of the ideal person, and when such personalized definitions were challenged by impersonal or depersonalized alternative definitions, the personalized accounts often prevailed.

From this premise further hypotheses seem to follow. It may well be that the persistent Buddhist tendency to elaborate on the path by dividing it into multiple and further subdivisible stages, although perhaps begun as a kind of "cartography" of the terrain of Buddhist religious experience, led retrospectively to creation of a spiritual pedigree for the ideal person such as might render that person worthy of emulation by others. Thus the process of mārga construction, whereby the path is built step by step, may be said to define a necessary stage in the evolution of a tradition, viz., the stage of transition from the category of the particular, the idiosyncratic, or the biographical to the category of the universal and the generic. In this way the experience of one person is made accessible, in principle, to all. By organizing experience into sequences of stages, the transcendent goal presumed to have been achieved by spiritual exemplars at the source of the tradition is objectified, codified, and made available to ordinary Buddhist practitioners. The detailed ordering of experience that these schemata of the path provide offers practitioners an explicit guide to achieving the original and archetypal goal for themselves. The path thus mediates between the enlightened and the unenlightened.

This bears on the question of whether mārga is descriptive or prescriptive. We know that some of the elaborate master-student genealogies created, for example, by the Ch'an and Tibetan Buddhist traditions as accounts of their own histories have only the most tenuous basis in historical fact. Their true purpose has been to shape the future rather than recount the past. So, too, the various stages outlined in highly schematized versions of mārga may have no direct connection with any real problems or experiences in the lives of real persons. They may apply only analogically and normatively, prompting students to mold their own life experiences according to the ideals of their religious heritage. Or they may be means by which individual experience can be made communal, to the extent that common prescriptions of practice may foster experiences similar to those of one's colleagues. Thus rather than only "mediate" Buddhist mystical experiences, as has sometimes been suggested, mārga schemes may actually shape those experiences, and also provide the means by which they may be shared.

Even in Tibet and East Asia, where the mārga received extensive scholastic exegesis, we see the persistence of Buddhism's earliest focus on the idealized person. Jeffrey Hopkins shows in his chapter that Tibetan exegetes continued to conflate the person with the path. In China, in that quintessentially Chinese soteriology which John McRae here studies under the label of "Ch'an encounter dialogue," Buddhist training culminates not in some abstract goal but in the formation of an idealized person, the enlightened Ch'an master. McRae describes classical Ch'an as a performative soteriology in which the archetypal drama of the practitioner's approach to, and realization of, salvation is reenacted through the medium of the dramatic and dialectical encounter. For the student, salvation is defined as the ability to act as an enlightened Ch'an master is thought to act. Notions of a chartable path and of progressive achievement by differentiable stages need not intrude upon Ch'an soteriology: the student confirms his enlightenment through his direct interactions with the idealized person. Such an interpretation, McRae suggests, implies a subitist soteriology, for there can be no intermediary stages in becoming a master or a patriarch—either one is such, or one is not. Ch'an soteriology also implies a view of Buddhist practice in which the community and the lineage of practitioners play especially important roles, thereby establishing a contrast with the stress on doctrinal exegesis and explication of theoretical issues that seems paramount in other indigenous schools of Chinese Buddhism, like Hua-yen. On this point, and on the larger issue of the tension between doctrine and meditative practice as a factor in the growth of Chinese Buddhism, Yoshizu Yoshihide has much to say in his chapter.

Inverse Mārga: The Path in Terms of Its Obstacles

Such conflation of practitioner and goal contributes to the decidedly pragmatic tenor of much Buddhist soteriological writing, and to the characteristically Buddhist concern to identify and distinguish the defilements by which persons fall short of the ideal, so as to explain the causes producing those defilements while also prescribing antidotes to them. Such interest in the defilements and their eradication is seen in mārga schemes ranging from the Indian Vaibhāṣika to the Chinese T'ien-t'ai and the Tibetan Dge-lugs-pa. In these systems, unlike Ch'an, we see a shift in soteriological emphasis away from the idealized person to the abstract qualities associated with the path.

Describing the various stages of the path in terms of the defilements destroyed by each stage thus became a major preoccupation of many traditions of Buddhist soteriological writing. This interest sometimes evolved into concern with wide ranges of conatively negative qualities, including *kleśa* (defilements), *āsrava* (fluxes), *anuśaya* (contaminants), *saṃyojana* (fetters), and so forth. Progress on the path came to be defined by some specifically in terms of the successive abandonment of defilements. The goal of practice was not some transcendent, experiential state but gradual separation from specific defilements, one after the other. This is what Collett Cox shows in her chapter on the Sarvāstivāda-Vaibhāṣikas. The disposition to "abandon" particular defilements served as the principle of continuity underlying the elaborate mārga schemes of those schools. By framing the path negatively in this manner, these traditions could define the goal privatively, as what is left once those defilements are abandoned. This helped Buddhists resist the temptation to conceptualize a state understood in their heart of hearts to be fundamentally nonconceptual. Such concern with defilements is what allows soteriologies with universalist claims to maintain hierarchies among practitioners. Thus the Tibetan formulations of mārga covered by Hopkins are arranged according to the various sorts of practices assigned to different types of beings.

Mārga as a Path of Knowledge versus Mārga as a Path of Purification

Many Buddhist mārga schemes arose from attempts to resolve a fundamental tension in Buddhism, and indeed in much of Indian religion, between the impulse toward knowledge and the drive to purification, these two being the counteragents, respectively, to ignorance and impurity. This polarity is adumbrated even in the two distinct soteriologies presented, as Burford shows, in one of the earliest of all Buddhist texts, the *Aṭṭhakavagga*. One of these is a purificatory system concerned with developing specific ethical virtues that were thought capable of destroying—incinerating, as it were—the various defilements. The other is an approach via insight or analysis that denies the value of reliance on any and all speculative views and so subjects defilements not so much to destruction as to epistemological sublation. The tension between these two methods remained unresolved in that early text and reemerged frequently in later Buddhist writings. As Cox suggests in her chapter, the distinction is rather more than that commonly drawn between rationality and mysticism. The Vaibhāṣikas, and later the Mahāyāna Buddhists of Yogācāra tendency, addressed this tension by developing a bipartite mārga that divided the path into two broad categories—*darśana* (insight) and *bhāvanā* (cultivation). The Vaibhāṣikas, characteristically, defined the defilements abandoned on the mārga in terms of those factitious dharmas—mistakes of understanding, really—that are removed by insight (the *avastukakleśa* of individuality, attachment to rites and rituals as a means of salvation, skepsis, etc.) and those real dharmas (such as greed, ill-will, and conceit) that must be removed, purged, or consumed by a persistent intensity of cultivation. Rather than resolve this tension, the bipartite mārga seeks to mediate between the path of purification through cultivation and that of sublation through analytical vision, acknowledging the soteriological efficacy of both.

This bifurcation of a path of knowledge which nullifies error and a path of purification which burns up defilement may have been the principal catalyst in the production of the Buddhist mārga as a diversity rather than a uniformity of disciplines. Thus at least two generic forms of mārga, and many subsidiary forms, seem to emerge in the different traditions of Buddhism represented in this volume: an approach concerned with mental purification (as in Theravāda and Vaibhāṣika) and an approach based on a direct, analytic vision of truth (as in Ch'an and Zen). As an indication of how sharp the difference between the two can be, consider the contrast between two attitudes toward the virtue or perfection of giving *(dāna)* fostered by Ch'an, a way of knowledge *par excellence,* and by the Abhidharma tradition, mother to all purificatory paths. For Ch'an we can let its putative founder, Bodhidharma, speak in his legendary role as the scourge of conventional piety. Few tales are better remembered in Ch'an than Bodhidharma's devastating verdict on the prodigious generosity of King Wu of the Liang dynasty: there was "no merit in it at all," he said, ruthlessly. And yet, as Robert Buswell shows in his essay on the eradication and restoration of wholesome roots in Abhidharma, Buddhists have also seen *dāna* as the ultimate foundation of mārga. It may be that no mere making of "merit" *(puṇya),* not even the merit of giving, can by itself accomplish liberation, but such moral effort—and perhaps it alone—can plant the deepest of "good roots" *(kuśalamūla),* out of which later progress toward liberation grows.

Even in one of the latest works treated in this volume, the thirteenth-century *Zazen ron* studied by Carl Bielefeldt, Buddhist practice is divided between the gradual accumulation of wholesome karmic effect and the Zen way of "becoming a buddha by seeing one's own nature." The polarity between these two broad approaches, sometimes even the paradoxical amalgamation of the two, both characterizes and vivifies, in one way or another, most of the treatments of soteriology considered in these pages. The matter can become even more complex, as when moderate forms of Ch'an are differentiated from extreme varieties according to the degree to which they preserve elements of the gradual purificatory path, deeming them necessary complements to the sudden analytical vision. This last is a theme touched on in Robert Gimello's contribution to the volume.

Two features in particular seem to be common to the progressive and purificatory visions of the path. These are both foreshadowed in the ancient and oft-repeated synopsis of the Buddha's teaching: "Avoidance of all evil,/Cultivation of the good,/Purification of one's mind,/This is the teaching of the Buddha."[9] On the one hand, traversing the mārga involves a gradual removal of various types of defilements, and this frames the soteriological process in essentially negative or privative terms. On the other hand, progress involves the cultivation of a full range of positive moral and psychological qualities as well. At the consummation of both these endeavors, mental purity is achieved, enlightenment realized, and salvation won. Even in the context of the mārga schemes of later Tibetan Buddhism, as Hopkins' analysis shows, the path involves a tension between withdrawal from negative phenomena and expansion of positive commitments. In his comments made during the conference that produced this volume, Bernard Faure referred to Bergson's idea of "twofold frenzy" *(loi de double frénésie),* in which two related views tend to dissociate and run to their own logical conclusions, producing a creative dichotomy that widens the range of discourse between extremes.[10] The multiplication of stages in scholastic discussions of mārga may have been made possible by opening up this expansive middle ground between ignorance and enlightenment. And as Donald Lopez explains in his chapter, once the mārga was so expanded, its terminus could be found to be so far in the future as to render saṃsāra—and practice of the path—virtually endless.

Of the "direct" path or paths of knowledge, by contrast, at least three different interpretations or interpretive metaphors seem possible. First, there is the view that the true path is a telescoping or a condensation of the total mārga into a single moment, a moment in which all the stages of the path are consummated simultaneously. Second, there is the conception of the direct path as a transcendence—or, in the Chinese phrasing, a "leaping over" *(ch'ao-yüeh)*—of all intermediary stages.[11] Finally, there is simply the progressive path as seen from the point of view of its consummation, a perspective that ignores all the prior progressive development of the mind. The Korean Sŏn/Hwaŏm syncretist Chinul (1158–1210), for example, held that sudden approaches consummate instantaneously all the experiences achieved in following the gradual path. He believed that the sudden approach of Sŏn (Ch'an) subsumes in a single moment of experience the complex, progressive mārga of Hwaŏm (Hua-yen) and so perfects instantly all the various qualities differentiated in Hwaŏm thought. Chinul accepted the need for the varieties of achievement thought to be sequentially possible in the course of mārga, but he sought to compress the whole process of development into the shortest possible period of time, even to the point of making it virtually instantaneous.[12]

In his chapter on Kamakura Zen, Bielefeldt likewise notes that subitism involves a "conflation of cause and effect" in which there is a "collapsing of the path and its fruit." Analogously, the Japanese Tendai tradition is shown by Paul Groner in his contribution to have sought to bring the realization of buddhahood down to lower levels of the path, so as to make the fruition of the path directly accessible even to ordinary folk just starting out in their practice. The Chinese Ch'an master Ta-hui Tsung-kao's (1089–1163) interpretation of the "shortcut" approach of Ch'an suggests instead that the path of knowledge is more a transcendence of stages than it is their compression. Finally, Tsung-mi's (780–841) interpretation of the radical subitism he saw as rife in the Ch'an of his day implies the third interpretive possibility, viz., that what is called "sudden awakening/sudden cultivation" is simply "sudden awakening/gradual cultivation viewed from the standpoint of this final lifetime," regardless of the many past lives of religious development that preceded it.[13]

Tsung-mi's argument, brought from China to Korea in the twelfth century, continues to be a focus of urgent controversy even today. There is ongoing now in Korea a rather strenuous and quite serious debate between, on the one hand, representatives of Tsung-mi's and Chinul's moderate and balanced amalgamation of what we are here calling the sudden path of knowledge and the gradual path of purification and, on the other hand, spokesmen for the more radical Lin-chi tradition, which seems entirely committed to the all-at-once path of knowledge (as embodied, for example, in *k'an-hua* or *kōan* practice).[14] In this debate the subitists adduce two kinds of arguments very much like those Bielefeldt discovered in the subitist soteriologies of medieval Japanese Zen: first, the reduction of all spiritual experience to the single transformative vision of the enlightened mind and, second, the inflation of practice so that all action becomes the spontaneous expression of this mind. Bielefeldt traces the sectarian splits in Japanese Zen and Chinese Ch'an to the tension created by this polarity, and we learn from contemporary Korean Buddhism that the polarity is still highly charged.

A similar tension is found in the history of later Indian and Tibetan Buddhism, where Vajrayāna was seen to threaten conventional views of mārga progression in much the same way that radical Ch'an or Zen did in East Asia. This is the subject of Matthew Kapstein's essay on "the illusion of spiritual progress." Drawing on (and translating parts of) a rare document written by the Indian female adept Niguma, Kapstein notes that, as a kind of shamaness as well as a tantrika, Niguma was able both to undercut or dissolve and also to reaffirm the traditional mārga categories by subsuming them all under the rubric of "apparition."

Attempts of a different sort to synthesize progressive and subitist programs of Buddhist soteriology occur in several scholastic traditions as well. The Chinese T'ien-t'ai school was born in one such effort. As Daniel Stevenson noted in his contribution to the conference from which this book derives,[15] T'ien-t'ai seeks to incorporate the direct approach into a broader progressive program of spiritual development. Such a synthesis was required because of the change in ontology prompted by the adaptation of Buddhism to the new Chinese worldview. Indeed, the system of Chih-i, founder of T'ien-t'ai, can be seen as a "sinicization" of Buddhist soteriology, i.e., as a new outline of spiritual development especially suited to the Chinese predilection for harmony and integration. Chih-i sought to develop a subitist soteriology that could operate within the confines of gradualist paradigms inherited from India. His "sudden and complete" approach embodied a soteriology in which a fundamentally stageless process was nevertheless stratified into several stages of spiritual development. This paradoxical synthesis was justified by the claim that progress did not consist in the sequential perfection of specific virtues, as the Indian mārga format suggested, but was instead, in Stevenson's words, "the incremental intensification of a singular vision of reality."

The purpose behind such a system was not merely to synthesize the variant systems presented in Indian texts but also to counter radically subitist perspectives, which Chih-i felt could foster attachment to one technique of praxis as superior to all others. This, it will be recalled from Burford's chapter, is a criticism implicit also in the anti-*diṭṭhi* polemic of the *Aṭṭhakavagga.* The same criticism also lurks in the "no-mind" of Ch'an, which Bielefeldt sees as "a refraining from judgment." In attempting to prescribe one soteriological technique for everyone, subitism can fail to recognize or appreciate the differences in people's spiritual capacities and the changing circumstances of practice. If one were to take it to its logical extreme, as some Ch'an schools eventually did, subitism could also lead to antinomianism, the implicit rationale being that there is no particular form of practice that can be judged necessary to the achievement of nirvāṇa. This threat of antinomianism is considered in both Gimello's and Bielefeldt's essays below.

Mārga and Scholasticism

The proliferation of vast numbers of negative and positive qualities, seen as either to be shed or to be acquired in traversing the path, engendered a concern among Buddhist exegetes for order and intellectual consistency. The desire for coherence and elegance within the vast array of Buddhist spiritual technologies is certainly one reason for the corresponding proliferation of stages and grounds in systematizations of the mārga, like those found in Buddhaghosa's *Visuddhimagga* or Asaṅga's *Yogācārabhūmiśāstra.* Buddhists sometimes approached this task of organizing the path with methodical zeal, inflating it into a multitude of specific stages. Yoshizu's chapter shows that they did this with particular vigor in medieval China. In the syncretic Hua-yen mārga scheme, for example, as many as fifty-two or fifty-three stages were stipulated, the first fifty of which are arranged in a series of five groups comprising ten steps each. While the notion of stages in spiritual evolution is not unknown in Western Christian thought, at least since the writings of the Psuedo-Dionysius in the sixth century, Christians typically did not claim that God comes to be known through any expenditure of human effort in traversing a path; rather, it is God who is believed to reveal himself to us. Thus the negative theology privileged in Thomism explicitly holds that if we were to rely only on our own efforts, we would never know what God is; the best we could do is discover something of what God is not.[16] As a rule, Buddhism is rather more ambivalent on the question of whether the path serves as a necessary or only a contributory cause of the experience of enlightenment. At certain times, mārga and the human effort expended in traversing it are held to be both necessary and sufficient unto liberation, but at other times (as when the unconditioned character of liberation is stressed), the goal can be made to seem quite beyond the reach of path or deliberate effort, as though it were somehow gratuitous or self-generating. The latter, of course, is puzzling in a nontheistic tradition like Buddhism.

Buddhist soteriological systems and the speculative philosophies of medieval Christianity share similar concerns with intellectual consistency and systematicity. Western thinkers of the Middle Ages sought to apply the logic and metaphysics of classical Greek philosophy to Christian theological concerns. Such representative philosophers as Boethius, Thomas Aquinas, and Bonaventure sought to reconcile faith and reason in what Joseph Pieper has called a "contrapuntally structured unity" that would reconcile the tension they perceived between the two.[17] This "balance of tension" (to use another of Pieper's phrases) is what led to the complex, synthetic philosophies of medieval European Christianity. Rather than faith and reason, however, Buddhist scholastics sought to balance the immediate experience of meditation with the modes of logical analysis commonly used in Indian philosophical exegesis.[18] Many of the more scholastic Buddhist schools, including the Indian Vaibhāṣika, the Tibetan Dge-lugs-pa, and the Chinese Hua-yen, attempted to apply rigorous standards of intellectual verifiability to questions of religious achievement. The mārga thus provided a convenient means of ranking different types of spiritual experience, and of weaving them into comprehensive systems of Buddhist thought and practice.

But medieval Christian scholasticism was not simply rationalism. Most scholastics did not claim that human reason could comprehend everything, nor did they deny the mysteries of faith or divine revelation, despite the ultimate opacity of such things to reason. Indeed, Aquinas understood rational "proof" *(demonstratio)* to be more a matter of providing a "reason of convenience," and he undertook such proofs in attempts "to show how the truth of faith 'accords with' and 'suits' what we know from our own experience or rational argument."[19] Likewise,

Buddhist treatments of mārga nowhere claim that the intellectual exercise of mapping the path can itself produce enlightenment. It is only grudgingly that many Buddhist schools accept the value of intellectual analysis in Buddhist praxis. Instead, meditation was generally considered indispensable if practitioners were to achieve salvation for themselves. Rational analyses of spirituality are useful for providing the student with coherent outlines of the path of practice; but walking that path, and achieving its fruits, ultimately demand the abandonment or transcendence of rationality.

A paradox was thus created in Buddhist soteriology: to be a true protagonist of the mārga, one must also be its antagonist. This paradox underlies much of the tension in Buddhist descriptions of soteriology. Indirect, rational understanding of the mārga may provide support for direct, experiential apprehension of Buddhist truths, but that direct experience can only come once rational understanding is transcended. A reflection of this paradox may be found in the Hua-yen distinction between awakening as understanding *(chieh-wu)* and awakening as realization *(cheng-wu),* and in that tradition's oft-repeated claim that the former, defined as the intellectual apprehension of truths formulated in doctrine, is prelude to the latter, understood as the sort of direct encounter with truth made possible in part by the prior understanding of doctrine.[20]

Buddhist scholastics may once have sought to link their descriptions of meditative experience to specific religious teachings, but as Cox suggests in her chapter on the Vaibhāṣikas, it was not only or always issues of praxis that underlay the construction of elaborate mārga schemes. Rather, there was a diversity of concerns—theoretical and scholastic issues prominent among them—that prompted these cartographies of the path. And the maps they produced, Lopez reminds us in his contribution, are fictive in the sense that they review a path not yet traversed from a vantage point not yet reached but only projected. Although the design of an intellectually consistent and logically indefeasible mārga, in which all stages of the path serve a necessary function, may have been an interesting scholastic exercise, it may also have had little if anything to do with actual meditative practice. In the minds of the Buddhist scholastics who created these elaborate schemes, personal spiritual experience need not always have been at issue. While this is no doubt a pejorative conclusion—and one that the scholastic traditions themselves would probably have rejected—the evidence demands that we make it.

Indeed, the elaborate and meticulous construction of hierarchies of religious understanding may derive from a breakdown in religious praxis. Such failure might well have forced the creation of conceptual systems as an attempt to explain religious transitions that seemed problematic because they were no longer being achieved. It may be, then, that in some cases hierarchically arranged and progressive māargas were not intended as guides to actual experience. The numerological preoccupations so often evident in many mārga schemes (such as the fifty-three-stage Hua-yen system noted above) may belie the assumption of their foundation in actual practice. However, such judgments should not be construed as indictments of the validity of Buddhist religious experience or as challenges to the authority of Buddhist texts. They are intended simply as cautions, as reminders that such attempts to order—and thus to authenticate—Buddhist religious experience need not always be first-person accounts of actual religious experience.

Mārga, Hermeneutics, and Polemics

This caveat on the interpretation of mārga is vital to an understanding of the many different types of issues mārga schemes were employed to resolve. One of the most important roles assigned to mārga was that of a hermeneutical device to be used in systematizing, and in interpreting between, the diverse doctrinal positions of various Buddhist traditions. For example, Buddhist schools often sought to associate particular stages along the mārga, usually lower ones, with various of their sectarian rivals, while holding the higher stages to correspond to their own doctrinal positions. The sequential listing of stages on the path was thus used to classify Buddhist schools hierarchically, sometimes invidiously, in what we might term a "soteriologically based" hermeneutic. The purpose of such rankings was not purely interpretive; it often had an implicit polemic thrust.

One of the most fully wrought hierarchies is that of the ten stages of realization devised by Kūkai (774–835), the Japanese founder of Shingon, who used an especially comprehensive mārga scheme to rank rival traditions, both Buddhist and non-Buddhist. His "ten abodes of the mind" *(jūjūshin)* borrows an old Chinese term for the ten *bhūmis* and gives each stage a new description and a new referent. The first abode of the mind is that of the immoral, irreligious person who is immersed in "goatish desires," i.e., totally dominated by cravings for sex and food. The fourth abiding mind corresponds to the Hīnayānists, who recognize the truth of no-self *(anātman)* but little more than that, whereas the sixth relates to the Yogācārins, who generate universal compassion for all. Kūkai's path then progresses through stages corresponding to the Sanron (Mādhyamika), Tendai (T'ien-t'ai), and Kegon (Hua-yen) systems, culminating in his own Shingon Esoteric school. At this tenth and final stage, it is said, the practitioner is able to act in a completely free and unhindered manner on behalf of all sentient beings.[21] Kūkai's soteriological system is thus explicitly hermeneutical and polemical, while it also serves as a curriculum for individual spiritual advancement.

Yoshizu, in his contribution to this volume, discusses the similar hermeneutical and syncretic roles played in the history of Chinese Buddhism by such systems for classifying doctrines according to progressive visions of the path *(p'an-chiao chih tu).* Several of these were precursors of Kūkai's system. Still another parallel is provided in the soteriological typology of persons created by Atīśa (982–1054) in his *Bodhipathapradīpa.* As Hopkins explains in his chapter, despite the explicitly inclusionary agenda of this typology, it has an implicitly exclusionary purpose as well: to keep non-Buddhists off the list of religious practitioners. The exclusionary implications of such a typology contrast sharply with the Mahāyāna notion of universal compassion, revealing once again the polemical intent behind some Buddhist soteriological formulations.

Mārga, Conditioning versus Deconditioning, and Faith

Some varieties of Buddhism—certain kinds of Ch'an and Zen, for example—commonly claim to offer direct, immediate experiences of truth which are said not to be products of any sequential practice. To be sure, these seemingly anti-mārga traditions often belie their own rhetoric by providing explicit orderings of experience that help to "domesticate the unknown" and make the process of liberation somewhat predictable (e.g., the five-ranks method of Ts'ao-tung Ch'an or the ox-herding pictures of the Lin-chi lineage). Nevertheless, we should not rush to dismiss their frequently repeated claims that the ultimate religious goal is somehow radically discontinuous with the path and not at all its product.

What is at work here is yet another paradox of mārga: If the goal (say, nirvāṇa) is averred to be unconditioned *(asaṃskṛta),* as seems always to be the case, how can it also be said to be in any sense achievable by following a conditioned and conditioning program of practice? How could any path be said to "condition" such a goal? Yet if the goal is not the product of the path, and if it is in that sense unconditioned by the path, what sort of causal efficacy or necessity can the path be said to have? And if it has none, what then is its value or relevance? Anne Klein raises these issues in her chapter in this volume. How is it, she asks, that a structured path can lead to unmediated, unstructured mystical experience? Drawing on exquisitely technical analyses of meditation argued in the Tibetan Dge-lugs-pa tradition, she shows that in that tradition the practice of meditation, especially at the intersection of calming *(śamatha)* and insight *(vipaśyanā),* is held to be a deconditioning process rather than a form of conditioning. As such, it is said to be an occasion when the constructed and constructing mind ceases its constructive activities and encounters the unconditioned directly, without mediation. Klein also notes that this view is not shared by other Tibetan traditions, such as Rdzogs-chen and Rnying-ma, which prefer to explain the efficacy of the path by recourse to the gratuitous activity of the absolute itself. We can add that similar recourse is taken by those various Indian, Tibetan, and East Asian Buddhist traditions which are based on such notions as tathāgatagarbha (womb or embryo of buddhahood), the intrinsic purity of the mind *(cittaprakṛtivaimalyadhātu),* and so forth. In these, moreover, we see intimations of the spirituality of faith that would take shape in East Asia as Pure Land Buddhism.

Another facet of the same problem emerges when one considers not the intermediary goals of meditative attainment but the final goal of nirvāṇa. Given the notorious difficulty of characterizing, let alone defining, that goal, how better to understand the concept than by appreciating the sense in which nirvāṇa is implicit in, and shaped by, the very path leading to it? Ninian Smart has offered the useful analogy of the relationship between the goal of a game and the rules of that game.[22] Any effort to define a "home run," for example, would inevitably lead to a systematic statement of the rules of baseball. Likewise, the only feasible description of an ineffable religious goal would seem to be an outline of the path leading to it. In both cases, the goal is implicit in the rules of behavior leading to its attainment, and thus may be said to be accessible only through such behavior. Conversely, the meaning of any one element on the path consists principally in the contribution it makes to the achievement of the goal. Hence the conditioned and unconditioned realms have meaning only in relation to one another (just as nirvāṇa and saṃsāra are said to entail each other); without a path there is no destination, and without a destination, no path.

This accords well with Buddhist, especially Mahāyāna, gnosiology, in which the point is variously made that nirvāṇa is not really a destination at all. Indeed, it cannot be, for the common-sense meaning and deeper implications of a metaphor like "destination" are quite incompatible with other essential claims Buddhists insist on making about nirvāṇa. In Mahāyāna, we must recall, nirvāṇa is said to be "nonabiding" *(apratiṣṭhita).* To "achieve" nirvāṇa, then, is not to "arrive at," much less to "settle," anywhere. Rather (if we may hazard some descriptions that are themselves only metaphors, but perhaps less misleading than the metaphor of "destination"), to "achieve" nirvāṇa is to be released from confinement, to embark on a continuing transformation, to participate in unfettered change and in unbounded interrelation with all things and beings. This, we suspect, is part of what Nāgārjuna meant when he said, famously, "the very limit of nirvāṇa is precisely the limit of saṃsāra; between the two there is not the least difference."[23] Seen in this light, the discontinuity that would otherwise appear to separate the goal of nirvāṇa from the path fades, and the path becomes more deeply involved in that goal than any mere conditioning would allow; indeed, it is constitutive of the goal.

Still another attempt to resolve this paradox is found in discussions of soteriology in the Chinese Tathāgatagarbha traditions, which claimed that the innate seed of buddhahood is the dynamic force that both encourages and enables the student to practice the mārga. Thus in texts like *The Awakening of Faith in Mahāyāna (Ta-sheng ch'i-hsin lun),* innate enlightenment *(pen-chüeh)* is said to permit and to support the process by which enlightenment is actualized *(shih-chüeh).*[24] The conflation of goal and path seen in systems like those found in Rdzogs-chen, Hua-yen, and Sōtō Zen may have been prompted by similar attempts to resolve the problematic relationship between the conditioned and the unconditioned.

The same paradox seems also to culminate in the Pure Land doctrine of "other power," in which personal effort is said to be deleterious—or, in some systems, like Shinran's, even antithetical—to liberation.[25] Rather than the spiritual practice of the aspirant, Pure Land claims, it is the grace of an enlightened buddha that brings that aspirant to salvation. But such an explicitly "anti-mārga" stance could not have evolved without advocacy by many rival schools of Buddhism of elaborate soteriological systems demanding personal purification and growth. And even this approach need not imply that the mārga has been jettisoned. Rather, grace could be seen as an expedient means *(upāya)* of perfecting the soteriological program during the age of the demise of the dharma *(mo-fa, mappō),* when even the best of intentions are so easily overcome by dire circumstances and the simple impotence of sentient beings.

Indeed, the Pure Land school went so far as to equate particular Pure Land charisms with specific stages on the traditional mārga. It was in this vein that the *Sukhāvatīvyūha-sūtra* (vow number 34) identified rebirth in Amitābha's Pure Land with what had traditionally been regarded as a bodhisattva's achievement of the perfection of "acquiescence to the nonproducation of dharmas" *(anutpattikadharmakṣānti),* a Mahāyāna term equivalent to nirvāṇa.[26] Hence even schools that do not at first glance seem to subscribe to progressive soteriological programs may have been responding in one way or another to the emphasis on method so characteristic of the rest of Buddhism. Even such radical responses to this fundamental emphasis do not in the end suffice to deny the integrity and centrality of mārga; instead, they developed ways of perfecting it that would be either faster or more timely.

Mārga and the "Anti-Mārga" Tradition in Buddhist Thought

Perhaps the centrality of mārga to Buddhism, and its ineluctability, are nowhere better confirmed than in those traditions of Buddhist thought which seem to challenge or deny mārga but which also seem to end up reaffirming it. If Buddhist mārga can be shown to survive even those threats to it posed by Buddhism itself, then its importance to Buddhism can be demonstrated beyond challenge. And just such affirmation of mārga, made in the teeth of its denial, can be shown often to be a defining characteristic of Buddhism.

At the heart of every religious tradition are certain fertile antinomies, certain rationally irresolvable oppositions of concept or value, that serve in their very irresolvability to keep the tradition alive, to foster its growth, and to prevent its closure or ossification. In the case of Buddhism, one of the most profound of these life-giving antinomies is the creative and persistent tension between that religion's fundamental cognitive claims and its most characteristic conative injunctions. On the one hand, Buddhism insists that the reality of the things and persons that comprise the world is fundamentally indeterminate and that all things and persons are thus devoid *(śūnya)* of any inherent structure or stable identity.[27] On the other hand, Buddhism has been equally adamant in claiming that particular patterns of effort and practice, both private spiritual practice and interpersonal moral conduct, are necessary to achieving the liberating realization that all things and persons are empty and indeterminate; necessary as well to achieving that abundance of compassion for all beings which is possible only for those who have realized emptiness.

In the Buddhist world of cognitive indeterminacy, all things or events are so thoroughly transient as to be actually instantaneous, so radically interdependent that none may be assigned its own fixed and discrete identity; thus is the lie given to all apparent differentiation and imagined substantiality. Yet in this unstructured and unstructurable world, some order, sequence, and stringency of disciplined practice are still deemed necessary. To be sure, Buddhists often warn themselves not to reify their practices. Any tendency to trust in the practical disciplines of Buddhism as though they were self-efficacious mechanisms, like any assumption that liberation is simply the conditioned *(saṃskṛta)* effect of certain efficient causes, is condemned as severely as those same disciplines are enjoined. Thus do Buddhist texts abound in such seeming self-contradictions as the claim that the fruit *(phala)* of practice is actually a prevenient cause *(hetu)* of its own causal practices,[28] the assertion that practice and realization are really indistinguishable from each other,[29] the claim that sudden realization precedes and enables gradual practice,[30] and even the conviction that all prideful confidence in the sufficiency of one's "own power" *(jiriki)* as exercised in "difficult practices" *(nangyō)* must be relinquished humbly in the "easy practice" *(igyō)* whereby one accepts the "other power" *(tariki)* of the transcendent.[31]

However, such warnings against the reification or exaggerated assessment of practice have seldom counted as warrants for the abandonment of practice. Whenever they have been misunderstood to be outright rejections of practice, as has occasionally happened, Buddhism has usually corrected the mistake promptly. In most cases it has managed to purge itself of the results of any attempt to transform its anomic *(nairātmya)* cognitive stance into practical antinomianism in the religious and ethical spheres of life. Thus early radical forms of Ch'an, like the Pao-t'ang school of eighth-century Szechwan, which is believed to have espoused literal non-practice,[32] were roundly condemned soon after their inceptions, and their stories lingered in Chinese and Tibetan Buddhist memory only as cautionary tales. A similar fate awaited extremely antinomian interpretations of Tantric texts and Pure Land principles. The repeated and consensual Buddhist judgment has been that the empty indeterminacy of things is not license for abandoning the deliberate Buddhist path, and that the very emptiness which some rash Buddhists have taken to validate such license cannot be realized except by assiduous practice of the path.

To say that Buddhism never succumbed to antinomianism, however, is not to say that the implicit tension between śūnyatā and mārga could simply be put out of mind, to be recalled only when heresy threatened. Rather, that tension functioned as a kind of spring, tightly wound at the core of Buddhism, providing the tradition with the kinetic energy necessary for its continued development. Its presence was remarked especially when Buddhism came into contact with other traditions that were wont to fix on one pole of the tension to the exclusion of the other and so, for example, to question or decry Buddhism's cognitive insistence on emptiness while ignoring the conative rigor and coherence of the Buddhist mārga. It was this failure to see the whole of Buddhism, we would suggest, which led orthodox Hindu thinkers often to accuse Buddhists of nihilism. The same misimpression characterized traditional Confucian (including "Neo-Confucian") reactions to Buddhism, in which the dharma was seen as a threat to the order and stability of social and political life, was excoriated as a conceptual caustic in which the bonds of moral responsibility were quickly dissolved, or was condemned as a seductive opiate that could lull one into the illusion that all things and beings are illusory.

Such issues are still the focus of lively debate within and about Buddhism. Recently, certain partial views of Buddhism reminiscent of those held by its ancient Hindu and Confucian critics have infected the dialogue between Buddhism and Christianity. The fault for this, we regret to say, lies more with the Buddhist parties to the dialogue than with their Christian interlocutors. Consider the following remarks by the Protestant Christian theologian Langdon Gilkey, made in his insightful review of Abe Masao's *Zen and Western Thought.*[33] Having discussed briefly the "progressive naturalism" of Dewey and Whitehead, to which Buddhism has often been compared, Gilkey notes, quoting Abe as he proceeds:

> In starkest contrast to this [the naturalists'] confidence in the developmental possibilities of temporal sequence, Abe negates the meaning of all sequences in which the self participates. Nothing builds to a fruition, a satisfaction, an achievement either personal or social. "Substantial thinking," a world made up of selves and objects, self and environment, past events and future projects, and the scientific intelligence built upon that world, is creative of estrangement and not of resolutions; attachment to ends, natural or appraised, must be overcome and eradicated. All sequences of events lead nowhere, only to more desire and duality and the suffering consequent on both. Instead of an intelligently directed *continuity* of moments from puzzled past to problem-free future, the continuity of the moments of time must be negated and the independence of each moment emphasized: "Only by being freed from aim-oriented human action both in practice and in enlightenment is Dōgen's idea of oneness of practice and end realized. . . . This indicates complete discontinuity of time which is realized through negating a transition from one state to another. . . . Only by the realization of the complete discontinuity of time and of the independent moment, i.e., only by the negation of temporality, does time become real time." The true self is not achieved by intelligent action over time within the world; it is rather emptied of sequences as it is of all else. Through its realization of outer endlessness and "pointless" impermanence, it empties itself of attachments to objects or to self, to memories and to projects alike, and so it empties itself of world and of self in time. In that cool emptiness it becomes identical with the endless process outside of it—it is both enlightened and released. Unattached to any worldly meanings, it has *become* the meaningless natural world in which it participates. Put this way, Abe's Buddhism seems, in truth, to be the more valid mode of "natural piety" in such a totally unstructured and transient universe than does the optimistic, rational, moral and progressivist humanism of Dewey.

Reflecting the concern with morality that presently (and properly) dominates the Buddhist-Christian dialogue, Gilkey is here giving voice to the perennial Christian (and also, perhaps, Jewish and Islamic) "supernaturalist" view that there can be no order in the world, certainly no teleological order, unless there is also a transcendent orderer. He is troubled by both the Buddhist and the Western "naturalist" rejection of a transcendent agent, fearing that lack of such an agent, and lack of belief in transcendence generally, deprives Buddhists and others of any possible foundation for the personal or communal moral life. Despite its distinctively Christian emphasis on the transcendent, however, Gilkey's reservations about Buddhism are not unlike those of its earlier Confucian critics, who saw similar dangers for morality in the Buddhist denial of immanent moral principles *(li).*[34] The Christian attributes the possibility of order and teleological progression to the work of a transcendent orderer, whereas the Confucian attributes it to the presence *in the world* of constitutive moral patterns. But whether the structure of things and human action is held to come from beyond or from within, Buddhism seems, in its claim that all is empty and indeterminate, to deny structure entirely, or to locate its origin in the ignorant craving of the deluded human mind. Thus has it incurred the incredulity or apprehension, and sometimes the hostility, of Christian and Confucian alike.

Part of the problem here, we would suggest, is that the Buddhism about which Gilkey is so apprehensive, represented in this case by Abe Masao, is a truncated, asymmetrical, perhaps even eccentric Buddhism. Abe and the "Kyoto school" of religious philosophy of which he is a prominent spokesman—probably in a less than fully conscious effort to accentuate just those aspects of Buddhism that are both most different from Western traditions and most distinctively Japanese—have fostered in the West the now widespread conception of Buddhism as a tradition of exclusively cognitive import, inordinately preoccupied with the most apophatic register of Buddhist doctrine. Thus in the current phase of the Buddhist-Christian dialogue there is relentless talk of śūnyatā, nonduality, "absolute nothingness," and the like, but precious little talk of karma, mārga, compassion, or even the "marvelous qualities of buddhahood." The Buddhism that so repulsed and alarmed Chu Hsi seven centuries ago was a similarly partial tradition, made to seem morally incoherent and dangerous by a refusal to see it whole. Such refusals consist in failures to give as much attention to the positive disciplines (including morality) that comprise the actual lives of Buddhists as one gives to those cognitive claims which, taken by themselves, suggest that Buddhists are unable to treat the world of human endeavor seriously. They also lead to an unfortunate deafness to the affirmative soteriological message of Buddhism, which is as much a part of the tradition as its metaphysical negation. These are failures, in other words, to appreciate the stubborn persistence and unavoidable centrality of mārga in even the most apophatic of Buddhist contexts.

Mārga and the Transcendent

An approach to Buddhism that gives mārga and Buddhism's conative import a value equal to that normally assigned to the cognitive message of śūnyatā and associated concepts—an approach, that is to say, which exploits the vital and productive tension between the two constituents of the tradition—will reveal, we would propose, a Buddhism that is at once less alien from the world of ordinary human concerns and more sensitive to the presence of the transcendent in that world. It is under the rubric of mārga or concerted and methodical practice that Buddhism addresses itself to such temporal matters as the regimen of daily life, the particular arts and sciences of self-cultivation, the values and norms of interpersonal relationships, institutional organization and authority, and so forth. Because the overriding concern in such matters must be with spiritual efficacy, with what "works" and what does not "work" unto liberation, it follows that attention to issues of mārga invites consideration of such questions as the source of spiritual efficacy. How is it that deliberate spiritual disciplines can be effective, given the inherent emptiness that must mark them all? How can obedience to the precepts, scriptural study, asceticism, calming of the mind and body, exercise of analytical insight, and so on collaborate to sustain a coherent course of spiritual development? How can they lead consistently to a single end? Were one to focus only on the cognitive message of Buddhism, the message of metaphysical indeterminacy, such efficacy would be inexplicable, perhaps even unlikely. But since Buddhists teach mārga as insistently as they teach śūnyatā, we have good reason to believe that the practical principles of structure, continuity, and efficacy implicit in the one are as important as the theoretical principles of indeterminacy, discontinuity, and structurelessness implicit in the other. If this is so, then the reality of things and actions is not exhausted by their emptiness but must consist equally in "the marvelous qualities of buddhahood" that are thought to quicken all things and actions, to energize them, and to endow them with their efficacy.

There is ample room in all this, we would suggest, for a more transcendentalist, even supernaturalist interpretation of Buddhism than is usually found in those readings of the tradition that stress only its world-withering vision of emptiness. One need not restrict oneself to purely immanentist or naturalist interpretations of Buddhism, like Abe Masao's and Langdon Gilkey's (or, for that matter, like Chu Hsi's), all of which puzzle and disturb those Buddhists who find evidence that the transcendent is active in the world and who believe that a coherent religious and moral life is impossible without such transcendent support. In other words, although Buddhism has good epistemological and dialectical reason to deny the cognitive validity of categories like "the transcendent," and therefore to argue that the world is empty and indeterminable, it has equally good soteriological and gnosiological reason to affirm the same categories as necessary supports or prerequisites of the full and coherent religious life. The "buddha-nature" that must be judged empty (along with everything else) must also be judged actual, apodictic, and efficacious; otherwise the very practices that enable the realization of emptiness would be otiose or impossible. Should this seem improbable in light of the rigorous apophasis of so much of Buddhism, let us cite a well-known but inexhaustible line from Nāgārjuna himself: "Ultimate truth is not taught except upon the foundation of conventional discourse" *(vyavahāraṃ anāśritya paramārtho na deśyate).*[35] Conventional transactional usage *(vyavahāra)* and its rough equivalent, conventional truth *(saṃvṛtisatya),* are but locutionary instances of emptiness and indeterminacy. For them actually to serve as a "support" or "foundation" *(āśraya,* Ch. *i)* of ultimate truth, or as a vehicle for the transmission thereof, they must have some efficacy, some supportive force. From what else could such efficacy or force derive, if not from the energizing presence of the transcendent (buddhahood, etc.) within the emptiness of transactional usage?[36] Such at least was a conclusion, Robert Gimello argues in his chapter, that was often drawn within the East Asian Buddhist traditions, and in this the East Asian traditions were quite in harmony with the still underappreciated kataphatic traditions of Indian and Tibetan Buddhism.[37]

Mārga and Culture

At least one other kind of consequence to Buddhism's emphasis on mārga deserves our attention. If Buddhism, as a religion of mārga, enjoins upon its adherents programs of discipline and structures of life that differ markedly from life as it usually lived in the secular world—and if mārga is as different as it seems to be from all secular life-forms, regardless of whether they be naturally evolved or deliberately constructed—then what kinds of relation are possible and desirable between mārga and the disciplines and activities of secular life? This, of course, is but a variation on the age-old, universal question of the relation of religion to culture, but if it is a question that we would ask of Buddhism, we must ask it apropos of mārga, explicitly and particularly.

Again Ch'an and Zen Buddhism would seem to qualify as a good case-study of this issue. As a form of Buddhism that tends, in one way or another, to emphasize practice or experience rather than, say, reflection or study, Ch'an/Zen would seem to be a partisan of Buddhism's emphasis on mārga. And yet we know it to be one of the most vociferously anti-mārga of all Buddhist traditions, at least in its rhetoric and in its frequent disavowal of routine, gradualist practice. To these two, somewhat contradictory, features of Ch'an and Zen we can add their intimate association, throughout their East Asian histories virtually since their inceptions, with traditions of secular art and literature (poetry, painting, calligraphy, *belles lettres,* Noh drama—even tea ceremony, flower arrangement, ritual archery, etc). Moreover, through such associations, Ch'an and Zen have often come into closer contact than have other schools with non-Buddhist traditions of religious thought and practice like Confucianism and Taoism.

These multivalent connections—between Ch'an's mārga or anti-mārga Buddhist postures, the secular cultures of the environments in which Ch'an flourished, and non-Buddhist traditions competing with

Ch'an—are the subject of Gimello's essay in this volume. That essay deals with an array of questions including the following: Can disciplines originally extrinsic to mārga, and often thought to be inimical thereto, nevertheless be incorporated into larger definitions of mārga that do not consist only of traditional Buddhist disciplines? If this is possible, as when Ch'an monks become painters and poets, under what kind of constraints and cautions must it proceed if it is not to threaten the integrity or distract from the proper goals of the Buddhist life? Can the disciplines of secular culture be sacralized and incorporated into Buddhist mārga, and what are the limits of that enterprise? How, in turn, can secular cultural traditions make creative use of the disciplines and attitudes implicit in mārga, without denaturing or otherwise abusing them? And how can mārga contribute to, or participate in, the dialogue that inevitably occurs when Buddhism and non-Buddhist traditions meet on the common ground of a shared secular culture? It is hoped that questions of this particular and historical kind may allow further, more universally focused questions about the relevance of mārga to wider ranges of human concern.

Conclusion

Against the background of issues like those sketched above, we wish to suggest that mārga is a factor pervading everything that is Buddhist, uniting not only its various practices and its various adherents, but also its disparate traditions and its conflicting attitudes toward its own and other forms of life.

We also believe that the possibilities for the general revisioning of religion suggested by Buddhism's emphasis on the path offer the further possibility of a more holistic assessment not only of Buddhism but of any religious tradition. Mārga, we would suggest, provides an especially integrative way of interpreting religion, an approach in which all elements of a tradition can be seen to collaborate in the service of the common goal of liberation. Under the template of mārga, a religion's doctrines can be seen to correspond to its concrete practices and to flow from them; its worldviews and axiologies can be seen as implicit in its regimens of practice; the popular piety of its common adherents can be seen to resonate deeply with the insights informing the conceptual systems of its more élite and reflective adherents. We propose that mārga —at least as much as, if not more than, doctrine—creates among the various strata of a religion's adherents a sense of community, of what Buddhists call "saṃgha," despite the variety of their many particular concerns and needs. Emphasis on a practical spirituality, even when framed in scholastic terms, has the effect of bringing the highest reaches of religious achievement within the purview of the most humble of adherents. It also demands that even the more basic of practices be directly preparatory to, if not actually reflected within, the most advanced disciplines. By making religious achievement measurable in terms relevant to daily life, all the activities of ordinary adherents are made to serve the soteriological process. The famous statement of the lay Ch'an practitioner P'ang Yün (d. 808)—really a comment on the pervasiveness of mārga—may therefore apply: "Mysterious power and marvelous function: carrying water and gathering kindling."

If our confidence in the potential of mārga as a category for the study both of Buddhism in particular and of religion generally seems unwarranted even after all we have said so far, we trust that the chapters which follow, in their more extensive arguments and documentation, will provide ample compensation and confirmation.

Notes

1. We must bear in mind, however, that although the concept of "path" may be more thoroughly developed in Buddhism than elsewhere, it is not exclusive to Buddhism. As Karl Potter and others have shown, it seems to be important in all the major Indian traditions. See Potter, *Presuppositions of India's Philosophies* (Englewood Cliffs, N.J.: Prentice Hall, 1963), esp. pp. 36–46 and 236–256. Nevertheless, when one considers both Indian Buddhism and Buddhism as it developed outside of India, the sheer quantity and variety of mārga discourse exceeds whatever may be found in, say, the varieties of Hinduism, Jainism, etc.

2. See, for example, the entries on "Soteriology" in James Hastings, general ed., *The Encyclopedia of Religion and Ethics* (Edinburgh: T. E. Clarke, 1908–1926) and Mircea Eliade, general ed., *The Encyclopedia of Religion* (New York: Macmillan, 1987). Note, too, that in its pre-Christian Greek etymology, *"soter"* actually means "healer"—a point worth pondering in view of Buddhism's common depiction of the Buddha as a healer or a physician, to which we refer below.

3. For example, when an adjectival form is needed. "Soteriological" is, after all, an acceptable locution, whereas we are reluctant to coin the term "mārgic." The term "soteriology" may also be advisable when introducing Buddhist notions of mārga into ongoing scholarly discussions of soteriology as instanced in other traditions.

4. *Dīghanikāya* II.156.

5. K. N. Jayatilleke, *Early Buddhist Theory of Knowledge* (London: George Allen & Unwin, 1963), chs. 7 and 8.

6. *Majjhimanikāya* I.134–135.

7. Joseph Pieper, *Scholasticism: Personalities and Problems in Medieval Philosophy,* trans. Richard and Clara Winston (New York: Pantheon Books, 1960), 39.

8. The "four noble truths," the "four approaches and fruits," and the "ten perfections" are treated in most general introductions to Buddhism. The *locus classicus* of the version of "ten stages" scheme given here is the *Daśabhūmika Sūtra,* which has been rendered into English from the Sanskrit by Megumu Honda and Johannes Rahder, "Annotated Translation of the *Daśabhūmika-sūtra,*" in *Studies in South, East, and Central Asia: A Memorial Volume for the Late Professor Raghu Vira,* Śata-Piṭaka Series, vol. 74, Denis Sinor, ed. (New Delhi:

International Academy of Indian Culture, 1968), 115–276. The "five paths" scheme, less well known in Western literature, is associated especially with the various Abhidharma traditions and was given one of its most influential classical formulations by Asaṅga in his *Abhidharmasamuccaya;* see Asaṅga, *Le Compendium de la super-doctrine (philosophie) (Abhidharmasamuccaya),* trans. Walpola Rahula, Publications de l'École Française d'Extrême-Orient LXXVIII (Paris: École Française d'Extrême-Orient, 1971). Several of the essays in this volume treat of the third and fourth of these five paths. For an English-language treatment of the Hua-yen path—listing its fifty-three stages and coordinating them with the fifty-three teachers whom the mythical pilgrim-bodhisattva Sudhana met on his journey in the *Gaṇḍavyūha Sūtra,* but dealing especially with the influence of the latter on Buddhist art—see Jan Fontein, *The Pilgrimage of Sudhana: A Study of Gaṇḍavyūha Illustrations in China, Japan, and Java* (The Hague and Paris: Mouton, 1967). The only extensive treatment of the "five ranks" theme in a Western language is Alfonso Verdu's rather obscure *Dialectical Aspects in Buddhist Thought: Studies in Sino-Japanese Mahāyāna Idealism,* International Studies, East Asian Series Research Publication No. 8 (Lawrence, Kans.: Center for East Asian Studies, The University of Kansas, 1974), 115–242.

9. These lines—*"sabbapāpassa akaraṇaṃ kusalassa upasampadā sacittapariyodapanaṃ etaṃ buddhāna sāsanaṃ"*—or close variations on them, are found in numerous canonical sources. Their most famous occurrence, perhaps, is as verse 183 of the *Dhammapada.*

10. See the treatment of this concept in Bernard Faure's *The Rhetoric of Immediacy: A Cultural Critique of Chan/Zen Buddhism* (Princeton, N.J.: Princeton University Press, 1991).

11. See Jacques May, "Chōotsushō," in *Hōbōgirin: Dictionnaire encyclopédique du bouddhisme d'aprés les sources chinoises et japonaises* (Paris: Adrien-Maisonneuve), quatrième fascicule (1967): 366–370 and cinquième fascicule (1979): 371.

12. On this, see Robert E. Buswell, Jr., "Chinul's Ambivalent Critique of Radical Subitism in Korean Sŏn Buddhism," *The Journal of the International Association of Buddhist Studies* 12.2 (1989): 20–44; also Buswell's translation of Chinul's major writings: idem, *The Korean Approach to Zen: The Collected Works of Chinul* (Honolulu: University of Hawaii Press, 1983), especially 56–61.

13. Buswell has discussed the implications of this interpretation in "Chinul's Ambivalent Critique."

14. A conference on this very topic, the most recent in a series, was held in October 1990 at the Songgwang Monastery in Korea. At the same time the conference was held, its proceedings, entitled *Pojo sasang* 4, were published by the monastery's Institute for the Study of Chinul's Thought (Pojo sasang yŏn'guwŏn).

15. See the summary of Stevenson's presentation in Robert E. Buswell, Jr. and Robert M. Gimello, "Buddhist Soteriology: The Mārga and Other Approaches to Liberation: A Conference Report," *Journal of the International Association of Buddhist Studies* 13-1 (1990): 97–98.

16. See Pieper, *Scholasticism,* p. 53. The original German version of Pieper's work, entitled *Scholastik,* was published in 1952, in Munich, by Koesel Verlag.

17. Ibid., p. 39.

18. The classical treatment of this issue is Louis de La Vallée Poussin, "Mūsila et Nārada: le chemin du *nirvāṇa,*" *Mélanges chinois et bouddhiques* 5 (1937): 189–222. More recent treatments of the topic are too numerous to list, but special notice should be taken of K. N. Jayatilleke, *Early Buddhist Theory of*

Knowledge (London: George Allen & Unwin, 1963), particularly chapters V through VIII.

19. Pieper, *Scholasticism,* p. 46.

20. For these two types of awakening, see Robert E. Buswell, Jr., "Chinul's Systematization of Chinese Meditative Techniques in Korean Sŏn Buddhism," in Peter N. Gregory, ed., *Traditions of Meditation in Chinese Buddhism,* Studies in East Asian Buddhism, no. 4 (Honolulu: University of Hawaii Press, A Kuroda Institute Boook, 1986), 204–207.

21. See Kūkai's *Jūjūshin ron,* as summarized in *Hizō hōyaku* (The Precious Key to the Secret Treasury), trans. in Yoshito S. Hakeda, *Kūkai: Major Works* (New York: Columbia University Press, 1972), 162–224. For convenient companion charts of the soteriological goals of each stage, together with their respective sectarian affiliations, see Miyasaka Yūshō and Umehara Takeshi, *Inochi no umi: Kūkai,* Bukkyō no shisō, no. 9 (Tokyo: Kadokawa shoten, 1968), 105–107.

22. Ninian Smart, *Reasons and Faiths: An Investigation of Religious Discourse, Christian and Non-Christian* (London: Routledge & Kegan Paul, 1958).

23. *Mūlamadhyamakakārikā* 25:20.

24. See T 32.575–583, or Yoshito S. Hakeda, trans. and commentator, *The Awakening of Faith in Mahāyāna* (New York: Columbia University Press, 1967).

25. The editors are keenly aware of, and very much regret, the fact that Pure Land Buddhism, consideration of which is essential to any full treatment of mārga, is glaringly absent from this volume.

26. *Wu-liang-shou ching* 1, *T* 12.268c18–20. *Anutpattikadharmakṣānti* is the realization gleaned by the bodhisattva on the seventh *bhūmi,* when he realizes that all dharmas are eternally uncreated and empty. Through his acquiescence to that fact, the bodhisattva is able to perceive directly the quiescence inherent to all phenomena and thus he overcomes all limited views about the conditioned nature of things.

27. We employ the term "indeterminate" here in the sense in which Bimal K. Matilal has used it in his discussions of Mādhyamika. See his *Epistemology, Logic, and Grammar in Indian Philosophical Analysis* (The Hague and Paris: Mouton, 1971), esp. pp. 146–167.

28. This classical Mahāyāna theme was given special emphasis in the Hua-yen tradition of East Asian Buddhism. It also served as part of the foundation of Hua-yen mārga theory. According to that theory, the bodhisattva's path is both complex and simple, both instantaneous and gradual. It comprises as many as fifty-three stages and stations (matching Sudhana's fifty-three *kalyānamitra*), but in each stage, even the most elementary, the final goal of buddhahood is proleptically and causally present. Li T'ung-hsüan's (635?–730?) expressions of this mystery are authoritative for much of the later tradition, and a typical example of them is the following, from the introduction to his *Exposition of the Flower Garland Scripture* (*Hua-yen-ching lun* 1, *T* 36.730a3–5): "And so with the ten stages and ten abodes among the five divisions of the bodhisattva's path, the fruit of buddhahood *(fo-kuo)* is present in each and all of them, just as the ocean is present in each droplet of sea water. This is because the various practices are not carried out apart from the buddha-nature and it is just by means of this buddha-nature that progressive cultivation *(chin-hsiu)* is possible." It became common for Hua-yen thinkers to discuss the various relations between cause and fruit by means of their analogy with the various relations (contrast, complementarity, difference, identity, interfusion, mutual support, etc.) among the "three sages," i.e., among Vairocana, Samantabhadra, and Mañjuśrī, the former representing the fruit or effect of attainment while the latter two represent

cause or practice. See, for example, the sententious and influential *San-sheng yüan-jung kuan-men* (Contemplations of the Perfect Interfusion of the Three Sages, *T* 45.671a–672b), attributed to Ch'eng-kuan (738–839?).

29. This is a view especially associated in modern East Asian Buddhist scholarship with Dōgen's (1200–1253) dictum, *shushō ittō* (unification of cultivation and realization), but of course it was not really original with him. See *Shōbōgenzō,* "Bendōwa."

30. The Hua-yen and Ch'an patriarch Tsung-mi (780–841) gave classical expression to this notion, which echoed repeatedly in the later history of Ch'an, Sŏn, and Zen. See Peter N. Gregory, "Sudden Enlightenment Followed by Gradual Cultivation: Tsung-mi's Analysis of Mind," in idem, ed., *Sudden and Gradual: Approaches to Enlightenment in Chinese Thought,* Studies in East Asian Buddhism 5 (Honolulu: University of Hawaii Press, 1987), 279–320.

31. We allude, of course, to Shinran's (1173–1262) version of Pure Land doctrine, the conventional interpretation of which holds that he had foresworn traditional notions of mārga and had discarded practice or cultivation in favor of faith. However, despite his claim that the faith expressed in the *nembutsu* is "non-practice" *(higyō),* it is clear that faith is itself a discipline, and a rather rigorous one at that, regardless of its unconventionality (elsewhere, in fact, Shinran calls it "the great practice" [*daigyō*], *Kyōgyōshinshō* II). On this point see Tokunaga Michio, "Shinran no daigyō ni tsuite," in Nihon Bukkyō Gakkai, eds., *Bukkyō ni okeru shūgyō to sono rironteki konkyo* (Kyoto: Heirakuji, 1980), 405–420. Moreover, reliance on faith rather than conventional practice falls short of being an entirely anti-mārga attitude insofar as it need not lead to absolute antinomianism. So Shinran himself explained when, in reply to someone who had interpreted Amida's vow as encouragement to commit evil, he noted that "it is not necessary to take poison just because there is a remedy available" (*Tannishō* XIII).

32. See Jeffrey Broughton, "Early Ch'an Schools in Tibet," in Robert M. Gimello and Peter N. Gregory, eds., *Studies in Ch'an and Hua-yen,* Studies in East Asian Buddhism 1 (Honolulu: University of Hawaii Press, 1983), 1–68.

33. *The Eastern Buddhist* 19 (Autumn 1986): 118–119. The book Gilkey is here reviewing, edited by William LaFleur, was published in 1985 by University of Hawaii Press.

34. There is a growing literature exploring these aspects of the issue of Buddhism and morality. The following are a few of the general works we have found useful on the subject, even though we do not agree with all the arguments they adduce:

Douglas A. Fox, "Zen and Ethics: Dōgen's Synthesis," *PEW* 21 (January 1971): 33–41.

George Rupp, "The Relationship between Nirvāṇa and Saṃsāra: An Essay on the Evolution of Buddhist Ethics," *PEW* 21 (January 1971): 55–67.

Luis O. Gómez, "Emptiness and Moral Perfection," *PEW* 23 (July 1973): 361–373.

Charles Wei-hsün Fu, "Morality and Beyond: The Neo-Confucian Confrontation with Mahāyāna Buddhism," *PEW* 23 (July 1973): 375–396.

A. D. Brear, "The Nature and Status of Moral Behavior in the Zen Buddhist Tradition," *PEW* 24 (October 1974): 429–437.

Thomas P. Kasulis, *Zen Action/Zen Person* (Honolulu: University of Hawaii Press, 1981), esp. 94–99.

Charles Wei-hsün Fu, "Chu Hsi on Buddhism," in Wing-tsit Chan, ed., *Chu*

Hsi and Neo-Confucianism (Honolulu: University of Hawaii Press, 1986), 377–407.

James Whitehill, "Is There a Zen Ethic?" *The Eastern Buddhist* 20 (Spring 1987): 9–33.

35. *Mūlamadhyamakakārikā* 24:10 (for the Chinese, see *T* 30.33a).

36. It was something like this, in part, to which the Hua-yen thinker Fa-tsang (643–712) was referring in his scholastic ruminations on the "six meanings of causation," as when he noted that in one sense any cause may have efficacy *(li)* while also being empty. See *Hua-yen wu-chiao chang* 4, *T* 45.502b. However, the issue of how *vyavahāra* or *saṃvṛti* may be efficacious is difficult and has long been controversial within Buddhism. The most thoroughgoing apophatic traditions were reluctant even to consider the matter. Thus, as David Ruegg has noted, "Candrakīrti evidently regards the surface-level processes of transactional usage as causally indeterminate—even as antinomic and unamenable to ontological construction." Ruegg goes on to note that this was a principal issue separating Candrakīrti and the Prāsaṅgika tradition of Mādhyamika from Bhāvaviveka and the Svātantrika tradition. One might also mention that the issue seems to have played a role in the differentiation of Yogācāra from Mādhyamika. See David S. Ruegg, *The Literature of the Madhyamaka School of Philosophy in India,* A History of Indian Literature, vol. VII, fasc. 1 (Wiesbaden: Otto Harrassowitz, 1981), 75.

37. For one of the more recent of his several astute and learned treatments of this theme, see David Seyfort Ruegg, "The Buddhist Notion of an Immanent Absolute as a Problem in Comparative Religious and Philosophical Hermeneutics," which comprises the first of its author's 1987 Jordan Lectures delivered at the School of Oriental and African Studies, University of London. These lectures have been published as idem, *Buddha-nature, Mind, and the Problem of Gradualism in a Comparative Perspective: On the Transmission and Reception of Buddhism in India and Tibet* (London: The School of Oriental and African Studies, University of London, 1989).

Glossary

Abe Masao 阿部正雄
Amida 阿彌陀
Butsu 佛
Ch'an 禪
ch'ao-yüeh 超越
cheng-chung-lai 正中來
cheng-chung-pien 正中偏
cheng-wu 證悟
Ch'eng-kuan 澄觀
chieh-wu 解悟
chien-chung-chih 兼中至
chien-chung-tao 兼中到
Chih-i 智顗
chin-hsiu 進修
Chinul 知訥
chu 住
Chu Hsi 朱熹
daigyō 大行
Dōgen 道元
ekō 廻向
Fo 佛
fo-kuo 佛果
goi 五位
gyō 行
Gyōnen 凝然
henchūshō 偏中正
higyō 非行
Hizō hōyaku 祕藏寶鑰
hsin 信
hsing 行
Hua-yen-ching lun 華嚴經論
Hua-yen wu-chiao chang 華嚴五教章
hui-hsiang 廻向
Hwaŏm 華嚴
i 依
igyō 易行

ji 地
jiriki 自力
Jōdo hōmon genryūshō 淨土法門源流章
jū 住
jūjūshin 十住心
Jūjūshinron 十住心論
k'an-hua 看話禪
Kegon 華嚴
kenchūshi 兼中至
kenchūtō 兼中到
kōan 公案
Kūkai 空海
Kyōgyōshinshō 教行信證
li 理
Lin-chi 臨濟
mappō 末法
miao-chüeh 妙覺
mo-fa 末法
myōkaku 妙覺
nangyō 難行
nembutsu 念佛
noh 能
p'an-chiao chih tu 判教制度
P'ang Yün 龐蘊
Pao-t'ang 保唐
pien-chung-cheng 偏中正
San-sheng yüan-jung kuan-men 三聖圓融觀門
shin 信
Shinran 親鸞
Shōbōgenzō 正法眼藏
shōchūhen 正中偏
shōchūrai 正中來
shushō ittō 修證一等
Sŏn 禪
Sōtō 曹洞
T'ien-t'ai 天台
Ta-hui Tsung-kao 大慧宗杲
Ta-sheng ch'i-hsin lun 大乘起信論
Tannishō 歎異抄
tariki 他力
Tendai 天台
teng-chüeh 等覺
ti 地
tōgaku 等覺
Ts'ao-tung 曹洞
Tsung-mi 宗密
wu-wei 五位
Yoshizu Yoshihide 吉津宜英
Zazenron 坐禪論
Zen 禪

Theravāda Buddhist Soteriology and the Paradox of Desire

GRACE G. BURFORD

Introduction

The path (mārga) to enlightenment has traditionally functioned as the focus of Buddhist practice and theory. As Robert Buswell and Robert Gimello have observed, each of the various Buddhist schools delineates and endorses a specific path, or pattern of religious behavior, that is seen as leading inevitably to a particular religious goal. In many cases we find quite a few points of disagreement among these different versions of Buddhist soteriology and the interpretations of reality they imply. The Buddhist tradition's lack of consistency with regard to the Buddha's most basic claims comes as no great surprise because of its long history and extensive geographical spread. Such inconsistency, although of some interest to the historian of religions, has little significance for the Buddhist believer-practitioners who are aligned with one of the many specific types of Buddhism. Inconsistencies between the doctrines and practices of any one school of Buddhism and those of another have little impact on the followers of either one. These inconsistencies are not used to challenge the basic truth-claim of the religion because no one takes the entire corpus of teachings attributed to the Buddha over the past twenty-five centuries—from the early Pali scriptures to the later Chinese, Japanese, and Tibetan texts—as a reliable record of the truth that the Buddha saw and taught.[1]

In contrast, the presence of inconsistencies within a particular Buddhist tradition raises serious questions. In this case inconsistencies are problematic both for the believer-practitioner in that tradition who attempts to implement the advice of the Buddha in daily practice and for the philosopher who seeks to evaluate this version of the Buddha's teachings as a description of a path to the highest human good. Every version of the buddhadhamma (truth, teachings of the Buddha) includes components we might distinguish as epistemology, metaphysics, cosmology, soteriology, and ethics. Some inconsistencies within this complex of teachings may actually pose no problem whatsoever. After all, a specific bit of practical advice is not generally expected to be universally applicable. For example, it does not seem unreasonable for the Buddha to have told one person to work hard and give alms and another to take up the life of a wandering mendicant and gather alms. This inconsistency does not pose a serious challenge to the validity of the Buddha's teachings because both pieces of advice reflect a consistent, underlying, normative value theory. The purpose of both giving and gathering alms is assumed to be the cultivation of selflessness, and the two practices can be seen as different stages of the path to eventual elimination of selfish attachment.

Indeed, even more theoretical points of doctrine may safely conflict as long as they are explained in terms of a common evaluation of what is fundamentally true and good. Insofar as the various teachings attributed to the Buddha concerning the path to the highest ideal reflect a consistent assessment of what is ultimately valuable, no particular inconsistencies among them seriously challenge either the believer-practitioner's ability to put them into practice or the philosopher's acceptance of the fundamental Buddhist claim that the Buddha discovered and taught the truth.

If the scriptures of any particular branch or school of Buddhism are truthful records of the Buddha's efforts to teach his followers how to reach, as he had done, the highest religious goal, they must contain answers to two crucial questions: (1) what is the highest religious goal? and (2) how does one attain it? Here I will consider what happens within one particular Buddhist tradition, the Theravāda, when one of its most ancient normative texts implies conflicting answers to these fundamental questions—when it presents two different explicit patterns of religious behavior that reflect contradictory concepts of the highest religious goal.

The Theravāda is the oldest known school of Buddhism, describing itself as not only the earliest but also the most conservative of the schools, the one that preserves unchanged the words *(vāda)* of the Buddha as remembered and codified shortly after his death in the sixth century B.C.E. by his immediate disciples, the elders *(theras)*. For the strictly orthodox Theravāda believer, there is no such thing as doctrinal development within the Theravāda canonical texts. In this view, the Pali scriptures record the very words of the Buddha *(buddhavacana)*, the fully enlightened one, whose teachings required no improvement or alteration.

The Theravāda did develop a long tradition of commentarial literature in which many skilled interpreters explained the teachings of the Buddha, as recorded in the Pali canon, in greater and greater detail.

Their aim is not to alter the Buddha's teachings, however, but to dispel any appearance of inconsistency or confusion within the recorded buddhadhamma. From this traditional Theravāda perspective, the Buddha's specific advice may have varied from time to time or follower to follower, but it all reflects a consistent and coherent worldview that an able commentator can elucidate. This commentarial tradition began even before the closing of the canon (ca. second century B.C.E.) and reached its peak during the fifth century C.E. in the literary activity of Buddhaghosa, whose work is considered normative in the traditional Theravāda interpretation of buddhadhamma.

The canonical Theravāda text I will examine here, the *Aṭṭhakavagga,* is one of the few Pali texts for which there is substantial evidence of its historical place within the early Buddhist literature. It appears in the Chinese *Āgamas* with contents almost identical to the Pali version.[2] In addition, the Bhabru edict of Aśoka refers to several suttas that appear to belong to the *Aṭṭhakavagga.*[3] Pali, Sanskrit, and Chinese texts refer often to the *Aṭṭhakavagga* by name.[4] The most convincing indication of its relative antiquity within Buddhist literature is the fact that a commentary on it (the *Mahāniddesa*) forms the major portion of the only commentary accepted as canonical by the Theravāda tradition. Thus the *Aṭṭhakavagga* seems to have been a popular text that has been preserved, referred to, and interpreted within the Buddhist tradition since its early history. By Buddhaghosa's time, it had long been treated as the fourth *vagga* of the *Sutta-nipāta,* and Buddhaghosa comments on it as such in his commentary on the *Sutta-nipāta* (the *Paramatthajotikā II*). By focusing on the *Aṭṭhakavagga,* we can consider not only a very interesting and relatively early Buddhist text, but also the Theravāda interpretations of that text dating from two significant periods in the history of this Buddhist tradition, namely, the late-canonical period and the time of Buddhaghosa.

The *Aṭṭhakavagga*

The Ideal and the Path

No one term emerges in the *Aṭṭhakavagga* as a label for the ultimate goal of the path therein prescribed. For example, one cannot examine all instances of the word "nibbāna" in this text and hope to understand the ideal goal according to the teaching it presents. Neither is it possible to understand this goal by examining all the other terms used in the *Aṭṭhakavagga* to designate the ideal goal, because that goal is for the most part discussed indirectly—through depictions of what exemplary persons do and avoid doing, and through contrasts drawn between such persons and others who represent less-than-ideal attitudes and behavior.

This linguistic feature of the text reflects a significant aspect of the religious worldview preserved in the *Aṭṭhakavagga:* the definition of the highest ideal is inseparable from the delineation of how persons can live life fully and well. That is, the *Aṭṭhakavagga* focuses primarily on the path, which it defines in terms of the person who cultivates it. Further, through its almost exclusive focus on explicit patterns of behavior and characteristics or qualities of persons (both ideal and less than ideal), it implies that the goal is equivalent to the path perfected (i.e., properly followed). If one does what ideal persons do, one has followed the path and attained the goal.[5] The summum bonum is neither transcendent nor categorically distinct from what is good to do and what is bad to do, for all people, in everyday life.

The terms the *Aṭṭhakavagga* uses most frequently to refer to the goal are *suddhi* (purity) and *santi* (calmness). According to the *Aṭṭhakavagga,* when one has achieved the ideal, one has achieved purity and calmness. Yet neither of these terms represents an abstract notion of a goal apart from the ideal person's qualities. In this text purity and calmness have no significance apart from pure or calm people.

Further, as characteristics of ideal persons, purity and calmness tend to reveal more about the less-than-ideal condition than about the ideal condition. Purity, as an ideal, points to the fact that nonideal persons are subject to certain specific impurities. Although the text discusses the impurities considered characteristic of less-than-ideal persons, the exact meaning of purity remains unspecified. Purity does not involve doing certain things or being a certain way, but rather consists of not behaving in specific ways. The same observation holds generally for calmness, which amounts to an absence of anxieties. Such anxieties can be pinpointed in the text, but calmness is just calmness (i.e., not being agitated, not being excitable, not being quick to anger, feel grief, etc.).

Several other terms that occur in the *Aṭṭhakavagga* could represent the goal that ideal persons have reached. *Viveka* (seclusion or separation) is used to refer to seclusion or separation of the individual person, rather than expressing a characteristic of the goal itself. It is not that the goal is isolated from the less-than-ideal world in any way; rather, the ideal person strives for seclusion (v. 822) and sees seclusion (v. 851). Likewise, *khema* (security) is used to refer directly to a condition of the ideal person. With both these terms, the *Aṭṭhakavagga* continues to elucidate the goal by contrasting it with qualities of less-than-ideal life.

The Theravāda tradition's primary label for the goal, nibbāna, occurs in the *Aṭṭhakavagga* three times. Verse 940 advises the person striving for the ideal to "train for his/her nibbāna";[6] v. 822 describes the one striving for *viveka* as "near nibbāna"; and v. 942 describes a trainee on the path to the ideal as one "having [his/her] mind [set] on nibbāna." These three instances of the term "nibbāna" are the only times the *Aṭṭhakavagga* uses labels for the ideal goal that do not refer to a particular attribute or quality of the person who has reached it. Since there is no definition of "nibbāna" in the *Aṭṭhakavagga,* we should not rule out the possibility that in this text the word does signify something specific about the ideal person that has been obscured by the later development of this word. The one occurrence in the *Aṭṭhakavagga* of its verb-form counterpart, *nibbāti,* indicates that even this goal-referent was understood in terms of the actions or achievements of an ideal person:

> Having seen what does a bhikkhu *nibbāti* [become cool?], not grasping anything in the world?[7]

All four of these examples are consistent with the *Aṭṭhakavagga*'s overall treatment of terms that refer to the goal, in that they focus on how the ideal person strives for the goal, rather than substantively describing the ideal condition itself.

In light of the *Aṭṭhakavagga*'s anthropocentric treatment of the goal itself, it comes as no surprise that almost every line of every verse in this text says something about the persons who have achieved this ideal or are striving for it. This information falls into two broad categories: positive terminology concerning what the ideal person has accomplished, and—by far the greater number of instances—negative vocabulary relating what such a person has eliminated or overcome.

We find a limited set of words in the *Aṭṭhakavagga* for ideal persons and—in verses in which the training that leads to the goal is recommended—for potential ideal persons. The terms that function in this way most often are *muni* (silent one), bhikkhu, and brāhmaṇa. *Dhīra* (wise one), *dhona, santa* (calm one), *vedagū* (knowledgeable one), *vidvā* (knowing one), *vimutta* (released one), *nāga, pāragū* and *pāraṃgata* (one gone beyond), *paṇḍita* (wise one), and *samaṇa* also occur.[8]

Most of these labels communicate something about the qualities and characteristics of the persons they designate, indicating that silence, wisdom, calmness, knowledge, and the like are exemplary features of ideal persons; indeed, these characteristics have been adopted to epitomize such persons. The remainder of the positive terminology relating to these persons emerges in the *Aṭṭhakavagga*'s descriptions of ideal persons' positive characteristics and in specific recommendations to persons who would strive to attain this ideal.

According to the *Aṭṭhakavagga,* ideal persons are mindful *(sata, satimā).* Their primary positive characteristics have to do with seeing and knowing. As we have seen, an ideal person sees *viveka* (seclusion, v. 851) and *khema* (security, v. 809); such a person has open eyes (v. 921), yet is not visually greedy (v. 922) and has downcast eyes (v. 972). Thus such a one controls vision and minimizes distraction. Observation of the unhappy consequences of less-than-ideal behavior provides a strong motivation to strive for the ideal (e.g., vv. 777, 817). Seeing is both the final prerequisite for attaining the goal (v. 915) and the ideal condition itself (v. 795).

The importance of knowing is clear in the *Aṭṭhakavagga,* both as a means to the goal and as an attribute of the ideal person. Several terms in the *Aṭṭhakavagga* signify knowing and knowledge or wisdom, such as *paññā* (wisdom), *ñatvā* (having known), many other forms of *jānāti* (to know), *veda* (knowledge), and *vidvā* (knowing—an old perfect active participle in *-vas*). Wisdom frees one from illusions (v. 847), and reverence for it leads one to strive for the ideal (v. 969). The ideal person knows dhamma as well as the dangers of less-than-ideal living (e.g., vv. 775, 792, 933, 943, 947). In v. 971 the trainee for the goal is encouraged to "know moderation for the sake of satisfaction here."[9] To know is both the chief means to the goal and the primary characteristic activity of one who has achieved it. To be wise is the highest good. Accordingly, in the one instance of the term "buddha" in the *Aṭṭhakavagga,* it functions as an adjective ("awakened"), applied to Gotama. Likewise, *sambodhi* (awakening or enlightenment) refers once in the *Aṭṭhakavagga* to the ideal goal itself, since the trainee for the goal is called "one desirous of awakening" (*sambodhikāma,* v. 963).

In addition to being alert and knowledgeable, the ideal person is unmoved by this seeing and knowing. This notion of equanimity is expressed with forms of *upekkha* and *sama.* Here equanimity is equivalent to mental composure (v. 972) and incompatible with selfish grasping (vv. 855, 911–912). Someone with equanimity is not affected by praise or blame (vv. 895–896). The ideal person is "the same in all circumstances" (v. 952).

Finally, the ideal person is released, liberated. We have seen that the ideal person is freed by wisdom (v. 847) and that such a person is sometimes designated as a *vimutta* (released one). In v. 877 release is said to come after knowledge and is described as concomitant to refraining from arguments. According to v. 975, the mindful person's *citta* (mind) is released. All in all, in the *Aṭṭhakavagga* release is associated with a mental state that is knowledgeable, yet free and not defensive.

Release or freedom, not unlike purity and calmness, defines the ideal person at least partly in negative terms, which leads us to inquire: from what exactly are these persons free? Although goal-referents are scarce and positive terminology rather vague in the *Aṭṭhakavagga,* it is full of negative vocabulary, which occurs in both specific ethical injunctions and in a complex, broader teaching against desire and grasping. Almost every sutta of the *Aṭṭhakavagga* includes a number of formulaically reiterated injunctions against particular types of behavior, including indulging in grief, lamentation, envy, greed, anger, false-speaking, doubt, pride, conceit, backbiting, and selfishness.[10]

Desire stands out as the primary problem, according to the *Aṭṭhakavagga.* A strong condemnation of desire—desire in and of itself, desire for particular persons and objects and ideas, all action that naturally follows upon desire (namely, grasping or acquiring), and any dependence that results from action motivated by desire—emerges from the rich and varied vocabulary relating to desire. The *Aṭṭhakavagga* describes a vicious circle of wrong behavior, a self-perpetuating series of events based on indulgence in desire. Once one desires and thereby binds oneself through grasping or attachment, that very bondage increases the likelihood of becoming involved in further attachment and desire. The ideal person desists from all such activity (grasping, attachment); having undermined its cause (desire), such a one eliminates its ill effect (dependence on or bondage to particular persons, objects, and ideas).

In the *Aṭṭhakavagga,* two types of persons are described: ideal and less than ideal. The two modes of living that they represent are contrasted for the benefit of those who would make the transition to the ideal by abandoning the ways of less-than-ideal persons and emulating the ways of ideal persons, thereby attaining the goal themselves. The less-than-ideal sort of life, led by selfish, deluded persons, is marked by desire, personal and interpersonal strife, grief, anxiety, attachment, and dependence. The ideal life, led by knowledgeable persons who clearly see life and the world as it unfolds and who live in accordance with wisdom, is characterized by harmony and calmness, purified of the negative qualities of ordinary life.

The goal described here is anthropocentric and individually oriented, in every way; whether one lives in the ideal or less-than-ideal manner is entirely one's own responsibility and affects only oneself. Although we might assume that social harmony naturally would result from everyone following the teachings this text prescribes, this is never cited as a motivation for doing so.[11] Even more significantly, the goal itself consists of living in the ideal way. The means recommended for achieving the ideal —being alert, watchful, and equable; seeing and knowing; avoiding conceit, greed, and slander; rejecting desire; not grasping; being free of dependence on any particular persons and things—are often utilized in the *Aṭṭhakavagga* as descriptions of the defining characteristics, attitudes, and behaviors of persons who have achieved the ideal goal. Indeed, the text never describes ideal persons or the condition they have achieved in terms other than these. On the basis of the evidence of the *Aṭṭhakavagga* itself, there is no way to distinguish between ideal and less-than-ideal persons except by the perfect consistency with which ideal persons behave in the ideal ways.

This continuity of path and goal reflects and expresses the continuity of values operative in this account of the ideal goal and how one achieves it. The values remain constant throughout; none is added at the point of reaching the ideal condition. The same attitudes and actions that are valued as good along the way to the goal, when they are but inconsistently maintained by the aspirant, prove to be valued as good ultimately, when they are maintained consistently by the ideal person.

Two Approaches to the Goal

The *Aṭṭhakavagga* emphasizes the problematic nature of desire and attachment. One object of desire that it singles out for special attention is view *(diṭṭhi).* In the first instance of the term, v. 781 says:

> How could one who is led by desire, intent on what s/he prefers,
> fulfilling his/her own [expectations],
> overcome his/her very own view?
> Just as that one would know, so would s/he preach.[12]

Here the *Aṭṭhakavagga* treats a less-than-ideal person's espousal of a particular view as a manifestation of desire. Due to desire, one prefers one view over all others and thus prevents oneself from seeing the truth and becoming truly knowledgeable. There is no worse barrier to mindful seeing than the belief that one has already seen and known fully.

Further, the *Aṭṭhakavagga* indicates that such a person prefers a view that legitimates and reinforces his or her desires. The less-than-ideal person substitutes a particular view for a direct apprehension of reality. If one does not refer to reality directly as its own truth, the *Aṭṭhakavagga* implies, one's only criterion for choosing among the competing formulations of truth is selfish desire: which view best states what one wishes were true? When one has found such a view, one will defend it with conviction born not of personal and direct apprehension of the truth, but rather of the fact that it meets that primary selfish criterion. Hence attachment to views epitomizes the viciously circular, self-perpetuating nature of desire, attachment, and dependence in general. A good number of verses in the text dwell on this topic, elucidating the dangerous consequences of attachment to views, such as being drawn constantly into quarrels and disputes, losing one's composure, and selfishly denigrating those whose views differ from one's own.

Several verses condemn all relative ranking of and preference *(purakkhata)* for things and people. This follows logically from the notion that desire and attachment are major obstacles to achieving the ideal goal. To evaluate any one thing or person as superior to another, this reasoning implies, is to indulge in desire and exclusive attachment. The *Aṭṭhakavagga*'s strong condemnation of attachment to *diṭṭhi* represents an application of this principle to preference for particular ideas and theories, as is evident in v. 796:

> In contrast to what a person stuck in views calls "highest,"
> and considers to be supreme in the world,
> all else is "inferior,"
> therefore s/he has not gone past disputes.[13]

Despite the anti-*diṭṭhi* condemnation of all preference and relative ranking, v. 969 presents preference in a positive light:

> Having preferred wisdom, having joy in [what is] lovely,
> one should destroy those dangers.[14]

In addition, the *Aṭṭhakavagga*'s disapproval (e.g., vv. 796–798) of holding one thing as supreme *(parama, uttari)* and of considering some persons superior to others clashes with its recommendation in v. 822 that one train in *viveka* (seclusion), since that is the highest *(uttama)* practice for noble ones *(ariyas)*.

There is a certain ranking in the very identification of particular persons as ideal and others as less than ideal. Thus it is not surprising that the text's anti-*diṭṭhi* position introduces some inconsistencies into its treatment of exemplary persons. Some verses cite experts or skilled ones *(kusalas)* as authorities, indicating that their words are truthful and should evoke respect (e.g., vv. 782, 783, 798, 830). Yet other verses, concerned with the *diṭṭhi* issue, refer to *kusalas* as argumentative fools (vv. 878, 879, 885). In addition, vv. 866 and 868 refer respectfully to the *samaṇa* as the teacher of dhammas (truths), and numerous verses portray brāhmaṇas as exemplary ideal persons (e.g., vv. 790, 802, 843, 911). But *samaṇas* are also portrayed as argumentative and closed-minded preachers (vv. 828, 883), while v. 859 groups *samaṇas* and brāhmaṇas with common persons and depicts their teaching activities as less than ideal.

In terms of specific actions, we have seen that v. 822 recommends training in seclusion as the highest practice for noble ones. We have also noted that the *Aṭṭhakavagga* frequently emphasizes seeing and knowing as the key attributes of an ideal person. Considering the text's numerous positive references to seeing, one might be surprised at its vehemently negative treatment of *diṭṭhi,* since the notion of a view is at least related to the process of seeing. Yet it is easy enough to infer the rationale underlying this argument. Although seeing is a good thing—leading to the goal, even constituting the goal, if it is done well—formulation of that vision into a view somehow betrays the value of it. However, in presenting the anti-*diṭṭhi* argument, the *Aṭṭhakavagga* occasionally takes the condemnation of views even further, to include seeing itself; it also contains several verses that condemn knowing and knowledge. Verses 788–789 reject knowing as a means to attaining the ideal condition, while v. 800 relates knowing to forming a view and advises the aspirant against attachment and dependence:

> Having abandoned assumption, not clinging,
> [an ideal person] does not depend even on knowledge.[15]

Verse 909 is the epitome of these verses that deny the efficacy of seeing and knowing as means to the goal:

> A person who sees, sees name and form,
> and having seen, will know them as such.
> Let him/her see as much or as little as s/he likes;
> the experts do not say that [one attains] purity by means of that.[16]

If one ought not to prefer any one teacher, exemplary person, or method for reaching the ideal goal, is there a particular teaching that conveys the ideal? The *Aṭṭhakavagga* wavers on this point, too, as its uses of "dhamma" illustrate. Verse 792 exalts knowing and wisdom and regards "dhamma" as the true teaching. In a number of other verses this term is also used to signify the correct teaching which, when known, frees one from dependence (e.g., vv. 856, 921, 947). Yet in v. 785 "dhamma" signifies a limited view that functions as an object of attachment, and v. 824 indicates that dhammas can be problematic as exclusive, limited teachings:

> They argue "just this is purity,"
> they deny that purity is in other dhammas.[17]

Teachings inherently exclude other teachings. Verse 886 states this directly by noting that if one follows a particular teaching, one inevitably depicts one's own view as true *(sacca)* and all others as false *(musa)*. To follow a particular teaching is to prefer or rank ideas and things in the world—which activity ultimately derives, this argument implies, from desire.

The most striking inconsistency that results from the anti-*diṭṭhi* argument concerns the ideal goal itself. We have just seen that v. 824 depicts less-than-ideal persons as defending their own dhamma in terms of its exclusive claim to purity *(suddhi)*. Similarly, vv. 898 and 906 argue that those who present their teachings or paths as true render purity exclusive and so, the text implies, invalid. If the ideal person is beyond all preferences and holds nothing as beyond or further (v. 795), it follows that s/he does not even prefer purity over impurity, or grasp calmness in preference to anxiety (v. 900). Yet the *Aṭṭhakavagga* itself—attributed to the most exemplary of all ideal persons, the Buddha—draws clear distinctions between ideal and less-than-ideal persons, practices, and teachings, and definitely teaches that the ideal is ultimately preferable to the less-than-ideal condition.

The specific inconsistencies concerning ideal persons and practices that occur within the teaching recorded in the *Aṭṭhakavagga* verses point to the presence in this text of two different approaches to the ideal. On the one hand, persons strive for an ideal condition that both consists of and is reached through (1) cultivating seeing and knowing, and (2) avoiding attachment and desire. Once they have attained this goal, such ideal persons teach others how to follow a similar path. On the other hand, to prefer certain persons, actions, or views over any others is itself to desire and to be attached. The ideal of desirelessness consists of defending no particular view or path, avoiding argumentation, and living entirely without preference—even for a revered teacher, respected teaching, or ideal condition.

The specific condemnation of attachment to *diṭṭhis* (views) follows logically from the general condemnation of desire. The *Aṭṭhakavagga*'s argument against *diṭṭhis* focuses on this type of attachment as particularly pervasive and dangerous. The issue is not whether one's particular view is true or false, but whether one is attached to any particular view.[18] Presumably, even if one were to discover a true *diṭṭhi*—and this possibility is never explicitly ruled out—aligning oneself with it, to the exclusion of conflicting views, would prevent one from attaining the ideal. In other words, despite all the talk about *diṭṭhis* recorded in the *Aṭṭhakavagga,* the discussion is not really about views and opinions, but rather about the formulation and defense of them. As Luis Gómez has observed, the *Aṭṭhakavagga* neither proposes a new view nor systematically rejects all views.[19] What is soundly rejected is attachment to views.

The *Aṭṭhakavagga*'s recommendations of certain means to a goal, exaltation of certain persons as exemplary of the ideal, and descriptions of certain conditions or qualities as of ultimate value raise two types of questions about the viability of the anti-*diṭṭhi* teaching. The first concerns the contradictions between the general anti-desire teaching and the anti-*diṭṭhi* teaching about the nature of the ideal and the path to it. The second concerns the status of the teaching of no-views as a view itself. Doesn't the no-views teaching unavoidably perpetuate the discrimination of "true" and "false" by its own contradiction of the claims —found in the *Aṭṭhakavagga* itself—that certain means lead to a particular ideal and that certain persons are exemplary of that ideal? Can a dhamma that consists of the rejection of all attachment, even to dhammas themselves, be presented coherently in oral or written form? Can the truth, so conceived, ever be expressed in words, as a specific teaching?

Although the latter type of question is a theoretical, intellectual problem, the former illustrates why it is a serious one, even in a fully practical setting. If one were to endeavor to achieve the ideal by means of the methods set out in the *Aṭṭhakavagga,* it would be crucial to be able to discern which means (if any) that text is actually recommending, which persons (if any) are to be regarded as exemplary role models, and which conditions or qualities (if any) one should aim to attain. It is difficult to see how such information could be derived from this teaching without transgressing the general principle, espoused in the anti-*diṭṭhi* argument, that no view, way, teaching, or teacher should be preferred over any other. If "choicelessness" is ideal, then how does one choose what to do?[20]

The danger of attachment to particular views concerning means to the goal, ideal persons, and the nature of the goal itself is the central concern of the anti-*diṭṭhi* teaching. The anti-views argument is not presented in order to replace all previous, untrue teachings with a new, improved teaching.[21] Consequently there is, at least in theory, no place within this teaching for particular advice to the aspirant for the goal. As long as the ideal is held to be complete detachment from preference for particular, exclusive teachings, no authority can be found for recommending that the aspirant follow particular means to particular ends. The view of no-views is a teaching of nonduality. As such, it cannot explicitly deny the validity of views that deny the validity of other views without undermining its own authority.

This paradox brings to mind another that is raised by the Buddhist teachings: the paradox of desire. The parallel amounts to more than mere coincidence of form. Briefly stated, the Buddhist paradox of desire is that desirelessness is ideal, yet one must cultivate one's desire to attain the ideal in order to be motivated to continue to strive for that goal. Every action one performs on the path to the goal is a manifestation of desire. If one is ever to attain desirelessness, it will be by means of desire-driven actions. Although ultimately one strives to be free of all desires, the only way to accomplish this is by means of desire.[22]

The focus of the anti-*diṭṭhi* teaching is, as we have seen, the less-than-ideal nature of attachment to particular views. As a philosophical stance, this teaching leads to self-contradiction in terms of the values it upholds. On the one hand, nonduality is ideal, and any preference for one teaching over another belies true understanding. On the other hand, the duality of desire versus nondesire, or of duality versus nonduality, reflects something real, and the preference for one (nondesire, nonduality) over the other (desire, duality) is ideal. This is simply a radical, extended form of the paradox of desire, in which both desire and the absence of desire are valued. It results from adding a very important component to the teaching that desire is characteristic of the less-than-ideal and must be eradicated in order to attain the goal. That component is views. By extending the objects of desire to include views, this teaching eventually forces the issue of the paradox of desire. By shifting the focus away from desire for things and people and existence—and toward attachment to views—it brings out the less obvious (and therefore even more troublesome) inconsistency of the teaching that identifies desire as the problem and then fails to show how the desire to end desire is different from any other sort of desire.[23] One cannot ignore the ease with which the anti-views argument is developed here: from the premise that desire is the root of all evil comes the argument that preference for any particular view, path, and even goal is counterproductive on the path to the ideal.

The Commentaries

The Ideal and the Path

In the course of defining and commenting on the *Aṭṭhakavagga*'s soteriological vocabulary, the *Mahāniddesa* commentator and Buddhaghosa present a highly developed understanding of the ideal goal and the path to it. They maintain a certain continuity with the *Aṭṭhakavagga*'s outlook, both in their emphasis on desire as the root cause of the problems of the less-than-ideal condition and in their descriptions of the path to the ideal in terms of specific negative actions and attitudes to be overcome by one aspiring to the summum bonum.

These commentators on the *Aṭṭhakavagga* interpret its contrasting depictions of less-than-ideal and ideal persons in terms of a complex path theory. The number of categories of persons goes from two (less than ideal and ideal) to at least three: ordinary persons, persons striving for the ideal, and ideal persons. Frequently these categories are even more numerous, as the commentators distinguish laypeople from monastics; those who might still backslide in their progress toward the ideal from those who have "entered the stream" and are assured of eventually attaining their goal; and those who have entered the stream from those who are "once-returners," "never-returners," and arahants (who have reached the highest goal). The path itself is marked by organized gradations of negative factors eliminated, is called "noble," and is described as eightfold. Here truth is encapsulated in another eightfold formula, that of the four noble truths concerning *dukkha* (discomfort, ill) plus the same four, but substituting *āsavas* (influxes, toxins) for *dukkha*. This constitutes a highly refined, complex soteriology that contrasts sharply with the simple notions of path and goal reflected in the *Aṭṭhakavagga*.[24]

Diṭṭhi *and the Paradox of Desire*

The *Aṭṭhakavagga*'s anti-*diṭṭhi* position takes to a logical extreme the notion that desire is the root cause of all that is wrong with the less-than-ideal condition, and concludes that all preferential ranking—even that of spiritual teachers, paths, and ideal goals—is ultimately a form of desire and therefore itself less than ideal. Although it is possible to see how the anti-*diṭṭhi* argument might have arisen from the general anti-desire view, which teaches a particular ideal, the presence of both in one text proves somewhat problematic. The two commentaries we are considering here are almost identical in their treatment of the specific inconsistencies raised by the juxtaposition of these two teachings in the *Aṭṭhakavagga,* and of the more theoretical paradox raised by the anti-*diṭṭhi* position itself.

The main difference between the two is that Buddhaghosa writes in a somewhat freer form. Not being limited, like the *Mahāniddesa,* to the task of explaining each term in the *Aṭṭhakavagga* with a separate gloss *(niddesa),* he can introduce new terms and draw connections among different words, lines, and verses. The *Paramatthajotikā II* often records noticeably smoother interpretations of particular verses than does the *Mahāniddesa,* but in most cases it provides a concisely reworded summary of the *Mahāniddesa*'s analysis.

The most problematic claim in the *Aṭṭhakavagga*'s anti-*diṭṭhi* argument is that preference or ranking is always a form of desire and therefore bad. This is problematic because the text itself clearly prefers some people, activities, and teachings over others. The commentaries encounter this problem even more obviously, since they are filled with complex rankings of types of behavior, persons, and even realms of existence.

The *Mahāniddesa* frequently offers a dual *(taṇhā-diṭṭhi)* definition of terms signifying desire, attachment, and dependence as both thirst *(taṇhā)* for a wide variety of objects and desire for (attachment to) a view *(diṭṭhi).* If this commentary were to follow the example of the *Aṭṭhakavagga,* we would expect it to explain the latter form of desire as the selfish attachment to any particular view. The *Mahāniddesa,* however, is very consistent in its interpretation of this form of desire as desire for specific wrong views, as opposed to allegiance to the one correct teaching (i.e., that of the Buddha).

Verse 781 of the *Aṭṭhakavagga* has already been quoted when examining the questions raised by the anti-*diṭṭhi* position:

> How could one who is led by desire, intent on what s/he prefers,
> fulfilling his/her own [expectations],
> overcome his/her very own view?
> Just as that one would know, so would s/he preach.[25]

The *niddesa* on v. 781 is equally useful for illustrating how the commentaries deal with this issue. It describes attachment to view in two ways. First, it refers to, but does not fully recount, a story in which some adherents of other sects try to lay the blame for a murder on the Buddha and his followers in order to regain their own lost possessions, fame, respect, and honor. Depicting these people as "having this view, indulgence, will, theory," as "intent on that and desiring that," the gloss says that they are "unable to overcome their own view, indulgence, will, theory, and intention," so their ill-repute returns. Therefore how could they overcome their own view?

Second, the *niddesa* lists ten views that such persons "hold as dogma, have grasped as complete, and so cannot relinquish." These ten views occur often elsewhere in the *Mahāniddesa,* in the following formulaic passage:

> The world is eternal, just this [is] truth, [all] else [is] delusion; the world is ephemeral; the world is finite; the world is infinite; the soul/life-principle [is] the body; the soul/life-principle [is] other than the body; the tathāgata is after death; the tathāgata is not after death; the tathāgata both is and is not after death; the tathāgata neither is nor is not after death—just this [is] truth, [all] else [is] delusion.[26]

Buddhaghosa also refers frequently to this list in the *Paramatthajotikā II.* According to the *Mahāniddesa,* these are the views the persons referred to in v. 781 "hold as dogma," and so forth. It cites these views again in its explanation of the last line of this verse. With reference to the idea that such persons fulfill their own expectations, the *Mahāniddesa* says they "render their views highest, best" and each claims

> This [i.e., my] teacher is omniscient; this teaching is well-taught; this group is well-practiced; this view is good; this way is well-attained; this path leads [one] out [of saṃsāra].[27]

But the problem here, judging from the commentaries' further explanations, is not the same problem the *Aṭṭhakavagga*'s anti-*diṭṭhi* argument raised. Here the problem lies in the fact that these particular persons have no right to make these claims precisely because their teacher is not omniscient, their teaching not well taught, and so on, so that their path is not one that leads them out of saṃsāra. Thus the *Mahāniddesa* (re: v. 790) explains that

> The brāhmaṇa does not say [etc.][28] that purity [etc.] is [accomplished] by means of an impure path, a wrong path, a path that does not lead [one] out [of saṃsāra], a path other than the foundations of mindfulness, other than the right exertions, other than the bases of psychic power, other than the faculties, other than the powers, other than the constituents of wisdom, other than the noble eightfold path.[29]

In numerous instances, when the *Aṭṭhakavagga* suttas devoted to explaining the *diṭṭhi* position condemn holding any one thing as highest, the *Mahāniddesa* explains that this means regarding any particular teacher, teaching, group, view, way, or path as right, and then goes on to attribute such reprehensible activity to persons who follow the wrong teachers, teachings, and so forth! This exemplifies the commentaries' treatment of this issue: when they try to preserve the *Aṭṭhakavagga*'s *diṭṭhi* argument, they produce extreme internal inconsistencies, precisely because they have so thoroughly opted for the other version of the teaching in the *Aṭṭhakavagga*—namely, the one that regards certain persons as exemplary and certain teachers as teaching the truth about the valid way to the true highest goal.

The commentaries ignore the *Aṭṭhakavagga*'s blanket condemnation of exclusive teachings and focus instead on determining which specific teachings are true and which are false. Thus at six negative instances of the term "dhamma" in the *Aṭṭhakavagga,* the *Mahāniddesa* identifies the term with the sixty-two theories *(diṭṭhigatas).*[30] Although the *Mahāniddesa* never lists the sixty-two theories, it refers to them often and frequently treats them as synonymous with the ten wrong views of the "This world is eternal" passage. In other negative instances the commentary defines "dhamma" as "teacher, teaching, group, view, way, or path," explicitly indicating that it is referring to teachers, teachings, followers, and paths other than the Buddha, dhamma, saṅgha, and noble eightfold path. Where the *Aṭṭhakavagga* uses "dhamma" positively, the commentary delineates the specific contents of this one true teaching, namely

> All *saṃkhāras* [(tendencies, compositions) are] impermanent; all *saṃkhāras* [are] *dukkha;* all dhammas [are] without self; *saṃkhāras* [are] dependent on ignorance; consciousness [is] dependent on *saṃkhāras;* name-form [is] dependent on consciousness; the six organs and objects of sense . . . ; touch . . . ; feelings . . . ; thirst . . . ; grasping . . . ; existence . . . ; birth . . . ; old age [and] death . . . ; cessation of *saṃkhāras* [is] due to cessation of ignorance; cessation of consciousness [is] due to cessation of *saṃkhāras;* [etc.] . . . cessation of old age [and] death [is] due to cessation of birth; this is *dukkha;* this is arising of *dukkha;* this is cessation of *dukkha;* this is the way leading to cessation of *dukkha;* these are *āsavas;* [etc.] . . . this is the way leading to the cessation of *āsavas;* these dhammas should be known; these dhammas should be understood; these dhammas should be abandoned; these dhammas should be cultivated; these dhammas should be realized; [there is] arising and disappearance, enjoyment, danger, and going out of the five contact spheres; [there is] arising and disappearance, enjoyment, danger, and going out of the five grasping [sensory] substrata; there is arising and disappearance, enjoyment, danger, and going out of the four great elements; whatever is capable of arising, all that is destructible.[31]

As for the particular means to the goal, the commentaries elaborate easily on the *Aṭṭhakavagga*'s positive uses of terms related to seeing and knowing. For example, the *niddesa* on v. 837 explains that the person who sees does not grasp views. The reason for this is not that the very act of grasping any view is itself less than ideal, but rather that this ideal person sees the dangerous consequences of grasping the views described in the "This world is eternal" passage, since they are characterized by *dukkha,* are not conducive to nibbāna, are conducive to continued becoming and rebirth in the unhappy realms, and are impermanent, interdependently arisen, and subject to cessation.

The commentaries' methods of avoiding concurrence with the *Aṭṭhakavagga*'s strongest condemnation of seeing and knowing are evident in their comments on v. 909:

> A person who sees, sees name and form,
> and having seen, will know them as such.
> Let her/him see as much or as little as s/he likes;
> the experts do not say that [one attains] purity by means of that.[32]

The *Mahāniddesa* simply defines this seeing and knowing as imperfect and inaccurate, thus leaving open the possibility of an accurate vision and knowledge that could see and know name-form *(nāma-rūpa)* as it really is and thus could lead to purity *(suddhi).*

Like the *Mahāniddesa,* the *Paramatthajotikā II* redefines old terms and—adding to the *Mahāniddesa*'s argument—introduces new ones to render v. 909 compatible with the ongoing commentarial interpretation:

> Who saw by means of knowledge of others' minds [etc.], that person who sees, sees name and form, and having seen other than that [i.e., other than (the true nature of) name and form], will know those names and forms as permanent and happy and not otherwise; thus seeing, let her/him see as much or as little name and form as permanent and happy as s/he likes; the experts do not say [one attains] purity by means of such a seeing *(dassana)* as hers/his.[33]

Thus the commentaries interpret the lines, "A person who sees, sees name and form,/and having seen, will know them as such" as saying, "[That person] does not see name and form, and knows them as they are not"—which is no mean accomplishment.

Certain verses of the *Aṭṭhakavagga* illustrate the logical conclusion of the anti-*diṭṭhi* theory in their negative assessments of the very attributes and accomplishments which the remainder of that text uses to define the ideal. Thus v. 794 says that ideal persons do not preach eternal purity. The *Mahāniddesa* handles this particular conflicting verse in a radical way, explaining that " 'eternal purity' means not-eternal purity, saṃsāra purity, ineffective purity, eternalism."[34] This presents a coherent argument—namely, that when less-than-ideal persons preach about eternal purity they are mistaken and are really talking about eternalism, not purity in the highest sense. Truly ideal persons, it implies, really do preach true, eternal purity. Yet this interpretation radically alters the *Aṭṭhakavagga* by stating that *accanta* (eternal) means *anaccanta* (not eternal), and in the process contradicts the point of the orginal verse, which is that exemplary persons do not preach or issue claims about the highest goal at all.

The *Paramatthajotikā II,* too, contradicts the *Aṭṭhakavagga* at v. 794, but in a slightly more subtle manner. Instead of simply substituting "not-eternal" for "eternal" in the line, "They do not preach 'eternal purity,' " Buddhaghosa remarks, "They do not preach supreme eternal purity as if it were the eternal purity of the ignorant eternalist view,"[35] but the end result is the same.

According to the *Aṭṭhakavagga*'s condemnation of holding particular views, no one should prefer one condition over another, for to do so is to discriminate, desire, and grasp. This is where the critical value of this position lies, because it points out the paradox inherent in the very ideal of desirelessness. The *Mahāniddesa*'s comment on v. 900 spells out the Theravāda treatment of this issue, by claiming that one must desire in order to become desireless. Commenting on the lines

> Not longing for purity (or) impurity,
> one should fare detached, not having grasped calmness,[36]

it states that persons training for the highest goal first long for entry into the path. Having accomplished that, they then long for the highest goal, arahantship. But arahants themselves do not long for any of the things called "purity" or "impurity."

This hierarchy interprets accomplishment of the goal according to the idea that training in the path is to arahantship what pre-path entry is to path training. It thus renders the transition from less than ideal to ideal parallel to the initial taking up of the path. This reasoning transforms the original, uncompromising anti-*diṭṭhi* argument's condemnation of discriminating anything as ideal compared to anything else into the observation that one does not desire what one has already attained. Ordinary persons want to enter the path; those who have accomplished that desire the next step: arahantship. But arahants have attained the ultimate goal, so there is nothing left for them to desire.

This amounts to saying that the ideal person's lack of desire is merely an incidental consequence of her/his attainment of the ideal. In the context of v. 900, this comment interprets the *Aṭṭhakavagga*'s negative assessment of longing for purity, as distinct from impurity, as the claim that once one has attained purity, one no longer desires it as distinct from its opposite. But this interpretation certainly does not condemn the trainees' desire for this specific ideal condition. On the contrary, it indicates that the trainees' desire is necessary and effective. Finally, where the original verse says one should not grasp calmness, the *Mahāniddesa* takes "calmness" to connote a limited, nonideal calmness rather than the true highest calmness, which we can infer is a legitimate object of longing for those training on the path to it.

The *Aṭṭhakavagga* simply presents two approaches to the ideal without any attempt to resolve the inconsistencies that result. To explain the teaching recorded in the *Aṭṭhakavagga* as true (consistent, coherent), the *Mahāniddesa* and the *Paramatthajotikā II* must somehow integrate both approaches. The two commentaries accomplish this in similar ways. In some of their definitions of the ideal person, and in their comments on certain anti-*diṭṭhi* verses, the commentaries superficially preserve the basic tension introduced by the anti-*diṭṭhi* position's negative critique of desire for anything, including the ideal goal. But for the most part the commentaries relegate such paradoxical elements of the Buddhist teaching to the realm of the perfected ideal person.

In this interpretation, the notion of pure desirelessness belongs to the ideal alone. Persons who have not yet achieved the ideal desire it as a matter of course. The commentators appear to assume that the fact that this may be paradoxical has no practical bearing on the path to the goal. It is for these aspirants to the goal that the commentaries define all paths, teachings, teachers, and goals other than their own as less than ideal, and their own as ideal. Similarly, the *Mahāniddesa* and the *Paramatthajotikā II* seem to assume that ideal persons may indeed have no need to express the truth, over and above the views of others. But the Buddha and his followers, who are interested in sharing their accomplishments with others, must do so by teaching the truth and by instilling a desire for the ideal in their followers. Thus the commentaries pay lip service to the anti-*diṭṭhi* claims while, at a deeper level, they radically transform this teaching by means of a "present company excepted" interpretation.

Theravāda Soteriology and the Paradox of Desire

The *Aṭṭhakavagga* both teaches a basic Buddhist soteriology, oriented toward the gradual elimination of desire, and presents—in its anti-*diṭṭhi* argument—an effective challenge to the legitimacy of any soteriology. This juxtaposition of views in an early Buddhist text is of historic interest, in part because it renders questionable the traditional Theravāda claim to preservation and consistent interpretation of the earliest version of the teachings of the Buddha. More significantly, this text, accepted and revered by the Theravāda as the word of the Buddha, clearly anticipates one of the most significant challenges the Mahāyāna would issue, centuries later, to the Theravāda understanding of the highest ideal and the path to it. Applying the paradox of desire, this critique asks why the ideal goal itself should be exempt from the fundamental condemnation of desirous attachment to all objects and conditions. If desire is characteristic of less-than-ideal persons and is left behind by ideal persons, how can desire for the ideal goal be salvific? The core of this critical application of the paradox of desire lies in the claim that every exclusive formulation of truth is an expression of selfish attachment that mistakenly posits a distinction between "true" and "false." Thus no one view (or teacher, practice, teaching, etc.) can distinguish itself as exclusively true.

It was Nāgārjuna, of course, who took up this argument anew in his formulation of the Mādhyamika interpretation of the Buddha's teachings. There he criticized the Theravāda (and other pre-Mahāyāna schools) for ignoring this important implication of the Buddha's teachings. Using his famous negative dialectic, Nāgārjuna interpreted those teachings as advocating a negative critique of all conceptual constructions; he argued that this negative critique does not thereby make its own specific conceptual claims. Thus he took the Buddha's teachings to be special by virtue of their ability to point toward a higher truth, without taking them to be conceptually substantial or exclusive. The *Aṭṭhakavagga* clearly presents the setup of this critique in its anti-*diṭṭhi* argument, adamantly condemning any attachment to exclusive individual views, but it does not anticipate Nāgārjuna's resolution of the problem.[37] Instead, it simply records two paths to the goal—one that focuses on eliminating desire by means of cultivating specific types of behavior, following the example of certain ideal persons, and another that recommends the elimination of desire by complete disassociation from any particular view, path, teacher, or goal. It includes no attempt to integrate the two into one coherent path.

It is impossible to determine, by analyzing the *Aṭṭhakavagga* itself, any chronological or even theoretical/doctrinal sequence of the development of these two approaches to the goal. Although we can speculate that one of the teachings follows logically on the other, the internal evidence provides no clear, objective basis for distinguishing which teaching precedes the other historically. Further, one certainly cannot presume to conclude from a study of the *Aṭṭhakavagga* alone whether either or both of these views actually represents the authentic teaching of the Buddha.

An analysis of the contents and structure of the *Aṭṭhakavagga* does show that one sample of what could be the earliest layer of Buddhist literature records a doctrinal conflict of the sort that proves quite significant in the later history of Buddhism. The *Aṭṭhakavagga* contains both the basic ideas of what would become a full-fledged soteriology in the Theravāda tradition, and the seeds of the attitude toward views and particular teachings that Nāgārjuna, for one, would later develop into a new Buddhist philosophy, and that the Zen masters would apply somewhat ruthlessly to their would-be disciples.[38] In a certain sense, even the Pure Land schools of Buddhism address the question of how one can act effectively to attain the highest goal, given the practical quandary posed by the paradox of desire.[39] In other words, an analysis of the soteriological stance(s) of the *Aṭṭhakavagga* indicates that one point of doctrinal disagreement that would later divide the major schools of Buddhism may date from the earliest layer of this tradition.

Tracing the development of the Theravāda response to the anti-*diṭṭhi* challenge raised by the *Aṭṭhakavagga* through examination of the two major normative Theravāda commentaries on this text, we have found evidence of some development of the Theravāda path soteriology, and in this development we have discovered the Theravāda resolution of the paradox of desire. As we have seen, this paradox, raised implicitly by the presence of the anti-*diṭṭhi* argument in the *Aṭṭhakavagga,* lies in the observation that any effort to become desireless itself belies a very basic desire: to attain this ideal of desirelessness. The commentaries' treatment of the *Aṭṭhakavagga*'s anti-*diṭṭhi* argument shows that the Theravāda generally finds the full anti-*diṭṭhi* response to this quandary untenable. To accept fully that resolution of the paradox of desire would require that it neither regard the Buddha as exemplary nor espouse his teachings as ultimately accurate and normative.

The Theravāda clearly did not recognize this solution—which would leave one with no path to the goal—as a solution at all. Instead, the commentaries opt to undermine the anti-*diṭṭhi* position, in order to retain the example of the Buddha and the guidance of his teachings. They accept the teachings concerning the path and the goal literally, and in the process accept the paradox inherent in them. This is exemplified by the *Mahāniddesa*'s comment on v. 900 of the *Aṭṭhakavagga,* which explains that trainees for the ideal aspire for entrance to the path and that entrants to the path long for arahantship, but that arahants do not hold anything as ideal. This implies that desire for the goal is a necessary part of the path to it, and also that those who desire anything other than path entry or arahantship (and thus nibbāna) do not qualify as Buddhist trainees; they are common folk whose objects of desire are less worthy than these. Such lower goals constitute the desire that entraps one in the less-than-ideal condition, while the higher desire, for attainment of the ideal goal, actually helps to raise one from that condition.[40]

Although it weakens the condemnation of desire that lies at the base of the early Buddhist worldview, this Theravāda resolution of the paradox of desire proves successful, philosophically speaking.[41] Challenged to show why preference for the teaching of one particular person (the Buddha) should be a good tendency when that teaching itself denounces desire as the root of all evil and such preference as a form of desire, the Theravāda eventually replies: because it is effective. Theoretically, this may be paradoxical, but it is not contradictory, and from a practical point of view, it is realistic. In practice, such preference is conducive to attainment of the highest good, which renders it—by definition—good.

Thus analysis of the *Aṭṭhakavagga* reveals that, although the Theravāda tradition's historical claims to the sole possession and only accurate interpretation of the earliest teachings of the Buddha may be questioned, its response to this particular, philosophically problematic issue manages to resolve it. When faced with the *Aṭṭhakavagga*'s evidence that the Buddha taught two incompatible teachings, the Theravāda opted for one and reinterpreted the other so as to contradict its original intent, thus rendering it consistent with what the Theravāda saw as the greater whole of the teaching.

The power of the Theravāda argument for this somewhat radical measure derives from its direct link with the experiential or empirical basis of Buddhist doctrine.[42] The paradox of desire relates, at least potentially, to every person's experience of the path to the highest goal. The Theravāda resolves that, paradoxical though it may be, the effectiveness of this path is proven by the successful practice of exemplary persons who have followed it. The paradox of desire challenges the very purpose of any path in Buddhism. The Theravāda treats this as a practical challenge that calls for a practical resolution.

Notes

1. With the possible exception of some Tibetan Buddhists, who accept all of the recorded scriptures of the Theravāda (and other "Hīnayāna" schools), Mahāyāna, and Vajrayāna as the authentic record of the Buddha's words, "All the canonical Sūtras and Tantras which form the basis of Buddha-dharma in Tibet were taught by Lord Buddha in person" (His Holiness Tenzin Gyatsho, the XIVth Dalai Lama of Tibet, *The Opening of the Wisdom Eye* [Wheaton, Ill.: Theosophical Publishing House, 1966], 10.) But even the great Vajrayāna philosophers of Tibet used later teachings to remedy the deficiencies of earlier texts.

2. See M. Anesaki, "Sutta-Nipāta in Chinese," *Journal of the Pali Text Society* 5 (1906–1907): 50–51, and N. A. Jayawickrama, "The Vaggas of the Sutta Nipāta," *University of Ceylon Review* 6 (October 1948): 236.

3. See Jayawickrama, "Vaggas," pp. 229–232.

4. See Sylvain Lévi, *Journal Asiatique* (1915): 401ff.; Anesaki, "Sutta-Nipāta," pp. 50–51; and Jayawickrama, "Vaggas," pp. 233–235 for examples and discussions of such references.

5. In this analysis, the terms "goal," "purpose," "ideal condition," and the like represent the condition that the text portrays as ultimately good, the summum bonum for which one should strive. Also, "positive" and "negative" in this context refer to "good" and "bad," respectively, judged by comparison to this ideal.

6. *Nibbānam attano.* There is no explicit reference to the Buddhist doctrine of anattā. When the term *"atta"* appears, it either functions reflexively (as in this example) or connotes something taken up, an assumption. Cf. N. A. Jaya-

wickrama, "Sutta Nipāta: Some Suttas from the Aṭṭhaka Vagga," *University of Ceylon Review* 8 (October 1950): 248, 249. In my translations, I have used forms that avoid the assumption that the persons (whether ideal or less than ideal) referred to in these verses are male. I can find no indication in the *Aṭṭhakavagga* that any of these descriptions or pieces of advice apply exclusively to males.

7. V. 915cd: *Kathaṃ disvā nibbāti bhikkhu/anupādiyāno lokasmiṃ kiñci.* Unless otherwise noted, all translations from the Pali in this essay are my own. Despite the recent plethora of translations of the *Sutta-nipāta,* I still find V. Fausböll's literal and straightforward early translation most useful (*The Sutta-Nipāta: A Collection of Discourses,* Sacred Books of the East, vol. 10, pt. 2 [Oxford: Clarendon, 1881]). Of the newer translations, H. Saddhatissa's is the most readable and K. R. Norman's the most interesting for its presentation of possible variant translations *(The Sutta-Nipāta,* trans. H. Saddhatissa [London: Curzon, 1985]; *The Rhinoceros Horn and Other Early Buddhist Poems (Sutta Nipāta),* trans. K. R. Norman, with alternative translations by I. B. Horner and Walpola Rahula [London: Pali Text Society, 1984].)

8. The translations offered parenthetically come from the literal meaning of these terms, where this can be surmised. In many cases, they are adjectives functioning as substantives, which makes literal interpretation of them possible. The terms that seem to refer to these persons *qua* exemplary persons pose a more difficult translation problem. "Bhikkhu," "brāhmaṇa," and *"samaṇa"* convey no clear literal meaning and thus must be taken to signify something like "monk," "wanderer," "ascetic," or "recluse." Jayawickrama argues that *"dhona"* cannot mean "wise one," as the commentaries interpret it (see "Some Suttas from the Aṭṭhaka Vagga," pp. 247–248). For a definition and etymology of *"nāga,"* see A. F. Hoernle, "The Sutta Nipata in a Sanskrit Version from Eastern Turkestan," *Journal of the Royal Asiatic Society* (1916): 722–723.

9. *Mattaṃ so jaññā idha tosanatthaṃ* (v. 971b).

10. See, e.g., vv. 809, 862, 866, and 951. Only the *Mahāviyūhasutta* fails to mention any of this type of recommendation.

11. Cf. Karl H. Potter, *Presuppositions of Indian Philosophies* (Englewood Cliffs, N.J.: Prentice-Hall, 1963), 259:

> So accepted is the distinction between egoism and altruism that it hardly seems possible to question its legitimacy. Yet the Indians did not recognize this distinction as particularly important and certainly not as obvious. Their assumption is that the good of all is served by the enlargement of a person's concern for himself, for his self eventually encompasses all selves.

In the specifically Theravāda Buddhist context, it would be more accurate to say that the good of all is served by the person's seeing to his or her own improvement, both because one cannot truly help anyone else until one sees the true nature of reality and because the conditions of all individuals are interdependent. Cf. Roy Perrett, "Egoism, Altruism and Intentionalism in Buddhist Ethics," *Journal of Indian Philosophy* 15 (1987): 71–85.

12. V. 781: *Sakaṃ hi diṭṭhiṃ katham accayeyya/chandānunīto ruciyā niviṭṭho/sayaṃ samattāni pakubbamāno/yathā hi jāneyya tathā vadeyya.*

13. V. 796: *Paraman ti diṭṭhīsu paribbasāno/yad uttariṃkurute jantu loke/hīnā ti aññe tato sabba-m-āha/tasmā vivādāni avītivatto.*

14. V. 969ab: *Paññaṃ purakkhatvā kalyāṇapīti/vikkhambhaye tāni parissayāni.*

15. V. 800ab: *Attaṃ pahāya anupādiyāno/ñāṇe pi so nissayam no karoti.*

16. V. 909: *Passaṃ naro dakkhiti nāmarūpaṃ/disvāna vāññassati tāni-m-eva/kāmaṃ bahuṃ passatu appakaṃ vā/na hi tena suddhiṃ kusalā vadanti.*

17. V. 824ab: *Idh eva suddhi iti vādiyanti/nāññesu dhammesu visuddhim āhu.*

18. Cf. Luis O. Gómez, "Proto-Mādhyamika in the Pali Canon," *Philosophy East and West* 26 (April 1976), n. 55.

19. Ibid., p. 146.

20. Cf. ibid., n. 57: "this 'choicelessness' creates a problem for the formulation of directives in the path."

21. Cf. ibid., p. 146.

22. Cf. A. L. Herman's description of this paradox ("A Solution to the Paradox of Desire in Buddhism," *Philosophy East and West* 29 [January 1979]: 91): "If I desire to cease desiring then I have not ceased all desire after all; I have merely replaced one species of desiring by another. The paradox of desire points to the practical contradiction or frustration involved in the desire to stop all desiring and states simply that those who desire to stop all desiring will never be successful."

23. This problem is evident in the *Aṭṭhakavagga* terminology of desire. In v. 963 the trainee for the ultimate goal is called *sambodhikāma* (desirous of enlightenment), lending one of the primary terms for desire in this text *(kāma)* a positive significance. Cf. the *Kāmasutta* (vv. 766–771), where all desire is deemed unsuitable and no such allowance for a middle term (i.e., desire *for something*) is made.

24. For more on this topic, see Grace G. Burford, *Desire, Death, and Goodness: The Conflict of Ultimate Values in Theravāda Buddhism* (New York: Peter Lang, 1991), esp. chaps. 5 and 7.

25. V. 781: *Sakaṃ hi diṭṭhiṃ katham accayeyya/chandānunīto ruciyā niviṭṭho/sayaṃ samattāni pakubbamāno/yathā hi jāneyya tathā vadeyya.*

26. *Sassato loko, idam eva saccaṃ mogham aññam, asassato loko, antavā loko, anantavā loko, taṃ jīvaṃ tam sarīram, aññaṃ jīvaṃ aññaṃ sarīraṃ, hoti tathāgato parammaraṇā, na hoti tathāgato parammaraṇā, hoti ca na ca hoti tathāgato parammaraṇā, n' eva hoti na na hoti tathāgato parammaraṇā, idam va saccaṃ, mogham aññan ti.*

27. *Ayaṃ satthā sabbaññū, ayaṃ dhammo svākkhāto, ayaṃ gaṇo supaṭipanno, ayaṃ diṭṭhi bhaddikā, ayaṃ paṭipadā supaññattā, ayaṃ maggo niyyāniko ti.* It is interesting to note that the specific claims the *Mahāniddesa* attributes to these less-than-ideal viewholders include most of the same areas in which inconsistencies arise in the *Aṭṭhakavagga* as a result of its teaching of the *diṭṭhi* position: teacher, teaching (dhamma), path.

28. Here the commentary offers a standard string of synonyms for the verb.

29. *Brāhmaṇo aññena asuddhimaggena micchāpaṭipadāya aniyyānapathena aññatra satipaṭṭhānehi aññatra sammappadhānehi aññatra iddhippādehi aññatra indriyehi aññatra balehi aññatra bojjhaṇgehi aññatra ariyaṭṭhaṇgikamaggena, suddhiṃ visuddhiṃ parisuddhiṃ muttiṃ vimuttiṃ parimuttiṃ, n' āha na katheti na bhaṇati na dīpayati na voharati.*

30. At vv. 784a, 785b, 801d, 803b, 837b, 907b.

31. *Sabbe saṃkhārā aniccā; sabbe saṃkhārā dukkhā; sabbe dhammā anattā; avijjāpaccayā saṃkhārā; saṃkhārapaccayā viññāṇaṃ; viññāṇapaccayā nāmarūpaṃ; nāmarūpapaccayā saḷāyatanaṃ; saḷāyatanapaccayā phasso; phassapaccayā vedanā; vedanāpaccayā taṇhā; taṇhāpaccayā upādānaṃ; upādānapaccayā bhavo; bhavapaccayā jāti; jātipaccayā jarāmaraṇaṃ; avijjānirodhā saṃkhāranirodho; saṃkhāranirodhā viññāṇanirodho; viññāṇanirodhā nāmarūpanirodho; nāmarūpanirodhā saḷāyatananirodho; saḷāyatananirodhā phassanirodho; phassanirodhā vedanānirodho; vedanānirodhā taṇhānirodho; taṇhānirodhā upādānanirodho; upādānanirodhā bhavanirodho; bhavanirodhā jātinirodho; jātinirodhā jarāmaraṇanirodho; idaṃ dukkhaṃ; ayaṃ dukkhasamudayo; ayaṃ dukkhanirodho; ayaṃ dukkhanirodhagāminī paṭipadā; ime āsavā; ayaṃ āsavasamudayo; ayaṃ āsavanirodho; ayaṃ āsavanirodhagāminī patipadā; ime dhammā abhiññeyyā, pariññeyyā, pahātabbā,*

bhāvetabbā, sacchikātabbā; channaṃ phassāyatanānaṃ samudayañ ca atthaṅgamañ ca assādañ ca ādīnavañ ca nissaraṇañ ca; pañcannaṃ upādānakkhandhānaṃ . . . ; catunnaṃ mahābhūtānaṃ . . . ; yaṃ kiñci samudayadhammaṃ sabban taṃ nirodhadhammaṃ.

32. See n. 16 above.

33. *Yv āyaṃ paracittañāṇādīhi addakkhi so passan naro dakkhiti nāmarūpaṃ tato paraṃ disvāna vāññassati tāni-m-eva nāmarūpāni niccato sukhato vā na aññathā; so evaṃ passanto kāmaṃ bahuṃ passatu appakaṃ vā nāmarūpaṃ niccato sukhato ca ath' assa evarūpena dassanena na hi tena suddhiṃ kusalā vadanti.*

34. *Accantasuddhī ti anaccantasuddhiṃ saṃsārasuddhiṃ akiriyasuddhiṃ sassatavādaṃ.*

35. *Paramattha-accantasuddhiṃ yeva akiriyasassataditthi accantasuddhī ti na te vadanti.* Literally: they do not call highest eternal purity "unwise eternal view eternal purity."

36. V. 900cd: *Suddhī asuddhī ti apatthayāno/virato care santim anuggahāya.*

37. Cf. Gómez, "Proto-Mādhyamika," p. 149.

38. The contemporary Thai Buddhist reformer Buddhadāsa also seems to espouse the anti-*diṭṭhi* notion, as well as its problematic ramifications, within the Theravāda path to the ideal. See Donald K. Swearer, "Bhikkhu Buddhadāsa on Ethics and Society," *Journal of Religious Ethics* 7 (Spring 1979): 60.

39. Cf. Alfred Bloom, *Shinran's Gospel of Pure Grace* (Tucson: University of Arizona Press, 1965), 30: "Shinran came to the conclusion that it was entirely impossible for a person to do a good act. Whatever good deed he appeared to do on the finite level was still evil, because it was done with a calculation in mind and was ultimately intended to redound to his benefit. Thus all good deeds performed by individuals were seen as essentially self-centered and involved in the entire web of passion."

40. This distinction is spelled out in the *Ariyapariyesana* (26th) sutta of the *Majjhimanikāya,* where desire for nibbāna is said to be different from desire for all other (i.e., conditioned) objects. Unlike desire for anything conditioned, desire for the unconditioned (nibbāna) is a noble *(ariya)* desire.

41. Cf. Herman, "A Solution," p. 92, where he rejects this resolution "because Buddhists themselves seem to reject it" in all its forms and functions.

42. Cf. the equally practical (and paradoxical), if different, Zen resolution described in ibid., pp. 92–94.

Attainment through Abandonment: The Sarvāstivādin Path of Removing Defilements

Collett Cox

Introduction

Even a cursory examination of religious praxis as described by the northern Indian Abhidharma texts reveals an exceedingly complex array of specific practices and attainments. The organizational patterns and exhaustive analysis that characterize Abhidharma texts in their treatment of all aspects of Buddhist doctrine reach a hypertrophic extreme in the case of the all-inclusive path-structure (mārga) into which this array of practices and attainments was incorporated. As elaborated by the later Sarvāstivāda-Vaibhāṣika school, this path-structure encompasses: numerous meditative states, cosmic realms, or cognitive stages; varieties of religious aspirants associated with each state, realm, or stage; specific techniques of religious practice; and, finally, attainments and powers that appear with these practices. Interpreting this intricate collection of affective and cognitive powers and attainments is a daunting and seemingly overwhelming task.

In addition to clarifying the function and significance of the various specific components of the path, a comprehensive interpretation of the path would, ideally, elucidate certain underlying historical and structural issues. Historically, the later Abhidharma texts adopted both terminology and structures for religious praxis from prior Buddhist accounts. In doing so, they attempted to incorporate rather than delete anything that may have been redundant or even contradictory. Consequently, many components of the path described in the Abhidharma texts contain the same factors or overlap in function. A systematic appraisal of the Sarvāstivādin path must therefore consider the following historical issues.

First, what were the specific sources for the components used to construct the Abhidharma path of praxis, and how did their operation or importance change, through association with other components, when they were incorporated into an expanding path-structure? Indeed, how feasible is it to answer this question, since doing so is limited by the degree to which text-historical and philological methods can be applied to the available materials? Second, how far can we proceed in the recovery and reconstruction of the religious and socio-historical intentions underlying the development of the path-structure? Can we presume that religious praxis was intended to conform to the path-structure described in Abhidharma texts, or were the Abhidharma descriptions the result of other concerns? Third, is there no dichotomy between doctrinal description and praxis in Abhidharma texts, but only the record of a shift in soteriology, which equated the analytical with the religious quest? If so, what does the available internal and external historical evidence (including evidence outside the Abhidharma texts themselves) allow us to conclude about the activities of those involved in the composition and transmission of Abhidharma texts?

In the spectrum between the extremes of philosophical speculation and effective praxis, a multiplicity of motives undoubtedly influenced these texts, including mediated religious motives such as the desire of sect members to assert sectarian identity by revising, expanding, and defending their canonical tradition vis-à-vis those of rival groups. Although modern scholars often regard these concerns as secondary to what are assumed to have been fundamental religious motives, we should not underestimate the actuality and immediacy of such concrete historical issues for the bearers of these traditions.

When viewed structurally, the complexity of the path also suggests a diversity of religious contexts and objectives. Even within the confines of a single Abhidharma text by a known author, the practices described are so diverse that they could hardly be followed by a single person. Indeed, by associating specific modes of practice with types of aspirants, the Abhidharma texts apparently offer not a single course but a set of parallel options for religious praxis. This complexity raises a number of important structural problems.

First, is it possible to identify a single underlying objective or principle that organizes the multifaceted components of the path, or to identify one component of the path as primary? If so, what is the intrinsic principle or inherent order that coordinates all the components and directs them toward this single ultimate objective? Second, should we assume instead that the apparent "structure" of the path in later Abhidharma texts is a product of self-conscious doctrinal systematization secondarily applied to a traditional aggregate of historical accretions, and that this structure therefore stems from doctrinal demands for coherence quite divorced from the expectations of actual practice? In other words, are the structure and elaboration of the path based on principles of practice or of doctrinal analysis? Or, third, does this path-structure indicate a bifurcation of religious life into an elite, intellectual, monastic enterprise that was superimposed on and parallel to an inherited, less systematic religious praxis? In this case as well, the later Abhidharma path-structure would represent the culmination of a tendency inherent within the earlier stages of Abhidharma—namely, the wish to provide an all-inclusive, taxonomically complete presentation of the doctrine, not simply for pedagogical purposes but as a direct form of soteriologically effective action.

Given the complexity of the path and the historical and structural issues that this complexity yields, interpretation cannot begin from the naive assumption that the path is an ahistorical harmonious whole, but must recognize both the diverse origins of the various components of the path and the existence of objectives in addition to the one claimed for the path as a whole. Concentrating on a single aspect of the path inevitably distorts the interpretation of the structural whole, whereas concentrating on the whole obscures the history of its development and fails to emphasize properly those components that may be most important in actual practice. Further, from the viewpoint of individual practitioners, the integrating path-structure may be only a heuristic and nominal overlay, whereas from the viewpoint of Abhidharma masters, the distinctions in practice may be negligible and readily harmonized. Thus interpretation of the Abhidharma path must be guided by a constant awareness of the interplay between the components and their integrating structure—and between their practical and theoretical purposes, as well. Perhaps attempts at interpretation must recognize that, within the perspective of Abhidharma, the theoretical enterprise is itself an integral part of practice.

Many prior studies of early Buddhist religious praxis have noted this interplay, expressing it in terms of a tension or even a fundamental dichotomy implicit in the textual descriptions of the path—that is, a tension or dichotomy between the acquisition of requisite knowledge and the meditative experience or cultivation of affective qualities. This tension has been described as (1) that between the rational and the mystical;[1] (2) that between methods of knowledge (jñāna) and of trance (dhyāna), which might be equated with discerning *(vipaśyanā)* and calming *(śamatha)*, respectively;[2] (3) that between insight meditation and concentrative meditation;[3] and (4) that between conflicting theories of praxis and liberation represented by a "negative-intellectual" current of philosophical theory and by a "positive-mystical" current of spiritual practice.[4] These treatments presume that the tension between knowledge and meditative concentration evident in certain textual descriptions of the path reflects an actual divergence in techniques and historical traditions of religious praxis. They also imply that either perfected knowledge or perfected concentration, whether alone or combined, constitute the final goal. This begs the question of whether the apparent divergence in praxis is a sign of different ultimate objectives that are historically distinct in origin, or whether knowledge and meditative concentration were intended to function together to elicit a single goal.

An examination of the path-structure in Abhidharma texts suggests an alternative explanation, neglected in previous studies, to this tension between the cognitive and meditative—namely, a final goal that subsumes knowledge and concentration as equally cooperative means rather than mutually exclusive ends.[5] This inclusive goal is the abandonment of specific defilements *(kleśaprahāṇa)* and the ultimate destruction of all fluxes *(āsravakṣaya);* extensive textual evidence both from early canonical texts and from Abhidharma materials argues that this—not concentration or knowledge alone—represents the final goal in many segments of the Buddhist tradition.[6] It would be instructive to examine the interplay among the components of the path and the apparent tension between cognitive and meditative techniques in this new light. If, then, the ultimate objective is recognized to be the abandonment of defilements, how do knowledge and concentration function in eradicating them?

This new perspective provides the first and essential key to resolving the numerous structural and historical issues encumbering a comprehensive interpretation of the path, for even a sampling of the available textual evidence suggests that abandoning defilements is indeed the goal of Abhidharma religious praxis and the organizing principle of its construction of the path. While acknowledging the tension between knowledge and concentration as recognized in previous studies,[7] I will demonstrate that Abhidharma texts attempt to harmonize these two tendencies, or at least incorporate them both on the path toward a different ultimate objective—that is, the abandonment of defilements. As will become clear, later Sarvāstivādin Abhidharma texts do not present either the practice of concentration or the acquisition of knowledge as the ultimate religious goal, but rather as means for abandoning and preventing the future arising of defilements.

The Goal of the Abhidharma Path

The northern Indian Abhidharma interpretations of modes of praxis, the religious goal, and the interrelation between praxis and goal naturally depend on antecedents transmitted through earlier Buddhist texts and traditions of practice. Unfortunately, there is little agreement in the scholarly interpretation of these early Buddhist sources. Given the difficulty of dating strata within the earliest texts and the divergent viewpoints that these texts represent, such lack of agreement is inevitable, but it also results, in part, from a tacit acceptance of differences in interpretative emphasis proposed by later Buddhist transmitters and compilers. This tacit acceptance, in turn, often reflects implicit scholarly biases—in this case, a predilection for interpretations that emphasize either knowledge or concentration.

Among the canonical materials that provide evidence for the putative goals of early Buddhist praxis are (1) scattered references to the methods and objectives of religious praxis, and (2) accounts of the enlightenment experiences of the Buddha and his disciples, including both biographical references and descriptions of the content of this realization as presented in the *Dharmacakrapravartanasūtra.*[8] There are multiple accounts of the enlightenment experience and evidence of historical accretions,[9] but abandoning defilements, attaining the destruction of the fluxes *(āsravakṣaya),* and knowing that this destruction has been accomplished play a central role in all accounts. For example, both in the biographical accounts of the Buddha's enlightenment and in separate discussions of the three clear intuitions *(vidyā),* which are accepted as the content of that enlightenment experience, the last intuition or culminating realization is that of the destruction of the fluxes *(āsravakṣaya)* or the knowledge of the destruction of the fluxes *(āsravakṣayajñāna).*[10] This particular knowledge is first elaborated as consisting of the sequential knowledge of the four noble truths—knowledge of the fact of suffering, of the origin of suffering, of the cessation of suffering, and of the path leading to this cessation. Next, this fourfold knowledge is applied to the fluxes themselves, yielding knowledge of the fact of the fluxes, of their origin, and so on.

Although there is much scholarly disagreement about whether these references to the destruction of the fluxes belong to the earliest accounts of the enlightenment experience,[11] the canon also positions the destruction of the fluxes as the culmination of a series of practices or cultivations,[12] often through the stereotyped formula, "thought is liberated from the fluxes" *(āsavehi cittaṃ vimuttam).*[13] The destruction of the fluxes is thus presented as the generalized goal of religious praxis and, subsequently, as the quality defining arhatship.[14]

The prominent role accorded the destruction of the fluxes in the elaboration both of religious praxis and of the soteriological goal within early Buddhist texts is continued within northern Indian Abhidharma texts.[15] The noble path of religious praxis is defined as that which is contrary to the arising of defilements,[16] and entering completely into the ocean of the Buddha's teaching is said to occur through the realization of complete nirvāṇa as a result of destroying the fluxes.[17] The aspirant progresses along this path by successively abandoning defilements that are associated with an established sequence of cosmic realms and cognitive stages,[18] and by attaining virtuous qualities, powers, paths, or fruits associated with each realm or stage.[19] Similarly, retrogression *(parihāṇi)* from a given level of religious attainment is possible given the reemergence of defilements specific to that level.[20] The final goal of enlightenment *(bodhi)* is defined as consisting of the two varieties of knowledge of the destruction of the fluxes *(āsravakṣayajñāna)* and knowledge of their absolute future nonarising *(anutpādajñāna)*.[21]

The ultimate state attained by religious praxis, that of arhatship, is also conceived in terms of the destruction of defilements. Abhidharma texts offer pseudo-etymologies for the word "arhat": for example, one by whom all defilements—that is, the enemies *(ari)*—are struck down *(han)* by the sword of insight, or one for whom there is distant separation *(āra)* from all evil, unvirtuous factors *(han)*, that is, from the defilements that obstruct virtuous factors.[22] The fruit of arhatship *(arhattvaphala)* occurs when an aspirant completely abandons, in the present life, all defilements of lust, hatred, and delusion; thereby, the aspirant's thought attains liberation from the three varieties of the fluxes—desire, existence in the three realms, and ignorance.[23] This destruction of defilements that constitutes the unconditioned fruit of arhatship is further specified in Sarvāstivādin Abhidharma texts as the past, present, and future possession *(prāpti)* of the cessation resulting from consideration *(pratisaṃkhyānirodha)*, which refers to cessation of defilements through consideration.[24] As will be explained, in later Sarvāstivādin Abhidharma texts, this mechanism of possession is used to explain both the ordinary condition of defilement and the process by which defilements are abandoned.

The Character of Defilements

The complexity of the terminology and taxonomic categories used by Abhidharma texts in the analysis of defilements defies attempts at summary characterization. This complexity results not only from the retention of virtually all terms and categories used in prior texts, but also from a systematizing elaboration characteristic of Abhidharma analysis. For example, the **Śāriputrābhidharmaśāstra*, an early northern Indian Abhidharma text, begins its discussion of defilements *(kleśa)* by listing over 530 individual defilements or categories of unvirtuous factors *(akuśaladharma)*.[25] The *Jñānaprasthāna*, a later Sarvāstivādin text, lists sixteen categories of defilements in numerical order from the least numerous category of three fetters *(saṃyojana)* to the most numerous category of ninety-eight contaminants *(anuśaya)*.[26]

Even though these categories represent different groupings of often identical defiling factors, the various terms for the individual factors and the categories themselves, as used in the sūtra, are not without historical differences in meaning and function. However, after being systematized by Abhidharma compilers, who arranged traditional categories in new schemata, often without respect to their original context, the traditional distinctions among these categories were blurred and can now be recovered only with great difficulty from the Abhidharma accounts. Also, the new interrelations among the various categories of defilements developed within the early Sarvāstivāda-Vaibhāṣika texts are ambiguous. For example, a stylized list is used frequently to refer generically to all varieties of defiling factors: fetters *(saṃyojana),* bonds *(bandhana),* contaminants *(anuśaya),* subsidiary defilements *(upakleśa),* and manifestly active defilements *(paryavasthāna).*[27] Although each of these terms undoubtedly had distinct contexts of use within the sūtras, such formulaic lists suggest that the terms were no longer clearly distinguished in Abhidharma texts. The *Mahāvibhāṣā* even states explicitly that any factor included in one of these categories should also be included in the others.[28] Commenting on the sixteen categories of defilements listed in the *Jñānaprasthāna,* the *Mahāvibhāṣā* suggests their interchangeability by identifying each category as a subset of the general category of defilements or *kleśas.* Despite this harmonizing and leveling of the categories of defilements, the *Mahāvibhāṣā,* possibly in deference to inherited traditional usage, also gives independent definitions of the names for each of these categories, often distinguishing the specific activity of a given category within the scope of the activity of defilements in general.[29] However, the *Mahāvibhāṣā* stops short of declaring either that all these terms for and categories of defilements are identical or that they are radically different in character or function.

Within post-*Vibhāṣā* Sarvāstivādin Abhidharma texts, categories of defilements come to be differentiated according to their functions, which in turn become the subject of heated sectarian controversy. This controversy reflects the further refinement of theories concerning the operation of both thought and defilements, as well as the methods by which defilements are to be abandoned. It is also interconnected with the development of more sophisticated ontological theories, which inevitably affected all aspects of Abhidharma doctrine. In particular, this controversy involves the possibility of a distinction between latent and active defilements, and the relation between these defilements (whether latent or active) and the thought processes of the individual life-stream that they characterize.

At issue is the development of a model that could successfully explain the apparent, persistent activity of certain defilements, the reemergence of their activity after an interruption, and the mechanism by which they are to be abandoned. For example, can unvirtuous defilements arise conditioned by a morally dissimilar virtuous factor? If not, then what is the causal mechanism by which defilements arise immediately after a virtuous moment of thought? Further, if defilements are associated with thought, since two associated thought-concomitants of differing moral quality cannot occur simultaneously, how can the virtuous counteragent that obstructs a particular defilement arise simultaneously with it? If, however, defilements are not understood to be associated with thought, their very activity of defiling thought is meaningless, and no abandonment is necessary. Finally, if defilements are understood to exist as real entities in the past and future as well as in the present, then they can never be destroyed in the sense that they become nonexistent, so in what sense can they be said to be abandoned?

One important focus for this controversy is the interpretation of the term "contaminant" *(anuśaya),* which is the primary word used for defilement in Sarvāstivādin Abhidharma texts.[30] The varying interpretations of this term depend on the possibility of a distinction between contaminants and another variety of defilements, the "manifestly active defilements" *(paryavasthāna).* The *Mahāvibhāṣā* records the views of certain northern Indian Abhidharma schools that define *anuśaya* as a latent phase of defilements, as distinguished from their overtly functioning phase, which is designated by *paryavasthāna.* The Vibhajyavādins, for example, in rejecting the possibility of retrogression for an arhat, claim:

> Contaminants are the seeds of manifestly active defilements. Contaminants are, by nature, not associated with thought; manifestly active defilements are, by nature, associated with thought. Manifestly active defilements are produced from contaminants. [Even if it were said that] one retrogresses from arhatship due to the present operation *(saṃmukhībhāva)* of manifestly active defilements, since manifestly active defilements would not arise when the contaminants have been abandoned, how could one be said to have retrogression?[31]

Here the Vibhajyavādins propose that contaminants are defilements in a latent phase and are, in that phase, dissociated from thought. These latent dissociated defilements are the seeds that give rise to a manifestly active phase, which, like all thought contaminants, is associated with thought. This distinction between a latent and active phase of defilements, represented by the terms "contaminants" and "manifestly active defilements," respectively, is further intimated by Upaśānta's *Abhidharmahṛdayaśāstra.* This text offers a pseudo-etymology to support the interpretation of *anuśaya* as meaning "subtle," that is, as operating only subtly *(sūkṣmapracāratvāt)* in contrast to manifestly active defilements *(paryavasthāna),* which are gross or overt in their operation.[32] Finally, Ghoṣaka's **Abhidharmāmṛtaśāstra* also implicitly supports this distinction between a latent and an active phase of defilements by dividing a maximum possible total of 108 defilements *(kleśa)* into two groups, including both contaminants (98) and manifestly active defilements (10).[33] Although later Kāśmīra Sarvāstivāda-Vaibhāṣika texts adamantly deny any such distinction between contaminants and manifestly active defilements, at several points in the course of arguments on other topics, the *Mahāvibhāṣā* records such a distinction based on the latency or manifestation of a defilement's activity. For example:

> Further, it is said that only when the defilements *(kleśa)* are in present operation are they called fetters belonging to the lower realm *(avarabhāgīyasaṃyojana);* [but] the Buddha has said that whether [they are] in the state of being manifestly active defilements or contaminants, they are still called fetters belonging to the lower realm.[34]

Another important focus for these controversies about the function of defilements concerns their association with or dissociation from thought.[35] The *Mahāvibhāṣā* records three pseudo-etymologies for the term "contaminant" *(anuśaya),* two of which—*aṇu* (subtle) and *anuśerate* (adhering closely, or, in later Sarvāstivādin texts, growing)[36]—are interpreted as reflecting its intrinsic association with thought. The third pseudo-etymology, which derives *anuśaya* from *anubadhnanti* (binding), is understood to refer to those contaminants that are dissociated from thought. For the Sarvāstivādins all contaminants are understood to be associated with thought, so this third sense of contaminants as binding and dissociated must refer, the *Mahāvibhāṣā* argues, not to the contaminant itself but to a separate factor intimately connected to its functioning: namely, possession *(prāpti),* which serves to connect a given contaminant to a particular life-stream. As a force dissociated from thought *(cittaviprayuktasaṃskāra),* this possession can therefore justifiably be referred to as dissociated.[37]

This issue of association with or dissociation from thought is raised explicitly in Dharmaśrī and Upaśānta's *Abhidharmahṛdayaśāstras* and the *Saṃyuktābhidharmahṛdayaśāstra.* These texts, in accord with the position that was to become standard for the Kāśmīra Sarvāstivāda-Vaibhāṣikas, give four explicit reasons for the necessary association of contaminants with thought. Contaminants must be associated with thought in order to perform their three activities: (1) that of defiling thought; (2) that of obstructing the arising of virtuous factors; and (3) that of opposing good factors already arisen. As a fourth reason, if contaminants were dissociated from thought, virtuous factors would never arise because these contaminants, being unrestricted by any association with thought, could always be in operation, thereby forever obstructing the arising of virtuous factors.[38] For the Kāśmīra Sarvāstivāda-Vaibhāṣikas, who accepted no distinction between latent and active defilements, contaminants or manifestly active defilements must then be associated with thought. However, certain opponents resorted to a distinction between contaminants and manifestly active defilements, attributing these activities not to contaminants per se but to their active phase as manifestly active defilements. As a result, whereas the manifestly active defilements that perform these activities must be associated with thought, the latent defilements may be dissociated from it.

Later Abhidharma texts, such as Vasubandhu's *Abhidharmakośabhāṣya,* Saṅghabhadra's *Nyāyānusāra,* and the *Abhidharmadīpa,* pursue these two points of controversy in their debates over the interpretation of the compound *kāmarāga-anuśaya,* the name of the first of the seven recognized varieties of contaminants.[39] One group, in an attempt to support the identity of manifestly active defilements and contaminants, interpreted the compound as a descriptive determinative *(karmadhāraya),* stating that it refers to "the contaminant *(anuśaya),* that is, [the manifestly active defilement called] lust for desires *(kāmarāga).*" This group included the Sarvāstivāda-Vaibhāṣikas, who rejected any latent form of defilements. A second group, in an attempt to support the position that manifestly active defilements are distinct from contaminants, interpreted the compound as a genitive dependent determinative *(tatpuruṣa)* referring to "the contaminant *(anuśaya)* of [the manifestly active defilement called] lust for sense pleasures *(kāmarāga).*" To this group belonged the Vibhajyavādins, Mahāsāṅghikas,[40] and Vātsīputrīyas, all of whom claimed that the term "contaminants" can be used in both a broad and a narrow sense: broadly to include manifestly active defilements, or more narrowly to refer only to the cause of manifestly active defilements—that is, latent contaminants.[41] The Sautrāntikas and Vasubandhu also interpreted the compound like this second group, and thus accepted some distinction between latent contaminants and manifestly active defilements. They claimed, however, that latent contaminants do not exist as independent, real entities.

The divergent positions of these groups concerning the relation between contaminants and manifestly active defilements paralleled their views on the issue of a contaminant's association with or dissociation from thought. All groups agreed that manifestly active defilements are factors (dharmas) associated with thought *(cittasaṃprayukta):* that is, a given active defilement and a given moment of thought share the same basis *(āśraya),* object-support *(ālambana),* features *(ākāra),* time *(kāla),* and existential occurrence in a single moment *(dravya).*[42] However, a contaminant's association with or dissociation from thought depends on the identification of or distinction between contaminants and manifestly active defilements. For the Sarvāstivāda-Vaibhāṣikas, who maintained the identity of contaminants and manifestly active defilements, a contaminant is always associated with a given moment of thought. However, the Vibhajyavādins, Mahāsāṅghikas, and Vātsīputrīyas, who distinguished contaminants from manifestly active defilements, maintained that contaminants are dissociated from thought.[43] Vasubandhu, following the position of the Sautrāntikas, adopted an intermediate position, claiming that because a contaminant is not a distinct, real entity *(adravyāntaratvāt)*, it cannot be said to be either associated with or dissociated from thought.[44] Rather, a contaminant is simply a latent defilement *(prasuptakleśa)*—that is, a seed-state *(bījabhāva)* not in present operation *(asaṃmukhībhūta)*. When that seed is awakened *(prabuddha)*, the defilement comes to present operation and becomes manifest as an active defilement. This seed-state itself arises from another, previous defilement and contains the power to produce a subsequent defilement, thereby forming a series *(bījabhāvānubandha)* that belongs to the material basis *(ātmabhāva, āśraya)* of a sentient being.

The problem of interpreting *anuśaya* may appear to be simply one of terminology. Indeed, all parties would agree that active defilements, regardless of what they are called, must be associated with thought if they are to be effective in defiling thought. Substantive and unavoidable difficulties ensue, however, in trying to explain the arising of an active defilement in the midst of a series of dissimilar virtuous moments of thought, or in trying to account for the process by which a defilement is abandoned. Here terminological distinctions reflect attempts to devise additional explanatory mechanisms to resolve these difficulties. The Vibhajyavādins' mechanism is a distinct contaminant *(anuśaya)* that is both distinguished from active defilements as their cause and dissociated from thought.[45] Because it is dissociated, it can condition the arising of active defilements regardless of the moral character of the preceding moment of thought.[46] Similarly, for Vasubandhu and the Sautrāntikas, this mechanism is the active defilement in its latent form as a contaminant or seed *(bīja)* that can either remain dormant or emerge under proper conditions as a functioning active defilement.

The Sarvāstivāda-Vaibhāṣikas attempted to resolve these difficulties with a dual mechanism. First, since defilements, like all factors, are claimed to exist and can function as conditions in the past, present, and future, a past defilement, though not presently active as such, can function as the condition for the arising of a different presently active defilement, regardless of the moral character of the preceding moment of thought. The Sarvāstivāda-Vaibhāṣikas thus obviate the need to assume the existence of a separate latent contaminant or seed from which presently active defilements emerge. Second, they account both for the connection between a given defilement and a life-stream during moments of varying moral quality and for the abandonment of defilements by positing a new mechanism: possession *(prāpti)*. Possession acts to connect a given defilement to a given life-stream, whether or not that defilement is actively functioning—that is, whether that defilement is present, past, or future. A defilement can be abandoned by severing this possession and thus terminating the connection between the defilement and the life-stream.

These models of a contaminant (1) as distinct from manifestly active defilements, (2) as a seed, and (3) as possession were all motivated by a need to resolve the same causal problems. These models also indicate that later Abhidharma texts were more specific in their analysis of the character and operation of defilements. Like the early texts, post-*Vibhāṣā* Sarvāstivādin Abhidharma texts use stylized lists of synonyms for defilements, but with an important difference in motivation: the synonymous use of all these terms for defilements now follows naturally from the Sarvāstivādin position that contaminants and manifestly active defilements are identical.[47] The taxonomic classification of defilements also reached an apex in the Sarvāstivādin schema of ninety-eight contaminants, which is not attested in the sūtra. Rather than reflecting any intrinsic difference among the contaminants themselves, this elaborate schema was assembled in accordance with the edifice of cosmic realms and cognitive stages, and mirrors the gradual process through which contaminants are to be abandoned. This schema of ninety-eight contaminants was generated from a basic set of seven contaminants mentioned in the sūtra and prominent among the lists of categories of defilements in Abhidharma texts: lust for sense pleasures *(kāmarāga),* hostility *(pratigha),* lust for existence *(bhavarāga),* pride *(māna),* ignorance *(avidyā),* views *(dṛṣṭi),* and doubt *(vicikitsā).*[48] By combining the two varieties of lust and dividing views into five varieties, ten contaminants result.[49] When these ten varieties are correlated with the three cosmic realms—the realm of desire, the realm of form, and the formless realm—and each contaminant in each realm is specified according to whether it is to be abandoned by the path of vision or by the path of cultivation, the schema of ninety-eight contaminants is produced.[50]

The Structure of the Path

Concomitant with the elaboration of this schema of defilements is a parallel elaboration of stages of religious praxis. The intricate path-structure characteristic of the later Sarvāstivāda-Vaibhāṣikas is not explicitly developed in early Abhidharma texts. Instead, evidence suggests that in these early texts, diverse traditional components of practice were incorporated from the sūtra and elaborated in accordance with newly emerging distinctions, which together gradually produced the structure that came to characterize the new Abhidharma path.[51] The absence of a single organizing principle and internally consistent path-structure in the earliest Abhidharma discussions may indicate that a distinctive Abhidharma path had not yet developed, or it may reflect a lack of concern with an overarching and coherent doctrinal structure. But this absence may also be, at least in part, a function of the implicit purposes underlying early Abhidharma exegesis. The authors of the earliest Abhidharma texts may have been motivated not to construct a coherent edifice of theoretical doctrinal interpretation, but rather to specify the character of the component factors of sentient experience by clarifying the distinctions among them in accordance with emerging categories of classification. By thus classifying all the components of sentient experience, those that are to be cultivated are differentiated from those that are to be abandoned, and the direction of proper praxis becomes evident. This classification is carried out by examining each factor in terms of formulaic questions and answers based on categories *(mātṛkā):* for example, the categorization of factors in terms of their character as conditioned and unconditioned; in terms of their moral quality as virtuous, unvirtuous, and indeterminate; and so on. Thus, in the early texts, abstract doctrinal positions are not explicitly stated but must be inferred from the categories used, the specific questions raised, and the answers given.

The path of praxis as developed in later Sarvāstivādin texts is characterized by a bipartite structure including a path of vision *(darśanamārga)* and a path of cultivation *(bhāvanāmārga).* Precedents for this distinction between vision and cultivation appear in the earliest northern Abhidharma texts in a threefold categorization *(mātṛkā)* of all factors in terms of their method of abandonment: certain factors are to be abandoned by vision *(darśanaheya, darśanaprahātavya),* others by cultivation *(bhāvanāheya, bhāvanāprahātavya),* and still others are not to be abandoned *(aheya, aprahātavya).*[52]

Further, in early Sarvāstivādin texts, the elaboration of the schema of ninety-eight varieties of contaminants and the descriptions of specific types of practice presume the existence of this bipartite structure.[53] For example, the *Vijñānakāya* classifies varieties of perceptual consciousness *(vijñāna)* and thought *(citta)* in terms of their relation to contaminants *(anuśaya);* it exhaustively enumerates those types of perceptual consciousness that support the growth of certain contaminants, and it specifies which of those contaminants are to be abandoned by vision *(darśana)* and which by cultivation *(bhāvanā).*[54] In this discussion, vision takes the four noble truths as its object, and this fourfold vision yields four distinct varieties of knowledge. The *Vijñānakāya* makes further reference to

> unvirtuous thoughts that belong to one who is not yet separated from lust in the realm of desire, but who has already given rise to the knowledge of suffering, and not yet to the knowledge of the origin of suffering. [Such unvirtuous thoughts] are to be abandoned through vision of the origin of suffering, of cessation, or of the path, or [they are to be abandoned] through cultivation.[55]

In this passage, both vision and its resultant knowledge as well as cultivation are designated as methods by which contaminants are to be abandoned, and this abandonment occurs by progressing through successive stages of the vision of the four noble truths to the practice of cultivation.

Another important component of the later Sarvāstivādin path-structure, which also has precedents in earlier texts, is that of two stages of knowledge: namely, knowledge of the doctrine *(dharmajñāna)*[56] and subsequent knowledge *(anvayajñāna)*.[57] These two are applied to each of the four noble truths, yielding eight varieties: the knowledge of doctrine with regard to suffering, the subsequent knowledge of suffering, and so on.[58] The *Saṅgītiparyāya* further subdivides each of these eight into two varieties, the presentiment of the knowledge *(jñānakṣānti)*[59] and the knowledge proper *(jñāna)*, yielding sixteen stages.[60] In this passage from the *Saṅgītiparyāya*, the description of praxis begins with the stage of the supreme mundane factors *(laukikāgradharma)*, from which one progresses to the presentiment of the knowledge of the doctrine with regard to suffering *(duḥkhe dharmajñānakṣānti)*. The remaining fifteen stages follow, culminating in the subsequent knowledge of the path *(mārge 'nvayajñāna)*.

Significantly, in contrast to the passage from the *Vijñānakāya* just cited,[61] the *Saṅgītiparyāya* does not append any reference to cultivation *(bhāvanā)* as necessary after the acquisition of these sixteen stages of presentiment and knowledge. It simply juxtaposes its discussion of these stages with a discussion of the two paths through which one attains the four fruits of religious praxis: the mundane path *(laukikamārga)*, through which one can attain only the fruits of the once-returner or the nonreturner; and the path not tending toward the fluxes *(anāsravamārga)*, through which one can attain any of the four fruits. This passage from the *Saṅgītiparyāya* may thus represent an early stage in the development of the Sarvāstivādin path-structure, in which the path of vision and the path of cultivation had not yet been combined sequentially in the manner of later texts.

The outline of the later Sarvāstivādin path-structure appears fully developed in the *Abhidharmahṛdayaśāstra*.[62] As presented there, this structure begins with four stages of penetration *(nirvedhabhāgīya)*, which are also identified with one form of the four virtuous roots *(kuśalamūla)*:[63] heat *(ūṣmagata)*, summit *(mūrdhan)*, presentiment *(kṣānti)*, and highest mundane factors *(laukikāgradharma)*. These four stages are traversed prior to the acquisition of the first moment of thought not tending toward the fluxes *(anāsravacitta)*, which constitutes the first moment of the path of vision. In this path of vision, one progresses through successive stages of presentiment and knowledge applied to each of the two stages of knowledge and subsequent knowledge of the four noble truths, until, in sixteen moments, correct vision is attained. In this sixteenth moment, various stages and noble fruits of religious praxis can be attained, depending on the categories of defilements that have been, or still need to be, abandoned through the practice of cultivation. Each of the nine stages of the cosmic realms (i.e., the realm of desire, four trance states in the realm of form, and four spheres in the formless realm) possesses nine varieties of defilements (weak-weak, weak-middle, weak-strong, and so on). After abandoning the eighth variety of defilements belonging to the ninth stage, one enters the equipoise of cessation *(nirodhasamāpatti),* in which one experiences with one's body *(kāyasākṣin)* the cessation of defilements.[64] Finally, within the ninth and final variety of the ninth stage—that is, the sphere of neither conception nor nonconception *(naivasaṃjñānāsaṃjñāyatana)*—one enters the adamantine concentration *(vajropamasamādhi)* and the final remaining variety of defilements is eliminated. The knowledge of the destruction of the fluxes *(āsravakṣaya)* arises together with the recognition that the process of abandonment is complete; one is then an arhat.

This basic path-structure, as presented in the *Abhidharmahṛdayaśāstra,* is further elaborated in later Sarvāstivāda-Vaibhāṣika texts, which interweave categories of virtuous qualities, meditative states, supernormal powers, or liberations, formerly distinct within the sūtra, into the stages of the new path-structure. Throughout, the organizing principle underlying this structure and directing the incorporation of these practices continues to be that of defilement and purification. Praxis consists of a gradual process through which one is sequentially disconnected from specific defilements through the application of vision and cultivation, culminating in the complete abandonment and future nonarising of all such defilements. The result of this interweaving is a massive edifice of progressive stages, each associated with specific defilements and qualities, all of which are directed toward the final goal of freedom from all defilements.

The Abandonment of Defilements

The Range, Mode of Operation, and Arising of Defilements

The conception of defilements found in the Abhidharma—specifically, the conception of their range, their mode of operation, and the conditions required for their arising—dictates the concrete methods proposed for their abandonment. As the *Prakaraṇapāda* makes clear, defilements operate within the limits of thought and thought-concomitants, and do not operate on material form *(rūpa),* unconditioned factors *(asaṃskṛtadharma),* or forces dissociated from thought *(cittaviprayuktasaṃskāra).*[65] Therefore, a defilement can be abandoned only through the manipulation or transformation of thought processes, not through any exclusively physical means. Defilements provide the basis for action *(karman),* and thus ultimately contribute to the continuation of rebirth.[66] The close connection between defilements and actions is further suggested by the *Saṃyuktābhidharmahṛdayaśāstra,* which specifies the operation of defilements in terms of ten functions, the majority of which detail how defilements act as causes generating and supporting action, thereby reinforcing entrapment in those conditions that result in future rebirth.[67] Conversely, one can of course alter the effect and future generation of defilements by manipulating action *(karman).*

The conditions for the arising of defilements also determine their methods of abandonment. The *Mahāvibhāṣā,* quoting the *Prakaraṇapāda,* gives three such requisite conditions, which are also cited and elaborated in the *Abhidharmakośabhāṣya* and *Nyāyānusāra.*[68] The first condition obtains when a contaminant *(anuśaya)* that is not yet abandoned *(aprahīṇa)* and not yet completely understood *(aparijñāta)* serves as the cause *(hetubala)* for the arising of another contaminant. As Saṅghabhadra explains, there are three reasons why a contaminant may be neither abandoned nor thoroughly known: (1) its possession is not yet cut off *(tatprāptyanucchedāt);* (2) its counteragent has not yet arisen *(tatpratipakṣasya cā 'nutpatteḥ);*[69] and (3) its object is not yet thoroughly known.

The second condition for the arising of defilements obtains when factors that are presently appearing *(ābhāsagata),* and that are conducive to the manifestation *(paryavasthānīya)* of a given contaminant, serve as the object-field *(viṣayabala)* for the arising of that contaminant.[70] In explaining this, Saṅghabhadra argues vehemently against the Dārṣṭāntika position that the object-field of defilements is not established as real, but rather is simply a product of discriminative thought *(vikalpa).*[71] For Saṅghabhadra, all object-fields are real entities by their very nature as object-fields; further, the particular character of an object-field, as conducive to lust, hostility, and so on, is intrinsic to it and not merely a product of discriminative thought. Therefore, in Saṅghabhadra's view, religious praxis actually severs one's connection to actually existing defilements and does not simply alter an erroneous or deleterious process of discriminative thought.

The third condition for the arising of defilements obtains when incorrect attention *(ayoniśomanaskāra)* with regard to the object-field of a contaminant serves as the impetus *(prayogabala)* for the arising of that contaminant. Saṅghabhadra identifies this incorrect attention as erroneous *(viparīta)* orientation *(ābhoga),* and compares the action of incorrect attention to an object-field to that of boring a piece of wood: when this orientation of incorrect attention occurs, the fires of lust are produced.[72]

Through its insistence on the cooperation of three requisite conditions for the arising of defilements, the *Mahāvibhāṣā* rejects the contentions put forth by non-Buddhists that defilements arise only due to an object-field, and thus no longer arise if the object-field is destroyed.[73]

Instead, the *Mahāvibhāṣā* claims that a particular manifestly active defilement *(paryavasthāna)* arises not simply as a result of an appropriate object-field, but also because contaminants *(anuśaya)* of the same type have not yet been abandoned, or because of incorrect attention. Accordingly, it holds that the destruction of the object-fields of defilements cannot be the sole condition for their abandonment. Although the object-field plays an important role in the process of abandonment, the removal of the object-field alone is not sufficient to guarantee that a defilement no longer arises.

The Meaning of Abandonment

What then does the abandonment of defilements entail, and what are its specific causes? As in the case of the character of defilements, the meaning of abandonment and the processes through which it is effected depend on the ontology and model of psychological functioning adopted by particular schools. For the Sarvāstivādins, who supported a realistic ontology in which factors exist in their intrinsic nature in all three time periods, abandonment cannot be equated with destruction, for a defilement, like any real entity, cannot be destroyed.[74] Instead, abandonment must entail some type of separation from or deactivation of a defilement, which, though continuing to exist, no longer contaminates a given moment of thought. However, due to the Sarvāstivādin position that there is no distinction between a latent and an active phase of defilements, deactivation cannot consist either of the suppression of active defilements or of the extirpation of latent ones. Further, given the Sarvāstivādin position that all defilements are associated with thought, and that this quality is an intrinsic characteristic that cannot be altered, an associated defilement cannot be abandoned in the sense that it becomes dissociated from thought, thereby changing its intrinsic character. Finally, for the Sarvāstivādins thought does not exist as an unchanging substratum that undergoes, by turns, association with or dissociation from specific defilements.[75] Rather, if a given moment of thought is associated with a defilement, that moment of thought will always be thus associated, even when it has passed away. Therefore, separation or deactivation cannot consist of dissociation from a previously associated defilement.

Thus the Sarvāstivādin ontology and theory of psychological functioning precludes any interpretation of abandonment as destruction or dissociation. Indeed, their interpretation of abandonment is revealed only by analyzing the fundamental mechanism through which thought is understood to be defiled. First, a contaminant does not become active in defiling a given moment of thought merely through association with it; rather, that contaminant must "adhere or grow" *(anuśerate)* within that moment of thought.[76] Accordingly, abandonment does not occur through mere dissociation, but through terminating a contaminant's adhering or growing, for even if abandoned (and hence no longer adhering or growing), a contaminant is still considered to be associated with thought.[77] Contaminants adhere or grow in two ways: either with regard to the object-support *(ālambanataḥ)* of a given moment of thought, or with regard to the factors with which that moment of thought is associated *(saṃprayuktataḥ).*[78] This adherence or growth is threefold: a contaminant projects the arising of the present possession of contaminants, obstructs the life-stream, and acts as the homogeneous cause *(sabhāgahetu)* in projecting the uniform outflow *(niṣyanda)* of similar moments of thought within that life-stream.[79] Abandonment of an associated contaminant does not mean that it becomes dissociated from thought, but rather that these three operations cease through the power of a counteragent that arises within the life-stream.

For the Sarvāstivādins, even past and future contaminants are considered defiling in the sense that they adhere or grow. Otherwise, since only one thought *(citta)* and its associated thought-concomitants *(caitta)* arise in each moment, and morally dissimilar thought-concomitants cannot occur simultaneously, when an undefiled moment of thought is in present operation, a person would be said to be without contaminants, making the further practice of the path unnecessary.[80] However, this adherence or growth of past or future contaminants must somehow be distinguished from their present activity *(kāritra).* Some Abhidharma masters suggested that past contaminants act to condition the arising of the present possession of contaminants, just as an extinguished fire is able to give rise to smoke. The Abhidharma master Ghoṣaka proposed that, even though a past contaminant does not exert the present activity *(kāritra)* of grasping an object-field, it still has the capability *(sāmarthya),* like a present contaminant, of binding one to an object-support or to other associated factors. Finally, another master, Kṣemadatta, offered a fivefold explanation of this adherence or growth of past and future contaminants: (1) the cause of the contaminants is not yet destroyed; (2) their possession is not yet abandoned; (3) their material basis *(āśraya)* is not yet transmuted *(*parāvṛtta);* (4) one has not yet known their object-support; and (5) one has not yet obtained their counteragent *(pratipakṣa).* Therefore, for the Sarvāstivādins, religious praxis consists of the abandonment of defilements, not only present, but also past and future.

Methods of Abandonment

The central role accorded to the object-support in the arising and operation of defilements is apparent also in the specific methods recommended for their abandonment. In the *Jñānaprasthāna,* contaminants are said to be abandoned "in dependence upon the object-support."[81] However, there are several interpretations of this phrase. The *Mahāvi-*

bhāṣā generally interprets this dependence as indicating that defilements can be said to be abandoned if, due to the activity of a counteragent, they no longer give rise to error with regard to an object-field. Others propose that a contaminant is abandoned only when one sees its object-support with insight.[82] Still others propose that in certain cases contaminants are abandoned through the abandonment of their object-support, or through the abandonment of other contaminants for which the original contaminants are the object-support.[83] Finally, the *Mahāvibhāṣā* quotes the views of yet other masters who, in addition to these methods employing the object-support, admit the possession of a counteragent alone, without the object-support, as a method for the abandonment of certain contaminants.[84]

These various interpretations are then subsumed within four distinct methods for the abandonment of contaminants listed in Upaśānta's *Abhidharmahṛdayaśāstra* and the *Saṃyuktābhidharmahṛdayaśāstra,*[85] and later adopted by Vasubandhu and Saṅghabhadra. These include abandonment of certain contaminants through: (1) the complete understanding of the object-support *(ālambanaparijñāna);* (2) the destruction of those contaminants that take the contaminant to be abandoned as their object-support *(tadālambanasaṃkṣaya);* (3) the abandonment of the object-support *(ālambanaprahāṇa);* and (4) the arising of the counteragent *(pratipakṣodaya).*[86] Each of these methods has as its scope the contaminants of distinct cosmic realms that are to be abandoned through specific stages of the path of vision or of the path of cultivation.[87] The first three methods expand the terse assertion made in the *Jñānaprasthāna* that contaminants are to be abandoned "in dependence upon the object-support." These methods are to be applied to contaminants that are to be abandoned by the path of vision *(darśanamārga),*[88] whereas abandonment through the arising of a counteragent is to be applied to those contaminants that are to be abandoned by the path of cultivation *(bhāvanāmārga).*[89] Cultivation is also divided into four types: the first two —the cultivation of acquisition *(pratilambha)* and the cultivation of habitual practice *(niṣevaṇa)*—are directed toward developing virtuous conditioned factors, while the last two—the cultivation of the counteragent *(pratipakṣa)* and the cultivation of escaping *(vinirdhāvana)*—are applied to all factors tending toward the fluxes, and hence refer specifically to the cultivation of methods for abandoning defilements.[90]

Therefore, from the terse directive of the *Jñānaprasthāna* that contaminants are to be abandoned "in dependence upon the object-support," numerous methods were developed that are applicable to all possible contaminants. First, contaminants are distinguished according to whether or not their object-support is involved in their abandonment. If the object-support is involved, contaminants are to be abandoned by the path of vision; distinctions are then drawn among them in accordance with (1) whether or not their object-support tends toward the fluxes, (2) the cosmic realm to which their object-support belongs, and (3) the noble truth with which their object-support is associated. If the object-support is not involved, contaminants are to be abandoned through cultivation alone; they are distinguished simply by their intensity and by the cosmic realm to which they belong. Thus later Sarvāstivādin texts enumerate contaminants in a complex matrix in accordance with qualifications concerning the role of their object-support, the cosmic realm to which they belong, and the consequent path through which their abandonment occurs.

The Paths of Vision and Cultivation

The differences among these four methods of abandonment and their correlation in the later Sarvāstivādin path-structure with the paths of vision or cultivation suggest that there are substantive differences between these two paths with regard to practice and expected goal. Furthermore, later texts, such as the *Abhidharmakośabhāṣya,* contain lists of various types of paths (mārga) that imply different modes of practice and that argue for a complex history leading to the Abhidharma systematization.[91] However, regardless of any historical differences in the contexts of use for these various paths, according to later Sarvāstivāda-Vaibhāṣika analysis, the paths of vision and cultivation do not correspond to radically different modes of practice or goals. Despite their names, the operations of vision, knowledge, and insight are not exclusively reserved for the path of vision, nor are trance, meditation, and repeated practice exclusively reserved for the path of cultivation.

How then are the paths of vision and cultivation to be distinguished from each other? The *Mahāvibhāṣā* itself raises this question:

> Question: Why [do we use the] terms "to be abandoned by the path of vision" *(darśanaprahātavya),* and "to be abandoned by the path of cultivation" *(bhāvanāprahātavya)?* Since vision is not separated from cultivation and cultivation is not separated from vision, how are these two [different] names for abandonment established?
>
> Answer: Though true cultivation can be attained even in the path of vision and true vision can be attained even in the path of cultivation, [since] vision [here refers to] insight *(prajñā)* and cultivation [here refers to] vigilance *(apramāda),* . . . [and since] in the path of vision insight is great and vigilance is slight, and in the path of cultivation vigilance is great and insight is slight, therefore the terms for these [methods] of abandonment are distinguished [from each other].[92]

The *Mahāvibhāṣā* continues by presenting more than thirty different theories concerning the distinction between abandonment by vision and by cultivation. In this range of theories, the following general points are emphasized: comprehensive observation *(abhisamaya)* of the four noble truths, knowledge (jñāna), and concentration (samādhi) characterize both paths; one progresses gradually through each stage of the path of vision only once, whereas one practices each stage of the path of cultivation repeatedly; ordinary persons *(pṛthagjana)* may practice only the path of cultivation, while noble persons (ārya) may practice both the path of vision and the path of cultivation; the four noble fruits are attained only on the path of cultivation; no retrogression occurs in the case of defilements abandoned through the path of vision, but retrogression is possible in the case of defilements abandoned through the path of cultivation; and the path of vision includes stages of both presentiment and knowledge, whereas the path of cultivation includes stages of knowledge alone.[93] Elsewhere, the *Mahāvibhāṣā* distinguishes the two paths by the cosmic realm and intensity of the defilements to be abandoned by each.[94] Thus the paths of vision and cultivation are demarcated not on the basis of mutually exclusive methods of abandonment but by various criteria, including the character of the defilements to be abandoned, the aspirants employing the path, and the frequency of praxis each path requires.

The Interdependence of Knowledge and Concentration

Hence the mere existence of the two paths of vision and cultivation does not justify the presumption of a strict dichotomy between knowledge and concentration inherent to the Sarvāstivādin path-structure. Instead, references in Abhidharma texts of all periods suggest that the application of vision (or knowledge) and the practice of cultivation (or concentration) are closely intertwined in all varieties of religious praxis, and specifically in the process by which defilements are to be abandoned on any path. This interconnection is demonstrated in the traditional list of the four cultivations of concentration *(samādhibhāvanā)*: the fourth cultivation, which occurs in the fourth trance state (dhyāna) within the realm of form, is directed toward the destruction of the fluxes *(āsravakṣaya),* which results from the comprehensive observation of the four noble truths as applied to each of the five aggregates.[95] This interconnection between knowledge and concentration is further demonstrated in the *Saṅgītiparyāya,* which distinguishes between two powers: the power of consideration *(pratisaṃkhyānabala),* which considers the dependence of future effects, specifically rebirth states, on present action; and the power of cultivation *(bhāvanābala),* which practices the limbs of enlightenment such as the applications of mindfulness and other meditative states.[96] The *Saṅgītiparyāya* affirms that both these powers equally result in "the abandonment of unvirtuous factors and the cultivation of virtuous ones." Similarly, in its discussion of calming *(śamatha)* and discerning *(vipaśyanā),* the *Saṅgītiparyāya* quotes an *Udānavarga* passage that states:

> There is no concentration without insight; there is no insight without concentration. Only when there is both concentration and insight does one attain nirvāṇa.[97]

In its interpretation of this passage, the *Saṅgītiparyāya* again asserts the interdependence of concentration and insight: the particular type of concentration attained is determined by the type of insight developed in it, and since insight takes concentration as its origin and arises from concentration, a given type of insight is produced by an appropriate concentration. Finally, nirvāṇa, defined as the cessation consisting of the destruction of craving, is attained only through both concentration and insight.

The *Mahāvibhāṣā* demonstrates that, for the later Kāśmīra Sarvāstivāda-Vaibhāṣikas also, knowledge and concentration were inextricably linked in the process by which defilements are abandoned. For example, it states that defilements can be abandoned in the applications of mindfulness *(smṛtyupasthāna),* but only in mindfulness produced through cultivation *(bhāvanāmaya),* not in that produced through hearing *(śrutamaya)* or through reflection *(cintāmaya).*[98] This is because only a path that is characterized by a state of concentration, and that is thus a form of cultivation, is capable of abandoning defilements. Further, in discussing those trance states (dhyāna) in which defilements are abandoned, the *Mahāvibhāṣā* notes that, according to the sūtra, the fluxes are destroyed "in dependence upon" *(āśrita)* a particular trance state, not by the trance state itself.[99] All interpretations offered in the *Mahāvibhāṣā* for this "dependence" emphasize that trance or concentration alone cannot cause the abandonment of defilements; knowledge, discernment, or insight are also necessary.

Although Sarvāstivādin Abhidharma texts present ample evidence for the interdependence of knowledge and concentration in religious praxis, certain passages attest to an ongoing historical and structural tension between them. The *Mahāvibhāṣā* refers several times to disagreements between two masters, Jīvala and Ghoṣavarman, whose divergent opinions on specific doctrinal issues reflect precisely this historical tension between knowledge and concentration.[100] In one such passage, the two masters disagree over whether insight (i.e., knowledge) or the equipoise of cessation (i.e., concentration) is more important for attaining the final religious goal of arhatship.[101] Jīvala claims that insight, because it has an object-support, is superior to the equipoise of cessation. The implication is that the superior efficacy of insight derives from its ability to undermine defilements associated with its object-support; the equipoise of cessation, being without an object-support, would be ineffective in counteracting such defilements. In contrast, Ghoṣavarman claims that the equipoise of cessation is superior to insight because it is, by definition, attained only by noble ones, whereas ordinary persons can possess certain varieties of insight.

The *Mahāvibhāṣā* also refers to Jīvala and Ghoṣavarman in a discussion of whether or not states of concentration are essential to the abandonment of defilements.[102] Defilements, it states, can be terminated only in dependence on a state of concentration, where "concentration" is explained as the path of the counteragent *(pratipakṣamārga)* and "termination" as complete abandonment *(prahāṇa)*. The views of Jīvala and Ghoṣavarman are then cited on the issue of the particular meditative stages in which defilements can be abandoned, and specifically on whether or not ordinary persons *(pṛthagjana)* can completely abandon defilements by means of the mundane path *(laukikamārga)*.[103] Jīvala contends that only the noble path *(āryamārga)* as cultivated by noble persons is effective in completely abandoning defilements, while Ghoṣavarman maintains that both the noble path and the mundane path practiced by ordinary persons are effective. The *Mahāvibhāṣā* supports Ghoṣavarman and concludes that both noble and ordinary persons, by means of the noble and mundane paths, respectively, are able to abandon defilements completely in the appropriate states of concentration.

The positions of various schools on the capability of ordinary persons and the efficacy of the mundane path in abandoning defilements usually correlate with their views on the relative importance of knowledge and concentration. For the Sarvāstivāda-Vaibhāṣikas, ordinary persons can abandon certain defilements by practicing the path of cultivation *(bhāvanāmārga)*, in their case referred to as the mundane path *(laukikamārga)*.[104] Abandoning defilements as an ordinary person on the mundane path obviates the need to abandon them once again as a noble person on the path of vision. Thus the path of cultivation can be practiced either by an ordinary person prior to entering the path of vision, in which case it is referred to as the mundane path, or by a noble one after completing the path of vision.

However, this ability of ordinary persons to abandon defilements was disputed by certain Abhidharma masters. Their view evinces a developing opinion that insight is the primary—if not the sole—determinant for the abandonment of defilements. This insight is understood to be pure, that is, not tending toward the fluxes. It enables one to observe the noble truths comprehensively and occurs only after one becomes a noble one by giving rise to a factor not tending toward the fluxes *(anāsravadharma)*, and thereby enters the path of vision *(darśanamārga)*.

These masters would claim that even though ordinary persons, or even non-Buddhists, may enter the various states of concentration within the Buddhist path-structure, they cannot be said to have abandoned defilements completely because they have not entered the distinctively Buddhist noble path of vision, and therefore have not given rise to the pure insight that is requisite before the defilements can be abandoned.

In the *Mahāvibhāṣā,* this view is attributed to the Dārṣṭāntikas, who argue that defilements cannot be abandoned by the mundane path of an ordinary person.[105] Opponents of the Dārṣṭāntikas cite a sūtra passage referring to Udraka Rāmaputra, who, though not a Buddhist, is said to have entered the sphere of neither conception nor nonconception *(naivasaṃjñānāsaṃjñāyatana)* after having abandoned defilements in the lower regions.[106] The Dārṣṭāntikas reject the applicability of this sūtra passage, claiming that the term "abandonment" is not being used in a strict sense. Applying a distinction between manifestly active defilements *(paryavasthāna)* and latent contaminants *(anuśaya),* they interpret this passage to mean that ordinary persons only temporarily suppress manifestly active defilements, without abandoning the underlying latent contaminants. This temporary suppression of defilements occurs in stages up to but excluding the final sphere of neither conception nor nonconception; at any time, these ordinary persons can fall back to an inferior stage.

This Dārṣṭāntika position appears to echo the position, attributed to the Vibhajyavādins and others, that there is no irreversible abandonment of defilements until the final stage of the adamantine concentration, when comprehensive observation and the complete abandonment of all defilements occur simultaneously.[107] For the Sarvāstivāda-Vaibhāṣikas, however, the final goal of the complete destruction of the fluxes is reached through the incremental abandonment of defilements, which results from stages of both concentration and knowledge. Though this final goal of the complete destruction of all defilements may be attained only by a noble one utilizing pure insight after completing the distinctively Buddhist path of vision, ordinary persons and even non-Buddhists can actually abandon individual defilements through cultivation characteristic of the mundane path, and can thereby progress gradually toward the same goal. The Sarvāstivādin insistence on the interconnection of knowledge and concentration at all stages of the path thus shows them to be resistant to the developing opinion that insight is preeminent.

The Role of Possession in the Abandonment of Defilements

For the Sarvāstivāda-Vaibhāṣikas, the mechanism by which defilements are abandoned cannot be reduced to a meditative attainment or to the emergence of insight. Although the term "abandonment" is recognized to have been used in a number of senses, including separation, termination, complete understanding, and so on,[108] for the Sarvāstivāda-Vaibhāṣikas, it comes to have a special sense intimately connected to their most important ontological assumptions.[109] If, as the Sarvāstivāda-Vaibhāṣikas claim, all factors, including defilements, always exist as distinct, real entities in the three time periods of past, present, and future, then abandonment cannot mean the destruction of a defilement itself. And since for the Sarvāstivāda-Vaibhāṣikas defilements are associated with thought, and hence can never become dissociated, abandonment also cannot mean dissociation from a defilement. Further, once a factor becomes the the object-support for a moment of thought and its associated thought-concomitants, including defilements, this status can never be altered. Therefore, one also cannot abandon past defilements in the sense that one separates those defilements from their object-support. Thus the Sarvāstivāda-Vaibhāṣikas were forced by their ontological premises to develop a new model to explain the process of abandonment.

The Sarvāstivāda-Vaibhāṣikas found the key to this model in the mechanism of possession *(prāpti)* or accompaniment *(samanvāgata),* which acts to connect factors that occur within a given life-stream to that life-stream.[110] As a distinct factor that is dissociated from thought *(cittaviprayuktasaṃskāra),* possession can connect a life-stream to any defilement, which then arises or becomes active due to other causes. Even when the present activity of a defilement and its possession cease and become past, they both continue to be connected to that life-stream through subsequent present possessions that arise conditioned by the original one. These possessions form a stream of effects of uniform outflow *(niṣyandaphala)* that not only connects the life-stream to that past defilement but also causes the arising of the possession of future defilements. Within the life-stream of each person, these streams of possession connecting one to past defilements continue without interruption, regardless of whether or not defilements are presently active.

However, this process of the continued connection with past defilements and the potential for the arising of new defilements can be terminated.[111] The uniform outflow of successive possessions of past and present defilements and the arising of future defilements can be interrupted through the present operation of other possessions—namely, the possessions of counteragents *(pratipakṣa).* According to the four methods of abandonment set forth by later Sarvāstivāda-Vaibhāṣika texts, the fourth method, via the counteragent, acts to obstruct those defilements to be abandoned by the path of cultivation. However, the term "counteragent" *(pratipakṣa)* is also used in a wider sense, to refer to the obstruction that constitutes the central event in the abandonment of all defilements, whether by the path of vision or the path of cultivation. For example, the arising of the counteragent for a given past object-support interrupts the causal stream of the possessions of both those defilements that arose dependent on that past object-support and those defilements that arise in dependence on those original defilements. Even though, like all factors, those original defilements and their object-support (as well as the defilements caused by those original defilements) continue to exist in themselves, since the causal stream of their possessions as connected to a particular life-stream has been interrupted, those defilements are said to be abandoned. Further, the arising of yet other defilements is prevented through the present operation of counteragents produced as a result of uniform outflow from the previous counteragents.

A specific type of knowledge, complete understanding *(parijñā),* has an indispensable role in this process of interrupting the stream of possessions. Because a defilement arises, and the stream of possessions of that defilement begins precisely when a given object-field is not completely understood, this stream can be interrupted through the arising of complete understanding with regard to that object-field.[112] Therefore, in the case of those defilements whose method of abandonment is said to be through the object-support, complete understanding is the effective method. This process of abandonment is summarized clearly in the *Mahāvibhāṣā:*

> The noble path does not produce the abandonment of various defilements like a knife cutting a plant, or a stone grinding incense. Rather, when the noble path is present, it causes the possession *(prāpti)* of the accompaniment *(samanvāgata)* of those defilements to cease, and also causes the possession of the nonaccompaniment *(asamanvāgata)* of those defilements to arise. At such a time, it is said that defilements have been abandoned.[113]

In other passages, the phrases "the possession of the accompaniment" and "the possession of the nonaccompaniment" are replaced with "the possession of connection" *(saṃyogaprāpti)* and "the possession of disconnection" *(visaṃyogaprāpti),* respectively.[114] Thus there are two steps in the procedure by which every defilement is abandoned: first, the cessation of "the possession of connection" to a particular defilement, and second, the arising of "the possession of disconnection" from that defilement. The first step serves as the cause for the arising of the second, and their respective activities are compared to throwing out a thief and closing the door, or catching an insect in a jar and plugging the jar's mouth.[115] The second step of disconnection *(visaṃyogaprāpti)* corresponds to the cessation resulting from consideration *(pratisaṃkhyāni-rodha),* which, for the Sarvāstivādins, is equated with nirvāṇa.[116] One progresses along the path by (1) abandoning the possession of connection to and (2) giving rise to the possession of disconnection from each separate defilement in turn; thus there are as many disconnections, cessations, or nirvāṇas as there are defilements or categories of defilements to be abandoned.[117]

Each of these two steps is also correlated, through the two paths of vision and cultivation, with specific types of paths, varieties of counteragents, and stages in the later Sarvāstivādin elaboration of the path-structure.[118] The first step, that of abandoning the possession of a given defilement, is referred to as the stage of the immediately successive path *(ānantaryamārga).*[119] The second step, that of the arising of the possession of disconnection *(visaṃyogaprāpti)* from that defilement, is referred to as the path of liberation *(vimuktimārga).* These two paths are also identified, respectively, with the counteragent that results in abandonment *(prahāṇapratipakṣa)* and the counteragent that results in maintenance *(ādhārapratipakṣa).* Both the immediately successive path and the path of liberation occur every time a defilement is abandoned on either the path of vision or the path of cultivation. On the path of vision, the immediately successive path corresponds to the eight stages of presentiment *(kṣānti),* while the path of liberation corresponds to the eight stages of knowledge (jñāna). On the path of cultivation, where there are no stages of presentiment; both the immediately successive path and the path of liberation correspond to stages of knowledge.[120]

The *Mahāvibhāṣā,* however, explicitly anticipates and rejects any interpretation that would turn this distinction between two steps in the process of abandoning defilements into a strict dichotomy of mutually exclusive processes.[121] It does this by emphasizing that the first step, the immediately successive path, also can be said to constitute disconnection *(visaṃyoga),* in that it projects the possession of disconnection that will be effectively present in the subsequent moment of the path of liberation. Through these correspondences between the two steps in the abandonment of defilements and specific types of paths, varieties of counteragents, and stages within the path, the Sarvāstivāda-Vaibhāṣikas underscore the importance of the abandonment of defilements as the basic dynamic underlying both the structure of the path and religious praxis. Moreover, by these correspondences they demonstrate that knowledge is important as a means for removing defilements, not as an end in itself.

Thus, for the Sarvāstivāda-Vaibhāṣikas, abandonment does not and cannot involve the destruction of a defilement, its dissociation from thought, or separation from its object-support; rather, abandonment is simply the interruption of the stream of its connective possessions. In considering the possibility of retrogression for an arhat, the *Mahāvibhāṣā* clearly illustrates the interdependence of Sarvāstivādin ontology and soteriological progress:

> An arhat who abandons defilements does not make them nonexistent since the characteristics and nature of past and future defilements still actually exist. If a path contrary to the defilements is not yet present in the arhat's life-stream, at such a time it is said that the defilements have not yet been abandoned. If a path contrary to the defilements is already present and the arhat abandons the possession of the connection [with those defilements] and attains the possession of [their] disconnection, then that arhat is no longer accompanied by those defilements and they are said to be abandoned.[122]

Hence even an arhat, in abandoning a given defilement, abandons only its possession and does not destroy the defilement itself. Under certain conditions, that past defilement may serve as the cause for the arising of another present defilement, causing the arhat to retrogress. Similarly, Saṅghabhadra explains abandonment as the arising of a factor contrary to a given defilement, the abandonment of the possession of that defilement, and the attainment of the possession of the disconnection from that defilement. When a defilement is abandoned, the path of the counteragent does not pluck the possession of the defilement out of the life-stream, thereby rendering the defilement forever unable to arise, for even abandoned defilements can arise once again for those whose knowledge is slight. The possibility of defilements arising is forever obstructed only in the final stage of arhatship, by the realization of the knowledge of the nonarising of defilements *(anutpādajñāna).*[123]

Conclusion

Underlying and organizing the intricate structure of the later Sarvāstivāda-Vaibhāṣika path is the core issue of early Buddhist practice—namely, the sequential abandonment of individual defilements, which culminates in final liberation from all defilements. This path-structure continues and elaborates a tension between knowledge and concentration found in the earliest canonical accounts of the enlightenment experience. Further research is needed to explore the roots of this tension in these early Buddhist materials and to describe its resolution in the post-Abhidharma period. Yet an examination of both earlier and later Abhidharma literature shows that this tension was not resolved in favor of either option. Instead, each of the extensions and refinements of the path-structure should be seen as a systematic elaboration of methods still guided by what appears to be the original soteriological goal of the destruction of the fluxes *(āsravakṣaya),* rather than as an attempt to displace this goal and erect either concentration or knowledge as the ultimate religious objective.

The defining characteristics of the later Sarvāstivāda-Vaibhāṣika path-structure unmistakably reflect the primacy of this soteriological goal of the destruction of the fluxes. First, religious praxis is a gradual and cumulative process on the path, and is open to both ordinary and noble persons; liberation is not a question of a sudden or privileged realization of a particular knowledge or meditative state. Second, since the goal is the abandonment of defilements, the path of cultivation *(bhāvanāmārga)* is accorded an importance equal to that of the path of vision *(darśanamārga)*. The Sarvāstivāda-Vaibhāṣikas assert that the path of cultivation can be practiced by both ordinary and noble persons through the repeated application of identical states of knowledge in concentration. As on the path of vision, the path of cultivation entails the application of knowledge to the four noble truths. However, only the path of cultivation results in the attainment of all the noble fruits of religious praxis, through the abandonment of defilements thought to pervade all realms and stages of the cosmos. Ordinary persons can practice the path of cultivation before entering the path of vision, but attain its ultimate fruits only after subsequently becoming noble ones and practicing the path of vision; noble persons first complete the path of vision, and can only attain the ultimate fruits of their praxis through the subsequent practice of the path of cultivation. Thus, in both cases, sudden insight into the four noble truths, which occurs on the path of vision, is insufficient for the attainment of the Sarvāstivāda-Vaibhāṣika ultimate soteriological goal.

Although they reached their apex in the later Sarvāstivāda-Vaibhāṣika path-structure, these same concerns to balance concentration and knowledge in a path directed, ultimately, toward the destruction of the fluxes are found throughout the entire historical period of Abhidharma literature. The contribution of the Sarvāstivāda-Vaibhāṣikas should be viewed not as discontinuous innovation, but rather as an integral part of their transmission and reconstitution of traditional doctrine and praxis in an ontologically consequent fashion. Specifically, their ontological position was shaped by demands for a coherent explanation of the arising and abandonment of defilements. And, in turn, their realistic ontology entails the refinement of the causal principle behind the arising and abandoning of defilements, also understood as real forces of contamination, and precludes any idealistic solutions in which these defilements are equated with cognitive error. Their need to find a coherent and realistic explanation of the abandonment of defilements is satisfied in the notion of possession, which forms the keystone of their theory of religious praxis. By erecting the concrete mechanism of an actually existent defilement, an actually existent possession, and an actually existent path, the Sarvāstivāda-Vaibhāṣikas integrated the traditional soteriological goal into their systematic metaphysics and thereby safeguarded, in their opinion, the authenticity, value, and accessibility of the original enlightenment experience.

Notes

1. Louis de La Vallée Poussin illustrates this tension using the disagreement between Musīla and Nārada, where Musīla represents the position that knowing and seeing *(jānāmi . . . passāmi)* are sufficient for the acquisition of arhatship, and Nārada represents the challenge of meditative experience, claiming that, in addition to nonexperiential "dry" knowledge, one must also "touch [the goal] with one's own body" *(kāyena phusitvā)*. See his "Musīla et Nārada," *Mélanges chinois et bouddhiques* 5 (1936–1937): 189–222; *Saṃyuttanikāya* 12.68, *Kosambisutta,* in M. Leon Feer, ed., The *Saṃyutta-Nikāya,* 5 vols. (London: Pali Text Society, Henry Frowde, 1884–1904; hereafter *SN*), 2:115ff.; *Tsa a-han ching (Saṃyuktāgama;* hereafter *SA),* 14 no. 351 *T* 2 (99) 98c1ff.

2. See Giyū Nishi, "Shikan to chi," *Indogaku Bukkyōgaku kenkyū* 5/2 (1957): 329–340, where these tensions are used to investigate the character of the Buddha's knowledge and its relation to religious praxis. See also Mauro Bergonzi, "Osservazioni su *Samatha* e *Vipassanā* nel Buddhismo Theravāda," *Rivista degli Studi Orientali* 54 (1980): 143–170, 327–357.

3. Paul Griffiths, "Concentration or Insight: The Problematic of Theravāda Buddhist Meditation-Theory," *The Journal of the American Academy of Religion* 59 (1981): 605–624.

4. Lambert Schmithausen examines this tension in relation to possible origins of the Yogācāra school. See his "On the Problem of the Relation of Spiritual Practice and Philosophical Theory in Buddhism," in *German Scholars on India, Contributions to Indian Studies* 2, edited by the Cultural Department of the Embassy of the Federal Republic of Germany, New Delhi (Bombay: Nachiketa Publications, 1976), 235–250. Schmithausen also details both currents from the perspective of "liberating insight" in early Buddhist texts. See idem, "On Some Aspects of Descriptions or Theories of 'Liberating Insight' and 'Enlightenment' in Early Buddhism," in *Studien zum Jainismus und Buddhismus. Gedenkschrift für Ludwig Alsdorf,* Klaus Bruhn and Albrecht Wezler, eds., Alt- und Neu-Indische Studien 23 (Wiesbaden: Franz Steiner Verlag, 1981), 199–250.

5. One notable exception is Schmithausen's "Liberating Insight," which discusses the relation between the destruction of the fluxes and concentration or knowledge in early Buddhist sūtras. Yet here even Schmithausen, apparently deemphasizing the concrete cessation of the fluxes in favor of an abstract liberating insight, states that in the stereotyped description of the enlightenment, "the special emphasis on the Cankers means a shift of the focus of attention from the final aim of Liberating Insight (viz. the cessation of Suffering) to the immediate one (viz. the cessation of the Cankers)" (ibid., p. 213). See *Majjhimanikāya* no. 4 *Bhayabheravasutta,* in V. Trenckner et al., eds., *The Majjhima-Nikāya,* 3 vols. (London: Pali Text Society, Henry Frowde, 1888–1925; hereafter *MN*), 1:21ff.

6. It is possible historically that the destruction of defilements is connected with concentration in contrast to knowledge. It is a topic for further research to determine how this connection may have contributed to the tension between concentration or the destruction of defilements on the one hand, and knowledge on the other.

7. In particular, this chapter builds upon Schmithausen's treatment of certain aspects of the problem raised in his "Liberating Insight." See note 4 above.

8. See ibid., pp. 202–207, for references to discussions of the various scriptural accounts of the enlightenment experience. Though it is generally acknowledged that Abhidharma texts postdate and presume the sūtra, it is of course

possible that any individual sūtra passage may, during the course of its ongoing transmission, have undergone revision and amplification, including influence by later Abhidharma analysis. I have drawn my references predominantly from the *Saṃyuktāgama* and *Madhyamāgama,* which have been proposed as representing the Sarvāstivādin school. See Egaku Mayeda, "Japanese Studies on the Schools of the Chinese Āgamas," in *Zur Schulzugehörigkeit von Werken der Hīnayāna-Literatur* 1, Heinz Bechert, ed., Abhandlungen der Akademie der Wissenschaften in Göttingen, Philologisch-historische Klasse 3-149 (Göttingen: Vandenhoeck & Ruprecht, 1985), 94–103; Ernst Waldschmidt, "Central Asian Sūtra Fragments and Their Relation to the Chinese Āgamas," in *Die Sprache der ältesten buddhistischen Überlieferung,* Heinz Bechert, ed., Abhandlungen der Akademie der Wissenschaften in Göttingen, Philologisch-historische Klasse 3-117 (Göttingen: Vandenhoeck & Ruprecht, 1980), 136ff. For a discussion of the complex problems involved in determining the sectarian affiliation of the *Āgamas* in general and in particular the possibility of Mūlasarvāstivādin and Sarvāstivādin recensions, see Lambert Schmithausen, "Beiträge zur Schulzugehörigkeit und Textgeschichte kanonischer und postkanonischer buddhistischer Materialien," in *Zur Schulzugehörigkeit von Werken der Hīnayāna-Literatur* 2, Heinz Bechert, ed., Abhandlungen der Akademie der Wissenschaften in Göttingen, Philologisch-historische Klasse 3-154 (Göttingen: Vandenhoeck & Ruprecht, 1987).

9. For a discussion of the versions of the *Dharmacakrapravartanasūtra* in Pali and Chinese translation, see André Bareau, *Recherches sur la biographie du Buddha dans les Sūtrapiṭaka et les Vinayapiṭaka anciens: de la quête de l'éveil à la conversion de Śāriputra et de Maudgalyāyana,* Publications de l'École Française d'Extrême-Orient 53 (Paris, 1963), 172ff., esp. 179–182, where Bareau suggests that the familiar structure of the four noble truths may have been a later development. For the central role of *āsravakṣaya* in at least one version, see *Fo-shuo san-chuan fa-lun ching, T* 2 (110) 504b1–2ff., passim, where the goal is described as one wherein "thought, having abandoned all defilements, attains liberation and is then able to realize supreme enlightenment."

10. See *Chung a-han ching (Madhyamāgama;* hereafter *MA),* 40 no. 157 *T* 1 (26) 679c12–13; 48 no. 184 *T* 1.729b21ff.; *Tseng-i a-han ching (Ekottarāgama;* hereafter *EA),* 23 *T* 2 (125) 666c15ff.; *MN* no. 4 *Bhayabheravasutta,* 1:23. Cf. P. Pradhan, ed., *Abhidharmakośabhāṣyam of Vasubandhu,* 2nd ed., Tibetan Sanskrit Works Series 8 (Patna: Kashi Prasad Jayaswal Research Institute, 1975; hereafter *AKB*), 2.44 p. 71.14: *na tāvat bhetsyāmi paryaṅkam aprāpte āsravakṣaye.* The close relation between knowledge or vision on the one hand and the destruction of the fluxes on the other is also found in *MA* 10 no. 54 *T* 1.490a1ff.: "One who has knowledge and vision then attains the destruction of the fluxes; not one who does not have knowledge and does not have vision." Knowledge and vision are then specified as knowledge and vision of the four noble truths. See also *MA* 2 no. 10 *T* 1.431c15ff.; *MN* no. 2 *Sabbāsavasutta,* 1:6; *SA* 10 no. 263 *T* 2.67a23ff., *SN* 22.101 *Vāsijaṭasutta,* 3: 152–153.

11. Bareau, *Recherches sur la biographie du Buddha,* pp. 75–91 suggests that the fourfold structure applied to the fluxes in accounts of the three clear intuitions *(vidyā)* is a later addition. Schmithausen, "Liberating Insight," pp. 205–206 responds that if we admit, as even Bareau does, the centrality of *āsrava* to these accounts, it is "preferable to consider the whole '*āsrava*-layer' as genuine"; hence the application of the fourfold structure to the *āsrava* would not be a later addition. However, one could accept both Bareau's and Schmithausen's suggestions by admitting that even though the application of the fourfold structure

to the fluxes may be a later addition, the destruction of the fluxes itself forms a central and original component of the early Buddhist religious goal. Cf. *SA* 31 nos. 884, 885, 886, esp. 885 *T* 2.223c1ff., which includes the formula describing the four noble truths but does not apply the fourfold structure to the fluxes. This disagreement concerning the priority either of the knowledge of the four noble truths or of the destruction of the fluxes is evident in the contrasting views of Erich Frauwallner (*Geschichte der indischen Philosophie,* 2 vols. (Salzburg: Otto Müller, 1953), 1:216), who claims priority for the fourfold structure of the noble truths, and Ludwig Alsdorf *(Les études Jaina, État présent et taches futures* [Paris: Collège de France, 1965], 4ff.), who suggests the priority of the fluxes and their destruction.

12. For example, *SA* 10 no. 263 *T* 2.67a28, 67b27ff., *SN* 22.101 *Vāsijaṭasutta,* 3:152ff. includes in this series the four applications of mindfulness *(smṛtyupasthāna),* the four right exertions *(prahāṇa,* P. *padhāna),* the four magical powers *(ṛddhipāda),* the five controlling factors *(indriya),* the five powers *(bala),* the seven members of enlightenment *(bodhyaṅga),* and the eightfold noble path, or all together, the thirty-seven limbs *(bodhipakṣyadharma)* of enlightenment, all of which are directed toward the final attainment, the destruction of the fluxes. Or, *MA* 27 no. 107 *T* 1.596c28ff., which lists correct mindfulness, concentration, liberation, the destruction of the fluxes, and nirvāṇa. Cf. also *SA* 41 no. 1140 *T* 2.301b6ff.; and *MN* no. 17 *Vanapatthasutta,* 1:104ff.

13. See *MN* no. 112 *Chabbisodhanasutta,* 3:30ff. The corresponding passage in the Chinese version of the *Madhyamāgama* reads "liberation of thought [through the] destruction of the fluxes." See *MA* 49 no. 187 *T* 1.732a28ff.

14. For example, see Dines Andersen and Helmer Smith, eds., *Sutta-nipāta* (1913; rpt. London: Routledge & Kegan Paul, 1984), no. 163 p. 29, no. 178 p. 31, no. 374 p. 65, no. 539 p. 100, no. 546 p. 101, nos. 1082–1083 p. 209. See also *SA* 22 no. 579 *T* 2.154a28; ibid. no. 581 *T* 2.154b24ff., *SN* 1.3.5 *Arahantasutta,* 1:14ff.; *SA* 5 no. 103 *T* 2.30a7, *SN* 22.89 *Khemakasutta,* 3:128; *SA* 45 no. 1199 *T* 2.326b11; ibid. 14 no. 351 *T* 2.98c1ff., *SN* 12.68 *Kosambisutta,* 2:117. See also Bareau, *Recherches sur la biographie du Buddha,* pp. 72–74.

15. For various histories and tentative chronologies of northern Indian Abhidharma texts, see Hajime Sakurabe, *Kusharon no kenkyū* (Kyoto: Hōzōkan, 1969), 41ff.; Ryūjō Yamada, *Daijō Bukkyō seiritsu ron josetsu* (Kyoto: Heirakuji shoten, 1959), 69ff.; Baiyū Watanabe, *Ubu abidatsumaron no kenkyū* (Tokyo: Heibonsha, 1954), 135ff.; and Erich Frauwallner, "Abhidharma-Studien II. Die kanonischen Abhidharma-Werke," *Wiener Zeitschrift für die Kunde Süd- und Ostasiens* 8 (1964): 59–99.

16. *A-p'i-ta-mo ta-p'i-p'o-sha lun (Mahāvibhāṣā;* hereafter *MVB)* 94 *T* 27 (1545) 487c19.

17. *MVB* 66 *T* 27.343a4ff., 47 *T* 27.244c6ff. See also *A-p'i-ta-mo chi-i-men tsu-lun (Saṅgītiparyāya;* hereafter *SP)* 4 *T* 26 (1536) 383a10–11: "If, monks, the [three] fluxes of desire, existence, and ignorance have been abandoned, then since all the fluxes are eternally destroyed, being without stain, one experiences nirvāṇa." See also the conclusion of the *A-p'i-t'an kan-lu-wei lun (*Abhidharmāmṛta) T* 28 (1553) 980b16–17: "When all fluxes are destroyed, one attains the destruction of all suffering, one attains the nectar of all knowledge."

18. For the four noble fruits of religious praxis *(śrāmaṇyaphala),* including that of the stream-enterer *(srotaāpanna),* the once-returner *(sakṛdāgamin),* the nonreturner *(anāgamin),* and the arhat, see *A-p'i-ta-mo fa-yün tsu-lun (Dharmaskandha;* hereafter *DS)* 3 *T* 26 (1537) 463c7ff.; Valentina Stache-Rosen, *Das Saṅgītisūtra und sein Kommentar Saṅgītiparyāya Teil 1. Dogmatische Begriffsreihen im älteren Bud-*

dhismus 2-1 (hereafter *SR-SP*), Sanskrittexte aus den Turfanfunden 9, Deutsche Akademie der Wissenschaften zu Berlin, Institut für Orientforschung 65, 1-2 (Berlin: Akademie Verlag, 1968), 98; *SP* 6 *T* 26.392c22ff.; *She-li-fu a-p'i-t'an lun* (**Śāriputrābhidharmaśāstra;* hereafter *ŚAŚ*) 4 *T* 28 (1548) 553c8ff.; *MVB* 51 *T* 27.236b20ff., 64 *T* 27.332b2ff., 65 *T* 27.335a29ff., 140 *T* 27.719b27. Each fruit is defined in accordance with the abandonment of specific defilements associated with specific realms or stages. The first fruit of the stream-enterer is attained when one has completely abandoned the three fetters *(saṃyojana),* or the eighty-eight varieties of contaminants that are to be abandoned within the path of vision *(darśanamārga),* and so on, up to the fruit of the sixth and final type of arhat, the unshakable arhat *(akopyadharman),* who has eradicated all the defilements of all realms and stages, and who gives rise to the knowledge of the nonarising of future defilements *(anutpādajñāna).* See Hajime Sakurabe, *Sonzai no bunseki. Abidaruma, Bukkyō no shisō* 2 (Tokyo: Kadokawa shoten, 1969), 121.

19. See *MVB* 46 *T* 27.239c10ff. For an analysis of this process according to the seven types of religious practitioners *(pudgala),* see *MVB* 54 *T* 27.278a8ff.

20. See *MVB* 60 *T* 27.312b6ff. The possibility of retrogression becomes a controversial point in Abhidharma texts that postdate the composition of the *Vibhāṣā* compendia.

21. See *MVB* 46 *T* 27.240b20, 96 *T* 27.496b18.

22. See ibid. 94 *T* 27.487b29ff., where other etymologies are also given. Cf. *Aṅguttaranikāya* 7.9.8 *Arahāsutta,* Robert Morris and E. Hardy, eds., *The Aṅguttara-Nikāya,* 5 vols. (London: Pali Text Society, Henry Frowde, 1885–1910; hereafter *AN*), 4:145.

23. See *DS* 3 *T* 26.464a1ff. See also *MVB* 47 *T* 27.246b29ff. See *AKB* 6.58b p. 376.18ff. for an implicit definition of arhatship as a state in which the fluxes are destroyed *(kṣīṇāsrava).* For the three varieties of fluxes, see *SR-SP* 68; *SP* 4 *T* 26.383a4ff., 425b23ff.; *DS* 3 *T* 26.465b8ff., 491a27ff.; *MVB* 47 *T* 27.243c20ff.; *A-p'i-ta-mo shun cheng-li lun (Nyāyānusāra;* hereafter *NAS)* 53 *T* 29 (1562) 640b18ff.; *AKB* 5.35 p. 306.2ff.

24. Each of the four noble fruits of religious praxis *(śrāmaṇyaphala)* has conditioned and unconditioned varieties, with the unconditioned variety in each case referring to the cessation of specific defilements that are abandoned with the attainment of that particular fruit. For this definition of the arhat, see *SP* 7 *T* 26.393a3ff. The *Dharmaskandha* (*DS* 3 *T* 26.465a17ff.) defines the unconditioned fruit of arhatship as "having forever abandoned all defilements of lust, hatred, and delusion, and so on, having crossed over all rebirth states, having abandoned all paths, having forever extinguished the three fires [of lust, hatred, and delusion], having crossed over the four floods [of lust, existence, views, and ignorance] . . . ," and so on. The *Prakaraṇapāda (A-p'i-ta-mo p'in-lei tsu-lun;* hereafter *PP),* 7 *T* 26 (1542) 719a5ff., cites the same definition, substituting the term "abandonment of fetters" *(saṃyojanaprahāṇa)* for the term "cessation resulting from consideration" *(pratisaṃkhyānirodha).* The *Mahāvibhāṣā* cites this definition of the arhat from the *Prakaraṇapāda* (*MVB* 65 *T* 27.337c2ff.) and another from the *Prajñaptiśāstra* (ibid. 65 *T* 27.338a1ff.), which is very similar to the definition found in the *Dharmaskandha.* Another early Abhidharma text, the **Śāriputrābhidharmaśāstra* (*ŚAŚ* 4 *T* 28.554a6ff.), offers a series of four definitions of the arhat, all of which involve the abandonment or destruction of defilements.

25. *ŚAŚ* 18 *T* 28.646a10ff. For a discussion of the dating and school affiliation of the **Śāriputrābhidharmaśāṣtra,* see Taiken Kimura, *Abidatsuma ron no kenkyū*

(Tokyo: Meiji shoten, 1937), 67ff.; André Bareau, "Les origines du Śāriputrābhidharmaśāstra," *Muséon* 43 (1950): 69–95.

26. *A-p'i-ta-mo fa-chih tsu-lun (Jñānaprasthāna;* hereafter *JP)* 3 *T* 26 (1544) 929b13ff. Cf. *MVB* 46 *T* 27.236b20ff.; *AKB* 5.35 p. 306.2ff. These sixteen are: three fetters *(saṃyojana),* three unvirtuous roots *(akuśalamūla),* three fluxes *(āsrava),* four floods *(ogha),* four connections *(yoga),* four attachments *(grahaṇa),* four ties to the body *(kāyagrantha),* five hindrances *(nivaraṇa),* five fetters *(saṃyojana),* five fetters belonging to the lower realms *(avarabhāgīyasaṃyojana),* five fetters belonging to the upper realms *(ūrdhvabhāgīyasaṃyojana),* five views *(dṛṣṭi),* the group of six desires *(kāmakāya),* seven contaminants *(anuśaya),* nine fetters *(saṃyojana),* and ninety-eight contaminants *(anuśaya).* The *Mahāvibhāṣā* (*MVB* 46 *T* 27.236b21ff.) notes that all of these categories appear in the sūtra with the exception of the five fetters, which are cited first in the *Jñānaprasthāna* (*JP* 3 *T* 26 (1544) 929b20ff.), and the ninety-eight varieties of contaminants, which are implied in sections of the *Dharmaskandha* (*DS* 3 *T* 26.464c25ff.) and first explicitly mentioned in the *Prakaraṇapāda* (*PP* 2 *T* 26 (1542) 698b6ff., 3 *T* 26 (1542) 702a8ff., passim). This disparity between the sūtras and the Abhidharma precipitates a lengthy discussion in the *Mahāvibhāṣā* on the role of Abhidharma texts as commentary on the sūtras, on their principles of interpretation, and on the differences between Buddhist and non-Buddhist methods of interpretation.

27. See *DS* 6 *T* 26.481a8–9, passim; *SP* 3 *T* 26.376a28, 4 *T* 26.383a7–8, 8 *T* 26.399c3, passim; *A-p'i-ta-mo shih-shen tsu-lun (Vijñānakāya;* hereafter *VK),* 1 *T* 26 (1539) 531b16–17, passim; *PP* 1 *T* 26 (1542) 692c3ff., passim. Cf. Ryōzaburō Sakaki, comp., *Mahāvyutpatti,* Suzuki gakujutsu zaidan, Reprint Series (1916; rpt. Tokyo: Suzuki gakujutsu zaidan, 1973), nos. 2134–2139, p. 160, which inserts *paryutthāna* between *anuśaya* and *upakleśa.* See *PP* 1 *T* 26 (1542) 693a27ff., where the individual members of each category are given. For the identification of *kleśa* with *āsrava,* see *A-p'i-t'an shin lun (*Abhidharmahṛdayaśāstra;* hereafter *AHŚ-D) T* 28 (1550) 809b13; *A-p'i-t'an shin lun ching* (**Abhidharmahṛdayaśāstra;* hereafter AHŚ-U) *T* 28 (1551) 834b27ff.; *Tsa a-p'i-t'an shin lun (*Saṃyuktābhidharmahṛdayaśāstra;* hereafter *SAHŚ)* 1 *T* 28 (1552) 871a23ff.

28. *MVB* 47 *T* 27.244a17ff.

29. See ibid. 47 *T* 27.244b4, 48 *T* 27.247a19, 48 *T* 27.249a6, 48 *T* 27.249c11, 48 *T* 27.250a27ff., 49 *T* 27.252b7ff.

30. "Contaminant," or *anuśaya,* is perhaps the term for defilement used least in the sūtras. See Sakurabe, *Sonzai no bunseki,* pp. 115ff. Frauwallner suggests that it is precisely because the term "contaminant" was loose in meaning and infrequently used in the sūtra that it became the convenient focus of Abhidharma elaboration. See Erich Frauwallner, "Abhidharma-Studien III. Der Abhisamayavādaḥ," *Wiener Zeitschrift für die Kunde Südasiens* 15 (1971): 75ff. For an examination of the definitions given for *anuśaya* in the versions of the *Vibhāṣā* and later texts, see Hiromichi Katō, "Zuimen no hataraki," *Bukkyōgaku kenkyū* 38 (1982): 33ff. Cf. Kenyō Mitomo, "Anuśaya no gogi to sono kaishaku," *Indogaku Bukkyōgaku kenkyū* 23/2 (1975): 1007–1002.

31. *MVB* 60 *T* 27.313a1ff. Cf. *NAS* 45 *T* 29.598c16ff. Étienne Lamotte discusses a distinction between defilements *(kleśa)* and their traces *(vāsanā)* in early Buddhist and Abhidharma texts. See his "Passions and Impregnations of the Passions in Buddhism," in *Buddhist Studies in Honour of I. B. Horner,* L. Cousins et al., eds. (Dordrecht-Holland: D. Reidel, 1974), 91–104.

32. That is, *anuśaya* means "subtle" as derived from *aṇu,* or "minute." *AHŚ-U T* 28 (1551) 846c27. The four pseudo-etymologies offered here for *anuśaya* are also found in *PP* 3 *T* 26 (1542) 702a24ff. Cf. *Tsun p'o-hsü-mi p'u-sa so-chi*

*lun (*Āryavasumitrabodhisattvasaṅgītiśāstra)* *T* 28 (1549) 774c14ff. These etymologies are not given in Dharmaśrī's *AHŚ-D* *T* 28 (1550) 817a9ff. Cf. *SAHŚ* 4 *T* 28.902c17ff.; *MVB* 50 *T* 27.257a26ff.; *Pi-p'o-sha lun (*Vibhāṣāśāstra;* hereafter *VB)* 3 *T* 28 (1547) 436a29ff.; *AKB* 5.39 p. 308.9ff.; Unrai Wogihara, ed., *Sphuṭārthā Abhidharmakośavyākhyā: The Work of Yaśomitra* (Tokyo: The Publishing Association of the *Abhidharmakośavyākhyā,* 1932; hereafter *SAKV*), 487.32ff.

33. *A-p'i-t'an kan-lu-wei lun (*Abhidharmāmṛta)* *T* 28.968c24ff. See *MVB* 179 *T* 27.899a23, and the references in Hiromichi Katō, "Zuimen no hataraki. 'Kusharon' shosetsu no zuimen no jyūji," *Shūgakuin ronshū* 53 (1982): note 1, pp. 17–20, which gives four interpretations of the method by which the number 108 is generated, all of which assume the addition of the ten manifestly active defilements to the ninety-eight contaminants. For the analysis of the fluxes *(āsrava)* into 108 varieties, see *A-p'i-t'an p'i-p'o-sha lun (*Abhidharmavibhāṣā;* hereafter *AVB),* 26 *T* 28 (1546) 189a19ff.; *VB* 2 *T* 28.425a1ff.; *MVB* 47 *T* 27.243c21. For this analysis applied to the floods *(ogha),* see *AVB* 26 *T* 28.192b6ff.; *MVB* 48 *T* 27.247a9ff. For this analysis applied to the varieties of grasping *(upādāna),* see *AVB* 26 *T* 28.192c27ff.; *MVB* 48 *T* 27.247b28.

34. See *MVB* 49 *T* 27.253b20–21. See also ibid. 22 *T* 27.113a27–28, 41 *T* 27.313c22ff., 162 *T* 27.819b27–28. The *Prakaraṇapāda* (*PP* 6 *T* 26 (1542) 715c17ff.) defines *kleśa* and *paryavasthāna* in terms of each other, but then uses *paryavasthāna* to refer to the functioning of *kleśa.* Though *anuśaya* is not contrasted with *paryavasthāna* in this passage, it is noteworthy that *paryavasthāna* is used for defilements in their active phase.

35. See *MVB* 50 *T* 27.257b18ff., *VB* 3 *T* 28.436b17ff. Cf. *NAS* 45 *T* 29.599b28ff. See also Genjun Sasaki, "Bonnō no honshitsu," in idem, ed., *Bonnō no kenkyū* (Tokyo: Shimizukobundo, 1975), 104ff., and Yukiō Sakamoto, "Bonnō to gō," in idem, *Abidatsuma no kenkyū* (Tokyo: Daitō shuppansha, 1981), 382ff.

36. The *Abhidharmakośabhāṣya* and later texts emphasize this sense of growing. Junshō Katō suggests an evolution of the meaning of *anuśerate* from an early meaning as "adhering," which was prevalent up to the period of the *Saṃyuktābhidharmahṛdayaśāstra* (*SAHŚ* 1 *T* 28.871a17), in which the new meaning of "growing" is used. Katō proposes that the first Sarvāstivādin text to use *anuśerate* in this new sense of "growing" is the *Ju a-p'i-ta-mo lun (*Abhidharmāvatāraśāstra)* *T* 28 (1554) 983c9ff. See Junshō Katō, "Uro muro no kitei," *Indogaku Bukkyōgaku kenkyū* 29/2 (1973): 637. There are indeed passages in the *Mahāvibhāṣā* (*MVB* 22 *T* 27.111c13ff.) that include both *anuśerate* and *vardhante,* or "growing," in the same phrase, thereby suggesting a meaning for *anuśerate* other than growing. Other passages (*MVB* 86 *T* 27.442c4ff.) gloss *anuśerate* with "binding." By comparing the translation of pertinent sections of the *Mahāvibhāṣā* and **Abhidharmavibhāṣāśāstra,* Hiromichi Katō concludes that the translation of *anuśerate* as "growing," which appears also in the translation of early Sarvāstivādin texts, may be attributable to Hsüan-tsang. See H. Katō, "Zuimen no hataraki," pp. 38–39.

37. For this third sense of contaminants as *anubadhnanti,* or "binding," and its relation to a fourth sense as *anugata,* or "pervasive," which is cited in the *Mahāvibhāṣā* as the view of Buddhist teachers from other regions, see H. Katō, "Zuimen no hataraki," pp. 42–45.

38. *AHŚ-D* 2 *T* 28 (1550) 817c27ff.; *AHŚ-U* 3 *T* 28 (1551) 848b1ff.; *SAHŚ* 4 *T* 28.907b20ff. Cf. the reference in *AKB* 5.2a p. 278.11: *cittakleśakaratvād āvaraṇatvāc chubhair viruddhatvāt.* For the second line of this verse, see ibid. p. 278.15: *kuśalasya co 'palambhād aviprayuktā atha ihā 'nuśayāḥ.* Cf. *SAKV* 443.17ff.

39. *AKB* 5.2a p. 277.17ff.; *SAKV* 442.28ff.; *NAS* 45 *T* 29.596c24ff.; Padmanabh S. Jaini, ed., *Abhidharmadīpa with Vibhāṣāprabhāvṛtti,* Tibetan Sanskrit Works Series 4 (Patna: Kashi Prasad Jayaswal Research Institute, 1977; hereafter *ADV*), nos. 261–262, pp. 220.5ff.

40. For the Mahāsāṅghika view, see Vasumitra's *I-pu-tsung lun lun (*Samayabhedoparacanacakra) T* 49 (2031) 15c28ff.

41. *AKB* 5.2 p. 278.5ff.; *SAKV* 444.15ff.; *NAS* 45 *T* 29.599b28ff.

42. See *MVB* 16 *T* 27.80c1ff.; *AKB* 2.34d p. 62.9; *SAKV* 142.6ff.

43. For the Vātsīputrīya position that contaminants are dissociated, see *MVB* 2 *T* 27.8b23. Cf. *NAS* 45 *T* 29.599b28ff.; *SAKV* 444.3ff.

44. *AKB* 5.2a p. 278.17ff.

45. See *NAS* 45 *T* 29.598c16ff. For the refutation of this view on the grounds that a cause and effect cannot be different from one another as dissociated and associated, see *SAHŚ* 4 *T* 28.907c12ff. Cf. *NAS* 45 *T* 29.597b27ff. for the position of the Dārṣṭāntika master Sthavira (or Śrīlāta), who identifies the contaminant with the secondary element *(*anudhātu),* which functions as the cause to produce active defilements.

46. Saṅghabhadra (*NAS* 45 *T* 29.599b27–28) notes that this Vibhajyavādin position is to be expected, given their rejection of the existence of past and future factors.

47. This list of synonyms includes the connections (yoga), grasping *(upādāna),* floods *(ogha),* and fluxes *(āsrava).* See Dharmaśrī's *AHŚ-D* 2 *T* 28 (1550) 817a13ff.; Upaśānta's *AHŚ-U* 3 *T* 28 (1551) 847a3ff.; *SAHŚ* 4 *T* 28.903b17ff.; *AKB* 5.35 p. 306.2ff.; *NAS* 53 *T* 29.640b18ff. Cf. ibid. 45 *T* 29.599b10ff. The *Abhidharmadīpa* (*ADV* no. 260 p. 219.10ff.) lists defilements *(kleśa),* contaminants *(anuśaya),* fluxes *(āsrava),* fetters *(saṃyojana),* ties *(grantha),* connections (yoga), and floods *(ogha)* as synonyms. See also *NAS* 2 *T* 29.340b1ff., where Saṅghabhadra explains that even though the sūtra only uses the term "fluxes" *(āsrava)* to describe those defilements from which an arhat attains liberation, it actually intends the other varieties of defilements as well, since an arhat is liberated from all defilements *(kleśa)* and subsidiary defilements *(upakleśa). NAS* 48 *T* 29.615b26ff. states explicitly that the various categories of defilements include one another.

48. See *EA* 34 *T* 2.738c23ff.; *AN* 7.8 *Saṃyojanasutta* 4:7, *AN* 7.11–12 *Anusayasutta* (1–2) 4:9; *SR-SP* 184; *SP* 17 *T* 26.439a18ff.; *PP* 1 *T* 26 (1542) 693b28ff.; *MVB* 50 *T* 27.257a18ff.; *AVB* 27 *T* 28.200a10ff.; *VB* 3 *T* 28.436a22ff.

49. *MVB* 46 *T* 27.239a5. Cf. Eduard Müller, ed., *Dhammasaṅgaṇi* (London: Pali Text Society, Henry Frowde, 1885), 197 for these ten identified as fetters *(saṃyojana).* For an interpretation of the transition from seven to ten contaminants, see Frauwallner, "Abhidharma-Studien III," pp. 75–76.

50. See Sakurabe, *Sonzai no bunseki,* (chart), p. 121. See *PP* 3 *T* 26 (1542) 702a8ff., 7 *T* 26 (1542) 719c15ff.; *JP* 14 *T* 26 (1544) 992b9ff.; *MVB* 50 *T* 27.259b18ff., 145 *T* 27.743a12ff. Among the ninety-eight contaminants, thirty-six belong to the realm of desire, thirty-one to the realm of form, and thirty-one to the formless realm. In accordance with the cognitive stages of the path, there are twenty-eight contaminants to be abandoned by vision of the noble truth of suffering, nineteen by vision of the noble truth of the origin of suffering, nineteen by vision of the noble truth of the cessation of suffering, twenty-two by vision of the noble truth of the path leading to this cessation, and ten by the path of cultivation. Combining the cognitive stages and the cosmic realms, eighty-eight contaminants are to be abandoned by the path of vision and ten by the path of cultivation. Among the thirty-six contaminants belonging to the realm of desire, thirty-two are to be abandoned by the path of vision and four by the

path of cultivation; among the thirty-one belonging to both the realm of form and the formless realm, in each case, twenty-eight are to be abandoned by the path of vision and three by the path of cultivation. Of interest here is a text entitled *A-p'i-t'an chiu-shih-ba chieh ching* in one volume (i.e., The Abhidharma Sūtra on the Ninety-eight Fetters or Contaminants) cited in the catalogue of the fifth- to sixth-century bibliographer Seng-yu, but apparently lost even in his time. See *Ch'u san-tsang chi-chi* 2 *T* 55 (2145) 6b1.

51. For an extensive discussion of practices attested in the sūtra, their relation to early Abhidharma practices, and the history of the development of the distinctive Abhidharma path in early Sarvāstivādin texts, see Yamada, *Daijō Bukkyō,* pp. 40–136.

52. See *SP* 8 *T* 26.401c24ff.; *DS* 4 *T* 26 472a7ff.; *PP* 2 *T* 26 (1542) 697b3ff., 3 *T* 26 (1542) 702a8ff., 7 *T* 26 (1542) 719c14ff., 12 *T* 26 (1542) 741c18ff., passim.

53. Cf. the account of the history and development of the later Sarvāstivādin path-structure proposed by Frauwallner (in his "Abhidharma-Studien III"), who concludes that this structure found its first expression in the *Abhidharmahṛdayaśāstra* as the innovation of the individual master, Dharmaśrī.

54. *VK* 4 *T* 26.548c4ff.

55. Ibid. *T* 26.551a21ff., passim. For the four varieties of knowledge as applied to the noble truths, namely, knowledge of suffering, of the origin of suffering, of its cessation, and of the path, see *SR-SP* 100; *SP* 7 *T* 26.393c27ff.; *PP* 5 *T* 26 (1542) 712b10–11.

56. The term *"dharmajñāna"* is ambiguous: "dharma" can refer to the doctrine, as possibly in *MVB* 106 *T* 27.549b21; cf. *AKB* 6.26c p. 350.20; *SAKV* 542.11ff.; Wilhelm and Magdalene Geiger, *Pali Dhamma vornehmlich in der kanonischen Literatur* (1920), in Heinz Bechert, ed., *(Wilhelm Geiger) Kleine Schriften zur Indologie und Buddhismuskunde,* Glasenapp-Stiftung 6 (Wiesbaden: Franz Steiner, 1973), 149–151. Or, "dharma" can refer to those factors belonging to the realm of desire specifically, as in the *Saṅgītiparyāya* (*SP* 7 *T* 26.393c14ff.), in which case *"anvayajñāna"* would refer to the subsequent knowledge of those factors belonging to the realm of form and the formless realm. Cf. *SAKV* 616.29ff., which quotes a śāstra passage, identical to the *Saṅgītiparyāya* passage referred to above: *dharmajñānaṃ katamat. kāmapratisaṃyukteṣu saṃskāreṣu yad anāsravaṃ jñānaṃ. . . . anvayajñānaṃ katamat. rūpārūpyapratisaṃyukteṣu saṃskāreṣu yad anāsravaṃ jñānaṃ.* Wogihara suggests that the śāstra referred to here is the *Jñānaprasthāna* (*JP* 8 *T* 26 (1544) 957b19ff.).

57. This pair appears in early Sarvāstivādin texts in a list of four varieties of knowledge including, in addition to the preceding pair, the knowledge of other people's thoughts *(paracittajñāna)* and conventional knowledge *(saṃvṛtijñāna).* See *SR-SP* 100; *SP* 7 *T* 26.393c14ff. Cf. *ŚAŚ* 23 *T* 28.672c3–4. These four varieties of knowledge are combined with the four knowledges of the noble truths, the knowledge of destruction *(kṣayajñāna),* and the knowledge of nonarising *(anutpādajāna)* to form the ten varieties of knowledge characteristic of later Abhidharma texts. See *PP* 1 *T* 26 (1542) 694b4ff. For various theories as to the number of knowledges, see *MVB* 148 *T* 27.756c20ff.

58. See *ŚAŚ* 10 *T* 28.598b20ff.

59. For the relation between presentiment *(kṣānti)* and knowledge (jñāna), see *MVB* 95 *T* 27.489b19ff., 95 *T* 27.490b17ff.

60. *SP* 4 *T* 26.383a27ff.; cf. *SR-SP* 68–69. This passage appears in an explanation of the objective of disciplined conduct or of the religious life *(brahmacaryaiṣaṇā),* which constitutes the last of the three objectives *(eṣaṇā).*

61. *VK* 4 *T* 26.551a15ff.

62. See *AHŚ-D* 2 *T* 28 (1550) 818a10ff.; *AHŚ-U* 3 *T* 28 (1551) 848b16ff.; *SAHŚ* 5 *T* 28.907c24ff. For the dating of the *Abhidharmahṛdayaśāstra* prior to the *Mahāvibhāṣā* and contemporaneous with the *Jñānaprasthāna*, see Yamada, *Daijō Bukkyō*, pp. 111ff.; Frauwallner, "Abhidharma-Studien III," pp. 71–72. For the provenance of the text, see Watanabe, *Ubu abidatsumaron*, pp. 123ff.

63. See Robert Buswell's chapter in this volume. See *MVB* 6 *T* 27.29c13, 6 *T* 27.30a2ff. The *Jñānaprasthāna* refers to only three of the four preparatory stages of penetration (omitting *kṣānti*) to be practiced prior to the path of vision: *JP* 1 *T* 26 (1544) 918a7ff. All four preparatory stages do appear in the *Mahāvibhāṣā* (esp. *MVB* 5 *T* 27.23c15ff.).

64. For a passage indicating that it is the cessation of defilements that is experienced with one's own body *(kāyasākṣin)*, see *MVB* 23 *T* 27.115b17ff.

65. *PP* 6 *T* 26 (1542) 715c22ff.: "What factors are actively defiled? Defiled *(kliṣṭa)* thought and thought-concomitants. What factors are not actively defiled? Undefiled thought and thought-concomitants, material form, unconditioned factors, and forces dissociated from thought."

66. See Sakamoto, "Bonnō to gō," pp. 380–381; H. Katō, "Zuimen no hataraki," pp. 29–32; Sasaki, "Bonnō no honshitsu," pp. 78–83, 98–104. Cf. *MVB* 47 *T* 27.244c1. The *Mahāvibhāṣā* (ibid. 50 *T* 27.257c5ff.) identifies the ultimate effect of each of the seven contaminants as a particular rebirth state: lust for sense pleasures results in rebirth as a dove, a small bird, or a mandarin drake or duck; hostility, in rebirth as a bee, a grub, or a poisonous snake; lust for existence, in rebirth in the realm of form and the formless realm; and so on. Similarly, the *Abhidharmahṛdayaśāstra* (*AHŚ-D* 2 *T* 28 (1550) 815b15ff.; *AHŚ-U* (1551) 843c24ff.) declares that contaminants are the root of all existences and accompany action to produce the one hundred varieties of suffering.

67. *SAHŚ* 4 *T* 28.899c20ff. This list of ten functions also appears in the *Abhidharmakośabhāṣya* (*AKB* 5.1aff. p. 277.3ff.; *SAKV* 441.1ff.), and the *Nyāyānusāra* (*NAS* 45 *T* 29.596a21ff.), which includes an additional six. For a detailed examination of these sixteen functions, see H. Katō, "Zuimen no hataraki. 'Kusharon' shosetsu no zuimen no jyūji," pp. 3ff.; idem, "Zuimen no hataraki," pp. 52ff.

68. See *PP* 3 *T* 26 (1542) 702b15ff.; *MVB* 61 *T* 27.313b18ff., 61 *T* 27.313c18ff.; *AKB* 5.34 p. 305.16ff.; *SAKV* 485.2ff.; *NAS* 53 *T* 29.638c29ff., 722b1ff.; *ADV* no. 359b–d p. 295.18ff. The context of this discussion in the *Mahāvibhāṣā*, but not in the *Prakaraṇapāda*, is the relation between the arising of defilements and the occurrence of retrogression *(parihāṇi)*. That the *Abhidharmakośabhāṣya* and *Nyāyānusāra* depend directly on one of the versions of the *Vibhāṣā* as their source for these three reasons is indicated by their subsequent reference to retrogression. See *AKB* 5.34 p. 306.1; *NAS* 53 *T* 29.639a26ff. Saṅghabhadra (*NAS* 53 *T* 29.638c9ff.) also lists as many as twelve specific causes for the arising of defilements, all of which, he claims, can be summarized by these three conditions: for example, good fortune, false teachings, sleeping too much, eating, one's stage in life, or one's habits, and so on.

69. Yaśomitra (*SAKV* 485.2–3) cites, without acknowledgement, the first two of these three reasons given by Saṅghabhadra, and correlates them with *aprahīṇa* and *aparijñāta*, respectively. Such a correlation is not evident in Hsüan-tsang's translation of the *Nyāyānusāra*.

70. Yaśomitra (*SAKV* 485.4–6) indicates his awareness of an ambiguity in the interpretation of the relation between *kāmarāgānuśaya* and *paryavasthāna* by providing two interpretations of this second condition: *kāmarāgasya paryavasthānīyā anukūlā iti. kāmarāga eva vā paryavasthānaṃ kāmarāgaparyavasthānaṃ. tasmai hitāḥ*

kāmarāgaparyavasthānīyāḥ. "[The compound] *'kāmarāgaparyavasthānīya'* [should be understood as] those [object-fields that] are conducive, [that is,] suitable to the manifestation of [the contaminant,] lust for sense pleasures. [Or, the compound] *'kāmarāgaparyavasthāna'* [should be interpreted as] the manifestly active defilement that is precisely [the contaminant,] lust for sense pleasures. [The gerundive *'paryavasthānīyā'* indicates] those that benefit that [lust for sense pleasures]; [therefore,] those that are conducive to the manifestly active defilement, lust for sense pleasures."

71. *NAS* 53 *T* 29.639b4ff. Cf. *MVB* 86 *T* 27.442c4ff.

72. Yaśomitra (*SAKV* 485.8–9) explains incorrect attention as "the contiguous condition *(samantarapratyaya)* that is erroneous with regard to a presently appearing object-field" *(tatra cā 'bhāsagateṣu viṣayeṣu viparītaḥ samanantarapratyaya ity arthaḥ)*.

73. *MVB* 61 *T* 27.313c22ff. Cf. *NAS* 55 *T* 29.650b13ff.

74. In contrast, the Dārṣṭāntikas reject this realistic ontology, denying that either the contaminants or the object-support actually exist as real entities in the three time periods. The object-support of a given defilement is therefore not an actually existent entity but merely the product of misapprehension. They also maintain a distinction between latent contaminants *(anuśaya),* which exist in the life-stream as seeds, and manifestly active defilements *(paryavasthāna)* produced by these seeds. As potentialities, these contaminants cannot be said to be either associated with or dissociated from thought. See *MVB* 22 *T* 27.110a22ff., 85 *T* 27.442a4ff. Cf. *NAS* 49 *T* 29.617a4ff., where these views are attributed to Śrīlāta.

75. For those who support the view that thought continues as an unchanging stream upon which defilements are superimposed, see *MVB* 22 *T* 27.110a10ff.

76. In general, a moment of thought can be said to have contaminants *(sānuśaya)* either because contaminants adhere or grow in dependence on it or because contaminants are associated with it. However, a moment of thought that has contaminants only as a result of association is not considered to be defiled. See *MVB* 22 *T* 27.110b13ff.; *AKB* 5.32 p. 304.5ff. Cf. *NAS* 53 *T* 29.637c7ff., which, referring to the *Jñānaprasthāna* (*JP* 1 *T* 26 (1544) 921a11ff.), states: "What is 'adhering' or 'growing' *(anuśerate)?* It refers to the fact that contaminants are associated with this [moment of] thought, are dependent upon thought, and not yet abandoned. What is 'not adhering' or 'not growing' *(na anuśerate)?* It refers to the fact that contaminants are [still] associated with this [moment of] thought, and yet one has already attained complete abandonment [of them]."

77. See *JP* 1 *T* 26 (1544) 921a19ff: "Are contaminants of a given [moment of] thought to be abandoned? They are either to be abandoned or not to be abandoned. Which are those to be abandoned? They are those contaminants that depend upon this [moment of] thought. Which are those that are not to be abandoned? They are those contaminants that are associated with this [moment of] thought." Cf. also *MVB* 22 *T* 27.113b11ff.: "In this [passage from the *Jñānaprasthāna*] it is indicated that contaminants [functioning] with regard to the object-support can be said to be abandoned, not [those functioning] with regard to associated [factors]. That is to say, one can regulate defilements [functioning] with regard to an object-support, making them not arise in the present and not construct error; it is not the case that one can regulate defilements [functioning] with regard to associated [factors,] making them no longer associated with thought." Cf. *AKB* 5.61 p. 320.17ff.; *NAS* 55 *T* 29.651a6ff. Cf. *MVB* 22 *T* 27.113b25ff.: "However, in this [passage] the statement, 'contaminants [func-

tioning] with regard to the object-support can be abandoned, and not those [functioning] with regard to associated factors,' is made from the perspective of [whether or not] thought is said to be possessed of contaminants, and not from the perspective of [the contaminant] functioning as adhering or growing, because this functioning as adhering or growing in both senses [with regard to the object-support and associated factors] can be abandoned."

78. For a discussion of these two types of contaminants and their basis either in the object-support or in associated factors, see *MVB* 22 *T* 27.111c17ff. esp. 22 *T* 27.112c28ff.; *AKB* 5.18 p. 289.16ff.; *NAS* 49 *T* 29.616b22ff.; *AKB* 5.39 p. 308.11–12; *NAS* 53 *T* 29.641c14ff. (parts of which are quoted, without attribution, by Yaśomitra, *SAKV* 488.2ff.); *ADV* p. 242.18ff.; H. Katō, "Zuimen no hataraki," pp. 36–42; and Sakamoto, "Bonnō to gō," pp. 387ff. For the interpretations of various Sarvāstivādin masters, see *MVB* 22 *T* 27.112a14ff.

79. See *NAS* 53 *T* 29.637c16ff. The *Mahāvibhāṣā* (*MVB* 22 *T* 27.113a10ff.) attributes to Vasumitra a fourfold explanation of the adherence or growth of contaminants: (1) they stimulate evil, as when the evil conduct of one person stimulates that in others; (2) they are like the heat of a fire, which pervades completely a small water vessel; (3) they are like smoke, as when clothes permeated by smoke become dirty; (4) they are capable of censure, as when an entire community of monks is punished for the offense of a single person. As H. Katō notes ("Zuimen no hataraki," p. 39), this fourfold explanation emphasizes the influence of contaminants on other thought-concomitants. For a later definition of growth or adherence as the fact that "contaminants are established and grow with regard to a certain factor: that is to say, they bind and increase stain," see *NAS* 49 *T* 29.616b12ff.

80. See *MVB* 22 *T* 27.113a23ff.

81. *JP* 1 *T* 26 (1544) 921a22; *MVB* 22 *T* 27.113b29ff.

82. See *MVB* 22 *T* 27.113c5ff., 22 *T* 27.114a9ff. Cf. *NAS* 55 *T* 29.649c18.

83. See *MVB* 22 *T* 27.113c21ff., 22 *T* 27.114a10ff., 22 *T* 27.114a18ff. Cf. *NAS* 55 *T* 29.650a3ff.; *ADV* nos. 385–386 pp. 317ff.

84. For the views of Kṣemadatta, who offers four methods, see *MVB* 22 *T* 27.114b2ff.; for the views of Vasumitra, who offers five, see ibid. *T* 27.114b6ff.

85. *AHŚ-U* 3 *T* 28 (1551) 847c27ff.; *SAHŚ* 4 *T* 28.906a13ff. This list does not appear in Dharmaśrī's *Abhidharmahṛdayaśāstra.* The *Saṃyukābhidharmahṛdayaśāstra* (*SAHŚ* 4 *T* 28.906a18–19) also includes a list of five methods, which are the opposite of Kṣemadatta's fivefold explanation of the adherence or growth of past and future contaminants cited previously (see *MVB* 22 *T* 27.113b4ff.): (1) the cause of the contaminants is forever terminated; (2) their possession is abandoned; (3) their material basis has been transmuted; (4) their object-support is known; and (5) their counteragent is obtained.

86. See *AKB* 5.60 p. 319.19ff.; *SAKV* 498.9ff.; *NAS* 55 *T* 29.649c18ff.

87. See Hiromichi Katō, "Danwakuron kara mita kujūhachi zuimen," *Indogaku Bukkyōgaku kenkyū* 30/1 (1981): 303–306.

88. Saṅghabhadra (*NAS* 55 *T* 29.650a27ff.) attempts to resolve the apparent inconsistency between these three methods, each appropriate in the case of certain varieties of contaminants, and his previous general statement (ibid. *T* 27.649c18ff.) that contaminants are abandoned as a result of insight observing their object-support.

89. Saṅghabhadra (*NAS* 55 *T* 27.650c2ff.) explains that even though the path of the counteragent is applied specifically to defilements that are to be abandoned by the path of cultivation, counteragents are operative in the aban-

donment of all contaminants. The *Mahāvibhāṣā* (*MVB* 151 *T* 27.264c27ff.) proposes a twofold distinction between the counteragent of the path of vision and that of the path of cultivation.

90. See *MVB* 79 *T* 27.408b2ff., 105 *T* 27.545a18ff. For alternative theories of six varieties of cultivation, see ibid. 105 *T* 27.545a20ff., 163 *T* 27.824b2ff.; *SAHŚ* 10 *T* 28.954a7ff.; *AKB* 7.27 p. 410.18ff.; *SAKV* 640.2ff.; *NAS* 74 *T* 29.745b26ff. Yaśomitra (*SAKV* 640.11) glosses *vinirdhāvana* as "severing the possession of the defilement" *(vinirdhāvanaṃ kleśaprāptichedaḥ).*

91. See *AKB* 6.65b–d p. 381.19ff., including paths that are mundane *(laukika),* supermundane *(lokottara),* characterized by vision *(darśana),* characterized by cultivation *(bhāvanā),* beyond training *(aśaikṣa),* preparatory *(prayoga),* immediately successive *(ānantarya),* characterized by liberation *(vimukti),* and special *(viśeṣa).* Cf. also *ŚAŚ* 15 *T* 28.625a7ff., which refers to eleven different paths, containing from one to eleven members, and including all practices and virtuous factors instrumental in religious praxis.

92. *MVB* 51 *T* 27.267a7ff. Cf. ibid. 144 *T* 27.742b13ff.

93. Cf. Giyū Nishi "Indo Bukkyō shijō ni okeru kendōron no tenkai," in idem, *Abidatsuma Bukkyō no kenkyū,* (Tokyo: Kokusho kankōkai, 1975), 601ff., where six major differences between the paths of vision and cultivation are given.

94. *MVB* 51 *T* 27.265a7ff.

95. *ŚAŚ* 16 *T* 28.635c21ff.; *DS* 8 *T* 26.489b2ff.; *SR-SP* 112ff.; *SP* 7 *T* 26.395c8ff.; *AKB* 8.27c–d p. 451.8ff.; *SAKV* 684.29ff. (which quotes the sūtra source at length); *ADV* no. 586 p. 425.16ff.

96. *SR-SP* 53ff.; *SP* 2 *T* 26.372a25ff. See also Müller, ed., *Dhammasaṅgaṇi,* p. 232.

97. *SP* 3 *T* 26.375b24–25. Cf. *Fa-chü ching (*Udānavarga) T* 4 (210) 572a18–19; *Ch'u-yao ching (*Udānavarga) T* 4 (212) 766b29–c1; *Fa-chi yao-sung ching (*Udānavarga) T* 4 (213) 796c20ff. Cf. Franz Bernhard, ed., *Udānavarga,* 2 vols., Sanskrittexte aus den Turfanfunden 10, Abhandlungen der Akademie der Wissenschaften in Göttingen, Philologisch-historische Klasse 3–54 (Göttingen: Vandenhoeck & Ruprecht, 1965), 1:439 (ch. 32, v. 25): *nā 'sty aprajñasya vai dhyānaṃ prajñā nā 'dhyāyato 'sti ca. yasya dhyānaṃ tathā prajñā sa vai nirvāṇasāntike.*

98. See *MVB* 187 *T* 27.937b25ff. Since the intrinsic nature of mindfulness is insight, it therefore, like insight, has these three varieties. See ibid. *T* 27.938b8ff.

99. Ibid. 161 *T* 27.818a19ff.

100. The disagreements between Ghoṣavarman and Jīvala cited in the *Mahāvibhāṣā* bear a striking resemblance to those between Musīla and Nārada in the *SN* 12.68 *Kosambisutta* 2:115ff., and to the controversy concerning the necessity of meditation for religious attainment found in the *SN* 12.70 *Susimaparibbājakasutta* 2:119ff.; *SA* 14 no. 347 *T* 2.96b25ff. It is significant, however, that the views of Ghoṣavarman and Jīvala are not attributed to the sūtra. The Chinese translation of the *Kosambisutta* (*SA* 14 no. 351 *T* 2.98c1ff.) refers to a Musīla and a Nārada, and not to a Ghoṣavarman or a Jīvala. These two figures could have been cited in a sūtra that is not preserved, or they may simply serve as representatives in the Abhidharma traditions of a fundamental tension between knowledge and concentration, under whose names controversies of distinct historical origins have been conflated.

101. *MVB* 143 *T* 27.734b29ff.

102. Ibid. 60 *T* 27.310c6ff. Here the *Mahāvibhāṣā* counters the position of the

Vibhajyavādins, who claim that certain defilements can be abandoned simply due to the end of one's life in a particular rebirth state, quite apart from any state of concentration.

103. Ibid. *T* 27.310c28ff.; *AVB* 32 *T* 28.234b9ff. Cf. *MVB* 129 *T* 27.671b3ff.; *NAS* 78 *T* 29.765c5ff. This involves the issue of whether or not defilements are abandoned only in the seven basic meditative states (the four trance states of the realm of form and three among the four spheres within the formless realm), or also in the preliminary stages or thresholds *(sāmantaka)* for these basic meditative states. See *AKB* 6.49 p. 368.8ff., 8.22 p. 447.18ff.

104. *MVB* 90 *T* 27.465a15ff.

105. See ibid. 51 *T* 27.264b19ff., 144 *T* 27.741c20ff., where this view is attributed to the Abhidharma master Bhadanta. Cf. ibid. 90 *T* 27.465a15ff., 140 *T* 27.719c21ff. See also Jīvala's view cited above that the mundane path practiced by ordinary persons is not effective in abandoning defilements, ibid. 60 *T* 27.310c29ff.

106. See *MN* no. 26 *Pariyesanasutta* 1: 165; *MA* 56 no. 204 *T* 1.776c6ff.

107. See *MVB* 47 *T* 27.246c19ff., 68 *T* 27.355a15ff., 103 *T* 27.533a21ff., 144 *T* 27.742a2ff. For similar views attributed to Sthavira (or Śrīlāta), see *NAS* 62 *T* 29.686b27ff. For the views of the Mahāsāṅghikas, see Nishi, "Indo Bukkyō shijō ni okeru kendōron no tenkai," pp. 617ff.

108. *MVB* 62 *T* 27.321b7ff. lists eight senses, including abandonment, separation, termination, truth, complete understanding, the noble fruits of religious praxis, nirvāṇa with remainder, and nirvāṇa without remainder. Cf. ibid. 162 *T* 27.819b23ff., 181 *T* 910a17ff.

109. See *NAS* 55 *T* 29.651a6ff.

110. See ibid. 53 *T* 29.637c16ff. For an explanation of the activity of possession, see *MVB* 93 *T* 27.479a8ff., 157 *T* 27.796a26ff.; *AKB* 2.36b–d p. 62.15ff.; *SAKV* 143.8ff.; *NAS* 12 *T* 27.396c21ff.

111. For a detailed description, see *NAS* 55 *T* 29.651a17ff., quoted by Yaśomitra, *SAKV* 500.7ff. Cf. Hiromichi Katō, "Danwakuron no tokushitsu," *Indogaku Bukkyōgaku kenkyū* 33/2 (1985): 471–476.

112. See *NAS* 55 *T* 29.651b3ff.; *SAKV* 500.19ff.

113. *MVB* 93 *T* 27.479c8ff. Cf. ibid. 157 *T* 27.796c28ff.

114. Ibid. 157 *T* 27.797a2ff. Cf. ibid. 155 *T* 27.788b19ff.

115. Ibid. 64 *T* 27.333c20ff.; *AKB* 6.28 p. 352.11ff.; *SAKV* 545.9ff.; *NAS* 63 *T* 29.689c12ff.

116. See *MVB* 158 *T* 27.803b2–3. For an extensive discussion of cessation resulting from consideration *(pratisaṃkhyānirodha)* and its relation to the possession of disconnection *(visaṃyogaprāpti)* and nirvāṇa, see ibid. 31 *T* 27.161a9ff., esp. 31 *T* 27.161a14–15, 31 *T* 27.161c11ff. Cf. ibid. 157 *T* 27.797b15ff., 158 *T* 27.803a5ff.

117. See ibid. 31 *T* 27.162a24ff. Cf. ibid. 158 *T* 27.802a18ff.

118. In the later Sarvāstivādin path-structure, the numerous paths are grouped under four types: (1) the path of preparation *(prayogamārga),* consisting of the four preparatory stages of penetration consisting of heat and so on, practiced prior to entering the path of vision; (2) the immediately successive path *(ānantaryamārga),* which removes obstacles and corresponds to the various stages of presentiment *(kṣānti)* in the path of vision, and to knowledge in the path of cultivation; (3) the path of liberation *(vimuktimārga),* which corresponds to the various stages of knowledge (jñāna) in the paths of vision and cultivation; and (4) the special path *(viśeṣamārga),* which is different from the preceding paths and corresponds to the path of cultivation through which one practices to attain

the four noble fruits of praxis. See *MVB* 166 *T* 27.344b8ff.; *AKB* 6.65b–d p. 381.21ff.; *SAKV* 597.32ff.; *NAS* 71 *T* 29.725c7ff. For the four varieties of counteragents *(pratipakṣa)* and their correlation with the various paths and stages in the Sarvāstivādin path-structure, see *MVB* 181 *T* 27.907c12–13; *SAHŚ* 10 *T* 28.953c24ff.; *AKB* 5.61a–c p. 320.7ff.; *SAKV* 499.4ff.; *NAS* 55 *T* 27.650c12ff. Cf. *MVB* 3 *T* 27.12c14ff., 141 *T* 27.725a11ff. for lists of five varieties of counteragents. Cf. ibid. 181 *T* 27.910a17ff., where different senses for the term "abandonment" are correlated with each of these four paths and four counteragents: namely, in this case, the immediately successive path produces abandonment as such, which is associated with the counteragent that results in abandonment; and the path of liberation produces separation, which is associated with the counteragent that results in maintenance. Both of these are declared to produce complete, as opposed to temporary, abandonment.

119. This first step of the immediately successive path is also referred to as the path of abandonment *(prahāṇamārga)*. See *MVB* 106 *T* 27.549c29ff.; *AKB* 4.87a–b p. 255.16.

120. See *AHŚ-D* 2 *T* 28 (1550) 819b18ff.; *SAHŚ* 5 *T* 28.913b2ff.; *MVB* 155 *T* 27.788b19ff.

121. The position that these two paths are strictly distinguished is attributed to certain groups within the Sarvāstivādin school: namely, the Westerners (*MVB* 90 *T* 27.465c8ff.) or the Outsiders (ibid. 108 *T* 27.557a18ff.).

122. Ibid. 60 *T* 27.312c10ff.

123. See *NAS* 68 *T* 29.716a1ff.

The Path to Perdition: The Wholesome Roots and Their Eradication

ROBERT E. BUSWELL, JR.

It has been typical in most scholarly treatments of Buddhist soteriology to focus on those points along the path where the religion proves its spiritual mettle, especially on those several stages of insight and cultivation at the upper reaches of the mārga where enlightenment is said to unfold. We find in this volume, for example, a number of chapters dealing with such rarified levels of achievement as the path of insight, the meaning of enlightenment, and the realization of buddhahood. This concern with factors crucial to consummating the mārga is entirely appropriate, of course, and such treatments tell us much about Buddhist contributions to soteriological discourse. I would like, however, to take a rather different tack toward Buddhist soteriology by exploring those factors that may prevent any further prospect for liberation. This focus on the other end of the path—where the beginning of the mārga recedes so far into the distance that it may seem to be lost forever—may help demonstrate what factors might render a person forever incapable of enlightenment in the Buddhist religious system. Perhaps just as important, it promises to reveal what soteriological factors are indispensable if a Buddhist is to retain any hope of setting out on the path, let alone completing that path and achieving enlightenment.

Buddhism most commonly portrays its religious discourse as being pervaded by "but one taste, the taste of liberation," as the Buddha states so eloquently in the famous simile of salt that we have used as the epigraph to our introduction to this volume.[1] This "taste of liberation" that Buddhism makes known to its followers was generally conceived to be accessible to all beings, provided they fulfill the preconditions necessary to its achievement. This Buddhist tendency toward universalism is perhaps best exemplified in the clarion call of the *Nirvāṇa Sūtra* that all beings have the capacity to achieve buddhahood, which I will examine later.

While espousing this ultimate goal of enlightenment for all, however, some Buddhist scriptures make the apparently conflicting claim that certain persons can be forever barred from salvation. Even more problematic, this claim is found even in universalist texts, such as the *Nirvāṇa Sūtra.* People who had engaged in the most heinous of evil actions were called "those whose wholesome roots are eradicated" *(samucchinnakuśalamūla,* Ch. *tuan shan-ken* [*che*], Tib. *dge baḥi rtsa ba* [*kun tu*] *chad pa).* In the vast majority of cases, such persons were condemned to subsequent rebirth in hell. The different schools of Buddhist thought grappled with the problem of reconciling these two contradictory claims of the religion: on the one hand, a universalist dogma of liberation; on the other, the tenet that some beings could be abandoned, perhaps irrevocably, to hell. Examining the doctrine of *samucchinnakuśalamūla* will thus help answer a question fundamental to Buddhist soteriology: what could cause the prospect of salvation to become forever out of reach?

But the notions of wholesome roots and their eradication also provide important input in answering the converse question: what factor is absolutely essential if people are to retain their capacities for religious cultivation? With the plethora of qualities that Buddhists emphasize in their writings, it is difficult to determine which is most fundamental—which is the "lowest common denominator," as it were, of the Buddhist spiritual equation, the sine qua non of the path. It is on this issue that the treatment of *samucchinnakuśalamūla* looms large. Our examination of the wholesome roots will reveal their association with the concept of merit-making, or *puṇya,* and will take us down to the very bedrock of Buddhist soteriology. The essential catalyst to cultivation will prove to be, not one of the several important concepts of doctrine and praxis for which Buddhism is renowned, but the simple practice of charity or giving *(dāna),* a specific type of merit-making.

Some of the most detailed examinations of all these issues appear in the texts of the Indian Vaibhāṣika school of Abhidharma, virtually all of which are now available only in Chinese translation. My focus here will be on the treatments found in that school's massive compendium of Abhidharma doctrine, the *Abhidharmamahāvibhāṣā* (Great Exegesis of Abhidharma; hereafter the *Vibhāṣā*). This treatise was compiled in northwest India around the second century C.E., but is now extant only in a Chinese translation made under the direction of Hsüan-tsang (d. 664) during the years 656 to 659.[2] The two hundred fascicles of this text are rich with material on virtually all the major doctrinal concepts and debates in early Indian Buddhism, and have been unconscionably neglected by most Western scholars of Buddhism (with the notable exception of Louis de La Vallée Poussin). I hope that by demonstrating the importance of the *Vibhāṣā*'s material in treating the concept of the *kuśalamūlas* and their eradication, others will be encouraged to make use of this important text in their own work. I will supplement my treatment of the Vaibhāṣika sources with other Śrāvakayāna and Mahāyāna materials in Sanskrit, Pali, and Chinese, in order to clarify the broader outlook of the Buddhist tradition as a whole toward *samucchinnakuśalamūla.* I will also consider the relationship between *samucchinnakuśalamūla* and the better-known doctrine of the *icchantika,* a related term for the spiritually bereft used in the Mahāyāna traditions. This broad approach to the wholesome roots and their eradication should elucidate a surprisingly wide variety of issues in Buddhist soteriology as well as verify the seminal place ascribed to giving in Buddhist praxis.

The Wholesome Roots

The wholesome "roots" or "faculties" *(kuśalamūla, shan-ken)* are considered by all schools of Buddhism to be fundamental to progress in religious praxis. Despite the central role that they play in Buddhist soteriology, they have been all but ignored in modern scholarship. Virtually the only mentions they have earned have appeared in discussions of related issues such as the doctrine of mental "seeds" *(bīja)* and spiritual lineage *(gotra).*[3]

The classification of the wholesome roots most familiar in Buddhism is a threefold one: nongreed *(alobha),* nonhatred *(adveśa,* P. *adosa),* and nonignorance *(amoha).*[4] These comprise nothing more than the converse of the three unwholesome roots *(akuśalamūla,* Ch. *pu-shan-ken),* which are even more pervasive in the literature. This same threefold arrangement is found in widely disparate strata of Abhidharma materials as well, including both the *Vibhaṅga* of the Theravādins and the *Śāriputrābhidharmaśāstra.*[5]

We find in Vaibhāṣika texts, however, considerable development in the meaning of the *kuśalamūlas,* which is subsequently mirrored also in Mahāyāna materials. In place of the simple threefold listing, the Vaibhāṣikas have three separate typologies of *kuśalamūlas*—and it is this wider threefold typology that is generally meant whenever they refer to three *kuśalamūlas (san shan-ken).* The first class is the "wholesome roots associated with merit" *(puṇyabhāgīyakuśalamūla, shun fu-fen shan-ken),* which involve the seeds or *bījas (chung-tzu)* that produce rebirth in the realms of humans or luminaries (devas).[6] The qualities developed through this kind of wholesome root involve compounded *(saṃskṛta)* wholesome dharmas that are associated with the outflows *(sāsravakuśaladharma)*—viz., such qualities as faith, energy, shame and blame, and so forth. Second are the "wholesome roots associated with liberation" *(mokṣabhāgīyakuśalamūla, shun chieh-t'o-fen shan-ken),* which involve the seeds of certain liberation *(*mokṣabīja, chüeh-t'o chung-tzu).*[7] It is this type of root that will eventually produce the attainment of *parinirvāṇa.*[8] The *mokṣabhāgīyas* yield qualities that correspond to compounded wholesome dharmas that are free from outflows *(anāsravakuśaladharma),* i.e., the truth of the path *(mārgasatya),* or various factors conducive to liberation.[9]

Third are the "wholesome roots associated with spiritual penetration" *(nirvedhabhāgīyakuśalamūla, shun chüeh-tse-fen shan-ken),* which are the four aspects of the direct path of preparation *(prayogamārga, chia-hsing wei):* heat *(ūṣmāgata, nuan),* summit *(mūrdhan, ting),* acquiescence *(kṣānti, jen),* and highest worldly experience *(laukikāgradharma, shih ti-i fa).* The *nirvedhabhāgīyas* culminate in the entry onto the path of vision *(darśanamārga, chien-tao),* where the first stage of sanctity is achieved, and thus constitute the crucial points in the transformation of an ordinary person into a saint. Curiously, the *nirvedhabhāgīyas* are the only type of *kuśalamūla* that does not have a corresponding *bīja* associated with it. The only plausible explanation for this lack is that the *nirvedhabhāgīyas,* as the mārga's proximate stage of preparation, refer to the culmination of the gradual process of development represented by the remote stage of preparation—i.e., the first two classes of wholesome roots.[10] In an immediate flash of insight *(nirvedha),* there would be no need to posit a fundamental seed that sustains that development, as a gradual process of maturation would demand. The *nirvedhabhāgīyas* differ so dramatically from the two earlier types of *kuśalamūlas* that they are often referred to independently as the four *kuśalamūlas (ssu shan-ken)* in the Vaibhāṣika texts. Describing their special role in spiritual culture would require much more space than I have available in this chapter, so I shall defer their discussion for now.[11]

As for the first two types of *kuśalamūlas,* the Vibhāṣāśāstrins devote the great majority of their discussion to the *mokṣabhāgīyas.*[12] They note that the inherent characteristic *(svabhāva, tzu-hsing)* of the *mokṣabhāgīyas* are the actions done via body, speech, and mind, though mental actions predominate. That this type of *kuśalamūla* is under the control of the mental faculty *(manendriya)* is also confirmed by their statement that the *mokṣabhāgīyas* reside in the mind-ground (*manobhūmi*[*ka*]), not in the five categories of consciousness *(pañcavijñānakāya).* The *mokṣabhāgīyas* are matured through the kind of consistent cultivation the Vaibhāṣikas term "sustained application" *(prayogalābhika, chia-hsing teh)* and are perfected by the wisdom that derives from learning *(śrutamāyīprajñā)* and reflection *(cintamāyīprajñā).*[13] They can be planted by acts that are based on nongreed, nonhatred, and nondelusion, such as giving, keeping precepts, or learning the dharma; however, the number and type of wholesome actions necessary to ensure the implantation of this root vary and depend on the mentality *(āśaya, i-le)* of the individual. The Vibhāṣāśāstrins' treatment suggests that the *mokṣabhāgīyas* derive from the very same meritorious acts that defined the *puṇyabhāgīyas.* The only difference is that the *mokṣabhāgīyas* involve a more mature outlook on merit, the focus of concern having shifted from mundane heavenly rewards to attainment of the unconditioned realm of nirvāṇa.

Certain types of personalities are said to be most conducive to generating the *mokṣabhāgīyas*. As an exchange in the *Vibhāṣā* relates:

> Question: Who is certain to be able to plant the *mokṣabhāgīyakuśalamūlas?*
>
> Answer: If there is a person who is of the highest capacity *[*adhipatyāśaya, tseng-shang i-le]*, who willingly seeks nirvāṇa and who turns his back on birth and death, then even with only a small amount of the wholesome [actions] of giving, keeping precepts, and hearing [the dharma], he is certain to be able to plant this *kuśalamūla*. However, if one is not such a person [repeated as above], then even with a large amount of such wholesome actions, one will still be unable to plant this *kuśalamūla*.[14]

A person can be sure that this wholesome root has been planted when certain signs appear:

> Question: The characteristics of the *mokṣabhāgīyakuśalamūlas* in the bodies of sentient beings are extremely subtle *(susūkṣma)*.[15] How is it that one can know for sure whether these [wholesome roots] have already been planted?
>
> Answer: There are signs by which one can know. What are these signs? If, at the time that one hears a spiritual mentor speak the right dharma, one's body hairs horripilate and tears flow freely; if one turns away from saṃsāra and is joyfully intent on nirvāṇa; and if one has deep love and respect toward that dharma teacher, then one can know that it is certain that one has already planted the *mokṣabhāgīyakuśalamūlas*.
>
> There is a simile in connection with this. It is like a man who may have sown seeds in a field but, after a long interval of time, comes to doubt whether or not he actually sowed seeds in that field, and becomes befuddled and uncertain. Someone might come up to him and ask, "What's the point of being like this? You need now only sprinkle the field with water and cover it with fertilizer; then, if sprouts come up, you will know that [the field] has already been sown; if nothing comes up, then it hasn't." The man did as he was advised and then found out for sure. In the same way, if a cultivator is uncertain whether or not he has already planted the seeds of the *mokṣabhāgīyas* in himself, a spiritual mentor will tell him, "Go to a place where the dharma is being spoken. If, when you hear that dharma, your body hairs horripilate and tears flow freely . . . and

> if you have deep love and respect toward that dharma teacher, then you will know that you have already planted the seeds of liberation. If these things don't happen, then you haven't." Hence, from these signs one can know [whether the *mokṣabhāgīyabījas* have already been planted].[16]

Once the *mokṣabhāgīyas* have been planted, a minimum of three lifetimes must pass before a person can progress to planting the *nirvedhabhāgīyas,* thereby reaching the threshold of liberating insight *(darśanamārga).* During the first lifetime, the seeds associated with liberation *(*mokṣabhāgīyabīja),* which will produce the *mokṣabhāgīyakuśalamūlas,* are planted; during the second, this type of wholesome faculty is matured, so that one is able to plant the *nirvedhabhāgīyas;* and during the third, liberation (viz., *darśanamārga*) can occur. This agenda is, however, far from determined, and depending on a person's karmic makeup, an eternity of kalpas can be required before liberation is finally achieved.[17]

Eradication of the Wholesome Roots in Non-Vaibhāṣika Sources

Most strata of Buddhist texts, from the earliest *Āgamas* onward, accept that there were beings whose *kuśalamūlas* might be eradicated, at least temporarily allaying, if not permanently subverting, their capacity for spiritual progress. The Theravāda school, for example, claimed that a person could become so utterly evil that he would be doomed to virtually eternal damnation. Support for this view was found in the *Puggalapaññatti* (Discourse on Human Types), probably the earliest of the six Theravāda Abhidharma texts: "Here a certain person is endowed with absolutely black *(ekantakāḷaka),* unwholesome dharmas. Thus that person, once drowned, is just drowned [viz., drowned forever]."[18] As Buddhaghosa interprets this passage,

> The term "absolutely black" means those grave wrong views [which deny the result of karman, such as] the theories of nonbeing *(natthikavāda),* noncausationism *(ahetukavāda),* and randomness *(akiriyavāda).*[19] A person like [the non-Buddhist fatalist] Makkhali Gosāla who holds those grave wrong views becomes the food of the fire of lower and lower hells. For such a person there is no emergence from worldly existence.[20]

Hence a person who had embraced such perverted views *(mithyādṛṣṭi)* no longer had any hope of attaining nirvāṇa. He had effectively become *aparinirvāṇagotraka* (divorced from the lineage of *parinirvāṇa*), close to the Mahāyāna definition of the *icchantika,* which I discuss later.

In its *Āgama* usage, the term *"samucchinnakuśalamūla"* commonly refers to wealthy householders *(gṛhapati)* who turn niggardly and refuse to make offerings to śramaṇas and brahmaṇas, or eventually even to their own parents, family, and friends. The *Ekottarāgama* (Sequentially Numbered Collection), for example, says: "He became niggardly and greedy and did not have any intention to give. He feeds only off his previous merit and makes none anew."[21] Such an attitude invariably led to moral and material profligacy, the result of which was perdition, as shown in another story of a rich man *(śreṣṭhin)* also found in the *Ekottarāgama.*

> King Prasenajit asked, "Is this *śreṣṭhi-gṛhapati* one whose wholesome roots are eradicated?"
>
> The World Honored One replied, "So it is, oh king. As the king said, that householder is one whose wholesome roots are eradicated, for his past merit *(puṇya, fu)* is already exhausted and he has made none anew."
>
> King Prasenajit asked, "Does that householder have any remaining merit?"
>
> The World Honored One replied, "No, he does not, oh king, he hasn't the slightest bit remaining. It is like a farmer who only harvests and doesn't plant. Eventually, he will become poor and destitute and slowly his life will come to an end. And why is this? [Because] he merely fed on his past merit and didn't make any anew. This evening, [upon his death], this householder will be living in the Hell of Tears and Lamentations (Mahārauravaniraka)."[22]

Samucchinnakuśalamūla seems not to have been regarded as an inviolable state in the *Āgamas,* however, and the Buddha specifically allowed provisions that would free one who had become *samucchinnakuśalamūla* from being condemned to hell. In one sūtra in the *Ekottarāgama,* the Buddha observes a wealthy householder named *Vilāsin (P'i-lo-hsien), who was also ignoring his charitable duties. Hearing him cavorting with his female musicians, the Buddha predicted,

> "Ānanda. After seven days this elder's life will come to an end and he will be born into the Hell of Tears and Lamentations. And why is this? This is the fixed dharma: at the time that the lifespan of a person whose wholesome roots are eradicated comes to an end, he will be born into the Hell of Tears and Lamentation. This householder's previous merit is now exhausted and he has made none anew."
>
> Ānanda addressed the Buddha, "Isn't there some means whereby this *śreṣṭhin* need not have his lifespan come to an end after seven days?"

> The Buddha replied to Ānanda, "There is no way that he can keep his life from coming to an end. The [meritorious] practices that he developed in the past have today been exhausted. His [fate] is sealed."[23]

Significantly, although it was fixed that the life of this *samucchinnakuśalamūla* must come to an end, the Buddha does provide one dispensation: he can avoid rebirth in hell provided he shave his head, take up the three robes of the monk, go forth into homelessness, and cultivate the mārga. In this case *Vilāsin, after delaying his ordination for six days, finally went forth on the seventh and final day of his life. While cultivating the ten recollections of the Buddha, dharma, saṃgha, and so forth, he was reborn among the Four Heavenly Kings (Caturmahārājikadeva). The Buddha foretells that, after that rebirth, he will continue up through the heavens to the Paranirmittavarśavartin gods (lit., "those who control enjoyments conjured by others"), whence he will return back down through the heavens, arriving once again at the realm of the Four Heavenly Kings. From there, he will be reborn one last time among humans and achieve an end to suffering. But ultimately his success in avoiding hell was "because he had faith in the Tathāgata."[24]

The premise that the *samuucchinnakuśalamūla* need not be destined to eternal damnation is also broached in passages in the *Nikāyas* and *Āgamas* where the Buddha refuses to address the various indeterminate *(avyākṛta)* questions.[25] As Vasubandhu noted in the *Abhidharmakośabhāṣya,* the Buddha's silence on the question of whether or not the universe is eternal, for example, has direct bearing on the problem of *samucchinnakuśalamūla.* If the Buddha had answered that the world is both eternal and noneternal, this would have implied that some beings are congenitally destined for liberation while others can legitimately be condemned to saṃsāra for an eternity. "If both [extremes] are accepted as valid, [then] for certain people, parinirvāṇa would be possible, [but] not for others."[26] Hence the Buddha's positivistic attitude toward language reflected the soteriological underpinnings of his teachings. By refusing to respond to these indeterminate questions, the Buddha denied that any type of being is to be regarded as eternally *samucchinnakuśalamūla.*

Eradication of the Wholesome Roots in the Vaibhāṣika School

Occasional references to *samucchinnakuśalamūla* are found in later neo-Vaibhāṣika compendia such as *Abhidharmakośabhāṣya, Abhidharmanyāyānusāra,* and *Abhidharmadīpa,* but no concerted effort is made in any of those treatises to define the term precisely or to spell out the process by which a person becomes condemned to such a fate.[27] We are, however, fortunate to find scattered throughout that seminal Vaibhāṣika handbook of doctrine, the *Abhidharmamahāvibhāṣā*, several detailed descriptions of *samucchinnakuśalamūla* that allow us to elucidate several of its ramifications. These include such crucial issues as the process by which eradication of the wholesome roots occurs and the means by which recovery from that state can be effected. The treatment of *samucchinnakuśalamūla* in the *Vibhāṣā* also illustrates the penchant of its authors, the Vibhāṣāśāstrins, to expand on the number of dissociated forces *(cittaviprayuktasaṃskāra)* found in the static dharma lists of later Sarvāstivādin handbooks; this discussion will therefore have important implications as well for our view of the development of the Vaibhāṣika doctrinal system.

Unlike proponents of several other contemporary schools of Buddhist thought, the Vaibhāṣikas refused to accept an eternal state of *samucchinnakuśalamūla*. According to the Vibhāṣāśāstrins, once the Buddhist adept had planted the *puṇyabhāgīya-* and *mokṣabhāgīyakuśalamūlas,* their resiliency was almost astounding, especially considering the power of evil *(akuśala)* to subjugate all activities within the desire realm *(kāmāvacara)*.[28] Persons who had planted the *mokṣabhāgīyakuśalamūlas* were destined eventually to perfect them: even though they might first perform many types of unwholesome actions and end up in hell, ultimately their seeds of liberation *(*mokṣabīja, chieh-t'o chung-tzu)* would find an opportunity to sprout and they would achieve perfection as śrāvakas, pratyekabuddhas, or buddhas. The Vibhāṣāśāstrins give a simile to show this resiliency of the wholesome roots:

> This can be compared to a person who was traveling and carrying two vessels: one made of metal, one made of clay. He tripped and fell, breaking both of his vessels. At that time, that person did not begrudge the loss of his metal vessel, but he did begrudge the loss of his clay vessel, and lamented over this. Another person came by and asked him what had happened, and the man told him the whole story. This person then told the traveler, "When you do not even begrudge the loss of your metal vessel, how instead can you begrudge the loss of this clay vessel?" And he said again to him, "You certainly are ignorant. Why do I say this? When a metal vessel is broken, even though it has lost the form of the vessel, it has not lost the substance of the vessel. If you take [that broken vessel] back to a metalworker, he can make it as good as new, or even better than new. But when a clay vessel is broken, both the shape and the substance are lost: although one returns it to a potter, he cannot even reuse the materials, let alone restore the original vessel!"[29]

The implication drawn elsewhere by the Vibhāṣāśāstrins is that *samucchinna* can refer only to the immediate present moment; it is devoid of any ontological intimations whatsoever:

> According to the explanations appearing in the *Prajñaptibhāṣya, kuśala* cannot continue in the present life *(dṛṣṭadharma)* [for the person who is *samucchinnakuśalamūla*]. It is fixed *(niyata/avaśyam, chüeh-ting)* that *kuśala* can regenerate only at the time of either birth or death in hell. As that *Bhāṣya*

says, "If a person destroys an ant's egg and does not feel even the slightest remorse, it should be said that that person has eradicated the *kuśala* of the three realms of existence. For him, the *kuśalamūlas* cannot continue in the present life. It is fixed that *kuśala* can regenerate only at the time of either birth or death in hell."[30]

This view that the *kuśalamūlas* can regenerate only after one's requisite destiny has been fulfilled is adumbrated above in the passages from the *Ekottarāgama,* which state that while the *samucchinnakuśalamūla* must die, he is not thereby barred from ever attaining *parinirvāṇa.* There the Vibhāṣāśāstrins insist that although rebirth in hell must take place, living out that existence will allow *kuśala* to revive.

This mitigation of the punishment due the *samucchinnakuśalamūla* is further indicated by a number of passages in the *Vibhāṣā* where such a person compares favorably even to arhats. Although they may be purified now, arhats had many flaws in the past and are tainted in the present by their desire to cultivate merit *(puṇya, fu).* "For this reason, this makes us revile them now. Who can consider them capable of rendering benefit to others?" The *samucchinnakuśalamūla,* in contrast—because of his humble status at the bottom of the spiritual heap—has nowhere to go but up, and is therefore ultimately capable of developing merit anew. In addition, he may have cultivated much merit in previous lives, so that "now [after the end of his present rebirth in hell] he would be capable of gaining birth in an aristocratic family, of having handsome features that everyone would admire, eloquence in speech that everyone would respect, and wisdom and learning that everyone would honor. For these reasons, we should consider him [rather than the arhat] capable of rendering benefit to others."[31] In a passage even more damning, the arhat is doomed to return to the defiled ways of action he presumed he had overcome forever, while the *samucchinnakuśalamūla* is not:

> The *samucchinnakuśalamūla* perforce is endowed with wholesomeness *(kuśalasamanvāgata);* the dispassionate [gods in the form and formless realms] perforce are endowed with unwholesomeness *(akuśalasamanvāgata)* [because of their attachment to the pleasures of meditative isolation]. All those who need no further training [i.e., the arhats] perforce are endowed with taints *(rāgyasamanvāgata).*[32]

The Mahāsāṅghikas are well known to have had a low opinion of the arhats,[33] and the Sarvāstivādins held some views that tarnished, however slightly, their pristine image.[34] But this praise of the *samucchinnakuśalamūla* over the arhat raises serious questions about the adequacy of the śrāvaka ideal and seems incongruous in a Śrāvakayāna text. One cannot help thinking that the Mahāyāna attitude toward the arhat is adumbrated here: since the arhats are fixed at one of the six arhat stages, they are in an ultimate sense inferior to the *samucchinnakuśala-mūla,* who at least has the potential to go forward and possibly progress all the way to buddhahood.

What creates *samucchinnakuśalamūla,* this most dangerous of all soteriological obstacles? Various interpretations concerning the fundamental quality *(svabhāva)* of *samucchinakuśalamūla* are noted by the Vibhāṣā-śāstrins. These cover the gamut of unwholesome dharmas, from lack of faith *(aśraddhā)* to wrong views *(mithyādṛṣṭi)* to being swayed by the defilements *(kleśasaṃyoga).* All dharmas *(sarvadharmāḥ)* are even called the *svabhāva* of *samucchinakuśalamūla,* because all dharmas are said to follow those *kuśalamūlas* to perdition.[35] As implied in the passages marshalled above, however, the judgment of the Vibhāṣāśāstrins is that

> the fundamental quality *(svabhāva)* of all *samucchinnakuśalamūlas* is lack of inherence *(asamanvāgama, pu-ch'eng-chiu).* It is included in the category of nonobstructing, neutral, dissociated forces *(anivṛtāvyākṛta-cittaviprayukta-saṃskāra-skandha)* and is one among the remaining [and unspecified] dharmas of similar type *(evañjātīyakadharma)* among the dissociated [forces].[36]

Eradication *(samucchinna)* for the Vaibhāṣikas therefore means only the temporary allayment of *kuśala,* not a permanent state of perdition.

Since *samucchinna* is not the permanent excision of the *kuśalamūlas* from a person's mental continuum, what does it in fact mean for the Vaibhāṣikas? Clearly, the Vibhāṣāśāstrins intend for *samucchinna* to refer only to the temporary allayment *(asamanvāgama)*[37] of the *kuśalamūlas* due to the overriding force of perverted views *(mithyādṛṣṭi):*

> Question: What is the meaning of *samucchinnakuśalamūla?*
> Answer: [Cutting off the wholesome roots] is not to be taken in the worldly sense of an axe cutting down a tree, etc., because *mithyādṛṣṭi* and *kuśala* cannot be in mutual contact *(saṃspṛṣṭa, hsiang-ch'u).*[38] Rather, at the time that *mithyādṛṣṭi* appears within the mental continuum *(santati, hsiang-hsü),* it results in the annihilation of any endowment with the wholesome faculties *(kuśalamūlasamanvāgama-vināṣa)* and brings about their nonendowment. Then what is meant by "eradication" *(samucchinna)?* If in an individual continuum there is no acquisition of the wholesome faculties *(kuśalamūlāprāpti),* then at that time it is said that the *kuśalamūlas* are already eradicated. . . . Moreover, at the time that *kuśala* is eradicated, wholesome dharmas are all abandoned *(parihāṇa, she)* and one gains the nonendowment *(asamanvāgamatā, pu-ch'eng-chiu hsing)* of all wholesome dharmas.[39]

This claim that perverted views bring an end to the wholesome roots is accepted only with debate in the *Vibhāṣā,* even though the weight of the Vaibhāṣika tradition is clearly behind that interpretation. Still, this passage clarifies the position of the Vibhāṣāśāstrins toward eradication. The Vibhāṣāśāstrins distinguish two principal stages in bringing an end to the wholesome roots. First, a peculiar kind of immaterial "force dissociated from mind" *(cittaviprayuktasaṃskāra)* interrupts the presence of the wholesome roots *(kuśalamūlāprāpti)* in the mental continuum of the person.[40] Second, an especially virulent type of unwholesome dharma, such as *mithyādṛṣṭi* or the most severe form of evil action *(akuśalakarman),* serves as the actual agent of excision *(upaghāta).* Because perverted views and wholesome dharmas cannot be in mutual contact, *mithyādṛṣṭi* itself cannot function as that agent. As the Vibhāṣāśāstrins consistently propose for equally complex transitional states, a totally dissociated causal force—a *cittaviprayuktasaṃskāra*—could best account for such a radical change in an individual mental continuum. This new dharma was given the technical designation *samucchinnakuśalamūla-cittaviprayukta-saṃskāra.* Hence, although *mithyādṛṣṭi* should be considered the actual agent of excision, its ability to perform this function is dependent on the presence of this accompanying *cittaviprayuktasaṃskāra.*

There would seem to have been no overriding need for the Vibhāṣāśāstrins to have posited the completely distinct dharma of *samucchinnakuśalamūla-cittaviprayuktasaṃskāra* to cover this eventuality. Because this dissociated force was defined as *asamanvāgama* (nonendowment), it could just have easily been considered the *aprāpti* (nonobtainment) of the *kuśalamūlas,* in the same way that the Vibhāṣāśāstrins interpret *pṛthagjanatva* (ordinariness) to be the nonobtainment of *arhattva* (sanctity). Hence the number of *viprayuktasaṃskāras* found in the *Vibhāṣā* could have been drastically limited.[41] Indeed, the fact that this and many other of the *viprayuktasaṃskāras* mentioned in the *Vibhāṣā* are not found in such neo-Vaibhāṣika works as the *Abhidharmakośabhāṣya* suggests that such a simplification of the Vaibhāṣika system had taken place by the time those texts were composed, sometime during the fourth century C.E. Nevertheless, the difficult soteriological questions raised by *samucchinnakuśalamūla* could be resolved—indeed, almost sidestepped entirely—by resorting to a peculiar kind of force, a *cittaviprayuktasaṃskāra,* that would prompt the temporary allayment of *kuśala.*

Samucchinnakuśalamūla and Its Relationship to the *Icchantika* Doctrine

Much more well known in Buddhist literature than *samucchinnakuśalamūla* is the related term *"icchantika,"* which is also used to refer to a person who is unable to attain nirvāṇa. Although *icchantika* is unknown to the Pali *Nikāyas* or the Chinese *Āgamas,* Mahāyāna texts employ both it and the synonymous *samucchinnakuśalamūla,* which should help to clarify their respective denotations. A close examination of the evolution of the conception of *samucchinnakuśalamūla* in Mahāyāna materials will also provide some insight into the contradictory views on the *icchantika* found in different strata of Mahāyāna literature.

The derivation of "*icchantika*" is obscure. It is generally presumed to be some variation on the present participle "*icchant*" (desiring),[42] a view supported by the translations of the term in Chinese and Tibetan. In addition to Chinese transcriptions, which render the term as *i-ch'an-t'i* or the abbreviated *ch'an-t'i,* the Chinese also translated it as *(ta-)shen-yü,* "greatly hedonistic (or dissipated)," a rendering suggestive of the Tibetan equivalent *hdod chen (po),* "subject to great desire." As we have seen in the *Ekottarāgama* story of the householder *Vilāsin, *samucchinnakuśalamūla* also involved such excessive forms of sensual desire, immediately suggesting the close connections between the two terms. Against this traditional interpretation, Wogihara Unrai derives *icchantika* from *itthaṃtvika* or *aitthaṃtvika* (worldly, or belonging to the world).[43] Although Wogihara's derivation has not been generally accepted, his view finds some substantiation in the *Ratnagotravibhāga*'s definition of the *icchantikas* as "those who cling to the worldly life *(bhavābhilāsin).*"[44]

One of the simplest Mahāyāna treatments of the *icchantika,* which recalls a number of Śrāvakayāna interpretations of *samucchinnakuśalamūla,* appears in the *Yang-chüeh-mo-lo ching* (*Aṅgulimālīyasūtra;* trans. ca. 435–443, by Guṇabhadra), a text closely associated with the Tathāgatagarbha tradition.[45] In this scripture, *icchantikas* belong to the spiritual lineage *(gotra)* of the "perverse determined" *(hsieh-ting),* while tathāgatas, bodhisattvas, and two-vehicle adherents (pratyekabuddhas and śrāvakas) are of "salutary determined" *(cheng-ting) gotra.* This distinction parallels the account in the Theravāda *Puggalapaññatti* that those of determined destiny include both the five types of hell-goers and people holding wrong views as well as the eight classes of saints.[46] The *icchantikas* are also said to be the most vile of beings, and to engage in all the ten evil types of conduct in the same way that the bodhisattvas perfect all ten pāramitās. For this reason, the *icchantikas* are born among the hungry ghosts, whose desires are equally intense. This is one of the few instances where the destinies of *icchantikas* or *samucchinnakuśalamūlas* are said to be other than the hells.[47]

It is Asaṅga in his *Abhidharmasamuccaya* (Compendium of Abhidharma) who first clarifies the close relationship between the concepts of *samucchinnakuśalamūla* and *icchantika:*

> He whose wholesome roots are eradicated may be considered as either endowed *(samanvāgama)* or not endowed *(asamanvāgama)* with the endowment *(samanvāgama)* with the seeds *(bīja)* of wholesome dharmas. As far as its extreme is concerned, [the *samucchinnakuśalamūla*] who is endowed with

> defilements *(saṃkleśa)* is to be classed among the *icchantikas* who lack the dharma of *parinirvāṇa.*[48]

In this interpretation, the *icchantika*'s complete segregation from all other living beings could not be clearer: "The extreme of those [*icchantikas*] is one who is not endowed with the cause [that leads to mokṣa], because he lacks the cause of mokṣa [and is thus indefinitely barred from gaining nirvāṇa]."[49]

Asaṅga's treatment here suggests that there are two types of *samucchinnakuśalamūlas:* one who is still endowed with the seeds of the wholesome dharmas and thus still has the potential to regenerate the *kuśalamūlas,* and another who is not. In extreme cases, the latter type no longer retains the capacity to achieve *parinirvāṇa* and is thus the true *icchantika,* who is presumably barred forever from enlightenment (though Asaṅga never states this explicitly). Because the former type continues to be endowed with the seeds of wholesome dharmas, he remains capable of regenerating the *kuśalamūlas,* and therefore may ultimately redeem himself. Hence, in the *Abhidharmasamuccaya,* the term *"icchantika"* refers to the extreme form of the most severe variety of *samucchinnakuśalamūla*—the one who is no longer endowed with the seeds of wholesome dharmas.[50]

Asaṅga's *Mahāyānasūtrālaṃkāra* also includes a brief discussion of the *icchantika*'s status within the *gotra* scheme. There, *icchantikas* once again are divided into two types.

> In this [verse no. iii.11], the sense is that those who are destitute of the *parinirvāṇa*-dharma are not part of the *gotra* [scheme]. In brief, they are of two types: those who are momentarily lacking the *parinirvāṇa*-dharma and those who are indefinitely so lacking. Those who are momentarily lacking the parinirvāṇa-dharma are of four types: [1] he whose evil conduct is absolute; [2] he who is *samucchinnakuśalamūla;* [3] he who lacks the *mokṣabhāgīyakuśalamūlas;* [4] he of inferior *ku śalamūlas* whose provisions are incomplete. But if they are indefinitely destitute of the *parinirvāṇa*-dharma, then they are deficient in its cause, for they lack the *parinirvāṇa-gotra.*[51]

This passage helps clarify a number of issues in the Yogācāra interpretation of *icchantika* and *samucchinnakuśalamūla.* First of all, the *samucchinnakuśalamūla* is only one of the subclasses of the less severe of the two types of *icchantikas.* Because the *samucchinnakuśalamūla* is distinguished from those who lack the *mokṣabhāgīyakuśalamūlas,* it appears that *samucchinnakuśalamūla* was used to refer exclusively to those whose *puṇyabhāgīyakuśalamūlas* were eradicated. In addition, as we saw above with the *Abhidharmasamuccaya,* only those beings who are indefinitely (i.e., eternally) *aparinirvāṇagotraka* are the true *icchantikas;* they presumably correlate with the above-mentioned type, who no longer possess the seeds of wholesome dharmas. Although Asaṅga hedged on stating the ultimate fate of this latter type in his *Abhidharmasamuccaya,* in the *Mahāyānasūtrālaṃkāra* he is more explicit, stating that the segregation of such *icchantikas* from *parinirvāṇa* will be indefinite *(atyanta).*

This distinction between two major types of *icchantikas* also resonates with their treatment in the *Nirvāṇa Sūtra,* which defines the *icchantika* in the following terms:

> He does not believe in the law of causality, he has no feeling of shame, he has no faith in the workings of karma, he is unconcerned with the present or the future, he never befriends good people, he does not follow the teaching of the Buddha.[52]

This definition is remarkably similar to one given previously by the Vibhāṣāśāstrins, in which *mithyādṛṣṭi* was regarded as the agent of eradication. There is some contradiction, however, in this sūtra's attitude toward the *icchantikas;* earlier portions state that they are utterly incapable of attaining nirvāṇa, whereas later sections allow that they still possess the innate buddha-nature *(buddhadhātu, fo-hsing)* and thus have not lost irrevocably all capacity for enlightenment.[53] Although this subsequent softening of views might be due to textual interpolations, the final result does leave us with two types of *icchantikas,* again close to Asaṅga's position on the problem. Yet the major difficulty with the notion of the *icchantika* in the *Nirvāṇa Sūtra*—a difficulty that consistently plagued the traditional Buddhist commentators—is that it contradicts the sūtra's fundamental message of the innate presence of buddha-nature in all sentient beings. As Takasaki Jikidō has noted, "The final solution of this problem seems to be the denial of the existence of such people from the ultimate point of view through introducing the idea of the Bodhisattva's compassion or the idea of the long time needed before their achieving Buddhahood."[54]

Furthermore, the *Laṅkāvatārasūtra* accepts two different subclasses among the *icchantikas:* those who are *icchantikas* "because they have abandoned all the wholesome roots" *(sarvakuśalamūlotsargata),* and those who are so "because they cherish certain vows for all beings since beginningless time" *(sattvānādikālapraṇidhānata).*[55] The former are defined as those

> who have abandoned the bodhisattva collection [of the canonical texts], making the false accusation that they are not in conformity with the sūtras, the codes of morality, and emancipation. By this they have forsaken all the stock of merit *(kuśalamūla)* and will not enter into nirvāṇa.[56]

Here the Mahāyānists give an explicitly sectarian interpretation of the *icchantika,* redefining him as an antagonist of their own doctrine. This view that an *icchantika* has enmity toward the Mahāyāna teachings is also found in other Mahāyāna texts, such as the *Ratnagotravibhāga,* where this antagonism is called the "obstruction of the *icchantikas,* and its antidote *(pratipakṣa)* is to cultivate conviction in the Mahāyāna teachings *(Mahāyānadharmādhimuktibhāvanā).*"[57]

This first type of *icchantika,* who has fallen into that state because of his conflict with Mahāyāna, can eventually attain nirvāṇa according to the *Laṅkāvatārasūtra,* in that he "might some day be influenced by the power of the tathāgatas and be induced at any moment to foster the stock of merit. Why? Because, Mahāmati, no beings are left aside by the tathāgatas."[58] However, the second type of *icchantika* found in the *Laṅkāvatāra* has voluntarily renounced forever all the wholesome roots because of the vow he took at the initiation of his spiritual quest:

> "So long as they [all beings] do not attain nirvāṇa, I will not attain it myself." . . . Knowing that all things are in nirvāṇa itself from the very beginning, the Bodhisattva-*icchantika* would never enter nirvāṇa.[59]

The bodhisattva-*icchantika* par excellence was Kṣitigarbha, who voluntarily assumed that state in order to save those sentient beings condemned to hell. In this sense, Kṣitigarbha was superior even to Amitābha who, according to the thirtieth of his forty-eight vows, was able to guarantee that devas, humans, and even insects could be reborn into his buddha land without having to pass through any of the three evil bournes.[60] But use of the adverb "even" in this phrase could be construed to imply that insects are the lowest species that can be saved through Amitābha's intercession; it is not stated that his grace extends as far as the denizens of hell, or specifically to the *samucchinnakuśalamūlas* who no longer retain the capacity to achieve nirvāṇa.

Despite the special dispensations given to *samucchinnakuśalamūlas* or *icchantikas* in both Śrāvakayāna and Mahāyāna literature, which sometimes frees them from irredeemable damnation, such freedom was, of course, not invariably guaranteed. As we saw with the Vaibhāṣikas, the regeneration of the *kuśalamūlas* takes place because of the *samucchinnakuśalamūla*'s continued endowment *(samanvāgama)* with the wholesome dharmas. However, because *samanvāgama* is also considered to be a dissociated force *(cittaviprayuktasaṃskāra)* in the *Mahāvibhāṣā,* that dharma is always present in the conditioned realm but need not come into operation until the proper conditions are present. Hence, in the Vaibhāṣika interpretation, only after the *samucchinnakuśalamūla-cittaviprayuktasaṃskāra* has vanished from a person's mental continuum can he again be endowed with wholesome dharmas, thereby allowing him to rise from his ignoble state.

The Vaibhāṣikas were not the only Buddhist school that accepted the possibility that the *kuśalamūlas* could be regenerated. Such a position was much more urgent, in fact, for the proponents of tathāgatagarbha doctrine. Their acceptance of the presence of an innate germ of buddhahood in all beings meant that they had to circumvent any eternal condemnation of the *icchantikas* to hell. In the *Ratnagotravibhāga,* this problem was resolved by interpreting statements such as that found in the *Nirvāṇa Sūtra* that "*icchantikas* belong to the lineage of those for whom *parinirvāṇa* is un[attainable] *(aparinirvāṇagotraka)*" as being of purely conventional validity, intended simply to point out that the *icchantikas* would remain in their ignoble state until they were able to overcome their antipathy toward the Mahāyāna:

> And also the saying: "the Icchantikas are by all means of the nature of no Perfect nirvāṇa" is taught in order to remove the hatred against the Doctrine of the Great Vehicle, this being the cause of their being Icchantikas and refers to a certain period of time. Indeed, as there exists the Germ *(garbha)* which is pure by nature, none could be of the absolutely impure nature. Therefore, . . . all living beings, with no difference, have the possibility of being purified.[61]

Perhaps the only recourse available to the Mahāyānists in attempting to reconcile such diametrically opposed doctrines as tathāgatagarbha and *icchantika* was this appeal to the skillful means *(upāya)* and compassion *(karuṇā)* of the Buddha.

Giving as the Basis of the Path

This treatment of the *kuśalamūlas* and their eradication has shown that the Buddhists presumed there was a close relationship between the *kuśalamūlas* and merit *(puṇya)*—and specifically, the meritorious practice of giving *(dāna)*. This conclusion can be drawn from the passages in the *Ekottarāgama* cited above about the rich householder becoming *samuchinnakuśalamūla* through his niggardliness. As is well known, the instruction on charity *(dānakathā)* was the first third of the graduated discourse that the Buddha commonly used in instructing laypeople; it is even more fundamental than the succeeding discourses on morality *(śīlakathā)* or the temporal joys of the heavens *(svargakathā)*.[62] This placement of *dāna* at the inception of his teaching suggests that the Buddha considered it to be the foundation of lay practice, presumably because of its value in weaning the layperson from interest in material acquisitions, one of the coarsest types of attachments. "Giving," as the *Ta-sheng i-cheng* (Entries on the Meaning of Mahāyāna) states, "produces the power of radical nonattachment, in which one gives constantly without resting."[63] The nonattachment engendered through giving would lead in turn to specific temporal and spiritual benefits in this life, including wealth[64] and long life,[65] as well as better rebirths in the future.[66] But giving also played an integral part in the practice leading to liberating wisdom for the Śrāvakayānists,[67] an innovation that would be of tremendous importance in the subsequent development of Buddhism.

The correlation drawn in Śrāvakayāna materials between *puṇya* and the *kuśalamūlas* is also suggested in the evolution of both terms in Indian Mahāyāna texts. This evolution can be gleaned from an examination of the various Chinese translations of the *Aṣṭasāhasrikāprajñāpāramitāsūtra,* the earliest Mahāyāna text, which Lewis Lancaster has studied in considerable detail. Lancaster's comparison of different Chinese translations of that scripture shows that where the word *"puṇya" (kung-teh)* is found in earlier renderings of this sūtra, *"kuśalamūla" (shan-ken)* appears in the later. Specifically, in passages translated before 382 C.E. the former is used, whereas after 408 we find the latter.[68] Hence the concept of the *kuśalamūlas* apparently evolved out of a practice that emphasized merit-making, and did not come to be used as a distinct term until around the beginning of the fifth century.

This relationship between *puṇya* and the *kuśalamūlas* may also explain why there was no extension of the meaning of *kuśalamūla* among the Theravādins, such as we find among the Vaibhāṣikas and the Mahāyānists. The Theravādins were perhaps reticent to consider supererogatory acts like charity to be *kuśalamūlas* in their own right, because such acts were considered to stem from the more fundamental faculty of "nongreed" *(alobha-kuśalamūla).* The presence of the underlying nongreed was the factor that allowed a person to undertake merit-making activities in the first place. Hence, *alobha* rather than *dāna* deserved to be regarded as the *kuśalamūla* proper.

Dāna is considered to be the first of the six (alt. ten) pāramitās in Mahāyāna and later Śrāvakayāna literature, presumably also because of its role in overcoming material cravings.[69] In Mahāyāna materials, the specific soteriological effect engendered by giving was considered to be mental control. The *Fo-shuo Hai-i p'u-sa so-wen ching-in fa-men ching* (The Buddha Speaks the Dharma Instruction Concerning Hai-i Bodhisattva's Question Regarding the Seal of Purity) tells us, for example,

> To control well the mind is the meaning of giving. . . .
> The control brought about through giving,
> Causes the inner recesses of the mind to become extremely firm.[70]

Such control would in turn produce that deep mental repose which is samādhi, leading eventually to bodhisattvahood, achievement of the thirty-seven factors of enlightenment and other important stages in praxis, the certitude of enlightenment, the ten *bhūmis,* and, eventually, all the physical and psychical powers of buddhahood.

Thus perfection of giving leads to the perfection of all the pāramitās, and finally even of *anuttarasamyaksaṃbodhi* (complete, perfect enlightenment).[71] The symbiotic relationship between the different pāramitās ensured that perfection of any one would lead to the perfection of all:

> Out of any one pāramitā issue forth innumerable pāramitās. Each and every pāramitā [is interconnected], like Indra's net. If you just know the

original emptiness of the one mind, then naturally the myriad practices will be complete.[72]

It is in Chinese materials that this focus on giving is taken to its inevitable conclusion: giving alone is said to be sufficient to bring about liberation, while the other pāramitās actually inhibit such progress. The San-chieh-chiao (Three Stages Teaching) sect of Chinese "popular" Buddhism, which was proscribed during the reign of Wu Chao (684–704) for its radical beliefs, taught a system of praxis that focused almost exclusively on "universal giving" *(p'u-shih)*. As the *Hsiang-fa chüeh-i ching* (Book of Resolving Doubts during the Semblance Dharma Age), a Chinese apocryphal scripture affiliated with the sect, states:

> All the buddhas of the ten directions also attained buddhahood through the practice of giving. This is why I [the Buddha] have stated at several places in the sūtras that the six pāramitās are all headed by giving.[73]

Monks actually delude themselves if they neglect charity and emphasize instead the cloistered activities of meditation and study. Indeed, the devaluation in monastic practice of the role played by giving could even lead monks to perdition:

> "Why should a renunciant give alms? He has only to cultivate the practices of dhyāna meditation and wisdom. What is the use of these hurly-burly, futile affairs?" Those who produce such thoughts belong to the retinue of Māra and at the end of their lives will fall into the great hell, where they will pass through progressive torments.[74]

And again:

> Although bhikṣus cultivate the [other] five pāramitās for kalpas as numerous as the sands of the Ganges, if they don't practice giving, they will be unable to attain the other shore of nirvāṇa.[75]

Another seminal text of the San-chieh chiao, the *Tui-ken ch'i-hsing fa* (The Teaching on Generating Practice that Accords with Capacity), explicitly notes that such practices as patience, dhyāna, and compassion are all variations on giving. Even the Buddhist soteriological goal of liberation itself is redefined as the breaking down of the traditional hierarchical relationship between the laity and the monks, a difference in status that earlier interpretations of giving sustained. This overarching role given to a practice identified since the inception of institutional Buddhism with the laity could therefore lead also to the breakdown of the barriers between lay and ordained practice.[76]

This reductionist view toward praxis, in which the whole range of Buddhist soteriological techniques is reduced to giving, suggests that for many Buddhists the concept of *dāna* was the very lifeblood of their religion, playing an even more crucial role than meditation and wisdom. A similar reductionism is seen in statements by the famous Ch'an master Ta-chu Hui-hai (d.u.; fl. ca. ninth century), who noted that all six pāramitās are contained in *dānapāramitā,* because if one cultivates an attitude of selflessness through charity, all the other pāramitās will automatically be perfected.[77] The soteriological value ascribed to giving in Chinese Buddhist materials attests to the continued importance of the concept in widely separate strata of Buddhist literature.

Based on the evidence presented here, the evolution of the original three *kuśalamūlas* (of nongreed, nonhatred, and nondelusion) into a concept that embraced both the *puṇyabhāgīya-* and *mokṣabhāgīyakuśalamūlas* occurred through the transformation of the conception of *puṇya,* and more specifically of *dāna.* Once that extension of *dāna*'s significance was made, it was easy to expand the range of the *kuśalamūlas* even further, so as to involve them in virtually all stages of spiritual development. Thus, as we saw in the Vaibhāṣika system, the *kuśalamūlas* come to be extended beyond their basis in such preliminary practices as *puṇya,* until, as *nirvedhabhāgīyas,* the stage leading into *darśanamārga,* they become the critical point of the mārga.

This progression from *dāna* to the *darśanamārga* is brought out well in a striking passage of the *Mahāsāṅghikavinaya.* There it is explained that giving produces a joyful mind, which leads to the purity of samādhi. Through that purity the constant production and cessation of the five skandhas are seen, which creates a disgust for sensual experiences, eventually leading to *vajrasamādhi* or "adamantine absorption," the initiation into sanctity.[78] The preceptory *Yu-p'o-sai chieh ching* (**Upāsakaśīlasūtra;* Sūtra on the Lay Precepts) even states that *vajrasamādhi* allows one to give equally to all and thus obtain infinite merit.[79] Thus this sūtra not only connects giving to the apex of Buddhist meditative development but also shows its limitless efficacy in religious praxis. Hence giving comes to be considered the catalyst for the full range of Buddhist soteriological experiences.

We may thus conclude from this examination of the *kuśalamūlas* that the quality most fundamental to the mārga is *dāna.* As long as people have a modicum of the detachment that is a byproduct of charitable aspirations—and thus the potential to develop the radical detachment that is a necessary precondition to enlightenment—they have the capacity to achieve salvation. But should that aspiration be lost, their wholesome roots would be eradicated and their destiny would be an indeterminate, and perhaps infinite, period of perdition.

Notes

1. *Seyyathāpi bhikkhave mahāsamuddo ekaraso loṇaraso, evam eva kho bhikkhave ayaṃ dhammavinayo ekaraso vimuttiraso. Cullavagga* ix.14. All references in Pali are to the Pali Text Society editions.

2. *A-p'i-ta-mo ta p'i-p'o-sha lun (Abhidharmamahāvibhāṣā;* hereafter *AMV), T*

1545, vol. 27, pp. 1a–1004a; hereafter cited only by fascicle, page, and line number. I also refer occasionally to two alternate recensions of the text, *A-p'i-t'an p'i-p'o-sha lun* (*T* 1546) and *Pi-p'o-sha lun* (*T* 1547).

3. For example, the *kuśalamūlas* have been treated tangentially in Padmanabh S. Jaini, "The Sautrāntika Theory of *Bīja*," *Bulletin of the School of Oriental and African Studies* 22 (1959): 236–249. See also the coverage in David Seyfort Ruegg, *La Théorie du tathāgatagarbha et du gotra: Étude sur la sotériologie et la gnoséologie du bouddhisme,* Publications de l'École Française d'Extrême-Orient, vol. 76 (Paris, 1969), cf. p. 80 n. 3, 458ff., 460 and n. 1, 462–463, 477, 478, 482, 493. There has yet to be any study of the role of the *kuśalamūlas* themselves and their place in Buddhist soteriology, such as I attempt in this chapter.

4. For selected translations of a number of the most important passages in Pali literature describing these three *kuśalamūlas,* see Nyanaponika Thera, trans., "The Roots of Good and Evil: Buddhist Texts," *The Wheel,* nos. 251–253 (Kandy, Sri Lanka: Buddhist Publication Society, 1978), 10–104. In the *Visuddhimagga*'s discussion of "root" in the term *"kuśalamūla,"* those things which achieve stability or skillfulness *(kuśala)* through that root are said to be "firm, like trees, and stable; but those without root-cause are like moss [with roots no bigger than] sesamum seeds, etc., [and are thus] unstable" (*Visuddhimagga* xvii.70; Bhikkhu Ñāṇamoli, trans., *The Path of Purification* [*Visuddhimagga*] *by Bhadantācariya Buddhaghosa* [Colombo: A. Semage, 1964], 612). See also *Atthasālinī* iii.293; noted in Herbert V. Guenther, *Philosophy and Psychology in the Abhidharma* (1957; rpt. ed., Berkeley, Calif.: Shambhala, 1976), 79.

5. See *Vibhaṅga,* pp. 169, 210ff.; *She-li-fu a-p'i-t'an lun (Śāriputrābhidharmaśāstra)* 6, *T* 28.570a27–572c15. The *Śāriputrābhidharmaśāstra* is generally attributed to either the Vātsiputrīyas or their Saṃmitīya subsect, though different theories have been proposed about the text's origins; see the summary of the various positions in Watanabe Baiyū, "*Sharihotsu-abidatsumaron* kaidai" (An Analysis of the *Śāriputrābhidharmaśāstra*), *Kokuyaku issaikyō,* Abidon-bu 19 (Tokyo: Daitō shuppansha, 1934), 8–11.

6. The benefits accruing from planting the *puṇyabhāgīyakuśalamūlas* are discussed in detail at *AMV* 31, p. 159b and ibid. 82, p. 426a.

7. Sanskrit reconstructions marked by an asterisk are my own tentative equivalencies, which are not attested in the *Abhidharmakośa* (Prahlad Pradhan, ed., *Abhidharmakośabhāṣyam* of *Vasubandhu,* Tibetan Sanskrit Works Series, vol. 8 [1967; rpt. ed., Patna: K. P. Jayaswal Research Institute, 1975]; hereafter *AK*), the only Sarvāstivāda text for which both Chinese and Sanskrit recensions are extant. Based on Hsüan-tsang's noted consistency in rendering Sanskrit technical terms, however, I believe most of these reconstructions to be reasonably accurate.

8. Cf. discussion in Jaini, *"Bīja,"* p. 248, where he speculates that *mokṣabhāgīyakuśala* corresponds to *anāsravakuśalabīja* in the Sautrāntika system. This hypothesis is borne out in this passage from *AMV,* though I have found no explicit statement in *AMV* positing this correspondence. This definition shows that when the *icchantika* is called *aparinirvāṇagotraka* in the *Mahāparinirvāṇasūtra* and Yogācāra texts, he is *samucchinna* from this type of *kuśalamūla.*

9. See *AK* i.4 and the commentary by Yaśomitra, *Sphuṭārthāvyākhyā,* in Swami Dwarikadas Sastri, ed., *Abhidharmakośa and Bhāṣya of Ācārya Vasubandhu with Sphuṭārtha Commentary of Ācārya Yaśomitra* (Varanasi: Bauddha Bhāratī, 1981), 1:16.

10. See Guenther, *Abhidharma,* p. 215, for the use of the terms "remote" and "direct" in relation to the *prayogamārga.*

11. The *nirvedhabhāgīyas* are treated in *AK* vi.17ff.; and see Franklin Edgerton, *Buddhist Hybrid Sanskrit Dictionary* (New Haven: Yale University Press, 1954), s.v. *"nirvedhabhāgīya,"* and Louis de La Vallée Poussin, trans., *L'Abhidharmakośa de Vasubandhu, Mélanges chinois et bouddhique* 16 (1971), 4:169. For these faculties as four aspects of the *prayogamārga,* see Guenther, *Abhidharma,* pp. 215, 220–221. The Pali antecedent appears at *Visuddhimagga* iii.22, Bhikkhu Ñāṇamoli, trans., *The Path of Purification,* p. 89. The most detailed treatment of the *nirvedhabhāgīyas* appears in Leon Hurvitz, "The Abhidharma on the 'Four Aids to Penetration,' " in Leslie Kawamura, ed., *Buddhist Thought and Asian Civilization,* Herbert Guenther Festschrift (Emeryville, Calif.: Dharma Publishing, 1977), 59–104.

12. The following material is taken from *AMV* 7, p. 35a7–35b18.

13. This type of *kuśalamūla* is said to be perfected by *śrutamāyī* and *cintamāyī prajñās* because it is associated with the desire realm *(kāmāvacarapratisaṃyukta);* other teachers, however, have advocated that it is also perfected via *bhāvanāmāyīprajñā,* which would extend its range of applicability into the material and immaterial realms as well. According to *A-p'i-t'an p'i-p'o-sha lun (Abhidharmavibhāṣā)* 6, *T* 28.40b17–19, cultivation wisdom is activated only on the material and immaterial realms, not on the desire realm; the only type of wisdom that operates in all three realms of existence is congenital wisdom *(upapattipratilābhikaprajñā).* Hence even in the highest stage of dhyāna (where the *nirvedhabhāgīyakuśalamūlas* would already have come to the forefront?), the *mokṣabhāgīyakuśalamūlas* would retain some sort of applicability.

14. *AMV* 7, p. 35b4–8.

15. Cf. Yaśomitra's commentary to *AK* i.1 (Dwarikadas Sastri, ed., *Sphuṭārtha,* 1:7): *mokṣabījam aham hy asya susūkṣmam upalakṣaye/ dhātupāṣāṇavivare nilīnam iva kāñcanam* ("I see his extremely subtle seed of salvation like a seam of gold hidden in metal-bearing rock"); translated in Jaini, *"Bīja,"* p. 248.

16. *AMV* 176, p. 886a5–19.

17. Ibid. 7, p. 35b8–16; and cf. Guenther, *Abhidharma,* p. 215. The Jainas also have a similar doctrine in which three lifetimes are required for the attainment of *kevalajñāna.* Even in Chinese Hua-yen theory a three-lifetime theory was proposed, in which the first life was one of learning, the second one of reflection and cultivation, and the third the stage of fruition; see Fa-tsang, *Hua-yen i-sheng chiao-i fen-ch'i chang* 2, *T* 45.489c4–15, noted in Robert E. Buswell, Jr., *The Korean Approach to Zen: The Collected Works of Chinul* (Honolulu: University of Hawaii Press, 1983), 93 n. 211.

18. *Idh'ekacco puggalo samanvāgato hoti ekantakāḷakehi akusalehi dhammehi, evaṃ puggalo sakiṃ nimuggo nimuggo va hoti. Puggalapaññatti,* 7.1, translation adapted from Bimala Churn Law, *Designation of Human Types (Puggala-Paññatti)* (1924; rpt. ed., London: Pali Text Society, 1969), 99; this passage is noted in Jaini, *"Bīja,"* p. 246 n. 2, and discussed on pp. 246–247; see also Ruegg, *Tathāgatagarbha,* p. 479.

19. The theory of nonbeing *(natthikavāda)* is attributed in Pali materials to Ajita Kesakambali, noncausationism *(ahetukavāda)* to Makkhali Gosāla, and randomness *(akiriyavāda)* to Pūraṇa Kassapa. See the discussion in David J. Kalupahana, *Causality: The Central Philosophy of Buddhism* (Honolulu: University of Hawaii Press, 1975), 40.

20. *Puggalapaññatti Aṭṭhakathā* 7.1, translated in Jaini, *"Bīja,"* p. 246.

21. *Tseng-i a-han ching (Ekottarāgama)* 34, *T* 2.739b.14–15; this particular sūtra in the collection has no Pali equivalent. Preserved only in Chinese translation, the *Ekottarāgama* is generally considered to be a Dharmaguptaka recension,

though some scholars, notably Akanuma Chizen, have proposed affiliations with the Mahāsāṅghika school or its Prajñaptivāda offshoot. See A. K. Warder, *Indian Buddhism* (rev. 2nd ed., Delhi: Motilal Banarsidass, 1980), 7-9.

22. *Tseng-i a-han ching* 13, *T* 2.612c, corresponding to the Pali *Saṃyuttanikāya* 3.2.10 "Aputtaka." For Mahāraurava-niraka, a hot hell, see Edgerton, *Buddhist Hybrid Sanskrit Dictionary,* s.v. *"mahāraurava-niraka";* William Montgomery McGovern, *A Manual of Buddhist Philosophy* (New York: E. P. Dutton, 1923), 62.

23. *Tseng-i a-han ching* 34, *T* 2.739b19-25.

24. Ibid., *T* 2.740a17.

25. For discussion of the unanswered questions, and scriptural citations to them, see K. N. Jayatilleke, *Early Buddhist Theory of Knowledge* (London: George Allen and Unwin, 1963), 243; lists of ten and fourteen such questions are common.

26. Pradhan, ed., *Kośa,* p. 471.2-3; translated in Theodore Stcherbatsky, *The Soul Theory of the Buddhists* (1920; rpt. ed., Delhi: Bharatiya Vidya Prakashan, 1976), 44.

27. Generally, only passing remarks are made about this sort of individual when discussing the endowment *(samanvāgama; ch'eng-chiu)* with certain faculties *(indriya),* dharmas, and so forth. See, for example, the discussion of *samucchinnakuśalamūla* with reference to the *indriyas* at Pradhan, ed., *Kośa,* p. 50.19.

28. Cf. *AMV* 3, p. 14b8-9, and *AMV* 20, p. 102b10-11.

29. *AMV* 176, pp. 885c18-886a3.

30. *AMV* 35, p. 184a2-7. This passage continues with a long description of which type of person can reestablish the *kuśalamūlas* at birth and which at death in hell. *AMV* 112, p. 966c7-8 states specifically that the fruition of *samucchinnakuśalamūla* is experienced in the great hell beneath Jambudvīpa. Cf. also *AMV* 14, p. 67a7-8 and 125, p. 653c, which both clarify the Vaibhāṣika view that a being must be in hell before the *kuśalamūlas* can regenerate. I have been unable to trace the quotation from the *Prajñaptibhāṣya* (*Shih-she lun;* *T* 26.514a-529c). This text was not translated into Chinese until sometime between 1018 and 1058, during the Northern Sung dynasty, four centuries after Hsüan-tsang's time; thus it is virtually impossible that the extant text would represent the recension that Hsüan-tsang consulted in preparing this translation.

31. *AMV* 82, p. 422a22-b4.

32. *AMV* 158, p. 801a21-22.

33. See Jiryo Masuda, "Origin and Doctrines of Early Indian Buddhist Schools: A Translation of the Hsüan-chwang Version of Vasumitra's Treatise *I-pu tsung-lun lun,*" *Asia Major* 2 (1925), p. 24, proposition no. 28.

34. Cf. ibid., pp. 42-49, propositions nos. 8, 9, 23, 24, 32, 34.

35. Cf. *mūrdhapatita* (fall from the summit), one of the *nirvedhabhāgīyas,* where operation of the *adhipatipratyaya* causes all dharmas to follow along; *AMV* 6, p. 27c.9-10. For the relationship between *samucchinnakusalamula* and *mūrdhapatita,* see *AMV* 6, p. 30b16-c16.

36. The different propositions about the *svabhāva* of the *samucchinnakuśalamūla* are given at *AMV* 35, p. 182b26-c4. The Vibhāṣāśāstrins' judgment is given at p. 182b4-6; *asamanvāgama* as the *svabhāva* of *samucchinnakusalamula* is noted also in *A-p'i-t'an pa chien-tu lun (Jñānaprasthāna)* 3, *T* 26.783c8.

37. *Samanvāgama* is consistently translated by Hsüan-tsang as "accomplishment" *(ch'eng-chiu);* Edgerton *(Buddhist Hybrid Sanskrit Dictionary,* s.v., *"samanvāgata")* gives the equivalents "endowed," "provided," "attended." It seems to have been the early Vaibhāṣika equivalent for their later theory of *prāpti* (posses-

sion); cf. the discussion in *AKB* iv.80b, where *samanvāgama* is equated with *prāpti;* noted in Jaini, ed., *Abhidharmadīpa,* p. 167 n. 1; and see the discussion in idem, *"Bīja,"* p. 245 about the synonymity of *samanvāgama* and *prāpti.* Apparently, *samanvāgama* was a sūtra term assimilated by the Vaibhāṣikas and eventually transformed into the full-blown theory of *prāpti.* See also *AKB* ii.36 (Pradhan, ed., *Kośa,* pp. 62–63), and Saṃghabhadra's *A-pi-t'a-mo-tsang hsien-tsung lun (Abhidharmakośakārikāvibhāṣya)* 6, *T* 29.803cff. For the role of *prāpti* in the Vaibhāṣika doctrinal system, see Collett Cox, "Controversies in Dharma Theory: Sectarian Dialogue on the Nature of Enduring Reality" (Ph.D. diss., Columbia University, 1983), 37–59.

38. Cf. the parallel discussion on the possibility of the coexistence of avidyā and prajñā in Padmanabh S. Jaini, "*Prajñā* and *Dṛṣṭi* in the Vaibhāṣika Abhidharma," in Lewis R. Lancaster, ed., *Prajñāpāramitā and Related Systems,* Berkeley Buddhist Series, vol. 1 (Berkeley: Institute of South and Southeast Asian Studies, 1977), 403–415.

39. *AMV* 35, p. 182b22–26 and 45, p. 233a18. Several Vaibhāṣika texts make the claim that *mithyādṛṣṭi* is the agent of eradication; see ibid. 7, p. 30b19; ibid. 146, p. 748b29; and cf. *A-p'i-t'an p'i-p'o-sha lun* 25, *T* 28.187b22–188a8; *AK* iv.79a and La Vallée Poussin, *L'Abhidharmakośa,* 4:170. There is a detailed discussion on this point in Saṃghabhūti's 383 C.E. translation of the *Pi-p'o-sha lun (Mahāvibhāṣā)* 2, *T* 28.423b18–424a7. The Vibhāṣāśāstrins clarify that both *sāsrava-* and *anāsravapratyaya-mithyādṛṣṭi* can cause *samucchinnakuśalamūla* in their treatment of the question at *AMV* 35, p. 183b12–20. Cf. also Saṃghabhadra's comments in *Shun cheng-li lun (Nyāyānusāra)* 12, *T* 29.397b.

This sense that *mithyādṛṣṭi* is the agent of eradication also occurs later in the *Abhidharmadīpa.* As Jaini has noted, the Vaibhāṣikas there posit three different grades of both *mithyādṛṣṭi* and the *kuśalamūlas,* each of which is further subdivided into three still finer divisions. The extreme *(adhimātra)* grade of *mithyādṛṣṭi* destroys the developed *prāyogika-kuśalamūlas* pertaining to the desire realm. However, the extremely grave *(adhimātra-adhimātra)* grade of *mithyādṛṣṭi,* such as *nāstikavāda, ahetukavāda,* or *akriyāvāda,* destroys the most subtle variety of the *kuśalamūlas*—the congenital *(upapattilābhika) kuśalamūlas* of the desire realm—thus rendering the person *samucchinnakuśalamūla.* See Jaini, ed., *Abhidharmadīpa,* p. 165.1–2: *tayā punar mithyādṛṣṭyā prakarṣaprāptayā navaprakārayā navaprakārāṇi kuśalamūlāni samucchidyante.* Quoted also in Ruegg, *Tathāgatagarbha,* 478. See, too, the discussion in Jaini, *"Bīja,"* p. 247.

40. The *cittaviprayuktasaṃskāras* are various anomalous forces that are emblematic of the Vaibhāṣika taxonomy of dharmas. They were considered to be neither mental, material, nor uncompounded, and therefore could not be readily subsumed within other dharma classifications. They include such qualities as origination, subsistence, decay, and extinction; possession; life force; and various linguistic and semantic forces. For a description of this category of dharmas, see Padmanabh S. Jaini, "Origin and Development of the Theory of *Viprayukta-saṃskaras,*" *Bulletin of the School of Oriental and African Studies* 22 (1959): 531–547; and Collett Cox, "Controversies in Dharma Theory," passim. See also the following note.

41. Among the *cittaviprayuktasaṃskāras* unknown in the *Kośa* but mentioned in *AMV* are *arhattvaparihāṇa* (regression from sainthood), *mūrdhapatita* (falling from the stage of summit), and *saṃghabheda* (causing schism in the order). I have discussed these in an unpublished paper, "The Proliferation of Forces Dissociated from Mind *(Cittaviprayuktasaṃskāra)* in the *Abhidharmamahāvibhāṣā,*" delivered at the American Oriental Society, 197th Annual Meeting, 25 March 1987, University of California, Los Angeles.

42. See Edgerton, *Buddhist Hybrid Sanskrit Dictionary,* s.v., *"icchantika."*

43. Cited in Daisetz Teitaro Suzuki, *Studies in the Laṅkāvatāra Sūtra* (1930; rpt. ed., Boulder. Colo.: Prajñā Press, 1981), 219n.

44. Takasaki Jikidō, trans., *A Study on the Ratnagotravibhāga (Uttaratantra): Being a Treatise on the Tathāgatagabha Theory of Mahāyāna Buddhism,* Serie Orientale Roma 33 (Rome: Istituto Italiano per il Medio ed Estremo Oriente, 1966), 202.

45. Aṅgulimālīya (He Who Has a Necklace of Fingers) waylaid travelers and cut off their fingers, which he strung into a necklace. He was made the subject of the *Yang-chüeh-mo-lo ching* (*T* 2.512b–544b) to illustrate that even this most evil of men still maintained the innate capacity for enlightenment through possessing the tathāgatagarbha. The text has been treated by Takasaki Jikidō in his *Nyoraizō shisō no keisei* (Tokyo: Shunjūsha, 1974), 191–233. Takasaki dates it to sometime before the middle of the fourth century (ibid., p. 220).

46. *Puggalapaññatti* i.15, 16.

47. *Yang-chüeh-mo-lo ching* 2, *T* 2.529c.

48. Pralhad Pradhan, ed., *Abhidharma-Samuccaya of Asaṅga,* Visva-Bharati Studies 12 (Santiniketan: Visva-Bharati, 1950), p. 35; cf. Walpola Rahula, trans., *Le Compendium de la super-doctrine (philosophie): (Abhidharmasamuccaya) d'Asaṅga,* Publications de l'École Française d'Extrême-Orient (Paris, 1971), 78:58.

49. Pradhan, ed., *Abhidharma-Samuccaya,* p. 35; Rahula, *Compendium,* p. 58.

50. See Jaini, *"Bīja,"* p. 246, for the parallel Sautrāntika denial that the *sūkṣmakuśaladharmabīja* can ever be lost, since they are innate *(upapattilābhika).*

51. *aparinirvāṇadharmaka etasminn agotrastho 'abhipretaḥ. sa ca samāsato dvividhaḥ. tatkālāparinirvāṇadharmā atyantam ca. tatkālāparinirvāṇadharmā caturvidhaḥ. duścaritaikāntikaḥ, samucchinnakuśalamūlaḥ, amokṣabhāgīyakuśalamūlaḥ, hīnakuśalamūlaś ca aparipūrṇasaṃbhāraḥ. atyantāparinirvāṇadharmā tu hetuhīno yasya parinirvāṇagotram eva nāsti.* Sylvain Lévi, ed., *Mahāyāna-sūtrālaṃkāra,* Bibliothèque de l'École des Hautes Études, no. 159 (Paris: Librairie Honoré Champion, 1907), 12–13; idem, trans., *Mahāyāna-sūtrālaṃkāra,* Bibliothèque de l'École des Hautes Études, no. 190 (Paris: Librairie Honoré Champion, 1911), 30.

52. *Ta-pan-nieh-p'an ching (Mahāparinirvāṇasūtra), T* 12.365a–603c; translated in Suzuki, *Studies,* p. 219n. A long description of what makes one an *icchantika,* as well as of the connection between *samucchinnakuśalamūla* and *icchantika,* appears in *Ta-pan-nieh-p'an ching* 3, *T* 12.562b3ff.

53. *Icchantikas* are referred to as *aparinirvāṇagotraka* in the *Mahāparinirvāṇasūtra;* see Takasaki, trans., *Ratnagotravibhāga,* Introduction, p. 39, translated at p. 224 n. 182.

54. Takasaki, trans., *Ratnagotravibhāga,* Introduction, p. 40.

55. Bunyu Nanjo [sic], ed., *Laṅkāvatārasūtra* (Kyoto: Ōtani University, 1923), 66; Daisetz Teitaro Suzuki, trans., *The Laṅkāvatāra Sūtra* (1932; rpt. ed., Boulder, Colo.: Prajñā Press, 1978), 58; idem, *Studies,* pp. 217–221.

56. Nanjo, ed., *Laṅkāvatāra,* p. 66; Suzuki, trans., *Laṅkāvatāra,* p. 59.

57. Takasaki, trans., *Ratnagotravibhāga,* p. 205.

58. Nanjo, ed., *Laṅkāvatāra,* p. 66; Suzuki, trans., *Laṅkāvatāra,* p. 59.

59. Nanjo, ed., *Laṅkāvatāra,* p. 66; Suzuki, trans., *Laṅkāvatāra,* p. 59; quoted at idem, *Studies,* p. 220.

60. *Ta A-mi-t'o ching (Sukhāvatīvyūhasūtra), T* 12.329c4–8.

61. Takasaki, trans., *Ratnagotravibhāga,* p. 224. The quoted passage is taken from the *Mahāparinirvāṇasūtra,* but Takasaki gives no page reference. "A certain period of time" is interpreted to mean that they remain *icchantikas* only until such time as they overcome their antipathy toward Mahāyāna.

62. For this progressive discourse, see *Dīghanikāya* i.110.2, i.148.7, cited, with discussion, in Har Dayal, *The Bodhisattva Doctrine in Buddhist Sanskrit Literature* (1932; rpt. ed., Delhi: Motilal Banarsidass, 1975), 169. For the role of *dāna* in procuring rebirth in heaven for the laity, see Fujita Kōtatsu, "Genshi bukkyō ni okeru seiten shisō" (The Ideology of Heavenly Rebirth in Early Buddhism), *Indogaku bukkyōgaku kenkyū* 19-2 (1971): 412. For the importance of giving in Indian culture in general, see Vijay Nath, *Dāna: Gift System in Ancient India, A Socio-economic Perspective* (New Delhi: Munshiram Manoharlal Publishers, 1987).

63. *Ta-sheng i chang* 14, *T* 44.755a20–21; note also: "If one gives, then the mind is without any defiling attachment" *(Lu-shan Lien-tsung pao-chien* 6, *T* 47.333a9–10).

64. "Because giving has no covetousness, one then gains tremendous wealth. Through that giving, one then guards the precepts and then becomes a lord among gods and humans." (*Fang-kuang po-jo ching* 17, *T* 8.120b22–23).

65. "[When the human lifespan was two thousand years], that person was utterly without covetousness and practiced giving. His lifespan was then extended to five thousand years" (*Chüan-lun-sheng wang hsiu-hsing ching,* in *Ch'ang a-han ching* 6, *T* 1.41c6–7).

66. The *Mahāprajñāpāramitāsūtra* specifies that giving produces rebirths in such superior castes as those of *kṣatriya* warriors and brahman priests (*Ta po-jo po-lo-mi-to ching* 3, *T* 5.14a8–b11). "If one gives, keeps precepts, and cultivates diligently, one can leave behind the defilement of sexual desire and gain rebirth in the pure heavens" (*P'i-p'o-shih fo ching* 2, *T* 1.157a4–5). "One who gives to the śramaṇas and brahmacārins will be reborn in the future in the heavens and gain long life and pleasant rewards" (*Chung a-han ching* [*Madhyamāgama*] 6, *T* 1.456c25–26).

67. "Respectfully keeping the required precepts, cultivating wide learning, and perfecting the practice of giving, one will gain wisdom" (*Chung a-han ching* 26, *T* 1.605c19–20, 24–25).

68. In the different recensions of this text in Chinese translation, where Lokakṣema (*T* 224, translating in 179 C.E.), Chih Ch'ien (*T* 225; trans. ca. 223-253 C.E.), and Chu Fo-nien/Dharmapriya (*T* 226; trans. in 382 C.E.) use *puṇya,* Kumārajīva (*T* 227, trans. in 408) uses *kuśalamūla.* See Lewis R. Lancaster, "An Analysis of the *Aṣṭasāhasrikāprajñāpāramitā-Sūtra* from the Chinese Translations" (Ph.D diss., University of Wisconsin, 1968), 58–62; a chart of references to the term *"kuśalamūla"* appears at pp. 68–76. For an outline of the place of this scripture in accounts of the evolution of Mahāyāna doctrine, see idem, "The Oldest Mahāyāna Sūtra: Its Significance for the Study of Buddhist Development," *Eastern Buddhist* 8-1 (May 1975): 30–41.

69. Giving as a pāramitā is discussed at Har Dayal, *The Bodhisattva Doctrine,* pp. 172–193; and for the evolution of the pāramitās, see ibid., pp. 165–269.

70. *Fo-shuo Hai-i p'u-sa so-wen ching-in fa-men ching* 4, *T* 13.482a15–26; *chüan* 12, p. 505ba21.

71. See passages in *Ta po-jo po-lo-mi-to ching* 3, *T* 5.14a8–b11, and for virtually identical passages, see *chüan* 402, *T* 7.9a–b, *Mo-ho po-jo po-lo-mi ching* 1, *T* 8.220a. *Fang-kuang po-jo ching* 17, *T* 8.120b23–27.

72. *Lu-shan Lien-tsung pao-chien* 6, *T* 47.333a12–14.

73. *Hsiang-fa chüeh-i ching, T* 85.1336b20–22. For a complete translation and extensive study of this important Chinese apocryphon, see Kyoko Tokuno, "A Case Study of Chinese Buddhist Apocrypha: The *Hsiang-fa Chüeh-i Ching*" (M.A. thesis, University of California, Berkeley, 1983). This section of the text

is translated by Tokuno at p. 83. See also Mark E. Lewis, "The Suppression of the Three Stages Sect: Apocrypha as a Political Issue," in Robert E. Buswell, Jr., ed., *Chinese Buddhist Apocrypha* (Honolulu: University of Hawaii Press, 1990), 207–238; and Jamie Hubbard, "The Inexhaustible Storehouse" (Ph.D. diss., University of Wisconsin, 1986). The definitive study of the San-chieh chiao sect is Yabuki Keiki's *Sangaikyō no kenkyū* (Studies in the Three Stages Sect) (Tokyo: Iwanami shoten, 1927).

74. *Hsiang-fa chüeh-i ching, T* 85.1336b12–15; translation adapted from Kyoko Tokuno, "The *Hsiang-Fa Chüeh-I Ching,*" p. 82. For her discussion of the peculiar interpretation of giving in this indigenous Chinese sūtra, see ibid., pp. 57–64.

75. *Hsiang-fa chüeh-i ching, T* 85.1336b20–24.

76. See *Tui-ken ch'i-hsing fa,* in Yabuki Keiki, *Sangaikyō no kenkyū, betsu hen,* pp. 121.13–124.9; the significance of this passage is discussed in Lewis, "Three Stages Sect," pp. 32–34.

77. *Tun-wu ju-tao yao-men lun, ZZ* 2, 15, 5, 422c/*HTC,* vol. 110.422b.

78. *Mo-ho-seng-ch'i lü (Mahāsāṅghikavinaya)* 21, *T* 22.397b8ff.

79. *Yu-p'o-sai chieh ching (*Upāsakaśīlasūtra), T* 24.1065a13–14.

Glossary

ai-hsing che 愛行者
A-p'i-ta-mo chü-she lun 阿毘達磨俱舍論
A-p'i-ta-mo ta p'i-p'o-sha lun 阿毘達磨大毘婆沙論
A-p'i-t'a-mo-tsang hsien-tsung lun 阿毘達磨藏顯宗論
A-p'i-t'an pa chien-tu lun 阿毘曇八犍度論
A-p'i-t'an p'i-p'o-sha lun 阿毘曇毘婆沙論
ch'an-t'i 闡提
ch'eng-chiu 成就
cheng-ting 正定
chia-hsing shan-ken 加行善根
chia-hsing teh 加行得
chia-hsing wei 加行位
chieh-t'o chung-tzu 解脱種子
chien-hsing che 見行者
chien-tao 見道
chih-hsing 志性
chüan-yüan 轉遠
chüeh-ting 決定
chüeh-t'o chung-tzu 解脱種子
chung-tzu 種子
fo-hsing 佛性
Fo-shuo Hai-i p'u-sa so-wen ching-in fa-men 佛說海意菩薩所問淨印法門
fu 福
hsiang-ch'u 相觸
Hsiang-fa chüeh-i ching 像法決疑經
hsiang-hsü 相續
hsieh-ting 邪定
Hsüan-tsang 玄奘
i-ch'an-t'i 一闡提
i-le 意樂
jen 忍
ken-pen 根本
kung-teh 功德
meng-li 猛利
Mo-ho-seng-ch'i lü 摩訶僧祇律
nuan 煖
P'i-lo-hsien 毘羅先
Pi-p'o-sha lun 鞞婆沙論
pu-ch'eng-chiu 不成就
pu-ch'eng-chiu hsing 不成就性
pu-shan-ken 不善根
p'u-shih 普施
San-chieh-chiao 三階教
san shan-ken 三善根
shan-ken 善根
she 捨
sheng-teh 生得
sheng-teh shan-ken 生得善根
shen-yü 深欲
Shih-she lun 施設論
shih ti-i fa 世第一法
Shun cheng-li lun 順正理論
shun chieh-t'o-fen shan-ken 順解脱分善根

shun chüeh-tse-fen shan-ken
順決擇分善根
shun fu-fen shan-ken 順福分善根
ssu shan-ken 四善根
Ta A-mi-t'o ching 大阿彌陀經
Ta-chu Hui-hai 大珠慧海
Ta-pan-nieh-p'an ching 大般涅槃經
Ta-sheng i chang 大乘義章
ta-shen-yü 大深欲
teng-ch'i 等起
ting 頂
tseng 增
Tseng-i a-han ching 增一阿含經
tseng-shang i-le 增上意樂
tuan shan-ken [che] 斷善根者
Tui-ken ch'i-hsing fa 對根起行法
Tun-wu ju-tao yao-men lun
頓悟入道要門論
tzu-hsing 自性
Yang-chüeh-mo-lo ching 央掘魔羅經
yin-yüan 因緣
Yü-ch'ieh-shih ti lun 瑜伽師地論
Yu-p'o-sai chieh ching 優婆塞戒經

On the Ignorance of the Arhat

PADMANABH S. JAINI

In the opening verse of his *Abhidharmakośa,* Vasubandhu (ca. 400), while commenting on the words *yaḥ sarvathā sarvahatāndhakāraḥ,* which describe the omniscience of the Buddha, speaks of two kinds of ignorance.[1] The first is called *kliṣṭasammoha* (defiled delusion), which means ignorance of the four noble truths. The pratyekabuddhas (those who attain arhatship without the aid of a buddha) and the śrāvakas (those disciples of the Buddha who attain arhatship) are free from such ignorance, since they have realized the true nature of all *(sarvaṃ)* that exists as being *duḥkha* (suffering), *anitya* (impermanent), and anātma (nonself). However, Vasubandhu claims that they have not overcome the second kind of ignorance, *akliṣṭa-ajñāna,* the "undefiled," ordinary ignorance of the infinite varieties of objects that are distant in space and time. Vasubandhu states in passing that the Buddha has achieved this total freedom from ignorance *(ajñāna)* through cultivating its counterpart, but fails to indicate what that counteragent *(pratipakṣa)* could be.[2]

Yaśomitra (ca. 700), in his commentary to the *Kośa,* the *Sphuṭārthāvyākhyā,* states that *pratipakṣa* means *āryamārga* (the noble path), since it is the opposite of the adversary called *kleśa* (defilement). Yaśomitra does not seem happy with this explanation, because the śrāvakas and the pratyekabuddhas have destroyed the *kleśas* and yet have not overcome all forms of *ajñāna.* He therefore gives an alternative meaning, saying that *pratipakṣa* is *anāsravaṃ jñānam,* knowledge freed from *āsravas* (influxes).[3] Whether this *anāsravajñāna* is merely the understanding achieved by the destruction of the *anuśaya* (disposition or defilement) known as avidyā (ignorance,) or whether it entails some additional achievement, is not explained by Yaśomitra. He is also silent on the precise difference between the *kleśapratipakṣa* and the *ajñānapratipakṣa,* and about the possible stage on the path (mārga) at which the latter may be cultivated. Yet there must be some distinction, since the *akliṣṭa-ajñāna* is defined as a deficiency that the arhats failed to overcome even when they were presumed to have followed the same noble path traversed by the Buddha, which was believed to culminate in the same kind of nirvāṇa. Neither Vasubandhu nor Yaśomitra addresses this issue specifically, but an investigation of the Vaibhāṣika rules on the mārga pertaining to the destruction of the *akliṣṭa-ajñāna* may yield a solution.

Yaśomitra is acutely aware of the anomaly of admitting in the arhat a form of ignorance that remains even in the absence of *kleśas:*

> Surely, [a questioner asks,] all that is considered *sāsrava* [affected by influxes] is destroyed by both the *śrāvakas* and the pratyekabuddhas as in the case of the Buddha; so how could you maintain that in their case only the *kliṣṭasammoha* is destroyed? Has it not been said in the sūtra: "I do not say that there is the complete destruction of suffering as long as even a single dharma remains without being known *(aparijñāya)* and abandoned *(aprahāya)*?" Therefore it must be admitted that this *akliṣṭa-ajñāna* was abandoned by the arhats and the pratyekabuddhas as well, analogous to their destruction of eye *(cakṣu)* and other dharmas [i.e., the ten material elements] by the method of overcoming delight *(chandarāga)* toward them. Otherwise there would be no total destruction of suffering in their case?[4]

Yaśomitra accepts this sūtra and concedes that, even in the case of the arhats and pratyekabuddhas, this so-called *akliṣṭa-ajñāna* must be considered destroyed *(prahīṇam)* like the *kliṣṭasammoha,* but nevertheless pleads that there is a difference: whereas the *akliṣṭa-ajñāna,* unlike the *kliṣṭasammoha,* can be destroyed, it is liable to reappear *(samudācarati)* and needs to be dispelled anew on each subsequent occasion. In the case of the Buddha, however, once his *chandarāga* is destroyed, it will not reappear *(buddhasya tu prahīṇaṃ san na samudācarati)* at each instance of a new perception. Yaśomitra adds that, for this very reason, Vasubandhu qualified the Buddha's destruction *(prahāṇa)* as not subject to reemergence *(punar anutpattidharmatvāt hatam),* and hence the Buddha alone is totally free from both kinds of ignorance. It is this excellence which distinguishes him from other arhats.[5]

What we glean from this rather obscure commentary is that there is a form of ignorance that pertains not to the true nature of dharmas (which is dispelled by the knowledge of the four noble truths) but to the worldly nature of things, and that persists even after one has become an arhat. An ordinary person can be consumed by curiosity (a form of desire or *chanda*) and will experience dejection at not knowing—or delight *(chandarāga)* at knowing—the desired object. For the arhat, however, his *kleśas* having been destroyed, ignorance of "things" is unable to obstruct the purity of his mind. When a need arises to know something hitherto unknown (i.e., when he becomes aware of his ignorance), the arhat will be mindful and will dispel any delight that may accompany the act of knowing the new object. In the case of the Buddha there is no such deficiency because he lacks all forms of curiosity and consequent delight, since the objects he wants to know become instantaneously known to him without any effort *(prayoga)* whatsoever.

What is the arhat ignorant of? Vasubandhu mentions three items: (1) the eighteen special *(āveṇika)* dharmas of the Buddha, which are extremely subtle *(paramasūkṣma);* (2) the infinite variety of gross and subtle material aggregates *(paramāṇusañcita)* that are distant in place *(viprakṛṣṭadeśa),* and (3) those that are remote in time *(viprakṛṣṭakāla).* Yaśomitra illustrates these with examples about the arhats Śāriputra and Maudgalyāyana.[6] When questioned by the Buddha, Śāriputra admitted that he had no knowledge of the extent of the Tathāgata's countless aggregates of the practices of *śīla* (moral precepts), samādhi (meditation), prajñā (wisdom), and so on. This is because, as Yaśomitra points out, the special *(āveṇika)* dharmas of the Buddha are extremely subtle and no one but the buddhas can know them.

Nor are the other material objects accessible to the cognition of arhats, even when they are not subtle but are distant—that is, separated *(antarita)* by different world systems *(lokadhātu).* This is illustrated by the Elder Maudgalyāyana's ignorance of the extremely distant world system called Marīci where his mother was reborn; only the Buddha knew her whereabouts. Similarly, remoteness in time can prevent an arhat from knowing a past incident, as happened when a certain person approached Śāriputra seeking renunciation. Śāriputra rejected him because he failed to discern any roots of good *(kuśalamūla)* in him that might lead to nirvāṇa, but the Buddha was able to perceive a subtle seed of salvation *(mokṣabīja)*—the result of a certain wholesome act—which lay hidden like a speck of pure gold in ore, and granted him ordination. As for the countless variety of material objects in their infinite details, only the buddhas, if they cared to, could know them all, for it is said that even the totality of causes that come together to produce the "eye" on a peacock's feather cannot be known by anyone but a buddha, since that is the realm of omniscient cognition. Of course, not all arhats need be equally deficient in all these areas; but all fall far short of that omniscience *(sarvajñabala)* which characterizes a buddha.[7]

The Theravādins shared the Vaibhāṣika belief that omniscience is that mark which distinguishes a buddha from arhats and pratyekabuddhas. We learn from the *Kathāvatthu* and its *Aṭṭhakathā* that the Pubbaseliyas held a view—similar to that of the Vaibhāṣikas—that the arhat may still possess ignorance *(aññāṇa)* and doubt *(kaṃkhā)* because he may be ignorant and doubtful about worldly things, such as names of men, trees, and so forth, and may be excelled in such matters by worldlings *(puthujjana).*[8] The Theravādins admitted this but concluded that since the arhat has eliminated the *anuśayas,* the ignorance of worldly things does not in any way affect his attainment of arhatship. This shows that, unlike the Vaibhāṣikas, the Theravādins did not take the term *"apari-jñāya"* quoted above literally (as "without having known") but interpreted it as "without truly having understood [every dharma]." They therefore had no dispute with the Pubbaseliyas as long as it was agreed that the arhat's ordinary ignorance did not imply any residual presence of the *anuśayas* of *vicikitsā* (skeptical doubt) and avidyā.

This explains why the expression *"akliṣṭa-ajñāna"* is not attested in the Theravāda Abhidharma, which also fails to provide any explanation (such as those given by Vasubandhu and Yaśomitra) for the absence of this particular form of ignorance in the historical Buddha. Thus we need only examine the Vaibhāṣika texts for a possible solution to the problems of determining (1) the dharmic nature of this *akliṣṭa-ajñāna;* (2) when and how the Buddha destroyed this particular ignorance; and (3) whether its persistence could in any way be detrimental to the status of an arhat.

As seen earlier, *akliṣṭa-ajñāna* is, by definition, ignorance of worldly things—that is, the absence in varying degrees of what is called *saṃvṛti-jñāna* (knowledge of conventional objects).[9] It is therefore not subsumed under avidyā (the foremost *kleśa*) or under such lesser ones as skeptical doubt *(vicikitsā),* all of which are annihilated through the process of mārga. Could the *akliṣṭa-ajñāna* be one of the *kleśavāsanās* (impregnations of passions) which, as Étienne Lamotte has so convincingly demonstrated, are destroyed only by the Buddha at the time of attaining perfect enlightenment *(samyaksambodhi),* but which are never destroyed by arhats and which persist to the end of their lives?[10] This does not seem possible because the *akliṣṭa-ajñāna* does not fit the description of an impregnation *(vāsanā).* The *kleśavāsanās* are said to be special potentials of past passions that reside in the mind (hence designated impregnations) and that cause a special distortion in vocal and bodily behavior in the arhat's present life. For this reason they are said to be morally indeterminate *(avyākṛta)* special thoughts *(cittaviśeṣa).*[11] The *akliṣṭa-ajñāna,* characterized merely as absence of the knowledge of worldly things, whether gross or subtle, can hardly be described as the source of special distortions of behavior. Nor can this *ajñāna* be a *vāsanā* because, as Yaśomitra states, arhats overcome *ajñāna* (albeit temporarily at the time of attaining arhatship), whereas the *kleśavāsanās* are never destroyed by them. This is further supported by Vasubandhu's statement that the eighteen qualities of the Buddha are called *āveṇika* (special) because he alone has destroyed the *kleśas* together with their *vāsanās.*[12]

If the *akliṣṭa-ajñāna* is neither a *kleśa* nor its *vāsanā,* yet is something that can be destroyed, then what is its dharmic nature? It must surely stand for some obscuration or obstruction *(āvaraṇa)* that is capable of preventing the mind from functioning to its fullest capacity—namely, cognizing, as the Buddha did, even the subtlest objects situated in distant space and time.

This obstruction evidently could not be of the nature of karma (present action), *vipāka* (the fruition of past actions), or *kleśas,* the three kinds of obstructions known to the Vaibhāṣikas.[13] The word that comes immediately to mind is, of course, *jñeyāvaraṇa,* which is often cited as the agent of such obstruction. But strange as it may seem, *jñeyāvaraṇa* is not attested in the works of Vasubandhu and Yaśomitra, although it is not unknown to the *Mahāvibhāṣā.*[14] We do not know the Vaibhāṣika meaning of this term, but they certainly could not have understood it in the manner of the Vijñānavādins, for whom the *jñeya* (the object itself, as separated from the subject, i.e., consciousness) was an *āvaraṇa* (obstruction).[15]

We are thus left with no specific dharma that can be identified with the *akliṣṭa-ajñāna.* Yet how could the Vaibhāṣikas have introduced this whole controversy over the destruction of the *akliṣṭa-ajñāna* without first introducing a separate dharma of that name into their dharma list?! Could it be that the *akliṣṭa-ajñāna* is indeed a kind of a hindrance—like *styāna* (torpor), for example—but a nonmental dharma of the *cittaviprayukta* (neither material nor mental) category, capable of preventing the mind from achieving its full potential of absolute clarity? The *kleśas* certainly contribute to the prevention of this clarity by creating impurities such as wrong views, doubt, lust, hatred, pride, restlessness, and avidyā; but the destruction of these passions alone does not seem to result in total clarity of mind. The *akliṣṭa-ajñāna* must therefore be conceived of as that (undesignated!) dharma that can survive even when the passions are removed, and that can hinder the mind from achieving its full potential of cognizing all that is knowable.

The ignorance that persists after achieving arhatship may rightly be called *akliṣṭa* because there are no defilements *(kleśas)* beyond that stage. But in the case of the Buddha this ignorance is said to be forever eliminated with the destruction of the *kleśas.* Hence it is appropriate to investigate the stage on the mārga (path) where this elimination occurs. Also, is the *akliṣṭa-ajñāna* destroyed at one stroke, like *satkāyadṛṣṭi* (personality-belief) at the level of *darśanamārga* (the path of vision), or is it overcome piecemeal, like the afflictions of *rāga* (desire), *māna* (pride), and avidyā, through the various stages of the *bhāvanāmārga* (the path of practice)? We know that the destruction of this ignorance cannot occur at the stage of *darśanamārga,* because according to the Vaibhāṣika Abhidharma anything that is of the nature of the unafflicted *(akliṣṭa)* cannot be destroyed by that path.[16] But it cannot be destroyed on the *bhāvanāmārga* either, because on that path a specific *anuśaya* is eliminated through the cultivation of its counteragent, and we have determined that *ajñāna* is not an *anuśaya.* Since both these supramundane or *lokottara* paths are not relevant here, it seems to follow that in the Vaibhāṣika system, the *akliṣṭa-ajñāna* can be destroyed only by the *laukikabhāvanāmārga,* that is, the mundane path of meditation, which can be practiced by any one, at any stage in one's yogic career, with or without the total destruction of the *kleśas.*

The Buddhist texts recognize a variety of meditative techniques, known as *samāpattis,* that can be employed to enlarge progressively the mind's range of cognition. The most important of these are those which confer the six superknowledges *(abhijñās),* five of which pertain to worldly knowledge *(saṃvṛtijñāna).*[17] The absence of this mundane knowledge, together with all the other minor varieties of ignorances, could properly be designated *akliṣṭa-ajñāna.* These knowledges include (1) magical powers *(ṛddhiviṣaya),* (2) the divine eye and ear *(divyacakṣuḥ/śrotra),* (3) penetration of others' minds *(cetaḥparyāya),* (4) remembrance of former existences *(pūrvanivāsānusmṛti),* and (5) knowledge of the births and deaths of others *(cyutyupapādajñāna).* Although they admittedly do not constitute "omniscience," these five do encompass a great many objects described by Vasubandhu as "subtle" and "distant in space and time," knowledge of which is blocked by *akliṣṭa-ajñāna.* If, as Yaśomitra states, an arhat temporarily overcomes *akliṣṭa-ajñāna* prior to attaining arhatship, this probably means that for a time he acquires these five *abhijñās,* together with the sixth *abhijñā*—namely, *āsravakṣayajñāna* (knowledge of the extinction of the influxes), which confirms his status as an arhat. Only this final *abhijñā* has a lasting effect, because it alone is accomplished by *pratisaṃkhyānirodha* (extinction through knowledge of the four noble truths); still, it has no effect on the arhat's ignorance in worldly matters, since the other five *abhijñās* are of only temporary duration. In the case of the Buddha, however, the Vaibhāṣikas claimed that even *akliṣṭa-ajñāna* is annihilated forever, because it is destroyed by the practice of its counteragent *(pratipakṣa)* and, in the words of Yaśomitra, through *anāsravajñāna.* Although the precise meaning of this rather unusual term is not known, Yaśomitra probably uses it as a synonym for *āsravakṣayajñāna,* the sixth *abhijñā* and terminus of the *bhāvanāmārga.*

Would it be correct to postulate, then, that whereas an arhat attains only the last *abhijñā* by the *lokottarabhāvanāmārga,* the Buddha achieves all the *abhijñās* by the same exalted path? The arhat, after all, aspires only to attain his own nirvāṇa and needs only sufficient worldly knowledge to help him toward that goal. The five mundane *abhijñās* should be adequate for his purposes—especially the fourth and the fifth, dubbed *vidyās* (knowledges), which remove any perplexity regarding his past and future.[18] In the case of the Buddha, however, who aspires to teach all beings, even his *saṃvṛtijñāna* would be infinitely wider in scope and would need to be achieved in a manner consistent with his role. Thus a buddha perfects his *abhijñās* to such an extent that he destroys the *kleśavā-*

sanās as well as the *akliṣṭa-ajñāna* and thus becomes omniscient forever. This explains the Abhidharma claim that in the case of the Buddha nothing is born of effort *(prayogaja),* that all knowledge is immediately present to him, and that he is called one who not only knows everything but also knows everything in its entirety.[19]

Although an apparent deficiency, the persistence of *akliṣṭa-ajñāna* is no more destructive of arhatship than the persistence of the *kleśavāsanās,* and both are automatically terminated when the final *apratisaṅkhyāni-rodha* (cessation without knowledge of the four noble truths) is attained. Although the Vaibhāṣika accepts the possibility of a fall from arhatship for a certain kind of arhat, the reason given is not the presence of this *ajñāna* or of the *vāsanās* in him, but a sūtra passage cautioning an arhat against "gain and honor," the true meaning of which is hotly disputed by the Sautrāntika Vasubandhu, who rejects the Vaibhāṣika interpretation.[20] The claim of the nonomniscient arhat that he has attained the same nirvāṇa as the omniscient Buddha has been suspect, therefore, only in later Buddhist schools, especially those which formulated the doctrine of Ekayāna. The authors of the *Saddharmapuṇḍarīkasūtra,* for example, do not hesitate to challenge openly the arhat's claim to nirvāṇa. They declare through the mouth of the Elder Śāriputra that the arhats were wrong and conceited in thinking that they had attained nirvāṇa, when what they had reached was only a state of rest *(viśrāma),* and conclude that there is no nirvāṇa without omniscient cognition *(sarvajñatva).*[21] Granted that the real aim of the Mahāyānists is to teach the realization of *sarvadharmaśūnyatā* (emptiness of all existents) when they talk of the Buddha's omniscience, it is nevertheless true that they place equal emphasis on the infinitude of his *saṃvṛtijñāna,* as if the two cognitions were inseparable. This is clear from several passages of the same sūtra, where the arhat is berated not only for his limited understanding of reality, but also for the infinitesimal range of his mental powers pertaining to worldy objects.[22]

It is debatable whether there is an invariable concomitance between the attainment of nirvāṇa and the possession of omniscience. Parallels to both models—that of the nonomniscient arhat and of the omniscient arhat (namely, the Buddha)—can be found in the Yoga and the Jaina traditions, respectively. The entire third book of the *Pātañjala Yogasūtra,* for example, is devoted to a description of the various powers of perfections *(vibhūtis)* that enable a yogin to acquire knowledge of the past and future *(atītānāgatajñāna),* of the speech of all beings *(sarvabhūtarutajñāna),* of his previous births *(pūrvajātijñāna),* of other people's minds *(paracitta-jñāna),* of regions *(bhuvanajñāna),* of the position of stars *(tārāvyūhajñāna),* and so forth. These knowledges are similar to the mundane *abhijñās* of the Buddhists.[23] All can be mastered prior to knowledge of the spirit *(puruṣajñāna),* the first stage in the yogin's progress toward isolation *(kaivalya),* and hence are comparable to the Buddhist *darśanamārga.* As a result of this *puruṣajñāna,* there arise unceasingly in the yogin vividness *(pratibhā)* and the organs of supernatural hearing, feeling, sight, taste, and smell. The commentator Vyāsa describes the first of these "knowledges," *prātibhajñāna,* as an intuitive knowledge of subtle *(sūkṣma),* concealed *(vyavahita),* or remote *(viprakṛṣṭa)* objects, whether past *(atīta)* or future *(anāgata)*—words that echo Vasubandhu's description of the Buddha's range of cognition.[24] Patañjali warns that these extraordinary perceptions are powers *(siddhis)* only for one whose mind is distracted *(vikṣipta);* otherwise they are obstacles *(antarāya)* in the way of samādhi.[25] When finally the yogin has attained full discernment into the difference between the matter (*prakṛti,* i.e., the *buddhi*) and the spirit *(puruṣa),* he attains "omniscience" *(sarvajñātṛtvam)* and there follows *kaivalya* or the nirvāṇa of the Sāṃkhya-Yoga system.

It is evident from these Yoga aphorisms that although possession of these knowledges and powers may be commendable, they are not prerequisites to *kaivalya.* The yogin is even advised to remain indifferent to them and treat some of them as inevitable byproducts of the practice of meditation. Commenting on the perfections a yogin acquires on his way to the goal of isolation, Vyāsa declares that it is immaterial whether the yogin has or has not attained these powers or knowledges, since one whose seeds of *kleśa* are burnt *(dagdhakleśabīja)* has no need of knowledge and the like.[26] This is the position followed in general by the Theravādins and the Vaibhāṣikas as well: the Buddha's omniscience is highly commendable, but the arhat's nirvāṇa is not dependent on overcoming the *akliṣṭa-ajñāna,* for the seeds of rebirth have been burnt forever equally by both.

The Jaina position appears to agree with the Ekayāna claim that nirvāṇa is inseparable from omniscience, and hence that only the Omniscient One gets the designation of an arhat or, as an Ekayānist would say, only the Buddha has attained nirvāṇa. I will not explain here the precise difference between the omniscience of the Buddha and that of the Jina, as I have dealt with this problem elsewhere.[27] Unlike the Buddhists, the Jainas maintained that ignorance of the true nature of things and other passions (e.g., delusion, attachment, aversion, etc., which correspond to the *anuśayas* in the Abhidharma) and ignorance of worldly objects *(ajñāna)* are two different kinds of defects caused by two distinct karmic forces, the *mohanīya* (deluding) and the *jñānāvaraṇīya* (knowledge-obscuring). The former is destroyed by the Jaina path called *guṇasthāna* (stages of spiritual progress), which is very similar to the *darśana* and *bhāvanā* mārgas of the Buddhists.[28] The consequent purity generated in the soul (ātman) affects its ignorance to some extent also, since the soul gains without any special effort certain supernatural knowledges called *avadhijñāna* (clairvoyance) and *manaḥparyayajñāna* (telepathy), comparable to some of the mundane *abhijñās* and *siddhis* mentioned earlier. With the total destruction of the *mohanīya,* the aspirant reaches the irreversible stage of liberation (mokṣa), appropriately called *kṣīṇamoha* (the stage of the destruction of delusion), comparable to the *āsravakṣayajñāna* attained by the Buddhist arhat. Yet this is not the final stage for the Jaina arhat; rather, with the destruction of the *mohanīya* the aspirant is for the first time able to engage in higher trances—an advanced stage of the Pure Meditation *(śukladhyāna)* that had commenced earlier—with which he is able to destroy the entire mass of the *jñānāvaraṇīyakarma* that had hitherto obstructed the soul's innate ability for omniscience. Thus he attains *kevalajñāna* (knowledge isolated from all karmic matter and freed from the constraints of the senses and mind) and is able to cognize all existents in their infinite aspects. He will remain in that state forever, even after his final death, which is called nirvāṇa in Jainism.[29]

All four schools discussed here appear to agree that although both avidyā and *ajñāna* are called ignorance, they do not necessarily spring from the same source and may partake of two different natures. Avidyā appears to be caused by some form of passion, whereas *ajñāna* seems to result from a certain lack of clarity, the cause of which cannot be easily determined. This probably explains the near unanimity in these schools' approaches to the problem of overcoming avidyā through almost identical paths. Their failure to devise an equally unanimous way to be rid of *ajñāna* probably derives from their inability to establish an invariable causal relationship between impurity and ignorance.

Notes

1. *yaḥ sarvathā sarvahatāndhakāraḥ// Abhidharmakośa,* i, 1a. *pratyekabuddhaśrāvakā api kāmaṃ sarvatra hatāndhakārāḥ/ kliṣṭasammohātyantavigamāt/ na tu sarvathā; tathā hy eṣāṃ buddhadharmeṣv ativiprakṛṣṭadeśakāleṣv anantaprabhedeṣu ca bhavaty evākliṣṭam ajñānam// Abhidharmakośabhāṣya,* Part I, p. 6. Dvārikadāsa Śāstrī, ed., *Abhidharmakośa and Bhāṣya of Ācārya Vasubandhu with Sphuṭārthā Commentary of Ācārya Yaśomitra* (Varanasi: Bauddha Bhāratī, 1970–1971), pts. 1–4.

2. *ajñānaṃ hi bhūtārthadarśanapratibandhād andhakāram/ tac ca bhagavato buddhasya pratipakṣalābhena sarvatra jñeye punaranutpattidharmatvādd hatam; ato 'sau sarvathā sarvahatāndhakāraḥ// Abhidharmakośabhāṣya,* Part I, p. 6.

3. *pratipakṣalābhenety āryamārgalābhena/ vipakṣaḥ kleśaḥ// vipakṣapratighātāya pakṣaḥ pratipakṣa iti kṛtvā/ . . . athavā jñānam anāsravam ajñānapratipakṣaḥ, tasya lābhena// atyantaṃ sarvathā/ sarvatra jñeye punarutpattidharmatvādd hatam/ asamudācāraprahāṇīkṛtam ity arthaḥ// Sphuṭārthāvyākhyā, Abhidharmakośabhāṣya,* Part I, p. 6.

4. *nanu ca sarvaṃ sāsravavastu śrāvakapratyekabuddhānām api buddhavat prahīṇam/ kim idam ucyate—kliṣṭasammohasya teṣām atyantavigama iti? . . . tathā hy uktam— . . . "nāham ekadharmam apy aparijñāyāprahāya duḥkhasyāntakriyāṃ vadāmi" iti/ tasmāc chrāvakapratyekabuddhānām api tad akliṣṭam ajñānaṃ cakṣurādivac chandarāgaprahāṇāt prahīṇam eva/ anyathā hi śrāvakapratyekabuddhānāṃ duḥkhāntakriyā na bhavet?* Ibid., Part I, pp. 6–7.

5. *satyam; asty etad evam/ prahīṇam eva teṣāṃ kliṣṭavad akliṣṭam apy ajñānam/ tat tu teṣāṃ cakṣurādivat prahīṇam api samudācarati/ buddhasya tu prahīṇaṃ san na samudācarati/ ata eva viśeṣitaṃ—"punarutpattidharmatvādd hatam" iti/ . . . ye tu vyācakṣate—"śrāvakapratyekabuddhānāṃ kliṣṭasammohamātravigamāt saṃkleśavinivṛttiḥ" iti, tad apavyākhyānam eṣāṃ yathoktam iti pratyācakṣate//* Ibid., Part I, p. 7.

6. Ibid.

7. *tāny etāni catvāry ajñānakāraṇāni bhavanti/ teṣāṃ kvacid ekam/ kvacid dve/ kvacit trīṇi/ kvacic catvārīti sambhavato yojyāni//* Ibid., p. 8.

8. Shwe Zan Aung and Mrs. Rhys Davids, trans., *Points of Controversy (Kathāvatthu),* (London: Pali Text Society, 1960), pp. 114–119.

9. *Abhidharmakośabhāṣya,* Part IV, p. 1108.

10. Étienne Lamotte, "Passions and Impregnations of the Passions in Buddhism," L. Cousins, ed., *Buddhist Studies in Honour of I. B. Horner* (Dordrecht: D. Reidel, 1974), 91–104.

11. *kā punar iyaṃ vāsanā nāma śrāvakāṇām? yo hi yatkleśacaritaḥ pūrvaṃ tasya tatkṛtaḥ kāyavākceṣṭāvikārahetusāmarthyaviśeṣaś citte vāsanety ucyate/ avyākṛtaś cittaviśeṣo vāsaneti bhadantĀnatavarmā// Sphuṭārthāvyākhyā, Abhidharmakośabhāṣya,* Part IV, p. 1093.

12. *kasmād ete āveṇikā buddhadharmā ucyante? savāsanaprahāṇāt// Abhidharmakośabhāṣya,* Part IV, p. 1093.

13. *trīṇy āvaraṇāny uktāni bhagavatā/ karmāvaraṇaṃ kleśāvaraṇaṃ vipākāvaraṇaṃ ca//* Ibid., Part II, p. 722.

14. I am indebted to Dr. Collett Cox for the information that the terms *"kleśāvaraṇa"* and *"jñeyāvaraṇa"* are found in the *Mahāvibhāṣā, T* 27.724b28. Mr. Nobuyoshi Yamabe has kindly drawn my attention to a passage in the *Mahāvibhāṣā* (*T* 27.42b24–c6) which seems to suggest that the concept of *mithyājñāna* (false knowledge—which may have some relation to *ajñāna*) was considered to be a form of *kliṣṭaprajñā* (defiled wisdom), and in the case of the arhat was applied only from the conventional *(saṃvṛti)* point of view.

15. It is not likely that the Vaibhāṣikas would have interpreted *jñeyāvaraṇa* as a *dauṣṭhulya* (depravity), as it is described by Asaṅga (*jñeyāvaraṇadauṣṭhulyaṃ sarvajñatāvipakṣaḥ,* i.e., a form of depravity that is the adversary of omniscience), since for the Vaibhāṣikas it would still constitute some form of *kleśa.* See Nathmal Tatia, *Abhidharmasamuccayabhāṣyam of Asaṅga,* Tibetan Sanskrit Works Series No. 17 (Patna: Kashi Prasad Jayaswal Research Institute, 1976), 93. It should be noted, however, that Sthiramati follows the Abhidharma tradition, since in his *Triṃśikāvijñaptibhāṣya* he does describe the term *"jñeyāvaraṇa"* as *akliṣṭa-ajñāna: jñeyāvaraṇam api sarvasmin jñeye jñānapravṛttipratibandhabhūtam akliṣṭam ajñānam//* Sylvain Lévi, *Vijñaptimātratāsiddhi* (Paris: Librairie Ancienne Honoré Champion, 1925), 15. But he fails to clarify the precise denotation of the term in this context. Our surmise is substantiated by Prajñākaramati's gloss on *jñeyāvaraṇa* as *"jñeyam eva samāropitatvāt āvṛtiḥ,"* an oppositional *karmadhāraya,* in his commentary on the following: *kleśajñeyāvṛtitamaḥpratipakṣo hi śūnyatā/ śīghraṃ sarvajñatākāmo na bhāvayati tāṃ katham//* See P. L. Vaidya, *Bodhicaryāvatāra of Śāntideva together with Prajñākaramati's Pañjikā,* Buddhist Sanskrit Texts Series, No. XII (Darbhanga: Mithila Institute, 1960), chap. 9, v. 55.

16. *na dṛṣṭiheyam akliṣṭaṃ na rūpaṃ nāpy aśaṣṭajam// Abhidharmakośa, Abhidharmakośabhāṣya,* Part I, p. 110.

17. Ibid., Part IV, p. 1106.

18. Ibid., Part IV, p. 1113.

19. *buddhasya nāsti kiñcit prāyogikam/ tasya sarvadharmeṣvaratvād icchāmātrapratibaddhaḥ sarvaguṇasampatsammukhībhāvaḥ// Abhidharmakośabhāṣya,* Part IV, p. 1106.

20. See ibid., Part III, pp. 986–1002.

21. *tathaiva śrāvakāḥ sarve prāptanirvāṇasaṃjñinaḥ/ jino 'tha deśayet tasmai viśrāmo 'yaṃ na nirvṛtiḥ// upāya eṣa buddhānāṃ vadanti yad imaṃ nayam/ sarvajñtvam ṛte nāsti nirvāṇaṃ tat samārabha//* See P. L. Vaidya, *Saddharmapuṇḍarīkasūtra,* Buddhist Sanskrit Texts (Darbhanga: Mithila Institute, 1960), chap. 5, vv. 74–75.

22. Ibid., vv. 65–73.

23. Ram Shankar Bhattacharya, *Pātañjala-Yogadarśanam together with the Bhāṣya of Vyāsa and the Tattvavaiśāradīvyākhyā of Vācaspati* (Varanasi: Bhāratīya Vidyā Prakāśana, 1963).

24. *tataḥ prātibhaśrāvaṇavedanādarśāsvādavārtā jāyante// prātibhāt sūkṣmavyavahitaviprakṛṣṭātītānāgatajñānam/ . - . . ity etāni nityaṃ jāyante//* Ibid., pp. 137–138.

25. *te samādhāv upasargā vyutthāne siddhayaḥ//* Ibid., p. 138.

26. *tārakaṃ sarvaviṣayaṃ sarvathāviṣayam akramaṃ ceti vivekajaṃ jñānam//* Ibid., p. 153. . . . *prāptavivekajñānasyāprāptavivekajñānasya vā/ . . . sattvapuruṣayoḥ śuddhisāmye kaivalyam iti// yadā nirdhūtarajastamomalaṃ buddhisattvaṃ . . . dagdhakleśabījaṃ bhavati tadā . . . śuddhiḥ/ etasyāṃ avasthāyāṃ kaivalyaṃ bhavatīśvarasya vā vivekajñānabhāgina itarasya vā/ na hi dagdhakleśabījasya jñāne punar apekṣā kvacid asti . . . //* Ibid., p. 154.

27. Padmanabh S. Jaini, "On the *Sarvajñatva* of Mahāvīra and the Buddha," in Cousins, ed., *Studies in Honour of I. B. Horner,* pp. 71–90.

28. For a description of the *guṇasthānas,* see Padmanabh S. Jaini, *The Jaina Path of Purification* (Berkeley: University of California Press, 1979), 272–273.

29. *mohakṣayāj jñānadarśanāvaraṇāntarāyakṣayāc ca kevalam// mohanīye kṣīṇe jñānāvaraṇadarśanāvaraṇāntarāyeṣu kṣīṇeṣu ca kevalajñānadarśanam utpadyate/ . . . mohakṣayād iti pṛthakkaraṇaṃ kramaprasiddhyarthaṃ yathā gamyeta pūrvaṃ mohanīyaṃ kṛstnaṃ kṣīyate tato 'ntarmuhūrtaṃ chadmasthavītarāgo bhavati/ tato 'sya jñānadarśanāvaraṇāntarāyaprakṛtīnāṃ tisṛṇāṃ yugapat kṣayo bhavati/ tataḥ kevalam utpadyate//* See Khubcandra Siddhāntaśāstrī, *Sabhāṣya-Tattvārthādhigamasūtra* (Agas: Rājacandra Jaina Śāstramālā, 1932), 437.

Paths Terminable and Interminable

DONALD S. LOPEZ, JR.

The imagination is always at the end of an era.
Wallace Stevens

Tracks—the signs of the past presence of another—become a path only in retrospect; a path is known to be true only by those who have reached its end, accurately charted only by those who have followed its course. All Buddhists, irrespective of doctrinal affiliation, profess that the Buddha reached the end of the path and that he also proclaimed its route to the world. But with the development of the tradition, the Buddha's achievement was seen less as revelation than as restoration, a retracing of the path trod by the buddhas of forgotten aeons. That path was increasingly seen as more and more protracted, encompassing lifetimes of practice, finally reaching, in the Mahāyāna, the generally accepted length of three periods of innumerable aeons (which Har Dayal has kindly calculated for us at 384×10^{58} years). The process of enlightenment was no longer the simple cultivation of social virtues suggested in the *Aṭṭhakavagga* but an intricate complex of specific antidotes for specific afflictions that were to be abandoned in sequence.

The mapping of the path became the purview of the savants of the Abhidharma, both Hīnayāna and Mahāyāna—the Buddhist scholastics. The term "scholasticism" here refers to the tradition of Buddhist commentary that is concerned above all with system. Like the scholastic philosophers of medieval Europe, the Buddhists made use of definition, division, and demonstration to identify problems of apparent inconsistency and to formulate answers that resolve such inconsistencies, armed with the twin weapons of scripture *(āgama)* and reason *(yukti)*. "Scholasticism" is used to connote not a method of inquiry marked by a closed formality but a form of reflection which assumes that reality is accessible to the human mind; that the premises of truth are contained in the pronouncements of the Buddha (which, for the thinkers examined here, include the Mahāyāna sūtras); and that every principle must be carried out to its logical conclusion (as defined by the system).[1]

The scholastic delineations of the path read not as records of personal experience but as the pronouncements of theorists and technicians, who do not speak from the end of a path that they themselves have reached. Étienne Lamotte observed that the Abhidharma was "the work of scholars labouring in cells, far from the noisy crowd which would be incapable of grasping the import of the work carried out and discussed among specialists."[2] Theirs is not a path that is traversed among the palm trees; rather, it is a path inscribed on the leaves of those trees, a path that is broken by writing.

What the scholastics describe is a path that is only strangely retrospective, constructed by looking backward from a projected goal. This strangeness is multiplied by the realization that a path requires a double absence—the absence of the being who made the tracks, and the absence which is the tracks themselves. A path is an intrusion into the forest, a violent rupture of the natural, and its marks are the broken branch and gouged earth, the absence of the pristine state. A path requires that the previous state be somehow effaced; what is present in a path is an absence. The tracks that collectively constitute that path immediately point away from themselves to what is not there, namely, the previous unbroken state and its breaker.[3] We cannot pause to consider the nature of the forest through which the Buddhist path is broken. But for the Buddhist the breaker is the Buddha, and Buddhist scholasticism is predicated on his particular absence—in the nirvāṇa without remainder for the Hīnayāna, in the dharmakāya for the Mahāyāna. The Ābhidharmikas thus made maps, present representations of a hypothetically future destination, that place from which one is now absent. Enlightenment could serve as the present and perpetual object of scholastic reflection only as long as it remained absent in meditative experience. So long as wisdom arose merely from hearing *(śrutamayīprajñā),* the wisdom arisen from meditation *(bhāvanāmayīprajñā)* could be continually exalted as supreme precisely because it was absent. (Perhaps, in the end, it is the differentiation of scholastic reflection and meditative experience, in which *vikalpa* (discursive thought) is devalued before samādhi, that needs to be called radically into question. It may be that both are burdened [*āropa*] with diffusion [*prapañca*].)

The discourse of Buddhist scholasticism, therefore, provides a place to explore present theoretical questions more than a guide for future practice or a memoir of past experience; tracking produces more tracks. The path became a description of a state rather than a process—a path that was so long, and whose end was so distant, that it became a map of the present and of all the questions that attend it. For the Mahāyāna scholastics, that map had at its center a detailed outline of the present nature of the mind, traced in terms of defilement and purification. It included attempts to control from the present those of the past who claimed to have already reached the destination by another route. And it contained projections from the present into the future, speculating about a time, whether real or hypothetical, when all beings would reach the terminus of the single true path aboard the single true vehicle. It is this present, past, and future that will be considered here: the present with its elaborate structure of defilements and their counteragents; the past with its problem of the arhats, who claimed to have reached enlightenment before the proclamation of the true path, the Mahāyāna; and the future with its question of whether the promise of the bodhisattva will someday be fulfilled, of whether the cycle of birth and death will ever end.

For the Indian Mahāyāna scholastics, the most important śāstra for the exposition of the path was the *Abhisamayālaṃkāra* (Ornament of Realization) of Maitreyanātha. Traditionally considered to be a commentary on the *Pañcaviṃśatisāhasrikāprajñāpāramitāsūtra* (The Perfection of Wisdom in 25,000 Stanzas), it is little more than a series of terms drawn from the sūtra, from which commentators sought to construct the components of the bodhisattva's path, the "hidden teaching" of the Perfection of Wisdom sūtras. The *Abhisamayālaṃkāra* is organized under eight headings. The first is the knowledge of all aspects *(sarvākārajñātā),* the omniscient mind of the buddha which is the goal of the Mahāyāna path, the knowledge of all the varieties of phenomena as well as their modes (i.e., their emptiness). The second topic is the knowledge of paths *(margajñātā),* said to be essential for the achievement of omniscience. The bodhisattva must know not only the entire structure of his or her own path but that of the paths of śrāvakas and pratyekabuddhas as well. The third topic is the knowledge of all *(sarvajñātā),* that is, of all the categories of phenomena by which the followers of the Hīnayāna gain liberation from rebirth. The relationship among these three knowledges is suggested in the expression of worship that opens the *Abhisamayālaṃkāra:*

> Obeisance to the mother of buddhas and the assembly of śrāvakas and bodhisattvas, [she] who, through the knowledge of all, leads śrāvakas seeking peace to peace; who, through the knowledge of paths, causes those [bodhisattvas] aiding transmigrators to accomplish the aims of the world; through being fully endowed with whom, the *munis* set forth the varieties of all aspects.[4]

The three knowledges are set forth in reverse order here. It is through the knowledge that there is no person among all the various categories of phenomena that śrāvakas find the peace of nirvāṇa. It is through the knowledge of the paths that bodhisattvas are able to lead sentient beings to the most appropriate path. And it is through their knowledge of all the varieties and modes of phenomena that buddhas are able to set forth the sūtras.

It is the second knowledge, knowledge of the paths, and some of its attendant issues that provide the doctrinal basis for this chapter. For the Dge-lugs-pa order of Tibetan Buddhism, the *Abhisamayālaṃkāra* is the first and most exhaustively studied of the five Indian works that comprise the basis of the monastic curriculum.[5] Among the twenty-one commentaries on it enumerated by the tradition,[6] the Dge-lugs-pas rely most heavily on two of the commentaries of Haribhadra, the *Abhisamayālaṃkārālokā* (Illumination of the "Ornament for Realization")[7] and the shorter *Sphuṭārtha* (Clear Meaning).[8] There is also a massive Tibetan commentatorial literature on the *Abhisamayālaṃkāra.* I will draw primarily on Tsong-kha-pa's *Legs bshad gser phreng* (A Garland of Gold Eloquence), which, according to tradition, he undertook in 1375 at the age of 18, but will also make reference to five widely used supplements to Tsong-kha-pa's work.[9]

The knowledge of the paths is defined as a realization *(abhisamaya)* by a Mahāyāna noble person (ārya), that realization being conjoined with the wisdom which understands intuitively that the three paths do not truly exist.[10] In other words, the knowledge of the paths is by definition possessed solely by bodhisattvas and, further, by *āryabodhisattvas,* those who have achieved the path of vision *(darśanamārga)* through direct realization of emptiness. What qualifies such understanding as a knowledge of the paths is that which the bodhisattva understands to be empty—namely, one of the three paths: the path of the śrāvaka, the path of the pratyekabuddha, or the path of the bodhisattva. To have knowledge of the paths (one of the three sublime knowledges set forth in the Perfection of Wisdom sūtras), a bodhisattva must have gained direct understanding of emptiness and be fully conversant with all the components not only of the Mahāyāna path but of the two Hīnayāna paths as well, this latter knowledge being essential for effectively teaching those of the Hīnayāna lineage. Thus the knowledge of the paths is of three types: the knowledge of the paths of śrāvakas, of pratyekabuddhas, and of bodhisattvas.

To know the śrāvaka path is to know its structure and to know that, like all phenomena, the śrāvaka path is ultimately empty.[11] The bodhisattva must know the path that śrāvakas follow, and this entails knowing both the afflictions that the śrāvaka must abandon and their antidotes. These are set forth for the Dge-lugs-pas in textbooks derived by Pan-chen Bsod-nams-grags-pa, Rje-btsun Chos-kyi-rgyal-mtshan, and 'Jam-dbyangs-bzhad-pa from earlier Indian and Tibetan commentaries on the *Abhisamayālaṃkāra.* Some of these are textbooks on the seventy topics *(don 'dun bcu),* for which these authors derived definitions *(mtshan nyid),* equivalent categories *(don gcig pa'i chos),* and perimeters *(sa mtsham).* A further process of extraction, interpolation, and conflation resulted in a genre of works known as *sa lam (*bhūmi-mārga),* which set forth the paths of śrāvakas, pratyekabuddhas, and bodhisattvas according to what the Dge-lugs-pas called the Yogācāra-Svātantrika-Mādhyamika school.[12]

Paths are states of mind to be consciously engendered in a specific order. For all three vehicles, this order begins with the path of accumulation *(saṃbhāramārga, tshogs lam)* and ends with the path of no further learning *(aśaikṣamārga, mi slob lam)*. The progression through these paths is delineated in the Dge-lugs-pa *sa lam* texts using a vocabulary of separation, abandonment, and destruction, of opposition between affliction *(nyon mongs, kleśa)* and antidote *(gnyen po, pratipakṣa)*. The list of afflictions is long and complicated, the antidotes relatively simple.

The śrāvaka on the path of vision abandons the artificial afflictive obstructions *(nyon sgrib kun btags)* through the periods of doctrinal forbearance *(chos bzod, dharmakṣānti)*, subsequent forbearance *(rjes bzod, anvayakṣānti)*, doctrinal knowledge *(chos shes, dharmajñāna)*, and subsequent knowledge *(rje shes, anvayajñāna)*.[13] Following the *Abhidharmakośabhāṣya*, the *sa lam* texts explain that the path of vision consists of fifteen moments of understanding of the four truths, the sixteenth moment marking the beginning of the path of meditation. According to Vasubandhu, there are four moments of understanding for each of the four truths. The first moment is that of doctrinal forbearance of the truth of suffering with regard to the desire realm, in which the afflictions of the desire realm associated with the truth of suffering are abandoned; it is followed by a moment of doctrinal knowledge of the truth of suffering with regard to the desire realm, which is the understanding that the afflictions of that level have indeed been abandoned. This is followed by a moment of subsequent forbearance in which the afflictions associated with the truth of suffering in the form and formless realms are abandoned, which is followed by subsequent knowledge of the truth of suffering with regard to the upper realms.

This sequence of four moments—doctrinal forbearance and doctrinal knowledge (with regard to the desire realm) and subsequent forbearance and subsequent knowledge (with regard to the upper realms)—is repeated for the remaining truths of origin, cessation, and path. In each case, the moments of understanding called forbearance are the times when the afflictions are actually abandoned; they are called uninterrupted paths *(bar chad med lam, anantaryamārga)*. The eight moments of knowledge are the states of realizing that the afflictions of that particular level have been abandoned; they are called paths of liberation *(rnam grol lam, vimuktimārga)*.[14]

In the Dge-lugs-pa *sa lam,* however, the sixteen moments of forbearance and knowledge do not occur sequentially but are conflated into two: an uninterrupted path, which comprises the eight moments of doctrinal forbearance and subsequent forbearance, and a path of liberation, which comprises the eight moments of doctrinal knowledge and subsequent knowledge. In the first moment, all the artificial afflictive obstructions are destroyed by a single antidote, the initial realization of personal selflessness *(gang zag gi bdag med, pudgalanairātmya),* which is the path of vision; in the second moment, the śrāvaka realizes that those afflictions have been destroyed. The distinction between "doctrinal" and "subsequent" is maintained with the explanation that doctrinal forbearance is the understanding that the four truths are devoid of a personal self, whereas subsequent forbearance is the understanding that the consciousness realizing that this is the case (i.e., doctrinal forbearance itself) is not a personal self.[15] But this distinction, as well as the sixteen moments of forbearance and knowledge themselves, seems to be preserved merely to maintain the Sarvāstivādin vocabulary. Dkon-mchog-'jigs-med-dbang-po writes:

> The sixteen moments of forbearance and knowledge of the path of vision occur in two periods: the eight forbearances are produced simultaneously and the eight knowledges are produced simultaneously. The length of time of the uninterrupted path and the path of liberation of a śrāvaka's path of vision is the smallest unit of time in which an action can be accomplished.[16]

On the path of meditation, the śrāvaka abandons eighty-one afflictions, nine for each of the nine levels of saṃsāra: the desire realm, the four concentrations of the form realm, and the four formless absorptions. In each case, however, the antidote is single—the realization of personal selflessness. The path of the śrāvaka ends when the subtlest of the afflictions, the smallest of the small associated with *bhavāgra* (the summit of existence), is destroyed by the eighty-first uninterrupted path on the path of meditation. The path of liberation that follows immediately afterward is the first moment of the path of no further learning.[17] The śrāvaka is now an arhat and has completed his or her path, or so it would seem.

The pratyekabuddhas receive the least attention among the three types of practitioners considered in the Dge-lugs-pa *sa lam.* They abandon the same eighty-one afflictions over the course of the path of meditation, but employ a different antidote. Drawing on *Abhisamayālaṃkāra* II.8, the Dge-lugs-pas hold that pratyekabuddhas understand something subtler than what is understood by śrāvakas, namely, the nonexistence of external objects. Maitreyanātha's text says:

> Understand that the path of the rhinoceros-like is comprised by abandoning the conception of objects, not abandoning the conception of subjects, and by a [special] foundation.[18]

This understanding that objects do not exist as entities separate from the consciousnesses that perceive them is termed "the realization of the coarse selflessness of phenomena" *(chos kyi bdag med rags pa).*[19] As in the case of the śrāvaka, a single antidote destroys myriad afflictions, but over a protracted path.

To attain buddhahood, bodhisattvas must abandon all the afflictive obstructions *(nyon sgrib, kleśāvaraṇa)* as well as all the obstructions to omniscience (*shes sgrib, jñeyāvaraṇa,* lit., "obstructions to [all] objects of knowledge"). Dkon-mchog-'jigs-med-dbang-po writes:

> On the occasion of the path of vision, there are 112 afflictions that are to be abandoned. There are also 108 obstructions to omniscience to be abandoned on the path of vision. There are sixteen innate afflictive obstructions that are abandoned on the first through the tenth levels *(sa, bhūmi)* of the path of meditation. The seeds of the 108 innate obstructions to omniscience are abandoned on these same levels.[20]

To arrive at the figure of 112 artificial afflictive obstructions, the Sarvāstivādin model of calculating afflictions by employing the four truths and three realms as constants in the equation is maintained. The variable is the number of afflictions associated with each of the three realms.[21]

The actual antidote to each of these afflictions, both artificial and innate, is the wisdom consciousness that knows all phenomena to be empty of true existence. Because this wisdom discerns the subtle selflessness of phenomena (as understood by the Svātantrikas), it destroys all forms of the afflictive obstructions and the obstructions to omniscience. It is the single panacea that effects the abandonment of the 84,000 afflictions.

I present these data in order to consider several questions. Given the significant quantitative imbalance between the obstructions and their antidote, why was the Sarvāstivādin model of various levels of misapprehension of the four truths in the three realms maintained, while the antidote to ignorance was understood to be the knowledge of selflessness alone (albeit in one of three forms)? A traditional positivist response would hold that the mind has been contaminated over countless births, and that the defilements are engrained from the surface to the depths and can be dislodged only through persistent and prolonged purification. As for the single antidote, there may have been a conflation, in the last phases of Buddhism in India, of the purificatory and the visionary models of the earlier tradition, with the purification of myriad discrete defilements held to be effected by the vision of a single truth.

For the Mahāyāna, the focus was not on three marks of existence but on one, selflessness, and there was an attendant reduction in antidotes from the sixteen aspects of the four truths to only one, the third aspect of suffering (albeit reinterpreted), emptiness. It was this vision of emptiness that was said to destroy, in one moment on the path of vision, all seeds for future rebirth in the unfortunate realms of animals, hungry ghosts, and hell beings. Yet this was only the beginning of the first of ten *bhūmis;* it would take the bodhisattva two periods of innumerable aeons to complete the path, aeons in which, along with performing the other five pāramitās, s/he was to enter repeatedly into direct yogic perception *(yogipratyakṣa)* of an emptiness no more profound than that which s/he had first seen. These repeated visions of the same emptiness were to serve as antidotes to a wide variety of afflictions and thus effect the removal of the entire range of obstructions—both those to liberation (the *kleśāvaraṇa*) and those to the omniscience of a buddha (the *jñeyāvaraṇa*).

Despite Avalokiteśvara's proclamation to Śāriputra in the *Heart Sūtra* that "in that way, all phenomena are empty, that is, without characteristic, unproduced, unceased, stainless, not stainless, undiminished, unfilled," the categories of the stainless *(vimala)* and the not stainless *(avimala)* persisted, able to withstand the radical critique of the Mādhyamika. An historicist might argue that the persistence of this complex of defilements as an essential component of the vocabulary of Buddhist scholasticism only testifies to the inability of Buddhist practitioners to become enlightened: there must be such obstructions because, despite the earnest efforts of meditators, no one seemed to be arriving at the further shore. This very argument was put forth in China to prove the presence of the degenerate age.

Such an argument presupposes that the path must be long because the defilements are complex. Let us consider for a moment whether the defilements are complex so that the path may be long. Might one account for the unwieldy length of the path by examining the general conservatism of those concerned with the preservation of system? If there are many claims to enlightenment, there will be, in the absence of adjudication by the founder, many claims to authority, and thus a challenge to scholasticism. If there are many claims to buddhahood, there will inevitably be conflicting claims about the nature of reality and how it is to be understood. This is a challenge to system, for the role of the Abhidharma was to express the inexpressible content of the Buddha's enlightenment, in doctrinal formulations of the nature of reality, in the categorization of veridical and deceptive states of consciousness, and in the delineation of a process of purification.

Indeed, the role of the Abhidharma was to domesticate enlightenment. The infinite prolongation of the path removed enlightenment from the hazardous present and placed it in the safety of the unforeseeable future as the sole possession of the exalted, absent Buddha, extracting from it the danger and power, risks and benefits associated with the possession of the truth and securing for the Ābhidharmikas, if not enlightenment, at least its discourse.[22]

If the primary task of scholasticism is the imposition and defense of consistency, then enlightenment can remain uniform only to the extent that it remains inaccessible, if not impossible. If we see the development of the mārga schema as representing a transition from autobiographical to universal experience, then it would seem that experience can become universal precisely to the extent that it is the experience of no one. But such an explanation has almost a scent of conspiracy about it; it is what E. A. H. Blunt might term a "voluntarist explanation," whereby the complex of defilements and their antidotes are viewed as a wholly artificial product of the Ābhidharmikas, the elite of the Buddhist order.[23] For the moment, let us make the more drastic move of separating the complex of defilements from the question of enlightenment.

Apart from the doctrine of selflessness, one of the principal means by which the Buddha seems to have sought to distinguish his dharma from that of the adherents of various sects that later came be called Hinduism was his questioning of caste hierarchy, and particularly its attendant claims to the hereditary purity of the brahmins. He also widely ridiculed purification rites as having any efficacy as means to liberation.[24] Yet the very language of defilement and purification, of contact and separation, that he repressed in the physical sphere returns in the sphere of consciousness. Consider *kleśa* (impurity, affliction), *mala* (dirt, filth, excretion), *anuśaya* (outflow, abscess), *āsrava* (discharge, contaminant), *viṣa* (poison, venom), *kaṣaya* (defect, decay), *pāpa* (vile, wretched). Their correlate states of purity *(śuddhi, viśuddhi)* are too numerous to list: the *Mahāvyutpatti* provides fifty-nine terms under the heading "names for abandoning and relinquishing" *(nisṛjāparyāyāḥ, spangs pa dang dor ba la sogs pa'i ming).*

If we are to postulate the isomorphic introjection of the language of caste defilement and purification from the physical into the mental realm, we should consider for a moment the theoretical basis of caste. In his classic study, *Homo Hierarchicus,* Louis Dumont argues that "the immediate source of the notion [of ritual impurity] is to be found in the temporary impurity which the Hindu of good caste contacts in organic life."[25] Elsewhere, he speaks of "the irruption of the biological into social life."[26] On this model, the Buddhist defilements *(kleśa)* would function as the organic states of mind that the Buddhist must avoid, for the impurity they discharge is not easily expunged and, once touched, can cause pain over lifetimes. The *kleśas* are organic to the extent that they are states of mind *(caitta)* that occur quite commonly, even naturally: desire, anger, pride, doubt, jealousy, lethargy, excitement, laziness, forgetfulness, distraction. It is contact with these states that must be avoided, and it is separation from them that is the goal of the path. Yet in the Buddhist psychological systems, these states are not regarded as natural, innate, organic to consciousness; as Dharmakīrti declares at *Pramāṇavārttika* I.210 (in a statement to which we will return), "The nature of the mind is clear light; the defilements are adventitious."[27]

This reversal should not seem surprising, for it is central to Buddhist soteriology that the mental state of quiescence (however variously interpreted), which is absent in ordinary states of consciousness, should be privileged as the natural, organic state, while those states that seem most commonly to occupy the mind should be denigrated as adventitious. The function of the path is very much one of separation from these adventitious states, and it operates, as Dumont observes about caste regulations, as a means of "organizing contact with purificatory agents and abolishing it with external agents of impurity."[28] Whether the Buddhists view the impure as organic or inorganic is perhaps less significant than the fact that the basic binary opposition of pollution and purity is maintained.

To gain a further perspective on the nature of this opposition in Buddhist path-structures, we must go beyond the position that the Buddhist is simply seeking separation from the organic, as useful as this position might be in understanding nirvāṇa as a variation on the *ayoga-kevala* (inactive isolation) of the Jainas and the *kaivalya* (isolation) of the Yoga school. Here is it useful to recall Lord Chesterfield's famous dictum that "dirt is matter out of place." This definition becomes epigrammic for Mary Douglas, serving as the basis for her reflections on pollution beliefs in *Purity and Danger.* For Douglas, that there is something that a society identifies as dirt implies the existence of system; dirt is that which does not fit, and beliefs about pollution identify the areas of greatest systematization in a society. She writes:

> For us dirt is a kind of compendium category for all events which blur, smudge, contradict, or otherwise confuse accepted classifications. The underlying feeling is that a system of values which is habitually expressed in a given arrangement of things has been violated.[29]

Is such a category applicable to the Buddhist case? Indeed, the *kleśas* are portrayed as states that disrupt, muddle, and confuse the mind, displacing virtuous states and inducing present agitation and future suffering. And, as we have seen, the vocabulary of taint, stain, and defilement is very much in evidence. If we follow Douglas, we must see the Buddhist preoccupation with the categories of separation and purification as an attempt to impose a system, not onto societal relations, as is the concern of the social anthropologist, but onto mental activity. The path thus becomes, with its afflictions and antidotes, a process of demarcation. But Douglas argues that the attitude to dirt goes through a two-stage process. Dirt comes into existence through the differentiating activity of the mind, as "a by-product of the creation of order." As a differentiated entity, it then functions as a threat to the established categories; it is at this point that dirt is dangerous. In the end dirt loses its identity and hence its danger; "where there is no differentiation, there is no defilement."[30]

This final stage appears to be absent from the Buddhist case (except perhaps in tantra), for it is through the very classification of the states of mind termed *kleśas* that control is gained and maintained, not through their loss of identity, which could only occur in the ever-distant enlightenment. Desire, the irrational, is classified so that it can be controlled; its ultimate demise is something only hypothesized by the scholastics. As we have seen, even Nāgārjuna's critique could not dislodge the obsession with category from Buddhist soteriologies. This may, on some level, account for the persistence of the notion of a specific antidote for a specific affliction, even when the antidote remained in each case the vision of selflessness; it is in binary opposition that structure is maintained, and among the many things that the Indian delineations of the path may be about, there seems to be nothing more important than structure.

We might ask how appropriate it is to apply categories derived from the analysis of society to the analysis of a religious path, how appropriate to apply criteria derived from the study of primitive cultures to Buddhism, one of the "great traditions." Yet the Buddhist conception of defilement and purity seems to differ only in degree from that which occurs in the primitive or social sphere. Dumont notes that in the tribal situation, contact with the impure acts directly on the person's health, causing disease or misfortune, whereas for the Hindu such contact entails a fall in social status.[31] For the Buddhist it is a case of deferral: contact with the impure plants the seed for suffering, either mental or physical, at some point in the near or distant future. And, if we follow Douglas, the Buddhist worldview remains primitive to the extent that its universe is personal, behaving "as if it was intelligent, responsive to signs, symbols, gestures, gifts."[32]

A more sophisticated view of what constitutes the primitive mentality is put forth by Paul Ricoeur in *The Symbolism of Evil.* For Ricoeur, the primary characteristic of the primitive stage is that "evil and misfortune have not been dissociated, in which the ethical order of doing ill has not been distinguished from the cosmo-biological order of faring ill: suffering, sickness, death, failure."[33] That is, suffering is seen as a symptom, the link between defilement and suffering being one of causality and rationalization. Such rationalization is the very function of the doctrine of karma, which accounts for present events with past deeds, a doctrine that Indian Buddhism sometimes ignored but never called into question. In Ricoeur's view, the mentality of defilement is transcended only when the rationalization of suffering is sacrificed, when suffering becomes inexplicable. This marks the move from the primitive to the ethical, and such a move appears to be absent in Buddhism; thus far, no Book of Job has been discovered among the sūtras. In a statement whereby we might ponder the persistence of the vocabulary of defilement in the discourse of the Buddhist path (that path of which the bodhisattva must have full knowledge in order to become a buddha), Ricoeur writes:

> Hence it is in the era before this crisis of the first rationalization, before the dissociation of misfortune (suffering, disease, death, failure) and fault that the dread of the impure deploys its anxieties: the prevention of defilement takes upon itself all fears and all sorrows; man, before any direct accusation, is already secretly accused of the misfortunes in the world; wrongly accused—thus does man appear to us at the origin of his ethical experience.[34]

The *Yāna* Controversy

With his or her knowledge of the paths, the bodhisattva sets forth to persons lacking *bodhicitta* the paths of the śrāvaka and pratyekabuddha, that they may thereby purify themselves of defilement. But if the bodhisattva has vowed to bring all beings to enlightenment, can s/he be content in leading them to the liberation of an arhat, or must s/he lead them all to buddhahood? And what of those arhats who have already entered nirvāṇa—can they emerge from the remainderless state? In other words, how are the Mahāyāna Ābhidharmikas to integrate the old routes and destinations into their new and improved map of the path to enlightenment? To put these questions in context, let us return to the chapter of the *Abhisamayālaṃkāra* devoted to the knowledge of the paths, which begins with the following cryptic verse:

> Light outshining the gods in order that they be suitable, certain object, pervasion, nature, and its function.[35]

The verse refers to a passage that appears in an abbreviated form in the *Aṣṭasāhasrikāprajñāpāramitāsūtra* (Perfection of Wisdom in 8,000 Stanzas) and in an extended form in the *Pañcaviṃśatisāhasrikāprajñāpāramitā* at the beginning of the Śakra chapter, in which the lustre of the assembled gods pales in comparison to the brilliance of the Tathāgata. This dispels the pride of the gods, making them suitable vessels for the teaching of the perfection of wisdom, and specifically making it possible for them to develop the aspiration to enlightenment, the "certain object" mentioned in the verse.[36] Subhūti then says:

> Those, however, who rest in the certainty of perfection do not create the aspiration to unsurpassed, complete, perfect enlightenment. Why? Because they have cut themselves off from the stream of saṃsāra; they do not take rebirth in saṃsāra and do not create the aspiration to unsurpassed, complete, perfect enlightenment. And yet, I will admire them as well if they will create the aspiration to unsurpassed, complete, perfect enlightenment. I shall not obstruct their roots of virtue, for one must hold onto the supreme among the supreme dharmas.[37]

Subhūti appears to contradict himself here. On the one hand, he disparages the arhats who have entered nirvāṇa, "those who rest in the certainty of perfection," suggesting that they are aloof from saṃsāra and thus cannot, or do not, create the altruistic aspiration to buddhahood. On the other hand, he promises to admire them if they do so, but without explaining how "those who have cut themselves off from the stream of saṃsāra" might reimmerse themselves. This apparent contradiction illustrates the Mahāyāna's ambivalence toward both the antecedent tradition and those who had already entered nirvāṇa, for the proclamation of the bodhisattva path in the Mahāyāna sūtras carried with it a reevaluation of the path that had been proclaimed before and of those who had followed it to its conclusion. It raised the question of the fate of the arhats.

For the commentators on the *Abhisamayālaṃkāra,* this question was addressed in their discussion of the term "pervasion" in the verse above, generally taken to mean that all sentient beings are pervaded by the buddha lineage. Two solutions to the problem of the fate of the arhat were set forth by the Indian masters, solutions that ultimately rested on the question of the number of vehicles. Some sūtras said that there are three, some that there is one. The authors of the sūtras seem for the most part to have been unconcerned with, if not unaware of, conflicting views; they were armed with their claim to *buddhavacana* (word of the Buddha), the pinnacle in the hierarchy of Buddhist discourse, that which having been spoken remains spoken.[38] But for the commentator (unlike the authors of the sūtras), the weapon of authority had to be wielded with both hands—a hand that sought to rewrite only what the sūtras really meant, and a hand that sought to create a new discourse by contriving a consistency among them. This conflict is not one to which the Buddhist commentator alone is subject; rather, it seems endemic to the operation of commentary, as Michel Foucault notes: "Commentary averts the chance element of discourse by giving it its due: it gives us the opportunity to say something other than the text itself, but on condition that it is the text itself which is uttered and, in some ways, finalized."[39]

Tsong-kha-pa, in the second chapter of his commentary to the *Abhisamayālaṃkāra,* adopting the posture of chronicler rather than commentator, catalogued the views of the Indian commentators who said three and those who said one. There were ample passages from the sūtras to support both sides of the issue. For those who championed one final vehicle, there was the prophecy in the *Lotus Sūtra* that Śāriputra would become the Buddha Padmaprabha and the statement in the *Laṅkāvatāra* (Descent to Śrī Laṅka) that śrāvakas are not liberated by the śrāvakayāna, but ultimately are followers of the Mahāyāna.[40] For the proponents of three vehicles, there was the *Akṣayamatinirdeśa* (Teaching of Akṣayamati), which said, "These three are the vehicles that bring about emancipation: the śrāvakayāna, the pratyekabuddhayāna, and the Mahāyāna."[41] The *Saṃdhinirmocana* (Untying of the Intention) explained why śrāvakas do not enter the Mahāyāna:

> Persons of the śrāvaka lineage only proceed to peace. Although all the buddhas try to establish them in the essence of enlightenment, they are unable to achieve unsurpassed and complete enlightenment. Why? It is because their compassion is meager and they are horrified by suffering and because they are naturally of an inferior lineage.[42]

Not wishing to deny utterly the possibility of śrāvakas becoming buddhas, the proponents of three vehicles could look to the *Saṃdhinirmocana* again, where a distinction was drawn between those śrāvakas described above and those who turn toward enlightenment. The Buddha declares:

> I teach that those śrāvakas who turn toward enlightenment are a type of bodhisattva. It is thus. Having been liberated from the afflictive obstructions, they are exhorted by the tathāgatas to free their minds from the obstructions to omniscience.[43]

Hence it would seem that some śrāvakas follow their path to its final destination while others transfer onto the Mahāyāna. Those who would transfer must do so before entering the remainderless nirvāṇa *(anupādhiśeṣanirvāṇa);*[44] those who have entered the nirvāṇa in which the aggregates no longer remain have severed the possibility of any further effort. This is the position of Asaṅga, as cited by Tsong-kha-pa from the *Nirṇayasaṃgraha* (Compendium of Determination):

> Do those śrāvakas who change [to the Mahāyāna] achieve perfect, complete enlightenment while they abide in the realm of the nirvāṇa with remainder, or do they do so while they abide in the realm of the nirvāṇa without remainder? They do so while they abide in the realm of the nirvāṇa with remainder. Those who abide in the realm of the nirvāṇa without remainder have severed the continuum of all initiative and all striving.[45]

A commentator of Tsong-kha-pa, Rje-btsun Chos-kyi-rgyal-mtshan, cites an unspecified Perfection of Wisdom sūtra that speaks of arhats who have entered the remainderless nirvāṇa, saying, "Those who have entered the faultless purity lack the power to create the aspiration to enlightenment."[46] Arhats who have achieved the nirvāṇa with remainder *(sopādhiśeṣanirvāṇa),* that is, those who have destroyed the afflictions but continue to experience the effects of the karma that caused their present lifetime, are able magically to lengthen that lifetime to enable themselves to begin the bodhisattva path. Tsong-kha-pa writes:

> It is explained that they bless their own body so as not to pass into nirvāṇa and, with a magically created body, they display to others the way to pass into [the nirvāṇa] without remainder. With their former bodies, which even gods cannot see, they remain in isolation and complete the collec-

> tions. At that time, they rejoice in their own welfare and are not conscientious about cultivating the path and [so] are exhorted [to do so] by buddhas and bodhisattvas.[47]

This elaborate scheme of dissimulation in which śrāvakas practice the Mahāyāna with invisible bodies is but one example of the price of consistency, demonstrating the length to which Mahāyāna scholastics would go to explain how the śrāvaka could merge onto the bodhisattva path.

The rationale for the doctrine of three vehicles seems to be as follows. Sentient beings differ in their personalities. Some delight in the sufferings of others, some are pained by them. These various dispositions are not the result of social conditioning nor of karma, but are, in effect, genetically determined by a seed possessed by each sentient being in the *ālayavijñāna* (storehouse consciousness). Pan-chen Bsod-nams-grags-pa, another of Tsong-kha-pa's commentators, writes:

> The seeds of uncontaminated wisdom in the minds of sentient beings [determine] the path of the individual vehicles to which it is suitable that they be led. [These seeds,] ultimately, are the individual lineages that establish the three different capacities of sentient beings, the three different interests, the three different practices, and the three different fruitions of sentient beings.[48]

Thus the presence of different dispositions and interests leads to the postulation of a spiritual determinism in the form of three lineages, and from the presence of lineages a corresponding set of ultimate destinations is inferred, these being the nirvāṇas of the śrāvaka and the pratyekabuddha and the unsurpassed enlightenment of the buddha. Because arhats who have entered the remainderless nirvāṇa by the śrāvaka and pratyekabuddha paths have abandoned all the causes for rebirth in saṃsāra, it is impossible for them to achieve buddhahood, which requires many more lifetimes of practice.[49] Hence there are three vehicles, and these vehicles are final.

This apparently commonsensical approach to enlightenment is not in itself sufficient to deal with the sūtras which state that the nirvāṇa of the śrāvaka is like an illusory city conjured by a skillful guide, a waystation for weary travelers to keep them from turning back on their long journey to a distant goal. This simile, best known from the seventh chapter of the *Lotus Sūtra,* is also mentioned by Candrakīrti in the *Madhyamakāvatāra* (Supplement to the Middle Way) at XI.38:

> Therefore, just as a wise [captain] created a pleasant city en route to alleviate the fatigue of those who had set out for a jeweled island, you [created] this vehicle to turn the minds of students to the way of complete peace. [You] set forth [the Mahāyāna] separately when they had given up [the afflictions] and trained their minds.[50]

There is also the statement in the *Śrīmālādevīsiṃhanāda* (Lion's Roar of Śrīmālādevī) that arhats are subject to something called "inconceivable rebirth" *(acintyacyutigata),* and the Buddha's exhortation to the arhats in the *Lotus Sūtra:* "You are liberated from suffering but you still have not passed into nirvāṇa. You must seek this buddhayāna."[51] These statements suggest that the nirvāṇa of the Hīnayāna is a penultimate achievement.

The proponents of three vehicles respond to these apparent contradictions by reiterating the distinction between śrāvakas who seek peace and śrāvakas who change, the former entering the nirvāṇa without remainder while the latter, freed from the afflictions, turn to the Mahāyāna before entering nirvāṇa and continue to take rebirth due to the latencies of ignorance and uncontaminated ignorance.[52] With this distinction in place, the proponents of three vehicles can claim that when the sūtras speak of śrāvakas taking inconceivable rebirth, they intend only the śrāvakas who change; śrāvakas who seek peace enter a nirvāṇa without remainder from which they never emerge. Thus when the sūtras speak of the śrāvaka nirvāṇa as a penultimate and illusory destination, they are speaking not to śrāvakas but to bodhisattvas, indicating to them the trifling nature of the Hīnayāna achievement, which they must eschew; the actual nirvāṇa is buddhahood. And when the *Lotus Sūtra* exhorts śrāvakas to nirvāṇa, it is the śrāvakas who change, not those who seek peace, who are addressed, and it is the nirvāṇa of the buddha, not the nirvāṇa without remainder, that they are urged to seek.[53]

It is not to be denied, however, that certain sūtras, most notably the *Lotus,* speak unequivocally of a single vehicle. The proponents of three vehicles must show these sūtras to be subject to interpretation *(neyārtha),* which requires that they demonstrate some intention behind the Buddha's proclamation of a single vehicle, some factual referent that he had in mind when he said, without really meaning it, that there is but one vehicle. The *Mahāyānasūtrālaṃkāra* (Ornament of the Mahāyāna Sūtras) provides seven such referents at XI.53:

> Because the *dharma*[*dhātu*], selflessness, and liberations are similar, because of different lineages, because of having two thoughts, because of emanation, because of finality, [there is] one vehicle.[54]

Vasubandhu, Asvabhāva, and Sthiramati, the Indian commentators on the *Mahāyānasūtrālaṃkāra,* interpret this to mean that the use of the term *"ekayāna"* is merely rhetorical, that the term *"ekayāna"* has seven figurative meanings. Let us briefly examine three of them.[55]

It can be said that there is one vehicle when the vehicle is taken to be the person, the one who proceeds to the goal. And the three persons—the śrāvaka, the pratyekabuddha, and the Bhagavan—are one, or the same *(eka),* in the sense that they are all selfless. Hence when the Buddha spoke of the "one vehicle," he was thinking of the fact that all persons who proceed on the path are similar in that they are selfless, not that there is a single vehicle in the sense of a means of traversing the path.[56]

A second referent, according to the *Sūtrālaṃkāra,* is magical creation *(nirmāṇa),* an allusion to cases in which emanated doubles of the Tathāgata and of śrāvakas display to the world the passage into nirvāṇa. The single vehicle in this case would seem to be the Hīnayāna. Sthiramati, evincing the doceticism of the Mahāyāna, emphasizes that when the Tathāgata displayed the passage into *parinirvāṇa* through the practice of the śrāvaka path, it was not the Tathāgata himself who passed away but only an emanation created by his magical powers. He thereby falsely suggested that there is but one vehicle whereby one may achieve final nirvāṇa in order that sentient beings might be subdued by his skillful methods.[57]

Finally, the term "ultimacy" *(paryanta)* is used to refer to buddhahood itself, and by extension to the Mahāyāna which is its cause. Because the Mahāyāna is the ultimate, supreme, and consummate cause, such that there is none other that surpasses it, and because buddhahood is the ultimate attainment beyond which one cannot proceed, it can be said that the Mahāyāna and its buddhahood are the sole vehicle, in the sense that there are no others that surpass them; all supremacy is exhausted there alone.[58]

Thus, with a range of rhetorical figures, including hyperbole, synecdoche, and metonym, the possible referents of the term "one vehicle" are accounted for, if not explained away, and the doctrine of three vehicles can be upheld. The seven referents are all in some sense metaphoric, with metaphor taken to mean a figure of speech in which a name is transferred to an object to which that term is *not* applicable, with the term retaining reference both to its original meaning and to the object for which is stands;[59] the Yogācāra commentators all conclude their discussions of the stanza by saying that the statements in the sūtras that there is but one vehicle are not definitive *(nītārtha)* but are provisional and subject to interpretation *(neyārtha),* and are not to be taken to mean that there are not three vehicles. Rather, the Buddha had something else—one of these seven things—in mind when he used the term *"ekayāna."*

However, for a statement to be judged provisional, it is not enough that there be some unspoken referent in the Buddha's mind; he must also have a purpose in making a statement that is inaccurate.[60] The *Mahāyānasūtrālaṃkāra* provides two such reasons: "In order to lead some, in order to hold others, the complete buddhas teach one vehicle to the uncertain."[61] Those to be led are śrāvakas and pratyekabuddhas of indefinite lineage, that is, those who have entered the Hīnayāna path but who are not predestined to complete it. They are told by the Buddha that there is but one vehicle, which begins with the practices of śrāvakas and then proceeds to the practices of bodhisattvas. Those to be held are bodhisattvas of indefinite lineage, who are in danger of forsaking the Mahāyāna because they become discouraged about saṃsāra when they see that sentient beings irrationally do each other harm. To keep them from despondently turning to the Hīnayāna, the Buddha tells them that there is but one vehicle, the Mahāyāna, that there is no other alternative.[62]

According to Haribhadra, it was Āryāsaṅga and his followers who held that there is a variety of vehicles.[63] Before investigating the motivations for such a position, let us consider the opposing view, that of a single vehicle, well known from the *Lotus* and from passages such as this from the *Laṅkāvatāra:*

> The vehicle of the gods, the vehicle of Brahmā, and the vehicles of śrāvakas, tathāgatas, and *svajinas* (pratyekabuddhas); these are the vehicles I set forth. Until the mind is arisen, one does not encounter the vehicles. When the mind is transformed, there are no vehicles and no transmigrators. Even the explanation of the vehicles does not exist. I speak of one vehicle. In order to lead the childish, I speak of different vehicles.[64]

The dilemma of the commentator is to find a rationale for the unequivocal and definitive nature of his own interpretation of an authoritative text, and a rationale for judging the opposing interpretation heuristic, if not simply wrong. Finding sūtras to support one or the other position is not the problem. But to supplement citations from scripture *(āgama),* there must also be reasoned arguments *(yukti).* Nāgārjuna states in his *Niraupamyastava* (Hymn to the Peerless [Buddha]) that the vehicles are undifferentiated because the *dharmadhātu* is undifferentiated.[65] This entails the position which, according to Candrakīrti, Nāgārjuna also holds, that in order to achieve liberation from rebirth by any vehicle, one must gain cognition of emptiness.[66] A vehicle that does not provide a path for the realization of reality *(tathatā)* is not, then, an authentic vehicle for passing beyond mundane existence.[67] Tsong-kha-pa glosses Nāgārjuna to say that if reality is undifferentiated, it cannot be understood in a variety of ways. Based on this argument from symmetry, the existence of one vehicle—the means of gaining knowledge of the undifferentiated reality—is then (perhaps prematurely) inferred, with pronouncements about three vehicles being identified as yet another example of the Buddha's skillful methods, "to provide rest to those wearied on the road of mundane existence," as Nāgārjuna says in the *Bodhicittavivaraṇa* (Essay on the Mind of Enlightenment).[68]

A further tactic in the commentator's strategy is to attack the opponent's logic. The argument presented by Tsong-kha-pa calls into question the existence of quantifiable lineages. Noting that the capacities and interests of sentient beings are beyond enumeration, he argues that should one wish to posit the existence of vehicles on the basis of such factors, the number of vehicles would perforce be limitless. Furthermore, interests and capacities are inconstant. How, he asks, can one prove the existence of only three lineages based on a variety of interests and desires and, from that, derive three invariable lineages?[69]

On the question of lineage, Pan-chen Bsod-nams-grags-pa argues that the presence of the tathāgatagarbha in all sentient beings provides further proof of one final vehicle, that all sentient beings are endowed with the buddha-nature, and consequently that all are of the buddha lineage. Glossing *Ratnagotravibhāga* (Delineation of the Jewel Lineage) I.27, he provides three reasons why all sentient beings are endowed with the buddha-nature: the activities of the buddha affect all sentient beings, the reality *(tathatā)* of the stained minds of sentient beings and the reality of the stainless mind of the tathāgata are ontologically indivisible, and the buddha lineage exists in all sentient beings. The śāstra itself says:

> Because the body of the complete buddha creates emanations, because reality is indivisible, and because the lineage exists, all embodied beings are permanently endowed with the buddha-nature.[70]

The proponents of one vehicle cannot simply confine themselves to such theoretical issues. They are also confronted with an historical dilemma, namely, the accounts of the great arhats of thc past who achieved liberation without recourse to the Great Vehicle. If they wish to uphold their position, the proponents of one vehicle must deny the existence of a nirvāṇa without remainder entered by the arhat, never to emerge. Following the *Śrīmālādevīsiṃhanāda,* they accept that arhats sever the continuum of birth and death brought about by karma and *kleśa,* but hold that they are subject to inconceivable birth and death. Indeed, the hallowed Abhidharma categories of the knowledge of non-production *(anutpādajñāna)* and the knowledge of extinction *(kṣayajñāna)* are declared to be themselves subject to interpretation *(neyārtha).*[71]

Having denied the ultimacy of the Hīnayāna goal, the paths of śrāvakas and pratyekabuddhas can be assimilated as yet another instance of the Buddha's *upāya;* as the *Śrīmālādevīsiṃhanāda* says, "This so-called *parinirvāṇa* is a method of the tathāgatas."[72] Indeed, it is argued that it is simply unseemly to think that the buddhas, knowing the supremacy of the Mahāyāna, would in the final analysis teach anything else. Thus it is claimed that there is but one vehicle because it is unthinkable that there be three. The *Satyakaparivartta* (Chapter on the True Ones) says:

> Mañjuśrī, if the Tathāgata taught the Mahāyāna to some and taught the śrāvakayāna and pratyekabuddhayāna to others, the mind of the Tathāgata would be most impure, he would be guilty of favoritism, his great compassion would be meager, he would be discriminatory, and would be a teacher who kept the dharma secret.[73]

But even if the nirvāṇa of the arhats is merely a contrivance of the compassionate Buddha, the Mahāyāna must provide some explanation of their attainment. To wit, arhats abandon the afflictions of the three realms and consequently are not born there. Instead, they take birth in a pure land in a body of samādhi in the middle of a lotus and abide in this uncontaminated realm *(anāsravadhātu)* for many aeons until they are roused from their samādhi by buddhas, who exhort them to enter the Mahāyāna.[74] In his *Abhisamayālaṃkārālokā,* Haribhadra cites stanzas 45–47 of Candrakīrti's *Triśaraṇasaptati* (Seventy Stanzas on the Triple Refuge) on this point, where the śrāvaka and pratyekabuddha arhats are described:

> Having attained the two types of enlightenment, those who are frightened by mundane existence rejoice in the cessation of life [and] think that they have attained nirvāṇa. They lack nirvāṇa. Yet they are not born in the three realms of existence; they abide in the uncontaminated sphere. Later, they are roused by the buddhas to abandon the unafflicted ignorance. They amass the collections of enlightenment and become leaders of the world.[75]

But that will take some time, as we shall shortly see.

Just as the proponents of three vehicles had to account for those sūtras which unequivocally declared that there is but one vehicle, so the proponents of one final vehicle must explain away those sūtras that speak of three vehicles (the very texts on the basis of which Asaṅga and his followers argued that there are three final vehicles). Here again, *upāya* is called upon for the answer. According to Tsong-kha-pa's disciple Rgyal-tshab, the Buddha taught that there are three final vehicles out of his compassionate concern for those disciples of the Mahāyāna lineage who are temporarily incapable of understanding the profound teaching. The profound path is, of course, the Mādhyamika, and those disciples for whom it is temporarily unsuitable are the Yogācārins. Such was the Buddha's intention. What he had in mind when he spoke of three vehicles was simply that disciples must occasionally be led along various paths because they differ in their interests and capacities. His purpose in teaching three vehicles was to care for those who must be led along the Mahāyāna path without denying the true existence of the lack of a difference of entity between consciousnesses and their objects. Put less technically, the Buddha, recognizing that certain bodhisattvas were temporarily incapable both of understanding the most profound emptiness and of understanding that there is but one vehicle, skillfully explained to them that emptiness means that there are no objects which are not of the nature of consciousness, and that this emptiness is ultimately real. He also taught these dull-witted bodhisattvas that there are three vehicles.

Here again, Rgyal-tshab refers to the Yogācārins, who, according to the Dge-lugs-pa doxographies, hold that emptiness is the absence of objects that are not of the nature of consciousness, but also hold that that emptiness is truly established *(bden par grub pa)*. Rgyal-tshab links the assertions on the number of vehicles with assertions on the nature of reality, and ranks the Mādhyamikas above the Yogācārins in the hierarchy of *siddhāntas* on the basis of the Mādhyamikas' holding (1) that emptiness is itself empty of *svabhāva,* and (2) that there is but one final vehicle. Rgyal-tshab does not attempt to draw a connection between these two positions, but one might speculate that because the Mādhyamikas, or at least the Prāsaṅgikas, hold that all persons who achieve the enlightenment of a śrāvaka, pratyekabuddha, or buddha do so by understanding the same reality (that is, emptiness), and because for the Mādhyamikas nothing, not even emptiness, is truly established, there cannot be three autonomous and separate vehicles.[76]

Tsong-kha-pa ends his section on the *yāna* controversy with a plea standard to the conclusion of the exposition of a difficult topic:

> Thus even the great charioteers appear to differ on the interpretability and definitiveness of the vehicles. Therefore, because this is something that those with clear minds should consider, I have merely planted a seed here; it should be known extensively from the oceanlike texts of the Mādhyamikas and Cittamātrins and from the statements of the supreme scholar Kamalaśīla.[77]

Why did the problem of the number of vehicles arise, and why did the Yogācārins and the Mādhyamikas differ in their answers? The first question is perhaps more easily addressed than the second. The problem of the number of vehicles arose out of the question of authority. How was the Mahāyāna to deal with a tradition that was temporally prior to it, and that thus claimed the authority gained from proximity to the founder? To wrest away that authority, at least to its own satisfaction, the Mahāyāna needed to displace the earlier tradition, and it employed many weapons in the attempt, the most effective of which were the doctrines of *upāya* and *gotra* (lineage). More than simply a hermeneutical device to accommodate conflicting views, the idea that the Buddha taught different paths to different persons was employed to appropriate the power of discourse and to control those from whom it had been appropriated by consistently consigning them to the paths the Buddha taught to those incapable of comprehending the most sublime of his teachings. Such persons were designated as the lower members of the hierarchy, called the Hīnayāna, with *hīna* not simply meaning "lesser," as it is euphemistically translated, but "deficient," "defective," "faulty," "vile," "base," "excluded," "defeated." This status could then be made organic through *gotra*—yet another instance of the irruption of caste into Buddhist rhetoric.

The Mahāyāna's subordination of the earlier tradition in order to establish and maintain its own authority took two forms, reflected in the positions of three final vehicles and one final vehicle, in defense of which the commentators performed a wide range of machinations to impose a consistency on the sūtras that seems at times tyrannical in its veiled usurpation of sovereignty. For the proponents of three vehicles, hierarchy was maintained and the earlier tradition subordinated through concretizing the paths and the lineages; the Hīnayāna was inferior in its aspiration and in the content of its wisdom, comprehending only the selflessness of the person and unable to penetrate to the deeper understanding of emptiness that was the exclusive purview of the bodhisattva. The proponents of one final vehicle took another tack, subjugating the earlier tradition through subsumption, going so far as to deny the existence of *parinirvāṇa,* and demoting the ultimate attainment of the arhat to a detour on the path. Rather than keeping the Hīnayāna wholly external, they sought domination through the appropriation of origin: it was the Buddha's intention that all eventually join the Mahāyāna path and understand the sole reality of emptiness, without which liberation is impossible.

Thus, while the Yogācāra employed lineage to maintain superiority, the Mādhyamika rejected lineage toward the same end. Their strategy was to conflate all paths into the Mahāyāna. It is tempting to ascribe the Mādhyamika's integrating view of vehicles and fluid view of lineages to the totalizing power of emptiness. But it is nonetheless crucial to note that the Hīnayāna does not disappear for the Mādhyamika; even here, Mary Douglas' dirt does not lose its identity. This is because without the Hīnayāna there can be no Mahāyāna, without the inferior member there can be no superiority. The Hīnayāna functions for the Mahāyāna as the Other in terms of which it defines itself; the Mahāyāna constructs its identity through rejection of the Hīnayāna.

It has been observed that differentiation is dependent on disgust, but that this disgust is always ambivalent, being accompanied by desire, a nostalgia for the Other that has apparently been expelled.[78] Thus the śrāvaka is often portrayed in the Mahāyāna sūtras with a certain affection. We need think only of Śāriputra in the *Vimalakīrtinirdeśa* (Teaching of Vimalakīrti). Yet our discussion thus far has been about the Indian strategies (unconscious though they may have been) of dealing with the Hīnayāna in an historical context where there were indeed adherents and defenders of the śrāvakayāna. How do we account for the persistence of concern with śrāvakas in Tibetan Buddhist literature, for the long and extensive study of the structure of the Hīnayāna path in a land where there were no śrāvakas to be found, at least none of the card-carrying variety? This fascination with the śrāvakayāna cannot be seen as a further case of the Tibetans aping Indian Buddhism, an argument burdened beyond usefulness. Rather, the need to study the śrāvaka path in Tibet (and the fascination with the lohan in China?) can be attributed, at least in part, to the role of the śrāvaka as the imaginary Other. As Peter Stallybrass and Allon White note in another context:

> The point is that the *exclusion* necessary to the formation of social identity at one level is simultaneously a *production* at the level of the Imaginary, and a production, what is more, of a complex hybrid fantasy emerging out of the very attempt to demarcate boundaries, to unite and purify the social collectivity.[79]

Part of that fantasy is played out, perhaps, in the penalty that the proponents of one vehicle imposed on the śrāvaka who follows the Hīnayāna path to its completion before turning to the Mahāyāna. There is a range of opinion as to how long it takes such an arhat to follow the bodhisattva path and become a buddha. The sinified Korean monk Yüan-ts'e (Wŏnch'ŭk, 613–696), one of Hsuan-tsang's chief disciples, makes the ostensibly sensible assertion, in his commentary on the *Saṃdhinirmocana,* that arhats who enter the Mahāyāna path do so at the eighth *bhūmi,* since they have destroyed the afflictive obstructions and now need only abandon the obstructions to omniscience.[80] Bhāvaviveka, in his *Tarkajvālā* (Blaze of Reasoning), seems to suggest that arhats begin the path at the first *bhūmi.*[81] But Tsong-kha-pa interprets a passage from Dharmamitra's commentary on Maitreyanātha's *Abhisamayālaṃkāra,* called the *Prasphuṭapadā* (Clear Words), so as to support the position that arhats enter the Mahāyāna at the very outset of the path—i.e., on the path of accumulation, which commences with the creation of *bodhicitta*—his point being that it is not the level of the arhat's understanding of selflessness that is in question but the arhat's motivation. The bodhisattva path begins with the creation of *bodhicitta,* the aspiration to become a buddha out of compassion for all sentient beings, and the creation of this aspiration marks the beginning of the path of accumulation. It is this aspiration, regardless of the understanding of selflessness, that serves as the motivating cause of the bodhisattva's long career.[82]

'Jam-dbyangs-bzhad-pa points out a certain infelicity entailed by the assertion that the arhat enters the path at the first or eighth *bhūmi.* He recalls that Haribhadra, in his *Abhisamayālaṃkārālokā,* explains that the bodhisattva spends one period of innumerable aeons on the paths of accumulation and preparation, a second period between the first and seventh *bhūmis,* and the third period going from the eighth *bhūmi* to the attainment of buddhahood, and he also recalls that Vasubandhu says in the *Abhidharmakośa* that śrāvakas can with great effort become arhats in as little as three lifetimes. Consequently, he calculates that the śrāvaka who became an arhat and then entered the Mahāyāna path at the first *bhūmi,* for example, would take one period of innumerable aeons (minus three lifetimes) less to become a buddha than would a bodhisattva. This is clearly unacceptable.[83]

Hence the path of the arhat must be longer than that of the bodhisattva, which is commonly calculated at three periods of innumerable aeons, but the precise length of the addendum seems to be in question. In his *Munimatālaṃkāra* (Ornament of the Mind of the Sage), Abhayākaragupta puts forth the position that śrāvaka and pratyekabuddha arhats become fully enlightened after four periods of countless aeons, whereas a commentary to Śāntideva's *Bodhicaryāvatāra* (Guide to the Deeds of Enlightenment) by one Dge-ba-lha (Kalyāṇadeva) takes a sterner view, holding that arhats who enter the Mahāyāna take forty periods of countless aeons more than bodhisattvas to become buddhas.[84]

Eventually, however, they will complete the path. Moreover, if there is but one vehicle that all beings will eventually be led to enter, then all will eventually achieve buddhahood and saṃsāra will end. Or will it?

The End of the Path

> Thus did I hear at one time. The Bhagavan was dwelling at Sāvatthi in Jetavana monastery in Anāthapiṇḍika's Park. Then drew near Vaccha, the wandering ascetic, to where the Bhagavan was; and having drawn near, he greeted the Bhagavan; and having passed the compliments of friendship and civility, he sat down respectfully at one side. And seated respectfully at one side, Vaccha, the wandering ascetic, spoke to the Bhagavan as follows, "How is it, Gotama? Does Gotama hold that the world is eternal, and that this view alone is true, and every other false?" "Nay, Vaccha, I do not hold that the world is eternal and that this view alone is true, and every other false."[85]

Thus does the Buddha refuse to answer the first of fourteen questions (repeated in similar forms elsewhere in the Pāli canon) known as the *avyākata* (indeterminables), rendered felicitously by Henry Clark Warren as "questions which tend not to edification." Like all such questions, the Buddha informs Vaccha that the question of whether the world is eternal "is a jungle, a wilderness, a puppet-show, a writhing, and a fetter, and is coupled with misery, ruin, despair, and agony, and does not tend to aversion, absence of passion, cessation, quiescence, knowledge, supreme wisdom, and nirvāṇa."[86] In short, a perfect topic for buddhological reflection.

Despite the Buddha's dismissal of the question in the Pāli canon, with the ascendancy of the Mahāyāna, the problem of the end of saṃsāra rises again.[87] The vow of the bodhisattva is sometimes construed according to the simile of the king who assumes the powers of a buddha and then leads all beings to enlightenment; sometimes according to the simile of the ferryman who arrives simultaneously with his passengers at the further shore; and sometimes according to the simile of the shepherd who follows his flock into the shelter of the pen and closes the gate behind him. But whether the vow takes the form of "Having become a buddha, I will lead all beings to enlightenment" or "I will not enter nirvāṇa until all beings have been freed from suffering," the question naturally arises as to whether this vow is but a noble boast or whether there is in fact a time when the round of birth and death will cease. Is there a time when the purpose of the Mahāyāna will be fulfilled, a Buddhist eschaton?

Some two millennia after the Buddha declined to answer Vaccha's question, Tsong-kha-pa took it up in his first major work, *Legs bshad gser phreng* (A Garland of Gold Eloquence), his commentary on Maitreyanātha's *Abhisamayālaṃkāra.* Here he considers the third of the five divisions of the knowledge of the paths, called "pervasion" *(vyāpti),* where Subhūti's statement that he will admire even the arhats who create the aspiration to supreme enlightenment is glossed to mean that all sentient beings are pervaded by the buddha-nature. It is in this context that the question of the end of saṃsāra arises. Tsong-kha-pa reports that Haribhadra, in his *Abhisamayālaṃkārālokā,* presents the positions of those who hold that saṃsāra is endless and those who hold that saṃsāra will end. Haribhadra writes:

> Some say, "The lineage of buddhas is beginningless [such that] when individual buddhas arise, countless sentient beings pass into final nirvāṇa. However, saṃsāra still is limitless because it is inexhaustible, like the sky. Even though it is impeded by mountains, the sky is utterly inexhaustible." [Others say,] "That which encounters its antidote appears to diminish.[88] If the antidote is greatly increased it will completely disappear, like stains on gold. If one actualizes the antidote, whose character is selflessness, saṃsāra also will disappear." By the power of a nature reason,[89] they assert that the continuum of saṃsāra is severed.[90]

Here we have two models of saṃsāra. In the first, saṃsāra is compared to the limitless sky which, although impinged upon by mountain ranges that seem to rise up on the horizon to violate its domain, can never be taken over by them. Similarly, even though the lineage of buddhas is without beginning (since buddhas have appeared throughout history to liberate innumerable sentient beings), buddhas are like the great mountains that rise and fall; they can never block the sky. Saṃsāra, like the sky, is a constant: it is nature and cannot be opposed. It is portrayed as neither positive nor negative but as the unlimited setting, the context, of the processes of suffering and enlightenment.[91]

The other model is more familiar. It is the oppositional model of contagion and antidote, with saṃsāra identified as the malady brought on by the contagion. The disease diminishes as the antidote takes effect, and when the antidote comes to have full effect the disease disappears. Saṃsāra is the disease brought on by poisonous ignorance, its symptoms are birth and death, and emptiness is its antidote. The simile here is not of mountains and sky but of stains on gold, suggesting that through proper application of the counteragent stains are effaced, leaving behind a pure substance whose taints were superficial. It is significant that gold is chosen over some other shiny metal, in that gold can be stained but cannot rust. Whereas other metals lose their lustre to rust and are permanently corroded in the process, beneath the stains on gold there remains a purity that can be uncovered.

Haribhadra appears to side with those who hold that saṃsāra will end—an attractive position indeed. Let us consider some further arguments put forth to support it. Numerous proofs can be made by citing scripture. For example, in his *Munimatālaṃkāra,* Abhayākaragupta quotes the *Samādhirāja* (King of Samādhi), which unequivocally states, "All of these transmigrators, without exception, will become buddhas."[92] But as became clear in Tsong-kha-pa's description of the *yāna* controversy, Māra can cite scripture for his purpose.

The arguments based on reason for the end of saṃsāra all seem to pivot on Dharmakīrti's famous declaration at *Pramāṇavārttika* I.210, "The nature of the mind is clear light; the stains are adventitious." Like mud in a pond, grime on a jewel, encrustations on a shirt of mail, or stains on gold, the defilements that give rise to the cycle of birth, aging, sickness, and death are superficial, accidental, "added on" *(āgantu),* implying what might seem to be a surprisingly substantialist position for a Buddhist thinker—namely, that while the defilements are accidental the mind is substantial; that that substance is pure, clear, and undefiled; that the nature of consciousness persists after the defilements have been expunged; and that the mind is somehow more real than the defilements. If the defilements are adventitious, it follows that there must be a way to remove them to reveal the clear light of the mind. The separation of the accidental from the substantial takes place through the proper application of the antidote, and the Tathāgata is present to ensure that the ailing find that antidote.

Dharmakīrti states the argument in a slightly different form earlier in the *Pramāṇavārttika* (at I.145–148),[93] where he holds that all beings will become enlightened due to the following sequence of propositions. If the obstructions in the minds of sentient beings were permanent, they could not be abandoned, but that is not the case; the obstructions have a cause and are therefore impermanent. Even though they are impermanent, if there were no way to abandon them, universal enlightenment would be impossible, but that is not the case; the way to destroy the obstructions is to cultivate wisdom, the antidote to the belief in self. Even though the antidote exists, if there were no one who knew of its existence, the enlightenment of all sentient beings would be impossible, but there is such a person, the omniscient Tathāgata. Even though he knows the method, if he did not teach it to others, it would be impossible for all sentient beings to become enlightened, but this is not the case; the Tathāgata sets forth the method unerringly out of his abundant mercy. Finally, even though he teaches the method, if his disciples did not seek the goal that he presented to them, there could be no enlightenment, but that also is not the case; they seek freedom from rebirth. Therefore, saṃsāra will end.[94]

This argument invokes many of the tenets, if not articles of faith, of Buddhist philosophy: most importantly, that the defilements are abandoned through the knowledge of selflessness and that the Buddha achieved such knowledge and persuasively taught the world how to gain it. Yet this argument, which has been read by the tradition as a logical progression, is in fact a series of hops of faith which together equal a great leap toward validation of the central trope of the Mahāyāna, that all sentient beings will be liberated from suffering.

The youthful Tsong-kha-pa was not seduced, and identified the gaps in the argument that he deemed unleapable:

> This proves that separation from faults, like desire, merely occurs in some minds. With regard to the question of whether saṃsāra ends, this certainly proves that individual sentient beings become enlightened. However, since it is not the case that something is certain to happen [simply] because it might happen, this does not serve as a proof [that saṃsāra will end]. Therefore, the final proof that saṃsāra has a terminus [would seem to be] that the stains are adventitious and that the nature of the mind is clear light, and that, consequently, if one encounters the appropriate conditions, it is fitting that the obstructions be abandoned and suitable that the antidote be produced. However, this alone cannot prove that saṃsāra will end, because it confuses the feasibility of the occurrence of an effect with the certainty of the occurrence of an effect. It is like [trying to] prove that a sprout will definitely grow because seeds exist.[95]

He goes on to consider an argument, derived from statements in various sūtras, that saṃsāra will be emptied. For example, it is said that the fifth of the five certainties of the *saṃbhogakāya* of a buddha is that it teaches the Mahāyāna to *āryabodhisattvas* until saṃsāra is emptied.[96] He writes:

> Furthermore, others hold that because each buddha and bodhisattva brings many sentient beings to nirvāṇa, saṃsāra becomes empty in [the

> sense that] that it[s population] diminishes and is not augmented, like a pile of grain [in which kernels are removed one at a time].[97] Those who hold this position are mistaken, because they have not demonstrated that [the number of] sentient beings is decreasing. In order to say that something is growing or shrinking [in number], one must have some definite measure [at the outset], but this is not the case with the realm of sentient beings, which is like the sky. With this meaning in mind, the *Saṃcayagāthā* [Condensed Verses of the Perfection of Wisdom, XXVIII.5] says, "This mechanism of ignorance is without extinction and without increase."[98] And the *Bhadracaryāpraṇidhāna* [Aspiration to the Deeds of Samantabhadra] says, "As long as it would take to reach the end of the sky, so it is with the end of all sentient beings." Therefore, the intention of the statement that all transmigrators will become enlightened is this: if they encounter the conditions, it is suitable that they become so. Asaṅga [in his commentary to the *Ratnagotravibhāga*] explains the statement from [the *Śrīmālādevīsiṃhanāda*] sūtra, "It is beginningless but it has an end," to mean that there is no difference among sentient beings in their capacity to become purified. It is similar here.[99]

Thus Tsong-kha-pa, who would become one of the most sophisticated and articulate expositors of the supremacy of the Mahāyāna, consistently resists the compulsion to ratify its most important claim, that it is the vehicle that will deliver all beings to the safe haven of buddhahood across the raging ocean of saṃsāra. Since saṃsāra is merely the environment created by the karma of the unenlightened, when the last sentient being has made port, the sea will suddenly evaporate and all conditioned existence will end.

But although Tsong-kha-pa rejects the claim that these arguments prove that saṃsāra will end, he does not immediately jump to the opposite conclusion, that saṃsāra is endless:

> The great scholars of more recent times have noted that the Bhagavan made statements to both [effects]: that saṃsāra ends and that saṃsāra has no end, and based on these [statements] the proponents of tenets wrote treatises explaining both that saṃsāra ends and that it does not end. There are proofs for both positions.[100]

Tsong-kha-pa makes no attempt to apply the categories of *neyārtha* and *nītārtha* (provisional versus definitive) to the sūtras that proclaim the end or endlessness of saṃsāra. But in apparent reference to the *avyākṛta,* he notes that when the Buddha was asked whether saṃsāra ends, he did not answer. Tsong-kha-pa's interpretation of this silence appears unique. He does not see it as a critique of reason and an anticipation of the Mādhyamika dialectic, as T. R. V. Murti does.[101] Nor does he feel, like Vasubandhu, that the Buddha could not answer affirmatively or negatively without being misunderstood: to say that saṃsāra is endless would suggest that there is no liberation; to say that saṃsāra ends would suggest that individual effort is unimportant.[102]

Tsong-kha-pa even seems to disregard Nāgārjuna's interpretation. In the *Ratnāvalī* (String of Jewels) II.7–9, it is asked why the Buddha remained silent about the end of the world when he knew that the countless buddhas will indeed end it through leading beings to enlightenment. Nāgārjuna answers that the Buddha remained silent because the world is illusory; its production and disintegration do not exist.[103] Tsong-kha-pa also seems to ignore *Yuktiṣaṣṭikā* 14 and Candrakīrti's commentary on *Madhyamakaśāstra* XXV.20, "It is not only because of the undifferentiability of saṃsāra from nirvāṇa that it is impossible to imagine its beginning or its end."[104] Rather, the Buddha's silence suggests to Tsong-kha-pa that he knew that saṃsāra would never end, almost as though he refrained from delivering that piece of bad news to spare the world further despair. But Tsong-kha-pa also acknowledges that silence is not a proof.

Yet Tsong-kha-pa finds proof for the endlessness of saṃsāra, and he finds it in an unlikely place, in an argument he calls "pleasant to uphold."[105] Among the myriad practices of the bodhisattva enumerated in the *Abhisamayālaṃkāra* is the acquisition of the collections (*saṃbhārapratipatti,* listed at I.46–47), of which there are seventeen. The twelfth of these is the collection of wisdom *(jñānasaṃbhāra),* which the commentators, drawing on the *Pañcaviṃśatisāhasrikāprajñāpāramitā,* explain as the bodhisattva's knowledge of the twenty emptinesses, the tenth of which is called "the emptiness of the beginningless and the endless" *(anavarāgraśūnyatā).*[106]

It is a commonplace of the Dge-lugs-pa view of Mādhyamika that, in order for there to be emptiness, there must be something which is empty. The substratum or basis of the emptiness of the beginningless and the endless—that which is beginninglessly and endlessly empty—is saṃsāra. Candrakīrti writes in the *Madhyamakāvatāra* (VI.194–195):

> Because saṃsāra has no beginning and has no end, it is called that which is without beginning and without end. This dreamlike existence neither comes nor goes. The very absence of that is referred to in the treatises as the emptiness of the beginningless and the endless.[107]

Thus Tsong-kha-pa concludes, almost parenthetically, that saṃsāra must be endless. The irony here should not be lost: saṃsāra cannot be emptied because of emptiness. For Tsong-kha-pa, emptiness is reality, and by knowing that reality one is liberated from suffering. Yet emptiness becomes implicated in the perpetuation of that which knowledge of it is said to destroy (i.e., saṃsāra). This could be read as another example of the persistence of the Other, and as the logical conclusion of the doctrine of *pratītyasamutpāda* (dependent origination), since it is precisely the proclamation of emptiness as the self-present reality of saṃsāra that ensures saṃsāra's endlessness. But emptiness also seems to function as both remedy and poison; the mantra that can be misused to which Nāgārjuna alludes at *Madhyamakaśāstra* XXIV.11.

It is Tsong-kha-pa's allusion to the logically rigorous necessity of saṃsāra that unleashes emptiness' other, somehow repressed, meaning —the meaning that must always resurface when a nonphilosopheme becomes a philosopheme—for along with its philosophic definition as the absence of own-being by the Śūnyavādins, *śūnya* means that which is unreal, vain, hollow, barren, desolate, empty (the very terms used to evoke saṃsāra). Emptiness comes to serve as a substitute for saṃsāra. The root cause of saṃsāra is said to be ignorance, which is the belief that things are not empty but full, brimming in their autonomy, their *svabhāva.* This ignorance is called a poison. Emptiness, which is offered as the panacea to the entire complex and hierarchy of ignorance and the defilements it engenders, and whose function is to annul saṃsāra, has in fact both that effect and its opposite: it displaces and multiplies saṃsāra, ensuring its presence. Because emptiness, the *dharmadhātu,* is immanent in saṃsāra, the end of saṃsāra can never be imminent.[108]

All of Tsong-kha-pa's major commentators reject his argument that saṃsāra is endless without, of course, mentioning the master by name. Before examining their rebuttals, we might consider what is at stake for the Mahāyāna exegete in the problem of the end of saṃsāra. This question is addressed by Tsong-kha-pa's disciple Rgyal-tshab, who poses the difficulties that attend both the assertion that all sentient beings will become buddhas and the assertion that they will not. He begins by pointing out how embarrassing it would be if saṃsāra did not end. The complete and perfect buddhas want to establish sentient beings in the position that they themselves have achieved, and they turn the wheel of doctrine by performing the twelve deeds of a buddha until saṃsāra is emptied. If all sentient beings were not to achieve buddhahood through those efforts, says Rgyal-tshab, the turning of the wheel of the dharma, the very teaching of Buddhism, would be fruitless. Even if sentient beings were to seek the mere pacification of the sufferings of saṃsāra (the goal of the Hīnayāna), the great compassion which is the defining characteristic of the Mahāyāna could not be fulfilled, and the Bhagavān himself would be guilty of the fault of secrecy and of the other four faults enumerated in the *Satyakaparivarttasūtra.*[109]

On the other hand, the attainment of the Hīnayāna goal might not be so bad: if all sentient beings were capable of putting an end to the sufferings of saṃsāra via the śrāvakayāna, Rgyal-tshab argues, they could easily become buddhas, because the existence of one final vehicle has been well established. To argue against this and say that there are some sentient beings who will never achieve even the liberation of the Hīnayāna is to contradict Āryavimuktisena's proof that the Buddha's statement that there are such doomed beings is not to be taken literally.[110]

Rgyal-tshab goes on to imagine the practical difficulties that would be entailed if saṃsāra were to come to an end. He points out that if all beings attained buddhahood, then the last bodhisattvas would have very few beings for whose welfare they could strive, thereby rendering their concern for others trifling and insignificant (implying that the quality of compassion is a function of the quantity of its objects). He thus worries that it would be impossible for the last bodhisattvas to amass the collection of merit *(puṇyasaṃbhāra, bsod nams kyi tshogs)* essential to the achievement of buddhahood.

Rgyal-tshab also contemplates that moment when all sentient beings have become buddhas, a time that he describes not with joyous expectation but with anxiety, for then there would not be a single sentient being for the buddhas to benefit. Rather than declaring that the purpose of Buddhism will have finally been fulfilled, he concludes that the welfare of others, the raison d'etre of the Mahāyāna, would be eliminated and that all buddhas would fall into the extreme of peace, the scorned goal of the Hīnayāna path.[111]

These kinds of concerns must strike us as strange. Did the Buddha not say that the dharma was a raft to be set aside when one has reached the other shore? Should not Rgyal-tshab see Buddhism (with its persistent medical rhetoric) as something akin to the modern medical researcher seeking a cure for AIDS, who works tirelessly for the day when his or her skills are no longer required? If Buddhism has an eschaton, is it not the moment of its obsolescence? Such questions are based on a conception of Buddhism promoted by its apologists, both ancient and modern, that Buddhism is above all "practical," such that all Buddhist doctrine is the articulation of the experience of the meditator, ideally of the ur-meditator, the Buddha himself. But we cannot understand the question of the end of saṃsāra in such terms: whether or not saṃsāra is endless should be of no concern to the practitioner. The issue has more to do with the agenda of Buddhist scholasticism.

In pointing out the problems entailed by the realization of the Mahāyāna's goal (i.e., the enlightenment of all sentient beings), Rgyal-tshab underscores the symbiotic relationship between the buddhas and sentient beings, a relation to which Śāntideva alludes at *Bodhicaryāvatāra* VI.113, where he says that the bodhisattva's enlightenment is indebted equally to the buddhas and to sentient beings—to the buddhas for teaching the dharma, and to sentient beings for serving as the field for cultivating the bodhisattva's harvest of merit. But beyond that, Rgyal-tshab seems to think that enlightenment makes sense only if there are the unenlightened—yet another example of how the two members of a hierarchy perform a mutually defining function: sentient beings are the Other that differentiates the category of the buddhas. What does it mean to be a buddha if there are no sentient beings? Rgyal-tshab's comments imply that there is Buddhism only as long as there is saṃsāra.

Rgyal-tshab thus rather tellingly points out that all positions on the question of the end of saṃsāra are somehow problematic, whether one holds that all sentient beings will become buddhas, that they will not become buddhas, that they will achieve liberation from rebirth, or that they will not achieve liberation from rebirth. His own answer is less interesting than the questions he raises. He offers a Mādhyamika elaboration of Dharmakīrti's argument outlined above. If the minds of sentient beings were not naturally pure, then one would have to assert that a truly established phenomenon existed among objects of knowledge. That is, the stains of the afflictions would be intrinsic to the mind, part of its very substance, its *svabhāva,* as the Mīmāṃsikas hold. However, if it can be proven with valid knowledge that the mind is naturally pure, then it can be shown that ignorance and its predispositions are adventitious.

It is obvious that here Rgyal-tshab understands purity to mean emptiness. To the extent that the attributes of all phenomena are merely conventional designations and, in that sense, accidental, the phenomena themselves are pure, in that their attributes, whether positive or negative, are not intrinsic to them. Rgyal-tshab goes on to say that if one concedes that the mind can be separated from the defilements but denies the possibility of creating an antidote in the mind that can destroy those defilements, then one must hold (1) that no method exists for destroying the defilements in the minds of sentient beings, (2) that the method exists but no one knows it, (3) that the method exists but it never occurs to anyone to seek it, (4) that although the desire to seek the method occurs, the person who knows the method is utterly lacking in mercy and does not teach it, or (5) that even though the method is taught and there are those who pursue it, they do not practice it sufficiently to bring about its effect.

Not surprisingly, Rgyal-tshab finds each of these options untenable. First, he argues that the method indeed exists: by cultivating the wisdom of selflessness, all defilements can be extinguished. Second, there is someone who knows this method because it is established by reasoning that the Teacher, out of concern for all sentient beings, fully cultivated the wisdom that understands selflessness. Third, it is not the case that no one seeks the method because, Rgyal-tshab says, there are no sentient beings who, when exhorted by the buddhas, do not seek high status (that is, a favorable rebirth). Even though they may temporarily not seek liberation from rebirth, they will soon become discouraged about saṃsāra and seek nirvāṇa, because all sentient beings are endowed with the buddha-nature, and because the Buddha's compassionate wish to establish all sentient beings in the state of buddhahood never wanes.

Here Rgyal-tshab introduces a factor of soteric destiny that seems closer to Jōdo Shinshū than to Dge-lugs-pa doctrine, attributing to the buddhas the extraordinary ability to cause all sentient beings to turn away from the concerns of this life in hopes of a better future state, as well as the further ability eventually to bring each of them to the path, aided by their genetic propensity, the buddha-nature. Thus, Rgyal-tshab argues, one need not be concerned that the Buddha will not teach the path to those who seek it, because when sentient beings seek enlightenment, they find that the Buddha's mercy for all sentient beings is like that of a mother for her only child. That mercy never wavers and the Buddha never stops teaching the dharma. Finally, it is not the case that those who set out on the path will not complete it, because Asaṅga argues in his commentary to the *Ratnagotravibhāga* that the buddha-lineage can be severed only temporarily and cannot be annihilated.

Rgyal-tshab attempts, then, to demonstrate that the position that all sentient beings will not become buddhas cannot withstand reasoned analysis, and that if one holds that there are no sentient beings for whom buddhahood cannot occur, then one must hold that it is certain that all sentient beings will become buddhas. He is willing to concede that there will be no sentient beings, that this, indeed, is the end which all buddhas seek. Rgyal-tshab concludes unequivocally that saṃsāra will end, eschewing the qualification that the specific saṃsāras of individual sentient beings will end but that saṃsāra in general is endless.[112] Yet it is not evident that he has shaken Tsong-kha-pa's contention that all this proves only that it is possible for all sentient beings to become buddhas, not that it is certain that they will do so.

'Jam-dbyangs-bzhad-pa also challenges Tsong-kha-pa, presenting essentially the same argument as Rgyal-tshab but adding two other points. He appropriates the seeds that Tsong-kha-pa used (to argue that the existence of a cause does not ensure the production of an effect) to comment on the statement in the *Śrīmālādevīsiṃhanāda* that saṃsāra has no beginning but has an end. The causal nexus that produces a seed is beginningless, but the chain of causation which produced the seed and which would produce a sprout from that seed is seen to end when the causes for its continuance are absent; just as the end of a seed is observed when it is destroyed by fire, says 'Jam-dbyangs-bzhad-pa, so saṃsāra is brought to an end by extinguishing karma and *kleśa*. But again, 'Jam-dbyangs-bzhad-pa's argument seems more pertinent to the enlightenment of individuals than to the end of saṃsāra, as the quotation he provides for support betrays. He cites Āryadeva's *Catuḥśataka*

(Four Hundred) VIII.25, "Just as the end of a seed is seen [but] its beginning is not, birth does not occur because its cause is not complete."[113]

'Jam-dbyangs-bzhad-pa also challenges Tsong-kha-pa's interpretation of the emptiness of the beginningless and the endless by examining two other emptinesses from the list of twenty, the third and the fifteenth. The third emptiness is that of both the internal and the external *(adhyātmabahirdhāśūnyatā)*. The internal refers to the sense faculties *(indriya)* and the external refers to the objects of the senses. That which is both internal and external is the physical bases of the senses (the eyes, ears, nose, tongue, and body)—internal to the extent that they are controlled by consciousness, and external to the extent that they are not the actual sense faculties (the subtle matter that is supported by the eyes, ears, nose, tongue, and body). These physical bases of the senses are empty, like all other phenomena; hence the emptiness of that which is both internal and external.[114]

The fifteenth emptiness is the emptiness of the unobservable *(anupalambhaśūnyatā)*, whose referents are the three times (past, present, and future), which are unobservable, or perhaps unidentifiable, in isolation but which can be defined only in terms of one another.[115] 'Jam-dbyangs-bzhad-pa challenges the degree to which these referents are to be accepted literally, noting that it is not the case that the physical bases of the senses are both internal and external, nor that the past, present, and future cannot be observed.[116] His point is that this same literalness is misapplied to the tenth emptiness (that of the beginningless and endless); even if saṃsāra is beginningless, it is not really endless. 'Jam-dbyangs-bzhad-pa's attempt to discredit Tsong-kha-pa's argument by forcing a shift to metaphor is a desperate one, and evades the more important philosophical question of the relation of emptiness to that which is empty.[117] It is an example of the kind of pedantry of which Dge-lugs-pa scholastics are so often accused.

It is interesting to note that although all of Tsong-kha-pa's commentators claim that saṃsāra will end, none takes up his point that such an end could only occur if there were a finite number of sentient beings. Indeed, Tsong-kha-pa's commentators, the conservators of Dge-lugs-pa scholasticism, seem intent on preserving the ultimate fulfillment of the bodhisattva's promise at all costs, as if the efficacy of the path rested on its facticity, while Tsong-kha-pa resists the appeal of scripture to which his commentators succumb and subjects each argument to the light of reason, finding them all lacking but finding none a reason for despair.

The vow of the bodhisattva is a paradigm rather than a promise, and it is as a paradigm that it derives its meaning, underlying the way in which the Buddhist, as both performer and beneficiary of the bodhisattva's deeds, makes sense of the world. But for the world to end, for saṃsāra to be emptied, would bring an all too predictable conclusion to the narrative of the Buddhist path, and would unemploy the myriad buddhas of the ten directions.

To learn that saṃsāra is endless is a case of *peripeteia* or peripety, a term that Aristotle uses in the *Poetics* to describe the reversal of an audience's expectations, an unexpected turn of events, a special shift in plot that all good tragedy must contain.[118] For Tsong-kha-pa to consider exhaustively all the views for and against an end to saṃsāra and conclude that the most compelling argument for its endlessness is to be found in its very antidote, in emptiness, not only confirms the need for the persistence of the Other—that there be that which is empty so that there can be emptiness—but is also a double case of peripety, "an unexpected yet logical shift in the events of the play."[119] This is so first because emptiness is the last vessel that we would expect to contain the reason for the endlessness of saṃsāra, and second because it provides an unexpected twist to our expectation about the bodhisattva path.

It is difficult to conceive of the question of the end of saṃsāra, of whether all sentient beings will eventually become buddhas, as a practical concern of the Buddhist. Even as a theoretical issue, the affirmation of the end of saṃsāra is little more than an expression of faith in the compassion of the buddhas and in the dedication of the bodhisattvas. But is it not better to conceive a path that takes a single being three periods of innumerable aeons to traverse not as normative but as narrative? It is as a narrative that Tsong-kha-pa's peripetic conclusion derives its power, playing on our confidence of the end so as to subvert it.[120] It is a subversion carried out with logic and illogic: with logic as Tsong-kha-pa resists the magnetic pull of the distant goal and its demand for fulfillment (if only in fantasy) and the push of the scholastic urge to control the end; with illogic as he allows emptiness to play out all its possibilities, even if this means affirming its Other.

It has been observed that apocalyptic thought belongs to rectilinear rather than cyclical views of the world.[121] Although it is a commonplace that the Buddhist view of time is cyclical, with cycles of the birth and death of individuals and cycles of evolution, devolution, and involution of universes, the graphic representation of the Buddhist path seems to be neither a straight line between two points nor a circle endlessly retracing itself but a cone, spiraling in smaller and smaller circles until it ends in a point—the *apratiṣṭhitanirvāṇa,* the nirvāṇa without location—and then continuing from that point, to line, to plane. But this model pertains only to individual sentient beings, as Tsong-kha-pa points out. We see in his analysis of the question of the end of saṃsāra a resistance to the compulsion toward origin and end time, toward genesis and apocalypse, confirming the observation of the modern critic that "there is a correlation between the sophistication and variety of our fictions and remoteness and doubtfulness about ends and origins."[122]

Afterword

The title of this chapter plays on that of Freud's 1937 paper, "Analysis Terminable and Interminable," in which the practical strategy of fixing a date for the termination of the Wolfman's analysis prompts reflections on the theoretical possibility of an end of analysis, of complete cure, that "by means of analysis it is possible to attain to complete psychical normality and to be sure that it will be maintained, the supposition being that all the patient's repressions have been lifted and every gap in his memory filled."[123] Freud identifies two sources of neuroses: excessively strong instincts, which are traced to the patient's archaic heritage, and trauma suffered at a time when the ego was insufficiently prepared to defend itself. Freud dismisses as optimistic the view that it is possible to resolve an instinctual conflict once and for all while also protecting against the chance of future conflict, concluding that if this goal be demanded of analysis, "we shall not shorten its duration whether as a means or an end."[124]

Of course, this is never an issue for the Buddhist scholastic, who sees the very function of the path as the destruction of the *kleśas* and the prevention of their recurrence. The enlightenment of the arhat is marked by this double knowledge *(kṣayajñāna* and *anutpādajñāna).* The fundamental claim of Buddhism is that it can bring suffering to an end; enlightenment is the termination of analysis. For Freud, the utter disappearance of instinctual demands is neither possible nor desirable. Despite these fundamental differences, the Buddhist view is what Freud would term "economic," to the extent that both the afflictions and their antidotes are invested with degrees of energy that are variously derived, but with the supposition, again contrary to Freud, that the greater power rests ultimately with the antidotal.

Hence, at the theoretical level of the Buddhist scholastic, there is no question that, for individual sentient beings, the path is terminable. But if we view all sentient beings as a whole—as the body sentient, a single analysand—the question is more complex. Those who would argue for an end of saṃsāra retain a particularistic perspective in which individual buddhas cause individual beings to create the specific antidotes for specific afflictions until, at the end, the defilements of all beings have been destroyed. The goal of Buddhism would be, then, to effect the total destruction of all *kleśas.* To hypothesize such a state is to master conceptually the transformative process by projecting into the unimaginable future a final moment of control, the goal of Buddhist scholasticism. As we have observed, at this point Buddhism would end. In Freudian terms we might view this Buddhism as a single organism, moving slowly but inexorably toward its own extinction but impeded, rather than aided, by the pleasure principle. For those who would argue for an end to saṃsāra, the causal model that pervades Buddhist doctrine extends into the realm of eschatology.

Tsong-kha-pa, as we have seen, disputes arguments for the end of saṃsāra not because he holds a dark view of the ubiquity of defilement but because, by recalling that there are limitless sentient beings, he introduces into the equation a factor of infinity. Beyond that, and perhaps more importantly, his observation of the consequence of the emptiness of the beginningless and the endless suggests that emptiness is not untainted by ambivalence. As much as one might like to discern an evolutionary movement from the "primitive" defilement/purification model to the "philosophical" ignorance/insight model, the language of impurity, separation, and abandonment remains resiliently persistent both in spite of and because of emptiness. It is due to this inherent ambivalence, in turn, that analysis, saṃsāra, and the path can not end; unlike Aristotle's peripety, Tsong-kha-pa's conclusion carries with it not closure but continuation. The very idea of a path bears the notion of arriving late. Tsong-kha-pa's reading of emptiness constantly defers that arrival, intimating, perhaps, that the end of the path is death.

Notes

1. Adapted from Sydney H. Mellone, "Scholasticism," in James Hastings, ed., *Encyclopedia of Religion and Ethics* (Edinburgh: T. and T. Clark, 1908–1926), 11:240. For extensive studies of Christian scholasticism, see Martin Grabmann, *Die Geschichte der scholastischen Methode,* 2 vols. (Berlin: Akademie-Verlag, 1956); C. Spicq, *Esquisse d'une histoire de l'exégèse latine au Moyen-Age* (Paris: J. Vrin, 1944); Henri de Lubac, *Exégèse Médiévale: Les quatres sens de l'écriture,* 4 vols. (Paris: Aubier, 1959–1964); and Jean Leclerq, *The Love of Learning and the Desire for God* (New York: 1961).

2. Étienne Lamotte, *History of Indian Buddhism,* trans. Sara Webb-Boin (Louvain: Peeters, 1988), 620.

3. This Derridean reading of the path is drawn from Richard Harland, *Superstructuralism* (London: Methuen, 1987), 148.

4. The Sanskrit is: *yā sārvajñatayā nayatyupaśamaṃ śāntaiṣiṇaḥ śrāvakān/ yā mārgajñatayā jagaddhitakṛtāṃ lokārthasaṃpādikā/ sarvākārāmidaṃ vadanti munayo viśvaṃ yayā saṃgatam/ tasyai śrāvakabodhisattvagaṇino buddhasya matre namaḥ//* See Th. Stcherbatsky and E. Obermiller, eds., *Abhisamayālankāra-prajñāpāramitā-upadeśa-śāstra,* Bibliotheca Buddhica XXIII (Osnabruck: Biblio Verlag, 1970), 1.

5. The other four texts are Candrakīrti's *Madhyamakāvatāra,* Dharmakīrti's *Pramāṇavārttika,* Vasubandhu's *Abhidharmakośa,* and Guṇaprabha's *Vinayasūtra.*

6. For a list of the twenty-one commentaries to the *Abhisamayālaṃkāra,* see E. Obermiller, "The Doctrine of Prajñāpāramitā as Exposed in the *Abhisamayālaṃkāra* of Maitreya," *Acta Orientalia,* vol. XI, 1-2 (1932): 9–12.

7. *P* 5192. Sanskrit edition by Unrai Wogihara, *Abhisamayālaṃkārālokā Prajñāpāramitāvyākhyā,* (Tokyo: Toyo bunko, 1973).

8. *P* 5191. Tibetan and reconstructed Sanskrit edition by R. S. Tripathi, *Abhisamayālaṃkāravṛtti-Sphuṭārtha,* Biblioteca Indo-Tibetica 2 (Varanasi: 1977).

9. In this chapter, I have used a reproduction of the 1897 Lhasa edition of Tsong-kha-pa's text. The full title of the work commonly referred to as *Legs bshad gser phreng* is *Shes rab kyi pha rol tu phyin pa'i man ngag gi bstan bcos mngon par rtogs pa'i rgyan 'grel pa dang bcas pa'i rgya cher bshad pa i legs bshad gser phreng.* It occurs in the thirteenth volume *(tsa)* of the Lhasa edition of his collected works. See *The Collected Works (gsuṅ 'bum) of the Incomparable Lord Tsoṅ-kha-pa bLo-bzaṅ-grags-pa (Khams gsum chos kyis* [sic] *rgyal po shar tsong kha pa chen po'i gsung 'bum)* (New Delhi: Mongolian Lama Guru Deva, 1978; hereafter *Tsong-kha-pa*). The five commentaries are: (1) *Mngon rtogs pa'i rgyan gyi tsa ba 'grel pa dang bcas pa'i rnam bshad snying po'i rgyan,* commonly referred to as *Rnam bshad snying po'i rgyan,* by Rgyal-tshab-dar-ma-rin-chen (1364–1432), blockprint in possession of the author, no date or place of publication provided; this work is traditionally considered to represent Tsong-kha-pa's mature positions on the topics of the *Abhisamayālaṃkāra,* and is referred to hereafter as *Rgyal-tshab;* (2) *'Grel pa don gsal gyi rnam bshad rtogs dka'i snang ba,* by Mkhas-grub Dge-legs-dpal-bzang-po (1385–1438), in *The Collected Works (gsuṅ 'bum) of the Lord Mkhas grub rje dge legs dpal bzaṅ po,* vol. 1 *(ka)* (New Delhi: Mongolian Lama Guru Deva, 1980), 731ff., referred to hereafter as *Mkhas-grub;* (3) *Shes rab kyi pha rol tu phyin pa'i man ngag gi bstan bcos mngon par rtogs pa'i rgyan 'grel pa dang bcas pa'i rnam bshad snying po rgyan gyi don legs par bshad pa yum don gsal ba'i sgron me,* commonly referred to as *Phar phyin spyi don,* by Pan-chen Bsod-nams-grags-pa (1478–1554), (Buxadour, India: Nang bstan shes rig 'dzin skyong slob gnyer khang, 1963; hereafter *Panchen*); (4) *Bstan bcos mngon par rtogs pa'i rgyan 'grel pa dang bcas pa'i rnam bshad rnam pa gnyis kyi dka' ba'i gnas gsal bar byed pa legs bshad skal bzang klu dpang gi rol mtsho zhes bya ba skabs gnyis pa'i spyi don,* by Rje-btsun Chos-kyi-rgyal-mtshan (1469–1546), (Bylakuppe, India: Serjey Dratsang, no date; hereafter *Rje-btsun-pa*); and (5) *Shes rab kyi pha rol tu phyin pa'i mtha' dpyod nor bu'i 'phreng mdzes mkhas pa'i mkul rgyan las skabs gnyis pa,* better known as *Skabs gnyis pa'i mtha' dpyod,* by 'Jam-dbyangs-bzhad-pa (1648–1721), (Sarnath, India: Mongolian Lama Guru Deva, 1965; hereafter *'Jam-dbyangs-bzhad-pa*).

10. 'Jam-dbyangs-bzhad-pa, *Dngos po brgyad don bdun cu'i rnam bzhag legs par bshad pa mi pham bla ma'i zhal lung,* in *The Collected Works of 'Jam-dbyaṅs-bzad pa'i rdo-rje* (New Delhi: Ngawang Gelek Demo, 1972), 116.2–3.

11. *Abhisamayālaṃkāra* II.2 states, "Regarding the mode of the knowledge of the path, one should understand the śrāvaka path via the aspect of the four noble truths without apprehending [those truths to be real]." The Sanskrit is: *caturṇāmāryasatyānāmākārānupalambhataḥ/ śrāvakāṇāmayaṃ mārgo jñeyo mārgajñatānaye//* See Stcherbatsky and Obermiller, eds., *Abhisamayālankāra,* 11.

12. For a Dge-lugs-pa exposition of the doctrines of this "school," see Donald S. Lopez, Jr., *A Study of Svātantrika* (Ithaca, New York: Snow Lion, 1987).

13. Dkon-mchog-'jigs-med-dbang-po, *Sa lam gyi rnam bzhag theg gsum mdzes rgyan,* in *The Collected Works of dkon-mchog-'jigs-med-dbang-po* (New Delhi: Ngawang Gelek Demo, 1972), 434.1–2.

14. This description follows Vasubandhu's commentary on *Abhidharmakośa* VI.26–28. See P. Pradhan, ed., *Abhidharmakośabhāṣya of Vasubandhu* (Patna: Jayaswal Research Institute, 1975), 350–353.

15. See Dkon-mchog-jigs-med-dbang-po, *Sa lam,* 434.2–435.1.

16. Ibid., 435.4–5.

17. Ibid., 437.4–439.2.

18. The Sanskrit is: *grāhyārthakalpanāhānād grāhakasyāprahāṇataḥ/ ādhāratāśca vijñeyaḥ khaḍgamārgasya saṃgrahaḥ//* See Stcherbatsky and Obermiller, eds., *Abhisamayālankāra,* p. 12.

19. Dkon-mchog-'jigs-med-dbang-po, *Sa lam,* 442.2–3.

20. Ibid., 457.2–4.

21. In the desire realm, there are ten afflictions for each of the four truths to be abandoned on the path of vision. These are the six root afflictions *(rtsa nyon, mūlakleśa),* the sixth of which, (wrong) view *(lta ba, dṛṣṭi),* has five varieties. The first five root afflictions are desire, anger, pride, ignorance, and doubt. The five varieties of wrong view are the view of the transitory collection *('jig tshogs la lta ba, satkāyadṛṣṭi),* extreme view *(mthar 'dzin pa'i lta ba, antagrāhadṛṣṭi),* holding a (wrong) view to be supreme *(lta ba mchog 'dzin, dṛṣṭiparāmarśa),* holding (wrong) ethics and conduct to be supreme *(tshul khrims dang brtul zhugs mchog 'dzin, śīlavrataparāmarśa),* and false view *(log lta, mithyādṛṣṭi).* Each of these ten afflictions occurs in the desire realm in connection with each of the four truths, resulting in forty artificial afflictive obstructions for the desire realm.

Anger *(khong khro, pratigha)* does not occur in the form and formless realms. Hence there are nine afflictions for each of the four truths in the two upper realms, or thirty-six afflictions for each. The 112 afflictive obstructions abandoned on the path of vision are the total of forty afflictions of the desire realm, thirty-six of the form realm, and thirty-six of the formless realm.

The number of 108 artificial obstructions to omniscience abandoned on the path of vision is arrived at by multiplying nine gradations of four forms of the conception of true existence *(bden 'dzin)* times the three realms. The four forms of the conception of true existence are the conception that things which bodhisattvas should pursue truly exist *('jug gzung rtog),* the conception that things which bodhisattvas should turn away from truly exist *(ldog gzung rtog),* the conception that the mind which conceives of the person to be substantially existent truly exists *(rdzas 'dzin rtog),* and the conception that the mind which conceives of the person to be imputedly existent truly exists *(btags 'dzin rtog).* Each of these has nine levels of strength, following the standard formula of the small of the small, intermediate of the small, through the great of the great, all thirty-six of which occur for each of the three realms, resulting in 108 artificial obstructions to omniscience to be abandoned on the path of vision.

It will be recalled that there are sixteen innate afflictive obstructions to be abandoned on the path of meditation. The first six, associated with the desire realm, are the root afflictions of desire, anger, pride, and ignorance, plus two forms of wrong view: the view of the transitory collection and extreme views. This seems to imply that doubt and the other forms of wrong view—that is, false view and the holding of wrong views and wrong systems of ethics to be supreme—are fully abandoned on the path of vision. Again, because anger is absent in the upper realms, there are five innate afflictions associated with the form and formless realms, resulting in sixteen innate afflictive obstructions abandoned by the bodhisattva over the course of the ten *bhūmis.*

Finally, there are 108 obstructions to omniscience abandoned on the path of meditation. These are the innate forms of the 108 artificial obstructions to omniscience that were abandoned on the path of vision. See Dkon-mchog-'jigs-med-dbang-po, *Sa lam,* 457.2–458.4. The ability to compute all this prior to the invention of the electronic calculator is itself testimony to the Mahāyāna claim that bodhisattvas have sharper intellects than the adherents of the Hīnayāna.

22. In works like the *Lotus Sūtra,* the control of enlightenment rests not with

the scholastics but with the Buddha himself. The person of the Buddha is exalted to cosmic proportions in the sixteenth chapter of the *Lotus,* with the implied consequence that a path that he began in the inconceivable past can be equaled by others only in the inconceivable future, at a time known only to the Buddha, as evidenced by his prophecy *(vyākaraṇa).* The early Mahāyāna is thereby able to preserve the unique authority of the savior of the Saha world.

23. Blunt uses the term "voluntarist explanation" in his discussion of various theories that seek to account for the origin of the caste system in India. See E. A. H. Blunt, *The Caste System of Northern India with Special Reference to the United Provinces of Agra and Oudh* (London: Oxford University Press, 1931), 11–12.

24. See, for example, *Saṃyuttanikāya* I.39 and *Majjhimanikāya* I.183. For a useful study of the Buddha's attitude toward caste, correcting the misconception that he was an unequivocal opponent of the caste system, see Y. Krishnan, "Buddhism and the Caste System," *Journal of the International Association of Buddhist Studies,* 9, no. 1 (1986): 71–83.

25. Louis Dumont, *Homo Hierarchicus: An Essay on the Caste System* (Chicago: The University of Chicago Press, 1970), 47.

26. Ibid., p. 61.

27. The Sanskrit is: *prabhāsvaramidaṃ cittaṃ prakṛtyāgantavo malāḥ.* See Swami Dwarikadas Shastri, ed., *Pramāṇavārttika of Acharya Dharmakīrti* (Varanasi: Bauddha Bharati, 1984), 73. I am following Shastri's ordering of the chapters here as follows: *pramāṇasiddhi* (chap. 1), *pratyakṣa* (chap. 2), *svārthānumāna* (chap. 3), *parārthānumāna* (chap. 4). The standard Tibetan ordering is 3-1-2-4. Dharmakīrti's statement that the defilements are adventitious *(āgantu)* stands in contrast to the Sarvāstivādin view of the defilements as having *svabhāva.* Dharmakīrti's view of the defilements as accidental to the mind has its antecedent at *Anguttaranikāya* I.5–11. For a masterful study of the theme of the luminosity of the mind, see David Seyfort Ruegg, *La théorie du Tathāgatagarbha et du Gotra,* Publications de l'École Française d'Extrême-Orient (Paris, 1969), 411–454.

28. Dumont, *Homo Hierarchicus,* pp. 59–60.

29. Mary Douglas, *Implicit Meanings* (London: Routledge and Kegan Paul, 1975), 51.

30. Both quotations in this passage are from Mary Douglas, *Purity and Danger: An Analysis of Concepts of Pollution and Taboo* (New York: Praeger, 1966), 160–161.

31. Dumont, *Homo Hierarchicus,* p. 49.

32. Douglas, *Purity and Danger,* p. 86.

33. Paul Ricoeur, *The Symbolism of Evil* (Boston: Beacon, 1969), 27.

34. Ibid., p. 32.

35. *Abhisamayālaṃkāra* II.1. The Sanskrit is: *syāmīkaraṇatā bhābhirdevānāṃ yogyatāṃ prati/ viṣayo niyato vyāptiḥ svabhāvastasya karma ca//* See Stcherbatsky and Obermiller, eds., *Abhisamayālankāra,* p. 11.

36. See Wogihara, ed., *Abhisamayālaṃkārālokā,* pp. 129–130.

37. Ibid., pp. 131–133. For an analysis of the interpretation of this passage by Haribhadra and others, see Ruegg, *La théorie,* pp. 191–205.

38. In his essay entitled "The Discourse on Language," Michel Foucault speaks of a class of discourse that seems to comprise the Buddhist category of the sūtra, "those forms of discourse that lie at the origins of a certain number of new verbal acts, which are reiterated, transformed or discussed; in short, discourse which *is spoken* and remains spoken, indefinitely, beyond its formulation, and which remains to be spoken." See his *The Archaeology of Knowledge and the Discourse on Language* (New York: Pantheon Books, 1972), 220.

39. Ibid., p. 221.

40. Both passages are cited in *Tsong-kha-pa* at 313a1-3. For an English translation of the prophecy concerning Śāriputra, see Leon Hurvitz, *Scripture of the Lotus Blossom of the Fine Dharma* (New York: Columbia University Press, 1976), 53-56.

41. Cited in *Rje-btsun-pa,* 8b1.

42. Cited in *Tsong-kha-pa,* 313a5-6. The passage occurs in the seventh chapter of the sūtra. See Étienne Lamotte, ed. and trans., *Saṃdhinirmocana Sūtra: L'Explication des Mystères* (Paris: Adrien Maisonneuve, 1935), 74.

43. Cited in *Tsong-kha-pa,* 313a6-b1. See Lamotte, ed., *Saṃdhinirmocana Sūtra,* p. 74.

44. For a useful study of Dge-lugs-pa views on the various nirvanas, see Eugene Obermiller, *Nirvāṇa in Tibetan Buddhism* (Delhi: Classics India Publications, 1988).

45. *Tsong-kha-pa,* 313b3-5.

46. *Rje-btsun-pa,* 9a1.

47. *Tsong-kha-pa,* 313b6-314a1.

48. *Pan-chen,* 187a2-4.

49. *Tsong-kha-pa,* 314b2-3.

50. The verse and autocommentary occur in Louis de La Vallée Poussin, ed., *Madhyamakāvatāra par Candrakīrti,* Bibliotheca Buddhica IX (Osnabruck: Biblio Verlag, 1970), 402. The passage is cited in *Rje-btsun-pa* at 12b6-7. The last two lines as cited by Rje-btsun-pa differ from La Vallée Poussin's edition. Rje-btsun-pa's version reads: *khyod kyi theg pa 'di ni slob ma nye bar zhi ba'i tshul las yid/ sbyar zhing rnam par dben pa'ang blos sbyangs rnams la logs su gsungs//*

51. Cited in *Tsong-kha-pa,* 315a1-2.

52. Tsong-kha-pa, citing Asaṅga, describes the predispositions of ignorance *(ma rig pa'i bag chags kyi sa, āvidyāvāsanābhūmi)* as the subtle assumption of negative contaminated states which can be abandoned solely by a tathāgata. Like the scent of musk that remains in a vessel after the musk itself has been removed, these are instincts that persist even though the primary and secondary afflictions have been abandoned. See *Tsong-kha-pa,* 321b2-4. On the uncontaminated ignorance, see Padmanabh Jaini's chapter in this volume.

53. *Tsong-kha-pa,* 315a4-b4.

54. The Sanskrit is: *dharma nairātmyamuktīnaṃ tulyatvāt gotrabhedataḥ/ dravyāśayāpteśca nirmāṇātparyantādekayānatā//* See S. Bagchi, ed., *Mahāyāna-Sūtrālaṃkāra of Asaṅga,* Buddhist Sanskrit Texts, 13 (Darbhanga, India: The Mithila Institute, 1970), 68. The passage is cited in *Tsong-kha-pa* at 315b6.

55. The clearest and most complete commentary on this stanza is that of Sthiramati, which is drawn on in what follows. Vasubandhu's commentary is available in Sanskrit in S. Bagchi, ed., *Mahāyāna-Sūtrālaṃkāra;* his commentary on this stanza occurs on p. 68. Asvabhāva's commentary on the stanza is preserved in Tibetan in *P* 5530, vol. 108, 162.1.1-162.3.3. Sthiramati's commentary is preserved in Tibetan in *P* 5531, vol. 108, 287.1.6-288.3.1. See also Ruegg, *La théorie,* pp. 185-187.

56. *P* 5531, vol. 108, 287.2.4-8. 'Jam-dbyangs-bzhad-pa, at variance with the three Indian commentators, interprets the term "selflessness" to mean that all who achieve enlightenment are the same in that they understand selflessness. He makes this point in *'Jam-dbyangs-bzhad-pa,* 15.8.

57. *P* 5531, vol. 108, 287.5.7-288.1.3. There are also cases of śrāvakas creating such doubles; Pan-chen Bsod-nams-grags-pa suggests that Śāriputra himself did so. See *Pan-chen,* 187b3.

58. *P* 5531, vol. 108, 288.1.3-7.

59. See Stanley Jeyaraja Tambiah, *Culture, Thought, and Social Action* (Cambridge, Mass.: Harvard University Press, 1985), 36.

60. On this topic, see D. Seyfort Ruegg, "Purport, Implicature and Presupposition: Sanskrit *abhiprāya* and Tibetan *dgoṅs pa/dgoṅ gźi* as Hermeneutical Concepts," *Journal of Indian Philosophy* 13 (1985): 309–325; idem, "An Indian Source for the Tibetan Hermeneutical Term *dgoṅs gźi* 'Intentional Ground,' " *Journal of Indian Philosophy* 16 (1988): 1–4; and idem, "Allusiveness and Obliqueness in Buddhist Texts: *Saṃdhā, Saṃdhi, Saṃdhyā* and *Abhisaṃdhi,*" in Colette Caillat, ed., *Dialectes dans les Littératures Indo-Aryennes,* Publications de L'Institut de Civilisation Indienne, 55 (Paris: Edition-Diffusion de Boccard, 1989), 295–327. See also Michael Broido, "Abhiprāya and Intention in Tibetan Linguistics," *Journal of Indian Philosophy* 12 (1984): 1–33, and Donald S. Lopez, Jr., ed., *Buddhist Hermeneutics* (Honolulu: University of Hawaii Press, 1988), 55–56.

61. *Mahāyānasūtrālaṃkāra* 11.54. The Sanskrit is: *ākarṣaṇārthamekeṣāmanyasandhāraṇāya ca/ deśitāniyatānāṃ hi sambuddhairekayānatā//* See S. Bagchi, ed., *Mahāyāna-Sūtrālaṃkāra,* p. 69.

62. *P* 5531, vol. 108, 288.2.3–288.3.1.

63. See Wogihara, ed., *Abhisamayālaṃkārālokā,* p. 134.

64. Cited in *Tsong-kha-pa,* 316b4–6. For the Sanskrit and various Tibetan translations, see Ruegg, *La théorie,* p. 181, and n. 4 on that page.

65. The twenty-first stanza of the *Niraupamyastava* states: "Because the *dharmadhātu* is undifferentiated, the vehicles are without differentiation, Mighty One. You set forth the three vehicles in order that sentient beings would enter it." The Sanskrit is: *dharmadhātorsambhedādyānabhedo 'sti na prabho/ yānatritayamākhyātaṃ tvayā sattvāvatārataḥ//* For Sanskrit and Tibetan editions of the text, see Giuseppe Tucci, "Two Hymns of the Catuḥ-stava of Nāgārjuna," *Journal of the Royal Asiatic Society* (1932): 308–325; this passage appears on p. 320. Tucci edited Amṛtākara's *Catuḥstavasamāsārtha,* but the section on the *Niraupamyastava* does not appear to include a commentary on this passage. See idem, *Minor Buddhist Texts: Parts I and II* (Delhi: Motilal Banarsidass, 1986), 235–246. Tsong-kha-pa cites *Niraupamyastava* 21 in *Tsong-kha-pa,* 317a2.

66. For a discussion of the positions of Bhāvaviveka, Candrakīrti, and Nāgārjuna on the question of whether knowledge of emptiness is necessary for liberation from rebirth, see Donald S. Lopez, Jr., "Do Śrāvakas Understand Emptiness?" *Journal of Indian Philosophy* 16 (1988): 65–105.

67. Tsong-kha-pa makes this point in *Tsong-kha-pa,* 317a3. However, this interpretation would seem to entail the consequence that emptiness *(tathatā)* is not set forth in the śrāvakayāna, a position that Tsong-kha-pa argues elsewhere that Nāgārjuna and Candrakīrti reject. See Lopez, "Do Śrāvakas Understand Emptiness?"

68. Cited in *Tsong-kha-pa,* 317a1. The closest *śloka* in the *Bodhicittavivaraṇa* to the passage cited by Tsong-kha-pa is 94, which says something quite different. It reads: *srid pa'i lam la skyo rnams la/ ngal so'i don du theg pa che/ 'byung ba'i ye she gnyis po yang/ gsungs pa yin te don dam min//* Lindtner's translation is: "Though it has been said, in order to comfort those who are disgusted with the way of life, that there are two [kinds] of knowledge *(jñāna)* arising [from] the Mahāyāna, [this, however] is not the ultimate meaning *(paramārtha).*" See Christian Lindtner, *Nagarjuniana* (Copenhagen: Akademisk Forlag, 1982), 210–211. Tsong-kha-pa's version reads: *theg pa gnyis po dag kyang ni/ theg pa chen por 'byung pas na/ srid pa'i lam gyis dub rnams la/ ngal bso'i don de de nyid min//* This might be translated as: "Although there are two vehicles, they arise from the Mahāyāna. Therefore, the purpose is to comfort those wearied by the mundane path; [they] are not real."

69. *Tsong-kha-pa,* 317b2.

70. Cited in *Pan-chen,* 189a5.

71. *Tsong-kha-pa,* 317b5. Vasubandhu says at *Abhidharmakośa* VI.67: "The knowledges of extinguishment and non-production are enlightenment" *(anutpādakṣayajñāne bodhiḥ).* See Pradhan, ed., *Abhidharmakośabhāṣyam,* p. 382.

72. Cited in *Pan-chen,* 188a5.

73. Cited in *Rgyal-tshab,* 146b2–4. According to an oral communication from Lozang Jamspal, this sūtra is also known as the *Bodhisattvagocaropāyaviṣayavikūvaninirdeśa.*

74. Tsong-kha-pa cites the *Laṅkāvatārasūtra* on this point: "Having attained a body of samādhi, they do not awaken for aeons. For example, a drunken person becomes sober if there is no wine. So they will attain my body, the knowledge of the *buddhadharma.*" The Tibetan, as it appears in *Tsong-kha-pa,* 318b2–3, reads: *ting nge 'dzin gyi lus thob nas/ bskal pa'i bar du mi sad do// dper na skyes bu myos pa ni/ myos 'gyur med na sangs pa ldar// de bzhin de dag nga yi sku/ sangs rgyas chos shes bya ba 'thob//* The last four lines differ markedly from the Peking edition's translation of the final stanza of the second chapter of the *Laṅkāvatāra,* which reads (at *P* 775, vol. 29 50.3.2): *ji ldar skyes bu ra ro ba/ chang dang bral nas sangs 'gyur bzhin/ de na de dag nga yi yang/ chos kyi sku ni thob par 'gyur//* A description of the arhats and their being roused from samādhi by the buddhas appears in the *Bodhicittavivaraṇa* (vv. 95–96), a work traditionally ascribed to Nāgārjuna. For an edition of the Tibetan and an English translation, see Lindtner, *Nagarjuniana,* pp. 212–213. This rehabilitation of the arhat recalls the harrowing of hell described in I Peter 3.19 and Dante's description in Canto IV.31–61 of the first circle of hell, wherein abide those who did not sin but who never were baptised, as well as those who, Virgil says (IV.37–39):

> Or, living before Christendom, their knees
> Paid not aright those tributes that belong
> To God; and I myself am one of these.

Christ descends into the first circle to save the patriarchs of the Old Testament (Adam, Abel, Noah, Moses, David, Abraham), leaving the pagan poets and philosophers to live forever without suffering, but also without hope.

75. Cited by Haribhadra at Wogihara, ed., *Abhisamayālaṃkārālokā,* p. 134, and in *Tsong-kha-pa* at 318a2–3. The Sanskrit is: *labdhvā bodhidvayam hy ete bhavād uttrastamānasāḥ/ bhavanty āyuḥkṣayāt tuṣṭāḥ prāptanirvāṇasaṃjñinaḥ// na teṣām asti nirvāṇaṃ kiṃ tu janma bhavatraye/ dhātau na vidyate teṣāṃ te'pi tiṣṭhanty anāsrave// akliṣṭajñānahānāya paścād buddhaiḥ prabodhitāḥ/ saṃbhṛtya bodhisaṃbhārāṃs te'pi syur lokanāyakāḥ//* For a critical edition and annotated translation of the *Triśaraṇasaptati,* see Per K. Sorenson, *Candrakīrti Triśaraṇasaptati: The Septuagint on the Three Refuges* (Wien: Arbeitskreis für Tibetische und Buddhistische Studien, Universität Vien, 1986), 42–44. (Tsong-kha-pa's version differs slightly from the edition prepared by Sorenson.) A similar statement appears in the *Ratnagotravibhāga* (II.58), which Tsong-kha-pa cites: "Those who abide in the path to peace think that they have attained nirvāṇa. Through being taught the reality of the doctrine, such as the *Saddharmapuṇḍarīka,* they are turned away from the conception of self and, embracing method and wisdom, come to fruition in the supreme vehicle" (*Tsong-kha-pa,* 314b6–315a1).

76. Rgyal-tshab's discussion of the Buddha's purpose in teaching three final vehicles occurs in *Rgyal-tshab,* 147a3–6. For a discussion of the Dge-lugs-pa ranking of the Indian Buddhist schools, see Lopez, *A Study of Svātantrika,* pp. 153–159.

77. *Tsong-kha-pa,* 318a5–6. Kamalaśīla discusses the *yāna* controversy and argues for one final vehicle in his *Madhyamakālokā* (Illumination of the Middle Way). For further insight on the *ekayāna* question, consult Ruegg, *La théorie,* pp. 177–235; idem, "The *gotra, ekayāna,* and *tathāgatagarbha* theories of the Prajñāpāramitā according to Dharmamitra and Abhayākaragupta"; and Arnold Kunst, "Some Aspects of the *Ekayāna,*" the latter two found in Lewis Lancaster and Luis O. Gómez, ed., *Prajñāpāramitā and Related Systems* (Berkeley, Calif.: Berkeley Buddhist Studies Series, 1977), 283–326.

78. See Peter Stallybrass and Allon White, *The Politics and Poetics of Desire* (Ithaca, N.Y.: Cornell University Press, 1986), 191.

79. Ibid., p. 193.

80. See *Tsong-kha-pa,* 318a6–b1.

81. Cited in *'Jam-dbyangs-bzhad-pa,* 27.

82. This point is made in *Pan-chen,* 193a2–4.

83. See *'Jam-dbyangs-bzhad-pa,* 25.

84. Ibid., 26.

85. *Majjhimanikāya* I.483. Translated by Henry Clark Warren in *Buddhism in Translations* (New York: Atheneum, 1969), 123.

86. *Majjhimanikāya,* I.485–486; Warren, trans., *Buddhism,* p. 124.

87. The question in the Pāli canon is about the end of the world *(loka),* whereas Tsong-kha-pa takes up the question of the end of saṃsāra. Although it may not be appropriate to equate these two terms, Tsong-kha-pa appears to do so when he says (in *Tsong-kha-pa,* 319a5–6) that when the Buddha was asked whether saṃsāra will end, he did not answer. Tsong-kha-pa may be drawing on Vasubandhu's glosses of the *avyākṛta* in the ninth chapter of the *Abhidharmakośabhāṣya,* where he provides saṃsāra as a possible reading of *loka* in the context of the Buddha's refusal to respond to the four questions about the eternity of the world. See Pradhan, ed., *Abhidharmakośabhāṣyam,* pp. 470–471.

88. The argument concerning the relationship between an entity and its opposite seems to be drawn from *Pramāṇavārttika* III.121. See Shastri, ed., *Pramāṇavārttika,* p. 325; *Tsong-kha-pa,* 319b1–2; and Ruegg, *La théorie,* p. 215.

89. A "nature reason" *(svabhāvahetu)* is one in which the sign *(liṅga)* and the predicate of the probandum *(sādhyadharma)* are of the same nature. In the statement, "The subject, sound, is impermanent because of being produced," the reason, "being produced," is a correct nature sign because being produced and being impermanent are of the same nature. It is not immediately evident why the argument here is identified as a nature sign unless Haribhadra is simply indicating the relation endemic to a thing and its opposite, such that as one increases the other naturally and concomitantly decreases. On nature signs, see Ernst Steinkellner, "On the Interpretation of the Svabhāvahetuḥ," *Wiener Zeitschrift für die Kunde Südasiens* 18 (1974): 117–129.

90. Cited in *Tsong-kha-pa,* 318b5–319a2. For the Sanskrit, see Wogihara, ed., *Abhisamayālaṃkārālokā,* p. 575.

91. This model of saṃsāra evokes the event described at the end of the first chapter of the *Vimalakīrtinirdeśa,* in which the Tathāgata touches the ground with his toe, transforming the world into a jeweled realm that resembles Anantaguṇaratnavyūha. He then explains to Śāriputra that the buddhafield is always pure, but that the Tathāgata causes it to appear to be contaminated in order to bring inferior beings to spiritual maturity.

92. Cited in *Tsong-kha-pa,* 319a4.

93. See Shastri, ed. *Pramāṇavārttika,* pp. 53–54.

94. Paraphrase provided in *'Jam-dbyangs-bzhad-pa,* 18–19. The reference for

Dharmakīrti's argument occurs in the previous note. For the views of Bu-ston and Nya-dbon Kun-dga'-dpal on the question of the end of saṃsāra, see Ruegg, *La théorie,* pp. 207–213.

95. *Tsong-kha-pa,* 319b2–5.

96. See, for example, Mkhas-grub's statement in his *Rgyud sde spyi'i rnam.* For an edition and translation, see Ferdinand Lessing and Alex Wayman, *Introduction to the Buddhist Tantric Systems* (Delhi: Motilal Banarsidass, 1978), 20–22.

97. This position is put forth and rejected in the *Mahāvastu.* See J. J. Jones, trans., *The Mahāvastu,* vol. 1 (London: Pali Text Society, 1973), 99.

98. The Sanskrit is: *na ca yantra kṣīyati avidya na cāsya vṛddhiḥ.* See Akira Yuyama, *Prajñā-pāramitā-ratna-guṇa-saṃcaya-gāthā* (London: Cambridge University Press, 1976), 110. Yuyama's edition of the Tibetan (*'khrul 'khor zad pa med cing ma rig 'phel ba med,* p. 185) differs from Tsong-kha-pa's citation and is closer to the Sanskrit, which seems to say, "The mechanism is not extinguished and ignorance does not increase."

99. *Tsong-kha-pa,* 319b5–320a3.

100. Ibid., 319a4–5.

101. See T. R. V. Murti, *The Central Philosophy of Buddhism* (London: Allen and Unwin, 1955), 36–54.

102. See Pradhan, ed., *Abhidharmakośabhāṣyam,* pp. 470–471.

103. Nāgārjuna, *Ratnāvalī,* in P. L. Vaidya, ed., *Madhyamakaśāstra of Nāgārjuna,* Buddhist Sanskrit Texts, 10 (Darbhanga, India: Mithila Institute, 1960), appendix 6, 301-302.

104. The Sanskrit is: *na ca kevalaṃ saṃsārasya nirvāṇenāvisiṣṭatvāt pūrvāparakoṭikalpanā na saṃbhavati//* See Vaidya, ed., *Madhyamakaśāstra,* p. 235.

105. *mtha' med kyi grub mtha' skyong bde bar bzhad pa ltar khas blang//* See *Tsong-kha-pa,* 319a6.

106. For Haribhadra's exposition of the twenty emptinesses, see Wogihara, ed., *Abhisamayālaṃkārālokā,* pp. 95–96, and E. Obermiller, *Analysis of the Abhisamayālaṃkāra* (London: Luzac and Co., 1933), 126–141. See also *Tsong-kha-pa,* 255b3–266a2. For a translation of the *Aṣṭadaśasāhasrikāprajñāpāramitā* on the twenty emptinesses, see Edward Conze, trans., *The Large Sūtra on Perfect Wisdom* (Berkeley: University of California Press, 1975), 144–148. On the sixteen emptinesses, see R. Pandeya, ed., *Madhyānta-Vibhāga-Śāstra* (Delhi: Motilal Banarsidass, 1971), 41, and G. Tucci, "Minor Sanskrit Texts on the Prajñāpāramitā: I. The Prajñāpāramitā-piṇḍārtha of Diṅnāga," *Journal of the Royal Asiatic Society* (1947): 56–57, 60–61. On the eighteen emptinesses, see La Vallée Poussin, ed., *Madhyamakāvatāra par Candrakīrti,* pp. 302–338, and Lamotte, ed., *Saṃdhinirmocana Sūtra,* pp. 108–110. The most extensive exposition of the eighteen emptinesses occurs in Étienne Lamotte, *Le Traité de la Grand Vertu de Sagesse de Nāgārjuna,* Tome IV (Louvain: Institut Orientaliste, 1976), 2027–2151. Lamotte's discussion of the emptiness of the beginningless and the endless occurs at pp. 2094–2105.

107. For an edition of the Tibetan text, see La Vallée Poussin, *Madhyamakāvatāra par Candrakīrti,* pp. 313–314.

108. Emptiness, like Plato's *pharmakon,* is ambivalent because, as Derrida writes, "it constitutes the medium in which opposites are opposed, the movement and the play that links them among themselves, reverses them or makes them cross over into the other." See Jacques Derrida, *Disseminations,* trans. Barbara Johnson (Chicago: University of Chicago Press, 1981), 127. The preceding paragraph is indebted to Derrida's essay, "Plato's Pharmacy," from which this quotation is drawn.

109. See the passage cited on page 166 above.

110. *Rgyal-tshab,* 148a6–148b3.

111. Ibid., 148a4–5.

112. Rgyal-tshab's argument occurs in *Rgyal-tshab,* 151a3–152a4 and 152b3. For a French translation of Rgyal-tshab's entire section on controversies concerning the *ekayāna* and end of saṃsāra, see Ruegg, *La Théorie,* pp. 219–235.

113. *'Jam-dbyangs-bzhad-pa,* 21. As is clear from *Rje-btsun-pa* at 16a5, 'Jam-dbyangs-bzhad-pa is here either paraphrasing Sa-skya Paṇḍita's *Tshad ma rigs gder* ("Although a seed has no beginning, when it is burned by fire its end is seen. Similarly, although saṃsāra is beginningless, its end is established by seeing selflessness") or he is drawing on Candrakīrti's commentary on *Catuḥśataka* VIII.25. For the Sanskrit and Tibetan of Āryadeva as well as the Sanskrit of Candrakīrti's commentary on the passage, see Karen Lang, *Āryadeva's Catuḥśataka* (Copenhagen: Akademisk Forlag, 1986), 86–87.

114. See Wogihara, ed., *Abhisamayālaṃkārālokā,* p. 95, and Obermiller, *Analysis of the Abhisamayālaṃkāra,* pp. 127–128.

115. See Wogihara, ed., *Abhisamayālaṃkārālokā,* p. 96, and Obermiller, *Analysis of the Abhisamayālaṃkāra,* pp. 137–138.

116. *'Jam-dbyangs-bzhad-pa,* 20–21.

117. A more cogent disputation of Tsong-kha-pa's interpretation of the emptiness of the beginningless and the endless is made by Mkhas-grub-rje in his *Rtogs dka'i snang ba.* He cites Candrakīrti's statement on the emptiness of the beginningless and the endless ("This dreamlike existence neither comes nor goes. The very absence of that is referred to in the treatises as the emptiness of that which is beginningless and endless") and a sūtra which states, "One did not come here from a former life and does not go from here to the next." His point is that these statements are made from the ultimate perspective: saṃsāra has no ultimately or intrinsically existent beginning or end, just as the movement from one lifetime to another is unfindable under ultimate analysis. To read these passages literally would be to deny the existence of rebirth, even on the conventional level. Therefore Tsong-kha-pa is mistaken in finding in the emptiness of the beginningless and the endless a proof that saṃsāra will never end. Like the other interpreters, Mkhas-grub-rje argues that all sentient beings will become buddhas. See *Mkhas-grub,* 908.1–3.

118. On *peripeteia,* see Gerald F. Else, *Aristotle's Poetics: The Argument* (Cambridge: Harvard University Press, 1957), 342–349.

119. Ibid., p. 344.

120. On peripety, Frank Kermode writes: "it is a disconfirmation followed by a consonance; the interest of having our expectations falsified is obviously related to our wish to reach the discovery or recognition by an unexpected and instructive route. The more daring the peripeteia, the more we feel that the work respects our sense of reality; and the more certainly we shall feel that the story under consideration is one of those which, by upsetting the ordinary balance of our naive expectations, is finding something out for us, something real." See his *The Sense of an Ending* (New York: Oxford University Press), 18.

121. Ibid., p. 5.

122. Ibid., p. 67.

123. Sigmund Freud, *Collected Papers,* vol. 5 (London: The Hogarth Press, 1952), 320.

124. Ibid., p. 325.

The Illusion of Spiritual Progress: Remarks on Indo-Tibetan Buddhist Soteriology

MATTHEW KAPSTEIN

I

The Tibetans have always been fond of origin tales. Every family, every religious tradition, and every branch of learning has its own story, beginning in the distant past and relating that past to the present. This chapter is in large measure concerned with one such tale, but before plunging into it, I will explain the origin of the chapter itself.

At some point in my own mythic past, I undertook to survey the extant corpus of historical and doctrinal literature belonging to a little known school of Tibetan Buddhism called the Shangs-pa Bka'-brgyud, "the spiritual succession of the Shangs valley," which flourished during the twelfth through fourteenth centuries but then virtually disappeared as an independent sect.[1] The Shangs-pa school interested me for several reasons: the founder, Khyung-po Rnal-'byor ("the yogin of the Khyung clan"),[2] seemed to exemplify one of the grand themes of eleventh- to twelfth-century Tibetan Buddhism—namely, the attempt to resolve the tension between indigenous Tibetan and Indian sources of religious authority; his foremost teacher, Niguma, was said to have been the wife or sister of the famous siddha Nāropā, and thus the tradition accorded unique reverence to an Indian Buddhist woman; Niguma's teaching placed notable emphasis on the doctrines of apparition *(māyā, sgyu-ma)* and dream *(svapna, rmi-lam),* and so promised to clarify some difficult topics in later Indian Buddhist theory and practice; and finally, despite the demise of the Shangs-pa as an independent sect, its teachings, or elements thereof, had resurfaced throughout the history of Tibetan Buddhism in remarkably varied settings: in the Rdzogs-chen ("Great Perfection") teachings of the Rnying-ma-pa master Klong-chen Rab-'byams-pa (1308–1363),[3] in the Dge-lugs-pa rites of the protective deity Ṣaḍbhuja-Jñānanātha,[4] in the revelations of the bridge-building sage Thang-stong rgyal-po (fifteenth century),[5] in the meditation teachings promoted by the brilliant sixteenth- and seventeenth-century exponents of the renegade (and eventually suppressed) Jo-nang-pa sect, and as one of the "eight great vehicles" *(shing-rta chen-po brgyad)* of Buddhist practice informing the eclectic *(ris-med)* tendencies represented above all by the massive literary production of 'Jam-dbyangs Mkhyen-brtse'i dbang-po (1820–1892) and Kong-sprul Blo-gros mtha'-yas (1813–1899/1900).[6]

Through my study of the Shangs-pa literature, I discovered that Khyung-po's teacher Niguma had written a formal verse treatise on the path *(mārga, lam),* together with a detailed autocommentary.[7] If authentic,[8] these texts would be, so far as I know, the only extant systematic doctrinal treatises by an Indian woman, though I shan't discuss now the interesting historical questions that might be raised in connection with this topic.[9] In any event, the **Māyādhvakrama* (The Sequence of the Path of Apparition) and its autocommentary attempt to provide an account of the relationship between the categories developed in Buddhist scholastic philosophy for analyzing the path—the five paths, ten bodhisattva stations, thirty-seven factors allied to enlightenment, and so forth—and the experiences occurring to an adept specializing in the yogas of apparition, dream, and luminosity *(prabhāsvara, 'od-gsal)* as taught in the traditions of Vajrayāna Buddhism. The texts thus belong to a corpus of pre-twelfth-century Indo-Tibetan Buddhist literature that interestingly presages an important but doctrinally controversial development within later Tibetan Buddhism: namely, the emergence of what we might term "philosophical Vajrayāna"—that is, philosophical speculation inspired in part by tantric Buddhism, and so not entirely reducible to the philosophy of one or the other of the four normative schools recognized in later Indian Buddhist scholasticism. These considerations, combined with the discovery that the *Path of Apparition* had significantly influenced Klong-chen Rab-'byams-pa, led me to edit it and to translate it, along with the autocommentary.

My work on the Shangs-pa Bka'-brgyud path-literature accentuated, for me, some of the difficult questions surrounding the relationships between "the path" as a well-formed Buddhist discourse category and "soteriology" as a broad category in recent Western discourse about religion that is just beginning to be employed in Buddhist Studies. In the remainder of this chapter, I examine aspects of the tale of Shangs-pa origins and Niguma's *Path of Apparition* so as to disclose some of the possibilities presented by these two categories in relation to a particular Indo-Tibetan esoteric Buddhist tradition.

II

For the Shangs-pa Bka'-brgyud, the essential origin tale is the life of its founder, Khyung-po Rnal-'byor. His biography is an exceptionally difficult work to interpret historically. It is chronologically chaotic, and Khyung-po could hardly have been a contemporary of all the many great persons mentioned in connection with his career, unless in fact he lived the full 150 years that the tradition declares to have been his span. That he died around 1135 seems fairly certain, and many of the figures mentioned as his teachers belong to the last half of the eleventh century, though some were active much earlier.

Like other Tibetan religious biographies, Khyung-po's is called a *rnam-thar,* a term literally meaning "liberation," and so perhaps best translated in the present context as "soteriography." As this suggests, the central theme in such works is the subject's salvation.[10] *Rnam-thars* are thus illustrative of soteriological praxis and attainment, written usually by authors well versed in Buddhist doctrine. The culminating moment in Khyung-po's *rnam-thar* occurs when he meets Niguma, who is referred to ambiguously as Nāropā's "lady" *(lcam-mo).* Before learning of Niguma, Khyung-po had encountered, mastered, and finally abandoned the doctrines of a host of other teachers, Tibetan and Indian, Bon-po and Buddhist. Like much of the *rnam-thar,* the episode with which we are here concerned is related in the first person (though the text's colophon makes it perfectly clear that this is not an autobiography):

> Taking with me 500 ounces of gold, I wandered throughout India, and asked, "Who among the accomplished masters seems to have come face to face with the Buddha himself?" The *paṇḍitas* and *siddhas* concurred, "That would be Nāro Paṇḍita's lady *(lcam-mo),*[11] the *ḍākinī* of enlightened awareness called 'Niguma.' She abides in the three pure stations [i.e., the eighth through tenth bodhisattva stations, from which there is no falling back], and she has really requested instruction in dharma from Mahāvajradhara [the primordial Buddha of later tantric Buddhism] himself." Asking where she was residing just then, I was told that those of pure vision might meet her anywhere but that one of impure vision could search everywhere for her without success, for she dwelt upon the pure stations and her embodied form had become the stuff of rainbows. Nonetheless, I was told, she sometimes came to the dense grove of the Sosadvīpa charnel ground to preside over the communal feasting of the *ḍākinīs.* As soon as Niguma's name was first mentioned to me I began to weep: my faith was such that my hair stood on end. Therefore, then and there, I traveled to the Sosadvīpa charnel ground, to the dense grove that was there, and I chanted *namo buddhāya* ["hail to the Buddha!"] as I went along. Then, in the sky, at a height equivalent to that of seven palm trees, there appeared a *ḍākinī* of dark brown complexion, wearing ornaments of bone, holding a *khaṭvāṅga* [a ritual lance or trident piercing a skull] and *kapāla* [skull-cup], and appearing at once in various ways, as one and at the same time as many.[12] Seeing her dance, I thought, "This must be the *ḍākinī* Niguma," and I prostrated myself at her feet and circumambulated her many times. Then I begged her to confer upon me her genuine esoteric instructions.

"How do you know," she said, "that I'm no cannibalistic witch? When my circle arrives, you'll be our dinner! You'd better be moving; be quick!" But I persisted in my prostrations, circumambulations, and prayers to receive her instructions concerning secret mantras. She said, "For the secret mantras of the Mahāyāna, you'll need gold. If you've got gold, things may work out." I offered up my 500 ounces of gold, but she just tossed it all into the forest.[13] I thought, "Could she be a cannibalistic witch after all? She's not greedy for gold." At that instant, the *ḍākinī* glanced suddenly about the sky and her circle of innumerable *ḍākinīs* appeared from space itself. In a moment, some of them built a maṇḍala palace of three stories, some arrayed a maṇḍala of coloured sand, while some gathered together the provisions for the feast. Then, late during the night of the full moon, she conferred upon me the empowerment of the Body of Apparition *(māyākāya, sgyu-lus)* and that of the Dream. When the empowerment ceremony was completed, she said, "Little monk from Tibet, arise!" and in a moment, relying on the *ḍākinī*'s miraculous powers, we traveled three *yojanas* [about 24 miles]. There, in the sky above a mountain of gold, the *ḍākinīs* had assembled for the feast, dancing. From the four sides of the mountain four golden rivers descended, and I had to ask, "Where in India is such a mountain as this to be found, or is this too the *ḍākinī*'s magical creation?" To this she said:

> These varied thoughts, full of passion and hate,
> Stirring saṃsāra's ocean,
> Are insubstantial; when you realize that
> All's a golden isle, my son.
> As for apparitional dharmas,
> Like apparition contemplate them to be;
> You'll become an apparitional buddha—
> By the power of devotion it will come to be.

And she added, "Now I will bless you. Grasp your dreams!" Having grasped my dreams, I journeyed to the land of gods and demigods, where a gigantic demigod just swallowed me whole. The *ḍākinī* appeared in space and said, "Do not try to wake up, my son." It was at that time that she taught me the six doctrines in their entirety.[14]

To this account is appended an exhaustive list of the texts that Niguma transmitted to Khyung-po Rnal-'byor, which the latter brought back to Tibet, and which are preserved to this day in Tibetan translation.[15] Foremost among them are the *Path of Apparition* and its autocommentary.

Following his meeting with Niguma, Khyung-po Rnal-'byor continues for some time to travel in India, receiving further instruction from various masters, having renewed visionary experiences, and so forth. But his own liberation is from this point assured. Increasingly, he acts as a perfected master in his own right, bringing the fruits of the way to worthy Tibetan disciples who congregate around him in large numbers.[16]

III

Examining the tale of Khyung-po Rnal-'byor, it should be clear that there is no single soteriological theme that it seeks to advance to the exclusion of others. It is, rather, an intricately designed fabric whose several soteriological threads are tightly interwoven. By way of provisional analysis, I shall describe in brief four distinct types of soteriological themes that we may draw out of the account. To save words, I shall refer to them as "soteriologies," though this is somewhat inaccurate: they are, of course, dimensions of a single soteriology. I believe that the four types discussed here are prominent throughout Tibetan Buddhist "soteriographical" literature, and that there were definite socio-cultural reasons for emphasizing some such mix; but in the scope of this presentation it will not be possible to argue these points in full detail.

The Soteriology of the Shamanic Vision Quest

Shamanic themes are well known in all Indian religious traditions, and Buddhism is no exception.[17] In Indian tantric religion, apparently shamanic elements seem particularly prominent. For this reason, it is always difficult for the student of Tibetan Buddhism to distinguish satisfactorily between Indian tantric motifs and those supposed to represent indigenous Tibetan shamanic traditions.[18] In any event, it seems certain that the powerfully shamanic tendencies of indigenous Tibetan religion would have encouraged the continuation, assimilation, and accentuation of related aspects of Indian religion as they were introduced into Tibet.

It has sometimes been maintained that the shamanic vision quest, an especially prominent element in North American Indian traditions, is less emphasized in Asiatic shamanism. Although this assumption is perhaps misleading, it does seem that, among the apparently shamanic motifs found in Indian Buddhism, the vision quest is not notably important.[19] Only one Indian Buddhist text that I know of can be said to turn unambiguously throughout on the vision quest theme—namely, the *Gaṇḍavyūhasūtra,* the great saga of Sudhana's wanderings throughout India in search of Maitreya. Several of the tales of the *mahāsiddhas* of the Vajrayāna tradition also describe vision quests, as do a number of *avadānas,* though this is by no means the dominant element in these episodes.[20] Whereas some would hold that the story of the Buddha's own renunciation and search for enlightenment conforms to a vision-quest paradigm, I would argue that the highly rationalized nature of that account reveals it to be a remarkably deviant example at best.[21]

It is, rather, in the Central and East Asian literature of Buddhist pilgrimage that we find the elevation of the vision quest to the point that it becomes virtually coextensive with Buddhist path.[22] In the case of Tibet, where Buddhism was always faced with the challenge of having to coerce indigenous spiritual powers, it seems certain that the *bla-ma*—the Buddhist guru—had to reveal his mastery of the shaman's traditional domains in order to establish his own authority.[23] This is suggested even by the term *"bla-ma":* at once the superior (i.e., preceptor) of the Indian religious tradition, he is equally the controlling source, *ma,* of the *bla,* the primordial energies sustaining the soul's vitality.[24] Thus in the Tibetan soteriography, it is essential that the subject's religious authority be authenticated in two traditions simultaneously. Several motifs are relied on to achieve this: success in the vision quest; displays of magical power and curative ability; the subjugation of fierce chthonic divinities. In Khyung-po Rnal-'byor's *rnam-thar,* all of these are in evidence.[25]

The object of Khyung-po's search is "one who has come face to face with the Buddha himself," and that search culminates in a realm of vision and dream with his meeting Niguma, a woman whose "embodied form had become the stuff of rainbows" and who could thus be found only by "those of pure vision." Their meeting takes place in a charnel ground, which is transcended in a magical flight to a golden mountain. Niguma is depicted as dancing and has innumerable female followers who feast and join in her dance. She threatens cannibalism and imparts her full teaching only when Khyung-po has been swallowed by an asura in a dream. If the book hadn't been written 850 years ago, you'd think that the authors were getting their material right out of Mircea Eliade.[26]

In short, despite the fact that many of the motifs just mentioned run throughout the literature of Indic esoteric Buddhism, and so cannot be attributed to Tibetan shamanism in particular, their superabundance in the culminating moments of a pilgrim's quest must be seen above all as authenticating the hero's attainment of a shaman's salvation, through power won from a woman during a dream-flight on a magical mountain of gold.

The Soteriology of the Guru's Grace

Indian Buddhism often seems to embody a highly rationalized soteriology in which the possibility of salvation by grace is systematically minimized. In devotional Mahāyāna and in Vajrayāna Buddhism, however, soteriological efficacy is attributed to the grace of a buddha or one's guru, although salvation through grace alone seems not to have been a possibility seriously countenanced by Indian Buddhists.[27] The inch given to grace in Indian Buddhism became, of course, the proverbial mile in both East Asia and Tibet, being most powerfully manifest in the former in the various Pure Land schools, and in the latter in the emergence of the distinctively Tibetan institution sometimes called "Lamaism," at least when this term is used (as I believe it should be) to describe a type of social-cum-religious institution rather than a body of religious belief.[28]

In the quasi-theistic milieu of late Indian Buddhism, which was carried over into Tibet, the ultimate source of saving grace was the Buddha, and above all the Buddha embodying the power of the tantric preceptor, namely, Buddha Vajradhara. The closer one's ties to Vajradhara, the more powerfully one may receive the living blessing of the tantras' message, through which one's liberation in this life and body may be secured. So it is that Khyung-po Rnal-'byor is not content to search in India for teachings that can ultimately be traced back to the Buddha, but is determined to meet one who has been the direct beneficiary of Vajradhara's blessing. Realizing that he has now heard of such a being, Khyung-po feels no ordinary faith but weeps and experiences horripilation. It is expressly through Niguma's blessing *(byin-gyis brlabs)* that he is able to grasp his dreams and so receive the transmission of the six yogas. It will be easier to examine this in greater detail in the next section, on yogic soteriology, for these two threads are here very tightly intertwined.[29]

It is because of the immediacy of Khyung-po's connection with Vajradhara that the successors to his lineage in Tibet were able to claim that a special power and purity inhered in the blessing of their tradition. The Shangs-pa Bka'-brgyud, however, remained somewhat anomalous among Tibetan Buddhist schools, in that it did not succeed in combining its claims to be a dispenser of Vajrayāna Buddhism's exceptional grace with extensive temporal power, this combination being generally characteristic of Lamaist institutions.

The Soteriology of Yogic Perfection

If it is a sort of shamanic quest that brings Khyung-po to the feet of his guru, the grace of the guru is concretely embodied in the transmission to him of a particular body of salvific technique, mastery of which will bring about his spiritual perfection. The literature of yoga, Hindu and Buddhist, may involve elements resembling shamanism and also devotional religion, but in the final analysis yoga is always a sort of perfectibilism, which is clearly indicated by the characteristic term used to denote the successful adept, "siddha" (Tib. *grub-thob*), which means "accomplished, perfected, completed."

Khyung-po's personal attainment of perfection through yogic practice is made explicit in the later sections of the *rnam-thar.* As his initiation into a particular body of yogic lore, however, his meeting with Niguma describes imagistically the path of inner development he will take.[30]

Vajrayāna Buddhism employs several alternative classificatory schemes to set out the connections among the vast number of tantras, sādhanas, yogic disciplines, and so forth that collectively form its "canon."[31] The most popular of these schemes depends on a hierarchical ordering of tantras based on the structure of their respective initiatory rites *(abhiṣeka);* particular sādhanas or yogic practices may then be classified according to their relationships with the fundamental tantras. Usually four main hierarchical divisions are enumerated; the highest, comprising the tantras of unsurpassed yoga *(anuttarayogatantra),* is distinguished from the rest in part by teaching a system of practice that involves two distinct but ultimately unified sequences. The first of these, the sequence of creation *(utpattikrama),* depends on the visualized recreation of the world as maṇḍala and the accomplishment of rites, pacific and wrathful, through which the enlightenment of all who dwell within the maṇḍala-realm (ultimately all sentient beings) can be secured; the second, called the sequence of perfection *(niṣpannakrama),* focuses on the yogin's or yoginī's actualization of his or her own enlightenment through the forcible transmutation of mind-and-body into embodied enlightenment *(jinakāya, vajrakāya,* or *jñānakāya).*

In the later stages of the development of tantric Buddhism in India, it appears that masters of the Vajrayāna devoted increasing attention to the redaction of well-ordered summaries of the practices of the sequence of perfection. One of the most influential of these was the *Ṣaḍdharmopadeśa* of the siddha Tilopā, which was later transmitted to Tibet through his disciple Nāropā's Tibetan disciple Mar-pa Chos-kyi-blo-gros, whose school, the Mar-pa Bka'-brgyud, has many affinities with Khyung-po Rnal-'byor's Shangs-pa Bka'-brgyud (so that they are sometimes inaccurately lumped together). It is Tilopā's teaching of the sequence of perfection that is often termed the *Six Doctrines of Nāropā.*[32] The teaching that Khyung-po received while in the belly of an asura in a dream is quite similar, and so is called the *Six Doctrines of Niguma (ni-gu chos-drug).* The two differ primarily in points of emphasis.[33]

The *Six Doctrines* consist of four through which to attain buddhahood in this very life and this very body, plus two fail-safe maneuvers, lest one expire before succeeding in the bid to achieve perfection here and now. These last two doctrines—transference of consciousness *('pho-ba)* and the precepts of the intermediate state *(bar-do)*—need not detain us, for in the present context we are concerned only with buddhahood achieved during this lifetime.

The first four doctrines are inner heat *(caṇḍālī, gtum-mo),* apparitional embodiment *(māyākāya, sgyu-lus),* dream *(svapna, rmi-lam),* and luminosity *(prabhāsvara, 'od-gsal).* The most striking difference between the traditions of Tilopā and Niguma is the relative emphasis in the former on inner heat and luminosity, and in the latter on apparition and dream. A later Tibetan adherent of Niguma's tradition summarizes the results of the successful practice of these four doctrines as follows:

> [By means of the inner heat] the warmth of well-being blazes naturally. By means of apparitional embodiment, attachment and aversion naturally dissolve. By means of the dream, the subtle bewilderment [underlying all bewilderment] is naturally cleansed. And by means of luminosity, ignorance is naturally dispelled.[34]

With this background in mind, we are in a position to see precisely how perfection in yogic discipline is revealed in the story of Khyung-po Rnal-'byor and Niguma: Khyung-po arrives in India so desiring the teachings of the Vajrayāna that he is prepared to purchase them with large sums of gold. Motivated by his desire but fearful that it will not be fulfilled (attachment and aversion), his initial encounter with Niguma is a reflection of his own conflicted condition: she appears at once in various ways, a bit sinister, possibly a cannibal—in short, in the threatening guise of a tantric dominatrix. Khyung-po's faith, however, keeps his emotional turbulence in check; it is this that demonstrates in part his worthiness as a disciple, as one who is to be granted *abhiṣeka,* whereby he experiences the transformation of the world into a maṇḍala, visibly instantiated in the golden mountain surrounded by four rivers of molten gold.

Thus we have been transported to a place of well-being and warmth, iconographically equivalent to the energy-center at the perineum from which the inner heat radiates upward. Khyung-po's attainment of the yogas of apparition and dream is then made explicit—the former through the two verses on apparition, in which the dissolution of attachment and aversion becomes manifest, and the latter when he is blessed to grasp his dreams. Note, too, that Niguma herself has been transformed in Khyung-po's vision; no longer the object of hope and fear, she appears not in many ways, but is altogether straightforward; no longer threatening, her maternal affection for her disciple ("my son") is undisguised. The fourth doctrine, luminosity, is revealed only implicitly, when, as the culmination of his discipleship, Khyung-po receives many texts, thus dispelling the final remnants of his ignorance in the blazing light of knowledge.

The Soteriology of Buddhist Insight

Paradigmatically, Buddhist salvation has always been equated with liberating insight—in the case of the Buddha himself, this insight was his discovery of the four noble truths. The profoundly devotional poet of the Mahāyāna, Śāntideva, insists that, with respect to the perfection of wisdom, all other perfections are instrumental.[35] The conception of enlightenment revealed in the *Dohās* of Saraha is similarly gnostic in character.[36] So, too, Khyung-po Rnal-'byor comes to possess saving knowledge of a peculiarly Buddhist character in the course of his encounter with Niguma.

The quintessential philosophical message of the Shangs-pa tradition is embodied in the two quatrains with which Niguma answers Khyung-po's query about the location of the golden mountain. Although we are not told explicitly that these verses are of signal importance for the tradition, we shall see below that there is ample reason for underscoring them in this context. Moreover, even if it were not a conclusion reinforced by the study of other texts belonging to the same tradition, we would be justified in assuming that the verses are somehow crucial because the text shifts from prose to verse at this point, thus recapitulating the pattern of the Indian tales of the siddhas, in which the siddha's unique realization is presented in a culminating verse.[37]

The gnostic character of Khyung-po's salvation is further brought to our attention when we are told that Niguma transmitted to him certain texts. Because two of these, the *Path of Apparition* and its commentary, summarize the full range of Buddhist path-doctrine, we are entitled to regard Khyung-po as liberated in the traditional terms of normative Buddhist scholasticism, that is, by virtue of his knowledge of the path and its fruit.

IV

Having provided a rough-and-ready classification of the main soteriological themes informing the tale of Khyung-po Rnal-'byor's salvation, we can return to a question raised earlier: how is the description of the adept's actual salvation found here related to the normative doctrinal literature concerning the path? The presence in the Shangs-pa corpus of a treatise on the path, said to have been transmitted to Khyung-po by Niguma, allows us to examine this question in specific, concrete terms. That there is a genuine relationship to be studied here is signaled above all by the close convergence of the verses on apparition, recited by Niguma after Khyung-po expresses his amazement concerning the golden mountain, with verses I.3 and I.4 of the *Path of Apparition:*

> Apparition, from the beginning not substantially real, the beginningless elemental stratum,
> is itself the seed of all the elements of existence:
> it is the nucleus of enlightenment, and is good,
> and is well known as the "nucleus," or the "universal ground."

> If one endowed with excellent faith, energy, and respect
> meditatively cultivates the realization
> that apparitional elements of existence are apparitional,
> buddhahood will really be attained, apparitionally.

The autocommentary reveals that these verses paraphrase a passage from a now apparently lost tantra, the **Jñānābhyudaya (ye-shes mngon-par 'byung-ba)*, which appears to have been one of Niguma's main sources of inspiration.[38] These verses provide, in essence, a summary of the three fundamental categories of ground *(āśraya)*, path *(mārga)*, and result *(phala)*. They represent the epitome of Shangs-pa ontology, praxology, and buddhology: what there are are apparition-like dharmas; the essential element of practice is to cultivate the realization of their apparitionality; and the enlightenment that is attained is an apparition-like buddhahood. Apparition is thus the mediating category, pervading and so unifying the continuum of ground, path, and goal. It is not taken here, as elsewhere it sometimes is, as the negatively valued māyā from which one must flee in order to know a reality dualistically opposed to it. Rather, to be apparition-like is simply to be as beings are. Rejecting the common equation of māyā and evil deception, Niguma declares māyā to be good *(dge-ba,* Skt. *śubha* or *kuśala)*, for it is by virtue of it that all beings may aspire to the attainment of buddhahood. This significantly characterizes Niguma's entire soteriology; she would have undoubtably approved of the general thrust of Paul Deussen's remarks on the soteriological significance of māyā:

> [The] three essential conditions of man's salvation—God, immortality, and freedom—are conceivable only if the universe is mere appearance and not reality, mere *māyā* and not the *ātman,* and they break down irretrievably should this empirical reality, wherein we live, be found to constitute the true essence of things.[39]

From early on, Buddhism was much concerned with the topography of spiritual paths: between here and nirvāṇa many new insights were to be gained, psychic skills to be mastered, traps to be avoided. In the Pāli *Nikāyas* and other relatively early scriptures, we find various enumerations of paths and aspects of the path, such as the famous teaching of the eightfold noble path or that of the stations *(bhūmi)* set forth in the *Mahāvastu.* Drawing on the alternative and sometimes conflicting enumerations found in canonical texts, the redactors of the several Abhidharma traditions sought to codify definitive lists of path-categories and to explicate, without apparent contradiction, the manner in which the alternative lists complemented or otherwise related to one another.

This process was continued in the Mahāyāna schools that drew most heavily on the Abhidharma traditions, such as the early "Yogācāra" school, as revealed in the *Yogācārabhūmiśāstra* and related works. Here two categories emerge as particularly important. The first of these, which is very old—its elements are all present in the *Nikāyas*—concerns the faculties that the practitioner must develop to guarantee his or her progress on the path: this list of thirty-seven factors of enlightenment pervades the literature of the Abhidharma. These are usually arranged in the same ascending order, beginning with the applications of mindfulness.[40]

A second main path-category elaborated in the Yogācāra Abhidharma is that of the five paths: those of provisions, application (or connection), seeing, cultivation, and no more learning (or the final path). These come to correspond directly to the thirty-seven factors allied with enlightenment—the first three groups, each of four factors, belonging to the path of provisions; the next two groups, of five factors each, to the path of connection; the seven limbs of enlightenment to the path of seeing; and the eightfold noble path to that of cultivation; the path of no more learning is identical to the achievement of the goal, nirvāṇa.

The sections of Niguma's *Path of Apparition* devoted to the path adopt the scheme just outlined in its entirety, preceded by an analysis of the category of the ground, and appending to it a detailed discussion of the characteristically Mahāyāna teaching of the ten bodhisattva stations. Clearly, the method of describing the path that is employed here represents the analytic-rational dimension of Buddhism; among the four soteriological themes sketched above, this represents the "soteriology of Buddhist insight." A complete outline of Niguma's treatise and its commentary, despite some highly interesting variants with respect to certain particular categories, conforms to a pattern well known to students of Indo-Tibetan scholasticism:[41]

I. Ground *(āśraya)*

II–VI. Path *(mārga)*

II. Path of Provisions *(sambhāramārga)*
- 1–4. Four applications of mindfulness *(smṛtyupasthāna)*
  - 1. to body *(kāya-)*
  - 2. to sensation *(vedanā-)*
  - 3. to mind *(citta-)*
  - 4. to phenomena *(dharma-)*
- 5–8. Four genuine renunciations *(samyakprahāṇa)*
  - 5. renunciation of nonvirtues that have not yet developed *(anutpannākuśala)*
  - 6. renunciation of those that have developed *(utpannākuśala)*
  - 7. development of virtues that have not yet developed *(anutpannakuśala)*

8. retention of those that have developed *(utpannakuśala)*
9–12. Four supports for the miraculous *(ṛddhipāda)*
9. volitional concentration *(chandasamādhi)*
10. energetic concentration *(vīryasamādhi)*
11. mental concentration *(cittasamādhi)*
12. investigative concentration *(mīmāṃsāsamādhi)*[42]

III. Connecting Path (or Path of Application, *prayogamārga*)
13–17. Five faculties *(indriya)*
13. faith *(śraddhā)*
14. energetic application *(vīrya)*
15. mindfulness *(smṛti)*
16. concentration *(samādhi)*
17. insight *(prajñā)*
18–22. Five powers *(bala)* recapitulate the designations of 13–17.

IV. Path of Seeing *(darśanamārga)*
23–29. Seven limbs of enlightenment *(bodhyaṅga)*
23. mindfulness *(smṛti)*
24. analysis of phenomena *(dharmapravicaya)*
25. energetic application *(vīrya)*
26. delight *(prīti)*
27. fitness *(praśrabdhi)*
28. concentration *(samādhi)*
29. equanimity *(upekṣā)*

V. Path of Cultivation *(bhāvanāmārga)*
30–37. The Eightfold Noble Path *(āryāṣṭāṅgamārga)*
30. right view *(samyagdṛṣṭi)*
31. right attitude *(samyaksaṃkalpa)*
32. right speech *(samyagvāk)*
33. right parameters of action *(samyakkarmānta)*
34. right livelihood *(samyagājīva)*
35. right effort *(samyagvyāyāma)*
36. right mindfulness *(samyaksmṛti)*
37. right concentration *(samyaksamādhi)*

VI. Result = Path of No More Learning *(phala, aśaikṣamārga)*

VII. Ten Bodhisattva Stations *(bodhisattvabhūmi)*

VIII. Further Discussion of Buddhahood

We have already seen that Indo-Tibetan Buddhist soteriology cannot be reduced to the category of doctrinal insight alone. It is noteworthy, then, that while adhering to a normative scholastic pattern of exposition, Niguma's *Path of Apparition* does attempt, in its particulars, to broaden its account to include soteriological motifs certainly not originating in the analytic Abhidharma traditions. This is apparent above all with respect to what I have called the soteriologies of the guru's grace and of yogic perfection. The former is evidenced in verses such as I.8 and I.9:

> The sequences of five paths and ten stations
> are traversed by the force of devotion.
> It is the supreme essence of the tantras' intention
> that one be not separate from the guru's presence.
>
> Thus, it is best to experience
> all things seen and heard
> as being of the nature of deity and guru.

It is essential that we distinguish this devotion *(bhakti)* carefully from the faith *(śraddhā)* enumerated above among, for example, the five forces and five powers, because although the Abhidharma traditions made room for faith as a faculty employed on the path, they did not regard it as the motive force governing progress on the path overall.[43] Niguma's assertion that "the five paths and ten stations are traversed by the force of devotion" must therefore be regarded as supplementing what was perceived to be a deficiency of the older scheme with respect to the actualities of Vajrayāna practice.

Nonetheless, the interpretation of Niguma's yogic teaching in terms of the abhidharmic path-categories is doubtless the main point of the text. The entire discussion of the path of seeing, given in the appendix, offers a sustained example in confirmation of this. It seems, then, that only the soteriology of the shamanic vision quest is not clearly represented. Does this offer further indirect support for our contention that this is preeminently an indigenous Tibetan contribution? Perhaps; but it is important to note that the text's emphasis on visionary experience (e.g., verses IV.14–19 in the appendix) suggests further possible extensions of the categories of the path, plausibly embracing the vision quest and similar phenomena.

The *Path of Apparition* thus illustrates the potential openness of the apparently rigid abhidharmic path-categories, and the possibility of generating a more comprehensive Buddhist soteriology on their basis. But we may yet wonder why Niguma chose to utilize these seemingly pedantic categories, quite foreign to freewheeling festivals on mountains of gold, at all. It will not do to suppose that she (or any other Māhāyānist, for that matter) ever regarded the path-categories as representing "real" categories of being, in an ontologically ultimate sense. Nor can we dispense with the problem by supposing her work to be merely an elaborate rationalization of a deviant sectarian tradition, for we would thereby only restate it, now asking why and how the path-categories are invoked to rationalize that tradition. Having puzzled over this problem for some time, there is only one conclusion that seems reasonable to me: Niguma relied on the scholastic path-categories simply because they are the categories of Buddhist thought. She chose to play a Mahāyānist language game rather than any other, and delighted in that particular language game. The choice is by no means arbitrary: the path-categories, themselves illusory just because they are not "real" categories of being, mirror the phenomenology of apparition and dream that they are employed to express. "Is this *really* the eightfold path?" The question echoes as hollowly as did Khyung-po's plaintive query as to whether or not the golden mountain was in India.

We have wandered from the multiple soteriologies of Indo-Tibetan Buddhism to the scholastic analysis of the path, and back again. In Niguma's *Path of Apparition* the relationship between Buddhist scholasticism and the Vajrayāna is still perhaps an uneasy one, but it is a relationship that continued variously to progress outside of India, in the schools of Tibetan Buddhism and Bon, as also in Japanese Shingon. What I have indicated here is that, when we approach the point at which late Indian Buddhism intersects with a growing tradition in Tibet, we find the beginnings of a transformation in dogmatic soteriology, which reflects, in part, changing soteriological practices.[44]

Appendix: Selections from Niguma's Māyādhvakrama (The Sequence of the Path of Apparition)

Note: Following are excerpts from Niguma's verse treatise on the path. The extant Tibetan text is composed in continuous seven-syllable lines, without marked chapter or verse breaks, and the prose autocommentary is similarly undivided, though its structure is very clear. For the convenience of contemporary readers, I have broken both works into eight parallel sections and have numbered "verses" and paragraphs according to logical rather than metrical breaks in the text. Selections from the first two sections and the complete text of the fourth section are found here. The autocommentary on section IV is also given in its entirety. I have supplied the italicized headings containing brief explanatory comments on the text. A complete outline of these texts is given above, pp. 204–205.

I. *The Ground*

The introductory obeisance:

1. Homage to mind, in and of itself,
   that is primordially luminous by nature,
   and provides all that is yearned for,
   like the wish-fulfilling gem.

Statement of purpose:

2. To benefit others I shall expound
   The Sequence of the Path of Apparition,
   the spiritual essence of the ocean of Jinas,
   the heart of expressible meaning.

Summary of the doctrines of ground, path and result:

3. Apparition, from the beginning not substantially real, the beginningless elemental stratum,
   is itself the seed of all the elements of existence:
   it is the nucleus of enlightenment, and is good,
   and is well known as the "nucleus," or the "universal ground."

4. If one endowed with excellent faith, energy, and respect
   meditatively cultivates the realization
   that apparitional elements of existence are apparitional,
   buddhahood will really be attained, apparitionally.

The primary subject matter:

5. Therefore, hear me well, for well I shall explain,
   the five paths and ten spiritual stations.

The ground according to the Vajrayāna:

6. Whatever there is, whether animate or inanimate,
   everything that appears to the five senses,
   is all the Body of the deity, [the coalescence of] appearance and emptiness;
   and the Body of the deity is limitless apparition.

The path according to the Vajrayāna:

7. The learned should undertake to experience
   all factors that are allies of enlightenment
   as indivisible from the deity's Body and apparition.

8. The sequences of five paths and ten stations
   are traversed by the force of devotion.

It is the supreme essence of the tantras' intention
that one be not separate from the guru's presence.

9. Thus, it is best to experience
all things seen and heard
as being of the nature of deity and guru.

10. Shape, color, and the five poisons,
and the classes of being determined by karma are the Five Families.
Whatever appears is appearance and emptiness:
Creation, Consummation, Coalescence.

The result according to the Vajrayāna:

11. Where there is bliss, transparency, and nonconceptualization
is the natural arising of Trikāya.
Transparent and nonconceptual, it is the dual cognition
[of the abiding nature of reality and of the entire extension of phenomena].

II. *The Path of Provisions*

Definition of "path":

1. Moreover, [the path] is called a path
because śamatha and vipaśyanā are conjoined,
and because [by it] one seeks to journey
to that which is unsurpassed.

IV. *The Path of Seeing*

Characteristic and definition of the Path of Seeing:

1. At the last instant of the Ultimate Mundane Attainment
the nondiscursive pristine cognition of the Path of Seeing [is born]:
it is the natural arising of apparition
and is characterized as infallible.

2. It is the pristine cognition of the Path of Seeing,
because you see what was not seen before.

The Seven Limbs of Enlightenment:

3. The Seven Limbs of Enlightenment
are the characteristic mode of concentration on the Path of Seeing.

4. Not needing to be deliberately mindful of apparition,
which lies beyond the range of the intellect,
one sees the actual nature of things:
therefore, this is mindfulness, as a limb of perfect enlightenment.

5. The analysis of the elements of existence
as a limb [of perfect enlightenment],
[is the realization that] the discernible characteristics
of the wholesome, unwholesome, or indeterminate,
may not be established or apprehended with reference to apparitional elements of existence.

6. Because all perceptions are demolished
[in the realization of] apparition, free from all subjective grasping,
one strives without accepting or rejecting anything.
Therefore, this is energetic application, as a limb [of perfect enlightenment].

7. Regarding apparition,
about which there is nothing to prove or negate,
delight and unhappiness are demolished.
Therefore, having a disciplined mind, not engendering happiness about any conditions,
is delight, as a limb [of perfect enlightenment].

8. Training the mind with reference to all things,
not adhering to mental objects as objective points of reference,
because they are apparition, not substantially real,
is mental fitness, as a limb of [perfect] enlightenment.

9. And apparition itself is not substantially real:
following the realization in which the elements of existence are demolished,
one does not adhere to mind as an objective point of reference at all.
This is concentration as a limb of [perfect] enlightenment.

10. Apparition, not abiding anywhere,
neither supports, nor adheres, nor binds up.
To be unpreoccupied with the elements of existence
is equanimity, as a limb of [perfect] enlightenment.

The yogin's experience of the Path of Seeing:

11. Having cultivated that mode of concentration,
then during the day, and halfway through the night, all things seen and heard
arise as apparition, not substantially real,
the limitless coalescence of appearance and emptiness.

12. As bubbles arise and dissolve in a pristine ocean,
so our bubbling thoughts exist nowhere but in the ocean of Reality.
Therefore, you must neither prove nor negate,
but establish a relaxed meditation.

13. At that time the mist of thoughts and feelings
    becomes baseless, can no longer disturb you.
    Having become certain and decisive,
    you must practice without negation or affirmation.

14. By welding this with devotion, the Body of the deity—
    transparent and nondiscursive, blissful and free from grasping, devoid of craving,
    naturally arising, naturally liberated, uncompounded,
    free from conceptualization, omniscient and luminous—
    emerges, either during the interval between sleep and dream,
    or when you seize the dream, or naturally arising.
    It is the Sambhogakāya, [and endures] so long as you do not waver.

15. You intermingle day and night indivisibly,
    and having unwaveringly experienced whatever appears
    as being endowed with three wheels,[45]
    you perform acts of worship and supplication.

16. Having thus attained mastery
    of the emanation and transformation of dreams,
    you practice the craft of apparition [with reference to everything that exists],
    from the Buddha down to mere insects.

17. In this way the apparitional body
    is revealed without qualification;
    apparition, the Body of the deity, and Luminosity become indivisible;
    and visionary clarity spreads forth.

Marks of success on the Path of Seeing:

18. Having completed the course of the "appearance of objects,"
    you abandon the hundred and twelve things to be abandoned on the Path of Seeing;
    attaining higher knowledge,
    you become joyous; and awesome things become manifest.

19. The sign that the visionary clarity of apparition
    has arisen [is this]:
    during sleep, and at other times,
    in even a single instant,
    twelve [groups] of one hundred qualities of enlightenment [arise]:
    you become absorbed in one hundred states of concentration;
    and behold the faces of one hundred Buddhas;
    attend the teachings of one hundred Buddhas;
    and shake one hundred world-systems;

travel to one hundred Buddha-fields;
and fill one hundred realms with light;
bring about the spiritual maturation of one-hundred beings;
and open one hundred Dharma-doors;
live through one hundred aeons;
and penetrate one hundred, previous and subsequent;
you can divide bodily into one hundred emanations;
and with each body encircled
by a retinue of one hundred, you teach [the Dharma].

20. Because you are able to abandon even life
for the sake of the Dharma,
the objects of desire become allies [on the path].

21. You perfect the four kinds of generosity,
and practice the remaining [Perfections] as much as possible.

22. Attaining this station you become free of five fears:
fear of no livelihood, death,
the vicious states of existence, ill-repute, and saṃsāra.
Free from them, you abandon the dispositions [underlying those fears].

23. Thus, the realization arises that everything seen or heard is truthless apparition.

The anticipation on the Path of Seeing of attaining the eighth station (from which there is no falling back), and the attainment of buddhahood on realizing the station called, in the Vajrayāna, "lotus-endowed" (padma-can):

24. If the impure, bewildering idiosyncracies
of daytime and of the dream,
do not remain on the eighth station,
then what need be said of the Lotus-endowed?

25. Therefore, [when] various things appear
[within the field of] transparent and pristine sensory consciousness,
mental grasping does not set in,
[but you realize instead] that that is the indivisible coalescence of transparency and emptiness,
the natural manifestation of apparition, free from craving.

26. You realize the elements of dream
to be supreme bliss, [the coalescence of] transparency and emptiness,
free from subjective grasping.

27. The pristine cognition of the Path of Seeing
is considered to be the sign that there can be no falling back.

The extent of the Path of Seeing:

28. You should know that the Path of Seeing [extends]
    from Ultimate Mundane Attainment to the second station.

Niguma's Autocommentary on the Path of Seeing

1. Then, [following the Connecting Path] the Path of Seeing must be explained.

2. The essential quality of the Path of Seeing is the unqualified realization of the Four Noble Truths. It is defined as the Path of Seeing because one directly sees the Reality that one has not seen before. Its divisions are [the Four Noble Truths]:

a. suffering;
b. origination;
c. cessation; and
d. the path.

3. The ground for the assignment of its divisions [is described with reference to the following divisions]:

a. Seeing the Four Noble Truths, suffering and the rest, as emptiness is Receptivity to the Knowledge of the Real.
b. After that, the knowledge of the subsequent instant, [in which] one sees that emptiness in an extensive manner, is seeing the Reality of the Path of Seeing [i.e., the Knowledge of the Real].
c. The realization through which one thinks that both that Receptivity and Knowledge of the Real are the infallible causes for the attainment of enlightenment is Receptivity to Subsequent Knowledge with reference to the Four Noble Truths.
d. The arising of decisive certainty that that realization is without error is Receptivity to the Subsequent Knowledge of the Real with reference to the Four Noble Truths.
e. They are seen by the pristine cognition of the Path of Seeing. They are distinguished by the four degrees of lesser, greater, still greater, and very much greater [realization of] Reality.

4. The deliberate meditative discipline consists of the Seven Limbs of Enlightenment. It says in the *Byang-chub-sems-dpa' Blo-gros 'byung-gnas-kyis zhus-pa'i mdo* (Sūtra of the Dialogue with Bodhisattva Blo-gros 'byung-gnas):

a. Blo-gros 'byung-gnas inquired: "Victorious Lord! How should one regard the seven limbs of enlightenment?"
b. The Victorious Lord declared: "Blo-gros 'byung-gnas! These are the seven limbs of enlightenment: All elements of existence are

empty with regard to particular intrinsic characteristics. Thus, seeing that no element of existence attains to substantial reality is mindfulness as a limb of perfect enlightenment, because there is neither the act of remembering, nor is there deliberation.

c. "Blo-gros 'byung-gnas! Discrimination of the elements of existence as a limb of enlightenment [is the realization that] all so-called elements of existence are apparitional, not to be adhered to as objective points of reference at all, for they are not by any means established as substantially wholesome, unwholesome, or indeterminate.

d. "Blo-gros 'byung-gnas! Energetic application as a limb of perfect enlightenment is enthusiasm, nondiscursive devotion, and non-abandonment of striving with reference to the intuitive realizations of the path, which are free from subjective grasping, whereby one neither accepts nor rejects any of the elements of either the three mundane realms or nirvāṇa, for one has demolished the perceptions of the elements of existence.

e. "Blo-gros 'byung-gnas! Delight as a limb of perfect enlightenment is the removal of negative conditions, without the arising of delight about any conditioning elements, because all delight and unhappiness have been demolished.

f. "Blo-gros 'byung-gnas! Mental fitness as a limb of perfect enlightenment is the mind abiding in an unobscured and unqualified state of meditative concentration, [having achieved] physical fitness and mental fitness [with respect to] all elements of existence, for one does not adhere to even a particle of any element of existence that is present as an objective point of reference as an objective point of reference.

g. "Blo-gros 'byung-gnas! Concentration as a limb of perfect enlightenment is balanced absorption that is free from subjective grasping, the mind not adhering to any objective point of reference because the subjective grasping of the elements of existence has been demolished, or [the nature of those elements] realized. So it has been said that 'the mind being established in a balanced absorption in reference to a given thing, the elements of existence may be realized, but not by the mind not established in a balanced absorption; and with the mind established in a balanced absorption Buddhahood may be attained, but not without that balanced absorption.'

h. "Blo-gros 'byung-gnas! Equanimity as a limb of perfect enlightenment is that which causes no element of existence to abide anywhere, or to depend on, or to adhere to, or to become bound to anything, and by which mind does not grasp subjectively any element of existence, be it of pleasant, painful, or neutral mental [sensation]. It is the delight that is obtained when [mind], not carried off by any element of worldly existence, becomes endowed with an equanimity that is not preoccupied with any element of existence.

i. "Blo-gros 'byung-gnas! One should regard the seven limbs of enlightenment in that way."

5. Thus, by the power of that mode of concentration:

One sees Reality directly,
and becoming endowed with higher perception,
knows delight to the point of tears.
Always continent,
one can transform one's body for the sake of living beings,
and renounce one's life for the sake of the Dharma.
This occurs to the intelligent on the Path of Seeing
and is explained as the sign of nonreturning.
There are one hundred and twelve qualities contrary to it.

6. It says in the *Avataṃsaka:*

As soon as one attains [the first] station,
one becomes free from five fears:
one is without [fear of] the lack of livelihood,
death, ill-repute, and the evil conditions,
and is free from fear of saṃsāra.
In those one finds nothing fearsome.
And why, one might ask, is that?
Because there ego has no abode.

Thus, it should be known that [the bodhisattva who attains the Path of Seeing] is free from five fears.

7. The 112 [negative qualities] to be abandoned in the attainment of the Path of Seeing, which is the first station, are particularities of the six projected negative affections. What are those six?

a. unawareness;
b. desire;
c. egotism;
d. anger;
e. doubt; and
f. opinion.

8. There are five [kinds of] opinion:

a. false notions of self;
b. extremist opinions;
c. perverse opinions;

d. conceit with regard to ethics and observances; and
e. conceit with regard to one's opinions.

9. Adding together the five opinions and the five that are not opinions, unawareness, etc., there are ten negative affections.

a. Because, in the Realm of Desire, those ten primary negative affections occur with reference to each of the Four Noble Truths, there are forty.
b. In the higher realms, the Realm of Pure Form and the Formless Realm, there are nine, anger being the exception, which, when applied to the Four Noble Truths, become thirty-six in the Realm of Pure Form and thirty-six in the Formless Realm, making seventy-two.
c. If the forty pertaining to the Realm of Desire are added to those, there are, [in all], 112 things to be abandoned by the Path of Seeing.

10. As for the manner in which they are abandoned: The very great negative affections that are to be abandoned by the Path of Seeing are like a great darkness, which is abandoned by the small lamp of pristine cognition. Furthermore, they may be abandoned either by [the realization of] the Four Noble Truths, as explained above, or all at once, by the realization of the absence of self.

11. Moreover, there is the manner in which the truth is seen according to the Tantras.

a. It says in the *Ye-shes mngon-'byung* (The Disclosure of Pristine Cognition):

   By the *karmamudrā,* who is supreme bliss,
   the internal knot, grasping things as existing in truth, is undone by day;
   the internal knot of bewilderment is undone by night.
   Thus is the way of enlightenment taught.

b. And in the same work:

   The bliss of the *mudrā,* bliss supreme,
   comes from the grace of the guru.
   It is seeing Reality directly,
   and is renowned as the primary truth.

c. It says in the *Dam-tshig bkod-pa'i rgyud* (Tantra of the Array of Commitments):

   By day apparition, [the coalescence of] appearance and emptiness,
   and by night, in dream, the embodiment of the deity naturally arise.
   When one does not wander from that [vision]

the Sambhogakāya of the Jina [is attained].
[Realizing this] for a moment,
one [will attain] nirvāṇa in the Intermediate State.
What, then, need be said of continually abiding in it?
The same may be said of Apparition and Luminosity.
One must not speak of this to others.

d. It says in the *Ye-shes gsal-ba'i rgyud phyi-ma* (Subsequent Tantra which Clarifies Pristine Cognition):
If the impure tendencies of bewilderment,
those of the day and of dream,
do not remain on the eighth station
what then need be said of the Lotus-endowed?

e. It says in the *Tshangs-pa kun-dga'i mdo* (Sūtra of Brahma Ānanda):
The qualities of the paths and stations
should be realized during occasions of dream.

12. The boundaries [of the Path of Seeing extend] from the end of the Ultimate Mundane Attainment to the arising of the second station.

Notes

1. I was first encouraged in my study of the Shangs-pa tradition by its leading contemporary representative, the late Venerable Kalu Rinpoche Rang-byung Kun-khyab (1905–1989), to whose inspiration I remain profoundly indebted. For a summary of my initial research on the Shangs-pa, see Matthew Kapstein, "The Shangs-pa Bka'-brgyud: An Unknown Tradition of Tibetan Buddhism," in Michael Aris and Aung San Suu Kyi, eds., *Tibetan Studies in Honour of Hugh Richardson* (Warminster: Aris and Phillips, 1980), 138–144. I am grateful to the Institute for the Advanced Study of World Religions, and above all to its founder and first president, Dr. C. T. Shen, for their generous sponsorship of my work on the Shangs-pa tradition in 1978–1979.

2. The traditional account of Khyung-po Rnal-'byor's life, as given in George Roerich, trans., *The Blue Annals* (Delhi: Motilal Banarsidass, 1976), 728–733, is surveyed in David Snellgrove, *Indo-Tibetan Buddhism: Indian Buddhists and Their Tibetan Successors,* vol. 2 (Boston: Shambhala, 1987), 499–504, although Snellgrove's attempt (p. 501, n. 194) to resolve simply the difficulties that (as I have suggested in "The Shangs-pa bKa'-brgyud") surround the dating of Khyung-po's activities cannot be accepted. This complicated matter requires careful analysis of the original text of Khyung-po's complete *rnam-thar,* not just of the synopsis of that text given in later, derivative documents such as *The Blue Annals.* Such analysis cannot be carried out here, but will be treated in the introduction to my forthcoming edition and translation of Niguma's **Māyādhvakrama.* The primary sources for the study of early Shangs-pa biography are found in *Shangs-pa gser-'phreng: A Golden Rosary of the Lives of Masters of the Shangs-pa dKar-brgyud-pa* (sic) *Schools,* Smanrtsis Shesrig Spendzod, vol. 15 (Leh: T. W. Tashigangpa, 1970), and *Śaṅs-pa bKa'-brgyud-pa Texts: A collection of rare manuscripts of doctrinal, ritual, and biographical works of scholars of the Śaṅs-pa bKa'-brgyud-pa tradition from the monastery of Gsaṅ-sṅags-chos-gliṅ in Kinnaur* (Sumra, H.P.: Urgyan Dorje, 1977), 2 vols.

3. The relationship between Niguma's **Māyādhvakramavṛtti* and Klong-chen Rab-'byams-pa's *Sgyu-ma ngal-gso'i 'grel-pa shing-rta bzang-po* is established beyond doubt by a thorough comparative analysis of the two texts, which will appear in my forthcoming study of Niguma's work. Klong-chen-pa probably became familiar with the Shangs-pa teaching through his master Kumarādza (1266–1343), who was active at Tsā-ri, a hallowed Central Tibetan site for meditational retreat much favored by the early Shangs-pa masters. Biographical accounts of Kumarādza and Klong-chen-pa are found in Dudjom Rinpoche, *The Nyingma School of Tibetan Buddhism: Its Fundamentals and History,* trans. Gyurme Dorje and Matthew Kapstein (London: Wisdom Publications, 1990), vol. 1, bk. 2, pt. 4.

4. The history of this protector within the Dge-lugs-pa tradition is given by the Fifth Dalai Bla-ma, Ngag-dbang blo-bzang rgya-mtsho, *Record of Teachings Received* [*Gsan-yig gang-gā'i chu-rgyun*] (New Delhi: Nechung and Lhakar, 1970), vol. 1, plates 401–424. An account of the same deity from the perspective of the rival Jo-nang-pa tradition, authored by Jo-nang Rje-btsun Tāranātha, is found in *Shangs-pa gser-'phreng*.

5. Janet Gyatso, "The Teachings of Thang-stong rgyal-po," in Michael Aris and Aung San Sun Kyi, eds., *Tibetan Studies in Honour of Hugh Richardson,* pp. 111–119.

6. The teachings of the Shangs-pa tradition as transmitted through the lineage of Mkhyen-brtse and Kong-sprul are collected in 'Jam-mgon Koṅ-sprul Blo-gros mtha'-yas, *Gdams ṅag mdzod* (Delhi: Gelek and Lungtok, 1971), vol. 8, plates 237–332 representing the tradition of Thang-stong rgyal-po, and plates 333–543, the foremost texts of the Jo-nang-pa transmission of Shangs-pa meditational and yogic instruction.

7. These are the *Sgyu-ma lam-gyi rim-pa (*Māyādhvakrama)* and the *Sgyu-ma lam-gyi rim-pa'i 'grel-pa (*Māyādhvakramavṛtti).* Four editions of these texts have come to light so far: nos. 4643–4644 in the Peking edition of the Tibetan Bstan-'gyur; the similar redaction found in the Snar-thang edition of the Tibetan canon; and two manuscript versions published in facsimile in *Śaṅs-pa Bka'-brgyud-pa Texts* and in *Encyclopedia Tibetica: The Collected Works of Bo-doṅ Paṇ-chen Phyogs-las-rnam-rgyal* (New Delhi: Tibet House, 1969–1972). These two works are not found in the Sde-dge or Co-ne canons. My edition-cum-translation of them is based on all four available versions, referring also to the citations given by Klong-chen Rab-'byams-pa.

8. My investigations have led me to question whether the historical reality of Niguma is to be understood literally, and hence I am perplexed about the exact origins of the texts attributed to her, though the case is by no means decided. The arguments on both sides will be summarized in the introduction to my forthcoming study of Niguma's works. Whatever the solution (if, indeed, the problem is ever solved), it remains certain that the texts in question well represent the milieu of eleventh- and twelfth-century Indo-Tibetan Buddhism, and that they were, in their early history, exclusively associated with the Shangs-pa school.

9. I would be very interested to learn of any other scholastic writings attributed to Indian Buddhist women, should readers of this chapter be aware of such materials. It is, of course, true that learned women are depicted in some Indian Buddhist scriptures, and in the Tamil romance *Manimekhalaī* the heroine is even made to study the logic of Dignāga. This intriguing product of Tamil Buddhism has recently been translated into English by Alain Daniélou in *Manimekhalaī (The Dancer with the Magic Bowl)* by Merchant-Prince Shattan (New York: New

Directions, 1989), but exactly how its evidence is to be interpreted historically remains problematic in the extreme. I have not yet had the opportunity to read Paula Richman's *Women, Branch Stories, and Religious Rhetoric in a Tamil Buddhist Text* (Syracuse, N.Y.: Maxwell School of Citizenship and Public Affairs, Syracuse University, 1988).

10. In *The Autobiography of 'Jam-mgon Koṅ-sprul Blo-gros-mtha'-yas* (Bir, H. P.: Kandro, 1973), plate 89, we find the term explained as follows: "In general, *rnam-thar* is from the [Sanskrit] term *vimokṣa,* [which signifies] release or liberation. It is thus a historical account, concerning release from the evil destinies owing to the possession of pure faith in the case of the least among aspirants, concerning release from the ocean of saṃsāra owing to the possession of pure renunciation in the case of the middling aspirant, and concerning liberation from the two extremes of mundane being and peace owing to the possession of purity of higher meditation in the case of the best aspirant. In brief, it refers to a remarkable history of one's own release from suffering and its cause, while bringing about the liberation of other minds from bondage" *(de la spyir rnam thar ces pa ni bi mokṣa'i sgra las rnam par thar pa'am rnam par grol ba ste gang zag tha ma dad pa rnam par dag pa dang ldan pas ngan 'gro'i srid pa las rnam par thar pa dang/ 'bring nges 'byung rnam par dag pa dang ldan pas 'khor ba'i rgya mtsho las rnam par thar pa dang/ rab lhag bsam rnam par dag pa dang ldan pas srid zhi'i mtha' gnyis las rnam par grol pa'i lo rgyus bshad pa ste/ mdor na rang nyid sdug bsngal dang de'i rgyu las rnam par thar zhing gzhan rgyud 'ching ba las grol par byed pa'i lo rgyus rmad du byung ba zhig la brjod pa yin).*

11. The term *"lcam-mo,"* which originally means "elder sister," is ambiguous in this context: it may retain its literal significance or be a polite term for "wife." The Shangs-pa tradition adheres to the former interpretation, whereas historians of other Bka'-brgyud traditions tend to adopt the latter. It is also possible for the term to be used in a purely metaphorical sense, to mean something like "spiritual sister."

12. The description of Niguma is, of course, a sort of trope, portraying a yoginī of the Śaivite Kāpālika sect. Compare the yoginī Kapālakuṇḍalā, a minor character in the drama *Mālatīmādhava* by Bhavabhūti (early eighth century):

> The speed of my flight through the sky endows me with a great and charming tumultuousness. Shrill small bells jangle as they strike against the garland of skulls swinging to and fro about my neck. My pile of matted locks, though fastened by firm knots, streams out in every direction. The bell on my *khaṭvāṅga* staff seems to ring out with a continuous piercing scream as it whirls round and round. The wind whistling through the hollows of the row of bare skulls constantly jingles the small bells and causes my banners to flap about. . . . I can tell that the nearby enclosure of the great cremation area is in front of me by the smoke from the funeral pyres.

Quoted in David N. Lorenzen, *The Kāpālikas and Kālāmukhas: Two Lost Śaivite Sects* (Berkeley/Los Angeles: University of California Press, 1972), 56. The Buddhist tantric appropriation of Kāpālika imagery was very extensive, and appears to have been deliberate and systematic rather than a product of the "corruption" of later Indian Buddhism. The motivations underlying this appropriation have yet to be adequately explained.

13. The "scattering of the gold" is a not uncommon motif: for example, in Dudjom Rinpoche's *The Nyingma School* we find Padmasambhava scattering the gold-dust he has been offered to encourage him to visit Tibet (vol. 1, bk. 2, pt.

3) and Guru Chos-kyi dbang-phyug scattering the gold he is given as a parting gift by his Newari disciple Bharo Gtsug-'dzin (ibid., pt. 6). Besides being indicative of the master's detachment, this motif can usually be related to the purified transformation of the mundane, as it is in the present account.

14. *Shangs-pa gser-'phreng, Khyung-po rnal-'byor-pa'i rnam-thar,* folios 15b–17a.

15. It is the Peking edition of the Tibetan Tripiṭaka that actually preserves the bulk of the works attributed to Niguma: nos. 4633–4634, 4637–4650, 4657.

16. It is important to note that after his encounter with Niguma Khyung-po meets another yoginī who also becomes his teacher—namely, Sukhasiddhi, whose yogas form a special collection within the Shangs-pa corpus, although a much less extensive one than those of Niguma. An attempt to interpret this peculiar recapitulation is found in Judith Hanson and Mervin V. Hanson, "The Mediating Buddha," in Barbara N. Aziz and Matthew Kapstein, eds., *Soundings in Tibetan Civilization* (Delhi: Manohar, 1985), 296–303.

17. There is, of course, much controversy surrounding the proper definition and application of the term "shamanism." As a tentative point of departure, at least, one must refer to the authority of the single most influential work on the topic: Mircea Eliade, *Shamanism: Archaic Techniques of Ecstasy* (Princeton, N.J.: Princeton University Press, 1972). In chapters 11 and 12 we find Eliade's approach to the question of shamanic dimensions of Indian and Tibetan (among other Indo-European and East Asian) religious phenomena. Although some particular difficulties encountered in applying Eliade's conceptions to the study of Tibetan Buddhism will emerge below, let us first note the general criticism of Eliade found in Amanda Porterfield, "Shamanism: A Psychosocial Definition," in *The Journal of the American Academy of Religion* LV/4 (1987): 721–739, namely, that his "transcendental conception of spirits as manifestations of the sacred order behind ordinary reality also prevents analysis of their psychosocial referents and functions" (p. 735). In elaborating a psychosocial definition, Porterfield argues that

> The emotionally compelling aspect of shamanism is its dramatization of the distress experienced by the shaman's patrons. . . . The shaman helps his patrons appreciate symbols that address, interpret, and contribute to the resolution of their most pressing problems and conflicts . . . [B]y manifesting in his own body symbols that represent the resolution of problems besetting his patrons, *the shaman's own body is the locus of symbol production and this aspect of shamanism distinguishes it from other types of religious activity that symbolically address psychological and social problems, such as prophecy and priestly activity* (pp. 725–726, italics added).

It appears to me to be just this distinctive somatic localization of symbol production that forges an immediate link between shamanism and tantric practice, permitting the latter to harmonize to some extent the interests of shamanic and priestly religion. That some such harmonization or mediation does characterize important aspects of Tibetan Buddhism has been maintained primarily among anthropologists; examples are Robert Paul, *The Tibetan Symbolic World: Psychoanalytic Explorations* (Chicago: University of Chicago Press, 1982), 82–89, and Geoffrey Samuel, "Early Buddhism in Tibet: Some Anthropological Perspectives," in Aziz and Kapstein, eds., *Soundings in Tibetan Civilization,* pp. 383–397.

18. Cf. Janet Gyatso, "The Development of the *Gcod* Tradition," in Aziz and Kapstein, eds., *Soundings in Tibetan Civilization,* esp. pp. 322–323. Such considerations have encouraged a general restraint among textually oriented Tibetologists about accepting "shamanism" as a useful category in the description of

Tibetan Buddhism, or even of non-Buddhist Tibetan religious phenomena. Thus Giuseppe Tucci, in *The Religions of Tibet* (Berkeley/Los Angeles: University of California Press, 1980), passim, makes free use of the term but qualifies this convention by noting, in the course of his discussion of the Bon religion: "In our description the word shaman has occasionally been used. There can surely be no doubt of the existence of certain similarities between the old Tibetan religion and shamanism; the ride through the air, the magical use of the drum, the calling back of the souls of the dead or dying—all these were duties of particular classes of *gshen*. . . . All the same one can scarcely find here definite traces of those ecstatic aspects of shamanism so well portrayed by Mircea Eliade" (pp. 241–242). Anthropologists working among Tibetan and neighboring Himalayan peoples have exhibited rather less reticence here: see, for instance, in addition to the works cited in note 17 above, J. Hitchcock and R. Jones, eds., *Spirit Possession in the Nepal Himalayas* (New Delhi: Vikas Publishing House, 1976). Of interest, too, is Reneé de Nebesky-Wojkowitz, *Oracles and Demons of Tibet* (The Hague: Mouton, 1956), chap. 27, "Some Notes on Tibetan Shamanism."

19. See Eliade, *Shamanism,* pp. 99–109, on the quest in native North American shamanic initiation and its contrast with Asiatic shamanism. Alan Sponberg has rightly reminded me that the accounts of Chinese pilgrims in India do report questlike phenomena, so that it is plausible that we are being somewhat misled by the Indian textual record. See, for example, Samuel Beal, *Si-yu Ki: Buddhist Records of the Western World* (Delhi: Motilal Banarsidass, 1981), pt. 2, pp. 221–227, on the tale of Bhāvaviveka and the palace of asuras. But we may also wonder whether the emphasis on such phenomena found in the writings of Chinese pilgrims does not reflect somewhat their own peculiar cultural and religious milieu.

20. Note, in particular, the hagiography of Nāgārjuna, as given in James B. Robinson, trans., *Buddha's Lions: The Lives of the Eighty-Four Siddhas* (Berkeley, Calif.: Dharma Publishing, 1979), 74–80. The *Maṇicūḍāvadāna,* as told by Kṣemendra (*Avadānakalpalatā,* P. L. Vaidya, ed., Buddhist Sanskrit Texts No. 22 [Darbhanga: Mithila Institute, 1959], 1:22–37), with its powerful imagery of a journey culminating in grotesque bodily self-sacrifice, also merits consideration in this context. The perception, however, that vision-quest motifs have been regularly accentuated by the Tibetans is much strengthened when we contrast the Indian version of Nāropā's hagiography, found in Robinson (*Buddha's Lions,* pp. 93–95) with the much elaborated Tibetan version translated in Herbert V. Guenther, *The Life and Teaching of Nāropa* (Oxford: Clarendon Press, 1963).

21. Eliade, who does not fail to remark on apparently shamanic aspects of the Buddha-legend (*Shamanism,* pp. 403–412), seems to concur with this assessment. In ibid., p. 407, he states that "in Buddhism it is no longer a question of a symbolic ascent to the heavens, but of degrees of meditation and, at the same time, of 'strides' toward final liberation."

22. I am indebted here to the remarks of Raoul Birnbaum concerning pilgrimage at Wutaishan, delivered at the 1988 national meeting of the Association for Asian Studies held in San Francisco. The great Chinese novel of visionary pilgrimage, *The Journey to the West,* provides perhaps the most graphic literary example.

23. This becomes quite clear in the tales of Padmasambhava's subjugation of the hostile gods and demons of Tibet, reenacted in annual dance-dramas (*'cham*) throughout the Tibetan Buddhist domain.

24. Cf. Turrell V. Wylie, "Etymology of Tibetan: *Bla-ma,*" *Central Asiatic*

Journal, vol. 21/2 (1977): 145–148. On *bla* generally, see R. A. Stein, *Tibetan Civilization* (Stanford, Calif.: Stanford University Press, 1972), 226–229.

25. These actions are often explicitly interrelated. Thus, for instance, Khyung-po declares, "I impelled all those demons that bring injury to men not to bring injury to men" (*Śaṅs-pa Bka'-brgyud-pa Texts,* vol. 1, plate 459).

26. Some examples: "[E]very Teleut shaman has a celestial wife who lives in the seventh heaven. During his ecstatic journey to Bai Ülgän, the shaman meets his wife, and she asks him to remain with her; she has prepared an exquisite banquet for them" (Eliade, *Shamanism,* p. 76). "[D]uring the initiation people dance, drink, and sing, exactly as they do at weddings" (ibid., p. 76). "[T]he ribbons employed in Buryat initiations are called 'rainbows'; in general, they symbolize the shaman's journey to the sky" (ibid., p. 135). "The Tatars of the Altai imagine Bai Ülgän in the middle of the sky, seated on a golden mountain" (ibid., p. 266). "Transmission takes place in dreams and includes an initiatory scenario. . . . Among the Maricopa initiatory dreams follow a traditional schema: a spirit takes the future shaman's soul and leads him from mountain to mountain" (ibid., p. 103). An Eskimo shaman tells the candidate, "Then the bear of the lake or the inland glacier will come out, he will devour all your flesh and make you a skeleton, and you will die. But you will recover your flesh, you will awaken" (ibid., p. 59). It may be objected that the relationship between the Siberian shaman and his celestial wife always has an erotic component, but this, too, is represented in the *rnam-thar* of Khyung-po Rnal-'byor, in his encounter with the *ḍākinī* Sukhasiddhi: "At first she was most gracious, fully conferring on me the four empowerments in an emanational maṇḍala. Intermediately she was most gracious, acting as my secret consort who was none other than a goddess. In the end she was most gracious, fully bestowing all the esoteric instructions upon me" (*Śaṅs-pa Bka'-brgyud-pa Texts,* vol. 1, plate 440).

27. Cf. Takasaki Jikido, *An Introduction to Buddhism,* trans. Rolf W. Giebel (Tokyo: Tōhō Gakkai, 1987), 191: "[F]aith in the Buddha was expounded in all the early Mahāyāna sūtras to a greater or lesser degree. Yet although the Buddha is thus elevated to absolute heights, at the same time Mahāyāna Buddhism is also characterized by a wish to emulate the Buddha, to tread the same path, and to attain the same spiritual heights, even if it means calling on his assistance." The perspective of Vajrayāna is well represented in an oft-quoted verse found in D. L. Snellgrove, *The Hevajra Tantra: A Critical Study* (London: Oxford University Press, 1959), I. viii. 35–36: "In that realization of the perfect truth there is neither Wisdom nor Means. (36) By no other way may it be told, and from no one may it be received. It is known intuitively as a result of merit and of honouring one's *guru* and the set observances."

28. I am thus taking exception to the manner in which the term "Lamaism" is used, for example by Stein (*Tibetan Civilization,* pp. 164–191) or Tucci (*The Religions of Tibet,* chap. 3), where doctrine is emphasized above the peculiar institutional features of Tibetan Buddhism. That doctrine is employed in the service of institutions is not to be questioned. But if we wish to mark Lamaism off from the later Indian Buddhism of, for instance, Nālandā and Vikramaśīla, doctrine does not serve as an adequate differentiating characteristic. To see what does distinguish it, we must attend closely to the conjunction of the propositions that "the entire political and cultural history of Tibet was dominated by the monasteries" (Tucci, *The Religions of Tibet,* p. 110) and that "in Mahāyāna and Vajrayāna Buddhism the *guru* . . . is enabled, through living, direct contact, to transmit the letter and the spirit of the teaching, and to awaken the

sparks out of which blaze forth the fire of mystical experience" (ibid., p. 44). It is in the mutual reinforcement of these two propositions within the Tibetan world that the essential character of Lamaism is determined.

29. Indeed, the strict relationship between devotion to one's guru and the practice of yoga within the Indo-Tibetan Vajrayāna tradition is given formal expression in the terms of the tradition itself through the ubiquitous practice of *guruyoga,* for a typical Bka'-brgyud-pa formulation of which, see Jamgön Kongtrül, *The Torch of Certainty,* trans. Judith Hanson (Boulder, Colo.: Shambhala, 1976).

30. That the *rnam-thars* of tantric adepts may often be read as allegorical accounts of specific paths of yogic practice is well known: see, for instance, Janice D. Willis, "On the Nature of *Rnam-thar:* Early Dge-lugs-pa *Siddha* Biographies," in Aziz and Kapstein, eds., *Soundings in Tibetan Civilization,* pp. 304–319; and Dorje and Kapstein, "Translators' Introduction," in Dudjom Rinpoche, *The Nyingma School,* vol. 1, bk. 2.

31. Works supplying useful background on the categories of Buddhist tantras include: Dudjom Rinpoche, *The Nyingma School,* vol. 1, bk. 1, pt. 4; Ferdinand D. Lessing and Alex Wayman, *Mkhas grub rje's Fundamentals of the Buddhist Tantras* (The Hague/Paris: Mouton, 1968); Snellgrove, *Indo-Tibetan Buddhism,* vol. 1, pt. III; and Tsong-kha-pa, *Tantra in Tibet: The Great Exposition of Secret Mantra,* trans. Jeffrey Hopkins (London: George Allen and Unwin, 1977), esp. pp. 151–164.

32. Detailed accounts of the six yogas are found in Chang Chen Chi, trans., *Esoteric Teachings of the Tibetan Tantra* (York Beach, Maine: Samuel Weiser, 1981), pt. 2, and Herbert V. Guenther, *The Life and Teaching of Nāropa,* esp. pp. 43–86, where the six are included among the teachings transmitted in connection with Nāropā's "twelve great acts of self-denial."

33. For a convenient survey of the yogas of Niguma, see Glenn Mullin, trans., *Selected Works of Dalai Lama II: The Tantric Yogas of Sister Niguma* (Ithaca, N.Y.: Snow Lion, 1985). Tāla'i Bla-ma II Dge-'dun rgya-mtsho (1476–1542) himself hailed from a family with strong ancestral connections to the Shangs-pa Bka'-brgyud tradition.

34. 'Jam-mgon Koṅ-sprul, *Gdams-ṅag mdzod,* vol. 12, plate 674.

35. *Bodhicaryāvatāra,* 9.1ab.

36. David L. Snellgrove, "Saraha's Treasury of Songs," in Edward Conze, ed., *Buddhist Texts Through the Ages* (New York: Philosophical Library, 1954), 224–239; Herbert V. Guenther, *The Royal Song of Saraha: A Study in the History of Buddhist Thought* (Berkeley/London: Shambhala, 1973).

37. Cf. the hagiographies given in Robinson, trans., *Buddha's Lions.*

38. One of the peculiar difficulties with which Niguma's autocommentary confronts us is its abundant citations from works not otherwise known to us.

39. Paul Deussen, *The Philosophy of the Upanishads,* trans. A. S. Geden (New York: Dover, 1965), 50.

40. In these remarks, and those immediately following, a great body of very complicated material, some of which is considered in proper depth in other contributions to the present volume, is summarized in few words. For present purposes, the abhidharmic doctrines of the path as interpreted in the early Yogācāra school are best represented in the *mārgasatya* section of the *Abhidharmasamuccaya* of Asaṅga: see Walpola Rahula, *Le Compendium de la Super-Doctrine (Philosophie) (Abhidharmasamuccaya) d'Asaṅga* (Paris: École Française d'Extrême-Orient, 1971), 104–130. Rahula's note 9 (p. 117) provides useful observations on the relationship between the postcanonical lists of the *bodhipakṣadharmas* and

the enumerations found in the Pali *Nikāyas.* Note, too, that popular literature on Buddhism in the West has almost universally failed to observe that, from the standpoint of the Abhidharma traditions, the eightfold path represents not an elementary guide to the Buddhist life but the practice of only the most advanced disciples. The characteristically Mahāyāna exposition of the relationship between the five paths and thirty-seven *bodhipakṣadharmas* emerges, for instance, in the *Bodhipakṣādhikāra* of the *Mahāyānasūtrālaṃkāra,* S. Bagchi, ed., Buddhist Sanskrit Texts 13 (Darbhanga, Bihar: Mithila Institute, 1970), 128–153.

41. In this outline the roman numerals I to VIII represent the eight "chapters" into which I have divided Niguma's work in my forthcoming edition and translation.

42. Here we encounter another of the peculiar difficulties raised by the extant Tibetan version of Niguma's work: *mīmāṃsā* is normally rendered in Tibetan as *dpyod-pa,* though this is often misspelled as *spyod-pa,* a homonym meaning "conduct, activity," and used in translation for the Sanskrit *caryā.* In Niguma's *Path* and its autocommentary, we indeed find the common orthographical variant *spyod-pa,* but with an additional twist—the text supports our understanding of the term as "conduct" *(caryā)* and *not* as "investigation" *(mīmāṃsā).* Further discussion of this and other, similar problems will appear in my forthcoming study of Niguma's work.

43. Compare, for instance, Edward Conze, *Buddhist Thought in India* (Ann Arbor, Mich.: University of Michigan Press, 1967), 47: "In all religions some assumptions are taken on trust and accepted on the authority of the Scriptures or Teachers. Buddhism, however, regards faith as only a preliminary step, a merely provisional state."

44. I wish to thank professors Carl Bielefeldt and Bernard Faure of the Department of Religion, Stanford University, for arranging the presentation of this paper to Stanford's Buddhist Studies Seminar in February 1989. The pleasant discussion on that occasion did much to guide my revision for the present publication.

45. Probably the "three wheels" of religious works *(las),* teaching and study *('chad-pa),* and meditative attainment *(sgrub-pa),* which become manifest in all aspects of the advanced practitioner's routine, and which correspond to the "three gates" of body, speech, and mind that are transformed through the practice of the Tantras.

A Tibetan Perspective on the Nature of Spiritual Experience

JEFFREY HOPKINS

Background

Buddhism began gradually to be introduced to Tibet in the seventh century C.E., more than a thousand years after Śākyamuni Buddha's passing away. The form it took in Tibet was greatly influenced by the highly developed form of the religion that was present in India through the twelfth century (and even later); the geographic proximity and relatively undeveloped culture of the region provided conditions for an extensive, systematic transfer of highly developed scholastic commentaries and systems of practice. Unlike its East Asian counterparts, Tibetan Buddhism is centered not on Buddha's word as found in sūtras and tantras, but on Indian commentaries, many of which never made their way to East Asia. Scholasticism, therefore, often occupies a more central place in Tibetan culture than it does farther east; however, Tibetan culture is by no means characterized solely by devotion to scholastic inquiry. Rather, one of the keys to approaching Tibetan culture is its fascination with extreme forms of religious expression, whether in devotion, solitary yoga, philosophical debate, art, social organization around exalted figures, or the like. Moderation, though seemingly central to Buddhist dictums, is not the dominant theme. A visit to a Tibetan temple with its hundreds of images or to a reliquary adorned with literally tons of gold speaks to the unmoderated vibrancy of the culture.

Soteriology

The term "soteriology" at first seems out of place when considering the "self-help" presentations of Buddhism that predominate in the Tibetan cultural region. "Soteriology," which is built from the Greek *sōter* (savior) and means a "doctrine of salvation" or "way of salvation,"[1] seems to require an external agency that saves and rescues beings, whereas the Buddhism of this area for the most part (exceptions to be discussed) emphasizes that the preconditions necessary for liberation from suffering are within each person, and also that the techniques of rescue are to be enacted by practitioners themselves, not by an external savior. Exalted beings may help by teaching the path and by providing booster-blessings, but the path can be put into practice only by individual people. Thus, in translating these systems' terminology for release from undesirable states, I prefer such terms as "liberation" over "salvation" and "liberative" over "soteriological."

There are indeed external rescuers who assume considerable importance in Tibet, such as the female deity Tārā, whose very name means "rescuer" or "savioress"; also, the purpose of a majority of mantras is to call on deities such as Mañjuśrī for help. However, the main brunt of the normative tradition, as it is explained in the lectures halls and debating courtyards of Tibetan religious orders, does not view the process of gaining freedom as coming from an external agency. Even though many cultural practices in the Tibetan-Mongolian cultural region turn this orientation on its head through almost countless forms of "other-help" remedies, ranging from attendance at cleansing rituals to purchasing charms, drinking holy water, merely seeing people purported to be holy, and propitiating mundane deities—the extreme extent of which flies in the face of the basic call to make effort at internal practice—the normative tradition as well as much informed practice of the path is founded on self-help, albeit with boosts from the outside. Thus "soteriology" seems, from many but not all viewpoints, to be out of place in discussing the Buddhism of this region.

Still, I shrink from using neologisms such as "lysiology," or even the simpler but awkward "liberatology." There are a number of uses of "saving" in English in a reflexive context (saving oneself from trouble, etc.). Also, *dharma*—the basic Sanskrit word that can be taken as meaning "religion," and that is built from the verbal root *dhṛ* (to hold)—is etymologized as referring to doctrines (or practices) that hold a practitioner back from fright, specifically from the frights (1) of being reborn in a bad transmigration; (2) of being trapped in the round of suffering, whether in a good or bad transmigration; (3) of all sentient beings' being limited by obstructions preventing full development; and (4) of ordinary appearances and the conception of ordinariness.[2] The practices of self-help hold practitioners back, rescue, and save them from unwanted states. Hence, with the proviso that "self-help" is accepted as an integral part of "soteriology" and that an external savior is not the primary concern, I will use the term here.

Ninian Smart makes just such an allowance for self-help when he says about soteriology:

> The implication of the idea is that human beings are in some kind of unfortunate condition and may achieve an ultimately good state either by their own efforts or through the intervention of some divine power.[3]

Despite its etymology, he does not limit the scope of soteriology to other-help but includes self-help as well.

However, I take issue with Smart's limiting the scope of soteriology to the achievement of "an ultimately good state," for an important distinction needs to made with respect to Buddhist traditions: The "good states" that are being sought are not necessarily ultimate because they are of two types, one provisional and the other ultimate—namely, (1) release from low levels of transmigration into higher levels as humans, demigods, or gods, and (2) release from the entire round of suffering.[4] The latter is also envisioned as having two levels—(a) attainment of a lower enlightenment that is mere liberation from the round of suffering, and (b) attainment of the supreme enlightenment of altruistically effective buddhahood. Because the levels of concern, or "unfortunate conditions" from which Buddhists are trying to free themselves, are both provisional and ultimate, soteriology in this context cannot be limited to the notion of leading practitioners to ultimate states. The lower limit of soteriology in many Buddhist traditions is rescue from certain unfavorable conditions in a future lifetime—the goal being a more favorable state but one that is still trapped within the round of suffering. Such saving is an important part of this tradition (as is discussed below), and thus it would be an unwarranted superimposition to limit its soteriology, its doctrine of salvation, to more profound levels.

Sources

To give a picture of the states and means of rescue that are described in Tibetan Buddhism, I will use both written and oral sources. The written material is from genres of literature called "stages of the path" *(lam rim),* "decisive analyses" *(mtha' dpyod),* and "grounds and paths" *(sa lam);*[5] the oral sources are commentaries by contemporary lama-scholars that bring the language of the texts—often stilted by strict rules of redundancy—to life. Both types of sources are drawn primarily but not exclusively from one of the most scholastic orders of Tibetan Buddhism, the dGe-lugs-pa (Dge-lugs-pa) sect, founded by the polymath and yogi Tsong-kha-pa (1357–1419), who was born in the northeastern province of Tibet called A-mdo. As I have explained elsewhere, his followers came to have great influence throughout a vast region stretching from Kalmuck Mongolian areas near the Volga River (in Europe), where the Volga empties into the Caspian Sea, to Outer and Inner Mongolia, the Buriat Republic of Siberia, and most parts of Tibet and Ladakh.

Tsong-kha-pa established a system of education centered in large universities, eventually in three areas of Tibet, but primarily in Lhasa, the capital, which was as Rome is for the Catholic Church. For five centuries, young men came from all the abovementioned regions to these large Tibetan universities to study, usually (until the Communist takeovers) returning to their native lands after completing their degrees. My presentation is largely from standard dGe-lugs-pa perspectives[6] on the sūtra vehicle and the tantra vehicle (also called the vajra vehicle; Tib. *rdo rje theg pa,* Skt. Vajrayāna), the two basic forms of what is traditionally accepted as Śākyamuni Buddha's teaching.

The first genre of written material, "stages of the path," belongs to a wider class of texts that have a practical rather than theoretical orientation. These texts are aimed at making more coherent and accessible the plethora of practices that were inherited from India and that are the topics of critical study in more theoretical texts. In the standard dGe-lugs-pa educational curriculum,[7] six years are spent studying Maitreya's *Ornament for Clear Realization (mngon rtogs rgyan, Abhisamayālaṃkāra),*[8] a highly elaborate compendium on the paths that is not practiced in its own form. Rather, the long period of study is used to enrich understanding of a complex structure of spiritual development that provides an all-encompassing worldview daunting in its intricacy. Though the structure of the path, as it is presented in this text, does not provide the rubric of actual practice, much of its import is brought over to "stages of the path" literature, the practical use of which is certified by the great number of short texts in this genre aimed at daily meditation. The more complex system, having 173 aspects, provides a perimeter within which the more practical teachings can be enacted.

The second genre that I shall cite, "decisive analyses," are monastic textbooks on seminal Indian texts, in this case Maitreya's *Ornament for Clear Realization.* In its more advanced forms, this genre provides active stimulation of the intellect through juxtaposing assertions that are or appear to be contradictory, and through making what are often highly elaborate and aesthetically attractive reformulations of assertions in order to create coherence. In this genre, the intellectual fervor behind these topics and the format of philosophical confrontation (which is not accompanied by concluding practical summations) suggests that the aim is not what would usually be considered practice (i.e., meditation cultivating what has been studied); rather, the goal is endless intellectual reflection. This perspective has resulted in the flowering of intellectual pursuits in Tibet, but calls into question the injunctions to practical implementation. It appears that internal practice has given way to external debate on major and minor issues, but the emphasis on intellectual development also stems from stark recognition that these matters are not easily penetrated, requiring much intellectual exploration, and that immersion in topics—even to the point of entering a maze of conceptuality—can bear fruit over lifetimes. This is, at least, the system's self-justification for pursuing ever more refined conceptualization.

The third genre, "grounds and paths," is generally comprised of fairly brief texts used to structure—in a technical but more accessible format—complex Indian texts, again in this case Maitreya's *Ornament for Clear Realization.* A straight reading of such a text can be an exercise in boredom, but with the oral commentary of a teacher who is versed in a lineage of exegesis, the technical vocabulary can come to life in a vivid realm of imagination, much like a novel about a mythic land. Such stimulation of the metaphysical imagination is at the heart of the process of study in this tradition; whereas it may seem dry and sterile to those for whom the terminology has not been enlivened through evocative commentary, for those who have undergone this process the same technical vocabulary reverberates with meaning and epiphanies of new connections. Exploration of the elaborate architecture of the path itself becomes an important phase of the path, not to the exclusion of actually generating these path-states in meditation, but as an important part of creating a worldview that itself exerts a transformative force on the mind. It also often serves as a substitute for meditative practice, but even in such a context, its power is not to be belittled just because it contradicts the system's own dictum that meditation is the goal.

The Topics

Making use of these three genres of literature as well as oral commentary, I will consider first a threefold typology of practitioners and paths; then the profound experience of the mind of clear light in Highest Yoga Tantra; and finally the meaning of "path," or spiritual experience, in a more general sense. These topics provide a structure for considering—in an ancillary way—doctrinal, ethical, and social dimensions of Buddhist soteriology in the Tibetan cultural region. Much of the impetus of the inquiry is derived from my fascination, for more than two decades, with four issues:

1. In dGe-lugs-pa literature on the path of the sūtra systems, which are considered foundational and preparatory to the tantra systems, great stress is put on generating a plethora of attitudes and relationships, whereas in the form of tantra that is mainly practiced the practitioner seeks explicitly to withdraw all levels of coarser consciousness so that the most subtle level of mind can manifest. On the surface, the two styles of practice seem to be at odds, on the one hand extending and developing more and more beneficial attitudes, and on the other hand purposely seeking to cease all usual

mental activity. I will contend that a basic harmony—between the earlier elaborative practices and the later practices that are aimed directly at manifestation of the fundamental innate mind of clear light—is that they both involve withdrawal of bifurcating attitudes and extension of homogeneous ones.

2. This highly developed Tibetan tradition presents an intricately formulated series of paths, the very orderliness of which gives an impression of smooth, methodical progress. The elegance of the architecture of the system suggests that with the will to perform a graded series of practices, like following a map to a city, enlightenment is sure to be found. The neatly ordered path-structure communicates few of the dangers with which mental transformation is fraught—the harrowing readjustments of perceptions and priorities, the stagnation brought on by psychological blockages, and the counterproductive illusions generated by misunderstandings and preliminary experiences. To bring to the fore these aspects of practice of the path, I will briefly examine Rudolph Otto's description of the *mysterium tremendum* in order to provide a mirror in which similar presentations within the tradition can be seen.[9] I will attempt to put the compellingly beautiful, symmetrical structure of the path in the asymmetrical perspective of actual experience.
3. The systemization of the Buddhist path that this school presents performs many functions: it provides a basic handbook for practitioners; it explicates spiritual experience by providing a map of its levels; it provides a structure for theoretic discourse the impetus for which comes from actual experience but also from demands of coherence, elegance of system, and an overriding agenda of providing a comprehensive worldview; and it also serves socio-economic purposes of providing favored group identification, isolating the "ins" from the "outs." I will touch on these interpenetrating layers, which are often at such cross-purposes that a message of universal compassion, for instance, becomes wrapped in a package of prejudiced parochialism.
4. Finally, I will suggest that, through studying this Buddhist system, we can find hints that soteriological experience in general may be a matter of acquiring (or uncovering) perspectives that are at first dramatically "other" but that, with acculturation, are felt to be one's own basic nature.

To explore these topics, it is necessary to set the scene by "letting the tradition speak for itself" in its own style and vocabulary. I will do this by utilizing the oral and written sources mentioned above to pursue detail that will ground the ensuing discussion in the culture's own postures.

A Typology of Religious Experience

What do Tibetan systems see as constituting religious experience? An avenue of approach to this difficult topic that provides a wide perspective is to consider a basic typology of religious persons offered by the Bengali scholar Atīśa (982–1054) in his *Lamp for the Path to Enlightenment (byang chub lam gyi sgron ma, Bodhipathapradīpa).*[10] This text, which Atīśa wrote in 1042–1043 in Tibet at mTho-gling Monastery in the central Himalayas near Mt. Kailas, was originally composed in Sanskrit while Atīśa "simultaneously" dictated a Tibetan translation,[11] and came to have great influence in most Tibetan orders. In the dGe-lugs-pa order, Tsong-kha-pa considered it to be the root text for his *Great Exposition of the Stages of the Path (lam rim chen mo),*[12] a text of paramount importance throughout the vast region of Inner Asia.

In the third through fifth stanzas of the *Lamp for the Path to Enlightenment,* Atīśa speaks of persons as being of three types:

> Persons who seek for their own sake
> The mere pleasures of cyclic existence
> By whatsoever techniques
> Are to be known as low.
>
> Persons who seek merely their own peace—
> Having a nature of turning their backs on the pleasures of cyclic existence
> And turning away from sinful deeds—
> Are to be called middling.
>
> Persons who thoroughly wish
> To extinguish thoroughly all sufferings of others
> [Through inference of such] by way of the suffering
> Included in their own continuum are supreme.[13]

This typology of three levels of beings—those of small, middling, and great capacity—served as the framework for Tsong-kha-pa's *Great Exposition of the Stages of the Path* and has formed much of the perspective from which his followers both wrote texts and viewed the world up to the present day.[14] Among Tsong-kha-pa's followers, 'Jam-dbyangs-bzhad-pa Ngag-dbang-brtson-grus, a late seventeenth- and early eighteenth-century scholar from the northeastern province of Tibet, formulated definitions for the three types of beings, basing his exposition on Atīśa's stanzas but, typical to his style, drawing on a wide range of Indian texts, sūtras, and treatises.

'Jam-dbyangs-bzhad-pa's presentation is found in the first chapter of his textbook[15] on Maitreya's *Ornament for Clear Realization,* in a section supplementary to a presentation of the "openers of chariot-ways" *(shing rta srol 'byed).* 'Jam-dbyangs-bzhad-pa went to Central Tibet at age twenty-one and became abbot of the sGo-mang (Many Doors) College of 'Bras-spungs (Rice Mound) Monastic University at age fifty-three. Six years later, in 1707 (one year after a Mongolian chieftain, who happened to be one of his followers, murdered the regent and became "King of Tibet"), he returned to A-mdo (perhaps because it was safer than Central Tibet?), founding in 1710 a new monastic university to the southeast of sKu-'bum, another monastic university built in 1588 at the site of Tsong-kha-pa's birthplace. 'Jam-dbyangs-bzhad-pa's new institution, which was called bKra-shis-'khyil (Auspicious Circle), came to have great influence in that region; today, with about seven hundred monks, it is the largest functioning Tibetan monastic institution, although it is not included in the Tibetan Autonomous Region or even in Ch'ing-hai Province, but has been put in Gansu Province due to the radical redrawing of the map of Tibet after the Chinese takeover in the early 1950's. 'Jam-dbyangs-bzhad-pa's textbook literature became the standard texts for bKra-shis-'khyil Monastic University and was also adopted by the Go-mang College of Dre-bung Monastic University, replacing those by Gung-ru Chos-'byung in what must have been an interesting confrontation of monastic forces, given the inflated status that authors of textbook literature acquire due to being the leaders of the basic educational units in a very parochial society.

Beings of Small Capacity

'Jam-dbyangs-bzhad-pa formulates the definition of a being of small capacity as "a person who seeks mere high status *(mngon mtho, abhyudaya)* in cyclic existence (*'khor ba,* saṃsāra)."[16] He draws this definition from Atīśa's third stanza ("Persons who seek for their own sake/The mere pleasures of cyclic existence/By whatsoever techniques/Are to be known as low"). 'Jam-dbyangs-bzhad-pa takes Atīśa's word "mere" in the phrase "the mere pleasures of cyclic existence" as eliminating the possibility that persons on this level seek anything beyond high status within cyclic existence—namely, the pleasures of this or future lifetimes as a human, demigod, or god within the round of birth, aging, sickness, and death—and he takes the mention of "for their own sake" as eliminating the possibility that such persons seek to bring about others' welfare.

Drawing on Asaṅga's *Compendium of Ascertainments (rnam par gtan la dbab pa bsdu ba, Nirṇayasaṃgraha/Viniścayasaṃgrahaṇī),* 'Jam-dbyangs-bzhad-pa divides those of small capacity into three levels: low of the small, middling of the small, and supreme of the small. As the definition of a being of the low level of small capacity, he gives: "a person who seeks the mere happiness of this lifetime through nonreligious *(chos min)* means."[17] He bases this description on Asaṅga's speaking of "the first of those partaking of desires" as "the lowest beings," and on his identification of them as "rash" *(bab col)* or lacking consideration of their own circumstances "due to partaking of desires through nonreligious means."

The definition of a being of the middling level of small capacity is "a person who achieves [the mere happiness of] this lifetime through religious and nonreligious means." As is clear in Asaṅga's *Compendium of Ascertainments,* the distinctiveness of persons on this level is that they also use religious means to bring about happiness in this lifetime. Asaṅga identifies them as both "rash" and "nonrash." Though the middling of the small use "religious" means in their pursuit of pleasure in this lifetime, Kensur Lekden, abbot of the Tantric College of Lower Lhasa just before he escaped Tibet in 1959, speaks of both the low and the middling of those having small capacity as beneath the count of religious practitioners due to their short-term motivation. In his *Meditations of a Tantric Abbot,* which I translated and edited from lectures that he gave in Wisconsin, he says:

> The small of the small do not practise any religion, but only strive for happiness in this present existence. Like animals, these beings do not achieve any virtue at all.
>
> The middling of the small engage in both religious and non-religious means to achieve happiness in the present for only themselves, not for their friends or even for their own future lives. Due to this low motivation, their activities cannot function as religious practice.[18]

Kensur Lekden was fond of relating stories from the oral tradition with such vividness that it almost seemed he had been present at these events, his great detail and sense of presence at once enlivening the account and suggesting that a great deal of it was fabrication (even his historical accounts did not take on the guise of objective reporting). On one occasion he told of a question put to Atīśa about the effects of using religious means with a motivation limited to improvement of the present lifetime. He reported that Atīśa's answer was that the effect was rebirth in a hell, because good karma was being consumed through directing its effects to the superficial affairs of this lifetime, thereby leaving bad karmas to manifest in the next lifetime. Whether or not his story relates an actual encounter with Atīśa, it is widely renowned in this tradition, and thus provides a boundary line between religious and nonreligious experience—and also between what can and cannot be included within the scope of Buddhist soteriology—as seen by this tradition. The crucial issue is motivation: the scope of the nonsoteriological is limited to the affairs of this lifetime, whereas the scope of the soteriological is more long term.

This perspective is seen in the definition of a being of the supreme level of low capacity: "a person who seeks the mere happiness of a future cyclic existence [i.e., a future lifetime] by only religious means, not emphasizing this lifetime."[19] Again, 'Jam-dbyangs-bzhad-pa's source is Asaṅga's *Compendium of Ascertainments,* where Asaṅga refers to this third level as "supreme" within the low and describes it "as partaking of desire without rashness due to solely [making use of] religious means." As Tsong-kha-pa's *Great Exposition of the Stages of the Path* says:

> A special being of small capacity, not being greatly interested in this life, is interested in and engages in the causes for the achievement of high states *(mtho ris)* in future lifetimes.[20]

The shift to a longer range perspective constitutes the first step in becoming a religious person.

Thus in this tradition the initial soteriological experience is of a change of motivation, in the sense not of turning away from happiness, but of recognizing that happiness needs to be achieved beyond the present lifetime and that appropriate means must be used to gain it. This requires turning away from sole involvement with the temporary pleasures of the present in order to ensure pleasure in the future. Instead of seeking pleasure through the direct activities of accumulating wealth, power, and friends, the ten virtues (abstaining from killing, stealing, sexual misconduct, lying, divisive talk, harsh speech, senseless chatter, covetousness, harmful intent, and wrong views) are viewed as a better means for gaining a high position, accumulating wealth, and so forth in the long run. Without the motivation of improved future lives, these same virtues are not included within the practice of religion and cannot constitute initial soteriological experience. But with such a motivation, the virtues rescue, save, and hold one back from the frights of lower transmigrations as hell-beings, hungry ghosts, and animals.[21]

Beings of Middling Capacity

Just as persons become of supreme small capacity by extending the perspective that forms the basis of their behavior to include seeking relief from suffering in future lifetimes, so persons advance to middling capacity by extending their concern for the plight of suffering to the entirety of cyclic existence. 'Jam-dbyangs-bzhad-pa's definition of a being of middling capacity is "a person who is posited from the viewpoint of mainly seeking liberation for their own sake by way of turning the mind away from the marvels of cyclic existence."[22] Again, 'Jam-dbyangs-bzhad-pa draws his definition from Atīśa's *Lamp for the Path to Enlightenment* ("Persons who seek merely their own peace—/Having turned their backs on the pleasures of cyclic existence/And having a nature of turning away from sinful deeds—/Are to be called middling").

'Jam-dbyangs-bzhad-pa takes Atīśa's phrase "merely their own peace" as indicating that persons on this level (mainly)[23] seek only their own welfare; he takes the mention of their "turning their backs on the pleasures of cyclic existence" as indicating that they have overcome their attachment to the marvels of cyclic existence; and he takes "having a nature of turning away from sinful deeds" as indicating a nature of avoiding sinful activities at all times.[24]

About this level, Tsong-kha-pa's *Great Exposition of the Stages of the Path* says:

> A being of middling capacity, having generated regret with respect to all of cyclic existence, has taken as the object of attainment the liberation that is a release from cyclic existence and engages in the three trainings as the technique and path for that.[25]

Again, Kensur Lekden's description is more vivid:

> The best among those of small capacity have much to think about at this point. They wonder if attainment of a good future life is sufficient; they see that even if, through seeking the help of the Three Jewels, they attain the life of a god or human in their next lifetime, they will be born, grow old, become sick, and die. They arrive at the great understanding that merely gaining happiness in the next lifetime is not sufficient.
>
> A person exceeds the thought of a being of small capacity when he/she realizes that there is no peace until he/she no longer has to be reborn through the force of contaminated actions and afflictions. Progressing, he/she decides to obtain liberation from all types of cyclic existence and seeks the bliss of the extinguishment of suffering. Further, since the causes of contaminated actions are the afflictions of desire, hatred, and ignorance, he/she identifies these as foes and, by aiming to overcome them, generates the attitude of a being with middling capacity. Through proper meditation he/she can then be liberated from cyclic existence as a Foe Destroyer *(arhan)*.[26]

The shift in perspective that takes place with this second level of soteriological experience is more long range, for it takes into account not just the next lifetime (or a few future lifetimes) but the whole series of lifetimes and the precariousness of one's situation. Through practice of the path one is seeking to be rescued, saved, and held back from the entire uncontrolled round of birth, aging, sickness, and death in all of its forms.

The difference in the scope of the soteriological perspective—the range of that from which one is seeking to be rescued—comes from more accurately penetrating the nature of appearances. This is done by understanding the pervasiveness of the suffering of being under the uncontrolled influence of karma and afflictive emotions, and by understanding that any state within cyclic existence, no matter how pleasurable, will eventually lead to lower states, given the undeniable presence of negative karma.[27] More accurate realization of the situation of cyclic existence leads to a reformation of motivation.[28]

On this level, soteriological experience is comprised predominantly of generating disgust for the entire round of uncontrolled rebirth. In the Autonomy School (*rang rgyud pa,* Svātantrika), which provides the predominant perspective of "grounds and paths" literature, this experience motivates realization of the emptiness and selflessness found among the attributes of the four noble truths, as well as development of a powerfully concentrated mind of meditation. In the Consequence School (*thal 'gyur pa,* Prāsaṅgika), which is the dGe-lugs-pa sect's own final system, it also motivates realization of the subtle level of emptiness, since the conception of inherent existence is considered to be the root of cyclic existence. As before, the advance comes not from turning away from happiness, but from recognizing a greater happiness and the means to achieve it. This greater perspective impels meditation on the actual status of persons and other phenomena—their emptiness of inherent existence—in order to undermine the afflictive emotions that are built on misperceiving that things inherently exist. Such meditation leads in turn to direct cognition of the true status of things, such that various levels of afflictive emotions are gradually removed from the mental continuum forever.

Beings of Great Capacity

Just as persons become of middling capacity by extending their motivational outlook to include seeking relief from all of cyclic existence, so persons advance to great capacity by extending their understanding of their own plight in cyclic existence to a realization that others are in a similar position. 'Jam-dbyangs-bzhad-pa's definition of a being of great capacity is

> a person who is posited from the viewpoint of seeking an exalted knower of all aspects *(rnam mkhyen, sarvākārajñāna)* [i.e., the omniscience of buddhahood] for the sake of the attainment of buddhahood in the continuums of other sentient beings by way of having come under the influence of great compassion.[29]

As before, he draws his definition from Atīśa's *Lamp for the Path to Enlightenment* ("Persons who thoroughly wish/To extinguish thoroughly all sufferings of others/[Through inference of such] by way of the suffering/Included in their own continuum are supreme").

'Jam-dbyangs-bzhad-pa takes the phrase "by way of the suffering/Included in their own continuum" as indicating how these persons infer others' suffering based on experience of their own. He takes Atīśa's mention of "others" as indicating their being intent on others' welfare, and his mention of "all sufferings" as referring to all levels of suffering in cyclic existence, both gross and subtle. He takes "extinguish thoroughly" as indicating the extinguishment of obstructions together with their predisposing latencies *(bag chags, vāsanā),* and he takes "thoroughly wish" as indicating that these persons wish to relieve other beings of sufferings through a variety of techniques.[30]

On this level, practitioners are said[31] to be concerned about four defective conditions in all sentient beings: (1) cyclic existence, (2) the seeking of a solitary peace that is mere liberation for their own sake, (3) obstructions to liberation, and (4) obstructions to omniscience. The shift in perspective that takes place with this third and last level of religious experience is of far wider scope, in that others' suffering has become the primary concern. In a series of lectures at the University of Virginia, Den-ma Lo-chö Rin-bo-chay spoke movingly of this universal responsibility:

> Sentient beings' births are limitless, without beginning. There is, hence, not a single being who has not been one's mother. At the time when they were our mother, they protected us with kindness just as our mothers of this lifetime did. It would be very bad if one had no thought to help these beings who have been one's mother and been very kind to oneself since beginningless time, but rather discarded them. For instance, take the case of a mother who was blind and crazy and who went walking along the edge of an abyss into which she could easily fall. If her only child, seeing this, remained playing and enjoying him/herself, this would be considered vulgar even in the world. In just this way, sentient beings, our aged mothers, are as if blind, not knowing the discarding of non-virtues and the adoption of virtues, how to practice the path. Although they want happiness, they do not know how to achieve the causes of happiness; although they do not want suffering, they powerlessly achieve its causes. Thus they are as if crazed. Moreover, because they have accumulated many non-virtues and continue to do so, they are walking alongside the abyss of bad transmigrations. Just as the child should try to stop his/her blind, crazed mother from wandering along the edge of an abyss, so we should develop the compassion that seeks to free sentient beings from this state in which, though wanting happiness, they do not know how to achieve its causes and hence are bereft of happiness, and though not wanting suffering, powerlessly achieve its causes again and again. It is not sufficient just to think, "How nice it would be if these beings were free from suffering"; rather one must assume the burden of doing this oneself.
>
> When one considers whether one has the capacity to free all sentient beings from suffering, one understands that at present one does not. Who has such a capacity? When one investigates, one sees that it is a buddha, a Supramundane Victor, one who has removed all faults and perfected all attributes. Thus beings of great capacity are those who generate an altruistic intention to become enlightened, thinking, "I will attain buddhahood in order to establish all sentient beings in the great liberation of the non-abiding nirvāṇa" *(mi gnas pa'i myang 'das, apratiṣṭhitanirvāṇa).*[32]

Den-ma Lo-chö Rin-bo-chay's use of the image of an only child's relationship to his or her helpless mother is typical of the teachings for inculcating this altruistic attitude. An ordinary attitude of filial concern is made extraordinary by extending its scope beyond its usual range, to all beings. Just as, on the level of the practices of a being of low and middling capacity, the quest for happiness is not forsaken but is reaffirmed with a higher goal, so here ordinary concern and compassion are not replaced by otherworldly attitudes but are extended far beyond their usual scope and are thereby transformed.

In the earlier phase, the scope of a practitioner's soteriological concern (and hence of spiritual experience) advanced from concern with suffering in a future life to concern with one's own cyclic existence in general; now it advances to concern with the plight of all sentient beings.[33] All beings are to be rescued, saved, and held back from all levels of suffering.

In terms of how such progress in an ever-widening perspective is made, first one passes from the level of ordinary low capacity to that of special low capacity by reversing the emphasis on the appearances of the present lifetime; this is done by realizing (1) that the present situation endowed with pleasurable features is valuable, (2) that one will not stay long in this life, and (3) that lifetimes as animals, hungry ghosts, and hell-beings are bereft of such fortunate circumstances.[34] Second, one passes to the level of a being of middling capacity by reversing the emphasis on the appearances of future lives, thereby developing an intention definitely to leave cyclic existence; this is done by reflecting on the inevitable effects of karma and the many varieties of suffering certain to be induced by one's own bad karma. It is necessary to meditate on (1) suffering, so that a wish to separate from cyclic existence will be generated; (2) impermanence, so that attachment to the mental and physical aggregates and to this life will be eliminated; and (3) selflessness, so that attachment to what belongs to oneself (including one's own body) will be overcome.[35] Through this process, an attitude seeking liberation can be generated in full form. Third, one advances to the level of a being of great capacity by developing the unusual compassion of being willing to take on the burden of freeing other beings from suffering and joining them with happiness. This is done by meditatively cultivating a sense of closeness with all beings and by becoming aware of their suffering, which is inferred from one's own situation as realized earlier on the paths of beings of small and middling capacity.

The paths of the three levels thereby serve as an integrated gradation of practices; it is not that they are mutually contradictory.[36] By removing the merely self-directed aspects of the paths of the lower levels, the paths of the three levels form a coherent, integrated whole, inducing advancement in soteriological perspective and spiritual experience. The higher levels do not cancel the lower ones, but rather are built on the lower and continue to be reinforced by them, since beings of middling and great capacity need a continuum of favorable lives in order to complete their respective paths, and thus still need the practices of a being of small capacity to ensure good rebirths. Also, the great compassion that is so central to the motivation of a being of great capacity is founded on the realistic appraisal of one's own plight in cyclic existence, as understood through the practices of a being of middling capacity. Even more important, the realization of emptiness—detailed on the level of practice for a being of middling capacity for gaining liberation from cyclic existence—is central to achieving liberation from the obstructions to omniscience, which is the primary intent of a being of great capacity.

Thus for a being of great capacity, the practices of all three beings are intertwined: the lower ones both form the foundation for the higher and remain important aspects of continual practice. Hence the lower levels of soteriological concern cannot be dismissed as merely preliminary, in favor of more ultimate concerns; they remain an important aspect of a practitioner's intentionality throughout the entire scope of practice. The picture that emerges from considering such a broad range of practices is far richer than what is gained from considering only ultimate concerns.

Classification of Beings

The doctrine of three types of beings forms an integrated series of practices for one person and also constitutes a typology supposedly applicable to all beings; anyone and everyone can be classified within this rubric. Most ordinary beings, including animals, are the low of the low capacity, since the scope of their concern is mainly limited to the temporary affairs of this lifetime; those who also employ religious means to achieve happiness in this lifetime are middling of the low; those who are about to generate a nonartificial form of an intention to leave cyclic existence in all its aspects are of middling capacity, as are all Low Vehicle practitioners right through to those who have attained the state of a Foe Destroyer. Those who have generated the unusual compassion described above are classified as beings of great capacity.

As a typology for humanity in general, this system has obvious faults. For instance, it cannot classify the most compassionate Christians as any of these, since they are not mainly seeking either (1) "an exalted knower of all aspects so that buddhahood might be attained in the continuums of other sentient beings," as a being great capacity would, (2) "liberation for one's own sake," as a being of middling capacity would, (3) "the mere happiness of a future lifetime," as a being of supreme low capacity would, (4) "the mere happiness of this lifetime through religious and nonreligious means," as a being of middling low capacity would, or (5) "the mere happiness of this lifetime through nonreligious means," as a being of low low capacity would. The typology has similar but not so severe difficulties with Hindu systems, adherents to which, because of being considered not to recognize properly the process of cyclic existence, would probably be classified as beings of the middling low variety, outside the realm of religious practitioners.

Though the typology is aimed at including all beings, its failure to recognize other traditions even as religions suggests that it has a hidden agenda to exclude their practitioners from the count of religious beings.[37] This is not surprising in such a parochial culture, but such harsh exclusivity does appear to run counter to the advocacy of universal compassion. Followers quickly learn to bifurcate their minds so that they are deeply moved by calls to unbiased compassion and yet participate with vigor in exaggerated discrimination against other groups. Confronted with such exclusivity, I have sometimes wondered whether the message of universal compassion is being wrapped in a package of parochialism, or whether a message of parochial prejudice is being wrapped in the package of universal compassion.

Nevertheless, the typology says much about Indo-Tibetan Buddhist religious experience and can be used within such a framework. To summarize: The process of self-education, self-help, and self-rescue is a withdrawal from lower involvements—first from seeking pleasures only within the scope of the present lifetime, next from seeking the pleasures of cyclic existence in general, and finally from self-centeredness. At the same time, it requires an extension to higher involvements—first to concern with future lifetimes, next to liberation from all of cyclic existence, and finally to others' welfare. These are the "saving from" and "saving to" aspects of the path.

Otto's *Mysterium Tremendum*

To gain a perspective on this Indo-Tibetan description of what it means to be religious, let us consider a radically different presentation: that of Rudolph Otto. I find that his work, though treating experience of the sacred within a theistic context, provides a means of unmasking facets of the *experience* of the practice of this Buddhist system. The seemingly great difference between the two systems has challenged me to notice descriptions of the emotionally harrowing nature of soteriological experience that are indeed to be found in the Tibetan tradition but that are buried under the format of a grand design of spiritual development, which easily fosters a sense that, with the proper will, certain practices will yield a predictable series of results. Let us first consider Otto's position in some detail, citing his text to a degree sufficient to get its flavor.

He describes religious experience as being of the *mysterium*—"that which is hidden and esoteric, that which is beyond conception or understanding, extraordinary and unfamiliar"[38]—under five headings: awefulness, overpoweringness, energy or urgency, wholly otherness, and fascination.[39] "Awefulness" is analogous to fear but "wholly distinct from being afraid,"[40] a "terror fraught with an inward shuddering such as not even the most menacing and overpowering created things can instil,"[41] "the feeling of personal nothingness and submergence before the awe-inspiring object directly experienced."[42] Similarly, about "overpoweringness" he says:

> Thus, in contrast to "the overpowering" of which we are conscious as an object over against the self, there is the feeling of one's own submergence, of being but "dust and ashes" and nothingness. And this forms the numinous raw material for the feeling of religious humility.[43]

And:

> For one of the chiefest and most general features of mysticism is just this *self-depreciation* (so plainly parallel to the case of Abraham), the estimation of the self, of the personal "I," as something not perfectly or essentially real, or even as mere nullity, a self-depreciation which comes to demand its own fulfillment in practice in rejecting the delusion of selfhood, and so makes for the annihilation of the self. And on the other hand mysticism leads to a valuation of the transcendent object of its reference as that which through plenitude of being stands supreme and absolute, so that the finite self contrasted with it becomes conscious even in its nullity that "I am naught, Thou art all."[44]

Otto describes the third attribute of the *mysterium,* "energy or urgency," as "a force that knows not stint or stay, which is urgent, active, compelling, and alive."[45] The *mysterium* is also characterized by being the "wholly other," namely,

> that which is quite beyond the sphere of the usual, the intelligible, and the familiar, which therefore falls quite outside the limits of the "canny," and is contrasted with it, filling the mind with blank wonder and astonishment.[46]

In addition:

> The truly "mysterious" object is beyond our apprehension and comprehension, not only because our knowledge has certain irremovable limits, but because in it we come upon something inherently "wholly other," whose kind and character are incommensurable with our own, and before which we therefore recoil in a wonder that strikes us chill and numb.[47]

And:

> Mysticism continues to its extreme point this contrasting of the numinous object (the numen), as the "wholly other," with ordinary experience. Not content with contrasting it with all that is of nature or this world, mysti-

> cism concludes by contrasting it with Being itself and all that "is," and finally actually calls it "that which is nothing." By this "nothing" is meant not only that of which nothing can be predicated, but that which is absolutely and intrinsically other than and opposite of everything that is and can be thought. But while exaggerating to the point of paradox this *negation* and contrast—the only means open to conceptual thought to apprehend the *mysterium*—mysticism at the same time retains the *positive quality* of the "wholly other" as a very living factor in its over-brimming religious emotion.
>
> But what is true of the strange "nothingness" of our mystics holds good equally of the *sūnyam,* the "void" and "emptiness" of the Buddhist mystics. This aspiration for the "void" and for becoming void, no less than the aspiration of our western mystics for "nothing" and for becoming nothing, must seem a kind of lunacy to anyone who has no inner sympathy for the esoteric language and ideograms of mysticism, and lacks the matrix from which these come necessarily to birth.[48]

About the fifth and final characteristic, "fascination," Otto says:

> Possession of and by the numen becomes an end in itself; it begins to be sought for its own sake; and the wildest and most artificial methods of asceticism are put into practice to attain it. . . . The *mysterium* is experienced in its essential, positive, and specific character, as something that bestows upon man a beatitude beyond compare, but one whose real nature he can neither proclaim in speech nor conceive in thought, but may be known only by a direct and living experience. It is a bliss which embraces all those blessings that are indicated or suggested in positive fashion by any "doctrine of salvation," and it quickens all of them through and through.[49]

Thus,

> what we have here to point out is the unutterableness of what has been yet genuinely experienced, and how such an experience may pass into blissful excitement, rapture, and exaltation verging often on the bizarre and the abnormal.[50]

For Otto, the sacred is overpowering, charged with energy, awe-inspiring, and shocking/fascinating. His description finds so little resonance with the Indo-Tibetan presentation of the threefold typology of religious practitioners that we could easily conclude that his theistic perspective makes comparison impossible.

However, such language is not entirely lacking in the Tibetan cultural region; there are similar but not so prominent explanations that run counter to the seeming ease and fluidity of the steps in the Buddhist structure of the spiritual path. For instance, with regard to approaching realization of emptiness, the late eighteenth- and early nineteenth-century Mongolian scholar bsTan-dar-lha-ram-pa describes a stage of fear that is eventually overcome through training:

> An object that appears to a nonconceptual [sense] consciousness is the object conceived to exist inherently by a conceptual consciousness [in the sense that a conceptual consciousness assents to the object's appearance of inherent existence]. Therefore, related with this object are (1) the appearance of existing from its own side, which is to be refuted, and (2) the mere appearance [of the object], which is not to be refuted. [However,] before attaining the view [of the absence of inherent existence,] these two appear confused as one. When the view is found, these two [i.e., the appearance of existing from its own side and the mere appearance] are discriminated, and it is well renowned in the words of the wise that the fact that the mere appearance is not refuted is an important essential. When mountains, fences, houses, and so forth appear to ordinary beings, they appear in all respects to exist from their own side. Therefore, one should meditate until, destroying this mode of appearance, it is canceled in all respects for one's mind, and the fear, "Now there is nothing left over," is generated.
>
> The generation of such fear is extremely rare. Kay-drup's *Opening the Eyes of the Fortunate* says: "If even arrival at the point of actual generation of fear and fright of the profound emptiness is extremely rare, what need is there to say that arrival at an actual ascertainment, which is an understanding of an emptiness through experience, is almost nonexistent?"
>
> Therefore, greatly superior to the present-day philosophers, to whom not even an image of the mode of [an object's] existing from its own side has appeared, are those in earlier times who overextended what is refuted [in the view of selflessness and held that objects themselves are refuted].
>
> There are reasons for not being frightened about emptiness. On the one hand, the stupid who do not know either the term or the meaning of emptiness are not frightened because they do not know any of its disadvantages or advantages. For example, the stupid who do not know about how one can fall from a horse are brave to mount a wild horse. On the other hand, those who perceive emptiness directly do not fear it because they lack the cause of fear, that is, the conception of inherent existence which is abandoned through seeing [the truth], like a being who has learned well the ways of controlling a wild horse.
>
> Then, who fears [emptiness]? It is suitable for fear to be generated in those who have understood emptiness a little and are investigating whether or not such and such a phenomenon exists, for suddenly the phenomenon appears to their minds to be totally nonexistent. An example is a person who has understood a little but not completely how to mount a wild horse.[51]

Emptiness seems to be incompatible with appearance, in that when one understands it a little, objects no longer seem positable. Emptiness becomes a threat, like a wild horse—the analogy resonating with Otto's description of the sacred as overpowering, charged with energy, awe-inspiring, and shocking/fascinating. Indeed, in their analysis of objects, meditators must bring themselves to a point of fright; otherwise, the implications of emptiness—realization of which is diametrically opposed to the ingrained assent to a false status of objects on which all emotional turmoil is built—are missed. However, with acculturation, like learning horsemanship, the fear is removed, for one becomes able to make the distinction between the appearance that is negated—the object's seeming to exist from its own side—and the mere appearance of the object itself, which is not negated. The problem, therefore, is not with emptiness; it is with the untrained mind's perception of it as negating appearances—both of oneself and everything else.

Similarly, according to descriptions in Highest Yoga Tantra, when the fundamental innate mind of clear light dawns, it seems to leave no room for appearances, even annihilating oneself and thus generating fright. Since the final aim of the spiritual path, as presented in the Tibetan cultural region, is to manifest this most subtle level of mind and to remain within it, all the while manifesting dualistically in order to be of service to others, let us consider what that mind is in some detail, so that its significance and relationship to the broad spectrum of paths presented earlier can be discussed.

The Fundamental Innate Mind of Clear Light in Highest Yoga Tantra

The mind of clear light is identified as the eighth in a series of increasingly subtle experiences that pervade conscious life.[52] It manifests at periods when the grosser levels of consciousness cease either intentionally, as in profound states of meditation, or naturally, as in the process of death, going to sleep, ending a dream, fainting, and orgasm.[53] Prior to its manifestation, there are several stages during which a practitioner experiences increasingly subtler levels of mind.

Through meditative focusing on sensitive parts of the body, the winds (or currents of energy; *rlung, prāṇa*) that serve as foundations for various levels of consciousness are gradually withdrawn, in the process of which one first has a visual experience of seeing an appearance like a mirage. Then, as the withdrawal is more and more successful, one successively "sees" an appearance like billowing smoke, an appearance like fireflies within smoke, an appearance like a sputtering butter-lamp when little wax is left, and then that of a steady candle flame. With the withdrawal of conceptual consciousnesses,[54] a more dramatic phase begins, at which point profound levels of consciousness that are at the core of experience manifest.

The first subtle level of consciousness to manifest is the mind of vivid white appearance. All coarse conceptuality has ceased, and nothing appears except this slightly dualistic, vivid white appearance, which is one's consciousness itself appearing as an omnipresent, huge, white, vivid vastness. When that mind is withdrawn, a more subtle mind of vivid red or orange increase dawns; nothing appears except this even less dualistic, vivid red or orange appearance. The consciousness remains in this state for a period, and when this mind is withdrawn, a still more subtle mind of vivid black near-attainment dawns; it is called "near-attainment" because one is close to manifesting the mind of clear light. Nothing appears except this still less dualistic, vivid black appearance. During the first part of this phase of utter blackness, one remains conscious, but in a second phase one becomes unconscious in thick blackness.

When the mind of black near-attainment ceases, the three "pollutants" *(bslod byed)* of the white, red/orange, and black appearances have been entirely cleared away, whereupon the mind of clear light dawns. This is the most subtle level of consciousness; it is compared to the sky's own natural cast without the "pollutions" of moonlight, sunlight, and darkness, and is called the fundamental innate mind of clear light *(gnyug ma lhan cig skyes pa'i 'od gsal gyi sems).*

It is said that ordinary beings are so identified with superficial states that the transition to deeper states involves fear of annihilation; when the deeper states begin to manifest, beings panic, fearing that they will be wiped out, and due to this fear they swoon. As the late eighteenth- and early nineteenth-century Mongolian scholar Ngag-dbang-mkhas-grub (1779–1838; also known as Kyai rdo mkhan po) says in his *Presentation of Death, Intermediate State, and Rebirth (skye shi bar do'i rnam bzhag),*[55] at the time of the clear light of death, ordinary beings generate the fright that they will be annihilated. (This recalls Carl Jung's account of a Swiss mystic who, upon the dawning of great illumination, bashed his face into a large rock in front of him.) The fear-inspiring aspect of its manifestation accords with the oft-described awesomeness and sense of otherness that not only Rudolph Otto but much of world culture associates with types of profound religious experience.

Thus, both for the experience of emptiness and for that of this fundamental mind, the Buddhist tradition speaks in terms of a harrowing ordeal, full of dread. Also, although the threefold typology of practices may make it seem that the progression from one level to another is a smooth process of gradually acquiring a new outlook, the very structure of tiers suggests that the soteriological experiences of each succeeding level are not accessible and are even foreign to those on a lower level. The upper levels are outside the experience of those on lower levels—they are dramatically "other." One may study about the upper levels, but actually being a person of a higher level is outside one's experience. A realistic appraisal of one's own motivation yields a self-identification as very low on the scale; the typology gives the practitioner both a means to assess accurately his/her present condition and goals to strive toward. The typology itself thereby exerts an influence on the practitioner, beckoning toward the development of a more profound perspective but also making it clear that those higher levels are foreign.

In contrast, the use of common concerns—first with one's own suffering and then with familial responsibility—to deepen and then broaden one's perspective suggests that the seeds of the higher levels are indeed common to all. Seen in this light, the higher attitudes are profoundly "other" in the sense that they are outside present manifestation, their implications being unbearable to the present personality structure; yet they are also present in a common seed-form which, through repeated training, can be extended in a process of development.

Similarly, with respect to the manifestation of the mind of clear light, the fact that this awesomeness is one's own final nature suggests that the otherness and fear associated with its manifestation are not part of its nature but are due to the shallowness of untrained beings. Much of the dGe-lugs-pa system of spiritual education, framed around the practices of beings of the three capacities, can be viewed as aimed at overcoming this fear of one's own most basic nature. The strangeness of our own nature is a function of misconception, in this case of the basic nature of the mind—specifically, the sense that afflictive emotions subsist in the nature of the mind[56] and the consequent identification with them, such that when their own basis starts to manifest, the fright of annihilation is generated.

That is how ordinary, untrained beings react to the manifestation of their own inner being, but a central tenet of this system is that training can overcome the sense of alienness. In the rNying-ma (Rnying-ma), or Old Translation, Order of Tibetan Buddhism, an accomplished yogi's experience of fundamental mind is even described as like "being set on mother's lap" *(ma pang bu 'jug).* The joy and sense of at-homeness that a child feels when (in a happy mood) he or she is set on mama's lap is an analog to highly developed yogis' sense of joyful naturalness when they identify in experience their own basic nature.[57] The at-homeness of the fundamental innate mind of clear light, when experienced by one who has overcome the initial, distorted fear and sense of annihilation, suggests that this fundamental mind is, in a sense, most common, most ordinary. Indeed, in rNying-ma literature, it is called "ordinary mind" *(tha mal pa'i sems).* In this way, the sacred (or an aspect of the sacred) is both awesomely "other" (when initially experienced) and intimately common (when recognized as the fundamental stuff of ordinary existence).

Path

Emerging from these descriptions of the paths of beings of the three capacities and of the experience of the fundamental innate mind of clear light is a perspective that beings are not familiar with their own nature and that training is required to overcome the obstacles preventing profound recognitions from being manifested. In Buddhist literature, the process of training is called the "path" (Skt. mārga), a term which has many meanings:

> way, road, path, course, passage, tract passed over; reach, range; scar, mark; path or course of a planet; search, inquiry, investigation; canal, channel, passage; means, way; right way or course, proper course; mode, manner, method, course; style, direction; custom, usage, practice; hunting or tracing out game; a title or head in law, ground for litigation; high style of acting, dancing, and singing; hinting or indicating how anything is to happen; section; anus, musk; a certain month; and a name of Viṣṇu.[58]

The goal-directed nature of many of these terms is reflected in its verbal root, *mārg,* which means "to seek, seek for; to hunt after, chase; to strive to attain, strive after; to solicit, beg, ask for; to ask in marriage; to seek through, trace out; to go, to move."[59]

In dKon-mchog-'jigs-med-dbang-po's *Presentation of the Grounds and the Paths,* the term mārga (Tib. *lam*) is said to refer to something that opens the way to higher states:

> The definition of a path is an exalted consciousness—of one who has entered the path[60]—which serves to open a passageway allowing an opportunity to progress to the enlightenment that is its result.[61]

Den-ma Lo-chö Rin-bo-chay brings the stilted language of the monastic textbook to life:

> For instance, opening a door reveals a passageway, allows a passageway. Or, in another way, if you are driving a car and there is a large boulder in the road, you would have to break it up into pieces and get it aside, thus opening up a passageway.[62]

Paths allow passage by removing obstacles. They also are tracks set down by earlier practitioners; Den-ma Lo-chö Rin-bo-chay renders the point in everyday terms:

> What is a path? In the world we call the tracks *(shul)* of someone who went before and which serve as a way to be followed by those who go afterwards a "path." We know many kinds of paths—a road such as is used by cars, the tracks used by a train, a footpath one might follow when walking in the mountains. The term "path" is used here in a similar manner. We call paths those ways of proceeding of the Buddhas, Bodhisattvas, and Superiors of the past—the kinds of thought they generated—which is how those who wish to generate such realizations in the present and the future must proceed.[63]

In addition to removing obstacles and opening a way, "path" has the connotation of a tradition, the tracks worn into the ground by the passage of predecessors (which is a reflection of the meaning of mārga as "scar" or "mark," given above).

dKon-mchog-'jigs-med-dbang-po lists the synonyms of "path" and an etymology:

> Path of liberation *(thar lam),* exalted knower *(mkhyen pa),* exalted wisdom *(ye shes, jñāna),* clear realizer *(mngon rtogs, abhisamaya),* mother *(yum, mātṛ),* and vehicle *(theg pa, yāna)* are mutually inclusive synonyms. They are called "paths" because they cause one to progress to the status of liberation.[64]

Den-ma Lo-chö Rin-bo-chay explains:

> A path of liberation *(thar lam)* is so called because it is a path that allows progress to liberation. An exalted knower *(mkhyen pa)* is so called because it is unmistaken knowledge of a method for proceeding to that enlightenment which is one's own object of attainment. Exalted wisdom *(ye shes, jñāna)* and clear realizer *(mngon rtogs, abhisamaya)* are the same. A path is called a mother *(yum, mātṛ)* because it produces or gives birth to that superior person which is its own effect. It is called a vehicle [or platform] *(theg pa, yāna)* because it is like a ladder. . . . All of these are called paths because they cause progress to the state of liberation. The word "liberation" here refers to both the liberation of a Foe Destroyer and the great liberation of a Buddha.[65]

Paths are goal-directed—leading to, producing, and ascending to a higher state.

Paths are also called "grounds" or "earths" *(sa, bhūmi)* in the sense that they serve as bases *(gzhi)* of high qualities of mind, just as the earth serves as the basis of innumerable activities. Den-ma Lo-chö Rin-bo-chay elaborates:

> A ground acts as a basis of the many qualities that are its fruit. . . . Just as the ground [or earth] acts as a basis of orchards, forests, and so forth, so these consciousnesses act as the basis of many qualities of those who have entered the path; therefore, they are called grounds. . . . A ground serves as a basis not only for producing that which has not been produced but also for maintaining what has been produced as well as causing non-degeneration of what has been produced.[66]

The term "ground" (or the French *terre* used by David Seyfort Ruegg), which seems so awkward and forced in a discussion of spiritual paths in English, is, surprisingly, explained by Den-ma Lo-chö Rin-bo-chay as employed because of its familiarity and ease of understanding:

> The reason why the paths of the three vehicles are called grounds is that they serve as bases of one's generating higher qualities in one's own mental continuum. If, in the designation of a name, one employs a term from common usage, then it is easily remembered and used. The term "ground" is known well, for if we are going, wandering, lying down, or

> sitting, our activities are involved with the ground [or earth]. Thus, through skill in means—using a term that is easy to understand—the term "ground" is used. The reason for designating the paths of the three vehicles as grounds is from the viewpoint of a similarity of function.[67]

Given the descriptions of spiritual practices as "paths" that are the tracks of predecessors leading to salutary aims, as "vehicles" or "platforms" reaching higher states, as "mothers" giving birth to high qualities, and as "grounds" that are the bases of growing favorable states of mind, it is clear that soteriological activities are viewed as goal-directed. The tantric system is said to use the fruit (or goal) as the path, in that a buddha's abode, body, resources, and activities are mimicked in the practice of deity yoga (i.e., the yoga of imitating an ideal being). Yet even in tantra, as described by Tsong-kha-pa and his followers,[68] it is emphasized that one is merely mimicking buddhahood in order more effectively to induce it.[69]

Paths are what make advancement possible; they allow passage forward by removing obstacles. The three levels of path rescue, save, and hold practitioners back from ever more subtle, counterproductive attitudes and rescue them toward ever more salutary concerns. The stages progress from short-term self-orientation to long-term self-orientation and then to other-orientation, each stage requiring a profoundly ethical transformation. Even the self-oriented stages are built on practices aimed at not harming others, and they culminate eventually, as a being of great capacity, in a commitment to helping others.

These phases all involve withdrawal from mental perspectives that are characterized by multiplicity and a fracturing of attention—namely, from being sunk in attachment to the manifold appearances and purposes of the presently appearing world and of future lifetimes, and in the inequality of self-cherishing. Carl Jung speaks to this fractured state and to religion's attempt to regather this energy:

> To be like a child means to possess a treasury of accumulated libido which can constantly stream forth. The libido of the child flows into things; in this way he gains the world, then by degrees loses himself in the world (to use the language of religion) through a gradual over-valuation of things. The growing dependence on things entails the necessity of sacrifice, i.e., withdrawal of libido, the severance of ties. The intuitive teachings of religion seek by this means to gather the energy together again; indeed, religion portrays this process of re-collection in its symbols.[70]

The over-valuation of objects that the ordinary consciousness suffers is reversed in this Buddhist system not only through its symbols (such as the central image of the contemplative Buddha withdrawn into internal contemplation) and rituals of severance of ties to the world, but also through a series of increasingly re-collective, meditatively reflective exercises. The meditations that cause withdrawal of energy from these counterproductive states are realizations of qualities that are universal, or at least applicable to broad categories of objects—the nature of suffering of all the bad transmigrations as animals, hungry ghosts, and hell-beings, and then of all transmigrations in general; the nature of impermanence that pervades all commonly experienced phenomena; the nature of selflessness that pervades all phenomena; and the suitability of concern for all other beings.

These meditations, whose basic structure is withdrawal of a certain type of involvement and expansion of another, higher level with more homogeneous involvement, are consonant with the practice in Highest Yoga Tantra of withdrawing all the winds (energies) that support the grosser levels of consciousness so that the meditator can expand consciously controlled usefulness to the level of the fundamental innate mind of clear light. The mind of clear light is viewed as the stuff of appearances, all appearances being viewed as the manifestation *(rnam 'gyur)* or sport *(rol pa, līla)* of the mind of clear light. The mind of clear light is viewed as the universal substrate of appearance on this expanded level of awareness, which is obviously beyond self-centeredness and is a constant expression of the equality of self and other.[71]

In this way, the paths of the beings of the three capacities, by withdrawing energy (wind) and applying realization of universal qualities, can be seen as consonant with and leading to the unfolding of the mind of clear light. As explained earlier, the ascent of these levels is effected by a process that expands common perspectives beyond their usual range: the common concern for one's own present happiness is expanded to future lives; the common concern for happiness is expanded to a type of happiness that is beyond the vicissitudes of the rapidly changing nature of cyclic existence; the common concern for relatives and close friends is expanded to all beings, seen as close by virtue of similarity in type, in that both oneself and others equally want happiness and do not want suffering, and by virtue of having been friends in former lifetimes. Similarly, the common nature of mind—its luminous and cognitive essence—is expanded in the sense that it becomes a primary focus of attention whereby it, rather than its contents, becomes the dominant factor of experience and is seen as the stuff of all appearances. The earlier practices lead to the later, since the radical withdrawal of the winds that operate the grosser levels of consciousnesses cannot be effected without the withdrawals brought about by the preceding practices; otherwise, the practitioner's attached involvement with appearances would be too firm to allow conscious stoppage of these levels of mind.

In all these practices, energies are withdrawn and elements common to the ordinary mind are emphasized and expanded, but despite the commonness of the basic element in the process, the experience of such withdrawal and expansion is fraught with uneasiness (except apparently for a few gifted persons).[72] Attempts to expand common attitudes of concern for one's own welfare and for friends are characterized by a sense of being alien because of the attachments that must be overcome to open the way for such new perspectives. Similarly, due to self-identification with mental and physical factors that are contrary to one's own nature, the manifestation of the mind of clear light—the inner nature of all conscious experience—can evoke such a great sense of being alien that it is feared as a force capable of annihilating oneself. Thus on many levels soteriological experience evokes a sense of dread—dread of the loss of directionality that pursuit of temporary pleasures affords, of the loss of permanence, of the loss of a solidly existent sense of self, and of the loss of one's very being—because it means facing what is awesomely other than one's present, very limited perspective. Nevertheless, after acculturation by means of paths of practice, the very insights that initially evoked a feeling of loss evoke instead the feeling of finding a lost treasure. As the Fifth Dalai Lama said about the experience of realizing emptiness:

> This initial generation of the Middle Way view is not actual special insight; however, like a moon on the second day of the month, it is a slight finding of the view. At that time, if you have no predispositions for emptiness from a former life, it seems that a thing which was in the hand has suddenly been lost. If you have predispositions, it seems that a lost jewel which had been in the hand has suddenly been found.[73]

What is experienced with a sense of loss at an early stage is later reexperienced with a sense of gain.

The frequent descriptions in rNying-ma literature, as well as in East Asian Buddhism, of identifying one's own actual nature, one's own face, suggest that the sense of at-homeness, of "being set on mama's lap," reveals religion not as something separate but as eventually most familiar.[74] One might even think that such an experience is not religious because it lacks the qualities of separateness and awe, but as we have seen, soteriological experience in this tradition is an acculturation to a state that is first viewed as foreign only because of the afflicted state of the practitioner. The experience of the fundamental innate mind of clear light as the "standard, everyday" stuff of basic mind indicates that this most profound of religious experiences in Indo-Tibetan tantrism is not of a realm of the sacred that is radically other; rather, it is one's own nature that is immanent in all consciousness but transcendent until its manifestation. When manifested it loses the distance of transcendence, much as in the case of the Vedānta dictum *Tat tvam asi* (You are that), in which an identification of oneself with ultimate reality, Brahman, is made.[75] The diseased nature of oneself and the distance of Brahman, the ultimate, are canceled in the immediacy and closeness ("at-home-ness") of recognizing one's own final nature.

Such lack of alienation is not limited to mature experience of the fundamental innate mind of clear light, for, as explained above, the practices of the beings of the three levels of capacity, though extensions of common experiences, pass through a phase of being alien but culminate in a sense of familiarity that results from cultivation of the path. The path is the bridge between an original, common endowment and a final expansion of such experience to a universal level; it opens a passageway by removing obstacles—namely, the inability to stand the implications of these profound states. This need for acculturation is reflected in the frequently repeated Tibetan oral teaching that "meditation" *(sgom)* is actually "familiarization" *(khoms)*—a matter of getting used to, or adjusting one's mind to, the implications of profound realizations.[76] With respect to the mind of clear light, the experience of this basic state as alien and dreadful is only relative to clinging to distorted notions about one's own nature. It is a function of a temporary inadequacy of the mind perceiving it—a failure that, according to this system, can be overcome through meditative cultivation of the path.

The fact of this final at-homeness, as well as the system's presentation of the compatibility of reason and experience of the sacred, could cause us to ignore the awe-inspiring, horrific, sometimes stultifying clashes with what seems to be one's own basic personality due to misidentifying the afflictive emotions as being the very fabric of the mind. However, the experience of the sacred (including not just the experience of the fundamental innate mind of clear light but also the path-experiences of beings of all three capacities) as dreadful, as so shattering that one cannot stand it, is not to be discounted, because when the sacred (i.e., these common experiences in their expanded meaning) impinges on a consciousness not yet ready for it, it is indeed dreadful, fraught with implications undermining and threatening distorted postures of personality.

To appreciate the significance of the path, we must realize that initial contemplation of (1) the plight of transmigrations as animals, hungry ghosts, and hell-beings, (2) the plight of cyclic existence in general, (3) the needs of the endless number of sentient beings, and (4) the implications of the basic nature of the mind is upsetting, because it is in such opposition to ingrained attitudes. When done effectively (and the tradition supplies many techniques to accomplish this), the impact of such contemplations on the pursuit of present and superficial pleasures—as well as on the pursuit of self-centered goals, which are so central to ordinary personality—is devastating in its demand for rearrangement of the personality. This is so because attachment is built on bias, and the extension of these more homogeneous attitudes requires a dramatic withdrawal of the energy of attachment. Thus, even though the awe-inspiring nature of the path is experienced only relative to attachment to biased states (i.e., to viewing the afflictive emotions as the basic nature of the mind), it should not be ignored in favor of the neat layout of stages, which does not communicate the painful clash between intimately held attachments and these higher attitudes. Only when we see these implications can we place the path in the context of its soteriological task.

This discussion of a Tibetan Buddhist tradition has brought to the fore three phases of experience of the sacred—dreadful, overcoming obstacles, and totally "at-home." All three must be emphasized in order to convey even a minimally rounded picture of the path. Otherwise, the enormity and momentousness of the religious enterprise cannot be appreciated. Our starting point was an Indo-Tibetan typology of three types of beings, an obviously inadequate format for categorizing religious persons and religious experience in general. As Wilfred Cantwell Smith says:

> Every comprehensive Weltanschauung, insofar as it achieves the coherence at which it aims, therein reduces every alternative one: misunderstanding, distorting, its neighbors' world-view.[77]

There is no question that this Buddhist typology, due to its own exclusivistic agenda, is similarly distortive, but it has provided an avenue for exploring forms of Buddhist soteriology. That avenue has, in turn, yielded a view of religious experience as not limited to concern with the ultimate, but as having a broader range; as having its roots in common experience, but as involving an extension far beyond its usual bounds; and as initially being radically "other," due to unfamiliarity caused by personality distortions, but as finally being most familiar, due to acculturation that removes those distortions.

The Mind of Clear Light and No-Path

From among the many regional Buddhisms, the dGe-lugs-pa presentation of the soteriological path contrasts most sharply with the no-path presentation found in Ch'an and Zen, where one is warned not to conceive of there being anything (such as levels of a path) to be produced. In the dGe-lugs-pa presentation, we do not find a perception of the need to undermine its own presentation of the path, as is so dominant in Ch'an/Zen. Theoretically, this stems from delimiting what is negated in the view of emptiness to inherent existence: wisdom does not refute the existence of objects in general, but rather a certain status of inherent existence; thus it is not necessary, after presenting a practice, to undercut it.[78] Since an absence of inherent existence does not contradict nominal existence, the entire structure of the path can be laid out within the philosophically unassailable rubric of nominal existence. In this light, realization of emptiness is said to be impossible without first identifying the object of negation—namely, inherent existence.

Such delineation of the object of negation makes it unnecessary to engage in the seeming contradiction of undermining one's own position, as is so often done in Ch'an/Zen: first presenting what certainly looks like a path, next claiming there is no path, and then saying that everything is as it always was. I view the process of the path in Ch'an/Zen as negating something that makes it seem as if existence itself is negated, after which there is another stage when the unity of appearance and emptiness dawns. This progression suggests that what emptiness refutes is not existence itself, although it seems so to a practitioner, after which a correction is needed.

In a similar vein, even the dGe-lugs-pas admit that, without having realized emptiness, it is impossible to differentiate with valid cognition between inherent existence and existence. This would seem to make their path to realization of emptiness impossible, since they insist that the first step on the long road to realization is to recognize the object of negation, inherent existence, yet this cannot be done without first having realized emptiness! However, they attempt to get around this difficulty by holding that the initial recognition of the object of negation is accomplished not by valid cognition but by a correctly assuming awareness. The very great danger is that, because of the admitted inability to distinguish between existence and inherent existence prior to realizing emptiness, the mere presentation of a path to be generated would induce the false conception that the path, its production, and the meditator all inherently exist, whereby realization of the true nature of things would become more distant. Thus, although there are definite conceptual and systematic advantages to verbally differentiating between existence and inherent existence, this posture—a cornerstone of dGe-lugs-pa doctrine—is not without problems. From this vantage point, one can appreciate the seeming refutation of production in Ch'an/Zen, which, for a mind not given over to nihilism, allows the nature of the mind to shine forth.[79]

The delineation of the object of negation in dGe-lugs-pa and its non-delineation in Ch'an/Zen appears to be the fork in the conceptual road that sends the dGe-lugs-pas down the path of intricate conceptual elaboration and the adherents of Ch'an/Zen down the road of seemingly contradictory (but very profound) conceptual undercutting. Still, even in the dGe-lugs-pa system, a practitioner must withdraw the mind and concentrate nonanalytically in order to induce the subtler levels of mind required in Highest Yoga Tantra. Just as, in the Zen presentation translated in Carl Bielefeldt's chapter, it is said that one should not imagine that there is anything to be produced, so in dGe-lugs-pa it is said to be impossible to manifest these subtler states when imagining that there is something to be produced. To understand the dGe-lugs-pa path, therefore, we must make a distinction between the study of the path-structure and what is required in meditation at certain points.[80]

Indeed, much as in the Ch'an/Zen dictum that there is nothing to be produced, if one seeks to produce a particular state of mind, one's imagination then prevents the manifestation of basic mind, which is found in the hiatus between states (but which, when found, is continuously realized to be the basis of all states). When one arrives at the point where such conceptually withdrawn meditation is required, as long as a path that needs to be generated is imagined, one cannot manifest a subtler level of mind. Also, when it manifests, it does not work on obstacles like a person removing a boulder or like hot on cold, but totally sublates the obstacle in a state utterly beyond it. It is said that in one moment of realizing emptiness with such a subtle mind, a practitioner overcomes the afflictive obstructions to liberation from cyclic existence that take two periods of countless aeons to overcome in the sūtra system.[81] Also, the third period of countless aeons is replaced by practices, achievable in the same lifetime, that blend this profound experience of emptiness with appearance, such that their utter compatibility is realized.[82] In this way, tantra becomes the quick path, with enlightenment becoming a viable, palpable goal within a practitioner's lifetime.[83]

When viewed as a whole, the variety of presentations in the regional Buddhisms—path and no-path in a great many forms—suggests that there is a danger of reifying particular states of mind to the point of preventing manifestation of the profound, due to not penetrating the impact of the dictum that there is nothing (inherently existent) to be done. In the context of meditative requirements at certain levels of the path, it is counterproductive to think that there is a state from which one is to be saved and a state to which one will be saved; thus *in this context,* a meditator's conceptualization of soteriology—the saving from and saving to nature of spiritual paths—would be inimical to enlightenment, even if not so either in general or on other levels of the path. This perspective may provide a way to see some degree of harmony between the path and no-path traditions of Buddhism.

Notes

1. See Ninian Smart, "Soteriology," in Mircea Eliade, *Encyclopedia of Religion* (New York: Macmillan, 1986), 13:418.

2. My source is oral explanations by Kensur Ngawang Lekden, abbot of the Tantric College of Lower Lhasa before 1959.

3. Ibid.

4. Alex Wayman (in an entry on "Buddhist Soteriology" in Eliade, *Encyclo-*

pedia of Religion, 13:423–426) makes this distinction between two soteriological goals, but he misidentifies the lower goal as "birth in heaven," whereas it is actually birth in any of the good transmigrations, i.e., as a human, demigod, or god.

5. In Tibet, a genre of monastic literature developed with the aim of getting a handle on the plethora of assertions on the nature, divisions, and mode of procedure of the spiritual paths presented in Indian Buddhism. Called "Grounds and Paths," it came to shape the manner in which much of Tibetan Buddhism views spiritual experience. For the sūtra path, the texts are for the most part written from the viewpoint of the Yogic Autonomy Middle Way School *(rnal 'byor spyod pa dbu ma rang rgyud pa, Yogācārasvātantrikamādhyamika),* to accord with what is perceived to be the main system of Maitreya's *Ornament for Clear Realization.* In this class, and among the precursors of dKon-mchog-'jigs-med-dbang-po's text, is one by rJe-btsun Chos-kyi-rgyal-mtshan (1469–1546). However, there is at least one such text written from the viewpoint of the Consequence School *(thal 'gyur pa, Prāsaṅgika):* bLo-bzang-rta-dbyangs (also known as bLo-bzang-rta-mgrin, 1867–1937), *Brief Expression of the Presentation of the Grounds and Paths of the Three Vehicles According to the System of the Perfection Vehicle, Essence of the Ocean of Profound Meaning (phar phyin theg pa'i lugs kyi theg pa gsum gyi sa dang lam gyi rnam bzhag pa mdo tsam du brjod pa zab don rgya mtsho'i snying po),* The Collected Works of Rje-Btsun Blo-Bzaṅ-Rta-Mgrin (New Delhi: Guru Deva, 1975), 4:65–190.

The genre of "Grounds and Paths" literature is not confined to sūtra but also extends to tantra. Two prominent instances of the latter are dbYangs-can-dga'-ba'i-blo-gros (eighteenth century), also called A-kya-yongs-'dzin, *Presentation of the Grounds and Paths of Mantra According to the Superior Nāgārjuna's Interpretation of the Glorious Guhyasamaja, A Good Explanation Serving as a Port for the Fortunate (dpal gsang ba 'dus pa 'phags lugs dang mthun pa'i sngags kyi sa lam rnam gzhag legs bshad skal bzang 'jug ngogs),* The Collected Works of A-kya Yoṅs-ḥdzin (New Delhi: Lama Guru Deva, 1971), 1:452–497; and a similar text by his student Ngag-dbang-dpal-ldan (b. 1797), also known as dPal-ldan-chos-rje, *Illumination of the Texts of Tantra, Presentation of the Grounds and Paths of the Four Great Secret Tantra Sets (gsang chen rgyud sde bzhi'i sa lam gyi rnam bzhag rgyud gzhung gsal byed),* (rgyud smad par khang edition, no other data).

6. Given the emphasis within the dGe-lugs-pa sect on individual colleges (even within larger monastic universities) and the general provincialism of Tibetan culture, it might seem impossible to speak of "standard" postures of the sect, but my meaning here points to generally recognizable, or at least representative, explanations.

7. The notable exception is the curriculum at the monastery of the Paṇ-chen Lama, bKra shis lhun po, where Dharmakīrti's *Pramāṇavārttika* is the topic of this initial long period of study.

8. For a translation into English, see Edward Conze, *Abhisamayālaṃkāra,* Serie Orientale Roma (Rome: Is. M.E.O., 1954).

9. Rudolph Otto, *The Idea of the Holy,* trans. John W. Harvey (London: Oxford University Press, 1923; paperback rpt., 1977); esp. chap. 4, *"Mysterium Tremendum,"* and chap. 5, "The Analysis of *Mysterium.*" See Donald S. Lopez, Jr., "Approaching the Numinous: Rudolf Otto and Tibetan Tantra," *Philosophy East and West* 29, 4 (October 1979): 467–476; Lopez sharply contrasts Otto's view of the holy with the dGe-lugs-pa emphasis on the compatibility between reason and profound religious experience. My agenda is different; I am using

Otto's presentation to get at the awe-inspiring (and even dreadful) experience of the path, which is largely hidden by the dGe-lugs-pa emphasis on reasoning.

10. *P* 5343, vol. 103. An English translation with Atīśa's autocommentary is available in Richard Sherbourne, S.J., *A Lamp for the Path and Commentary* (London: George Allen and Unwin, 1983).

11. Sherbourne, *A Lamp for the Path,* pp. x–xii.

12. A translation of the first part of the section on special insight is available in Elizabeth Napper, *Dependent-Arising and Emptiness* (London: Wisdom, 1990). An English translation of the sections on calm abiding and special insight is available in Alex Wayman, *Calming the Mind and Discerning the Real* (New York: Columbia University Press, 1978; rpt. New Delhi: Motilal Banarsidass, 1979).

13. For Sherbourne's translation, see his *A Lamp for the Path,* p. 5. Our only substantial difference is with respect to the fifth stanza, which he translates as: "One who wholly seeks a complete end/To the entire suffering of others because/Their suffering belongs to his own [conscious] stream,/That person is a Superior." Sherbourne sees this level of person as understanding that others' suffering is included within their own mental continuum; this is both unlikely and differs from 'Jam-dbyangs-bzhad-pa's more cogent interpretation of this stanza, given below.

14. See, for instance, Kensur Lekden's presentation in the first part of Tsong-ka-pa, Kensur Lekden, and Jeffrey Hopkins, *Compassion in Tibetan Buddhism* (London: Rider and Company, 1980; rpt. Ithaca, N.Y.: Snow Lion, 1980), 17–21. The levels from the supreme of the low through those of great capacity can be viewed as three levels of ideal personhood—personality-goals to which practitioners aspire; see Grace Burford's chapter in this volume for an early Buddhist description of ideal persons. Using the approach of Peter Gregory's paper (Mārga Conference, UCLA, June 1988) about Tsung-mi's *p'an-chiao* (doctrinal classification), we can see that Atīśa's classificatory system similarly has (1) hermeneutical, (2) sectarian, and (3) soteriological functions, in that it (a) organizes diverse practices under one rubric, (b) legitimates the claim of this tradition to present the full teaching, and (c) provides a map of the Buddhist path.

15. 'Jam-dbyangs-bzhad-pa's *Decisive Analysis of the Treatise "Ornament for Clear Realization"* [*by Maitreya*]: *Precious Lamp Illuminating All of the Meaning of the Perfection of Wisdom (bstan gcos mngon par rtogs pa'i rgyan gyi mtha' dpyod shes rab kyi pha rol tu phyin pa'i don kun gsal ba'i rin chen sgron me),* The Collected Works of 'Jam-dbyaṅs-bźad-pa'i-rdo-rdo-rje, vol. 7 *(ja),* (New Delhi: Ngawang Gelek Demo, 1973), 34.4–42.6; also (Sarnath: Guru Deva, 1965), 25.14–33.4. The running citations are to the Sarnath edition (hereafter *Sarnath*), since it is clearer, although occasionally the New Dehli edition (hereafter, *New Delhi*) is used as well (see notes 34 and 35 below).

16. "High status" refers to the elevated *(ud)* states of happiness of humans, demigods, and gods relative to animals, hungry ghosts, and hell-beings. *Sarnath,* 25.15: *'khor ba'i mngon mtho tsam don du gnyer ba'i gang zag de.* A definition *(mtshan nyid, lakṣaṇa)* in this system is not a verbal description; it is the actual object, viewed in one way as being the meaning *(don, artha),* whereas the definiendum is the name *(ming, nāma),* and in another way as a "defining property" that characterizes an object. For an interesting discussion of this topic, see Georges Dreyfus, "Some Considerations on Definition in Buddhism: An Essay on the Use of Definitions in the Indo-Tibetan Epistemological Tradition" (Master's thesis, University of Virginia, 1987).

17. *Sarnath,* 25.20: *chos min gyis tshe 'di'i bde ba tsam don du gnyer ba'i gang zag de.*

18. Tsong-ka-pa, Kensur Lekden, and Hopkins, *Compassion in Tibetan Buddhism,* p. 17.

19. *Sarnath,* 26.10: *tshe 'di la ched cher mi byed par chos kho nas phyi ma'i 'khor ba'i bde ba tsam don du gnyer ba'i gang zag de.*

20. Tsong-kha-pa, *Great Exposition of the Stages of the Path (lam rim chen mo),* cited from an unpublished translation by Elizabeth Napper, chap. 10, "The Three Types of Beings," 2. Kensur Lekden's description of the supreme of the small (Tsong-kha-pa, Kensur Lekden, and Hopkins, *Compassion in Tibetan Buddhism,* pp. 17–18) is more vivid:

> The great of the small engage in virtue, seeking happiness, comfort, food, drink, resources, and so forth mainly for future lives. Because they practise not for the sake of others but for their own temporary welfare in cyclic existence—the beginningless round of birth, ageing, sickness, and death—they are the lowest among actual religious practitioners, but due to their longer perspective are included within the count of actual devotees.
>
> They have identified the cause and effect of actions as well as their own virtues and non-virtues. They know that in their next lifetime they will experience pleasures as gods or humans from virtuous deeds done in this lifetime and will experience sufferings as hell-beings, hungry ghosts, or animals from non-virtuous deeds done in this lifetime. They realize that at best this existence will not last more than a hundred years and that there are innumerable births in the future. Therefore, rather than seek their own welfare in this lifetime, which is so short, they begin to engage in religious practice for the sake of future lives.

21. dKon-mchog-'jigs-med-dbang-po (1728–1791), recognized as 'Jam-dbyangs-bzhad-pa's reincarnation, reformulated his predecessor's definition of a *person* of supreme small capacity in terms of the *path* of a being of supreme small capacity. (At the end of his presentation of the three types of persons, 'Jam-dbyangs-bzhad-pa [*Sarnath,* 29.9] says, "The paths of the three persons are easily understood from those three definitions." dKon-mchog-'jigs-med-dbang-po may have taken his cue from this suggestion.) In his *Presentation of the Grounds and Paths, Beautiful Ornament of the Three Vehicles (sa lam gyi rnam bzhag theg gsum mdzes rgyan,* The Collected Works of dKon-mchog-'jigs-med-dbang-po, vol. 7, [New Delhi: Ngawang Gelek Demo, 1972], 422.3; this work was used extensively in Eugene Obermiller, "The Doctrine of the Prajnā-pāramitā as exposed in the Abhisamayālaṃkāra of Maitreya," *Acta Orientalia* [Lugduni Batavorum: E. J. Brill, 1932], 14ff.), dKon-mchog-'jigs-med-dbang-po says:

> The definition of a path of a special being of small capacity is a thought posited from the viewpoint of mainly seeking mere high status within a future cyclic existence for one's own sake alone. Illustrations of this are, for instance, an awareness in the continuum of a being of small capacity that realizes the impermanence [i.e., precariousness] of death and an awareness of ethics in the continuum of a being of small capacity that is an abandoning of the ten non-virtues. These are called paths of a being of small capacity because—in dependence upon them—persons who possess [such awarenesses] in their continuum are caused to proceed to a state of high status [i.e., as a human or god].

dKon-mchog-'jigs-med-dbang-po refines 'Jam-dbyangs-bzhad-pa's definition by adding the word "mainly," thus suggesting that a person on this level is principally involved in seeking happiness in a future lifetime but could also seek liberation from cyclic existence or even altruistic buddhahood, albeit in a minor way. As illustrations of the path of such a being, he gives an awareness realizing the impermanence or imminence of death and an ethical awareness involved in renouncing the ten nonvirtues, but he qualifies these illustrations as being "in the continuum of a being of small capacity." These awarenesses themselves are not necessarily limited to those of supreme small capacity; rather, they are suitable illustrations only if accompanied by the particular motivation of such a person.

22. *Sarnath,* 26.18: *'khor ba'i phun tshogs la blo log pa'i sgo nas rang kho na'i don du thar pa gtso bor don gnyer gyi cha nas bzhag pa'i gang zag de.*

23. Following dKon-mchog-'jigs-med-dbang-po's refinement; see note 28 below.

24. However, 'Jam-dbyangs-bzhad-pa points out that such a strict description does not hold true for all persons of middling capacity, since some beings on this level still engage in sinful deeds (*Sarnath,* 27.5):

> There are beings of middling capacity of indefinite lineage who, although they have an intention to leave cyclic existence which [is seen as] like a blazing fire, engage in sinful deeds through the force of afflictive emotions or [bad] friends. Not only that, but also there are beings of great capacity who do such.

As sources for such waywardness, 'Jam-dbyangs-bzhad-pa cites Maitreya's *Ornament for the Great Vehicle Sūtras,* "Through the afflictive emotions oneself is destroyed, sentient beings are destroyed, and ethics are destroyed," and the *Nirvana Sūtra,* "Bodhisattvas are not as concerned with crazy elephants and so forth as they are with bad friends." He also cites the *Compilations of Indicative Verse (ched du brjod pa'i tshom, Udānavarga):*

> Do not company with sinful friends.
> When those not committing sins
> Acquaint with those committing sins,
> The qualm is generated that they will commit sins.

(This is likely the fourth line of the first stanza and the first three lines of the tenth stanza of the section called the compilation on intimate friends; see Gareth Sparham, *The Tibetan Dhammapada: Sayings of the Buddha* [London: Wisdom, 1986], 95–96.) The indefiniteness that is the result of not having reached an irreversible level of the path may be the reason for 'Jam-dbyangs-bzhad-pa's using, in the definition of a being of middling capacity, the phrase "posited from the viewpoint of," which is usually stipulated in order to include exceptions.

25. Tsong-kha-pa, *Great Exposition,* trans. Napper (unpub.), p. 2.

26. Tsong-ka-pa, Kensur Lekden, and Hopkins, *Compassion in Tibetan Buddhism,* p. 19. I have taken the liberty of changing my own translation as "he" to "he/she." With respect to the translation of *arhan arhant (dgra bcom pa)* as "Foe Destroyer," I do this to accord with the usual Tibetan translation of the term and to assist in capturing the flavor of oral and written traditions that frequently refer to this etymology. Arhats have overcome the foe which is the afflictive emotions *(nyon mongs, kleśa),* the chief of which is ignorance—the conception (according to the Consequence School) that persons and phenomena are established by way of their own character.

The Indian and Tibetan translators were also aware of the etymology of *arhant* as "worthy one," since they translated the name of the "founder" of the Jaina system, Arhat, as *mchod 'od,* "Worthy of Worship" (see 'Jam-dbyangs-bzhad-pa's *Great Exposition of Tenets,* ka 62a.3). In addition, they were aware of Candrakīrti's gloss of the term as "Worthy One" in his *Clear Words: sadevamānuṣāsurāl lokāt pūnārhatvād arhannityuchyate* (Louis de La Vallée Poussin, ed., *Mūlamadhyamakakāikās de Nāgārjuna avec la Pasannapadā Commentaire de Candrakīrtī,* Bibliotheca Buddhica IV [Osnabrück: Biblio Verlag, 1970], 486.5), *lha dang mi dang lha ma yin du bcas pa'i 'jig rten gyis mchod par 'os pas dgra bcom pa zhes brjod la* (*P* 5260, vol. 98, 75.2.2), "Because of being worthy of worship by the world of gods, humans, and demigods, they are called Arhats." Finally, they were aware of Haribhadra's twofold etymology in his *Illumination of the Eight-Thousand-Stanza Perfection of Wisdom Sūtra.* In the context of the list of epithets qualifying the Buddha's retinue at the beginning of the sūtra (see Unrai Wogihara, ed., *Abhisamayālaṃkārālokā Prajñā-pāramitā-vyākhyā, The Work of Haribhadra* [Tokyo: Toyo bunko, 1932–1935; rpt. ed., Tokyo: Sankibo Buddhist Book Store, 1973], 8.18), Haribhadra says:

> They are called *arhant* [= Worthy One, from root *arh,* "to be worthy"] since they are worthy of worship, religious donations, and being assembled together in a group, etc.
>
> (W9.8–9: *sarva evātra pūjā-dakṣiṇā-gaṇa-parikarṣādy-ārhatayarhantaḥ; P* 5189, 67.5.7: *'dir thams cad kyang mchod pa dang// yon dang tshogs su 'dub la sogs par 'os pas na dgra bcom pa'o.)*

Also:

> *They are called arhant* [= Foe Destroyer *arihan*] because they have destroyed *(hata)* the foe *(ari).*
>
> (W10.18: *hatāritvād arhantaḥ; P* 5189, 69.3.6: *dgra rnams bcom pas na dgra bcom pa'o.*)

(My thanks to Gareth Sparham for the references to Haribhadra.) Thus we are not dealing with an ignorant misconception of a term, but a considered preference in the face of alternative etymologies—"Foe Destroyer" requiring a not unusual *i* infix to make *ari-han—ari* meaning enemy and *han* meaning to kill, and thus "Foe Destroyer." Unfortunately, one word in English cannot convey both this meaning and "Worthy of Worship"; thus I have chosen what clearly has become the predominant meaning in Tibet. (For an excellent discussion of the two etymologies of Arhat in Buddhism and Jainism, see L. M. Joshi's "Facets of Jaina Religiousness in Comparative Light," L.D. Series 85, [Ahmedabad: L.D. Institute of Indology, May 1981], 53–58.)

27. Den-ma Lo-chö Rin-bo-chay, commenting on dKon-mchog-'jigs-med-dbang-po's *Presentation of the Grounds and Paths,* states the development of increasing scope clearly (unpub. lectures, University of Virginia, 1978, trans. Hopkins, p. 6):

> Beings of small capacity have concern for the sufferings that would take place in their own future lifetime; this is the limit of their thought, and thus it is not vast. Beings of middling capacity know that it will not help at all merely not to undergo the suffering of a bad transmigration in the next lifetime. They realize that even if they live at the peak of cyclic existence *(srid rtse, bhavāgra)* it is like living in a hell in a pot of molten copper, because they are about to fall into that. There is no difference between the peak of cyclic existence and a hell with respect to the suffering of pervasive condi-

tioning *(khyab pa 'du byed kyi sdug bsngal).* Even if, at the peak of cyclic existence, there is no suffering of mental or physical pain or suffering of change, when the actual meditative absorption that a person has in that state degenerates, then the person will fall from that state and be reborn in a state of the manifest suffering of physical and mental pain and the suffering of change. Thus, they understand that even in the best of rebirths within cyclic existence one has not passed beyond a state having the nature of the three sufferings. Hence, in order to attain a liberation in which none of these three sufferings will have to be experienced, persons of middling capacity cultivate paths such as realization of the sixteen aspects of the four noble truths and so forth. Their thought is vaster than that of beings of small capacity.

28. As before, dKon-mchog-'jigs-med-dbang-po reformulates 'Jam-dbyangs-bzhad-pa's definition of a person of middling capacity in terms of the path of a being of middling capacity (see note 22 above). In his *Presentation of the Grounds and Paths,* he says (423.1):

> The definition of a path of a being of middling capacity is a thought posited from the viewpoint of mainly seeking liberation for the sake of oneself alone, from the viewpoint of having turned the mind away from the marvels of cyclic existence. An illustration of a path of a being of middling capacity is, for instance, an awareness in the continuum of a being of middling capacity that realizes the sixteen [attributes of the four noble truths], impermanence and so forth. These are called paths of a being of middling capacity because in dependence on them persons who possess them in their continuum are caused to progress to the state of liberation.

29. *Sarnath,* 27.17: *snying rje chen po'i gzhan dbang du gyur pa'i sgo nas sems can gzhan rgyud la sangs rgyas thob phyir du rnam mkhyen don du gnyer ba'i cha nas bzhag pa'i gang zag de.*

30. About this level, Tsong-kha-pa's *Great Exposition* (trans. Napper [unpub.], p. 3) says:

> A being of great capacity, due to being under the other-power of great compassion, for the sake of extinguishing all the sufferings of sentient beings has taken Buddhahood as [his or her] object of attainment and trains in the six perfections, the two stages [of Highest Yoga Tantra, i.e., the stages of generation and completion], and so forth.

31. See Kensur Lekden's description of persons of great capacity in Tsong-ka-pa, Kensur Lekden, and Hopkins, *Compassion in Tibetan Buddhism,* p. 20.

32. Den-ma Lo-chö Rin-bo-chay, unpub. lectures, trans. Hopkins, p. 7.

33. As before, dKon-mchog-'jigs-med-dbang-po reformulates 'Jam-dbyangs-bzhad-pa's definition of a person of great capacity in terms of the path of a being of great capacity (see note 29 above). In his *Presentation of the Grounds and Paths,* he says (423.3):

> The definition of a path of a being of great capacity is a thought that is posited by way of seeking [to attain] an exalted knower of all aspects for the sake of other sentient beings' attaining buddhahood from the point of view of having come under the influence of great compassion. Illustrations of a path of a being of great capacity are the great compassion or the pure unusual altruistic attitude in the continuum of a being of great capacity. These are called paths of a being of great capacity because in dependence

upon them persons who possess them in their continuum are caused to progress to unsurpassed enlightenment.

34. *New Dehli,* 31.1–31.4.
35. Ibid., 30.4–30.8.
36. Tsong-kha-pa's *Great Exposition* (trans. Napper [unpub.], pp. 5–6) makes this point clearly:

> Since the paths of the other two types of beings are included in complete form within the stages of the path of a being of great capacity, those two [i.e., the paths of beings of small and middling capacity] are parts, or branches, of the path of the Great Vehicle. . . . Here, one is not being led to the path of a being of small capacity who takes as the object of attainment merely the happiness of cyclic existence nor to that of a being of middling capacity who takes as the object of attainment mere liberation from cyclic existence for his or her own sake alone. Rather, having taken some of the paths shared with those two as prerequisites for being led to the path of a being of great capacity, they are to be taken as branches of the deeds of the path of a being of great capacity.

Later, Tsong-kha-pa explains what these shared paths are (ibid., pp. 10–11):

> At the time of [the practices of] a being of small capacity, one contemplates the way in which the harm of the suffering of the bad transmigrations befalls one, and at the time of [the practices of] a being of middling capacity, one contemplates the way in which even if [one attains] high status there is suffering and there is no bliss of peace. Then, through meditation within inferring one's own experience with respect to other sentient beings who are close to one, this serves as a cause for generating love and compassion, and, from that, there is generation of the mind of an altruistic intention to become enlightened. Therefore, training in the thoughts shared with beings of small and middling capacity is a technique for generating a non-artificial mind of an altruistic intention to become enlightened, and it is not the case that one is being led on some separate path.

37. Much as in the case of the doctrine of beings "whose wholesome roots have been eradicated," discussed in Robert Buswell's chapter in this volume, the possibility of being excluded exerts an influence on practitioners to keep from falling into such a group by engaging in practice. In this way, the effect of the seemingly *exclusionary* doctrine is to induce persons to practice so that they can be *included* within the group.
38. Otto, *Idea of the Holy,* p. 13.
39. These are the section headings of chaps. 4 and 5 of ibid.
40. Ibid., p. 13.
41. Ibid., p. 14.
42. Ibid., p. 17.
43. Ibid., p. 20.
44. Ibid., p. 21.
45. Ibid., p. 24.
46. Ibid., p. 26.
47. Ibid., p. 28.
48. Ibid., p. 29.
49. Ibid., p. 33.
50. Ibid., p. 37.
51. bsTan-dar-lha-ram-pa, *Presentation of the Lack of Being One or Many (gcig du*

bral gyi rnam gzhag legs bshad rgya mtsho las btus pa'i 'khrul spong bdud rtsi'i gzegs ma), Collected gsung 'bum of Bstan-dar Lha-ram of A-lak-sha, vol. 1 (New Delhi: Lama Guru Deva, 1971), 425.1ff.

52. The material on the levels of consciousness is drawn from Lati Rinbochay's and my translation of a text by dbYangs can dga' ba'i blo gros; see Lati Rinbochay and Jeffrey Hopkins, *Death, Intermediate State, and Rebirth in Tibetan Buddhism* (London: Rider, 1979).

53. The traditional way of explaining the process of proceeding from grosser to subtler states is in the context of dying. In Highest Yoga Tantra, the explanation of the stages of dying and of the physiological reasons behind them is based on a complicated theory of winds (or currents of energy) that serve as foundations for various levels of consciousness. Upon the serial collapse of the ability of these "winds" to serve as bases of consciousness, the internal and external events of death unfold. The same experiences also can be induced by consciously withdrawing the winds in the practice of Highest Yoga Tantra.

54. In the Guhyasamāja system of Highest Yoga Tantra, as presented in Nāgārjuna's *Five Stages (rim lnga, Pañcakrama),* conceptual consciousnesses are detailed as being of eighty types, which are divided into three classes. The first group of thirty-three conceptions is composed of conceptual consciousnesses that involve a strong movement of "wind" to their objects—conceptions such as fear, attachment, hunger, thirst, compassion, acquisitiveness, and jealousy. The second group of forty conceptions is composed of conceptual consciousnesses that involve a medium movement of "wind" to their objects—conceptions such as joy, amazement, generosity, desiring to kiss, heroism, nongentleness, and crookedness. The third group of seven conceptions is composed of conceptual consciousnesses that involve a weak movement of "wind" to their objects—namely, forgetfulness; mistake, as in apprehending water in a mirage; catatonia; depression; laziness; doubt; and equal desire and hatred. Although the difference between the first two groups is not obvious (at least to me), it is clear that in the third group the mind is strongly withdrawn; on the ordinary level of consciousness, the three groups represent increasingly less dualistic perception.

55. This work is found in Ngag-dbang-mkhas-grub's *Collected Works* (Leh: S. Tashigangpa, 1973), vol. 1, 466.2. Cited in Lati Rinbochay and Hopkins, *Death, Intermediate State, and Rebirth,* p. 47.

56. This is a central theme of Enni's exposition of Zen as presented in Carl Bielefeldt's chapter in this volume, in which Enni indicates that the source of suffering is the misidentification of afflictive emotions as the very nature of the mind. Enni says:

> Those injured by this spirit of the afflictions, believing that their deluded thoughts are the original mind and taking delight in the seeds of desire, revolve through the four [kinds of] rebirth in the three evil [destinies].

The importance of faith in the basic purity of mind is clear in Han Ki Doo's paper on sudden awakening (Mārga Conference, UCLA, June 1988), in which he quotes Hui-neng as saying, "Don't doubt that your own mind is Buddha." In contrast, the dGe-lugs-pas stress reasoned affirmation of the basic purity of the mind, and frequently reiterate their conviction that well-reasoned faith is far stronger than unreasoned faith. However, this dictum may not take into account the very great power and effectiveness of faith that is built not on reasoning but on inklings, on glimpses; such faith seems to be a central element in leading a practitioner, consciously and unconsciously, to profound experience.

57. The analogy recalls Freud's descriptions of drives to return to earlier pleasant states, and of his "insight" into the meaning of the infant Jesus on Mary's lap, staring at his mother, as a depiction of a basic unconscious thrust of the religious enterprise. For Freud such insights undermined religions' claims, whereas I have yet to decide whether the metaphors are using the religions or the religions, the metaphors. Consider, for example, Jung's description of the search for wholeness as disguised in the form of incest (*The Collected Works of C. G. Jung* [Princeton, N.J.: Princeton University Press, 1971, second printing 1974], vol. 16, 471 [the latter is the paragraph number used for coordination between editions]):

> Whenever this instinct for wholeness appears, it begins by disguising itself under the symbolism of incest, for, unless he seeks it in himself, a man's nearest feminine counterpart is to be found in his mother, sister, or daughter.

Taken Jung's way, the image of the mother indicates a yearning for wholeness, which is naturally associated with the mother because of warm childhood experiences. Thus the primary motivating force is the striving for wholeness; the feminine image is the medium of its expression.

58. Vaman Shivaram Apte, *Sanskrit-English Dictionary* (Poona: Prasad Prakashan, 1957), 1264–1265.

59. Ibid., p. 1264.

60. This is a necessary qualification to eliminate similar experiences by those who have not reached a level of a formal path, i.e., any of the five paths of accumulation, preparation, seeing, meditation, or no more learning.

61. dKon-mchog-'jigs-med-dbang-po, *Presentation of the Grounds and the Paths,* 428.3.

62. Den-ma Lo-chö Rin-bo-chay, unpub. lectures, trans. Hopkins, p. 46.

63. Ibid., p. 8.

64. dKon-mchog-'jigs-med-dbang-po, *Presentation of the Grounds and the Paths,* 428.3.

65. Den-ma Lo-chö Rin-bo-chay, unpub. lectures, trans. Hopkins, p. 8.

66. Ibid., p. 26.

67. Ibid., p. 18.

68. I am drawing on H. H. the Dalai Lama, Tsong-ka-pa, and Jeffrey Hopkins, *Tantra in Tibet* (London: George Allen and Unwin, 1977; rpt. Ithaca, N.Y.: Snow Lion, 1987).

69. This does not seem to be the case in certain rNying-ma and certain East Asian teachings, in which it is more that one is uncovering an enlightenment already primordially present.

70. *The Collected Works of C. G. Jung,* vol. 6, p. 422.

71. See the final chapter, "Union of the Old and New Translation Schools," in The Fourteenth Dalai Lama, His Holiness Tenzin Gyatso, *Kindness, Clarity, and Insight* (Ithaca: Snow Lion, 1984), 200–224, esp. 210–221.

72. About sudden enlightenment in the rNying-ma school, see Khetsun Sangpo, *Tantric Practice in Nyingma* (London: Rider, 1982), 187.

73. Fifth Dalai Lama, Ngak-w̄ang-l̄o-sang-gya-tso (1617–1682, also known as Ngag dbang blo bzang rgya mtsho), *Instruction on the Stages of the Path to Enlightenment, Sacred Word of Mañjushrī (byang chub lam gyi rim pa'i khrid yig 'jam pa'i dbyangs kyi zhal lung),* (Thimphu: kun-bzang-stobs-rgyal, 1976), as found in Hopkins' translation in "Practice of Emptiness" (Dharamsala: Library of Tibetan Works and Archives, 1974), 17.

74. In a different context, Wilfred Cantwell Smith has said that religion is, in a sense, most common, its isolated separateness being a fabrication of our current secularism. In his presidential address at the 1983 annual meeting of the American Academy of Religion, Smith said ("The Modern West in the History of Religion," *JAAR,* LII/1, 9):

> For the fact is that reasonably well-informed perceptive awareness of the history of our planet over the past thirty or so millennia makes clear that modern Western secularism is an aberration; and that its attempt to interpret religion as some sort of extra in human life is dogmatic, is ideological eisegesis. The notion that human nature and truth are fundamentally secular, are the norm, from which most human beings have, whether for good or other reason, deviated, is sheer projection.
>
> By this I do *not* mean that humanity is, rather, fundamentally *homo religiosus.* That is an error that further illustrates my thesis, by its perpetuating the idiosyncratic outlook that the Modern West has defensively constructed. It took us some time to detect this. The concept "religion" has itself been developed by Western secularism as naming something that is supposedly over and above the standard everyday. Religion is in fact not something special, the historian can now see; it is secularism that is odd. "Religion" is a secularist notion, a conceptual element in that particular worldview—but a misleading one, setting up a dichotomy that secularists need in order to justify their own separate peculiarity, but normal people do not and cannot. The dichotomy is retained, in inverted form, in that phrase *homo religiosus.* Actually, there is rather just plain *homo sapiens,* and then a minority of those not quite *sapientes* enough to have sensed what kind of universe we live in and what kind of being we are.

Admittedly, Smith is not making the points that I am making, but it strikes me that once it is held that religion is not separate, its nonseparateness must be grounded in a reality that is at the very root of existence, as is the case with the fundamental innate mind of clear light. Smith's point is not just that at a different cultural period religion was not separated out; he is suggesting that this is the case *in fact*—that religion is rooted in "what kind of universe we live in and what kind of being we are."

75. For a lucid exposition of this dictum, see Śri Sureśvarācārya, *Naiṣkarmyasiddhi,* trans. S. S. Radhavachar (Mysore: University of Mysore, 1965).

76. A study of usage of the term "forbearance" *(bzod pa, kṣānti)* for levels of the path, to indicate an overcoming of nonfacility with profound doctrines, would add to the force of this point.

77. Smith, "The Modern West in the History of Religion," p. 6.

78. For an illustration of the tension created by not delimiting the object of negation of śūnyatā, see Robert Gimello's chapter in this volume on the "irresolvable opposition" and "creative tension" between śūnyatā and mārga.

79. See Grace Burford's chapter in this volume, in which she documents an early Buddhist position in the *Aṭṭhakavagga* that for reality to manifest "no view" is needed.

80. Although I am aware of the tendency in dGe-lugs-pa training to endless, conceptual proliferation, it is unwarranted to assume that because the path-structure is complicated, no one ever actually meditates it. There is a small but significant number of persons who, after much arduous study over many years, practice what, at superficial reading, seems to be a hopelessly complicated series of paths. This is not to say that *all* complicated structures are actually

practiced; my point is that the assumption that *none* of them can be practiced springs from a lack of awareness of cultures that put as least as much energy into these topics as we do into learning about football, road complexes, and so forth—and from a lack of appreciation of the fact that, for some people, the content of these highly elaborate presentations has an inner dynamic impelling them toward practice. Anne Klein's chapter in this volume provides insights into the dynamics of a very high level of the path—dynamics that take such presentations out of the realm of mere abstract proliferation of high states; I am referring specifically to her explanation of the theme of the bodhisattva's developing greater realization of the compatibility between appearance and emptiness, method and wisdom, conventional and ultimate truths.

81. This means that the first through the seventh bodhisattva grounds are traversed in an instant. Such sudden progress can be viewed as an extension of the sudden abandonment discussed in Collett Cox's chapter in this volume. The function of the path of seeing to remove artificially acquired obstructions and that of the path of meditation to remove innate obstructions are combined in one instant of a very subtle, and thus very powerful, consciousness realizing emptiness. Still, as Dan Stevenson discussed in his paper on the pathless path posited by T'ien-t'ai Chih-i (Mārga Conference, UCLA, June 1988), concrete stages are presented for what is experienced in a "non-successive, non-gradualistic, instantaneous, complete, and, it would seem, utterly 'stageless'" manner. This cultivation of levels leading to the path of seeing is in contrast to Alan Sponberg's presentation (Mārga Conference, UCLA, June 1988) of the path of seeing as essentially a noncultivative insight into the truth, after which cultivation is begun. Still, the point here is whether the presentation of levels of the path to be produced in practice is counterproductive to generating the manifestation of the essential nature of the mind. It is perhaps in this vein that Tibetan scholars sometimes speak of the inappropriateness of superimposing the vocabulary of stages, such as the bodhisattva grounds, on such a stageless experience, even though this is frequently done.

In the rNying-ma tradition, such dramatic cleansing of appearance is called the "utter eradication of cyclic existence" and is compared to arriving in a land of gold in which stone (suffering) is utterly unfindable. In rNying-ma, it can be brought about in a "sudden" or "simultaneous" manner through an encounter with a deeply realized being (see John McRae's chapter in this volume on encounter dialogues in Chinese Ch'an), such that in one session a practitioner passes from a pre-path-of-accumulation level either to the path of seeing or to buddhahood.

82. It is in this phase of the path that the obstructions to omniscience are overcome in the Guhyasamāja system of Highest Yoga Tantra. In his chapter in this volume, Padmanabh Jaini raises the intriguing question of just how nonafflictive ignorance is overcome in the classical Abhidharma systems. The specific practices implemented at this point in Highest Yoga Tantra address this topic, which came to be a focal issue in Mahāyāna treatises.

83. This is sometimes called "enlightenment in one lifetime in one body." Atīśa is said to have been quizzed by Tibetans—who probably were testing him to see whether he knew the most profound doctrines—about whether there was any such thing as enlightenment in one lifetime in one body. He answered that there was enlightenment in one lifetime but not in one body. The Tibetans are said to have assumed, therefore, that he did not know of this most profound doctrine of Highest Yoga Tantra. However, one of the Paṇ-chen Lamas is reported to have explained that Atīśa was making a very refined answer

because, to achieve enlightenment in one lifetime, it is necessary to achieve a second body made of "wind" and mind, at which point the usual body can be either retained or discarded. Thus enlightenment can be achieved within one lifetime, but it is necessary to develop a second body. See Ngag dbang dpal ldan (born 1791), *Illumination of the Texts of Tantra, Presentation of the Grounds and Paths of the Four Great Secret Tantra Sets (gsang chen rgyud sde bzhi'i sa lam gyi rnam bzhag rgyud gzhung gsal byed),* (rgyud smad par khang edition, no other data), 54.6. This story shows how literally the doctrine of "enlightenment in one lifetime in one body" is taken in this tradition, in contrast to the Tendai tradition of "realization of buddhahood with this very body" *(sokushin jōbutsu),* discussed in Paul Groner's chapter in this volume.

Mental Concentration and the Unconditioned: A Buddhist Case for Unmediated Experience

ANNE C. KLEIN

Amazing, stunning, marvelous doctrine
Secret of all the perfect buddhas
That everything is born from the birthless
When that very birth is unborn.

—*The Secret Essence*[1]

Overview

Theories about the relationship between the born and the unborn, or the conditioned and unconditioned, animate much of Buddhist writing, ritual, and meditation. The way such apparently antipodal categories coexist and make each other possible is a central issue in the literature of Indo-Tibetan Mādhyamika. Its descriptions of a path to enlightenment frame the issue largely in epistemological terms: How can the ordinary mind, variously described as conditioned, deluded, or defiled, experience a state that is unconditioned, omniscient, and pure? Any Buddhist position on this question depends, in good measure, on which of these paired antinomies it emphasizes.

As a case in point, Tibetan sūtra literature such as the Dge-lugs-pa material discussed below emphasizes the incremental progression from a deluded to an omniscient state, characterized by a movement from conceptual to direct experience of the final or ultimate nature of things. The Rnying-ma Rdzogs-chen, in contrast, emphasizes purification of adventitious defilements to reveal the buddha-nature, considered the actuality of every mind *(sems gyi chos nyid, *cittadharmatā)*. The culmination of both Dge-lugs-pa and Rnying-ma paths can be described as "unconditioned" in some sense, but the process by which this state is actualized, descriptions of the state itself, and the particular conundrums entailed in reaching it are framed quite differently. For Dge-lugs-pas, "unconditioned" is above all a description of the emptiness that is the *object* of the nondualistic wisdom consciousness. This emptiness is an unqualified voidness, a mere negation *(prasajyapratiṣedha, med dgag)*. The mind that knows this unconditioned emptiness is, like all minds, conditioned. This is a curious point, and one we shall refer to again. For Rnying-ma, the significant "unconditioned" is not a mere negation but an affirming negative *(paryudāsapratiṣedha, ma yin dgag).*[2] Unlike in Dge-lugs-pa, the "unconditioned" can in special circumstances also describe a *subject,* a consciousness spontaneously and beginninglessly endowed with certain qualities.

From these positions, different types of path structures take shape. For Dge-lugs-pa, knowledge of the "unconditioned" rests on the availability of that unconditioned object to experience, and especially on the possiblity of perceiving it "immediately." The mind itself, even the omniscience of a buddha, always remains a "conditioned phenomenon." However, as we shall see, the term "conditioned" here refers to the mind as an impermanent, momentary phenomenon (even when its moments are all of the same type, as in the case of a buddha's omniscience); it is not necessarily a statement about the mind's amenability to epistemological shifts due to changing external or internal "conditions."

The mind most completely experiences the unconditioned emptiness when it knows it "immediately." One criterion of such immediate or direct perception is that the object be known without the intervening presence of an image *(arthasāmānya, don spyi)* that characterizes all forms of conceptual thought *(kalpanā, rnam rtog).* In describing the Dge-lugs-pa position on such cognition, I also make use of select Rnying-ma material in order to introduce something of the Tibetan Buddhist context in which Dge-lugs-pa positions take shape.

When some of these same issues are placed in the frame of our own contemporary intellectual traditions, broader questions can also be raised. Most significantly, when we investigate mārga literature, we confront some of the fundamental issues that divide us, as contemporary Euro-Americans, from the worldview in which it was conceived. How are we to understand a literature whose fundamental theses are anathema to most contemporary Western intellectual traditions? For example, both Dge-lugs-pa and Rnying-ma, and Buddhism generally, claim that one can become a knower or self whose agency is free from the constraints of language (compare Lacan), who gains some form of unmediated knowledge (compare Kant), and—most antithetical of all—that this knowledge and its object are unconditioned by particularities of history and thus accessible in the same form, albeit through different means, to all persons regardless of cultural or psychological particularity (compare Foucault). In looking at one particular Buddhist tradition's way of handling mārga theory, I will suggest some connections between the different ways in which "they," the voices of tradition, and "we," the inheritors of modernity, find mārga theory a problematic endeavor.

The primary focus of this chapter is the way in which Dge-lugs-pa sūtra-path literature frames and attempts to "solve" the tensions between conceptual and nonconceptual, and between conditioned and nonconditioned, as well as the role that various forms of mental concentration play in this resolution. Secondarily, I suggest how this material plays into Dge-lugs-pa assumptions about the unmediated and presumably universal nature of this experience.

To this end I examine the changing juxtapostion of concentration and insight, and insight's own shift from conceptual to nonconceptual. Some of this material is very technical, for Dge-lugs-pa represents one of the extreme poles of Buddhist scholasticism, but I hope the larger issues remain in view, and that the summarizing statements which close each section provide an accelerated pathway through the discussion for those who would dispense with the Geshe's-eye view of the issue. (Scholars, like Buddhists, may be gradualists or subitists—important evidence that we are dealing with a fairly fundamental set of human preferences here, not just with religious esoterica.)

Objections to the Dge-lugs-pa Perspective

For Dge-lugs-pas, the most significant conundrum of the path has to do with how conceptual conditioning yields a nonconceptual experience of the unconditioned. This can be read as a particular instance of the more general conditioned-unconditioned problematic already noted. The response most characteristic of Dge-lugs-pa sūtra literature is to invoke two different mental gestures that must themselves be reconciled: opening consciousness to encompass the spacelike, unconditioned emptiness; and withdrawing the mind from sense objects through cultivating various stages of concentration *(dhyāna, bsam gtan)* and absorption *(samāpatti, snyoms 'jug)*. The intertwining of these epistemological styles or meditative strategies culminates, at buddhahood, in the ability to have immediate cognition of sense objects and their emptinesses at one and the same time. This is how Dge-lugs-pa, for all its emphasis on the purely empty status of the unconditioned, valorizes an attitude that the editors of this volume refer to as "at once less alien from the world of ordinary human concerns and more sensitive to the presence of the transcendent in that world."

The particular claims Dge-lugs-pa makes in its description of the path were often disputed in Tibet. Some of the most telling objections derive from Rnying-ma Rdzogs-chen's quite different formulation of the relationship between path and goal, conditioned and unconditioned. Whereas Dge-lugs-pas sutra literature must explain how conceptual thought, which is both conditioned and conditioning, can lead to nonconceptual experience of the unconditioned, Rdzogs-chen reflects on how the manifold qualities of the buddha-nature, which is unconditioned and permanent, can be conjoined with the mind, which is impermanent, and on the precise relationship of the buddha-nature, which is ever-present and unchanging, to the temporally locatable achievement of enlightenment.[3]

Briefly, three important premises shape the Dge-lugs-pa problematic, all countered by the Rnying-ma material considered here: (1) Emptiness, the unconditioned, becomes an object of consciousness on the path; (2) this object is a mere negative *(paryudāsapratiṣedha, med dgag)* with no positive qualities, in part because (3) the teachings on emptiness associated with the Perfection of Wisdom are to be taken literally. There are other important differences, of course, but these suffice to frame the issues at hand. Because emptiness is considered an object, and one that is accessible only upon careful analysis, Dge-lugs-pa must conceive of a complementary relationship between conceptual analysis and a nonconceptual, nondualistic experience of emptiness. Moreover, because such experience is not readily available to ordinary persons, a path for gradual development of this ability must be laid out. In contrast, Rnying-ma holds that although the Perfection of Wisdom sūtras find it necessary to identify the unconditioned, they never say to take it *as an object.*[4] Moreover, the buddha-nature must be experienced as not only pervading objects but as a form of subjectivity as well.[5]

Dge-lugs-pas often equate the emptiness which is a mere negative with the buddha-nature, but Mipham crystallizes the views of much of earlier Rdzogs-chen literature when he urges that these not be confused and observes that the buddha-nature is not a mere emptiness devoid of qualities.[6] According to Mipham, the former view is given to beginners as an antidote for mistaken views of the self; the final view takes literally, not the Perfection of Wisdom teaching on emptiness of the second wheel, but the buddha-nature teachings of the third wheel.[7] These cannot be understood merely through expounding upon emptiness.[8] Although like emptiness in being unconditioned, this buddha-nature is not a mere negative because it possesses spontaneously established *(anābhaga, hlun grub)* good qualities, none of which are appropriate to a mere negative.[9] Such qualities, like the buddha-nature itself, are not created through practice, and thus a developmental path is not appropriate. Indeed, the claim that an impermanent cause can give rise to an unconditioned nonproduct is, for Mipham, nothing short of amazing.[10]

This latter, as we have seen, is not precisely the Dge-lugs-pas' claim, since they emphasize epistemological rather than ontological terms in this context, and since the status of the mind as a conditioned phenomenon does not change in the process of the path. However, the gradual progression that Dge-lugs-pa does describe is entirely counter to Mipham and Rdzog-chen's perspective. Mipham is emphatic that the buddha-nature is not something to be achieved incrementally. It is not like a seed that eventually becomes a sprout, destroying itself in the process,[11] nor does it exist sometimes and not others. Moreover, being unconditioned, buddha-nature is unaffected by whether or not a person is enlightened. When the adventitious defilements that obscured it are purified, the buddha-nature *gets the name of an effect,* but it is not newly produced.[12]

These opening positions can also be read as an instance of the tension in Buddhism between "the impulse toward enlightement and the drive to purification" noted in this volume's introduction. Because Dge-lugs-pa's sūtra soteriology expressly equates buddha-nature with the emptiness that must be realized, and because emptiness itself, being a mere negative, is utterly devoid of qualities, Dge-lugs-pa must theorize how positive qualities such as concentration participate in the nondualistic and immediate cognition of this very special type of object, and the stages by which a mind that is both concentrated and cognizant of emptiness—the two gestures mentioned above—is developed. Thus the categories associated with mental calming and concentration become central to Dge-lugs-pa claims regarding the "immediate" cognition of the "unconditioned" at crucial stages of the path. This way of framing mārga gives rise to the issues discussed below.

Such considerations alone would give the topic of concentration significant claims on our attention, and yet the importance given to the topic of concentration in Buddhist traditions is not the only reason to take interest in it. The Buddhist discussions of path summarized here are, above all, reflections on epistemology. If we wish eventually to relate Buddhist path and epistemological rubrics to Western categories, calming and concentration are among the most difficult to place. This is especially true of those forms associated with the higher levels of "calming" the mind—calm abiding *(śamatha, zhi gnas)* itself, the four concentrations *(dhyāna, bsam gtan),* and the four formless absorptions *(samāpatti, snyoms 'jug).* By examining these, it may be possible to access something unique to Buddhist understandings of human mental systems. More specifically, I want to suggest that Dge-lugs-pa makes its case for what it considers an unmediated and culturally autonomous cognition partly by the way it finds that mental calming and concentration (1) ameliorate the tensions and differences between conceptual thought and direct perception and (2) reduce the experienced power of conditioned objects over their conditionable perceiving subjects.

Calming and the Path

To this end, I will analzye two segments of the Prāsaṅgika-Mādhyamika path structure wherein a claim for unmediated perception is elaborated: namely, the first and the sixth bodhisattva grounds. It is said that a union of calm abiding and special insight makes possible the initial direct cognition of emptiness (i.e., the first instance of unmediated and errorless cognition), and that the special concentration of the fifth ground makes possible the surpassing perfection of wisdom accomplished on the sixth ground, which in turn results in the uncommon absorption of cessation. In both cases, a particular form of mental calm is integrated with a nonconceptual cognition of emptiness; at that time any impingement on direct perception by conceptual thought is said to be removed. Concentration is also instrumental in the special union of method and wisdom that characterizes the seventh ground. This is the first time the bodhisattva can enter into direct, nondualistic cognition of emptiness *without first accessing conceptual imagery.* "Immediacy" as the absence of reliance on mental imagery now gains a new force.

In discussing the particular role of concentration at each of these junctures, I will highlight Dge-lugs-pa exegeses of Candrakīrti's classic discussion of ten bodhisattva grounds in his *Entrance to the Middle Way (Madhyamakāvatāra, Dbu ma la 'jug pa),* partly because these comprise a particularly detailed description of a gradualist path and partly because they introduce a category of calming, the uncommon absorption of cessation, that partakes of wisdom in such a way as to highlight the relationship between concentration and wisdom, the two central features of the gradual path.

Since the unconditioned emptiness is first directly cognized on the path of seeing, the first bodhisattva ground, and since this cognition is described as a wisdom consciousness, it might seem that any tensions or issues associated with differential mental functionings are resolved by this point on the path. To a certain extent they are. For example, special insight and calm abiding are united, and no conceptual or other perceptual errors are operative. However, the nature of this relationship again becomes an issue on the sixth ground, where a further integration of calming and wisdom is considered imperative. At this time one gains an enhanced perfection of wisdom which in turn makes possible a new type of mental focus known as the uncommon absorption of cessation *(*āsadhārananirodhasamāpatti, thun mong ma yin pa'i 'gog snyoms),* a category unique to Prāsaṅgika, and probably to Dge-lugs-pa Prāsaṅgika. In Tsong-kha-pa's *Illumination of the Thought, An Extensive Explanation of [Candrakīrti's] "Entrance to the Middle Way" (Dbu ma la 'jug pa'i rgya cher bshad pa dgongs pa rab gsal),*[13] and in later Dge-lugs-pa commentaries on Candrakīrti by Pan-chen Bsod-nams-grags-pa, Rje-btsun Chos-kyi-rgyal-mtshan, and 'Jam-dbyangs-bzhad-pa, the uncommon absorption of cessation forms a crucial part of mental functioning on the sixth ground.

Before passing on to this, we might note that, even in this Buddhist context, the suggestion of unmediated, universally accessible knowledge is a bit anomalous. After all, Tibetan scholarship distinguishes the higher philosophical systems from the lower (with Prāsaṅgika generally seen as the highest) in good measure by the extent to which the former understand the mental subject as constructive of its own experience. However, in contrast to contemporary theories (Derrida's *différance* comes immediately to mind), the participation of thought and direct perception in such constructions is considered erroneous precisely to the extent that it contradicts or interferes with cognition of that which is unconstructed, namely, with the unconditioned, emptiness. (Failing to take account of *différance,* by contrast, presumably interferes with an understanding of *différance,* not with something which transcends it.)

In Dge-lugs-pa Prāsaṅgika, unmediated, unmistaken direct perception must circumvent the errors of thought as well as those of ordinary direct perception. Thought, by its very nature, fails to properly distinguish its referent *(*adhyavasayaviṣaya, zhen yul)* from an image *(arthasāmānya, don spyi)* of the same. Ordinary direct perception, though valid regarding the specific characteristics of its object, is deceived by the false appearance of solidity, continuity, and so forth of that object. Most human experience involves an inchoate combination of conceptual and direct cognitions; consequently, although ordinary direct perception is free from the errors of thought, it tends to be closely associated with them and in any case, according to Prāsaṅgika, is not free from errors of its own. Thus, even though ordinary direct perception is unmediated in the sense of having no intervening image between subject and object, it is not said that anyone having direct perception of, for example, an orange would have an identical experience of that orange.

Why, then, is the experience of emptiness implicitly presumed to be the same for everyone? It is curious and notable that such universality is implied in the context of a system that recognizes ordinary direct perception, like conceptual thought, to be a product of the vagaries of human experience. However, there are ethical and epistemological differences posited between ordinary direct perception and the direct experience of emptiness that address this issue, albeit obliquely. Whereas ordinary direct perception can be associated with a nonvirtuous, virtuous, or neutral mind (someone wants to steal an orange, someone wants to give it to a friend), the nondualistic experience of emptiness is possible only for a virtuous mind. Still more significant, however, are the ways in which direct perception of emptiness is said to be structurally different from ordinary direct perception.

We can discern at least three senses in which the direct cognition of emptiness is "unmediated," and only one of these is true of ordinary direct perception as well. First, as already mentioned, this is a time when emptiness is known without an intermediary mental image. The direct experience of emptiness is also unmediated in that there is no experienced difference between subject and object. Despite Dge-lugs-pa insistence on calling emptiness an "object" of the wisdom consciousness, it is a nondualistically apprehended object, which signifies, among other things, that the mind is not being "conditioned" by its object as other forms of direct perception are conditioned by their objects.

Although emptiness is an object, it is not considered an object condition *(ālambanapratyaya, dmigs rkyen),* and there appears to be some debate about whether or not the consciousness observing emptiness "is produced in the aspect of emptiness" *(rnam ldan du skyes)* in the way that an eye consciousness is produced in, or takes on, the aspect of its object. The point is that the mind observing emptiness does not depend on emptiness in the manner that sense consciousnesses depend on their objects.[14] Finally, although mental preparation is crucial to the gradual development of this state, direct cognitions of emptiness are considered immediate and unconditioned insofar as such cognition does not perpetuate characteristics of the "causal" states leading up to it, such as mental imagery, coarse analysis, or a division between subject and object.[15]

All three of these—the absence of a mental image (necessarily the product of one's own unique experience),[16] the mind's not being produced through response to a specific object, and the mind's nonreplication of characteristics associated with cognitions that precede and lead up to direct cognition of emptiness—suggest that the usual ways in which experience is particularized no longer operate. Each of these attributes of "immediate" cognition tends toward a universalization of the cognitive experience, even if it does not do away with objections to claims for complete universality.

The experience of emptiness is also "universal" in the sense that the epistemological parameters for its cognition are rather narrow, apparently allowing for little diversity of experience. As already noted, emptiness is considered a mere negative, and thus it arguably will not imprint data on the mind. Further, we have seen that emptiness is not an "object condition" with causal efficacy. There are different ways to directly perceive an orange—in the shade, in full light, when hungry, and so forth—but only one way to fully understand emptiness. In Prāsaṅgika, the claim of unmediated, errorless direct perception is made only in connection with an object whose appearance is nondeceptive, and the only such object is emptiness. (Perhaps, to paraphrase Tolstoy, it is felt that all errors are different, but all completely correct perception is correct in the same way.) By implication, the mind that realizes emptiness inferentially or directly experiences union with it has an experience that can be considered universal. Moreoever, both in this state and subsequent to it, cultural as well as conceptual conditioning lose their characteristic power to govern experience.[17] Just how complete such cognitive independence might be is a question that underlies much of this discussion.

In the path approaching buddahhood, thought processes are undone. Thus, although Buddhist and contemporary Western intellectual traditions share a general emphasis on the constructed nature of experience as well as an acute awareness of the limitations intrinsic to language and other conventions, they seem to reach diametrically opposite conclusions regarding the possibility of an unmediated, complete, universally available and objective perception, at least within their different understandings of these terms. Buddhist philosophers do this in part by the kinds of epistemological distinctions noted above, and in part by elaborating dimensions of mental experience that receive relatively little attention in the West, such as the various forms of mental calming discussed below. To come to terms with specific Buddhist claims about cognition,it is thus vital to consider not only the role of concentration but the relationship it bears to other mental functions with which it is associated.

The First Bodhisattva Ground

Calm Abiding and Nonconceptual Analysis

Classic Indian Mahāyāna literature emphasizes that calm abiding is foundational to special insight. For example, Śāntideva's *Engaging in the Bodhisattva Deeds (Bodhisattvacaryāvatāra, Spyod 'jug),* 8.4:

> Having understood that the afflictions are overcome
> Through special insight thoroughly endowed with calm abiding,
> One should first seek calm abiding.[18]

In Tibet, Dge-lugs-pa sūtra-system texts paid particular attention to the relationship between analytical meditation *(dpyad sgom),* an analogue of insight, and stabilizing meditation *('jog sgom),* an analogue of calm abiding. This interest arose at least partly because of their claim that analysis can induce a state which is a union of calm abiding and special insight. (Many of us would agree that analysis induces attention and focus, but that it actually stills the mind so as to reduce conceptualization is a different and more difficult proposition.)

This claim, important as it was to the fourteenth-century Tsong-kha-pa and subsequent writers, did not originate with them. Pan-chen Bsod-nams-grags-pa notes that, at least as early as the twelfth century, the Ka-dam-pa Geshe Dol-pa-shes-rab-rgya-mtsho (1059–1131) stated that only a moment intervenes between the attainment of special insight and a union of calm abiding and special insight.[19] Tsong-kha-pa was slightly more radical in maintaining that, from its very first moment, a special insight on emptiness comprises a mind in which calm abiding and special insight are united.[20] In other words, the experience of the "unconditioned" depends on a particular consonance of subject and object, and this requires a mind of unusual composure, intensity, and clarity, the very qualities associated with calm abiding and higher levels of concentration.

Still, even when "united," calm abiding and special insight remain functionally distinct. They are not one entity *(ekadravya, ngo bo gcig);* whatever is one is not the other. Pan-chen Bsod-nams-grags-pa points out that those who say these become one at the time of attaining a bodhisattva ground are mistaken; the two mental gestures of withdrawing the mind in one sense and expanding its horizons in another are entwined, not blended. Nonetheless, the oral tradition offers a delicate caveat here: whereas in earlier stages of the path, analytical and stabilizing meditation are different, they later become "as if" one entity insofar as they neither manifest different functions nor require different forms of effort.[21]

The point for us is that accounting for the association of analysis with the first-ground bodhisattva's nonconceptual wisdom realizing emptiness is seen as a taxing and critical matter, as evidenced by the difficulty of drawing clear boundaries around each of these functions. Having said that analysis brings on a state of calm abiding on emptiness, a profound compatability between these should be supportable in some way. One area of compatability is that "calming" or "concentration" in part signifies that the mind is no longer involved with thought and thus, arguably, is temporarily beyond the reach of at least conceptual carriers of cultural experience. Thus when "analysis" is, however problematically, assimilated to the function of concentration, it is brought one step farther from its initial function of conditioning.

On the uninterrupted Mahāyāna path of seeing, attained simultaneously with the first bodhisattva ground, the mind combines stabilizing with analytical meditation; that is, it unites calm abiding with special insight. This is a mind for which all conceptual, dualistic appearances have vanished. In the absence of conceptuality and duality, the mind cannot engage in any new analysis.[22] Thus the case has to be made either that wisdom is compatible with a collapse of conceptual cognition, or that the analytical understanding associated with wisdom can occur in the absence of conceptual functioning. The Dge-lugs-pa exegesis favors the latter position. Nonconceptual experience of emptiness is an essential characteristic of all the bodhisattva grounds. In describing these grounds, therefore, Dge-lugs-pa finds it crucial to wed the element of analysis to the element of nondualistic cognition.

In Dge-lugs-pa literature, a Mahāyāna path of seeing is defined most succinctly as "a Mahāyāna clear realization of truth."[23] Somewhat less succinctly, but making the same point about the cognitive import of this stage, 'Jam-dbyangs-bzhad-pa calls it "a clear realization of the truth which is a cessation of the two extremes of existence and peace."[24]

To be a "clear realizer" of emptiness is a function of special insight. Since Dge-lugs-pa frames emptiness as an object that becomes available to direct perception only when analysis has prepared the way, it becomes crucial that Dge-lugs-pa account for the analytical capacity even of the nonconceptual direct cognition of emptiness. The function of calming is both the problem and the solution. It facilitates an absence of conceptual movement *and* it also enhances special insight and analysis.

How can there be nonconceptual analysis? I do not think this is merely a logistic or syntactical corner into which Dge-lugs-pa soteriology has painted itself, although it may be that in part. At the same time, it raises broader questions for us about the nature of knowledge: Can the mind know something undistortedly? If so, would all minds know undistortedly in the same way? The Dge-lugs-pa insistence that emptiness is an object and that there is nondualistic cognition of it raises the further question of how a mind can "know" an object without simultaneously distancing itself from that which is known. Is a state of powerful calm a necessary, if insufficient, factor for accomplishing this? If so, why? In Kantian terms, the above asks whether it is possible to know fully and undistortedly just what is, and whether such could occur if subject-object distinctions are collapsed. In Lacanian terms, this discussion probes the possibilty of a knowledge that, unlike the knowledge that operates through language, does not signify a loss or distance from that which it knows.

Much of Indo-Tibetan Buddhist epistemology outside Prāsaṅgika considers full and undistorted cognition to qualify direct perception in general, labeling it a "complete engager" *(*vidhipravṛttibuddhi, sgrub 'jug gi blo).* Direct perception, in this view, takes on the aspect *(ākāra, rnam pa)* of an object and thereby gains undistorted awareness of it. This completeness, in addition to the absence of an intervening mental image, is what most fundamentally distinguishes direct perception from conceptual thought. Thought always accesses its object by eliminating what is other than that object; for this reason thought is labeled an eliminative or "partial engager" *(*apohapravṛttibuddhi, gsel 'jug gi blo).*[25] On entering the path of seeing, emptiness, until then known only conceptually and thus through partial engagement, is first engaged with fully.

Calm abiding is the lowest level of mental quiescence that can support a direct cognition of emptiness. Thus the direct experience of emptiness is concomitant with a form of meditative equipoise *(samāhita, mnyam bzhag).* This term literally means "placed equally"; oral scholarly tradition understands the "equally" to signify that when the mind is in equipoise, consciousness and object are coextensive (and thus equal) in the sense that any emptiness is necessarily the object of an uninterrupted Mahāyāna path of seeing, and any object of such a consciousness (on the first ground) is necessarily an emptiness.[26] Because conceptual investigation *(vitarka, rtog pa)* and analysis *(vicāra, dpyod pa)* are part and parcel of the first concentration, calm abiding, too, can be understood as compatible with these. The various factors that are one entity with the consciousness cognizing emptiness are also said to cognize it. These twenty-three factors include two of the changeable mental factors *(*anyathābhāvacaitta, sems byung gzhan 'gyur),* namely, investigation and analysis.[27] A path of seeing gained on the basis of calm abiding or the first concentration can therefore be understood as compatible with analysis, since it itself contains factors of investigation and analysis—and all the more so since analysis itself induces calm abiding.

However, the path of seeing is most commonly gained in conjunction with the fourth concentration, not calm abiding.[28] At this level, unlike with the lower forms of concentration, conceptual investigation and analysis are regarded as "faults of fluctuation" *(g.yo ba'i skyon).*[29] In what sense, then, if any, can we speak of analysis at the time of a direct cognition of emptiness as associated with a mind of the fourth concentration? To discuss this is to reflect on the extent to which this tradition finds a specific cognitive experience to be separable from conceptual meditation, as well as from the nonconceptual habits of perception which affect, and in that sense mediate, ordinary direct perception. Without such meditations, I would argue, cultural and personal conditioning become so ephemeral as to be virtually nonexistent. Thus, to investigate Dge-lugs-pa claims regarding cognition of emptiness at the fourth concentration or higher is to probe the parameters of their view of experiencing the unconditioned.

Dge-lugs-pa oral tradition on this issue opines that (1) the mind on the uninterrupted path of seeing is engaged in analytical meditation, and (2) analysis associated with direct cognition of emptiness is to be distinguished from the ordinary form of investigation and analysis incompatible with the fourth concentration.[30] In the former, there is no sense that the observing mind is here and the observed emptiness is there. Unlike analysis that reflects "this is" or "this is not," the nonconceptual wisdom, like an eye consciousness, is said to engage its object fully, but unlike an eye or other sense consciousness, is able to ascertain all that appears to it. The implication is that this ascertainment is considered a form of analysis. Moreover, although there is no movement of thought, this mind is said to comprehend the reasons through which emptiness itself became known. It is thus deemed possible to have analytical meditation without conceptualization. The result is a dissipation of nonconceptual conditioning and of the appearance of inherent existence associated with ordinary sensory perception.

Indeed, the oral scholarly tradition takes the uninterrupted Mahāyāna path of seeing to be a highly superior type of analytical meditation *(dpyad sgom),* as well as the first instance, in their path sequence, of nonconceptual wisdom *(nirvikalpajñāna, rnam par mi rtog pa'i ye shes).* In short, the relationship betweeen concentration and insight, which in earlier stages are antithetical, becomes, to borrow Gregory Bateson's term, complementary—meaning that the increase of one fits with and engenders development in the other. This is expressed in a variety of ways. Not only, as we have seen, is calm abiding said to induce special insight, but nonconceptual analytical meditation in general is considered a form of a yogi's discriminative wisdom *(pratyavekṣaṇājñāna, so sor rtog pa'i ye shes),* and any instance of special insight is also an analytical meditation.[31]

The wisdom directly realizing emptiness is a form of yogic direct perception, and it is nonconceptual in two senses. It lacks conceptual thought *(kalpanā, rtog pa)* and is also free of mistakenly aspected thought *(avikalpa, rnam par mi rtog pa),* meaning that it is not prey to the mistaken appearances *('khrul snang yod mkhyan)* that accompany most sensory direct perception. All yogic direct perception is not necessarily nonconceptual in both these ways. The yogic direct perception of impermanence is, of course, without conceptual thought *(nirvikalpa, rtog med),* but is still associated with mistaken aspects of thought because the impermanence which it directly realizes appears to inherently exist, although it does not.[32]

Thus we have noted how Dge-lugs-pa sūtra texts construe the relationship between calming and analysis on the first bodhisattva ground. These are regarded as thoroughly complementary, given that a distinction is made between the kinds of analysis associated with ordinary direct perception and the kind associated with the direct perception of emptiness. In this way a case is made for a nonconceptual knowing—that is, for a state that is unmediated insofar as no image or distorting tendencies intervene between knower and known. The unconditioned emptiness is its only possible object. As we will see below, such specific claims about the nature of the nonconceptual state become relevant to descriptions of how this nonconceptual experience is construed in relation to its subject.

The Nonconceptual Subject: Knowing without Knowing "Difference"

One of Tsong-kha-pa's teachers, the Sagya scholar Red-mda'-ba (1349–1412), is unique among the *Entrance* commentators consulted here in taking up the issue of nonconceptual thought early in his discussion of the sixth bodhisattva ground. The use he makes of this issue contrasts with subsequent Dge-lugs-pa perspectives. He observes that the nature *(svabhāva, rang bzhin)* of the perfection of wisdom is a nonconceptual final wisdom *(nirvikalpajñāna, rnam par mi rtog pa'i ye shes),* and that it is nonconceptual in the sense that "when a yogi's mind is free of all signs of elaboration, becoming the nature of thusness, then it is nonconceptual."[33]

The clear distinction between subject and object that Tsong-kha-pa and his followers were to make axiomatic is foreign to Red-mda'-ba, as it is to Mipham and to Rdzogs-chen. Red-mda'-ba quotes Śāntideva's *Guide to the Bodhisattva's Way of Life* to support his own perspective (IX.34):

> When knower and object known
> Do not dwell before the mind,
> At that time, because no other aspect occurs,
> Objectless, [the mind] is fully pacified.[34]

According to Buddhist hagiography, Śāntideva began his ascent skyward while reciting this verse.[35] Perhaps this accounts for the interesting discrepancy in the first line of this stanza. In other versions of Śāntideva's text, this line makes no reference to knower and known but speaks of things and non-things.[36] However, Red-mda'-ba's rendition supports his subsequent explanation that a (wisdom) consciousness, indistinguishable from its object, is "the nature" of that object. (There is then, of course, no place for eliminative or partial engagement, or what Bateson calls "the difference that makes a difference." This is his definition of an idea, and in Buddhist terms it could be understood to refer to the eliminative process by which thought accesses its image.)[37]

Is such a nonconceptual wisdom a consciousness or not? If it is, then it would know its object and thus could not be described as pacified of the elaborations of subject and object. But if this nonconceptual wisdom is not a consciousness, how can it realize reality? For Red-mda'-ba, to say that it does so means this wisdom is not realizing anything that could be designated merely by the statement that "it realizes reality."[38] However, unlike other forms of nonconceptual consciousness such as sleep, fainting, and the like, this one is preceded by a yogi's discriminative wisdom that analyzes the nature of all things. At that time, not even a single atom of inherent existence is taken as an object and thus, after having done such analysis, the yogi's mind "becomes of the nature of reality."[39]

Postulating such fluidity between subject and object, and claiming that what is known is the subject itself, is certainly one way to suggest the possibility of an errorless, immediate, and nondualistic cognition. We have seen that Mipham and the Rnying-ma Rdzogs-chen tradition in general also choose this. But it is not Tsong-kha-pa's way. His discussion of Prāsaṅgika, and the Dge-lugs-pas' after him, emphasizes that the powerful nondualistic experience of mind and emptiness as like "water poured into water" does not mean that mind and emptiness actually become utterly one. As with Kant, the categories of subject and object do not dissolve, even though the experience of them does disappear. This is as true on the first bodhisattva ground as it is on the sixth.

The nondual wisdom of the first ground is a form of special insight[40] simply by virtue of being wisdom. For Tsong-kha-pa, as for Red-mda'-ba, wisdom is not associated with "elaborations" *(prapañca, spros ba),*[41] because "elaborations" are ingredients of error. At the same time, Tsong-kha-pa and other Dge-lugs-pas do not take the functioning of wisdom to be merely an absence of error or corrective of ignorance. Emptiness is a mere and complete negative, but knowing emptiness is not. It is wisdom. Moreover, the mind is said to have positive abilities of its own even after ignorance and its predispositions have been eliminated. This view of wisdom's capacity is significant for the Dge-lugs-pa understanding of a how flawless, complete, and immediate understanding of the unconditioned can occur.

For Tsong-kha-pa, this claim is another way of saying that wholly correct knowledge is possible; if all knowledge were linked with ignorance, all ability to know—wisdom itself—would disappear when ignorance was extinguished.[42] Thus, on the path of seeing and afterward, one has analytical meditation without conceptualization, without "movement of thought." At this time one has a calm abiding concordant *(dang tshung ldan)* with one-pointedness on emptiness.[43] Such nonconceptual analytical meditation occurs for the first time on the Mahāyāna uninterrupted path of seeing.

Because no conceptual superimpositions *(āropa, sgro 'dogs)* are operative, analysis is said to function by way of direct perception. Such can only be accomplished in connection with emptiness, it is said, because only emptiness exists as it appears, and thus no analytical corrective is required. Having emptiness as an object means that the mind does not cast up images or presuppositions of any kind during the meditation session. To have post-sessional wisdom *(pṛṣṭhalabdhajñāna, rjes thob ye shes)* means that the relationship of consciousness to any such images, as well as to the objects of direct perception, has shifted to such a degree that they no longer impinge on the mind in the same way, insofar as they are understood as illusory-like and so forth. In terms of whether subject or object now governs experience, the greater influence proceeds from the side of the subject, despite it being said that objects are at this time perceived with increasing accuracy and validity.

The first bodhisattva ground is the first time on the path when one is considered in unmediated contact with "reality" and knows it, without distortion, "just as it is." Two items are of interest here. First, by calling such a direct, noncognitive perception a refined form of analysis, the way is prepared for theorizing a kind of transfer to direct perception of some of the capacity of conceptual power when the conceptual function itself is inoperative. Our discussion of the uncommon absorption of cessation that occurs at the sixth ground suggests a further permutation of this theme. "Nonconceptual analysis" is, of course, a quite different order of business than either conceptual analysis or other forms of direct perception. It is distinguished from these because it does not operate through either conceptual or sensory difference. That is, gradations in the object (like the loudness of music or the strength of a scent) play no part in such perception. Ordinarily, as Bateson observes, "the mind can receive news only of difference."[44] For Bateson (as well as for Kant, and most of the rest of us), therefore, "nonconceptual analysis" is a *sine qua non* contradiction in terms. But the Buddhist point here is that significant gradations or "differences" now occur primarily in the subject, not in its special object, emptiness. This brings us to a second point of interest.

Despite claims that on the path of seeing one knows reality "just as it is," such knowledge improves considerably over the remainder of the path. As the mind cognizing emptiness becomes more subtle—especially, more concentrated—the appearance of emptiness itself becomes "clearer."[45] Such further development no longer depends on changes in the object, but in capacities intrinsic to this type of consciousness and set in motion by it.[46]

In short, even though the initial direct cognition of emptiness is a complete and correct engager, there is room for improvement. Here, however, the usual sequence of perceptual events is reversed: It is changes in the subject that give rise to changes in experience of the object. The mind on the path of seeing does not respond to an external object; in this sense, at least, the mind is not conditioned by its object. Nor is it conditioned by the ordinary internal states, such as mood or quixotic interest, that generally govern experience. Such a mind is not referred to as unconditioned; it is called a stainless meditative equipoise *(myams bzahg zag med).*[47]

The Dge-lugs-pa distinction between a wisdom consciousness and its object, a logically pristine but counterintuitive point, supports their charting of a progressive clarification of both subject and object. The relative autonomy of the consciousness from its object at this time becomes qualified, however slightly, by the Dge-lugs-pa insistence that the categories of subject and object do not actually converge, even in valid, nondualistic experience. This emphasis stands in contrast to Red-mda'-ba and to vast bodies of Rnying-ma and other Tibetan literature. The Dge-lugs-pa scenario also raises questions about whether or not the initial direct perception of emptiness, or only the ultimate one, can be considered immediate and undistorted perception. In any case, the dimensions along which "improvement" takes place (some of which are examined further below) by and large lie outside the issue of mediated versus unmediated cognition as it is examined in the West.

Thus claims regarding the possibilities of immediate cognition do not apply to knowledge in general, but have to do with the features particular to this nondual awareness, including its quality of calm, its special object, and its special relationship to that object. On the uninterrupted Mahāyāna path of seeing, the mind observing emptiness cannot have any new analysis,[48] but is said to have the function of analysis without the exertion (or fluctuation) of newly analyzing the object. Such lack of exertion is crucial to the claim that analysis can operate even when the mind observing emptiness has as its basis the meditative stabilization of the fourth concentration, in relation to which analysis is considered a fault.

Thus we have considered two issues associated with the "unmediated" cognition of emptiness on the first bodhisattva ground: the question of how analysis is associated with it, and the related matter of whether subject and object are construed as different. The category of mental calm pertains to both issues. A mind of calm abiding or greater concentration forms the ground of analytical insight and stills the constructs and elaborations of conceptual thought. In the process, it becomes a positive capacity associated with wisdom, providing the mental basis *(sems rten)* by which wisdom's special object can be cognized nondualistically, at the same time that calm abiding's very existence supports the distinction between subject and object.

The Sixth Bodhisattva Ground

The Uncommon Absorption of Cessation

In 1402, Tsong-kha-pa wrote the *Great Exposition of the Stages of the Path (Lam rim chen mo),* a classic of Tibetan Mādhyamika soteriology that, like his other *lam rim* texts, focuses on practices just antecedent to the accumulating path *(saṃbhāramārga, tshogs lam)* up to those by which the seeing path *(darśanamārga, mthong lam)* is attained. Sixteen years later, in his final work on Mādhyamika, *Illumination of the Thought,* Tsong-kha-pa turned detailed attention to the upper reaches of the path. Here he follows Candrakīrti's *Entrance to the Middle Way (Madhyamakāvatāra, Dbu ma la 'jug pa)* in describing the ten stages or grounds by which a bodhisattva progresses to buddhahood. In contrast to the *lam rim* genre, this text begins with the seeing path and describes the enhancement of the bodhisattva deeds: the perfection of giving on the first ground, and the perfections of ethics, patience, effort, concentration, wisdom, method, prayer, power, and initiation on the second through tenth grounds, respectively. Discussion of the sixth ground occupies over half the pages of this text.

Candrakīrti uses the term "cessation" to express an attainment unique to the sixth ground; Tsong-kha-pa glosses this as "an uncommon absorption of cessation," a term he uses only at the beginning of his three-hundred-page discussion of the sixth ground.[49] Monastic textbooks on the stages of the path *(sa lam)*, tenets *(siddhānta, grub mtha')*, and the Collected Topics genre *(bsdus grva)* do not discuss this category. Virtually the only significant sources for the topic of an uncommon absorption of cessation come from monastic texts that comment on Candrakīrti's *Entrance* and draw on Tsong-kha-pa's discussion of this. Notable among this group are the *General Meaning of the Middle Way (Dbu ma'i spyi don)* and *Responding to Queries on the "Entrance" (Dbu ma la 'jug pa'i brgal lan)* by Pan-chen Bsod-nams-grags-pa (1478–1554), a major author of Drebung-Loseling textbooks;[50] the *Good Explanation of the General Meaning, Clarifying the Difficult Points of [Tsong-kha-pa's] "Illumination of the Thought" (Bstan bcos dbu ma la 'jug pa'i rnam bshad dgongs pa rab gsal gyi dka' gnad gsal bar byed pa'i spyi don legs bshad skal bzang mgul rgyan)* by Rje-btsun Chos-kyi-rgyal-mtshan (1469–1546); and the *Great Exposition of the Middle Way (Dbu ma chen mo)* by 'Jam-dbyangs-bzhad-pa (1648–1721).

The uncommon absorption of cessation, gained in dependence on the wisdom of the sixth ground, is also central to descriptions of the seventh and eighth grounds, whose special perfections—subcategories of the perfection of wisdom—are special method *(upāya, thabs)* and prayers *(praṇidhāna, smon lam)*, respectively. Tsong-kha-pa's discussion builds directly from Candrakīrti, incorporating not only the *Entrance* verses but significant portions of Candrakīrti's own commentary on the *Entrance* as well.

The uncommon absorption of cessation is thus a category to which only a limited, albeit important, group of texts calls attention in Dge-lugs-pa, as well as a rubric that apparently gained increased attention after Tsong-kha-pa's day. The term appears to exist at least in part as a way of exploring how wisdom simultaneously (1) is completely united with its object, (2) is a knower of that object, and (3) improves or develops in the absence of any thought-imagery. Tsong-kha-pa may well have been the first to use the term; his own teacher Red-mda'-ba does not mention it in his commentary on Candrakīrti's *Entrance*.[51] It is also a category critical to understanding central aspects of the "improvement" that occurs without the benefit of "difference," as mentioned above, and that is said to characterize the subject knowing emptiness.

Tsong-kha-pa explains that on the fifth ground the bodhisattva's concentration, no longer impeded by distraction and other faults incompatible with the perfection of concentration, becomes surpassing. This surpassing concentration, in turn, enhances wisdom. Tsong-kha-pa, echoing Śāntideva's remarks on calm abiding quoted above, opens his discussion of the sixth ground with an observation on the relationship between calming and wisdom:

> As much as calm abiding is enhanced, so much is special insight enhanced. On the fifth ground the bodhisattva attained full development of the perfection of concentration so that, in dependence on this, here [on the sixth ground] the perfection of wisdom is fully developed.[52]

The power of what we might call a language-associated faculty—namely, insight—is increased through the development of a faculty not associated with language at all—namely, mental calming and concentration. To put this another way, calming, though it forms part of a cognitive process, is not itself altered by "ideas" or "difference." The mind of mental calm (technically, "calm abiding") does have an object, but its relationship to that object is distinguishable from that of most other cognitive processes. Here, the object is important as a support *(āśraya, rten)* rather than as an object of observation *(ālambana, dmigs pa).* Thus the object is not considered a cause of subjective experience during the upper stages of concentration; rather, the subjective process unfolds through a power of its own. The same is true of the wisdom consciousness, which can exist only when conjoined with such a calmed mind.

Indeed, although the wisdom of insight is famous for being "inexpressible," its function is far more language-associated than the faculty of concentration that forms its basis. It is the wisdom of insight, after all, that is characterized as analytical, albeit nonconceptually so. The sixth ground, a supreme form of nonconceptual analysis according to Dge-lugs-pa, is attainable only after the perfection of concentration on the fifth ground has been activated. This wisdom is a substantial cause *(upadāna, nyer len)* of the uncommon absorption of cessation.[53] The precise nature of this causality is not explained as fully as one might hope, but both Candrakīrti and Tsong-kha-pa clearly suggest such a sequence. Their doing so supports the idea that such a consciousness is not impinged upon in the usual way by its object, but that this subjective experience is construed to proceed almost entirely from the side of the subject. In the *Entrance* itself, Candrakīrti writes (VI.1d), "By dwelling in wisdom [the bodhisattva] attains[54] cessation." His own commentary elaborates:

> Because on the fifth ground the Bodhisattva attained the completely pure perfection of concentration, on the sixth ground the bodhisattva dwells in

> a mind of meditative equipoise and sees the nature of the profound dependent-arising; due to the thoroughly pure perfection of wisdom, the bodhisattva achieves a cessation that did not occur previously.[55]

Tsong-kha-pa develops this briefly:

> Because [the bodhisattva] attained the thoroughly pure perfection of concentration on the fifth ground, on the sixth ground, the Approaching or Manifest, s/he dwells in a fully developed mind of meditative equipoise. With this as a basis s/he abides on the sixth bodhisattva ground seeing the profound suchness which is mere conditionality, or dependent-arising. Due to this, s/he abides in the fully developed perfection of wisdom, whereby s/he attains cessation. Prior to this, on the fifth ground and below, s/he did not attain cessation because of lacking the surpassing form of the fully developed perfection of wisdom. One cannot attain cessation merely through the five fully developed perfections of giving and so forth.[56]

Immediately following this statement, Tsong-kha-pa identifies the cessation in question as "an uncommon absorption of cessation."[57] Commenting on this passage two centuries later, 'Jam-dbyangs-bzhad-pa points to Candrakīrti's own emphasis on the sequential relationship between the sixth-ground attainment of wisdom and this form of cessation:

> The bodhisattva, seeing the suchness of profound dependent-arising, attains [the uncommon absorption of] cessation through the thoroughly pure perfection of wisdom, not before, because he did not have the surpassing form of the perfection of wisdom.[58]

One gets the impression of two mounting spirals of mental functioning, each suporting and furthering the other. This internally stimulated energy continues to operate when thought disappears, revealing and expressing something about the nature of consciousness in the process, just as a bird that flies at the sight of a cat reveals and expresses something about the nature of bird.

What distinguishes a common from an uncommon absorption of cessation? The scholastic literature provides definitions of both. Pan-chen defines a common absorption of cessation as

> a nonassociated compositional factor included in the nine serial meditative absorptions, a category distinguished as free from desire for the peak of cyclic existence; it is attained in dependence on (1) the supermundane path that attains it, and (2) a mind of the peak of cyclic existence.[59]

Rje-btsun Chos-kyi-rgyal-mtshan defines a common absorption of cessation similarly, as

> the wisdom directly realizing emptiness that is distinguished as free of desire for the peak of cyclic existence, which is attained in dependence on

(1) a supermundane path, which is the method for attaining it, and (2) the meditative absorption, which is the actual basis for the peak of cyclic existence.[60]

Pan-chen also offers a briefer definition of a common absorption: "a meditative absorption of cessation that is included in the nine serial concentrations and absorptions."[61] Thus, according to Pan-chen Bsod-nams-grags-pa, the wisdom of meditative equipoise of the first five grounds is neither a common nor an uncommon absorption of cessation.[62] It is not a common one because, being a consciousness, it is hardly a category outside the categories of form and consciousness *(viprayukta-saṃskāra, ldan min 'du byed)*. Here Pan-chen, unlike 'Jam-dbyangs-bzhad-pa, seems to concede that certain cessations are not consciousnesses. Yet even he would agree that this is not the Prāsaṅgika view.

In Prāsaṅgika, there can be no question of any absorption of cessation being a nonassociated compositional factor. The issue has to do with the referent of "cessation" in the phrase "absorption of cessation." According to Prāsaṅgika, the lower systems use this term to refer to the cessation of "coarse feeling and discrimination"; for Prāsaṅgika, a consciousness so qualified is one for which "all elaborations" have ceased.[63] The term can also refer to the object of the uncommon meditative absorption of cessation—namely, "thusness" or emptiness. But 'Jam-dbyangs-bzhad-pa points out that Prāsaṅgikas do not take the absorption of cessation to be a mere negative of feeling and discrimination. He implies that those non-Prāsaṅgika systems which consider an absorption of cessation itself to be a category outside of form or consciousness are at fault in thinking that, because coarse feeling and discrimination is absent, the mind is not operating at all.[64] Similarly, Rje-btsun Chos-kyi-rgyal-mtshan observes that although sūtras common to both vehicles speak of a meditative absorption in which coarse consciousnesses have ceased, Prāsaṅgika would not assert such a mind as an absorption of cessation any more than it would accept as correct the non-Prāsaṅgika descriptions of the view that the transitory is a real self *(satkāya-dṛṣṭi, 'jig tshogs la lta ba)*.[65]

The point for Prāsaṅgika, of course, is that consciousness does not cease in absorption; only coarse forms of consciousness do. It is this assertion that allows us to consider cessation a mental process. Accordingly, Blo-bzang-rta-dbyangs observes that after attainment of the eighth meditative absorption, when the object is the cessation known as thusness, "coarse feelings and discrimination, the appearance of subject and object, and the movement of mind and mental factors are ceased."[66] Similarly, 'Jam-dbyangs-bzhad-pa writes that neither feelings, discriminations, nor the other aggregates are extinguished in such a meditative equipoise, except insofar as they fail to appear to the mind of a practitioner engaged in direct cognition of emptiness.[67] It is from this point of view that we can speak of an absorption of cessation.

In other words, Pan-chen's remarks notwithstanding, later Dge-lugs-pa Prāsaṅgika maintains that such an absorption must be a consciousness. By implication, it is only those who do not understand the extent of calm or the full potential of the internally engendered energy associated with consciousness who are susceptible to misinterpeting the cessation of coarse minds as cessation of consciousness.

The increasing subtlety of consciousness is a crucial ingredient in the developmental path proposed by Dge-lugs-pa Prāsaṅgika; it is essential to achieving the kind of unmediated cognition that characterizes much of a practitioner's experience over the ten grounds and finds its most complete expression in the consciousness of a buddha. These differences are expressed in epistemological, not ontological terms, insofar as all minds are technically "conditioned phenomena." However, the wisdom consciousness is not "conditioned" in the more ordinary sense of the term, which signifies the impact on the mind of afflictions, conceptual processes, or adventitious causes and conditions.[68]

As a type of meditative equipoise, this uncommon absorption is a form of the calming-and-focusing function; it is also, by definition, a wisdom consciousness. For example, Pan-chen defines an uncommon absorption of cessation as "a wisdom of meditative equipoise that is directly poised equally on reality, [and] induced by the surpassing practice of the perfection of wisdom."[69] This occurs, Pan-chen adds, from the sixth ground through to buddhahood. His definition of the meditative equipoise specifically indicated on the sixth ground is: "The wisdom of meditative equipoise on the sixth ground that is induced by the surpassing practice of the perfection of wisdom."[70] Pan-chen also offers a slightly broader definition of the absorption of cessation discussed here: "A wisdom of meditative equipoise of the sixth ground that is induced by that [surpassing] practice [of the perfection of wisdom] which does not come earlier, on lower paths."[71]

In any case, as Pan-chen further observes, the first five grounds are not uncommon meditative absorptions because they are not induced by a surpassing practice of the perfection of wisdom. It is not until the sixth ground that one has what Tsong-kha-pa calls a "surpassing, fully developed perfection of wisdom" *(shes phyin phul du byung ba'i lhag pa).*[72] Thus every instance of a bodhisattva's meditative equipoise on emptiness is not an uncommon absorption of cessation.[73]

Like all wisdom consciousnesses of the first and subsequent grounds, the wisdom of emptiness possessed by a sixth-ground bodhisattva is also a mind of collective engagement. By dwelling in this understanding, the bodhisattva can attain a cessation not possible previously. Why not?

Because, say Candrakīrti and Tsong-kha-pa, until that time one did not have the surpassing or fully developed perfection of wisdom, and one cannot gain such a cessation merely through the five perfections of giving and so forth.[74] In other words, without an increased level of concentration which frees the mind from dependence on difference supplied by the object—that is, from differentiating a single object over time, or even from differentiating it from other objects with the same force as before—there is an increase in the insight that undermines the impact of the object, so that the subject becomes increasingly free from a differentiation between itself and the emptiness that is its special object.

Even though the direct wisdom of emptiness begins on the first ground, we have seen that the "surpassing, fully developed perfection of wisdom" begins only at the sixth ground. One of the features of this wisdom is its special understanding of emptiness itself as dependently constituted, a dependent-arising. At this time, one "sees emptiness to be like a reflection in the sense that it exists but is not truly established."[75] It is a dependent-arising in the sense that, for example, the emptiness of a table depends on the emptinesses of the parts of the table, but at the same time it is "unconditioned" because it does not change from moment to moment in dependence on causal conditions, and thus does not exhibit the most telling symptoms of ordinary conditionality: production, aging, and destruction. Therefore, although beyond dependence on at least the more obvious forms of conditioning, including culturally conditioned functions such as language, emptiness is not independent in general; nor is the "inexpressible" mind that cognizes it. Inexpressibility has to do with a new relationship between subject and object, such as the subject's experienced fusion with its object, and between certain of the subject's cognizing functions, such as the full complementarity between concentration and insight. It also has to do with the ascendance of concentration, a mental state that is even less moored in language than the "inexpressible" wisdom it makes possible.

The uncommon absorption of cessation on the sixth ground and above has as its mental basis the highest level of concentration included within cyclic existence. Thus the calming side of the insight/calming equation is considerably more developed than at the initial union of calm abiding and special insight. More significantly, as already mentioned, the uncommon absorption of cessation is a wisdom consciousness. Its being a consciousness is the most obvious way in which the uncommon absorption of cessation is distinguished from the cessation of discrimination and feeling *(saṃjñāveditanirodha, 'du shes dang tshor ba 'gog pa)* described by Buddhaghosa in the *Path of Purification,* wherein nothing mental endures, and by Vasubandhu in the *Treasury of Knowledge,* where a cessation is described as neither mind nor form.[76]

This latter type of cessation could be considered unconditioned, according to Asaṅga's *Compendium of Knowledge (Abhidharmasamuccaya, Mngon pa kun btus).*[77] But as Pan-chen dryly observes, there are other types of absorptions of cessation than those mentioned in the *Treasury,*[78] and the uncommon absorption of cessation is said to culminate the four concentrations and formless absorptions.[79] In any case, the historical roots of this debate should not obscure the fact that the crucial epistemological issue here is the extent to which consciousness can become distanced from usual modes of sensory, conceptual, and other culturally or conceptually specific input, and still function as consciousness in some meaningful way.[80] As a category, this uncommon absorption of cessation furthers the interconnection of the functions of calm abiding and special insight, which first combined on the preparation path. To call the union of these "special insight" is to assimilate, at least linguistically, the function of calming to insight; by contrast, on the sixth ground, the name "meditative equipoise" assimilates, or even masks, the function of wisdom. In both cases, differential categories are maintained, despite their differences becoming less important than their mutuality.

Absorption of Cessation on the Seventh and Eighth Grounds

The category of cessation is also given a significant role in explaining the increased power of the unmediated cognition of emptiness over the sixth through eighth grounds. 'Jam-dbyangs-bzhad-pa, partly paraphrasing Nāgārjuna's *Precious Garland (Ratnāvalī, Rin che'i phreng ba),* describes several of the remaining steps to buddhahood in terms of the uncommon absorption of cessation:

> On the sixth ground one attains the absorption of cessation; on the seventh one attains power over the absorption of cessation; on the eighth one enters absorption in the sense of manifesting it, and the Conquerors raise one from cessation.[81]

Thus continues the tale of consciousness' functioning at an increased distance from the mediated and particularized, as its collateral or internally engendered activity continues to unfold.

Having initially gained the uncommon absorption of cessation on the sixth ground, on the seventh ground the bodhisattva becomes able to enter into and rise from it quickly, and on the eighth ground gains the surpassing perfection of prayer—specifically, a prayer that one not lose these good qualities. Powerful prayer is also deemed necessary because on the seventh ground one developed such an affinity for the absorption of cessation that no less than a buddha must rouse one from it—perhaps the only time on the sūtra bodhisattva path that Dge-lugs-pa finds outside intervention to be required. Thus the process or system is depicted as for a brief period in (hypothetical) danger of collapsing in on itself, due to the calming function overwhelming the insight function.

To restore and develop their complementarity, an "external" intervention (which, however, is a direct response to subjective processes) is framed. The danger is itself the result of a crucial change in the relationship between "subject" and "object." Candrakīrti writes:

> On [the seventh ground, called] Gone Afar, moment by moment [the bodhisattva] enters into cessation and attains the excellent, sparkling *(legs 'bar ba)* perfection of method. Because this absorption into cessation is an absorption into the excellent culmination *(bhūtakoti, yang dag pa'i mtha')*, it is known as a cessation into thusness *(tathatā, de bzhin nyid)* because all elaborations here are ceased.[82]

Commenting on this point, Tsong-kha-pa quotes from the *Sūtra on the Ten Grounds* the statement that from the seventh ground onward, the bodhisattva enters and arises from absorptions in cessation in a single moment of mind.[83]

The description of this cessation as a lack of elaborations and a cessation into "thusness" seems to indicate that the cessation which the seventh-ground bodhisattva enters into and rises from with such alacrity is the uncommon absorption of cessation mentioned in the sixth ground.[84] Yet Pan-chen observes that the cessation attained through abiding in the wisdom of the sixth ground and the cessation which is entered into in a single moment and departed from in the next are not the same, because the former is a subjective cessation *(yul can 'gog pa'i snyoms 'jug)* and the latter an objective one, correlative with thusness *(yul 'gog pa de bzhin nyid)*.[85] This accords with Tsong-kha-pa's observation that the seventh-ground bodhisattva's meditative equipoise is characterized by a cessation of all elaborations of dualistic appearance into thusness; hence the shifting referent of "cessation" from subject to object mentioned above. Perhaps it is inevitable that, with the line of demarcation between subject and object grown increasingly evanescent, a single term comes to point to both.

Why the increased agility on the seventh ground? What prevents the mind from quickly entering into and arising from this particular state of absorption as quickly when it is first attained? Two crucial elements are lacking. First, on the sixth ground the mind is slower, relatively speaking, because the practitioner still needs to enter direct cognition of emptiness by way of a mental image of such. This idea born of difference is still the revolving door by which one accomplishes the desired *mise-en-scène*. Put more traditionally, mental images are objects of conceptual thought; thus they are incompatible with direct perception, and reliance on them slows one down.[86] Second—and almost certainly related to the increased ability to bypass the conceptual apparatus—one acquires the "skillful means" that are the special perfection of the seventh ground and a subcategory of the surpassing perfection of wisdom. Mere meditative equipoise directly realizing emptiness is insufficient to provide such agile entering and arising as occur on the seventh ground; the skillful means attained here consists of "a wisdom of meditative equipoise induced by the surpassing method and wisdom which are of the entity of the uncommon absorption of cessation."[87] The particular skills of the seventh ground include an unprecedented ability to unite method and wisdom in a variety of ways.[88] One can, for example, combine a nondualistic realization that objects are like illusions with an intention to accomplish an immeasurable variety of activities and objectives.

'Jam-dbyangs-bzhad-pa lists three types of power that give rise to the agility of the seventh ground: (1) the power of possessing ten unions of special method and wisdom; (2) the power of cultivating a hundred thousand meditative stabilizations, and so forth; and (3) the power of a compassion induced by these.[89] Directly or indirectly, all three of these capacities appear to derive from the mind's growing independence from thought processes, and especially from those aspects of it which oppose the union or full complementarity of the conventional *(saṃvṛti, kun rdzob)* components of method and the ultimate *(paramārtha, don dam pa)* components of wisdom.

Both concentration and wisdom are described as contributing to the mind's ability to function in the absence of thought. The conception of true existence, in all its permutations, is represented as the first barrier to such unified cognition. On the seventh ground, the level at which one overcomes all conceptions of true existence, there is an increased facility with compassion and the wisdom of emptiness. One is able to enter and rise from meditative stabilization on either with equal agility. This suggests that the calming of the subject, combined with the seventh ground's final dismantling of conceptions incongruent with the view of emptiness, is at least as significant as having emptiness as the object of mental stabilization. Put another way, the religious significance of emptiness has as much to do with the special characteristics of the mind that observes it as with emptiness' own unique status as an unconditioned phenomenon.

Concluding Remarks

It is clear that the Dge-lugs-pa mārga literature goes to great lengths to explain how the two mental gestures of insight and calming intersect experientially. My contention is that the category of mental quiescence is crucial to their understanding of how the mind, itself a conditioned phenomenon, becomes divested of certain culturally and psychologically determined forms of conditioning. More specifically, the mind arguably becomes free, or at least freer, of the language that conditions conceptual formations, and free or freer from the impact of material culture through cessation of the sense consciousnesses by which material culture is apprehended. That is, both thought and ordinary sensory experience are quiescent in deep concentration. This is how the conditioned mind of insight comes to know the unconditioned emptiness.

The centrality of the categories associated with the calming function is partly a consequence of the Dge-lugs-pa insistence that emptiness is an object of the wisdom consciousness. This premise makes it necessary to explain how a conditioned consciousness can become experientially integrated with an an unconditioned object. Thus Dge-lugs-pa incorporates discussion of calming in its descriptions of this experience as (1) nondualistic, (2) nonconceptual, (3) and analytical. Calming the mind aids withdrawal from dualistic sensory perception; it also frees the mind from the usual impingement by conceptual thought. When such a nondualistic, nonconceptual state becomes the basis for insight, it bequeaths a steadiness of mind whereby analytical understanding can remain even after the conceptual processes of analysis have been left behind.

The significance of concentration as a category of path structure can also be inferred through observing that concentration becomes an issue at points of incremental change in the nonconceptual wisdom—namely, at the first and sixth bodhisattva grounds. The stilling of conceptual movement and of images allows the mind fully to take on the aspect of the unconditioned emptiness, even though, as categories, subject and object remain distinct. By exploring in some detail the role that specific forms of mental quiescence have at the first and sixth bodhisattva grounds, we can conclude that calm abiding and the uncommon absorption of cessation are crucial in explaining how "insight" is assimilated to a nonconceptual mind, and how such a consciousness, though technically "conditioned," is not subject to conditioning in the usual way. "Conditioned" and "unconditioned" are famous as mutually exclusive categories, and often spoken of as if there were no gray area between them; nevertheless, a close examination of the role of mental quiescence indicates that there are indeed "degrees" of conditioning. All mental states are not conditioned in the same way or to the same degree, and thus there is an ameliorating connection between these two oppositionally framed categories. It seems to me that this is a meaningful way to understand how, from the Dge-lugs-pa perspective, a bodhisattva's wisdom of the unconditioned "improves" over the path, even though no further analysis, correction, or conceptual development takes place.

It is also significant that, although posed in oppositional-sounding terms, "conditioned" and "unconditioned" do not, for the Dge-lugs-pas, describe a difference in existential status or ontology. Both the conditioned and unconditioned are dependent-arisings and conventionally existent, characteristics which allow them to participate with each other as objects in general and as objects of meditative processes in particular. In Dge-lugs-pa texts, this participation is often discussed in ontological terms as the union of the two truths—that is, of the unconditioned emptiness and the conditioned objects which it qualifies. In epistemological terms, the case is made that a properly conditioned mind can experience the unconditioned, and that it can do so with such force and immediacy that the effect of ordinary conditioning is negligible.[90]

Rnying-ma's discussion of Rdzogs-chen would fault Dge-lugs-pa for failing to recognize that the unconditioned can in fact characterize the subject itself. Mipham speaks of a primordial wisdom that knows the natural state of things and pervades everywhere. Not being separate from anything, it does not take an object in the Dge-lugs-pas' sense of the term. This primordial wisdom is not impermanent or changeable like ordinary consciousnesses. It is beyond being either conditioned or unconditioned, and therefore Mipham calls it the "Great Unconditioned."[91] Although he agrees with Dge-lugs-pa that consciousness in general is impermanent and conditioned, Mipham holds that "the primordial wisdom in which consciousness and object of consciousness are of one taste . . . is not like this";[92] rather, it "has the nature of the unconditioned and changeless."[93] Mental quiescence is just one of the many splendid qualities spontaneously associated with this primordial wisdom; unlike in the Dge-lugs-pa path described here, there is in Rdzogs-chen no need to speak of or cultivate it separately. Even such a very brief reference to a Rnying-ma perspective indicates how, within the Tibetan Buddhist context, there are dramatic differences regarding how the categories of conditioned and unconditioned are mapped onto a path of religious engagement.

Important as mental calming is for Dge-lugs-pas in resolving what they see as problematic in mārga theory, it is also an important category in relation to how contemporary Western thinkers might approach this presentation. We have noted that both Dge-lugs-pa and Rnying-ma presume that their practices facilitate an experience free from the imprint of ordinary conditioning, whether cultural or psychological. In the Dge-lugs-pa context especially, it seems fair to say that mental calm frees the mind of some layers of conditioning. Neither the usual internal dialogue nor sensory objects—both bearers of particular cultural circumstance—have the usual effect on the mind. Moreover, during cognition of emptiness, their influence does not intervene between the cognizing subject and its object, and the resultant meditative experience does not carry forward the full imprint of its conditioning causes. For these reasons, a bodhisattva's cognition of emptiness, made possible by mental quiescence, can be considered immediate.

If calming frees the mind from moving among different objects, special insight frees it from all experience of differentation. The mind, now capable of staying with only one object, focuses on an object without qualities, a mere negation. Particularity has no part in this direct cognition. Moreover, the impetus for both insight and calming derives from the side of the subject; unlike other "objects," emptiness is not a cause of the mind's perception of it. In this sense the mind is not conditioned by its unconditioned object. Moreover, the subjective conditions of mental clarity, intensity, stillness, and so forth, which make this perception possible, are regarded as attributes of consciousness that, once achieved, are the same for everyone. This leads to an implicit—and, for many of us, problematic—claim that conditioning by the path leads to a universal, transcultural experience.[94] At the same time, and somewhat paradoxically, the final effect of experiencing the unconditioned is not to make one more distant from environmental exigencies, but rather more responsive to them. The particularities that formerly limited one's perspective, or were so reified as to obscure the changing nature of a situation, are now experienced as insubstantial and transient. Constant attention is required.

The experience of emptiness is also presumed to be universal on the grounds that emptiness itself has no particular characteristics but is simply an absence of reified particularity. The mind has a capacity to "take on the aspect of," or mirror, this absence of specific images and thoughts. Whether we look at Rnying-ma descriptions of being "freed into the empty nature of your own mind" or Dge-lugs-pa descriptions of mind and emptiness as like "fresh water poured into fresh water," we find the distinct implication that here is an experience located in but not affected by personal, cultural, or social history.

This may seem like an extreme example of the point, noted in the introduction to this volume, that mārga literature sometimes favors the abstract at the expense of the person. The texts I have discussed here certainly do that. However, it must be remembered that the kind of training these texts describe was carried out in an intensely "personal" setting—typically while living closely with others in a monastery or small village. Even the solitary meditator in his mountain cave is understood to be part of this social context. Moreover, the texts themselves were important not only for their elucidations of the path, but because they provided a forum for intense, extended teacher-student relationships and for much peer interaction in the debating courtyard. In short, the mārga texts are evidence of the intellectual but not the social context for the practices they describe.

The unconditioned or transcultural nature of emptiness is a powerful assumption in the Buddhist context, and especially in its understanding of meditative experience. That such experience is discerned and expressed only through culturally specific language, art, and so forth does not undermine its power as a category of Buddhist thought. Unpalatable as it may be to contemporary sensibilities, the possibility of experiencing the unconditioned remains a crucial and irreducible element of Buddhist soteriology.

Claims of universal relevance characterize most traditional religions and are central to the complex tensions between traditional and modern (or post-modern) perspectives. As products of the contemporary Western world, we cannot understand our relationship to this literature without acknowledging that tension. Oddly enough, it is a tension that roughly parallels the antipathy Tsong-kha-pa observes between conditioned, conceptual analyses of emptiness and the nonconceptual experience of the unconditioned that is its result. In both cases the question is how a perspective grounded in conditionality responds to claims that possibilities exist outside that realm. However, whereas Tsong-kha-pa holds that a conditioned mind can have an unmitigated experience of the unconditioned, and thus is satisfied to resolve the tension epistemologically, contemporary theorists are not.

Virtually no contemporary Western thinker would take seriously, much less agree with, the notion that conditioned persons can have an experience outside of historical, cultural, psycho-social, and other sets of conditionings. Neither Derrida, Foucault, Lacan, nor those following Kant, for example, would postulate or even seek a resolution between their own positions and the Buddhist claim that there are states of mind unaffected either by personal or cultural histories or by epistemic limitations. Here, the conditioning role of social and personal histories is emphasized in ways that are foreign to Buddhism. From the viewpoint of contemporary theories, Buddhist soteriological categories are but one more example of cultural construction, with Tsong-kha-pa's "nondualistic experience of the unconditioned emptiness" or Mipham's "Great Unconditioned" included among culturally mediated constructs.

From the Buddhist perspective, such a viewpoint is limited and reductionistic in its fascination with conditionality. The Buddhist position also emphasizes conditionality but does not subsume all other perspectives to it. For Buddhists, the unconditioned is epistemologically meta to the conditioned—not the other way around.[95] For them, the emphasis that Foucault and Lacan put on cultural and linguistic constructions of experience is like theorizing the existence of dependent-arising without positing the emptiness that is its inseparable counterpart.[96]

Moreover, "unconditioned" does not, in Dge-lugs-pa sūtra systems, refer to a mind, a subject, but to an object that the mind can know. To the extent that imagistic and other interferences are set aside, one has an experience of the unconditioned. Although the unconditioned itself has no causes, the experience of it clearly does: it comes about through intentional behavior encouraged in certain cultural milieux, but from the Dge-lugs-pa perspective, as we have seen, this does not in and of itself make it a cultural construct.

The current scholarly emphasis on understanding all experience and beliefs, especially religious ones, as a product of human culture is in part a response to various kinds of traditionalist positions in the West, especially the Judeo-Christian emphasis on symbols and mores once claimed as universal but now unmasked as culture-bound. In some quarters, claims of universal truth inevitably became associated with imperialistic tendencies. Partly because of this history, it has become meaningful in the contemporary West to think of human behavior as necessarily mediated through culture. Buddhist vocabulary, however, reforms the issue as an examination of how concepts, language, and the process of differentiation itself filter and impinge on direct experience—and the extent to which this filter is removable. Again, the calming function is important in this process, even if we outside the tradition cannot assume that, because thought no longer impinges in the same way, cultural constraints and associated psychological ones are utterly in abeyance.

It is important to note, therefore, that the Buddhist claims discussed here are most appropriately understood as claims about mental process rather than about the nature of truth, even if such claims significantly inform one another. In their traditional context, premises about the universality of these experiences are less signifcant than Buddhist conviction in the salvific efficacy of these states. The issue of universality gains new significance as these ideas come into contact with contemporary Eurocentric sensibilities.[97]

The unification of method and wisdom that the uncommon absorption of cessation makes possible on the sixth bodisattva ground seems to offer a model of the conditioned and unconditioned as intertwined elements of an intersubjective dialogue. Together they form not a dichotomy but an intricate pattern of mental engagement. The Dge-lugs-pa emphasis on the role of calming at the first and sixth bodhisattva grounds suggests that the development of mental quiescence is crucial in reducing culturally specific impressions, making possible an experience that is immediate in being nonconceptual and nondualistic. Rnying-ma criticizes this model, suggesting that qualities such as mental quiescence are intrinsic to the "Great Unconditioned" mind rather than a means to it. For all their diversity, these two sets of Buddhist assumptions agree on the transcultural nature of the experiences they describe. Read closely, I hope they will stimulate reflection on the claims associated with the categories of the conditioned and unconditioned in a cross-cultural context.

Notes

Thanks to Harvey Aronson, Robert Buswell, George Dreyfuss, Bernard Faure, Van Harvey, Rob Gimello, Jeffrey Hopkins, and Lee Yearley for helpful comments at the Conference or at various stages of writing this article.

1. Quoted by Ngag-dbang-bstan-'dzin-rdo-rje in *Klong chen snying gi thig le'i mkha' 'gro bde chen rgyal mo'i sgrub gzhung gi 'grel pa rgyud don snang ba* (New Delhi: Sonam Kazi, Ngagyur Nyingmay Sungrab, 1972), vol. 28, 15.3. According to Ven. Tulku Thondup, this is probably from the *Rdor je gsang ba'i snying po rtsa ba'i rgyud de kho na nyid nges pa* from the *Rnyingma'i rgyud 'bum,* vol. 16, pp. 1–137.

2. For example, Mipham opens his commentary on Candrakīrti's *Entrance to the Middle Way* (*Madhyamakāvatāra, Dbu ma la 'jug pa;* see note 13 below) with an obeisance to "naturalness *(tathathā, de bzhin nyid)* free from the clouds of elaboration in the birthless sky of the dharma sphere *(chos dbyings).*" Mipham, *Commentary on* [*Candrakīrti's*] *"Entrance,"* in *Collected Writings of 'Jam-mgon 'Ju Mi-pham-rgya-mtsho* (Gangtok: Sonam Topgay Kazi, 1979), 1:340.1.

3. Mipham, *The Lion's Roar of the Great Synopsis of Topics on the Tathāgatha Essence (Bde gshegs snying bo'i stong thun chen mo seng ge'i nga ro),* (Delhi: Ngagyur Nyingma Sungrab, 1976), vol. 62, 575.1, "Consciousness does not occur in common locus with the permanent." See also ibid., 574.3–4 for a list of errors which are entailed if the tatāgatha essence, or buddha-nature, is construed as impermanent.

4. Khetsun Sangbo, July 1986, San Jose Ca., in comment on Mipham, *Lion's Roar,* 571.1–4.

5. Mipham, *Lion's Roar,* 568.1–2, and Khetsun Sangpo, oral comment, July 1986. Indeed, Mipham's own commentary on Candrakīrti's *Entrance* opens its sixth-chapter discussion of wisdom by noting that "the explanation of the sixth ground, the Manifest, has three parts, a brief indication of the subject which is the entity of the ground, an extensive explanation of the emptiness which is the object, and a conclusion which expresses the good qualities of the ground" (Mipham, *Commentary on* [*Candrakīrti's*] *"Entrance,"* 1:367.5). These first two "parts" do not occur in commentaries on the *Entrance* by Tsong-kha-pa and other Dge-lugs-pa writers. Mipham's mention of emptiness as an object indicates that in this text he entertains the categories of classic Indian Mādhyamika, whereas *Lion's Roar* expresses a Rdzogs-chen perspective.

6. Mipham, *Lion's Roar,* 568.2.

7. Ibid., 566.2.

8. Ibid., 568.2.

9. Ibid., 564.4; see also ibid., 568.3.

10. Ibid., 569.4.

11. Ibid., 560.2, 571.4ff., 575.5.

12. Ibid., 571.4ff.

13. Candrakīrti, *Madhyamakāvatāra (Entrance to the Middle Way, Dbu ma la 'jug pa), P* 5261, vol. 98; *P* 5262, vol. 98, and Tsong-kha-pa, *Illumination of the Thought, An Extensive Explanation of* [*Candrakīrti's*] *"Entrance to the Middle Way" (Dbu ma la 'jug pa'i rgya cher bshad pa dgongs pa rab gsal), P* 6143, vol. 154.

14. Informal discussion with Ganden Shartse scholars, including Kangyur Rinboche Lobsang Topgyal, Geshe Lobsang Tenzin, Lobsang Yarphel, and Geshe Tshultrim Gyeltsen, January 9, 1989, Houston, Tex. Compare with note 47 below.

15. Thanks to an anonymous reviewer of this volume who made several helpful suggestions on this point.

16. See Anne C. Klein, *Knowledge and Liberation* (Ithaca, N.Y.: Snow Lion, 1986), 183–189, 193–197.

17. The principle of nonlinearity may be helpful here. It means, among other things, that the act of playing the game has a way of changing the rules; there is no linear reproduction of causal characteristics in their "effects." Such occurs because neither the "game" nor the "person" is a closed or limited system, just as s/he is not in the thinking of Lacan, Foucault, and others. That the self is a variable cluster of processes which are themselves parts of larger processes is certainly a dominant contemporary theme; cybernetics and chaos theory in the "hard" sciences, and, in the "human" sciences, the influential writings of Lacan and Foucault can all be considered important variations on this theme. Nevertheless, despite an arguably similar "systems" approach, it is immediately obvious that important claims associated with classical Buddhist path-structure seem inexorably at odds with important principles of contemporary understanding.

18. Quoted by Pan-chen Bsod-nams-grags-pa (1478–1554) in *General Meaning of [Maitreya's] "Ornament for Clear Realization" (Phar phyin spyi don/Shes rab kyi pha rol tu phyin pa'i man ngag gi bstan bcos mngon par rtogs pa'i rgyan 'grel pa dang bcas pa'i rnam bshad snying po rgyan gyi don legs par bshad pa yum don gsal ba'i sgron me),* (Buxaduor: Nang bstan shes rig 'dzin skyong slob gnyer khang, 1963), 155a.1; see also the translation in Lati Rinbochay, Lochö Rinbochay, Leah Zahler, and Jeffrey Hopkins, *Meditative States in Tibetan Buddhism* (London: Wisdom Publications, 1983), 167.

19. Lati Rinbochay et al., *Meditative States,* p. 176; Pan-chen Bsod-nams-grags-pa, *General Meaning,* 156b.3–4. Pan-chen reports these texts' assertion that "the meditative stabilization that is a union of calm abiding and special insight is the attainment of a mind that abides non-conceptually on emptiness after special insight is induced through the power of having done analysis by reasoning from within calm abiding observing an object such as emptiness."

20. Tsong-kha-pa observes that "from the initial attainment of special insight one attains [this] union [of calm abiding with special insight]." Quoted in Pan-chen Bsod-nams-grags-pa, *General Meaning,* 156.b; translated in Lati Rinbochay et al., *Meditative States,* p. 176.

21. Denma Lochö Rinbochay (Geshe of Drebung, Loseling), quoted in Lati Rinbochay et al., *Meditative States,* p. 177.

22. Denma Lochö Rinbochay, quoted in ibid., p. 178.

23. Dkon-mchogs-'jigs-med-dbang-po (a.k.a. 'Jam-dbyangs-bzhad-pa II, 1728–1791), *Grounds and Paths: An Ornament Beautifying the Three-fold Presentation of the Grounds and Paths (Sa lam gyi rnam bzhag bsum smdzes rgyan),* (New Delhi: Ngawang Gelek Demo [reproduced from blocks of Gomang Bkra-shis-'khyil], 1971), 446.3.

24. 'Jam-dbyangs-bzhad-pa (1648–1721), *Srid zhi'i mtha' gnyis 'gog pa'i bden pa mngon rtogs,* in *The Seventy Topics: Sacred Word of the Indomitable Lama Explaining Well the Eight Categories and Seventy Topics [of Maitreya's "Ornament for Clear Realization" (Abhisamayālaṃkāra, Mngon rtogs rgyan)] (Dngos po brgyad don bdun [b]cu'i rnam bzhag legs par bshad pa mi pham bla ma'i zhal lung),* (New Delhi: Ngawang Gelek Demo [from blocks of Gomang Bkra-shis-'khyil], vol. 15 ba of the Collected Works, 1972), 131.5–6. In the same text, 'Jam-dbyangs-bzhad-pa also defines *mthong lam rtse sbyor,* which he explains (164.6) is a synonym for the path of seeing, as "a Mahāyāna manifest realization which is set forth in terms of being an

antidote to the conception of true [existence] that is abandoned by [the path of] seeing" (*mthong spang bden 'dzin gyi gnyen po byed pa'i cha nas bzhag pa'i theg chen gyi bden pa mngon rtogs,* 163.6).

25. This can profitably be related with Gregory Bateson's famous statement that "an idea is a difference which makes a difference" (*Steps to an Ecology of Mind* [New York: Ballantine Books, 1972], 318). Culture, too, is a process of differentiation. The Buddhist categories of complete and partial engagers and their relationship to direct and conceptual perception, respectively, are discussed in Klein, *Knowledge and Liberation,* and by Elizabeth Napper in *Mind in Tibetan Buddhism* (Ithaca, N.Y.: Snow Lion, 1980).

26. Loling Kensur Yeshay Tupden, oral commentary, spring 1980, Mundgod, India. This part of the etymology strictly applies only to the first bodhisattva ground because on the uninterrupted paths of the path of meditation—and hence of the second through tenth bodhisattva grounds—it is possible to have true cessation as an object, and thus the objects of equipoise on those grounds are not necessarily emptinesses. For example, the true cessation of afflictions that occurs on the first ground can be an object of the uninterrupted path of the second ground (Loling Kensur Yeshay Tupden, oral commentary, spring 1980).

This kind of parity, which does not have a parallel in ordinary direct perception, can be read as an attempt to theorize away "distance" between subject and object. It thus addresses one of Mipham's objections to "other viewpoints" such as Dge-lugs-pa—namely, that they understand the wisdom *dharmakāya* as coextensive mainly with objects, not subjects (Mipham, *Lion's Roar,* 567.4–568.3, and oral comment by Khetsun Sangpo, summer 1986, San Jose, Calif.)

27. The twenty-three also include: the five omnipresent factors of feeling, discrimination, intention, mental engagement, and contact; the five determining mental factors of aspiration, belief, mindfulness, stabilization, and wisdom; the eleven virtuous mental factors of faith, shame, embarrassment, nonattachment, nonhatred, nonignorance, effort, pliancy, conscientiousness, equanimity, and nonharmfulness; and the two changeable mental factors of investigation and anlaysis. Presumably, however, investigation and analysis would be absent if, for example, one were at the level of the fourth concentration.

Only those factors of mind that are one entity *(ngo bo gcig)* with the wisdom consciousness are said to cognize emptiness; however, there are qualities—such as the impermanence and emptiness of that consciousness—that, though one entity with it, do not cognize emptiness. Similarly, the compassionate intention of *bodhicitta* is not itself the wisdom realizing emptiness, but is a good quality of that wisdom, in the sense that both it and the perfection of wisdom embellish the same mental continuum (main points from Loling Kensur Yeshay Tupden, oral commentary, spring 1980). In this system, the mental factor of investigation is said to engage its object in a general manner, whereas analysis involves a more detailed investigation. See Lati Rinbochay et al., *Meditative States,* p. 116.

28. Geshe Gedun Lodrö (Geshe of Drebung, Gomang), "Calm Abiding and Special Insight," unpub. ms., p. 342.

29. Pan-chen Sö-nam-drak-pa, *General Meaning,* 162.a6; Lati Rinbochay et al., *Meditative States,* p. 197.

30. Tara Rinboche, oral commentary on 'Jam-dbyangs-bzhad-pa's *Dbu ma chen mo,* April 1988, Charlottesville, Va. At the same time, both Tara Rinboche and (Geshe) George Dreyfuss observe that the texts are not very clear on what the precise difference is here; Tara Rinboche also noted that insofar as neither Prāsaṅgika nor Svātantrika discusses the relationship between the categories of

"special insight" and "analytical meditation," this, too, is difficult to assess. The remainder of this paragraph and the next one are from Loling Kensur Yeshay Tupden in oral commentary on Tsong-kha-pa's *Illumination of the Thought,* summer 1986, Tibetan Buddhist Learning Center, Washington, N.J.

31. Thus a yogic direct cognition of impermanence does not depart from Lacanian, Kantian, or other contemporary epistemologies in the way that claims about direct perception of emptiness do. Other forms of direct perception, however religiously significant they may be, still do not know things just as they are. It remains to be investigated whether the sense in which they superimpose error on reality has much of significance in common with the kind of limits that Kant or Lacan observe in knowledge and language. In any case, for Prāsaṅgika, only the latter is claimed to be free of any area of mistake regarding appearances *(sang ba la 'khrul sa yod ma red).*

32. Thanks to George Dreyfuss on this point.

33. Red-mda'-ba Gzhon-nu-blo-gros, *Explanation of* [*Candrakīrti's*] *"Entrance to the Middle Way," A Lamp Illuminating Reality (Dbu ma la 'jug pa'i rnam bshad de kho na nyid gsal ba'i sgron ma),* (Delhi: Ngawang Topgay, 1974), 77.6–78.1.

34. Ibid., 78.1–2.

35. Michael Sweet, *Śāntideva and the Mādhyamikas: The Prajñāparamitā-Pariccheda of the Bodhicaryāvatāra* (Ann Arbor, Mich.: University Microfilms [University of Wisconsin diss.], 1977), 82.

36. Both the Shes-rig-bar-khang edition (Dharamsala, n.d.) of *Spyod 'jug,* p. 95 and Gyel-tsap's commentary on this, *Explanation of* [*Śāntideva's*] *"Entrance to the Bodhisattva Deeds," A Passageway for Buddha's Offspring (Spyod 'jug rnam bshad rgyal sras 'jug ngogs),* (Sarnath: Pleasure of Elegant Sayings Press, 1973), 228 render this first line as *gang tshe dngos dang dngos med dag;* Gyel-tsap goes on to specify that the lack of conceptual aspect here refers to the absence of any conception of true existence. See also Sweet, *Śāntideva and the Mādhyamikas,* pp. 82ff., 296.

37. See especially Gregory Bateson, *Mind and Nature* (New York: Bantam Books), 97, 100–107, and idem, *Steps,* pp. 272, 317–318, 402–405. One immediately begins to think of connections between Bateson's formulation here and Buddhist uses of *apoha* theory; one important distinction between them, however, is that Bateson applies the rubric of difference to both direct and conceptual processes, whereas the Dge-lugs-pa distinction between these as complete and partial perceivers means that only the partial engagers, i.e., conceptual ones, actually proceed *by way of* difference.

38. Red-mda'-ba (*Explanation,* 79.5–6) observes that there are two types of perfections of wisdom, those with and without (dualistic) appearances *(snang ba dang bcas pa* and *snang ba med pa).* He designates only the latter as "nonconceptual" and calls it a "meditative equipoise that is free from all elaborations."

39. Red-mda'-ba, *Explanation,* 78.1–6.

40. Tsong-kha-pa, *Illumination of the Thought* (Sarnath: Ge-den Chi-lay-kang, 1973), 115.13; see also Candrakīrti, *Autocommentary on "Entrance to the Middle Way" (Madhyamakāvatārabhāṣya, Madhyamakapatharabasuyanama* [sic]; *Dbu ma la 'jug pa'i rang 'grel),* (Sehore, Bhopal M.P.: The Tibetan Publishing House, 1968), 11.13; partial translation by Louis de La Vallée Poussin, *Museon* 8 (1907): 249–317; 11 (1910): 271–358; and 12 (1911): 235–328.

41. Red-mda'-ba, *Explanation,* 79.5–6.

42. Translated by Jeffrey Hopkins in Tsong-ka-pa [sic], Kensur Lekden, and Jeffrey Hopkins, *Compassion in Tibetan Buddhism* (Ithaca, N.Y.: Snow Lion, 1980), 132.

43. It is is interesting that Tsong-kha-pa mentions calm abiding in connec-

tion with this issue. Calm abiding is generally said to be the lowest level of stabilizing meditation with which emptiness can be realized on the seeing path. Calm abiding is easily made commensurate with analysis and insight. However, according to Geshe Gedun Lodrö, a peerless specialist in this topic, most persons attain the path of seeing using the fourth concentration (Geshe Gedun Lodrö, "Calm Abiding," unpub. ms., University of Virginia, Charlottesville, 1978, p. 342) and analysis is regarded as a *fault* in relation to this level of concentration, though not in relation to the first three. Thus it may become problematic to claim that a nondualistic wisdom with the fourth concentration as its basis is yet an analytical consciousness. It would not be problematic if the analysis associated with this concentration were explictly said to be nondualistic. We can infer that this is the case from what we know about the nature of concentration (even at the level of calm abiding, the sense of subject and object is absent), but such is not clearly stated in any text I have seen to date.

44. For an elaboration of this idea, see Bateson, *Mind and Nature,* pp. 100–107, who quotes a "quasi-scientific fable that if you can get a frog to sit quietly in a saucepan of cold water, and if you then raise the temperature of the water very slowly and smoothly so that there is no moment *marked* to be the moment at which the frog should jump, he will never jump. He will get boiled" (ibid., pp. 104–105). Bateson substitutes the concept of differences for Kant's "potential facts" *(Tatsachen).* Just as Kant observes that only a very few "potential facts" contained in an object come to affect the behavior of entities capable of responding to facts, so Bateson observes that only a very few of the infinite *potential* differences associated with an object become *effective* differences—that is, information—in the mental process of any larger entity.

45. Tara Rinboche, oral commentary on 'Jam-dbyangs-bzhad-pa's *Dbu ma chen mo,* April 1988.

46. This observation is inspired by Bateson's category of "collateral" energy, "the energy already available in the respondent, in advance of the impact of events" (*Mind and Nature,* p. 108). For example, in kicking a stone, energy is imparted to the stone and it moves with that energy alone; when I kick a dog, "it responds with energy got from metabolism." I would add that if the dog runs down the street as a result of this encounter and then gets involved with chasing its tail, that chasing (especially as time goes on) has less and less to do with the instigating kick, and more and more to do with the dog's own internal proclivities.

47. The Dge-lugs-pa contemplative and scholar Gen Lam-rim-ba, who made this observation, also noted that the term "unconditioned" *('dus ma byas, saṃskṛta)* applies only to the unchanging mental continuum of a tantric practitioner; the wisdom of the first, or the sixth, bodhisattva ground is *not* called unconditioned. Gen Lam-rim-ba, discussion, March 1988, Stanford, Calif.

48. Denma Lochö Rinbochay, quoted in Lati Rinbochay et al., *Meditative States,* pp. 177–178.

49. Tsong-kha-pa, *Illumination of the Thought,* 115.15–16.

50. Pan-chen Bsod-nams-grags-pa's works still form a major part of the curriculum at Loseling College of Drebung Monastic University. He himself studied at Sera, where Yongs-'dzin-don-yod-dpal-ltan was his teacher, and later became a Khenpo (abbot) of Loseling and Ganden Shardzay. In modern times it would be inconceivable that one man should be abbot at two different colleges, especially ones other than his alma mater (bio-data from Loling Kensur Yeshay Tupden, oral commentary, summer 1986, Washington, N.J.).

51. Red-mda'-ba, *Explanation,* 76.2ff., comments on verse VI.1d.

52. Tsong-kha-pa, *Illumination of the Thought,* 115.13ff. Adapted from an unpublished translation by Jeffrey Hopkins and Anne Klein.

53. Pan-chen Bsod-nams-grags-pa, *General Meaning,* 126.6–127.1.

54. The Bhopal edition of Candrakīrti's *Autocommentary* (61.4) gives *'thob* here, whereas when this text is quoted in Tsong-kha-pa's *Illumination of the Thought,* both the Dharamsala edition (62.14) and the Sarnath edition (114.29) have *thob.* A modern edition of the root text itself, Candrakīrti's *Dbu ma la 'jug pa,* also has *thob* (Sarnath: Legs bshad gter mdzod par khang, 1978, p. 69). I doubt that any difference in tense is to be construed.

55. Candrakīrti, *Autocommentary,* 61.4–8.

56. Tsong-kha-pa, *Illumination of the Thought,* Sarnath ed., 114.14–115.1. Based on an unpublished translation by Hopkins and Klein.

57. Ibid., 115.16. The earliest post-Tsong-kha-pa Dge-lugs-pa commentator on the *Entrance,* Dge'dun grub, later known as the First Dalai Lama (1391–1475), glosses the meditative equipoise of the sixth ground as an uncommon absorption of cessation and then, unlike slightly later commentators such as Pan-chen Bsod-nams-grags-pa and Rje-btsun Chos-kyi-rgyal-mtshan, says no more about it. Dge'dun grub, *Mirror Thoroughly Clarifying the Treatise "Entrance to the Middle Way" (Dbu ma la 'jug pa'i bstan bcos kyi dgongs pa rab tu gsal ba'i me lon),* (n.p., n.d; block print from private collection of L. T. Doboom Tulku), 10b.3–4.

Meditative equipoise itself has historically been associated with analysis. Jang-gya, in the context of discussing the analytical reasoning by which emptiness comes to be understood, quotes Bhāvaviveka:

> With the mind in meditative equipoise
> Wisdom analyzes in this way
> The entities of these phenomena
> That are apprehended conventionally.

(translated in Jeffrey Hopkins, *Emptiness Yoga* [Ithaca, N.Y.: Snow Lion, 1987], 137, 376).

58. Candrakīrti, *Autocommentary,* 61.6–9. Also cited by 'Jam-dbyangs-bzhad-pa, *Great Exposition of the Middle Way (Dbu ma chen mo),* (Buxaduor: Gomang, 1967), trans. Jeffrey Hopkins, unpub. ms., p. 1.

59. Pan-chen Bsod-names-grags-pa, *Response to Queries regarding* [*Candrakīrti's*] *"Entrance to the Middle Way," A Lamp Fully Illuminating the Profound Meaning (Dbu ma la 'jug ba'i brgal lan zab don yang gsal sgron me),* in *The Collected Works (Gsung 'Bum) of Pan-chen Bsod-nams-grags-pa* (Mundgod, Karnataka: Drebung Loseling Library Society, 1985; rpt., vol. 7 [vol. 27 in Pan-chen Bsod-nams-grags-pa Literature Series]), 54a.2–4. *Rang thob byed kyi 'das lam dang srid rtse'i sems la brten nas thob cing srid rtse la 'dod chags dang bral bas rab tu phye ba'i rigs su gnas pa'i mthar gnas snyoms 'jug dgu'i nang tshan du gyur pa'i ldan min 'du byed de thun mong ba'i 'gog snyoms kyi mtshan nyid.*

60. Rje-btsun Chos-kyi-rgyal-mtshan, *Clarifying the Difficult Points of* [*Tsong-kha-pa's*] *"Illumination of the Thought" (Dgongs ba rab gsal dka' gnad gsal bar byed pa),* 89a.6–89b.1. *Rang 'thob byed kyi thabs su gyur pa'i 'jig rten las b'as pa'i lam dang srid rtse'i dngos gzhi'i snyoms 'jug la brten nas thob cing srid rtse la 'dod chags dang bral ba'i rigs su gnas pas rab tu phye ba'i stong nyid mngon sum du rtogs pa'i ye shes.*

61. Pan-chen Bsod-nams-grags-pa, *Response,* 54a.5.

62. Ibid., 52a.5ff. Pan-chen Bsod-nams-grags-pa also makes this point in his *General Meaning,* 127.4, but there adds that it is a matter "to be analyzed."

63. See, for example, 'Jam-dbyangs-bzhad-pa, *Great Exposition,* 102b.4, 104a.2; Candrakīrti, *Autocommentary,* 261.

64. 'Jam-dbyangs-bzhad-pa, *Great Exposition,* 104a.2.

65. Rje-btsun Chos-kyi-rgyal-mtshan, *Clarifying the Difficult Points,* 90b.2–3. *Dgag gzhi yid kyi rnam shes phra mo'i steng du dgag bya tshogs drug rags pa 'khor bcas bkag pa'i snyoms 'jug de theg pa thun mong ba'i mdo nas 'gog snyoms su bshad pas de la thun mong ba'i 'gog snyoms zhes gsungs pa yin gyi de 'gog snyoms su khas mi len pa'i phyir dper na Tik-chen las gang zag rang sgya thub pa'i rzas yod du 'dzin pa'i blo la thun mong ba'i 'jig lta shes gzungs kyang de 'jig lta yin par rang lugs la mi bzhed pa bzhin no.*

66. Blo-bzang-rta-mgrin (a.k.a. Blo-bzang-rta-dbyangs, 1867–1937), *Annotations on [Pan-chen Bsod-nams-grags-pa's] "General Meaning of Mādhyamika," A Lamp Illuminating the Profound Meaning (Dbu ma'i spyi don gyi mchan 'grel),* (New Delhi: Tibet House, 1974), 161.3–5.

67. 'Jam-dbyangs-bzhad-pa, *Great Exposition,* 104a.2ff. Mipham also, in his *Commentary to [Candrakīrti's] "Entrance,"* glosses Candrakīrti's term "cessation" as a "correct position free from elaborations" and, like the Dge-lugs-pa texts we have noted, distinguishes this from Hearer and Solitary Realizer assertions about cessation (1:366.3).

68. Ven. Tenzin Gyatso, the Fourteenth Dalai Lama, October 10, 1989, San Jose, Calif.

69. Pan-chen Bsod-nams-grags-pa, *Response,* 53.b6–54a.1. *Sher phyin gyi nyams len ches lhag pas zin pa'i chos nyid la mngon sum du mnyam par gzhag pa'i mnyam gzhag ye shes de.*

70. Ibid., 54a.1–2.

71. Ibid., 54a.2–3.

72. Tsong-kha-pa, *Illumination of the Thought,* 114.20–115-1; Candrakīrti, *Autocommentary,* 61.9–10. Only Tsong-kha-pa uses the epithet "fully developed" *(phul tu byung ba)* to describe the meditative equipoise or perfection of wisdom; this term appears to be a gloss on Candrakīrti's term "surpassing" *(lhag pa),* which Tsong-kha-pa also incorporates.

73. Rje-btsun Chos-kyi-rgyal-mtshan, *Clarifying the Difficult Points,* 89a.4.

74. Tsong-kha-pa, *Illumination of the Thought,* 114.20.

75. Loling Kensur Yeshay Tupden, oral commentary on Tsong-kha-pa's *Illumination of the Thought,* 115.12ff, spring 1980, Mundgod, India.

76. See, for example, Pan-chen Bsod-nams-grags-pa, *Response,* 51a.3ff.; "whatever is an absorption of cessation is not necessarily a nonassociated compositional factor" (ibid., 52b.1; 53a.4–54a.6); see also idem, *General Meaning,* 127.6ff., where he distinguishes between subject *(yul can 'gog snyoms)* and object *(yul 'gog snyoms)* cessations; and Rje-btsun Chos-kyi-rgyal-mtshan, *Clarifying the Difficult Points,* 89a.3ff.

77. Asaṅga's *Compendium of Knowledge (Abhidharmasamuccaya, Mngon pa kun btus)* lists eight types of unconditioned phenomena *(bdus ma byas brgyad).* These are the three suchnesses (i.e., the actuality or *chos nyid* of phenomena distinguished as virtuous, nonvirtuous, and neutral); the two occasions when the mind is ceased, namely, during the lack of discrimination *('du shes med)* and the period of the cessation of meditative equipoise *('gog snyoms 'jug gi dus);* as well as the three unconditioned phenomena mentioned in the *Abhidharmakośa:* analytical cessation *(pratisaṃkhyanirodha, so sor brtags 'gog),* nonanalytical cessation, and space. (Lists cited in *The Great Tibetan-Chinese Dictionary* [*Bod rgya tshig mdzod chen mo*], Chengdu: Mi rigs dpe sgrun khang, 1984, pp. 1287 and 1409.)

The middle category is, of course, problematic, insofar as consciousnesses generally are included among unconditioned phenomena. The Dge-lugs-pa

Prāsaṅgika writers would dispute this classification, but it accords with other views known to them. In this regard, see Paul Griffiths, *On Being Mindless: Buddhist Meditation and the Mind-Body Problem* (La Salle, Ill.: Open Court, 1986), p. xivff., and his treatment there of absorption of cessation in the Theravāda, Vaibhāṣika, and Yogācāra traditions. Griffiths frames a tension between "knowing" and "unconsciousness," a fruitful perspective on his material, but one which does not map as well onto Dge-lugs-pa soteriology as it does onto the Theravāda and other schools he considers.

78. Pan-chen Bsod-nams-grags-pa, *Response,* 51b.2; see also Griffiths, *On Being Mindless,* p. 58ff.

79. However, the absorption of cessation attained at levels lower than the sixth ground (but exclusive of the meditative equipoise associated with the first five grounds) by never-returners, arhats, or on the seeing path or peak path of preparation are said in the lower systems to be the meditative absorption at the end of the series of concentrations and absorptions, and are nonassociated compositional factors (Rje-btsun Chos-kyi-rgyal-mtshan, *Clarifying the Difficult Points,* 89a.3–5). See also Pan-chen Bsod-nams-grags-pa, *General Meaning,* 126.4–5.

80. An interesting historical question is why the Dge-lugs-pas chose to use the traditional term "cessation" in association with this particular state, since the very use of the term necessitates considerable clarification to distinguish it from other types of cessation, especially from the cessation that exists at the end of the series of concentrations and absorptions *(Navānupūrvavihārasamāpatti, mthar gyis gnas pa'i snyoms par 'jug pa dgu).* Partly, no doubt, it was used out of obligation to Candrakīrti, but this does not really explain the expansion of meaning. One clue may lie with the significance this category has for postulating unmediated, nondualistic, analytical cognition.

81. 'Jam-dbyangs-bzhad-pa, *Great Exposition,* 97b.1–3. Similarly, Nāgārjuna's *Ratnāvalī,* quoted by 'Jam-dbyangs-bzhad-pa, describes the seventh as a time when "Moment by moment one can enter/The Equipoise of cessation," and the eighth as "the Immovable, the youthful stage/Through nonconceptuality one is immovable" (453–455, translated by Jeffrey Hopkins and Lati Rinbochay in *The Precious Garland and Song of the Four Mindfulnesses* [New York: Harper & Row, 1975], 86).

82. Candrakīrti, *Autocommentary,* 261.1–5.

83. Tsong-kha-pa, *Illumination of the Thought,* 442.4–13.

84. The oral commentary of Loling Kensur Yeshey Tupden also supports this interpretation, summer 1986.

85. Pan-chen Bsod-nams-grags-pa, *General Meaning,* 127.5–6. See also idem, *Response,* 51a.3–5.

86. 'Jam-dbyangs-bzhad-pa, *Great Exposition,* 101b1ff.

87. Blo-bzang-rta-dbyangs, *Annotations on "General Meaning,"* 96.1–2.

88. The ten special unions of method and wisdom listed by 'Jam-dbyangs-bzhad-pa (*Great Exposition,* 100b.5ff.) are:

> (1) much meditation on the three doors of liberation, and accumulating great collections of merit; (2) meditation on selflessness, and achieving the four immeasurables, (3) achieving the six perfections, and having no adherence to them as tru[ly existent]; (4) a separation from the three realms, and achieving a continuum of that [birth in the three realms, where helpful]; (5) pacifying [one's own] afflictions, and pacifying the afflictions of all sentient beings; (6) a nondualistic consciousness [of

objects] as like illusions and so forth, and an intention for an immeasurable variety of activities and objectives; (7) meditation on a skylike pure land, and achieving the ornaments of a [pure] land; (8) meditation on the abiding state *(gnas lugs)* [i.e., emptiness] of a Conqueror's form, and achieving the signs and marks of such a body; (9) knowledge of the exalted speech of a Conqueror as naturally pacified, and achieving the sixty branches [of a buddha's] speech; (10) entering into an understanding of the sameness of the three times for a Conqueror, and entering into an understanding [of the times] as different nature [of the three times] in sentient beings' thoughts.

89. Ibid., 100a.2–4.

90. This is true even when concentration itself reveals former "conditions." It is well known that concentration, as Buddhists typically understand it, does not simply pacify concepts; at certain junctures it causes the mind to teem with memories, feelings, and visions. The Buddha's recollection of his past lives while entering the concentrations that preceded his enlightenment is perhaps the most famous example of this. Still, such memories have no power to distract, and in that sense one is unconditioned by them.

91. Mipham, *Lion's Roar,* 575.5.

92. Ibid., 575.2.

93. Ibid., 576.2.

94. Also tending toward an assessment of this experience as universal is the relationship between calming and physical sensations. Even the most neophyte meditator can attest that calming the mind a bit changes the breath. With further development, other physical sensations may follow. Tibetan and other descriptions of calming and concentration point out the physical experiences associated with various levels of quiescence. Just prior to achieving calm abiding, for example, the "head tingles" and the body feels "light, like cotton" [Lati Rinbochay et al., *Meditative States,* p. 73]. Such experiences are arguably relatively free of cultural imprinting, partly because they are not significant in most cultural contexts. The same cannot be said for expressions of this experience, whether they be actions subsequent to meditation, textual descriptions such as the above, or artistic representations associated with a particular tradition. In the words of Jorge Luis Borges, "Ecstasy does not repeat its symbols."

95. Thanks to Harvey Aronson on this point.

96. Conversation with Elizabeth Napper, February 1990, Houston, Tex.

97. One might ask how claims of a universally applicable episteme or mental dynamic differ in implication from claims for, say, a universal God. Are they equally triumphalist, for example, or does the private sphere of the former make it intrinsically less threatening to those on its margins? All universalistic claims may not be equally dangerous.

The Relation between Chinese Buddhist History and Soteriology

YOSHIZU YOSHIHIDE

TRANSLATED AND EDITED BY PAUL GRONER

Introduction

My recent research has focused on the development of Fa-tsang's (643–712) doctrinal thought, especially his view of soteriology and its relation to one of the key doctrinal categories he posited, the Distinct Teaching of the One-vehicle. Fa-tsang's views have been compared with those of his teacher Chih-yen (602–668) and the Korean monk Ŭisang (625–702), who also studied under Chih-yen. Here I would like to discuss a different theme, namely, my view of the overall development of Chinese Buddhism, although I will return to Hua-yen and Fa-tsang later in this chapter. I have chosen this topic because from the time of Gautama Buddha's enlightenment until the present day, any group that called itself Buddhist has focused its soteriology on explaining the realization of buddhahood. Their explanations, however, have varied in form, content, and metaphors used.

For example, in India, the Abhidharma tradition and early Perfection of Wisdom literature clearly exhibit different soteriological stances. Abhidharma thought stressed the four noble truths; of the four, the path *(mārga-satya)* was especially important because of its soteriological significance. The first two truths, suffering and the cause of suffering, concern conditioned *(saṃskṛta)* and tainted *(āsrava)* existence, but the third noble truth, nirvāṇa, concerns the unconditioned *(asaṃskṛta)* and untainted *(anāsrava)*. Thus the world we live in and the ideal were separated. The fourth truth, which is both conditioned and untainted, serves as a bridge between the two by specifying religious practices. The eightfold noble path was generally considered to be the content of the fourth truth, but it was often interpreted so that all the various practices found in the threefold studies (morality, meditation, wisdom) could be included.

Because the path (mārga) specified in the fourth truth served as the basis for Abhidarma soteriology, this form of Buddhism may be called "mārga-Buddhism." Many people embraced it; its vitality is amply demonstrated by the survival of Theravāda Buddhism in Sri Lanka and Southeast Asia. However, mārga-Buddhism was not without problems. Although Śākyamuni Buddha had advised people to depend on both the Dharma and themselves as a lamp or guide, people were willing to sacrifice themselves in order to protect the Dharma. Thus while their actions could serve as examples of using the Dharma as a lamp, they did not remember the Buddha's admonition also to rely on themselves. Perhaps the Buddha's emphasis on no-self contributed to this situation. Many practitioners did not stop with simply eliminating their selves, but also refused to pay much attention to society, perhaps believing that they had done enough by receiving alms from lay believers.

Early Mahāyāna, especially Perfection of Wisdom, arose partly as the result of criticisms of mārga-Buddhism.[1] Although the earliest occurrence of the term "Mahāyāna" (great vehicle) in extant texts is found in the *Aṣṭasāhasrikāprajñāpāramitāsūtra* (Perfection of Wisdom in 8,000 Lines), the Mahāyāna movement started even earlier. Because so much of early Perfection of Wisdom thought was expressed in terms of "vehicles" *(yāna),* early Mahāyāna could also be called a "vehicle movement." For example, when Mahāyānists (those of the great vehicle) called the Abhidarma tradition "Hīnayāna" (small or inferior vehicle), they were using the term to criticize their opponents and exalt themselves.

The great vehicle was defined by using the teaching of nonsubstantiality or emptiness to criticize and evaluate various concepts. Thus Perfection of Wisdom sūtras directed bodhisattvas to practice the six perfections and advance through the ten grounds one by one, starting from the three realms and progressing to omniscience. Yet at the same time, all these concepts were empty. The bodhisattva who practiced even as he realized the emptiness of dharmas exemplified the revival of relying on oneself as a guide, a teaching that had been lost in the minutiae of Abhidarma. By basing his practice on the emptiness of dharmas, the bodhisattva obtained a freedom that allowed him to carry his teachings anywhere. That freedom, the essence of the *yāna* movement, was revolutionary when contrasted to the standardized and fixed elements of the Abhidarma systems. Although the use of such terms as "mārga" and *"yāna"* to characterize these trends in Buddhist soteriology is clearly a broad overgeneralization, their usefulness should become evident through the following survey of Chinese Buddhist history and soteriology.

In most textbooks on Chinese Buddhism, Ch'an, Pure Land, T'ien-t'ai, and Hua-yen are singled out as representative traditions of Chinese Buddhism. Ch'an and Pure Land are said to emphasize practice while T'ien-t'ai and Hua-yen stress theory. But this type of generalization is so broad that it tells us little or nothing. When T'ien-t'ai and Hua-yen are compared, T'ien-t'ai is said to have included practice while Hua-yen did not. Although this may seem reasonable at first, nothing is stated about whose version of T'ien-t'ai included practices and whose version of Hua-yen did not.

Before such broad generalizations are made, we must clarify the positions held by the various figures in a lineage. For example, in the Hua-yen lineage, enough common elements can be found among the Tu Shun (557–640), Chih-yen, Fa-tsang, Hui-yüan (n.d.), and Ch'eng-kuan (738–839) to justify calling it a lineage. However, if the individual figures are studied, major doctrinal differences clearly exist between teachers and their students. The researcher soon learns that the argument that Hua-yen had no tradition of practice is clearly unjustified. Some Hua-yen masters emphasized practice and others did not.

Rather than relying on such generalizations, we should grasp the general "movement" or "course" *(nagare)* of Chinese Buddhist history, the broad outline of how it develops over time. Although I already have written about the importance of understanding the "movements" of Buddhist history, I develop this topic in the next section.[2] Chinese Buddhist history can be divided into three major movements or ways of understanding Buddhism: teachings *(chiao),* personal standpoint (Ch. *tsung,* J. *jibun no tachiba*), and teachings and personal standpoints conjoined *(tsung-chiao).*

The historical period from the introduction of Buddhism to China until the early T'ang can be characterized as emphasizing *chiao.* Monks devoted themselves to defending Buddhism against Confucian criticisms, arguing that their tradition was a *chiao,* the "teaching of the Buddha," and that it was comparable to Confucianism, "the teaching of the scholars" *(ju-chiao).* Eventually, the Buddhist position was officially recognized. The lineages that appeared from the Northern and Southern dynasties through the early T'ang—Pure Land, San-lun, the Sect of the Three Stages, T'ien-t'ai, the Lü (Vinaya) school, Hua-yen, and Hsüan-tsang's Yogācāra (Fa-hsiang) tradition—all shared an interest in systematic "teachings."

The Ch'an tradition criticized the emphasis these traditions placed on the systematic exposition of doctrine by proclaiming that Ch'an was "a special transmission outside of the teachings *(chiao)* that did not rely on words."[3] Ch'an monks thus criticized the overemphasis on words that they perceived in establishment Buddhism. Later, Tsung-mi (780–841) would conjoin teachings, especially the Hua-yen tradition, with the personal emphasis *(tsung)* of Ch'an. In doing so, he established his own tradition of Hua-yen Ch'an and opened the way for those who argued that the three teachings (Confucianism, Taoism, and Buddhism) had the same purport.

Before T'ien-t'ai, Hua-yen, Ch'an, and Pure Land are compared, and before the individual representatives of a tradition such as Hua-yen are contrasted, the doctrinal and soteriological stances of the three major movements mentioned above must be explained. In doing so, the importance of this approach will become more evident. For example, Ch'an and Pure Land, the two traditions usually grouped together as "practical," can be differentiated because Ch'an emphasized personal standpoints *(tsung)* whereas the Pure Land tradition interpreted Buddhism as a teaching *(chiao)*. Hua-yen and T'ien-t'ai, often contrasted according to whether or not they have a practical aspect, can both be considered teachings. After the major movements of Chinese Buddhism are understood, the student can better comprehend the relationships and comparisons of the traditions of Chinese Buddhism. If comparisons are attempted ignoring the characteristics of these three movements, then Chinese Buddhism (which has a weak tradition of sectarianism) may well be interpreted in the light of the sectarian characteristics of Japanese Buddhist tradition.

In considering the development of Buddhism in China, Korea, and Japan, we must remember that Buddhism always began as an imported tradition. In doing so, two paradoxical problems emerge. First, Indian and Central Asian forms of Buddhism were transmitted to China. Later, distinctive Chinese forms of Buddhism were promulgated in Korea. Finally, Buddhist traditions characteristic of China and Korea were brought to Japan. In analyzing the spread of Buddhism, students are prone to think of the dissemination of a pure form of Buddhism, but this has never been the case. An understanding of the broad development of Buddhism helps to clarify this problem.

The second problem concerns the manner of transmission of Buddhism. Frequently, Buddhism was promulgated in a fortuitous, almost random manner, rather than as part of a systematic effort to spread the tradition. For example, T'ien-t'ai was established before Hua-yen in China; Hua-yen was thus influenced by T'ien-t'ai. At about the time Hua-yen was established, Ch'an was emerging as an important tradition in China. But when these traditions were transmitted to Japan, Hua-yen was brought over first. T'ien-t'ai was transmitted a number of decades later, and Ch'an was not established until several centuries later, during the time of Eisai (1141–1215). In India, Mahāyāna Buddhism arose approximately five hundred years after the death of the Buddha. It immediately had to compete with the established Abhidarma tradition. Thus in India the chronological relation of the appearance of Abhidarma and Mahāyāna was clear, but in China the two traditions were transmitted in an almost random manner, without any regard to the way they had arisen in India. When Buddhism, an exotic foreign tradition, was introduced in China, even as it maintained much of its original character, it was adopted with hiatuses because of the circumstances of its transmission. The story of Chinese Buddhism is replete with both important continuities and discontinuities.

In the remaining sections of this chapter, the transmission of Indian Buddhism to China is examined first. As Indian Buddhism was being transmitted to China, major differences with Indian Buddhism became evident. These differences contributed to the formation of distinctive forms of Chinese Buddhism that can be characterized as the three major movements mentioned above. I conclude with a consideration of the transmission of Chinese and Korean Buddhism to Japan and the emergence of unique forms of Japanese Buddhism.

The Course of Chinese Buddhism and Its Soteriology

The Establishment of Buddhism as a Teaching: Kumārajīva and Hui-yüan of Mt. Lu

Chinese Buddhism was affected by both the mārga and *yāna* movements of Indian Buddhism. Although these movements developed in a chronological sequence in India, they were introduced to China at virtually the same time.[4] During the reign of King Huan (146–167) of the Later Han, An Shih-kao (n.d.) translated Abhidarma texts in China. A few years later, during the reign of Emperor Ling (167–189), Chih Lou-chia-ch'an (Lokakṣema?) translated Mahāyāna works such as the Perfection of Wisdom sūtras. Thus An Shih-kao introduced mārga-Buddhism at about the same time that Chih Lou-chia-ch'an was translating texts presenting yāna-Buddhism.

Even though the texts they translated were from opposing traditions, Chinese Buddhists respected both movements as the preaching of the Buddha. For example, Tao-an (312–385) studied Perfection of Wisdom texts but was also interested in An Shih-kao's translations of Abhidarma works. His student Hui-yüan (338–416) adopted the same attitude; until he corresponded with Kumārajīva (344–413 or 350–409) late in his life, Hui-yüan had not decided whether Hīnayāna or Mahāyāna was superior.

Kumārajīva's arrival in China had a major effect on the development of Chinese Buddhism.[5] As a youth, Kumārajīva had gone to Kashmir to study Sarvāstivādin doctrine, but on his way home had spent time in Kashgar, where he was converted to Mahāyāna by Sūryasoma. From that time on, he advocated Mādhyamika as espoused by Nāgārjuna and Āryadeva. As soon as he arrived in Ch'ang-an, he began translating Mahāyāna works such as the Perfection of Wisdom sūtras and *Lotus Sūtra.* He also translated Mādhyamika texts by Nāgārjuna and Āryadeva, including the *Madhyamakakārikā* (Verses on the Middle Way), *Ta-chih-tu lun* (*Mahāprajñāpāramitāśāstra;* Commentary on the Greater Perfection of Wisdom Sūtra), and *Śatakaśāstra* (Treatise in One Hundred Verses). Hui-yüan soon began to write letters to Kumārajīva asking about a variety of issues, including discrepancies between the Hīnayāna and Mahāyāna positions. Like his teacher, Hui-yüan regarded both Hīnayāna and Mahāyāna as the word of the Buddha; but he also recognized that the two traditions contradicted each other on a number of points. Kumārajīva carefully answered each of Hui-yüan's questions, repeatedly pointing out that Hīnayāna and Mahāyāna were fundamentally different. He explained that, as their names implied, Mahāyāna (great vehicle) was superior to Hīnayāna (inferior vehicle). Their correspondence was eventually collected into a text entitled the *Ta-sheng ta-i chang* (Essay on the Great Meaning of Mahāyāna).[6]

Kumārajīva's translations and his correspondence with Hui-yüan convinced Chinese monks of the superiority of Mahāyāna. However, the contents of such texts as the *Ta-chih-tu lun* and Kumārajīva's letters strengthened the conviction of the Chinese that both Hīnayāna and Mahāyāna were the word of the Buddha.[7]

Tao-sheng and Hui-kuan

Two thousand monks are said to have come to Ch'ang-an to study under Kumārajīva. Because they adopted Kumārajīva's doctrinal position, Mahāyāna became the major Buddhist tradition in China. However, Mahāyāna texts contained many contradictions and discrepancies. To explain how the Buddha could have preached all these texts without contradiction, Chinese monks developed their own systems of classification of doctrine *(chiao-p'an).* Their early classifications are known through the presentation and criticism of "the three systems of the South and the seven of the North" made by the de facto founder of the T'ien-t'ai school, Chih-i (538–597).[8] The systems of categorization proposed by Tao-sheng (355–434) and Hui-kuan (n.d.) are discussed below.

Tao-sheng is famous for advancing a theory of sudden enlightenment. His classification of doctrines is presented at the beginning of the *Fa-hua i su* (Commentary on the Meaning of the Lotus Sūtra) as "the four turnings of the wheel of dharma":[9]

1. The dharma wheel of goodness and purity
2. The dharma wheel of expedient means
3. The dharma wheel of truth
4. The dharma wheel without residue

These probably corresponded to (1) teachings that enable a person to be reborn as a human being or a god and Hīnayāna, (2) the three vehicles, (3) the One-vehicle of the *Lotus Sūtra,* and (4) the *Nirvāṇa Sūtra.*

Tao-sheng's views were criticized by an exponent of gradual enlightenment, Hui-kuan. His classification system, known as "the two teachings and five periods," is presented below:[10]

1. Sudden teaching *(Avataṃsakasūtra)*
2. Gradual teachings
   a. The distinct teaching of the three vehicles *(Prajñāpāramitāsūtra)*
   b. The pervasive teaching of the three vehicles *(Vimalakīrtinirdeśa* and *Brahmaviśeṣacinīparipṛcchā)*
   c. The restraining and praising teaching (Perfection of Wisdom)
   d. The identical-goal teaching *(Lotus Sūtra)*
   e. The teaching of eternal abiding *(Nirvāṇa Sūtra)*

In the classification systems of both Tao-sheng and Hui-kuan, the dissimilar teachings of Hīnayāna and Mahāyāna have been arranged so that they fit within Śākyamuni's biography without any apparent contradiction.

The first major purpose of such systems was to determine which of the many Buddhist texts was the ultimate teaching of the Buddha. Kumārajīva had convincingly argued that Mahāyāna was superior to Hīnayāna; but when additional Mahāyāna texts were translated after his death, Chinese monks argued about which Mahāyāna teachings should be considered the Buddha's ultimate teaching.

The second major purpose of these classification systems was to respond to criticisms of Buddhism by outsiders, especially by Confucians and Taoists. These criticisms attacked Buddhism as a foreign religion from a variety of positions. For example, the Southern Ch'i Taoist Ku Huan (420–483) wrote a text entitled *I-hsia lun* (Treatise on the Barbarians and Chinese). In it, he argued that although Buddhism might be of value to barbarians, it certainly would not benefit the Chinese. Moreover, when Buddhists were ordained, they rejected filial piety because they chose to be celibate and did not have children. Their practice of honoring only the Buddha and refusing to pay obeisance to the emperor violated Confucian dictums on loyalty. Their doctrines of no-self and emptiness led to the teaching that the soul perished, a position that contradicted their views on karma. Mahāyāna Buddhist texts were filled with nonsensical talk that should not be trusted. Such attacks on Buddhism were a concerted effort to discredit the Indian tradition from a broad array of perspectives. These criticisms focused on whether Buddhism was to be considered a "teaching."

The term "teaching" *(chiao)* occupied a special position within Confucian ethics. According to one view, a teaching had to have the following three characteristics.[11] First, the founder of a teaching had to be an exceptional human being, a sage or superior man (such as Confucius). Second, a teaching's contents had to be worthy of belief and trust, of being included in a "classic" *(ching).* Third, a teaching had to benefit society in important ways. This last point was often used against Buddhists in China, most recently during the Cultural Revolution. Buddhist monks were said to be unproductive members of society; they did not work, pay taxes, or serve in the military. Moreover, the upkeep of their temples consumed large amounts of resources.

From the Northern and Southern dynasties through the early T'ang period, Chinese monks repeatedly argued that their founder was worthy of being called a sage, that the contents of Buddhism were correct, and that it benefited society. Their claims are found in commentarial and apologetic literature as well as in records of face-to-face debates. Classification of doctrines must also be considered in terms of the Buddha's biography. If all the various sūtras were the Buddha's words, then despite their apparent contradictions, monks had to claim that all the Buddha's teachings could be arranged within a biographical framework so that any discrepancies were resolved. If the Buddha's teachings were not consistent, then he could not be viewed as a sage. Far from being seen as classics *(ching),* Buddhist scriptures would then be exposed as containing falsehoods, and Buddhism would be revealed as undeserving of the trust given to a "teaching" that could benefit society. Thus classifications of doctrine should not be seen only as the product of debates within Buddhism; they also were directed toward Confucian and Taoist critics of Buddhism.

The Significance of Criticisms of Classifications of Doctrine

Criticisms of these early classification systems began to appear in Buddhist writings during the Sui and early T'ang periods. Examples of these critiques can be found in Ching-ying ssu Hui-yüan's (523–592) *Ta-sheng i-chang* (Essays on Mahāyāna Doctrines), Chih-i's *Miao-fa lien-hua ching hsüan-i* (Profound Meaning of the Lotus Sūtra), and Chi-tsang's (549–623) *Fa-hua hsüan-lun* (Profound Discussion of the Lotus Sūtra) and *San-lun hsüan-i* (Profound Meaning of the Three Treatises). Slightly later examples are Hsüan-tsang's disciple Chi's (632–682) *Ta-sheng fa-yüan i-lin chang* (Essays on the Mahāyāna Garden of Dharmas and Grove of Doctrines), Wŏnch'ŭk's (613–696) *Chieh-shen-mi ching su* (Commentary on the Saṃdhinirmocanasūtra), Fa-tsang's *Hua-yen wu-chiao chang* (Essays on the Five Teachings According to the Hua-yen Tradition) and *Hua-yen-ching t'an-hsüan chi* (Record of Investigations into the Mysteries of the Avataṃsakasūtra), Fa-tsang's disciple Hui-yüan's (n.d.) *Hua-yen-ching k'an-ting chi* (Record of Corrections of [Interpretations of] the Avataṃsaka), and Ch'eng-kuan's *Hua-yen-ching su* (Commentary on the Avataṃsaka).[12]

The purpose of these criticisms of classification schemes was not to deny the validity of such systems but to make them more inclusive and convincing, to strengthen the conceptual basis of Buddhism as a "teaching." As the systems suggested by Tao-sheng and Hui-kuan reveal, texts with a wide variety of teachings were arranged to demonstrate how the Buddha had appealed to beings with diverse capacities. The Buddha's teachings were arranged so that they seemed to fit into his lifetime without any contradictions. However, when these classification systems were examined carefully many problems arose, seriously reducing their value for Buddhists. As a result, monks felt compelled to criticize the old classification systems and develop new, more convincing ones.

The self-confidence of the monks who devised these new systems is amply displayed in Chih-i's discussion of the canonical sources for his classification system of the four types of teaching. In the *Ta-pen ssu-chiao i* (Doctrines of the Four Teachings), after he explained the Hīnayāna, Pervasive, Distinct, and Perfect teachings, Chih-i discussed the canonical sources for his system in the following question and answer.

> Question: If clear passages from sūtras and śāstras cannot be found supporting the classification into four teachings, how can we accept such a system?
>
> Answer: Were the lectures of the masters of the past all based on passages from the sūtras and śāstras? K'ai-shan [Chih-tsang, 458–522] and Kuang-tse [Fa-yün, 467–529] used a system of five periods to clarify the teachings. Chuang-yen [Seng-min] classified teachings according to four periods. [Among the current classification systems are] the Ti-lun [tradition's] use of four, five, or six tenets. [Other examples are from the San-lun tradition, such as] She-shan's [Seng-ch'üan, n.d.] classification [of the Buddha's teachings] according to whether they are simple or multiple and middle or provisional. [His disciple] Hsing-huang [Fa-lang, 507–581] categorizes [the Buddha's teachings] according to four aspects of provisional [existence]. None of these is based on clearly stated scriptural passages; all of them were established in accordance with the feelings [and opinions of the author] in order to help and support the Buddha in teaching and converting [sentient beings]. Any who had karmic affinity with a teaching were to practice, believe, and propagate it.[13]

In this passage, Chih-i rhetorically asked whether clear scriptural support was required for people to accept his classification system. He replied by asking whether the major teachers of the past had scriptural authority to support their systems, and noted that they did not. Instead, they taught in accordance with people's thoughts and feelings in order to benefit Buddhism. But Chih-i's attitude differed from that of earlier scholars, who had supplied as much scriptural support as possible to justify their classification systems so that they could withstand criticisms. Chih-i demonstrated his self-confidence by announcing that aiding the Buddha's transforming work was more important than carefully eliminating any contradictions in his system and amassing scriptural passages to support his claims.

Behind this shift in attitude lay the persecution of Buddhism under Emperor Wu (r. 560–578) of the Northern Chou. After witnessing debates between Confucians, Taoists, and Buddhists, Emperor Wu decided that Buddhism was not a "teaching" and persecuted it. To respond to such events, Chih-i decided that rigorously sticking to the formalistic requirements of doctrinal analysis would not work; instead, Buddhists must put the contents of those teachings into effect.

Fa-tsang's Matching of Vehicle and Teaching

Once classification systems had been established and refined, even rulers recognized Buddhism as a "teaching." Emperor Wen (r. 581–604) of the Sui dynasty used it as an ideology for ruling the country.[14] Both he and Emperor T'ai-tsung (r. 626–649) of the T'ang praised Buddhism as a "great teaching." The latter even issued a proclamation with the title "Preface to the Sagely Teaching of the Tripiṭaka," in which Buddhism was referred to as both a great teaching and, as the title indicated, a sagely one.[15]

Hsüan-tsang's translations called the attention of the Chinese back to the significance of Indian Buddhism. Hsüan-tsang argued that many of the previous translations had been done incorrectly. With his massive translation project, he strove to revolutionize Chinese Buddhism. Although the Fa-hsiang (Tz'u-en) school based on Hsüan-tsang's translations survived for several generations, Hsüan-tsang's translations were not as influential as he had hoped. Instead, the teachings he propagated were sternly criticized almost from their inception. In contrast to the One-vehicle Buddhism that had become popular in China, Hsüan-tsang propagated a form of Buddhism that may be called "Buddhism of the three vehicles." Although many of the texts he translated included the term "Mahāyāna" in their titles, Hsüan-tsang also translated a large amount of Hīnayāna Abhidarma material, partly to demonstrate the superiority of Mahāyāna. Hsüan-tsang's Buddhism was typical of the Indian Buddhist emphasis on categories such as mārga and *yāna*.

Ever since Kumārajīva had come to China, Chinese Buddhists had generally recognized Mahāyāna as being superior and had based their classifications of doctrine on that premise. However, Hsüan-tsang had called many of their presuppositions into question, especially the emphasis on the One-vehicle and the universality of buddha-nature. Instead, Hsüan-tsang argued for the three vehicles, five separate types of religious potential for humans, and the position that some people could never realize buddhahood. As a result, disputes over the interpretation of buddha-nature continued for a long period.[16]

One of the major reasons that Hsüan-tsang's translations did not have more impact on Chinese Buddhism is that Buddhism had already been accepted as a "teaching" by the Chinese on the basis of previously translated texts. Hsüan-tsang pressed for the importance of interpreting Buddhism in terms of vehicles *(yāna)* by retranslating the *Saṃdhinirmocanasūtra* (Sūtra Explaining the Profundities [of Doctrine]). On the basis of that text's classification of the Buddha's teachings into three periods, he argued for the reality of the three vehicles. However, as Chih-i's writings demonstrate, Chinese Buddhism already had a five-hundred-year history of establishing Buddhism as a "teaching." Even Hsüan-tsang's massive translation project, which included many texts of major doctrinal importance, had little effect on that tradition. As a result, Hsüan-tsang's interpretation of Buddhism had relatively little lasting impact on Chinese Buddhism.

After Hsüan-tsang had promulgated his view that Buddhism should be interpreted as a system of vehicles, many scholars criticized it and defended the tradition of interpreting Buddhism a "teaching." An example of this trend is found in Fa-tsang's *Hua-yen wu-chiao chang,* particularly in the fifth chapter ("Matching the Vehicles and Teachings"). The *Hua-yen wu-chiao chang* is composed of ten chapters. The first, "Establishing the Vehicles," is an examination of such Indian Buddhist terms as Hīnayāna, One-vehicle, and three vehicles from a Hua-yen perspective. Even though Fa-tsang eventually argued for the superiority of the Distinct teaching of the One-vehicle found in the *Avataṃsaka,* he did not reveal his conclusion in the first chapter. However, in the second chapter, "The Benefits of the Teaching and Its Objective," he argued that the *Avataṃsaka*'s Distinct teaching of the One-vehicle was superior to the *Lotus Sūtra*'s Pervasive teaching of the One-vehicle. Thus the teachings of the *Avataṃsaka* must be much better than Hsüan-tsang's three-vehicle system.

In the third chapter, "Doctrines Expounded in the Past and Present," Fa-tsang considered ten classification systems; of the ten, he praised nine of them, including Chih-i's classification. Only Hsüan-tsang's system of the three turnings of the teachings was criticized. For Fa-tsang, the *Avataṃsaka*'s authority rested at least partly on the claim that it was the first teaching expounded by the Buddha immediately after his enlightenment. In contrast, according to Hsüan-tsang's system, the Hīnayāna teachings expounded at Deer Park were the first teachings, a direct contradiction of Fa-tsang's system. Although Hsüan-tsang's position is closer to that revealed by modern historical scholarship, Fa-tsang's faith was more important to him than textual evidence. As Chih-i had stated, "helping and supporting the Buddha in teaching and converting [sentient beings]" was more important than scriptural evidence.

In the fourth chapter, "Analyzing the Teachings and Explaining the Tenets," Fa-tsang explained his system of five teachings and ten tenets for the first time. The superiority of the *Avataṃsaka*'s doctrines was emphasized by calling them Perfect teachings or the teachings of the Distinct One-vehicle. The fifth chapter, "Matching the Vehicles and Teachings," is particularly relevant to our theme here. In it, Fa-tsang took the summary of Indian Buddhism he had elaborated in the first chapter, "Establishing the Vehicles," and explained how it is matched up with the five teachings. In doing so, he recapitulated the process by which the Chinese had progressed from the Indian emphasis on vehicles to stressing teachings, and concluded with his own system of five teachings. His analysis had three parts. In the first, "Matching the Teachings," he explained how the five teachings could be derived through the five steps illustrated below.

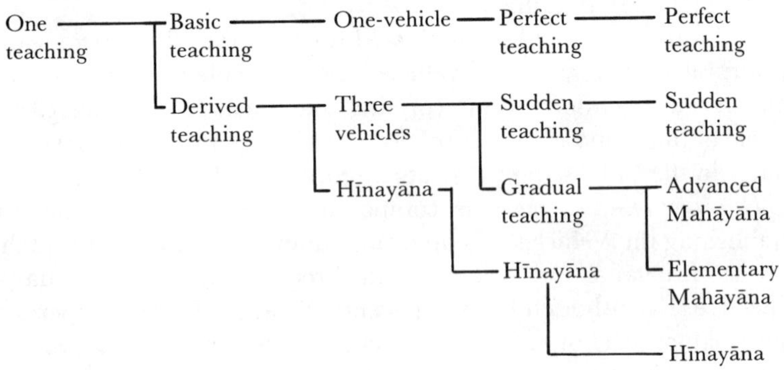

In the second part of the chapter, Fa-tsang demonstrated how the One-vehicle, three vehicles, and Hīnayāna were encompassed by the five teachings.[17]

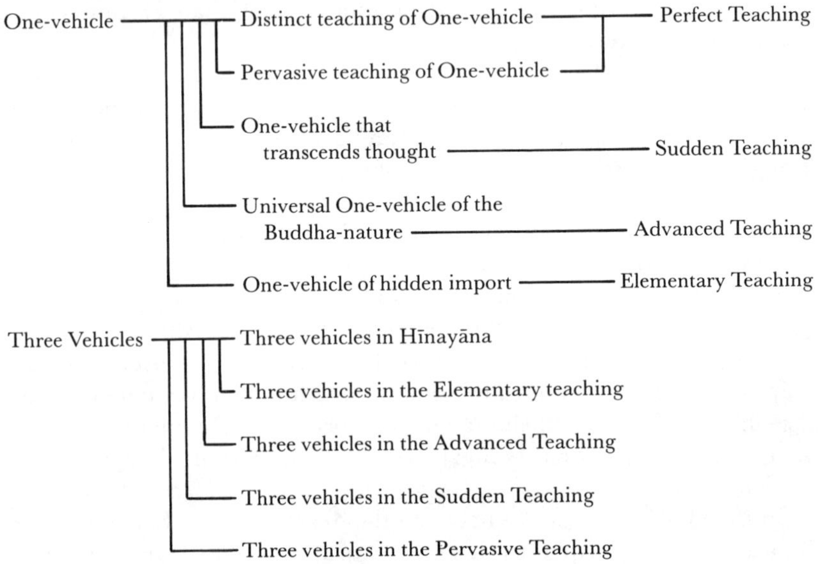

Fa-tsang's explanation of the One-vehicle, three vehicles, and Hīnayāna in terms of the five teachings is diagrammed in the above charts. In the third section of the chapter, the relations among the five teachings are analyzed. Fa-tsang did not hesitate to criticize both Hsüan-tsang's interpretation of Buddhism as a system of vehicles and various theories of the One-vehicle in terms of his own five teachings. The following chapters of the *Wu-chiao chang* (from the sixth, "The Sequence of the Teachings," onward) are primarily devoted to an explanation of the five teachings. Fa-tsang's discussion of Hsüan-tsang's interpretation of Buddhism as vehicles was intended only to supplement the analysis into five teachings.

Hsüan-tsang's campaign to emphasize the importance of the concept of vehicles did not have a major influence on Chinese Buddhism. Fa-tsang's criticisms once again established the concept of the "teachings" as the major idea for categorizing Buddhism. The appearance of the term *"chiao"* (teachings) in the titles of Chih-i's *Ta-pen ssu-chiao i* (Doctrine of the Four Teachings) and Fa-tsang's *Wu-chiao chang* (Essays on the Five Teachings) epitomizes the recognition of Buddhism as a teaching by both Buddhists and non-Buddhists.

The Characteristics of the Soteriological Stance of Buddhism as a Teaching

Buddhism gradually came to be accepted as "the teaching of the Buddha" *(fo-chiao)* by many Chinese. This was due not only to the efforts of monks such as Chih-i and Fa-tsang; the Three Stages movement, Tao-hsüan's (596–667) Lü (Vinaya) school, and the Pure Land movement, led by such figures as T'an-luan (476–542), Tao-ch'o (562–645), and Shan-tao (613–681), also played a role. Eventually some Chinese came to regard Buddhism as a teaching that was superior even to Confucianism.

The monks who maintained that Buddhism was a "teaching" held various soteriological positions; however, a common theme can be recognized in their writings in their use of the term *"kuan."* If a person followed, upheld, investigated, mastered, and preached the teachings of the sage called the Buddha, his personal expression of the teaching might be called his "view" or *kuan*. In addition, *kuan* is often used to refer to insight meditation *(vipaśyanā)* in contrast to calm abiding *(śamatha* or *chih)*. Later, however, with the exception of T'ien-t'ai, most Chinese Buddhists came to regard meditation and wisdom as essentially identical; as a result, *kuan* was thought to include both calm abiding and insight meditation. In the following discussion, it is interpreted as including both.

T'ien-t'ai thought includes a convincing and thorough analysis of the relation between teaching *(chiao)* and meditation *(kuan)*. Although Chih-i's *Mo-ho chih-kuan* ([Treatise on] Great Calm Abiding and Insight Meditation) includes exhortations to practice both teaching and meditation, an exemplary short statement of the relationship between meditation and teaching is found in the beginning of the *Chiao-kuan kang-tsung* (Outline of the Teachings and Meditation) by the Ming-dynasty T'ien-t'ai monk Chih-hsü (1599–1655):

> The teaching of the Buddhas and patriarchs lies only in teaching and meditation *(kuan)*. If meditation is not in teaching, it is incorrect; if teaching is not in meditation, it is not transmitted. Teaching without meditation is obscure; meditation without teaching is not trustworthy.[18]

Similar sentiments are found in the writings of other monks. In the encyclopedic *Ta-sheng i-chang* (Essays on Mahāyāna Doctrines) by Hui-yüan (523–592) of Ching-ying ssu, the doctrinal focus is found in the chapter on the eight consciousnesses. That chapter is divided into ten sections *(men);* the seventh concerns discarding delusion and cultivating enlightenment. In that section, three meditations are established for each of the sixth, seventh, and eighth consciousnesses.[19] The heart of Hui-yüan's doctrine, his discussion of the true and deluded, is thus not merely a discussion of epistemological issues but a soteriological treatment with meditations on the true and deluded states of mind.

Chi-tsang of the San-lun school also recognized the importance of *kuan.* He chose to call the most important text in his school, the *Madhyamakakārikā,* the *Chung-kuan lun* or *Cheng-kuan lun* (Treatise on the Middle [or Correct] View), instead of the more common title, *Chung lun* (Treatise on the Middle). In the *San-lun hsüan-i* (Profound Meaning of the Three Treatises), his summary of the San-lun position, he described his reasons for choosing to call it the *Chung-kuan lun:*

> Question: Why have you used these three characters to refer to the text?
>
> Answer: Through the middle *(chung),* meditation *(kuan)* emerges. Through meditation, the treatise is narrated. When these three elements are present, the meaning [of the text] is perfect and replete.[20]

Chi-tsang developed his theme of correct views *(sheng-kuan)* by analyzing each of the three characters in the title *Chung-kuan lun* in terms of their subjective and objective aspects. He then explained how correct views saved sentient beings.

Tao-hsüan, the systematizer of the Ssu-fen lü (Vinaya) school, also was interested in *kuan,* as is evident in the title of his text, the *Ching-hsin chieh-kuan fa* (The Procedures for Purifying the Mind through Following the Precepts and Meditation),[21] in which he examined some of the elements of monastic discipline and meditation maintained in common by both Hīnayāna and Mahāyāna.

In the Pure Land tradition, the character *"kuan"* is found in the title of Shan-tao's *Kuan Wu-liang-shou-fo ching su* (Commentary on the Sūtra on the Contemplation of the Buddha of Immeasurable Life), a text that concerns meditation on the Pure Land. As Shan-tao declared in summarizing the essentials of the scripture, "This *Contemplation Sūtra (Kuan-ching)* has the concentration of discerning the Buddha *(kuan-fo san-mei)* as its essence *(tsung)*; it also has the concentration based on recitation of the Buddha's name *(nien-fo san-mei)* as its essence."[22] Thus even Shan-tao, who was noted for encouraging people to recite the Buddha's name, considered meditation with recitation to be his basic practice.

Although Hsüan-tsang's disciple Chi strove to develop the Yogācāra tradition in China, he was not fully satisfied with Hsüan-tsang's emphasis on "vehicles." In the *Ta-sheng fa-yüan i-lin chang* (Essays on the Mahāyāna Garden of Dharmas and Grove of Doctrines), he enumerated the various vehicles mentioned in Indian Buddhism but then continued by noting that "When the innate nature *(t'i-hsing)* [of vehicles] is explained, teachings *(chiao)*, principle *(li)*, practice *(hsing)*, and the effect of practice *(kuo)* are discussed. These we collectively call vehicle."[23] Like Fa-tsang, Chi turned away from the concept of "vehicle" toward that of "teaching."

In the beginning of his "Chapter on Ideation-Only," Chi stated,

> There are two aspects to examining the essence *(t'i)*: (1) the essence of the object discerned, and (2) the essence of the subject that discerns. The essence of the object discerned in ideation-only is all dharmas. The practitioner performs a fivefold discernment on their existence and nonexistence in order to ascertain that they are ideation-only.[24]

Chi continued by explaining that the subjective aspect was the mental concomitant, wisdom. Since the objective aspect, all dharmas, had varying degrees in which they seemed to exist, a fivefold discernment had to be devised. However, this discernment was not based directly on Indian texts, but rather was devised by Chi on the basis of the three natures and the four aspects of consciousness.[25]

In the Hua-yen tradition, Tu Shun's (557–640) *Fa-chieh kuan-men* (Contemplation of the Dharmadhātu) deserves special attention. His disciple Chih-yen is the purported author of another meditation *(kuan-men)* text, the *Hua-yen i-sheng shih-hsüan men* (The Ten Profundities of the One-Vehicle of the Avataṃsaka), but the authenticity of this text has been questioned.[26] However, since the ten profundities are emphasized in Chih-yen's *Hua-yen sou-hsüan chi* (Record of Seeking the Profound in Hua-yen), they are clearly a vital part of his teachings. One of the most common terms in Hua-yen texts is "distinguishing between teachings and meaning" *(chiao-i fen-ch'i)*. The term "meaning" *(i* or *i-li)* refers to the basis of the teachings, that which the teachings point toward. Meaning thus constitutes the contents of the meditations or discernments. In works such as the *Wu-shih yao-wen-ta* (Fifty Essential Questions and Answers) and *K'ung-mu chang* (Essays on Articles within the Hua-yen ching), Chih-yen considers the doctrinal aspects of some of the most important passages of the *Avataṃsaka,* but at the same time that he discusses classification of teachings, he also considers meditations and discernments of the meaning elucidated in those passages.

Fa-tsang was more interested in the classification of doctrine than in meditation, but did not completely ignore meditation. The *Wang-chin huan-yüan kuan* (Contemplation of the Exhaustion of Defilements and the Return to Origins) is usually cited as a text representative of Fa-tsang's concern with practice; however, its authenticity has recently been questioned.[27] Among his other extant works, the *Yu-hsin fa-chieh chi* (Record of the Mind's Play amongst the Dharma-Realms) is noteworthy as a text on practice. The rough draft of this work seems to have been circulated as Tu Shun's *Wu-chiao chih-kuan* (Calm Abidings and Discernments of the Five Teachings), a text that is primarily a discussion of meditation in terms of the five teachings.[28] However, because Fa-tsang generally suggested that people rely on Chih-i's *Hsiao chih-kuan* (Short Treatise on Calm Abiding and Insight Meditation) in their practice, he was clearly more interested in doctrinal issues than in practice.[29]

Subsequent Hua-yen adherents reacted to Fa-tsang's emphasis on classification of doctrine by stressing the role of meditation. In doing so, they were both reacting to and resisting the increasing influence of Ch'an. The *Wang-chin huan-yüan kuan* attributed to Fa-tsang can be considered as part of this movement. Fa-tsang's disciple Hui-yüan (n.d.) was particularly concerned with the "discernment of the nature of dharmas" *(fa-hsing kuan);* unfortunately, none of his works on meditation is extant. Another disciple, Wen-ch'ao (n.d.), enumerated ten gates of meditation in his *Tzu-fang i-wang chi* (Compilation on Guarding against Forgetfulness). Among the disciples of Hui-yüan's student Fa-hsien (718–778) were Ch'eng-kuan and Hui-chi Shen-hsiu (n.d.). The latter was the author of a work on meditation entitled *Miao-li yüan-ch'eng kuan* (Contemplation of the Wondrous Principle and the Perfectly Accomplished).[30]

Ch'eng-kuan's teachings were based on the four *dharmadhātus* (dharma realms), but were actually a synthesis of Tu Shun's *Fa-chieh kuan-men* and Fa-tsang's ten profundities. The *dharmadhātu* of the interpenetration of phenomena was, in fact, a meditation. Ch'eng-kuan practiced under a number of Ch'an teachers. At times he was critical of Ch'an teachings, indicating that he was very much aware of that tradition. Yet he wrote a number of texts on meditation, such as the *San-sheng yüan-jung kuan-men* (Contemplation of the Perfect Interfusion of the Three Sages), *Shih-erh yin-yüan kuan-men* (Contemplation of the Twelve Links of

Dependent Origination), and *Wu-yün kuan* (Contemplation of the Five Aggregates). The first was influenced by the writings of the lay Hua-yen scholar Li T'ung-hsüan (646–740), whose meditation on the Buddha's light influenced a number of later Buddhist practitioners.[31]

Many of the monks who interpreted Buddhism as a teaching also emphasized meditation. Even though this tendency varied among monks, those who stressed the importance of teaching would often meditate on the teaching to gain a personal understanding of it, realize enlightenment, and then urge others to follow their example. In many ways, their approach was similar to the soteriological stance of those followers of Indian mārga-Buddhism who emphasized Abhidarma. The element *"abhi"* in the term "Abhidarma" can be interpreted as meaning "facing" or "discerning" the Dharma.[32] This interpretation closely resembles the relation between teaching *(chiao)* and meditation *(kuan).*

Establishment of the Ch'an School

The Personal Aspect of the Term "tsung"

Ch'an arose in part as a protest against the systems of teachings discussed in the previous sections. Ch'an monks objected to the political implications of the concept of "teaching" as a tradition founded by a sage whose teachings had been edited into classics and were of benefit to the state. Buddhism in China had so thoroughly adopted these criteria that it was sometimes regarded as more of a teaching than Confucianism. Buddhism's acceptance as a teaching required that the opinions and views of those above be conveyed to those below. This model applied to both the political realm, in which the emperor's commands were conveyed to the masses, and to the religious realm, in which the beliefs of the teacher were studied by his pupils.

Although this system often had much to recommend it in both the political and religious spheres, it did violate the dying Śākyamuni's instructions to his students that they both be a lamp unto themselves and take the Dharma as a lamp. Although the practitioner could rely on both the self and the Dharma, he could also choose to rely on only one of them. For example, just as self-reliance was lost in the mārga-Buddhism of Abhidarma, so it was lost in many of the Chinese traditions that emphasized "the teaching." By relying on the authority of the Buddha and his scriptures, Chinese monks gained the self-confidence to promulgate their teaching to the people; but because of their respect for their founder and his teaching, they tended to forget the Buddha's dictum that the practitioner should rely on himself.

Those people who wished to revive the Buddhist tradition of self-reliance were critical of the use of Buddhism to indoctrinate people. Their dissatisfaction is expressed in the following verses, sometimes said to epitomize the Ch'an position:

> A transmission outside the teachings,
> Not relying on words and characters,
> Directly pointing at man's mind,
> Seeing one's nature and realizing buddhahood.

The first two lines are typical of Ch'an's critical attitude toward Buddhism as a teaching.[33] Those who advocated the teachings proclaimed their contents through the use of characters. (When the characters were written on large signs they seemed to carry more authority; in recent years in mainland China, signs to instruct the people were erected on mountaintops.) Ch'an practitioners, however, wished to rely on something other than teachings and thus claimed that they did not rely on words.

In fact, Ch'an practitioners had to rely on words to reveal their personal standpoints *(tsung),* but those personal standpoints were based on their own minds rather than on external authorities such as systems of teachings. In an inscription commemorating the ordination and tonsure of Hui-neng, later known as the sixth patriarch, the author Fa-ts'ai describes Hui-neng's teaching as "the personal and profound principle of the simple transmission" *(tan-ch'uan tsung-chih).*[34] The direct and simple mind-to-mind transmission of Ch'an differed radically from the indirect transmission based on hierarchical distinctions between teachers and students or the emphasis on scripture found among those who interpreted Buddhism as teachings. The basic attitude of the Ch'an movement is expressed through its use of the character *tsung* (personal standpoint) in the compound *tsung-chih* (profound principle). When scholars read the term *"Ch'an tsung,"* they may well think of the Ch'an school. The term certainly did have a sectarian nuance when it was employed by figures such as Shen-hui (684–758), who attacked Northern-school Ch'an in favor of his own Southern school. Tsung-mi (780–841) also used the term in a sectarian manner when he advocated the Ho-tse school (of Shen-hui). Later on, the term was used to refer to the "five houses and seven schools" *(wu-chia ch'i-tsung).*

In Japanese Buddhism, once *tsung* (J. *shū*) had been used to refer to the six Nara schools *(Nanto rokushū),* the sectarian nuances of the term were inescapable. However, Dōgen disliked the sectarian sense of "Zen school" *(Zenshū)* and refused to call his own tradition the Sōtō school. He referred to the words of the various patriarchs and teachers as "profound principles" (J. *shūshi,* Ch. *tsung-chih*), the same term used to refer to Hui-neng's teachings.[35]

I believe that we can detect a new movement in Chinese Buddhism through the way in which Chinese monks regarded doctrines, and that this movement can be characterized by the term *"tsung."* Suzuki Daisetsu translated this term into English as "principle."[36] But Suzuki's explanation is easily confused with Tsung-mi's emphasis on terms such as "nature" *(hsing)* or "principle" *(li),* leading to a loss of the sense of *tsung* as a personal interpretation of Buddhism which reflects the Buddha's dictum that practitioners should be a lamp unto themselves. Translating *tsung* as "personal or subjective standpoint" indicates how certain terms came to characterize the position of individual Ch'an masters. For example, in comparing Shen-hsiu and Hui-neng, Suzuki noted that Shen-hsiu was scholarly, whereas Hui-neng seemed to have a personal sense of his religious mission that was expressed in the frequency with which *tzu* (self) appeared in the *Platform Sūtra.*[37] Similarly, *jen* (human) appears frequently in the *Record of Lin-chi,* in expressions such as "the true man of no rank" *(wu-wei chen-jen).*[38] The use of these terms to characterize the individual perspectives of the protagonists of these texts reflects the sense of *tsung* as personal standpoint.

The Ch'an protest against the emphasis on teachings can be expressed through the tension between the statements, "Take the Dharma as your lamp" and "Be a lamp unto yourselves." Ch'an monks respected the Dharma by honoring the buddhas and patriarchs, but at the same time they sought to develop their own individual understanding of Buddhism. As a result, they often used seemingly rough or coarse expressions in Chinese instead of Buddhist technical terms that had originated in India. Everyday events were often taken as the subject of their discourse. The meetings and clashes between the individual standpoints *(tsung)* of various Ch'an masters appear repeatedly in the genre of literature known as "records of the sayings [of masters]" *(yü-lu).*[39]

Ch'an Soteriology

The soteriological stance of those who advocated Buddhism as a "teaching" was characterized by the term *"kuan."* In contrast, Ch'an soteriology can be summarized through the words "mind" *(hsin)* and "transmission" *(ch'uan).* The term "mind" is found in the last two of the four lines quoted above ("Directly pointing at man's mind *(hsin),*/ Seeing one's nature *(hsing)* and realizing buddhahood"). These verses are often used to epitomize the Ch'an view of liberation. The term "transmission" has also been introduced above, in Fa-ts'ai's description of Hui-neng's teaching as "the personal and profound principle of the simple transmission" *(tan-ch'uan tsung-chih).*

The term "mind" is often misinterpreted as referring only to one's own mind. The phrase "seeing [or realizing] the nature *(hsing)* [of one's mind]" in the second line just cited has contributed to this explanation.

Instead, "mind" should be understood in accordance with the definition in the *Ta-sheng ch'i-hsin lun* (Awakening of Faith in the Mahāyāna), which equates the principle *(fa)* of Mahāyāna with the minds of sentient beings.[40] Thus early Ch'an practitioners saw the locus of practice as including all sentient beings. Rather than being concerned with the authority of words and scriptures, they strove to open their own minds in order to speak directly to and about the minds of other people. Hence "realizing the nature of mind" could be interpreted as meaning "directly pointing to society."

Practice directed toward sentient beings was expressed as "seeing the nature and realizing buddhahood." Although this phrase eventually was interpreted to mean that enlightenment was identical to seeing one's own nature, it was originally an exhortation to bodhisattva practices. When figures such as Shen-hui used the phrase, they did so with the sense of "seeing the buddha-nature" *(chien fo-hsing),* a phrase that was interpreted through texts such as the *Nirvāṇa Sūtra,* according to which a ninth-ground bodhisattva could hear about the buddha-nature and practice *(wen-chien fo-hsing),* but only a tenth-ground bodhisattva or a buddha could actually see the buddha-nature *(yen-chien fo-hsing).*[41] Thus the term "buddha-nature" could be interpreted as referring to the activities of bodhisattvas and buddhas. "Seeing the nature" *(chien-hsing)* indicated the practices of bodhisattvas and buddhas as they saw the buddha-nature of all sentient beings. Understanding the phrase "seeing the nature" as suggesting that the individual thoroughly saw his own nature was clearly a later interpretation.

The self-confidence evident in the Ch'an soteriological position is expressed through their frequent use of the term "transmission." Among the phrases already mentioned, "a special transmission outside of the teachings" and "the profound principle of the simple transmission" clearly indicate the importance of this term. In addition, the phrase "not dependent on words and phrases" is often associated with the expression "a transmission from mind to mind." Ch'an monks claimed that they transmitted the Buddha's teachings directly, without recourse to scriptures, because they were confident that their actions could serve as transmissions. In this sense, their use of the word "transmission" suggests the freedom in their actions and interpretations of Buddhism, much as the earlier use of "vehicle" in India had indicated the independent views of early Mahāyānists.

The term "transmission" was used in the titles of many texts. Beginning with early texts such as the *Ch'üan fa-pao chi* (Annals of the Transmission of the Treasure of the Dharma), this tendency continued with works such as the *Ch'üan-hsin fa yao* (Essentials of the Transmission of the Dharma That Can Only Be Passed from Mind to Mind), *Ching-te ch'uan-teng lu* (Records of the Transmission of the Lamp Compiled during the Ching-te Period), and the *Ch'üan-fa cheng-tsung lun* (Treatise on the Transmission of the Dharma and the True Essence). The transmission of specific pieces of clothing, such as robes, or the composition of verses concerning the transmission of the dharma were also emphasized. However, when the transmission of a robe came to be seen as proof of some sort of enlightenment, the original significance of the term was weakened. Similarly, when Ch'an traditions boasted of the length of correct transmission, the original meaning of the term was diluted. The initial emphasis on transmission had nothing to do with length of time or the conferral of an object; rather, it arose naturally out of the Ch'an focus on relying on the self rather than on external authorities.

Although the heart of Ch'an soteriology lies in the bodhisattva practices directed toward sentient beings and in the transmission of the lamp of enlightenment, another important aspect of Ch'an soteriology must also be mentioned: the use of all aspects of everyday life, even farming, as religious practice. This approach would have been unthinkable in the Indian Buddhist tradition. In Ch'an, however, leaving home to become a monk was not seen as a necessity for practice. Ch'an attitudes developed in part as an answer to Chinese criticisms that Buddhism was not productive and was immoral (especially when considered in the light of Confucianism's emphasis on filial piety). Thus Ch'an offered salvation to lay believers through everyday activities.

Hua-yen Ch'an: The Third Movement

The Identification of Personal Standpoint (tsung) *and Teaching* (chiao)

The differences between monks who stressed teaching and practitioners who emphasized their personal standpoints has been described above. Each of these choices had certain soteriological consequences. Tsung-mi's efforts to reconcile these two movements constitutes the third movement in Chinese Buddhism. Some of the reasons behind his efforts can be found in a summary of his biography. In his youth Tsung-mi was a Confucian, but then was ordained as a Buddhist monk, practiced Ch'an meditation, read the *Yüan-chüeh ching* (Sūtra of Consummate Enlightenment), and was instructed in Hua-yen by Ch'eng-kuan. In his *Ch'an-yüan chu-ch'üan-chi tu-hsü* (Preface to the Collected Writings on the Source of Ch'an), Tsung-mi contrasted Ch'an and the teachings in a variety of ways and then proceeded to bridge the gap between the two. He argued that the origins of Ch'an were to be found in the teachings, and that the essence *(t'i)* of the teachings was Ch'an.

Although earlier scholars have usually described Tsung-mi's position as "the convergence of Ch'an and the teachings" (J. *kyōzen itchi*), I believe that it may be more accurately called "Hua-yen Ch'an."[42] This term reflects the way Tsung-mi combined the Ch'an of Ho-tse Shen-hui with Hua-yen doctrine (as it had developed up to the time of Ch'eng-kuan) to formulate his position on the realization of innate buddhahood *(pen-lai ch'eng-fo).* The earlier description of Tsung-mi's position as "the convergence of the teachings and Ch'an" suggests that he had simply combined Ch'an and the teachings. Although this is one aspect of Tsung-mi's thought, his interest in developing the theme of the convergence of Buddhism, Taoism, and Confucianism must also be noted. This latter aspect of his thought might be described as "neither the teachings nor Ch'an." As a result, I have created the new term "Hua-yen Ch'an" to describe Tsung-mi's position.

Tsung-mi's thought can be traced by arranging his works in the order in which he composed them: his commentaries on the *Yüan-chüeh ching;* the *Ch'an-yüan chu-ch'üan-chi tu-hsü* (Preface on the Source of Ch'an); the *P'ei Hsiu shih-i wen* (P'ei Hsiu's Questions);[43] and the *Yüan-jen lun* (Essay on the Origins of Man). In his commentaries on the *Yüan-chüeh ching,* Tsung-mi examined the idea of "realization of innate buddhahood," a term mentioned only in passing in the *Yüan-chüeh ching* itself. In explaining it, Tsung-mi cited Ch'eng-kuan's views on the relationship of the realization of buddhahood to the discernment of the dharma-realm of unhindered interpenetration of phenomena *(shih-shih wu-ai fa-chieh).* The term "realization of innate buddhahood" came to refer to the realization of an innate nature that transcended any consideration of whether or not buddhahood had actually been attained. In developing his argument, Tsung-mi shifted the interpretation of the phrase "realization of innate buddhahood" from focusing on the term "realization" *(ch'eng)* to emphasizing "innate" *(pen-lai).* His interest in this problem is reflected in the use of "origins" *(yüan),* a term similar to "innate," in the titles of two of his major works, the "Preface to the Origins of Ch'an" and the "Essay on the Origins of Man." For Tsung-mi, recognizing these origins was sudden enlightenment, but even if the practitioner did not recognize his origins, he would not lose them.

In the "Preface on the Origins of Ch'an," Tsung-mi demonstrated how the teachings and Ch'an were identical in purport. Ho-tse Shen-hui's Ch'an was called "the personal standpoint *(tsung)* that directly reveals the nature of mind" *(chih-hsien hsin-hsing tsung).* The teachings found in the *Hua-yen ching, Yüan-chüeh ching,* and tathāgatagarbha literature were all called "teachings that reveal the true mind is the nature [of all]" *(hsien-shih chen-hsin chi-hsing chiao).* The similarities of both positions were disclosed through terms such as "nature of the mind" and "origins."

Two aspects of Tsung-mi's thought can be characterized as "neither the teachings nor Ch'an." First, although advocates of both the teachings and Ch'an might sometimes be concerned with the innate nature of things, Tsung-mi's emphasis on the innate nature seemed to deviate from both these traditions. Advocates of Buddhism as a system of teachings would have found little room for a discussion of the innate nature of things in the elaborate edifice of the Buddha's teachings they constructed. Ch'an practitioners, with their practices based on concrete behavior, would not have been interested in Tsung-mi's discussions of innate nature. Tsung-mi's position thus represented a third movement in Chinese Buddhism.

Tsung-mi's advocacy of the convergence of the three teachings (Confucianism, Taoism, and Buddhism) is illustrative of a second aspect of his views that can be called "neither the teachings nor Ch'an." Of course, many Ch'an advocates as well as scholars who considered Buddhism to be a system of teachings had been attracted by either Confucianism or Taoism. Although some of them had argued that Buddhism or Ch'an was essentially identical with Confucianism or Taoism, they had ended up rejecting Buddhism or Ch'an. Tsung-mi advanced beyond them by positively avowing the convergence of the three teachings.

Tsung-mi argued forcefully for his position in the *Yüan-jen lun* (Essay on the Origins of Man), in which he developed his case in two phases. First, he demonstrated the superiority of the "One-vehicle teaching that reveals the nature" over all other teachings. Thus Confucianism and Taoism were rejected as superstitious views concerned only with life in this world. The four Buddhist traditions of lay teachings, Hīnayāna, and Mahāyāna Fa-hsiang and San-lun were rejected as one-sided and shallow. Thus only the "One-vehicle teaching that reveals the nature" was accepted as the supreme correct teaching.

In the second phase of his argument, in a section called "Reconciling *(hui-t'ung)* the Roots and Branches," Tsung-mi revealed that Confucianism and Taoism were incorporated into and encompassed by the "One-vehicle teaching that reveals the nature." When the original nature of all was thoroughly understood, all previously rejected teachings were seen to be encompassed by the teaching that reveals the nature. Only then could the virtues of each teaching be appreciated. Thus Confucianism and Taoism were ultimately in agreement with Buddhism, and the three traditions converged.

This aspect of Tsung-mi's thought, described above as "neither the teachings nor Ch'an," does not directly contradict his insistence on combining Ch'an and the teachings. The combination of Ch'an and the teachings eventually contributed to the theories that led to Ch'an's cultural influences on art and literature.[44] Tsung-mi's insistence on the ultimate agreement of Buddhism with Confucianism and Taoism enabled adherents of the latter two traditions to associate more easily with

Buddhists. At the same time, Tsung-mi did not subordinate Ch'an or Buddhist systems of teachings to Confucianism or Taoism. Although the interaction and mutual criticisms of these traditions led to Ch'an's influence on culture, abuses resulted when the various traditions did not interact in a positive manner and keep each other's excesses in check.

Thus Chinese Buddhism eventually developed into a confused mix of various traditions without much vitality, in part through later developments of Tsung-mi's innovations. In particular, neither those who interpreted Buddhism as a system of teachings nor Ch'an adherents were critical enough of the tendency toward indiscriminate syncretism. Because they failed to check the confused mingling of religious traditions, they must bear the responsibility for the current state of Chinese Buddhism.

Soteriology in Hua-yen Ch'an

Tsung-mi is known for combining the systematic presentation of Buddhism as a teaching *(chiao)* with Ch'an's emphasis on personal standpoint *(tsung);* his soteriological stance is often summed up with the phrase "sudden enlightenment followed by gradual cultivation" *(tun-wu chien-hsiu).* The details of his view of practice and ritual are found in a text called the *Yüan-chüeh-ching tao-ch'ang hsiu-cheng i* (Rituals for Practice and Realization at the Place of Practice According to the Sūtra of Consummate Enlightenment). Since research on this text has already been done by earlier scholars, I will limit myself to summarizing its main points.[45] Although the phrase "sudden enlightenment followed by gradual cultivation" implies that Tsung-mi's views might be summarized by referring to terms such as "enlightenment" *(wu),* "practice" *(hsiu),* or "realization" *(cheng),* the character "reveal" *(hsien),* found in phrases such as the "teaching that reveals [innate] nature" *(hsien-hsing chiao),* is more central to his thought. In addition, the character *i* (ritual), found in the title of the text mentioned above, played a key role in his views. For Tsung-mi, gradual cultivation required the daily practice of worshiping the Buddha, confessing wrongdoing, and meditation *(tso-ch'an).* As the practitioner continued to perform these rituals, his innate buddhahood would gradually be revealed.

The influence of Chih-i's *Hsiao chih-kuan* (Short Text on Meditation) can be found in Tsung-mi's *Yüan-chüeh-ching tao-ch'ang hsiu-cheng i.* However, important differences between the two texts also exist. Through rituals, Chih-i argued that the practitioner could discern the three thousand realms in his everyday, polluted mind; in contrast, Tsung-mi used ritual to reveal the true nature of everything. T'ien-t'ai meditation is directed toward the deluded mind, whereas Tsung-mi is interested in revealing the true nature of mind. The differences between the two traditions are found in the two characters they employ repeatedly: "discern" or "meditation" *(kuan)* for T'ien-t'ai, and "reveal" *(hsien)* for Tsung-mi.

Differences existed between Tsung-mi's version of sitting meditation *(tso-ch'an)* and that advocated by many Ch'an masters. One view of sitting meditation within Ch'an circles is exemplified in the famous dialogue between Nan-yüeh Huai-jang and Ma-tsu Tao-i about polishing a tile to make a mirror.[46] The point of this story is that sitting meditation is ultimately nothing more than sitting and meditating, and is not to be used with the intention of becoming a buddha. Although meditation was certainly a valid practice, by itself it would not lead to buddhahood; the other practices of a bodhisattva were also needed. For Tsung-mi, the various bodhisattvas and gods were to be invited to the practice hall where meditation was performed; only then could the practitioner's true nature be revealed through sitting meditation. At the very least, Tsung-mi's attitude was markedly different from that of practitioners like Nan-yüeh and Ma-tsu.

Conclusion

Soteriology in Chinese Buddhism shifted through the ages as monks used different concepts to provide a framework for their views. However, even as they developed new positions, they also adopted themes from many of the movements that had occurred in Indian Buddhism. Of these themes, that of the tension between external authority and self-reliance was particularly important.

This approach can be extended to other cultures. If Japanese Buddhism were considered, the same tension between external authority and self-reliance that is important in Indian and Chinese Buddhism would be seen in the emergence of the Kamakura schools. The Japanese emphasized soteriological elements that were not as important in Indian and Chinese Buddhism. For example, the Japanese insistence on sectarianism *(shū,* Ch. *tsung),* the rapid realization of buddhahood, the worship of the founders of the schools, and the emphasis on a single practice were all major influences on Japanese Buddhist soteriology. However, these are themes for another paper.

Notes

1. In recent years, many scholars argued that Mahāyāna arose from the Mahāsaṅghika school. However, Hirakawa Akira has demonstrated that many peculiarly Mahāyāna characteristics arose around Buddhist *stūpas* (*Shoki Daijō Bukkyō no kenkyū* [Tokyo: Shunjūsha, 1965]). Shizutani Masao (*Shoki Daijō Bukkyō no seiritsu katei* [Kyoto: Hyakkaen, 1975]) has developed Hirakawa's research further by discussing "primitive Mahāyāna" Buddhist orders.

2. Yoshizu Yoshihide, *Kegon Zen no shisōshiteki kenkyū* (Tokyo: Daitō shuppansha, 1985).

3. For a discussion of these lines, said to epitomize the Ch'an position, see Yanagida Seizan, *Shoki Zenshū shishō no kenkyū* (Kyoto: Hōzōkan, 1967), 471–484.

4. For a thorough description of early Chinese Buddhism, see Kamata Shigeo, *Chūgoku Bukkyōshi,* vol. 1, *Shodenki no Bukkyō* (Tokyo: Tokyo daigaku shuppankai, 1982).

5. For Kumārajīva and Hui-yüan, see Kamata Shigeo, *Chūgoku Bukkyōshi,* vol. 2, *Juyōki no Bukkyō* (Tokyo: Tokyo daigaku shuppankai, 1983).

6. Kimura Eiichi, *Eon no kenkyū: Ibun-hen* (Tokyo: Sōbunsha, 1962).

7. For example, in the *Ta-chih-tu lun* 100 (*T* 25.756b14–16), Mahākāśyapa is said to have compiled the Hīnayāna canon while Mañjuśrī and Maitreya entrusted Ānanda with the compilation of the Mahāyāna canon. The text also notes that both Hīnayāna and Mahāyāna are the "word of the Buddha" (*T* 25.756b22).

8. For a survey of Buddhism under the Northern and Southern dynasties, see Kamata Shigeo, *Chūgoku Bukkyōshi,* vol. 3, *Nambokuchō no Bukkyō, jō* (Tokyo: Tokyo daigaku shuppankai, 1984).

9. *Miao-fa lien-hua ching su, Hsü-tsang-ching* (Taipei: Hsin-wen-feng ch'u-pan kuang-ssu, 1977; hereafter *HTC*), 100.396d13.

10. Hui-kuan's views are described in Chi-tsang's *San-lun hsüan-i* (*T* 45.5b4). In Ching-ying ssu Hui-yüan's *Ta-sheng i-chang* (*T* 44.465a), a similar classification system is attributed to Liu Ch'iu (438–495). Hui-yüan's statement was probably based on Liu Ch'iu's *Wu-liang-i-ching hsü* (Introduction to the Sūtra of Innumerable Meanings), included in the *Ch'u san-tsang chi chi* (*T* 55.68a). Liu Ch'iu's classification system was presumably based on that of Hui-kuan.

11. I have benefited from the discussion of *chiao* in Kobayashi Masayoshi, "Sangyō kōshō ni okeru kyō no kannen," in Yoshioka Yoshitoyo hakase kanreki kinen ronshū kankōkai, ed., *Yoshioka hakase kanreki kinen: Dōkyō kenkyūronshō: Dōkyō no shisō to bunka* (Tokyo: Kokusho kankōkai, 1977), 249f.

12. *Ta-sheng i-chang* 1, *T* 44.465a; *Miao-fa lien-hua ching hsüan-i* 10a, *T* 33.801a; *Fa-hua hsüan-lun* 3, *T* 34.382b; *San-lun hsüan-i, T* 45.5b4; *Ta-sheng fa-yüan i-lin chang* 1, *T* 45.245a; *Chieh-shen-mi-ching su* 1, *HTC* 34.298b; *Hua-yen wu-chiao chang* 1, *T* 45.480b; *Hua-yen t'an-hsüan chi* 1, *T* 35.110c; *Hua-yen ching k'an-ting chi* 1, *HTC* 5.8b; *Hua-yen-ching su* 1, 35.508a.

13. *Ta-pen ssu-chiao-i* 1, *T* 46.723a29–b5. The English translation, with minor changes, is based on Robert Rhodes, "Annotated Translation of the *Ssu-chiao-i,* chüan 1," *Annual Memoirs of the Otani University Shin Buddhist Comprehensive Research Institute* 3 (1985): 54–55.

14. *Chi ku-chin fo-tao lun-heng* 2, *T* 52.378b.

15. *Kuang hung-ming chi* 22, *T* 52.258a.

16. See Tokiwa Daijō, *Busshō no kenkyū* (Tokyo: Meiji shoin, 1944) for a detailed examination of these debates.

17. In *Hua-yen wu-chiao chang* 1 (*T* 45.482a23), Fa-tsang does not define both the Distinct and Pervasive teachings of the One-vehicle as the Perfect teaching. However, in following Chih-yen, he seems to relate the Pervasive teaching of the One-vehicle to the Perfect teaching. The Distinct and Pervasive One-vehicle are not equal, though; the Distinct One-vehicle teaching is identified with the *Avataṃsakasūtra,* while the Pervasive One-vehicle teaching is identified with the *Lotus Sūtra.* Thus even though the Pervasive One-vehicle teaching is not specifically defined as the Perfect teaching, the identification is implied in Fa-tsang's complex classification system.

18. *T* 46.936c.
19. *Ta-sheng i-chang* 3b, *T* 44.536b10.
20. *T* 45.13b29–c2.
21. *T* 45.819b.
22. *Kuan wu-liang-shou-fo ching su* 1, *T* 37.247a18.
23. *Ta-sheng fa-yüan i-lin chang* 1, *T* 45.264c17.
24. Ibid., *T* 45.258b19. For an English-language discussion of the fivefold meditation, see Alan Sponberg, "Meditation in Fa-hsiang Buddhism," in Peter Gregory, ed., *Traditions of Meditation in Chinese Buddhism* (Honolulu: University of Hawaii Press), 30–34. Sponberg's analysis of the term *"kuan"* comes close to my views.
25. Nemu Kazuchika, "Gojū yuishikikan no shisō to sono seiritsu," *Bukkyōgaku kenkyū* 38 (1982).
26. Ishii Kōsei, "*Ichijō jūgenmon* no shomondai," *Bukkyōgaku* 12 (1981).
27. Kojima Taizan, "*Mōjin gengenkan* no senja wo meguru shomondai," *Nanto Bukkyō* (1982).
28. Yūki Reimon has argued that the *Hua-yen wu-chiao chih-kuan* (*T* 1867), usually said to have been based on Tu Shun's talks, was in fact not by Tu Shun at all. Instead Yūki claimed that it was a draft of Fa-tsang's *Hua-yen yu-hsin fa-chieh chi* (*T* 1877). See Yūki Reimon, "*Kegon gokyō shikan* senjussha ronkō: *Gokyō shikan* no Tojun senjutsu setsu wo hitei shi, Hōzōsen *Yūshin hokkaiki* no sōkō nari to suitei su," *Shūkyō kenkyū* new 7.2 (1930).
29. Fa-tsang, *Ta-sheng ch'i-hsin lun i-chi* 3b, *T* 44.283b4, 284b16.
30. *Sung kao-seng chuan* 5, *T* 50.763b. The *Miao-li yüan-ch'eng kuan* is cited often in the works of the Korean monk Kyunyŏ (923–973).
31. For example, see Myōe Shōnin Kōben's (1173–1232) *Kegon Bukkō zanmaikan hihōzō* (*T* 72.87–100). For a study of Li T'ung-hsüan, see Robert Gimello, "Li T'ung-hsüan and the Practical Dimensions of Hua-yen," in Robert Gimello and Peter Gregory, eds., *Studies in Ch'an and Hua-yen* (Honolulu: University of Hawaii Press, 1983), 321–389.
32. *A-p'i-ta-mo chü-she lun* 1 *(Abhidharmakośa)*, *T* 29.1b9.
33. For a discussion of the compilation of these lines, see Yanagida Seizan, *Shoki Zenshū shisho no kenkyū* (Kyoto: Hōzōkan, 1967), 470–476.
34. For the inscription, known as the *Kuang-hsiao-ssu i-fa t'a-chi,* see Yanagida, *Shoki Zenshū shoshi no kenkyū,* pp. 535–538.
35. Yoshizu Yoshihide, "Shūshi no gaku ni tsuite," *Shūgaku kenkyū* 29 (1987).
36. *Suzuki Daisetsu zenshū* (Tokyo: Iwanami shoten, 1968), vol. 2: *Zen shisō kenkyū, 2. Daruma yori Enō ni itaru,* pp. 229, 371. Suzuki explains *tsung* as *"genri"* (principle).
37. *Suzuki Daisetsu zenshū,* vol. 3: *Zen shisōshi kenkyū,* 3. "Enō shijaku chokugo no Zen shisō," p. 72.
38. For Suzuki's view of Lin-chi, see *Suzuki Daisetsu zenshū,* vol. 3.: *Rinzai no kihon shisō,* pp. 337–560.
39. John McRae has argued that the "encounter dialogues" between Ch'an practitioners may be considered their soteriology. In these exchanges, each participant had his own point of view, but their confrontation sometimes resulted in a more profound understanding on the part of at least one of the participants. I agree with McRae's analysis, but note that the later tendency to base practice on Ch'an problems *(kung-an)* probably represents a return to a stance in which "teachings" are emphasized.
40. *T* 32.575c20; Yoshito Hakeda, trans., *The Awakening of Faith* (New York: Columbia University Press, 1967), 28.
41. *Ta-pan-nieh-p'an ching* 27, *T* 12.527c29.

42. See Yoshizu Yoshihide, *Kegon Zen,* pp. 269–336.

43. This text is often called the *Chung-hua ch'uan-hsin-ti ch'an-men shih-tzu ch'eng-hsi t'u* (Lineage Chart of the Masters and Students of Ch'an in the Transmission of the Mind Ground in China). However, Ishii Shūdō has argued that the phrase *"ch'eng-hsi t'u"* (lineage chart) is used only for diagrams of dharma lineages and has suggested that the title *P'ei Hsiu shih-i wen* is more appropriate ("Shinpukuji bunko shozō no *Haikyū shūimon* no honkoku," *Hanazono daigaku Zengaku kenkyū* 60 [1981]).

44. For a discussion of these developments during the Sung dynasty, see Robert Gimello's chapter on Wen-tzu Ch'an in this volume.

45. For more on Tsung-mi, see Kamata Shigeo, *Shūmitsu kyōgaku no shisōshiteki kenkyū* (Tokyo: Tōkyō daigaku shuppankai, 1975). Peter Gregory has written a number of thorough articles on Tsung-mi; see especially his excellent study, "Sudden Enlightenment Followed by Gradual Cultivation: Tsung-mi's Analysis of Mind," in idem, ed., *Sudden and Gradual: Approaches to Enlightenment in Chinese Thought* (Honolulu: University of Hawaii Press, 1987).

46. *Ching-te ch'uan-teng lu* 5, *T* 51.240c.

Glossary

An Shih-kao 安世高
Ch'an 禅
Ch'an tsung 禅宗
Ch'an-yüan chu-ch'üan-chi tu-hsü 禅源諸詮集都序
ch'eng 成
ch'eng-hsi t'u 承襲図
Ch'eng-kuan 澄観
Cheng-kuan lun 正観論
Chi 基
Chi-tsang 吉蔵
chiao 教
chiao-i fen-ch'i 教義分斉
Chiao-kuan kang-tsung 教観綱宗
chiao-p'an 教判
Chieh-shen-mi ching su 解深密経疏
chien fo-hsing 見仏性
chien-hsing 見性
chih 止
chih-hsien hsin-hsing tsung 直顕心性宗
Chih-hsü 智旭
Chih-i 智顗
Chih Lou-chia-ch'an 支婁迦讖
Chih-yen 智儼
ching 経
Ching-hsin chieh-kuan fa 浄心誡観門
Ching-te ch'uan-teng lu 景徳伝灯録
ch'uan 伝
Ch'uan fa-pao chi 伝法宝記
Ch'uan-fa cheng-tsung lun 伝法正宗論
Ch'uan-hsin fa yao 伝心法要
Chuang-yen Seng-min 荘厳僧旻
Chung-hua ch'uan-hsin-ti ch'an-men shih-tzu ch'eng-hsi t'u 中華伝心地禅門師資承襲図
Chung-kuan lun 中観論
Chung lun 中論
Ch'u san-tsang chi chi 出三蔵記集
Dōgen 道元
Fa-chieh kuan-men 法界観門
Fa-hsiang 法相
Fa-hsien 法銑
fa-hsing kuan 法性観
Fa-hua hsüan-lun 法華玄論
Fa-hua i su 法華義疏
Fa-ts'ai 法才
Fa-tsang 法蔵
fo-chiao 仏教
Hirakawa Akira 平川彰
Ho-tse Shen-hui 荷沢神会
Hsiao chih-kuan 小止観
hsien 顕
hsien-hsing chiao 顕性教
hsien-shih chen-hsin chi-hsing chiao 顕示真心即性教
hsin 心
hsing (practice) 行
hsing (nature) 性
Hsing-huang Fa-lang 興皇法朗
Hsüan-tsang 玄奘
Huan 桓
Hua-yen-ching k'an-ting chi 華厳経刊定記
Hua-yen-ching su 華厳経疏

Hua-yen-ching t'an-hsüan chi 華厳経探玄記
Hua-yen i-sheng shih-hsüan men 華玄一乗十玄門
Hua-yen sou-hsüan chi 華厳捜玄記
Hua-yen wu-chiao chang 華厳五教章
Hui-chi Shen-hsiu 会稽神秀
Hui-kuan 慧観
Hui-neng 慧能
hui-t'ung 会通
Hui-yüan (of Ching-ying-ssu) 慧遠(浄影寺)
Hui-yüan (Fa-tsang's disciple) 慧苑
Hui-yüan (of Lu-shan) 慧遠(廬山)
i 儀
I-hsia lun 夷夏論
i-li 義理
Ishii Shūdō 石井修道
jen 人
ju-chiao 儒教
K'ai-shan Chih-tsang 開善智蔵
Kegon Bukkō zanmaikan hihōzō 華厳仏光観三昧観秘宝蔵
kuan 観
Kuan-ching 観経
kuan-fo san-mei 観仏三昧
Kuang-hsiao-ssu i-fa t'a-chi 光孝寺瘞髮塔記
Kuang-tse Fa-yün 光宅法雲
kuan-men 観門
Kuan wu-liang-shou-fo ching su 観無量寿仏経疏
Ku Huan 顧歡
kung-an 公案
K'ung-mu chang 孔目章
kuo 果
kyōzen itchi 教禅一致
Kyunyŏ 均如
li 理
Lin-chi 臨済
Li T'ung-hsüan 李通玄
Liu Ch'iu 劉虬
Lü 律
Ma-tsu Tao-i 馬祖道一
men 門
Miao-fa lien-hua ching hsüan-i 妙法蓮華経玄義
Miao-li yüan-ch'eng kuan 妙理円成観
Mo-ho chih-kuan 摩訶止観
Myōe Shōnin Kōben 明恵上人高弁
Nanto rokushū 南都六宗
Nan-yüeh Huai-jang 南岳懐譲
nien-fo san-mei 念仏三昧
P'ei Hsiu shih-i wen 裴休拾遺問
pen-lai ch'eng-fo 本来成仏
San-lun 三論
San-lun hsüan-i 三論玄義
San-sheng yüan-jung kuan-men 三聖円融観門
Shan-tao 善導
Shen-hsiu 神秀
Shen-hui 神会
She-shan Seng-ch'üan 摂山僧詮
Shih-erh yin-yüan kuan-men 十二因縁観門
shih-shih wu-ai fa-chieh 事事無礙法界
Shizutani Masao 静谷正雄
Ssu-fen lü 四分律
Suzuki Daisetsu 鈴木大拙
Ta-chih-tu lun 大智度論
tan-ch'uan tsung-chih 単伝宗旨
T'an-luan 曇鸞
Tao-an 道安
Tao-ch'o 道綽
Tao-hsüan 道宣
Tao-sheng 道生
Ta-pen ssu-chiao i 大本四教義
Ta-sheng ch'i-hsin lun 大乗起信論
Ta-sheng fa-yüan i-lin chang 大乗法苑義林章
Ta-sheng ta-i chang 大乗大義章
t'i 体
T'ien-t'ai 天台
t'i-hsing 体性
Ti-lun 地論
tso-ch'an 坐禅
tsung 宗
tsung-chiao 宗教
tsung-chih 宗旨
Tsung-mi 宗密
tun-wu chien-hsiu 頓悟漸修
Tu Shun 杜順
tzu 自
Tz'u-en 慈恩
Tzu-fang i-wang chi 自防遺忘集
Ŭisang 義湘
Wang-chin huan-yüan kuan 妄尽還源観
Wen-ch'ao 文超
wen-chien fo-hsing 聞見仏性
Wen-tzu Ch'an 文字禅
Wŏnch'ŭk 円測
wu-chia ch'i-tsung 五家七宗
Wu-chiao chang 五教章
Wu-chiao chih-kuan 五教止観

Wu-liang-i-ching hsü 無量義経序
Wu-shih yao-wen-ta 五十要問答
wu-wei chen-jen 無位真人
Wu-yün kuan 五蘊観
yen-chien fo-hsing 眼見仏性
Yoshizu Yoshihide 吉津宜英
yüan 源
Yüan-chüeh ching 円覚経
Yüan-chüeh-ching tao-ch'ang hsiu-cheng i 円覚経道場修証儀
Yüan-jen lun 原人論
Yu-hsin fa-chieh chi 遊心法界記
Yūki Reimon 結城令聞
yü-lu 語録

Encounter Dialogue and the Transformation of the Spiritual Path in Chinese Ch'an

John R. McRae

Introduction

The Rejection of the Path in Chinese Buddhism

Instead of discussing some variant of the Buddhist notion of the mārga or spiritual path, I will consider a case involving the rejection, or at the very least a radical reworking, of the concept of mārga itself. The emergence in medieval China of the Ch'an school, with its distinctive style of spontaneous "encounter dialogue" between masters and students, represents just such a situation: the appearance of Ch'an and its development into a major school signals a major transformation in Chinese Buddhism—one that appears to have been based in part on a shift away from a primarily mārga-based perspective. Indeed, the practice of encounter dialogue derived much of its creative energy from the iconoclastic rejection of traditional Buddhist formulations of the spiritual path, and the incredible popularity of the Ch'an methodology meant, at least in part, a rejection of the concept of mārga itself.

The originally Indian concept of mārga was never completely uprooted from Chinese soil, and it is not my intent to argue that Chinese Buddhism underwent some sudden and total revolution in consciousness, some Foucauldian epistemological shift, at one particular point in time. Rather, the emergence of Ch'an implies a gradual metamorphosis in the Chinese religious and intellectual consciousness, and the mārga and encounter models of spiritual training, if I may use those terms, were reciprocally engaged in a mutually interactive evolution over a period of several centuries.

There are still many unresolved historical issues pertaining to the emergence of the classical style of Ch'an practice, which as much as possible will be relegated to some later forum. The texts of Ch'an encounter dialogue, as they exist today, are not journalistic accounts of actual events, although centuries of Chinese readers and practitioners have assumed that they are. Rather, they are literary re-creations of how the enlightened masters of the past must have spoken and acted. Although the narrative realism of many of the accounts about Ma-tsu, Pai-chang, and other famous masters should not be taken as evidence of historical accuracy, it is my current hypothesis that the style of dialogue represented in woodblock text was created in imitation of actual practice, and that the popularity of the printed texts eventually informed actual oral practice.

At present, the use of Ch'an stories within the context of monastic training during the T'ang is not well understood. Are we to believe that the T'ang masters actually functioned according to the style of spontaneous creativity depicted in the records? Or should we read the stories as firmly bounded by the precisely defined ritual contexts of the Sung, when the spontaneity and intuitive acumen of Ma-tsu and his associates and successors was a firmly accepted myth? My current feeling is that the "golden age" of the T'ang existed only in the mythic consciousness of later times, but this does not in any way eliminate the power of the images involved. Because of the very nature of time in the Chinese cultural context, the act of retrospective attribution was more than a powerful force within the Ch'an tradition; the process of re-creation and communion with the sages of the past was absolutely fundamental to the process of Ch'an spiritual endeavor.

I am not concerned here with the evolution of this oral practice or with its progressive creation (and re-creation) in written texts. Instead, I would like to focus on the theoretical implications of the bimodality between the encounter and mārga models in Chinese Buddhism. This discussion will have important implications for understanding the social, intellectual, and religious changes that mark what we now tend to call the "T'ang-Sung transition," that is, the period from roughly 750 to 1350 C.E. It may also complement the other discussions in this volume by showing some of the potential ramifications of themes deriving from the mārga concept, as well as the possibilities for approaches to Buddhism created in counterpoint, if not outright opposition, to the idea of the spiritual path itself.

"Encounter dialogue"[1] refers to the spontaneous repartee that is said to take place between master and student in the process of Ch'an training. This type of communication includes both verbal and physical exchanges that are often posed in the form of sincere but misguided questions from Ch'an trainees and perplexing, even enigmatic, responses from the masters. Instead of students, the questioners are sometimes monks with high monastic positions, specialists in Buddhist academics, or devotees of particular forms of religious devotion, all of whom are gleefully lampooned and often depicted as eventually giving up their mistaken preoccupations with the trappings of Buddhism in favor of true spiritual endeavor. And instead of the usual sort of master —that is, the seasoned religieux who administers a training center for young trainees—we often find exotic characters of unorthodox behavior who engage more traditional masters as equals and, more often than not, tweak the tendencies of the latter toward stuffiness and formulaic responses.

This is by no means a complete description of encounter dialogue, but it should suffice as a working definition.[2] The general understanding of modern scholarship is that this form of practice came to the fore with the Hung-chou school of Ma-tsu Tao-i (709–788). Certainly, Ma-tsu's school does represent a new form of Ch'an developing in a newly expanding area of the provincial South, and the extent to which his first- and second-generation successors blanketed what was then Chiang-hsi nan-tao (roughly, modern Kiangsi) is truly remarkable.[3] However, as I have shown elsewhere, the antecedents of encounter dialogue are apparent earlier in the Ch'an tradition.[4] In addition, my more recent research into the documents surrounding Ma-tsu and the Hung-chou school has yielded the preliminary suspicion that encounter-dialogue material may not have appeared as a genre of Ch'an literature until sometime during the tenth century. For the present purposes I will place only the broadest of limits on the emergence of this important style of Ch'an practice.

Locating an Important Development

Yanagida Seizan's landmark study of the historical works of early Ch'an Buddhism,[5] which was published just over twenty years ago, opens with the description of his research agenda as aimed at filling in a gap between the *Hsü kao-seng chuan* (Continued Lives of Eminent Monks; hereafter *HKSC*), written by Tao-hsüan in 645 and augmented until his death in 667, and the *Sung kao-seng chuan* (Lives of Eminent Monks [Compiled during the] Sung; hereafter *SKSC*), completed by Tsan-ning in 988. The first of these texts contains biographical entries on Bodhidharma, Hui-k'o, and Tao-hsin as well as other scattered information, all of which is crucial for our understanding of the early phases of Chinese Ch'an Buddhism, but which does not in any sense dominate Tao-hsüan's text as a whole. By the time the *SKSC* was written, however, the Ch'an school had become perhaps the single most important force in Chinese Buddhism, so that the number of Ch'an masters introduced in this text far exceeds that of any other category of monk.[6] Clearly, a major sea change had taken place in Chinese Buddhism, one that Professor Yanagida navigated with stunning expertise in his 1967 magnum opus. But since our purpose here is slightly different from Professor Yanagida's, a set of texts taken from the Chinese Buddhist meditation tradition itself will better serve as comparative reference points for the emergence of the classical Ch'an approach to religious training.

The first of these reference points is actually a set of texts: the prodigious output on the subject by the great T'ien-t'ai Chih-i (538–597) and his amanuensis Kuan-ting. The *Tz'u-ti ch'an-men* (Graduated Teaching of Meditation), *Mo-ho chih-kuan* (Great Concentration and Insight), and other shorter works by Chih-i constitute an encyclopedic repository of practical instructions and analyses regarding meditation. Although the T'ien-t'ai school suffered a temporary eclipse after the fall of Chih-i's patron Sui dynasty, his works in many ways represent both the font of knowledge and the springboard for the formation of Ch'an, both the wellspring from which Ch'an drew its sustenance and the template against which it rebelled.[7]

The complementary bracket to Chih-i's works is the *Tsu-t'ang chi* (Anthology of the Patriarchal Hall; hereafter *TTC*), the oldest of the mature and comprehensive "transmission of the lamp" texts to survive in complete form. Compiled in 952 by two obscure figures during the Five Dynasties period in what is now Fukien, the *TTC* survives only in a crude xylograph edition prepared as a supplement to the Korean canon. Organized according to the religious genealogy of Ch'an, the *TTC* traces the transmission of Ch'an from the Seven Buddhas of the past through a series of Indian and Chinese patriarchs and their successors, right down to earlier contemporaries of the compilers.

In contrast to the entries in the *HKSC* and *SKSC*, only rarely does the *TTC* attempt to create complete hagiographical portraits of its subjects. This is especially true for the more recent masters, for whom the legacy of earlier works is absent and about whom the editorial perspective of the compilers is most obvious; as in literary anthologies, only the most rudimentary of background information is given. The Ch'an masters included in the *TTC* are introduced primarily—it is almost fair to say solely—on the basis of their participation in memorable encounter-dialogue exchanges. In an editorial decision that was probably quite natural but extremely significant, it is left to the reader to visualize the contexts of those exchanges.[8]

Chih-i's works were in many ways the culmination of a long tradition of textual erudition and practical training. His synthesis is unique but could not have been accomplished without long years of study in the *Ta chih-tu lun* (Great Treatise on the Perfection of Wisdom; *Mahāprajñāpāramitopadeśa*) and training under the meditation master Hui-ssu. The *TTC*, in contrast, was but one of a long series of Ch'an "transmission of the lamp" texts, a genre that begins with two products of the Northern school in the second decade of the eighth century, climaxes with the appearance of the *Ching-te ch'uan-teng lu* (Records of the Transmission of the Lamp [Compiled during the] Ching-te [Period]; hereafter *CTL*) in 1004, and continues with a succession of works written during the Sung, Yüan, and Ming dynasties. The *TTC* is the oldest such text still extant to be so intensely devoted to the transcription of encounter dialogue.

The extreme contrast between the reference texts—namely, Chih-i's writings (chiefly the *Tz'u-ti ch'an-men* and the *Mo-ho chih-kuan*) and the *TTC*—is intentional; they have been chosen for heuristic purposes. My first task will be to summarize the salient characteristics of the approaches to spiritual training and of the path to liberation implicit in these texts, that is, the Chinese mārga paradigm implicit in Chih-i's writings and the encounter-dialogue model revealed in the *TTC*. For some aspects of encounter-dialogue practice I will refer to a seminal Ch'an text known as the *Pao-lin chuan* (Transmission from Pao-lin [ssu]; hereafter *PLC*), written in 801 C.E., which is the earliest extant product of the Hung-chou school of Ma-tsu. I will conclude with some general remarks on the historical and theoretical implications of the emergence of encounter dialogue, both in terms of the Buddhist tradition as a whole and for the role of Ch'an in the transformation of medieval Chinese society.

The Conception of the Path in the Meditation Manuals of Chih-i

Progressive and Hierarchical

The traditional paradigm implicitly predicated by the Ch'an school to pre- or non-Ch'an schools of traditional Chinese Buddhism was based on the Indian Mahāyāna conception of the mārga or spiritual path. This path is traversed by each sentient being from the initial moment of inspiration to achieve enlightenment on behalf of all other sentient beings *(bodhicitta)*, through potentially countless lives of spiritual discipline and compassionate service, to a theoretical culmination in the attainment of buddhahood. Indian texts—and their Chinese translations—define explicit stages along this path with great precision and detail; meditation practices are defined and assigned according to specific dispositional problems that occur at different stages, with the appropriate remedies assigned by a teacher who has progressed farther along the path than the student. The temporal extent of this paradigm can only be described as monumental and grandiose.

The first and most basic achievement of Chih-i and his master Hui-ssu in the field of meditation theory was the organization of the extensive variety of Buddhist meditation techniques into a rationalized system.[9] Chih-i's basic formulation of the "graduated meditation" *(chien-tz'u chih-kuan)* occurs in the *Tz'u-ti ch'an-men,* which was transcribed from lectures probably given around 571 at Wa-kuan ssu in Chin-ling.[10] Here occurs Chih-i's first formulation of what came to be called the twenty-five expedient means *(erh-shih-wu fang-pien),* which define the prerequisites of meditation practice. Even more important, this work contains the sequential explanation of the following list of techniques:

Four dhyānas *(ssu-ch'an)*
Four unlimited states of mind *(ssu wu-liang hsin)* or pure abodes (Skt. *brahma-vihāra*)
Four formless dhyānas *(ssu wu-se ting)*
Six wondrous teachings *(liu miao-men)*
Sixteen excellent dharmas *(shih-liu t'e-sheng fa)*
Three penetrative illuminations *(san t'ung-ming)*
Nine contemplations *(chiu hsiang)* of physical impurity
Eight remembrances *(pa nien)* of the Buddha, Dharma, Saṃgha, breathing, etc.
Ten contemplations *(shih hsiang)* of impermanence, suffering, the lack of a self, etc.
Eight renunciations *(pa pei-she),* more often known as the eight emancipations *(pa chieh-t'o)*
Eight excellences *(pa sheng-ch'u)* or distinctions in the treatment of craving by contemplating various aspects of form in this world
Ten totality-spheres *(shih i-ch'ieh ch'u)* of earth, water, fire, wind, etc.
Nine successive dhyānas *(chiu tz'u-ti ting),* the ability to pass through each stage of dhyāna without any extraneous intervening thoughts
Samādhi of the lion's charge *(shih-tzu fen-hsun san-mei),* which allows one to enter rapidly into an uninterrupted state of concentration
Samādhi of transcendence *(chao-yüeh san-mei),* the ability to proceed directly from normal consciousness to *nirodha-samāpatti* and back again without any intervening stages[11]

The order of the practices listed in the *Tz'u-ti ch'an-men* is derived in part from passages in the *Ta chih-tu lun* and, ultimately, the *Great Perfection of Wisdom Sūtra,* but the overall achievement is Chih-i's. The comprehensive approach taken by Chih-i in this work goes beyond a simple ranking of individual techniques, however. As Andō Toshio writes:

> [The *Tz'u-ti ch'an-men*] took a variety of Hīnayāna and Mahāyāna meditation techniques that had been given nothing more than a sequential ranking ever since the *Great Perfection of Wisdom Sūtra* and distinguished them on the basis of their being tainted or untainted, worldly in purpose or conducive to emancipation, and whether they emphasized phenomena or absolute principles, etc. [Chih-i] grasped the essential character of each prac-

> tice and validated the existence of every variety of meditation technique on the basis of research into a great number of Hīnayāna and Mahāyāna scriptures. On the basis of this, Hīnayāna meditation techniques were positively correlated with the Mahāyāna techniques. . . . Such a systematic classification of the graduated practice was truly unprecedented.[12]

Of course, the scope of Chih-i's work is such that no one practitioner could hope to master all the methods described. The important point is that Chih-i achieved a new synthesis of the Buddhist spiritual path, a schematization which suggests that any single meditation practice is part of a larger spiritual quest. This prioritization of meditation technique is similar in some ways to the "doctrinal taxonomies" *(p'an-chiao)* created by Chih-i and others. Although other masters might quibble over the details, Chih-i thus established the basic template of the Chinese mārga paradigm.

As defined by Chih-i, the spiritual path is inherently hierarchical, even cartographic, in its conception. Although not a pyramidal structure, it is highly segmented and articulated vertically, a detailed map of the pathway to emancipation. Paralleling the Indian understanding of this world as a realm of saṃsāra, this Chinese explication of the path explicitly categorizes the ranks of sentient beings, their innate abilities, their dispositional tendencies or problems, and the meditation techniques appropriate to their situations. Because one is always inferior to some others on the path, spiritual practice means following the guidance of one's superiors; and because these dispositional problems frequently, if not always, involve some function of ignorance, great importance is given to the teacher's instructions.[13]

Like the Indian conception of the path from which it is derived, Chih-i's formulation is based on a grandiose and abstract conception of time—grandiose, in that it assumes extraordinarily long periods of time for the cultivation of positive spiritual virtues, and abstract, in that this vast temporal span is not linked to any historical framework and its truths are applicable universally. Chih-i's path is necessarily progressive and intrinsically gradualistic. Students move gradually up a ladder of stages, a progressive structure that goes back to the stages of dhyāna in the primitive and sectarian periods of Indian Buddhism. Chih-i's meditation manuals discuss real developments, even if in the abstract, and assume the Buddhist notion of saṃsāra, the endless round of rebirth. Against this background the individual practitioner also becomes an abstract, almost hypothetical, agent.

Unipolar and Radial

Chih-i's greatest work on meditation, the *Mo-ho chih-kuan,* was recorded from lectures given at Yü-ch'üan ssu in Ching-chou in 594, just two and a half years before his death. Whereas the *Tz'u-ti ch'an-men* may be thought of as a self-study project undertaken after departing from Hui-ssu's side, the *Mo-ho chih-kuan* is much more intimately based on Chih-i's own religious experience—or at the very least on his later intellectual and spiritual development.

Chih-i's approach in the *Mo-ho chih-kuan* differs from that of the *Tzu-ti ch'an-men* in significant ways, although the same attention to comprehensive structure obtains. Practice of the "perfect and sudden meditation" *(yüan-tun chih-kuan)* explained within this work is organized into three stages:

1. The twenty-five expedient means, preparatory moral and procedural considerations drawn almost entirely from the *Tz'u-ti ch'an-men;*
2. The four types of samādhi, from which the practitioner selects the one most appropriate to his/her own needs and interests, as a more advanced but still preliminary stage;
3. The ten realms *(shih ching)* and ten modes of contemplation *(shih-sheng kuan-fa),* which alone constitute true contemplation.[14]

Even granting this overall structure, the most significant aspect of the *Mo-ho chih-kuan*'s system of perfect and sudden meditation is the allowance made for spontaneous, even instantaneous, freedom in the application of different meditation techniques.

Although in the *Tz'u-ti ch'an-men* Chih-i did not insist that practitioners master each of the listed techniques in serial order, the emphasis of that text was unmistakably on the overall contour of the spiritual agenda. In a text written slightly later, the *Liu miao-men* (Six Wondrous Teachings), Chih-i defines what is generally called the "indeterminate meditation" *(pu-ting chih-kuan).*[15] According to Chih-i, the practitioner can choose any technique at any given moment on the basis of individual needs and circumstances. Traditional meditation theory posited that certain techniques were appropriate responses to different problems, but never before, as far as I am aware, were the techniques to be chosen and applied in such an immediate, short-term framework. In addition, traditional meditation theory required that the student perform techniques chosen for him by an accomplished master, whereas in Chih-i's system this responsibility was shifted to the student.

In the *Mo-ho chih-kuan*'s explication of the perfect and sudden meditation, this allowance for momentary, instantaneous spontaneity in the application of different meditation techniques is incorporated into the very heart of the system. The beginning point of that system is contemplation of the first of the ten realms, the realm of cognitive reality or, more literally, the realm of the skandhas, *āyatanas,* and *dhātus (yin-ju-chieh ching).* This is nothing less than one's complete personal system of physical form, sensory capabilities, mental activities, and realms of sensory perception. This realm is present during every moment of contemplation—indeed, during every moment of sentient existence. Although the entire human cognitive apparatus is included in this category, Chih-i indicates that one's meditation should begin with concentration on the mind itself: "If you wish to practice contemplative investigation [of reality] you must cut off the source [of your illusions], just as in moxabustion therapy you must find the [appropriate physical] point."[16] The goal of this inspection of the mind is the comprehension of the first mode of contemplation, the contemplation of the inconceivable realm *(kuan pu-k'o-ssu-i ching)*.

Chih-i's elaborate explanation of the inconceivable realm is summarized by Leon Hurvitz; there is no need to expand on that summary here. What is significant at present is not Chih-i's description of the ultimate realization, but the substantial allowances he makes for those who do not achieve that realization immediately. Although the first of the ten realms is present in every moment of consciousness, the others occur adventitiously, based on the karmic propensities of the individual. In other words, the very effort of intense contemplation may agitate the *kleśas* (afflictions or illusions), generating various feelings and desires that would not occur during normal consciousness. Such agitation may lead to physical illness or to awareness of former events' karmic implications, both of which occurred during Hui-ssu's course of practice, or even to apparitions, both fearful and enticing, tempting the practitioner away from his practice, as supposedly happened to Chih-i.[17] Due to the practice of different states of dhyāna in previous lives, the practitioner may now experience any number of the concomitants of those states.

In other words, the latter nine realms are all manifestations of the impediments associated with meditation. They may occur in any order or combination and continue for any length of time. As they occur they are to be made objects of contemplation. Their nonarising would indicate the relative aptitude of the practitioner for the ultimate goal.

The ten modes of contemplation, in contrast, are a preconceived sequence of practices aimed at ensuring achievement of ultimate enlightenment. The goal of the entire system is success in the first mode, that of the contemplation of the inconceivable realm, but failing this at the outset, the practitioner is to avail himself of each successive mode until he achieves success. Thus he renews his dedication to the bodhisattva ideal, reposes his mind in the *dharmatā,* frees himself of attachments, distinguishes between that which hinders and that which aids his progress, and so on (these are a few of the ten modes), to the extent necessary and in the appropriate order.

The fundamental stance of the practitioner in this type of endeavor is one of autonomy and spontaneity: fixing his aspirations firmly on the highest goal, he draws from his broad knowledge of meditation techniques whatever means are appropriate to bring him nearer to success. As Kuan-ting writes in his introduction to the *Mo-ho chih-kuan:*

> In the Perfect and Sudden [Meditation], from the first one focuses *(yüan)* on the True Characteristic, the realms [all being] the Middle, there being nothing that is not True. One fixes one's focus on the *dharmadhātu;* one is completely mindful of the *dharmadhātu.* Of all the forms and fragrances (i.e., all reality) there is not a single bit that is not the Middle Path. One's own realm, the realms of the Buddhas, and the realms of sentient beings are also similarly [the Middle Path]. The skandhas and *āyatanas* are all "such-like" and without suffering that can be rejected. The illusions of ignorance are enlightenment and without any accumulation that can be eradicated. . . . Saṃsāra is nirvāṇa, with no extinction that can be realized. . . . The serenity of the *dharmatā (fa-hsing)* is called concentration *(chih, śamatha).* Serene yet permanently reflecting is called insight *(kuan, vipaśyanā).* Although the terms "beginning" and "later" are used there are no dualities, no distinctions. This is called the Perfect and Sudden Meditation *(yüan-tun chih-kuan).*[18]

There is an undeniably gradualistic cast to the design of the perfect and sudden meditation, in the self-evident sense that achievement of the goal requires the expenditure of effort in a prescribed set of contemplations. Nevertheless, the distinction between this and manifestly gradualistic systems such as that of the *Tz'u-ti ch'an-men* is clear: here one is not eradicating attachments, illusions, and the like in order to gain greater and greater individual perfection, but seeking for the one moment of realization that will obviate the entire framework of one's conceptualized ignorance. Hallucinations, recurrent swells of feeling, mental agitation, and so on are obstacles to success, but not in the sense that they must be eliminated or forcibly suppressed. Since one's illusions are fundamentally no different from enlightenment, they become objects of one's contemplation; one seeks to understand and not be unduly moved by them rather than to annihilate them.

What additional inferences can we now make about Chih-i's formulation of the path? First, there is a fundamental contradiction inherent in the concept of the gradual path: even though the overall process may be described as a progressive development, actual performance of the many exercises involved requires that the practitioner focus exclusively on the moment, the immediate present. This contradiction is, I believe, inherent in the earliest Indian formulations of the spiritual path, in which the stages of dhyāna are perceived as a vertical progression preparatory to but not sufficient for a lateral leap into a moment of prajñā. Of course, many Chinese were skeptical of the implicit requirement to continue spiritual training for lifetime after lifetime, and this awareness may have abetted Chih-i's description of the highest form of meditation as instantaneously malleable.

In addition, Chih-i's formulation of the path may harbor within its most basic structure an admission of its own inadequacy and a prescription for the articulation of an alternate paradigm. The wider implication of these qualifications is that, although the elaboration of the encounter model of spiritual training was a unique innovation of Chinese Ch'an, the very construction of earlier Buddhist models of the path virtually necessitated that some such dialectically superior paradigm be enunciated. Thus it is not merely adventitious that the sudden/gradual distinction arose in the Ch'an school, nor that that distinction embodied value-laden and polemic judgments similar to the Mahāyāna/Hīnayāna dichotomy. Such distinctions were inherent to the Buddhist conception of the path, at least as received in China, from its earliest stages.

Second, Chih-i's description of the perfect and sudden meditation highlights the peculiar role of the individual practitioner in his system. The focus of Chih-i's system was on spiritually gifted individuals. It was individual human beings, whether trainees, bhikṣus, bodhisattvas, or buddhas, who performed the practices necessary to propel them upward along the path.

I find it significant that these individual people are unnamed. The practitioner who navigates Chih-i's path is anonymous, and we never hear examples drawn from Chih-i's experience as a meditation instructor. The practitioner is a piece on the playing board, so to speak, who must make his or her own decisions on the basis of universal rules, rather than on inferences drawn from specific cases (as in the Indian literature) or through the contemplation of anecdotes intended not simply to instruct but to propel the listener or reader past the current obstacle (as in later Ch'an literature). Indeed, in Chih-i's system the present moment on which the practitioner is to concentrate is an abstraction constructed out of psychological categories and metaphysical principles. Judging in part from a draft paper by Daniel Stevenson, Chih-i's criticisms of contemporary meditation masters were largely based on their identification with individual approaches to meditation—that is, on their refusal to adopt a systematic approach to Buddhist meditation. He may also have resented them because they refused to subordinate their identities to the path as a whole, and thus become anonymous.

Perhaps it is only a result of the "dark age" that the T'ien-t'ai school entered after the fall of the Sui, but I get the impression that all the practitioners surrounding Chih-i were dressed in the invisible black of Nō stage assistants, like supporting characters attendant to the grand theater of his lectures. Indeed, his disciples are known chiefly for their service to him. Even the biography of the scribe Kuan-ting, who must have played a large role in the compilation and editing of Chih-i's writings, is largely unknown. The same situation prevails in Chih-i's theoretical descriptions of the path: the theoretician is glorified and the actual practitioner is reduced to a virtual cipher.

Third, implicit in the hierarchical structure and the focus on gifted if anonymous individual practitioners is the exaltation of the teacher or guru. In traditional meditation texts, the master is specifically given the responsibility for intuiting the student's dispositional tendencies and assigning the appropriate meditation technique or sequence of techniques.[19] Indian texts set out rules and guidelines for the master's input that make his role as instructor to students seem somewhat mechanical and automatic. Perhaps this is the source of Chih-i's tendency to deal with students' problems in the abstract: in traditional meditation theory, students have the autonomy to seek different teachers, but they themselves play only a secondary role in the cultural expression of the religion. To put it differently, practitioners are virtually invisible within the system until they achieve the status of master or teacher.

Of course, the master's training gives him special insight into Buddhist doctrine, and it is this facet of the Buddhist monk's identity that was most highly valued in the Chinese tradition. In China the teacher is often perceived as the great expounder, the theoretician, either delivering the authoritative interpretation of the text or generating brilliant theories for the consumption of lay and ordained followers.[20] These great teachers were, in effect, independent entities due to their perceived status as figures who towered over the rest of the religious community (this was, at least, a favored descriptive). Like lesser buddhas, they radiated their teachings outward and downward to their spiritual inferiors. There was competition among teachers for this role of ascendency and cooperation among those who recognized themselves to be at similar spiritual levels (usually considered out of humility to be uniformly low relative to the buddhas), but the radial and unipolar model held even in these situations.

Chih-i was, of course, the ultimate example of such an exalted teacher: his brilliance was transcribed in roll after roll of abstruse treatises and commentaries, he lectured to large audiences of monks and laypeople, and he ministered to princes and courtiers. Although his instructions on meditation are magnificent, it is simply not known how he taught his own students. Whereas traditional meditation texts place great emphasis on the role of the instructor in analyzing the student's temperament and assigning techniques to him, the role of the teacher is recognized but not emphasized so explicitly by Chih-i.

Mechanistic, Artisanal, and Elitist

I suspect that meditation practice in China prior to the advent of the Ch'an school was based primarily on the paradigm of Chih-i's graduated system. This is not to say that all meditators used his texts, nor that they restricted themselves to the techniques he described or the way he described them. Although his work was very influential, we have no means of tabulating the statistics that would be implied by such assertions. Rather, Chih-i's work was the dominant example of the kind of religious paradigm presupposed and superseded by the Ch'an school (according to its own perspective) in its creation of a "transmission outside the teachings."

In the most positive sense, meditation practice according to Chih-i's writings was the most subtle of crafts, a spiritual trade learned through self-effort by gifted students practicing predetermined techniques. But the mārga paradigm was so well elaborated in Indian texts that it often seemed to the Chinese to be mechanistic in its application and not a little overwhelming in its requirements. Authority was granted to the meditation instructor, but the relationship between instructor and trainee was mechanistic in that the master used preestablished rules to select among known meditation techniques on the basis of the student's dispositional problems. In Chinese biographies, however, individual masters appear devoted to a certain style or interpretation of religious practice. In cases where their training is described, the identities of their teachers is often unclear. And in accord with the invisibility of practitioners who are not (yet) teachers, in many cases their training is hardly mentioned and never described in any depth or detail. (In this the meditation master Seng-ch'ou [480–560] of the Northern Ch'i is much more representative than Chih-i.)[21]

As a spiritual craft, the practice of meditation as conceived by Chih-i was intrinsically elitist, being limited solely to the spiritually advanced. Essentially, it was open only to monks and others who had given up all family ties. This was in part due to the great dedication of time and energy involved, but it was also presumed that those with great moral impediments, such as a large store of negative karma from past lives, simply could not participate in the process described. Hence monks and the occasional layperson with the capacity for dedication to a long-term process of self-transformation were the intended audience of Chih-i's meditation texts.

The Encounter Paradigm as Manifested in the *Tsu-t'ang chi*

A Comprehensive, Reiterative Genealogical Structure

The *Tsu-t'ang chi (TTC)* was compiled in 952 by two students of Ching-hsiu Wen-t'eng, who provided a preface for the work. Although the two students are otherwise unknown, Wen-t'eng himself was the author of a series of verses for each of the Indian and Chinese patriarchs from

Kāśyapa to Hui-neng, and for a few other major figures up to Shih-t'ou and Ma-tsu. In addition to being incorporated into the *TTC,* Wen-t'eng's verses were discovered as a separate text among the finds from Tun-huang.[22] The *TTC* itself, though, does not occur at Tun-huang, nor was it widely circulated in China, where it seems to have merited only a reference or two in the annotation of Ch'an scholiasts. Fortunately, woodblocks for the text were carved in 1245 as a supplement to the Korean canon; since the text itself was not printed along with the canon, presumably due to its supplementary status, it was only in the twentieth century that the existence of the *TTC* became known.

Although the *TTC* is markedly different in character from the writings of T'ien-t'ai Chih-i, its high degree of structural integrity as a single text is at least as striking as the drive toward conceptual systematization apparent in Chih-i's writings. The *TTC* traces the "transmission of the lamp" of Buddhist enlightenment from the Seven Buddhas of the past through a series of Indian and Chinese patriarchs, thus connecting the historical present (i.e., tenth-century southeastern China) with its spiritual roots in a most comprehensive and compelling fashion. More specifically, the structure of the *TTC* is as follows:

1. The Seven Buddhas of the past: each buddha is identified by very brief name and family information, followed by a transmission verse for each (written by Wen-t'eng).
2. The historical Buddha: Śākyamuni receives a long entry, probably summarized from an earlier Ch'an text, the *Pao-lin chuan* (Transmission from Pao-lin [ssu], or *PLC*), but deriving from various canonical sources. The customary verse is included.
3. The twenty-eight Indian patriarchs from Kāśyapa to Bodhidharma: these sections are also drawn from the *PLC,* although they are abbreviated somewhat. Transmission verses are included.
4. The six Chinese patriarchs from Bodhidharma to Hui-neng: the verses for these patriarchs first appeared in the *Platform Sūtra.* (Bodhidharma receives only one *TTC* entry, of course.)
5. Eight generations of successors of Ch'ing-yüan Hsing-ssu through Shih-t'ou Hsi-ch'ien (700–790): this line of succession devolves to Hsüeh-feng I-ts'un and after him to Ching-hsiu Wen-t'eng; hence it is the lineage of the compilers of the *TTC.*
6. Seven generations of successors of Nan-yüeh Huai-jang through Ma-tsu Tao-i (709–788): this line of succession includes Lin-chi I-hsüan. The *TTC* adds transmission verses for several figures (in both this and the previous category) not included in Wen-t'eng's separate text.

As indicated by the references to the *PLC*—an extremely important work that will come up again later—the *TTC* was not the first text to utilize this comprehensive genealogical structure. Nor was the *TTC*'s version of the tradition history of Ch'an destined to become orthodox; this status was accorded the presentation found in the *CTL,* a text submitted to the imperial Sung court in 1004. The *TTC* is used here because it represents the earliest extant version of this comprehensive vision.

Whereas Chih-i's system involves a graduated set of practices set in a grandiose cosmological context, the structured nature of the *TTC* derives from a sequence of biographies, or at least biographical vignettes. This text was not written for practitioners who are conceived of as game pieces moving across a playing board and performing consciously selected sequences of spiritual exercises. In fact, the *TTC* may not have been written for living practitioners at all, for it describes a community of spiritual masters of the near and distant past. It was no doubt written for living aspirants to use as a guide to spiritual cultivation, but in form, at least—and this is an important qualification—the *TTC* is dedicated to the past. Here is a conception of time that is fundamentally different from that of the Indianesque framework of Chih-i's writings.

Yet it would not be fair to say that the *TTC* looks backward to the past. Rather, like many other works of Chinese literature, it acknowledges the supreme greatness of figures of antiquity. The Seven Buddhas of the past are concessions to the infinite regression of human history; the real beginning of this text (as, perhaps, of all Buddhist scriptures) is the historical Buddha Śākyamuni. The biography of Śākyamuni is the most complete hagiographical portrait in the *TTC,* and in many ways it is the root metaphor of the enlightened sage.

Although the Ch'an biography of the Buddha is an intriguing subject,[23] Śākyamuni represents only the beginning node of an interconnected chain of sages. By virtue of the transmission or certification of enlightenment that each patriarch bestows on his successor, each one of the subsequent Indian and Chinese sages is Śākyamuni's spiritual equal. This is a purportedly historical list, yet its impact is distinctly ahistorical: the transmission is perfect, each successor is the spiritual equivalent of his predecessor, and the distinctions of synchronic time are eliminated. Time is flattened into a single continuous, participatory moment—not a present moment, but a continuous expression of a golden moment of the past, whether from the hoary ancient age or from the poignant memory of one's recently departed master.

The primary feature of this temporal continuity is its participatory nature: to receive certification of enlightenment from a Ch'an master is to join the succession of patriarchs and enter into dynamic communion with the sages of ancient times. The primary goal of this training is not an exalted state of spiritual attainment but reenactment of the archetypal drama that takes place between each patriarch and his successor.

The "transmission of the mind with the mind" described in the anecdotes involving Hung-jen and Hui-neng, Bodhidharma and Hui-k'o, and eventually the historical Buddha and Mahākāśyapa, are scripts of the primal event in the Ch'an religious sensibility. This pristine moment of ancestral time was intended for repetition, over and over, within each teacher-and-student combination throughout the extended genealogy of Ch'an.

It was through the reenactment of this primal script that Ch'an derived its emphasis on sudden personal transformation: with the cast limited to teacher and student, there could be no in-between category of "almost-enlightened" or "rather like a master." One either belonged within the lineage of enlightened masters or one did not, and the religious transformation from one status to the other could only take place suddenly.

Bipolar and Collaborative

In encounter dialogue, the locus of spiritual practice shifted from the individual realm of yogic meditation exercises to the interpersonal interaction between master and student. Teachers sometimes wrote essays, poems, and gave sermons, but their primary source of identification lay in their interaction with students. It was impossible to express the truth in words radiated outward from a high seat in the lecture hall; rather, truth could be alluded to only in the spontaneous and natural activities of daily life. This critical importance of a teacher's ability to interact with students is a direct continuation of the emphasis on expedient means or salvific technique *(fang-pien,* Skt. *upāya)* in early Ch'an.

The cast of characters in the encounter-dialogue texts is essentially limited to master and students, and there is a remarkable degree of near-parity between these two statuses. I find it extremely significant that in this literature both masters and students are defined almost entirely through their mutual interaction. For example, although Ma-tsu is known for a few basic positions—"this mind is the Buddha" and "the ordinary mind is enlightenment"—the major emphasis is on the fact that he taught in the context of intimate interpersonal interaction. The very number of students, both named and anonymous, that appear in this literature, and the emphasis placed on the master's interaction with them, indicates a remarkable shift in Chinese Buddhist literature. In the theoretical works of previous centuries, a master's students were mentioned rarely, if at all, and then only as incipient exegetes, gifted translators, or future teachers whose presence proved the master's ability to attract followers.

In classical Ch'an texts, however, the gifted exegete or great theoretician is no longer the universal cynosure. Although it is still the master who is "on stage," he is depicted in terms not of doctrinal soliloquy but of his varied and creative responses—his mastery of *upāya*—in relation to a number of students. (A graphic example of this is the painting discussed by Robert Gimello in this volume, in which the Ch'an master Fa-hsiu appears with an anonymous lay student.) In other words, in Ch'an texts masters attain individual identity only through their group identity, that is, through their interaction with students and the rest of the Ch'an community.[24]

Unstructured and Creative

Encounter-dialogue anecdotes are presented as having been unrehearsed, and such exchanges are taken as the very nexus of spiritual cultivation. In the *TTC,* encounter-dialogue exchanges are sometimes preceded by a sermon or pronouncement of the master's; in many cases the student's inquiries are standardized. Nevertheless, and even though we can now posit rules to explain the master's strategic jumps, the dialogue itself proceeds in a spontaneous and unique fashion. There are no explicit rules that the student can follow.[25] Indeed, if the master detects any predication of logical structure (e.g., rules, preconceptions, or projections) on the part of the student, rejection is sure to follow. Any attempt by the student to impose logical structure on the dialogue is exploded by the master in a superior verbal parry or nonverbal thrust. Obviously, the most common type of logical structure students applied in their questions was that derived from the traditional conception of the Buddhist mārga.

It bears repeating that the locus of religious endeavor defined in these texts is not seated meditation practice, of whatever style, but engagement in encounter dialogue itself: it is in such exchanges that religious truth is to be found. The student is not allowed to rely on any explicit method or technique, including any form of meditation practice. The antiritualism of Ch'an toward traditional Buddhist activities is well known, but the most significant aspect of this was the school's iconoclasm toward meditative and contemplative exercises. It is virtually certain that such exercises continued to have wide currency, but they were removed from center stage. The impression given in the text—although it is an impression that probably would not have occurred to the actual participants in ninth- and tenth-century Ch'an training regimens, as opposed to the literary constructs who appear in the *TTC* itself—is that the locus of spiritual self-cultivation has shifted from the realm of private yogic endeavor to a more public realm of informal, interpersonal linguistic exchange.

Finally, the goal of spiritual endeavor had changed, perhaps irrevocably. Entering the confraternity of masters may have required a total and instantaneous transformation, but it did not require the laborious cleansing away of unwanted defilements. The prelude to the moment of transformation was a process not of self-improvement but of self-discovery: namely, recognition of one's own identity as a buddha or patriarch. This is graphically demonstrated by the internal structure of the *PLC*, in which each patriarchal successor is discovered by his predecessor but undergoes no training prior to his accession to the status of patriarch. In fact, the text does not contain a single description of the enlightenment experience of any of the Indian patriarchs.

The first patriarch whose enlightenment is described in the *PLC* is Hui-k'o, but even here the treatment is unusual. Before meeting his teacher Bodhidharma, Hui-k'o underwent an inner transformation that is depicted in amusingly physical terms: he experiences what is literally an exchange of skeletons prior to his encounter with Bodhidharma.[26] Thus to become a patriarch he had to be totally transformed. The suddenness of the encounter paradigm implies a transformation of self, awareness, or one's total being into a different mode of existence. As Robert Gimello has noted, sudden enlightenment was perceived as a transformation into a world totally different and absolutely separate from, but at the same time identical with, ordinary reality, yet immediately at hand.[27] This was a leap similar to that of prajñā, a lateral jump off the vertical ladder of the stages of dhyāna. In other words, the encounter model of Buddhist practice is intrinsically subitist. In addition, it makes no claims regarding the validity of saṃsāra as a description of sentient existence.

Conclusion

The Implications of Chronology

In this chapter I have described the T'ien-t'ai and Ch'an approaches to spiritual practice with a variety of terms, such as paradigms, models, and templates. Since this is a preliminary statement of findings that will change as my research continues, the reader is justified in considering the multiplicity of terms a function of the experimental nature of this paper. However, there is another more profound reason for the avoidance of a rigid terminology—namely, that the emergence of Ch'an was a complex process that should not be treated by the social and intellectual historian with artificially precise theoretical categories.[28]

To explain this dictum, let me briefly address the issue of the historical emergence of encounter dialogue itself. Earlier writers, including Professor Yanagida, have treated the existence of this unique form of spontaneous Ch'an dialogue as a given, with the explicit assertion that it emerged in conjunction with the Hung-chou school of Ma-tsu in the last part of the eighth century in south-central China.[29] It would seem, in fact, that singleminded devotion to encounter dialogue distinguishes the "classical Ch'an" of Ma-tsu from the "early Ch'an" of the Northern, early Southern, and Oxhead schools, the last of which was almost contemporaneous with the Hung-chou school. Indeed, the distinction between early and classical Ch'an, which I posed in an earlier article as the primary discontinuity in the development of Chinese Ch'an, was based on this identification of encounter dialogue with Ma-tsu's community.[30]

Although Robert Buswell recently made the very cogent suggestion that we identify early, middle, classical, and postclassical phases of Chinese Ch'an, the precise delineation of these stages is still subject to further consideration.[31] More important is the question of whether we can actually use the occurrence of encounter dialogue as a distinguishing characteristic of a specific chronological period. When did it emerge as the central style of Ch'an practice? Was there ever a period in which the primary activity of Ch'an students and masters was spontaneous religious dialogue, or is the image of such a period only an enabling myth generated by later generations of Ch'an devotees?

The orthodox texts of Ch'an would clearly have us believe that such a period did exist, and that it existed during the careers of Ma-tsu and his immediate students and successors. But examination of these sources indicates that none of the stories involved can be traced back earlier than the *TTC*. While some of the anecdotes seem quite obviously to be artificial reconstructions—for example, Huai-jang's mimicking the young Ma-tsu in meditation by trying to polish a piece of tile into a mirror—others carry a sense of vivid realism that makes us want to believe they really happened. However, we must not allow ourselves to be misled by this impression of credibility, which is an essential function of fictional writing.

Examination of the contemporary sources for Ma-tsu's Hung-chou school, which include a number of epitaphs and texts such as the *PLC*, supposedly from 801, and the *Ch'üan-hsin fa-yao* (Essential Teaching of the Transmission of Mind), from around 850, has led me to believe that the school did have a significant emphasis on oral practice, or at least oral instruction. But was the type of oral encounter emphasized the same as that evoked by the classical Ch'an encounter dialogue that appears in the *TTC* and later texts? At this point, I am uncertain. I suspect that all the famous stories we have about Ma-tsu and his students are later reconstructions rather than edited transcriptions of contemporary, first-person observer accounts. This is not to say that spontaneous dialogue did not occur, but that the examples we have of it are less journalistic reports than creative imitations.[32]

To support the assertion that encounter dialogue arose only with the Hung-chou school, it has usually been said that the absence of such material among the Ch'an literature discovered at Tun-huang shows a basic lack of conformity with early Ch'an. But although there was no encounter-dialogue material at Tun-huang, there were several Hung-chou school and later texts of the "classical" or "middle" periods. Significantly, the latest of these consists of Wen-t'eng's verses, which formed the backbone of the *TTC,* as mentioned earlier.[33]

Although further research is needed, the implication is clear: encounter dialogue was published for the first time in Chinese history with the *TTC.* No doubt there were private transcriptions circulating within the monastic community, but we know of nothing prior to this text, which was compiled more than 150 years after the death of Ma-tsu. Given this passage of time, the accounts that we have of Ma-tsu and his early generations of students must be edited reconstructions at the very least, rather than first-person accounts.

In the present context, we need not specify exactly when encounter dialogue came to dominate Chinese Ch'an. But notice that the question is not solely one of chronological obscurity. A larger issue is involved: the appearance of encounter-dialogue material in the *TTC* must be considered as a phenomenon of literary genre. We should think not only about masters and students of the late eighth and early ninth centuries engaging in spontaneous dialogue, but about their successors during the middle of the tenth century pondering the implications of the anecdotes of spiritual parry and riposte handed down from generations before.

The *TTC* was compiled during the relatively peaceful southeastern regime of Wu-Yüeh, and its very creation implies that its editors were on a mission to preserve a tradition that had become tenuous due to the difficult military and social conditions of the Five Dynasties period. If the urge to compose the text was essentially conservative, in the primary meaning of the term, then the attitude of the editors and their cohorts toward the patriarchs of earlier years was inherently retrospective. Whatever the facts of the eighth and ninth centuries, it was at the hands of these editors that the "golden age" of the T'ang Ch'an masters was created; it was from their text, and later ones like it, that students of Ch'an reenvisioned the wondrously enlightened actions of Bodhidharma, Hui-neng, and Ma-tsu. And it was in this process of creative visualization that the genealogical structure of the *TTC* is of absolutely fundamental significance.

The Attractions of Living in Ancestral Time

The masters and students of the postclassical Ch'an of the Five Dynasties and Sung periods read, pondered, discussed, and sermonized about the anecdotes contained in the *TTC,* and in so doing they defined both their own religious identities and the contour of their own spiritual endeavors. Meditating on the *hua-t'ou* or "critical phrase" *wu* (J. *mu*) according to the instructions of Ta-hui Tsung-kao (1089–1163) was not merely a psychological device, it was a method for visualizing oneself as a full-fledged member of the numinous world of the ancient patriarchs, a way of entering into dialogue with the patriarchs on their own terms, of entering a particular moment in ancestral time.

Why did Ch'an become so popular within Chinese Buddhism? No doubt there are many answers to this question, including the identity of the school as a movement of spiritual revitalization within Chinese Buddhism. However, I suggest that at least part of the reason is that its mode of practice and its entire self-understanding were inherently and intrinsically genealogical, in a way that echoed the extended family social structure and that mirrored some of the dominant concerns of post-T'ang Chinese society. This is not to say that the genealogical structure of Ch'an is intrinsically Chinese; as I have pointed out elsewhere, the nucleus of the transmission theory, whereby the true teachings of Buddhism are handed down from Śākyamuni Buddha through a succession of patriarchs, was brought into China by the Kashmiri masters who established the foundation of the meditation tradition in China.[34]

Roughly contemporaneous with the efflorescence of Ch'an was another movement in the Chinese intellectual world: the reclamation of the native civil tradition by a movement that began with the search for *ku-wen* (ancient texts)—a movement that later came to be called *tao-hsüeh* (study of the Way) or *li-hsüeh* (study of principle), and that is known in modern English writings as Neo-Confucianism. The de facto originator of this movement is thought to have been Han Yü (768–824), a scholar-official known both for his brilliant literary style and for his famous memorial attacking the worship of a relic of the Buddha. Han Yü's contemporaries did not share his xenophobic interest in reviving the Confucian tradition to the exclusion of Buddhism, but he became a cultural hero to Chinese literati during the Sung.

Although the group of thinkers now identified as Neo-Confucian did not go unchallenged during their own lifetimes, the dominant move during the Sung was to look back through Han Yü to the sages of the Chou dynasty and create a Confucian *tao-t'ung* (succession of the Way). This mirrored the Ch'an perspective, which looked back through the patriarchs of the T'ang to Śākyamuni.[35] In addition, most Sung literati held that the Way should be recovered by seeking within the ancient classics of the Chinese tradition to understand the principles known to the sages. Although it was generally recognized that the contemporary world was too complex to witness the perfect re-creation of ancient institutions, the golden age of the past and the wisdom of the ancient sages were to be used as models in reforming the present.[36]

If the Neo-Confucians and other Sung dynasty intellectuals were seeking to redress China's contemporary problems by returning to the rediscovered ideals of its past, postclassical Ch'an represents a more radical version of the same move. By meditating on famous anecdotes from Ch'an literature, Ch'an trainees were, in effect, visualizing the golden age of the T'ang, thus re-creating in their own minds the enlightened actions of the ancient sages and affecting the same style of intuitive repartee in their responses to their own living masters. What is more, masters such as Yüan-wu K'o-ch'in (1063–1135) and Ta-hui Tsung-kao effectively entered into dialogue with the ancient sages in their commentaries and sermons on Ch'an "public cases" *(kung-an,* J. *kōan).* The status of Ch'an master allowed one to communicate on an equal footing with the buddhas and patriarchs, so that time was flattened along the family tree of Ch'an in practice as well as in the organizational structure of the Ch'an legitimizing myth. Both Ch'an and Neo-Confucianism were innovatively conservative movements, in that they introduced new features to Chinese culture under the guise of re-creating a golden age of the past. Both monk and scholar idealized their respective forebears, but each wished to emulate rather than merely study them.

Elaboration of these very brief comments on the relationship between Ch'an and Neo-Confucianism will have to await another occasion; what is significant at present is that, for the Ch'an school, the imaginative re-creation of and communion with the past were not mere literary tropes but fundamental characteristics of Ch'an religious practice. It is thus no accident that Chinese texts do not talk openly about techniques of mental concentration, processes of spiritual growth, or dynamics of the experience of enlightenment. These subjects had already been covered in detail in the writings of Chih-i and others, and perhaps did not need repeating; there were also taboos against describing individual religious experience in ways that could be construed as self-aggrandizement. Nevertheless, I am convinced that if the members of the Ch'an movement had been more interested in exploring these areas they could have found ways to improve or expand on Chih-i and to avoid breaking the taboos.

Mārga and Encounter as Creative Bimodality

The very different proclivity of Ch'an—to the reproduction of almost endless quantities of encounter dialogue—suggests that the Chinese were intensely interested in exploring the new encounter paradigm, in deliberating over its famous cases in the meditation hall, and in emulating the style of untrammeled activity and discourse implicit in its famous exemplars. Does this mean that the mārga paradigm was completely discarded? I think not. The vitality of the originally Indian version of the spiritual path may have been mitigated through its reformulation by Chih-i and thoroughly undercut by Ch'an, but in the latter case the very dynamism of Ch'an spiritual practice depended on the contrast between the dualistic formulations of the student and the perfect spontaneity of the master. If there was a decline in the dynamism of Chinese Buddhism after the Sung, it may have occurred in part because the nature and quantity of new Buddhist translations completed during the Sung allowed the creative tension between the mārga and encounter paradigms to be lost.

It would be foolish to suggest, however, that the mārga approach to Buddhist spiritual practice disappeared from the Chinese world. It may be true that the impact of Indian Buddhism declined gradually from the mid-T'ang onward, but I suspect that Indian Buddhist conceptions were far more vital than has generally been thought to have been the case within the Chinese religious and intellectual life of the late T'ang, Five Dynasties, and Sung, and probably even later in Chinese history as well. Our task as historians of religion is to remain sensitive to the interplay between the two models. We may be inspired by Bernard Faure's very suggestive interpretation of Bodhidharma as only one element within a binominal religious and literary motif,[37] and we may take a cue from David Pollack's luminous if sometimes controversial work, *The Fracture of Meaning.* In a fashion similar to the interplay between foreign and native themes in Japanese culture, where China represented the richly complex versus the innocent simplicity of indigenous sensibilities, the mārga paradigm represented a logically ordered set of abstract priorities that was juxtaposed to the nondualistic illuminations of encounter dialogue.[38] That the former came to seem contrived and the latter natural is an indication of the dominant structure of later Chinese cosmology.

What are the ramifications of this development for our understanding of Buddhist soteriology in general? Grace Burford's discussion of the *Aṭṭhakavagga* implies that there may be very deep continuities between the Chinese case and the earliest Buddhist tradition. She describes two distinct approaches to Buddhism present in the *Aṭṭhakavagga*—one that encouraged the adoption of correct views *(diṭṭhi),* and another that suggested that only the absence of views was correct. When we consider the possible relationship between this set of approaches and the distinction between the mārga and encounter models in Ch'an, two separate questions arise.

First, is the Ch'an polarity of mārga/encounter a distant echo of the contradiction between right views and no views found in the *Aṭṭhakavagga?* Although the fully elaborated spiritual path is considerably more complex philosophically than the simple views discussed in the Pāli text, and although the encounter model of spiritual practice is considerably richer than the basic insight that one should be without views, the parallelism is there: to cultivate correct views is to engage in self-improvement, whereas to eliminate views is the sudden achievement of wisdom. In this sense, the congruence between Ch'an and the Indian tradition goes back not only to the *Aṭṭhakavagga,* but to the two traditions discussed by Alan Sponberg—the ecstatic, visionary perspective of the Upaniṣads and the enstatic, purificatory approach of the śrāmaṇa groups.[39]

In the Buddhist context, of course, these two traditions percolate out as the *śamatha* (concentration) and *vipaśyanā* (insight) branches of meditative endeavor. Even though the Indian conception of the path embraced both gradual and sudden, *śamatha* and *vipaśyanā,* in Ch'an the path is redefined as entirely gradualistic, entirely *śamatha.* Any gradual progress was but the cultivation of positive qualities, which, as shown in Collett Cox's chapter, was the preferred choice in the *Mahāvibhāṣa* system. It is thus possible to line up the different subtraditions of Buddhism according to how they treat the basic polarity between views or no views, *śamatha* or *vipaśyanā,* mārga or encounter; the delineation of precisely how these variants resemble, relate to, and differ from each other is an important task of future research.

Second, we might take a hint from the Chinese material and suggest that, no matter what set of alternatives is being considered, the relationship between the two is probably not so much one of absolute opposition as one of creative tension or mutual interrelation. For instance, is it possible that the two views apparent in the *Aṭṭhakavagga* were not independent viewpoints but different poles of a single continuum, or at least alternatives that constituted an interdependent pair? There does not seem to be any direct evidence of this in the text, and it would be difficult to find explicit, incontrovertible evidence that differing approaches to spiritual practice, when offered roughly simultaneously, necessarily represent pairs of alternatives operating as a single system. Nevertheless, this is an attractive interpretive perspective to which we must remain sensitive.

Within the Ch'an tradition, I am reminded of the introductory manual attributed to Hung-jen, the *Hsiu-hsin yao lun* (Treatise on the Essentials of Cultivating the Mind), which displays a palpable sensitivity in its simultaneous exhortations to vigorous practice and cautions against predicating enlightenment as a goal to be desired and achieved.[40] This same delicate touch is apparent in the Japanese *Zazen ron,* discussed in this volume by Carl Bielefeldt, which displays a delicate balance between zazen as a goal-oriented technique and as an expression of inherent buddhahood. Since the *Zazen ron* draws heavily on early Ch'an ideas, it is not surprising that it also records interest in two separate models of the religious life—one that suggests working to attain enlightenment, and another that advocates simply manifesting the enlightenment already inherent within.

In a similar fashion, Chinese texts from the late seventh and early eighth centuries seem to espouse two separate models of spiritual practice and enlightenment—one based on the doctrine of the buddha-nature obscured by ignorance (likened to the sun obscured by clouds), and the other based on the image of the mind of the sage reacting perfectly to the needs of sentient beings (depicted by the perfectly reflecting mirror).[41] As Gimello and Buswell suggest in their introduction to this volume, these are manifestations of Buddhism's maintenance of a vital balance between the apophatic thrust of the doctrine of śūnyatā and the theoretical implications of mārga. By restraining the urge to reify or routinize practice, the doctrine of śūnyatā mitigated spiritual enervation and the decay of mārga.

Thus for Chinese Buddhism to have sustained two different models of spiritual practice is consonant with the Buddhist tradition as a whole. Of course, the specific nature of that pair of models, not merely the paradigm of encounter dialogue but the antinomy between the mārga and encounter models, evolved within the context of the Chinese historical and cultural situation. Hence it is entirely valid to consider the parallels between the mārga/encounter opposition and themes native to Chinese culture, such as the different views of human nature in Chou dynasty Confucianism, the contrast between Taoist naturalism and Confucian moral training, and the differing approaches to self-cultivation in Sung and Ming dynasty Neo-Confucianism.

However, in at least two respects the mārga/encounter polarity seems unique. First, the encounter paradigm is based on an iconoclastic rejection of the very notion of mārga itself. Although such antinomian tendencies may be latent in other subtraditions of Buddhism, one suspects that the Ch'an example is the most pronounced. Second, the encounter paradigm involves an image of human interaction that derives jointly from Indian and Chinese sources. Not only did the genealogical model of the "transmission of the lamp" theory grow out of a coincidence of Indian and Chinese ideas, but the dialogic style of discourse used in Ch'an literature derived from a combination of Indian logical dilemmas and stylistic tendencies going back as far as the Chinese classics.

Notes

This paper was prepared while I was a postdoctoral fellow at the John King Fairbank Center for East Asian Research, with financial support from both the Fairbank Center and the American Council of Learned Societies. In addition to the participants at the UCLA conference on Buddhist soteriology, large measures of gratitude are due to Professors Masatoshi Nagatomi of Harvard University and Robert M. Gimello of the University of Arizona, both of whom made insightful suggestions on earlier drafts.

1. The term "encounter dialogue" is used to render *kien mondō,* as in "The Development of the 'Recorded Sayings' Texts of the Chinese Ch'an School,"

trans. from Yanagida Seizan, "Zenshū goroku no keisei," in Whalen Lai and Lewis R. Lancaster, eds., *Early Ch'an in China and Tibet,* Berkeley Buddhist Studies, no. 5 (Berkeley, Calif.: Lancaster-Miller Press, 1983), 185–205. The basic components of the corresponding Chinese, *chi-yüan wen-ta,* are attested, but the phrase is not widespread. The term *"wen-ta"* ("questions and answers," or simply "dialogues"), is quite general and may refer to any text with a question-and-answer structure.

2. Other than virtually any of the works of D. T. Suzuki, the most convenient source for examples of encounter dialogue is probably Chung-yuan Chang, *The Original Teachings of Ch'an Buddhism: Selected from the Transmission of the Lamp* (New York: Pantheon Books, 1969; rpt. New York: Grove Press, 1982).

3. See Suzuki Tetsuo, *Tō Godai no Zenshū—Konan Kōsei hen—,* Gakujutsu sōsho • Zen Bukkyō (Tokyo: Daitō shuppan sha, 1984), 112–138, 359.

4. See John R. McRae, *The Northern School and the Formation of Early Ch'an Buddhism,* Studies in East Asian Buddhism, no. 3 (Honolulu: University of Hawaii Press, 1986), 91–97.

5. Yanagida Seizan, *Shoki Zenshū shisho no kenkyū* (Kyoto: Hōzōkan, 1967).

6. There was a steady increase in the percentage of meditation specialists in successive "Biographies of Eminent Monks" texts, i.e., the *Kao-seng chuan* of 518, the *HKSC* of 645/667, and the *SKSC* of 967. As compiled by Mizuno Kōgen, only 16+ percent of the subjects were listed as meditators or thaumaturges (the power for whose feats came through meditation) in the first of these texts, whereas successive versions had 45+ and 36+ percent. The last figure may actually be adjusted to some 60–70 percent due to the suffusion of meditation specialists throughout the other categories. Mizuno suggests that the ultimate prevalence of meditation in Chinese Buddhism resembled that in primitive Indian Buddhism, where only certain monks were listed as especially proficient in meditation but all were well versed in it. See Mizuno Kōgen, "Zenshū seiritsu izen no Shina no zenjō shisōshi josetsu," *Komazawa Daigaku kenkyū kiyō* 15 (March 1957): 17–18. I would note that the increased number of figures bearing the title "Ch'an master" and identified within Ch'an genealogies does not immediately imply an increased devotion to the practice of meditation per se, but rather the greater currency of Ch'an as an ideology of religious identity.

7. The discussion of Chih-i's writings here is distantly based on work included in my doctoral dissertation, *The Northern School of Chinese Ch'an Buddhism* (Yale, 1983), 51–76.

8. The *TTC* is a quintessentially "hot" medium, as the term is defined in the dialogue surrounding the classic work by Herbert Marshall McLuhan and Quentin Fiore, *The Medium Is the Massage* (New York: Random House, 1967). That is, it provides only the bare narrative thread, forcing the reader to imagine the background information. This is in contrast to "cool" media (such as television), which supply enough information to supplant the process of creative imagination.

9. Hui-ssu's own curriculum of training seems to have paralleled a later T'ien-t'ai scheme of four types of meditation, and it is probable that he also initiated the process of rationalization that culminated in Chih-i's system of the graduated meditation *(chien-tz'u chih-kuan).* This inference is based on Chih-i's heavy dependence on the *Ta chih-tu lun* in explicating this graduated meditation, this being a text he studied under Hui-ssu. Unfortunately, there is very little direct evidence with which to gauge the extent of Hui-ssu's contribution, so for the purposes of this discussion I consider only the most relevent themes of T'ien-t'ai meditation theory, which become manifest in Chih-i's writings.

10. The *Tz'u-ti ch'an-men* is Chih-i's most important early work; there are a number of abstracts or commentaries based on it compiled by Chih-i and/or Kuan-ting. I have used an abbreviated title for this work, which occurs at *T* 46.475a–548c. For an analysis of its background and importance, including its relationship to other T'ien-t'ai texts, see Satō Tetsuei, *Tendai daishi no kenkyū—Chigi no chosaku ni kansuru kisoteki kenkyū*—(Kyoto: Hyakkaon, 1961), 103–127. For a discussion of the origins and date of this text, see Takahashi Shūei, "Dai ikkai Kinryō dendō jidai ni okeru Tendai daishi no kōsetsu ni tsuite—toku ni *Shidai zemmon* o chūshin to shite—, *Komazawa Daigaku Daigakuin Bukkyōgaku kenkyūkai nempō* 5 (June 1971): 125–126. Chan-jan's date for the compilation of this work is given in Ono Gemmyō, *Bussho kaisetsu daijiten,* 13 vols. (Tokyo: Daitō shuppan sha, 1933), 5:21a.

11. The four dhyānas, the four unlimited states of mind, and the four formless dhyānas are discussed at length in Paravahera Vajirañāna Mahāthera, *Buddhist Meditation in Theory and Practice: A General Exposition According to the Pāli Canon of the Theravāda School* (Colombo, Sri Lanka: M. D. Gunasena, 1962), 35–42, 263–317, 332–340. For a shorter explanation, see Stephen Beyer, "The Doctrine of Meditation in the Hīnayāna," in Charles Prebish, ed., *Buddhism: A Modern Perspective* (University Park: Pennsylvania State University Press, 1975), 138–139, 142–144. The six wondrous teachings refer to stages in the practice of meditation on breathing. The three penetrative illuminations refer to the four dhyānas, four formless dhyānas, and the attainment of extinction *(nirodha-samāpatti),* so named because they lead to the three illuminations *(ming)* into past, future, and the exhaustion of the defilements, as well as the six penetrations or supernatural powers *(t'ung* or *shen-t'ung,* Skt. *abhijna).* See Nakamura Hajime, *Bukkyōgo daijiten,* 2 vols. (Tokyo: Tōkyō shoseki, 1975), 2:972d. For the nine contemplations, eight remembrances, ten contemplations, eight renunciations, and eight excellences, see Mochizuki Shinkō, *Mochizuki Bukkyō daijiten,* 10 vols. (Tokyo: Sekai seiten kankō kyōkai, 1933–1936), 1:678b–79a, 5:4223a–c, 3:2284c–85b, 5:4206b–207b, 5:4213c–14b. For the totality-spheres, see Vajirañāna, *Buddhist Meditation,* pp. 139–165, and *Mochizuki* 3:2374a–75b. For the nine successive dhyānas, samādhi of the lion's charge, and the samādhi of transcendence, see ibid., 1:664c–65a, 2:1788a–c, and Nakamura, *Bukkyōgo,* 2:965c.

12. Andō Toshio, *Tendaigaku—kompon shisō to sono tenkai*—(Kyoto: Heirakuji shoten, 1968), 430.

13. Exceptions are lives of solitary practice or singleminded dedication to an ideal, such as the forbearance of suffering, that a practitioner may choose to emphasize for a particular lifetime. Such lifetimes are conceived of as individual steps along the path. A somewhat related exception must be made for the case of Mahāyāna texts that posit a single key to the entire panoply of Buddhist practices, such as the perfection of wisdom or the *śūraṁgamasamādhi.*

14. See Leon Hurvitz, "Chih-i (538–597): An Introduction to the Life and Ideas of a Chinese Buddhist Monk," *Mélanges chinois et bouddhiques* 12 (1960–1962): 318–331.

15. This text occurs at *T* 46.549a–55c under the title *Liu miao-fa men.* (The three-character title is apparently older.) See Satō, *Tendai daishi,* pp. 151–172; Andō, *Tendaigaku,* pp. 438–462; and Mochizuki, *Mochizuki,* 6:5077b–58a. Andō, *Tendaigaku,* pp. 434–436, discusses the status of this work as a forerunner to the *Mo-ho chih-kuan.*

16. *T* 46.52a–b, as quoted in Andō, *Tendaigaku,* p. 219.

17. See *T* 50.563a for the events cited for Hui-ssu.

18. *T* 46.1c–2a, quoted in Mochizuki, *Mochizuki,* 1:311c–12a. The "accumulation" of illusions and its eradication refers to the four noble truths.

19. This paradigm was described in detail in Chinese texts derived from the Kashmiri meditation tradition, e.g., Kumārajīva's *Tso-ch'an san-mei ching* (Scripture of Seated Meditation and Samādhi).

20. The theories proposed by these theoreticians are often very long on abstraction, categorization, and hierarchical evaluation, as is shown by the popularity of the *p'an-chiao* tradition of classifying Buddhist doctrines according to a systematic ranking of theoretical and heuristic principles.

21. See McRae, *Northern School of Chinese Ch'an,* pp. 31–50.

22. This is the *Ch'üan-chou Ch'ien-fo hsin-chu chu tsu-shih sung (i-chuan),* Stein 1635 or *T* 85.1320c–1322c.

23. My analysis of Śākyamuni's biography in the *TTC* is still not complete, but suffice it to say that the text explicitly cites a large number of early Chinese sources here. Presumably, this is drawn from the *PLC,* although the *TTC* does omit the *Sūtra in Forty-two Sections,* used in the *PLC* as the Buddha's "recorded sayings." See Yanagida Seizan, "Zen no Butsuden" (The Ch'an Biography of the Buddha) *IBK* 13, no. 1 (25; January 1965): 124–128.

24. Eventually, of course, the proliferation of Ch'an led to a very hierarchical arrangement of encounter-dialogue material according to generations and lineages. This may be viewed as a natural function of the institutionalization of the original charisma of early Ch'an, although hierarchy may also be inherent to the act of textual re-creation.

25. Encounter-dialogue exchanges may be analyzable into more or less regular patterns that were internalized by their participants, but the lack of explicit rules remains a relative distinction made in comparison with other forms of Buddhist spiritual endeavor. I refer to the notable efforts by William Frederick Powell, *The Record of Tung-Shan: An Analysis of Pedagogic Style in Ch'an Buddhism* (Ph.D. diss., University of California, Berkeley; Ann Arbor, Mich.: University Microfilms, 1983), and Alan Sponberg, "Puttin' the Jump on the Master: Nāgārjuna and the Tactics of Emptiness in Ch'an Encounter Dialogue" (unpub. draft, 1987).

26. Similar skeletal exchanges are noted in shamanic religions. See Mircea Eliade, *Shamanism: Archaic Techniques of Ecstasy,* trans. Willard R. Trask, Bollingen Series, no. 76 (Princeton, N.J.: Princeton University Press, 1964), 57.

27. I am recalling oral comments made at the Kuroda Institute conference on sudden and gradual approaches to enlightenment in Chinese Buddhism, held in Los Angeles, March 1982. For a more detailed and somewhat different statement, see Luis O. Gómez, "Purifying Gold: The Metaphor of Effort and Intuition in Buddhist Thought and Practice," in Peter N. Gregory, ed., *Sudden and Gradual Approaches to Enlightenment in Chinese Thought,* Studies in East Asian Buddhism, no. 5 (Honolulu: University of Hawaii Press, 1987), 67–71, 131–135.

28. In addition to Robert Gimello's lament, made in his role as respondent to an earlier reading of this paper, that the Kuhnian terminology of "paradigm shift" has been used ad nauseum and with insufficient discrimination in the humanities and social sciences, my criticism of the oversimplifications and distortions implicit in Hu Shih's work on Ch'an has rendered me more sensitive to the problems implicit in gross periodization schemata. Hu Shih's dichotomy between gradual/Indian/complex and subitist/Chinese/simple resembles that between the mārga and encounter paradigms, and the problems inherent in the former may thus apply to the latter. Although I believe the latter comparison to be more sophisticated and of greater analytical utility, the potential for error remains.

29. See Yanagida Seizan, "Goroku no rekishi" (The History of Recorded Sayings) *Tōhō gakuhō Kyōto* 57 (March 1985): 211–663, esp. 453–454.

30. See John R. McRae, "The Ox-head School of Chinese Buddhism: From Early Ch'an to the Golden Age," in Robert M. Gimello and Peter N. Gregory, eds., *Studies in Ch'an and Hua-yen,* Studies in East Asian Buddhism, no. 1 (Honolulu: University of Hawaii Press, 1983), 169–253.

31. See Robert E. Buswell, Jr., "The 'Short-cut' Approach of *K'an-hua* Meditation: The Evolution of a Practical Subitism in Chinese Ch'an Buddhism," in Gregory, ed., *Sudden and Gradual,* 321–377.

32. It is clear from Northern school texts that Chinese meditation masters had long emphasized spontaneous interaction as a means of both understanding and teaching their students. Hung-jen (600–674), remembered posthumously as the fifth patriarch of Ch'an, seems to have been adept at this, and his important but soon-forgotten student Fa-ju (638–689) certainly was. Northern school texts include quite a few "questions about things" *(chih-shih wen-i)* that masters posed to students, although the responses are not given, and there are other citations in eighth-century texts suggesting that Ch'an involved a unique and recognized form of teaching. See McRae, *Northern School and Formation,* 91–97.

33. See note 22 above.

34. See the conclusion to John R. McRae, "The Legend of Hui-neng and the Mandate of Heaven," *Fo Kuang Shan Report of International Conference on Ch'an Buddhism* (Kao-hsiung, Taiwan: Fo Kuang Publisher, 1990), 69–82. For the passage on which the comments in the article just cited are based, see idem, *Northern School and Formation,* 80–82.

35. Actually, the term *"tao-t'ung"* was used by Han Yü. Charles Hartman, *Han Yü and the T'ang Search for Unity* (Princeton, N.J.: Princeton University Press, 1986), 160, notes that "although there can be no doubt that the idea of transmission lineages in the Chinese scholarly tradition dates from at least the Han Dynasty and probably before, Ch'en Yin-k'o has suggested that Han Yü derived his concept of the *tao-t'ung* from the more immediate example of the Ch'an practice of the 'transmission of the dharma' *(ch'üan-fa).*" Hartman is citing an article by Ch'en called "Lun Han Yü" (1954), 105–106; the article is reprinted in *Ch'en Yin-k'o hsien-sheng lun-wen chi* 2:589–600. A recent and as yet unpublished manuscript by Peter Bol of Harvard University suggests that the concept of the *tao-t'ung* is also indebted to that of political succession *(cheng-t'ung).*

36. This summary is necessarily brief and overly general. In fact, the intellectual world of the Northern and Southern Sung, not to mention the Chin (which was contemporaneous with the latter), was complex and multivalent. To cite only the broadest of major currents, Sung dynasty intellectuals disagreed on whether the Way was real and universal, being transparently expressed by the sages through language and ritual (this was Ou-yang Hsiu's position), or whether it was an understanding or interpretation by the sages of the patterns of human affairs (Chu Hsi's position). They also disagreed on whether one could achieve wisdom by exploring the world on one's own and relying on the natural ability of the mind (the position taken by Ch'eng I), or whether one had to probe the ancient classics of the Chinese tradition to understand the principles known to the sages (Chu Hsi's interpretation). The latter, more absolutist position is that taken by Neo-Confucianism; the former, more epistemological one is that of Ou-yang Hsiu and others. Although still highly speculative at this point, it is possible to correlate the two major streams of Sung dynasty Ch'an practice with these differing currents within the civil Chinese tradition. Ch'eng

I's reliance on the natural ability of the mind resembles the "silent illumination" *(mo-chao)* approach to Ch'an meditation, while Chu Hsi's access to the Way through the mediation of the Confucian classics parallels the "observing the critical phrase" *(k'an-hua)* style of Ch'an. In this summary I am paraphrasing the formulation of Peter Bol, as expressed in several private conversations and stated during the Chinese religions workshop at Harvard, April 1988. In addition, I have referred to Bol's presentation at the Harvard Buddhist Studies Forum of February 1988, "Ch'eng Yi was not a Confucian"; I responded to these remarks with "And so the Ch'an monks weren't Buddhists?"

37. See Bernard Faure, "Bodhidharma as Textual and Religious Paradigm," *History of Religions* 25, no. 3 (February 1986): 187–198.

38. David Pollack, *The Fracture of Meaning: Japan's Synthesis of China from the Eighth through the Eighteenth Centuries* (Princeton, N.J.: Princeton University Press, 1986). For an extremely critical review of this book, see Naoki Sakai, "Modernity and Its Critique: The Problem of Universalism and Particularism," in Masao Miyoshi and H. D. Herootunian, eds., *Postmodernism and Japan,* a special issue of *South Atlantic Quarterly* (1988): 475–504, esp. 481–487. The reader should also consult Pollack's rejoinder, in his "Modernism Minceur, or Is Japan Postmodern?" *Monumenta Nipponica* 44-1 (Spring 1989): 75–97, esp. 83–86.

39. This discussion occurred in a paper Alan Sponberg presented at the Buddhist soteriology conference held at UCLA in June 1988 but not submitted for inclusion in this volume.

40. See McRae, *Northern School and Formation,* 136–138.

41. Ibid., 132–136, and 144–147, where I discuss these two models as complementary but separate "conceptual matrixes" of early Ch'an thought.

Glossary

Andō Toshio 安藤俊雄
chao-yüeh san-mei 超越三昧
cheng-t'ung 政統
Chiang-hsi nan-tao 江西南道
chien-tz'u chih-kuan 漸次止觀
chih 止
Chih-i (see T'ien-t'ai Chih-i)
chih-shih wen-i 指事問義
Ching-chou 荊州
Ching-hsiu Wen-t'eng 浄修文僜
Ching-te ch'uan-teng lu 景德伝灯録
Ch'ing-yüan Hsing-ssu 青原行思
chiu hsiang 九想
chiu tz'u-ti ting 九次第定
chi-yüan wen-ta 機緣問答
Ch'üan-chou Ch'ien-fo hsin-chu chu tsu-shih sung i-chuan 泉州千仏新著諸祖師頌一巻
ch'uan-fa 伝法
Ch'uan-hsin fa-yao 伝心法要
erh-shih-wu fang-pien 二十五方便
fa-hsing 法性
fang-pien 方便
Han Yü 韓愈
Hsiu-hsin yao lun 修心要論
Hsü kao-seng chuan 続高僧伝
Huai-jang 懷讓
hua-t'ou 話頭
Hui-k'o 慧可
Hui-neng 慧能
Hui-ssu 慧思
Hung-chou 洪州
Hung-jen 弘忍
k'an-hua 看話
kien mondō (see chi-yüan wen-ta)
kōan (see kung-an)
kuan 觀
kuan pu-k'o-ssu-i ching 觀不可思議境
Kuan-ting 灌頂
kung-an 公案
ku-wen 古文
li-hsüeh 理学
Lin-chi I-hsüan 臨済義玄
Liu miao-fa men 六妙法門

Liu miao-men 六妙門
Ma-tsu Tao-i 馬祖道一
ming 明
mo-chao 黙照
Mo-ho chih-kuan 摩訶止觀
mu (see wu)
pa chieh-t'o 八解脱
Pai-chang 百丈
p'an-chiao 判教
pa nien 八念
Pao-lin chuan 宝林伝
pa pei-she 八背捨
pa sheng-ch'u 八勝処
pu-ting chih-kuan 不定止觀
san t'ung-ming 三通明
Seng-ch'ou 僧稠
shen-t'ung 神通
shih ching 十境
shih hsiang 十想
shih i-ch'ieh ch'u 十一切処
shih-liu t'e-sheng fa 十六特勝法
shih-sheng kuan-fa 十乗觀法
Shih-t'ou Hsi-ch'ien 石頭希遷
shih-tzu fen-hsun san-mei 獅子奮迅三昧
ssu-ch'an 四禅
ssu wu-liang hsin 四無量心
ssu wu-se ting 四無色定
Sung kao-seng chuan 宋高僧伝
Ta chih-tu lun 大智度論
Ta-hui Tsung-kao 大慧宗杲
Tao-hsin 道信
Tao-hsüan 道宣
tao-hsüeh 道学
tao-t'ung 道統
T'ien-t'ai Chih-i 天台智顗
Tsan-ning 賛寧
Tso-ch'an san-mei ching 坐禅三昧経
Tsu-t'ang chi 祖堂集
t'ung 通
Tz'u-ti ch'an-men 次第禅門
wen-ta 問答
Wen-t'eng (see Ching-hsiu Wen-t'eng)
wu 無
Yanagida Seizan 柳田聖山
yin-ju-chieh ching 陰入界境
yüan 縁
yüan-tun chih-kuan 圓頓止觀
Yüan-wu K'o-ch'in 圓悟克勤
Yü-ch'üan ssu 玉泉寺
Zazen ron 坐禅論

Mārga and Culture: Learning, Letters, and Liberation in Northern Sung Ch'an

ROBERT M. GIMELLO

Introduction: Mārga and History

The concept of "the path," and any soteriology consisting principally in designs of the path, would seem to be inherently and by definition systematic. All paths, in at least an elementary sense, have "steps," and where there are steps there must also be direction, sequence, coherence, continuity, priority, posteriority, and so on. Now Buddhism is, par excellence, a religion of "the path." It is surely not the only such, but it may well be the one among the world's major religions of which consistent and pervasive concern with "the path" can be said to be most characteristic. And more often than not Buddhism has treated its notions of the path—the topic of mārga—in a decidedly systematic manner. Thus, as several of the other chapters in this volume demonstrate, Buddhists have tended to focus on the necessary rather than the contingent properties of mārga, on its inner structure, on the complex relations among its many parts, on its intrinsic efficacies—in short, on its systematicity. It is therefore neither surprising nor inappropriate that most modern scholarship on the Buddhist concept of mārga should focus on these same features.

However, we must remember that the topic of mārga also has important historical dimensions. No matter what may be learned from careful study of the ideal and normative descriptions of the path to liberation that Buddhists have so variously and intricately constructed, and regardless of how profitable investigation of the inner logic of such descriptions may be, if we cannot also learn something of the actual implementation of the schemes so described—if we have no access to their manifestations in particular times and places or to their real employment in the lives of particular men and women in specific cultures, and especially if we can know nothing of their relationships to other ranges and patterns of human action—then we may lose sight of the fact that mārga is not only a convenient frame for posing interesting theoretical problems but also, and most importantly, a prescription for life. There are questions, in other words, that we might too easily neglect if we were to ignore the issue of how mārga actually was, so as to be able more singlemindedly to consider the issue of how it should or must be.

Among such questions—more often implied than asked outright, and then in tones suggesting suspicion or incredulity—are these: Were the exquisitely complex and meticulously sequential regimens of spiritual practice that are so characteristic of Buddhism ever actually followed, and were they based on real experimentation, or were they only creations of an imagination working assiduously to deny, conceal, or tame the relentlessly refractory and finally unchartable territory of religious experience? And if they were ever actually employed, did they work? And if they did work (i.e., if they did really effect certain kinds of experiential change in those who followed them), were they simply self-fulfilling prophecies, predictable mechanisms which induced just those experiential consequences that their own inner structures and operations prefigured, or did they somehow engender genuinely unconditioned change of the kind Buddhism finally promises?[1]

Of course, consideration of mārga in history does not guarantee answers to such basic questions. One must even acknowledge that at the purely theoretical level it cannot do so; it is the philosophical, not the historical, perspective that holds ultimate judgmental authority in such matters. Nevertheless, attention to the historicity of mārga—to mārga as *parole* rather than *langue,* as performance rather than competence—may lend urgency and specificity to such questions. Moreover, it is usually history, rather than the normative structures of prescriptive texts, that prompts the asking of such questions. This it does by sowing seeds of curiosity or suspicion. I have especially in mind certain of those frequent episodes in the history of Buddhism when practitioners themselves noted sharp disparities between the texts they read and the times in which they lived, between the apparent orderliness or implied predictability of the formal procedures of religious life they strove to follow and the all too common disorder, frustration, or doubt they actually experienced in the effort.

On such occasions, Buddhist history often reveals, the practitioner finds that one must deliberately relinquish any mārga that is understood as normative or prescriptive, must cease to depend on such presumptively efficacious instrumentation, and must surrender to the immediacy and unpredictability of contingent experience, or to the power of "other," perhaps transcendent factors beyond his or her deliberate control. To be sure, the theoretical literature on mārga itself tells us that disengagement *from* mārga as formal and artificial procedure is in the end a paradoxical requirement *of* mārga, but the point of that paradox is lost, or becomes innocuous, if one accepts it too quickly. To grasp the full measure of its consequence, we must move from the realm of assured efficacy, normative theory, and systematic praxis into the realm of contingency. Such a move takes us inevitably into history (the proper domain of the contingent), and it is there that we find the Buddhist tradition itself calling mārga into question in ways that are sure to sharpen our efforts to assess the theoretical claims made for mārga's efficacy and relevance to real life.

What follows, then, is an exercise in the historical study of Buddhist mārga and Buddhism's mārga-based soteriology—an approach distinct from the textual, systematic, or philosophical investigation of the same. By "history" we mean not only a diachronic tracing of the internal evolution of Buddhist ideas and practices but also (and chiefly) a sustained investigation of the synchronic, multivalent, and densely circumstantial connections between Buddhism and the other values and events that comprise the full life experiences of particular Buddhists. Focusing on a particular period in the history of Chinese Buddhism, we shall consider a particular constellation of controversies carried on among certain Buddhists who displayed rather high levels of historical consciousness and who were explicitly concerned more with the historical ramifications of the issues involved (i.e., their relevance to the immediate historical situation) than with their purely theoretical or systematic implications.

The central questions under discussion were two, and yet inseparable. First, which (if any) of the components of the larger Buddhist tradition are to be classified as mārga, in the sense of being deemed necessary and sufficient unto liberation, and which may be regarded as extraneous, dispensable, or even deleterious? Second, how (if at all) may mārga be integrated into the general structures of value and action that make up a society; or to what extent (if at all) may mārga be understood to encompass the larger patterns of private and public practice that comprise a whole culture? These questions, I believe, are telling. The importunate way in which they were posed and answered by particular persons in particular historical situations reveals something more about mārga than is disclosed in any prescriptive statement thereof—this despite, or perhaps because of, the way in which the untidy particularity and unruly contingency of history and biography always resist neat, balanced, and rigorously consistent exposition as resolutely as they resist final closure.

Ch'an Buddhism and the Question of the Value of Tradition: The Pertinacity of Mārga

Perhaps there is no feature of Ch'an Buddhism better known, or more commonly regarded as definitive, than its claim to be "a special transmission outside of the theoretical teachings, which does not establish or depend upon words and letters" *(chiao-wai pieh-ch'uan/pu-li wen-tzu).*[2] Not so well appreciated, however, are the many different interpretations to which this self-characterization has been subjected over the course of Ch'an history. Nor are we sufficiently aware of how frequently it has incited serious controversy within Ch'an as well as between Ch'an and other traditions, both Buddhist and non-Buddhist.

One implication of this customary self-definition, according to at least one strain of interpretation, bears directly on the general subject of this volume: namely, the notion that Ch'an simply rejects traditional Buddhist notions of mārga. If Ch'an eschews all verbal and conceptual formulations of truth in favor of direct, unmediated experience, and if it thereby stands apart from the rich textual and doctrinal heritage of the rest of Buddhism, claiming not to need it, then the elaborate formulations of the path that fill the libraries of Buddhism—including both the diverse and intricate "technologies" of cultivation accumulated over centuries and the theoretical implications thereof codified in subtle systems of doctrine—are all to be denied or at least devalued. They are at best distractions or burdens, and at worst actual barriers or traps. This implies that Buddhism is really not a matter of path, direction, sequential progress, and so forth—really not, therefore, a matter of mārga at all. It suggests that the true Buddhist *sōtērion* is simply not amenable to "soteriology."

Clearly, this is an extreme interpretation of the character of Ch'an, a radical reading of its self-characterization.[3] Nevertheless, it is one that has been taken literally and radically several times in the course of Ch'an history, and we should not render it insipid by hasty and anodyne judgments that its intention was merely rhetorical. On those occasions when it was, or was seen to be, literally promulgated, this interpretation usually prompted conservative reaction in the form of pleas for moderation and balance, praise for the abundance of spiritual resources preserved in the broader Buddhist heritage, and warnings that heedlessness of that heritage was both foolish and dangerous for practitioners of Ch'an. The danger lay, it was said, in failure to understand just how difficult it is to find—and, once one has found it, how difficult it is to face—the terrible "truth of things as they really are" without the canny guidance and wise support of tradition. The folly consisted in not realizing how very easy it is, without such guidance and support, to become disoriented and so to stumble into bogus forms of spirituality like quietism or antinomianism. This conservative reaction led either to an outright rejection of the idea that Ch'an was singular and autonomous, or to the more moderate argument that Ch'an's apparently subversive posture is actually an attack not on tradition itself but only on the ossification of tradition that comes from slavish dependence on it. In contrast, those practitioners of Ch'an who persisted in asserting its singularity and autonomy were wont to retort that the scriptural and doctrinal tradition of Buddhism, like its vast repertoire of profound symbols and subtle techniques, is more likely to prove an affliction than a guide or a support; that its very richness and diversity can stultify; and that it is too susceptible to abuse as a false surrogate for true self-discovery or as a refuge from the rigors of genuine and immediate religious experience.

When the proponents of a radical and anti-mārga Ch'an felt it necessary (oddly enough) to offer theoretical justification for their position, they usually had recourse to the deep resonance of the doctrine of emptiness that is audible in any form of Buddhism if one but listens for it. The original Buddhist discovery of the emptiness of all things was a kind of doctrinal "Big Bang," the cognitive "radiation" from which has always been and still is coursing through the Buddhist universe like a low-frequency basal pulse. The more radical Ch'an Buddhists were therefore always able to cite the anomic implications of emptiness—the way emptiness dissolves the world of orderly progression and reveals it to be "like a mirage"—as a compelling reason to call the path into question.[4] Thus they could hark back, for example, to Ch'an's *"Urtext,"* the *Er-ju ssu-hsing lun* (Treatise on the Two Entrances and the Four Practices), and note that, according to that virtually scriptural authority, those who were capable of the superior "entrance of principle" *(li-ju)* thereby transcended all duality, even that of effort and goal or cause and effect, to realize that there is nothing to be attained, no difference between worldling and sage, no distinction between progress and non-progress, and thus no reason for an effortful path.[5] Their more conservative opponents, in turn, could draw on the various "non-emptiness" *(aśūnyatā)* strains of Mahāyāna (e.g., the manifold Tathāgatagarbha tradition, or Hua-yen, or T'ien-t'ai) to justify their position that there is indeed an efficacious path that can be relied on to lead to the goal of liberating realization, and that this path is effectively salvific precisely because it is empowered by the prior presence of buddhahood even in the imperfect realm of effort and practice.[6]

The argument, of course, was old even when Ch'an was young, and it would persist. Its persistence requires that we take it seriously. Although there were sincerity and goodwill to be found on each side, there was also, often enough, an absence of both. In any case, it does not suffice to say, as many have, that each side had a portion of the truth, that each argued against a mere caricature of the other's position, that one side spoke from an absolute perspective while the other adopted a relative point of view,[7] or that in the end Ch'an surmounted the controversy by finding a sane and sensible middle way between the two extremes. The issues were too urgent and deep for such facile resolution, and the tension between conflicting views of those issues was never really relaxed, but kept reappearing in various guises and in ever-narrowing frames of dispute. Thus, even among Ch'an traditions that were more or less in agreement on the question of Ch'an's "separateness" from the rest of Buddhism (scholastic doctrine, scripture, etc.), conflicts repeatedly erupted between two kinds of Ch'an. On the one hand, there were those who seemed to retain confidence in the mārga-like utility of particular devices—uniquely Ch'an devices like *k'an-hua* (inspecting the *hua-t'ou* [caption] or *kung-an* [precedent, J. *kōan*])—employed in a deliberately dynamic practice. Ch'an practitioners of this sort believed that such tecniques helped precipitate a distinct and unconditioned liberating experience *(wu, satori)* essential to final liberation. On the other hand, there were those who criticized all reliance on external, makeshift devices. They believed that such contrivances necessarily implied duality, and insofar as they felt it essential to deny all dualistic distinctions—including those between soteriological means and soteriological end—they declared null any notion of a distinct liberating experience to which any formulae of practice could lead.

This latter tack led to the claim that liberation does not follow from, but simply consists in, a life of assiduous practice understood as its own end. But those who made this claim were accused by their opponents of having sunk into mere routine, doltish passivity, or sheer inertia of spirit.[8] Further, even among advocates of *k'an-hua* Ch'an, and thus in still narrower polemical contexts, the same tension could reemerge in the form of distinctions between the proper use of *kung-an* as "living words" *(huo-chü)* and their abuse as "dead words" *(ssu-chü)*,[9] or between those whose *kung-an* practice was still at the reputedly elementary stage of "investigating the intention" *(ts'an-i)* of the *hua-t'ou* and those who had gone beyond such meditative conceptualizing to the purportedly metaconceptual "investigation of the word" *(ts'an-chü)* itself.[10] Perhaps the best known of these intramural arguments among various radical and moderate versions of Ch'an are the many changes rung on the difference between subitism and gradualism, a distinction which could further ramify in such a way that, among subitists (and everyone considered himself a subitist), there could be those who spoke only of sudden enlightenment, followed or preceded by gradual practice, and those who spoke of practice itself as sudden.[11]

Finally, this tension could appear in the most narrow and specific polemical contexts of all, that is to say, in the context of ambivalence or vacillation in the life of a particular individual. Thus we have the famous story (perhaps only a legend) about Ta-hui, foremost advocate of *k'an-hua* Ch'an, who is said to have grown concerned late in life that the *kung-an,* created originally as dynamic alternatives to routinized mārga schemes, were themselves succumbing to routinization and becoming mere literary distractions from true practice. This concern took the dramatic form of his burning the printing blocks of his revered teacher's famous *kung-an* collection.[12] So it goes. The tension between Ch'an as an utterly singular *(tan)* spirituality quite divorced from conventional Buddhist notions of the path and Ch'an as a vehicle for that path's concentration, amplification, and perfection—between, as it were, the revolutionary and conservative, or the "Protestant" and "Catholic" impulses in Ch'an—was irrepressible. In whatever guise and at whichever level it operated, it continued to enliven the Ch'an tradition and propel it through history.

Nevertheless, it is important to recognize that today we know one side of this story, one vector of this tension, far better than we know the other. The romanticized vision of Ch'an as a renegade school of Buddhism—that is, its common depiction as a subversion of mārga, as an abrogation of doctrine and theory, and as a renunciation of Buddhist learning—is quite familiar to us. But Ch'an as the conscientious husbander of a commodious Buddhist orthodoxy, as the reverent guardian of learned tradition, and as the generous sponsor of ever more expansive and accommodating designs of the path—this we find strange and tend to doubt. Yet this side of the story is available for the telling, particularly when we venture beyond later (often Japanese) reconstructions of earlier Ch'an history, and when we are willing to draw not only on the Buddhist historiographical tradition but also on secular literary, historical, and philosophical sources, thus placing Ch'an in its "Chinese" as well as its "Buddhist" contexts.

Throughout Ch'an history there have been periods in which committed Ch'an practitioners—some recoiling from real or perceived spasms of Ch'an antinomianism, others moved by impatience with the recurrent stagnation of Ch'an quietism, still others distressed by attacks on Ch'an from non-Buddhist quarters—have reasserted the claim that Ch'an, for all its singularity, is nonetheless Buddhist. Thus, it was said, Ch'an practitioners need not feel or cultivate any alienation from their Buddhist heritage but rather should fully avail themselves of it, for what is genuinely distinctive about Ch'an is not its simple rejection of traditional Buddhist text, doctrine, and path but its intensification, enhancement, and experiential fulfillment of the orthodoxy conveyed therein.

The Northern Sung was one such period. I would argue that the strains of Ch'an predominant during the eleventh and early twelfth centuries in one way or another rejected extreme or literalist interpretations of the standard Ch'an self-image as "a special transmission outside the theoretical teachings"; instead, they vigorously advocated the systematic integration of traditional or orthodox Buddhist doctrine and practice into a mature, self-confident Ch'an. This advocacy included frequent and eloquent reiteration of the older calls to "unify Ch'an and the teachings" *(Ch'an-chiao ho-i)* or to "practice Ch'an upon the foundation of the teachings" *(chieh-chiao hsi-Ch'an).* But it did not simply repeat such recommendations; it also proceeded in new directions. It led, for example, to a renaissance of scriptural study in Ch'an circles, a development not unrelated to the appearance of printed editions of the canon and to the general explosion of education and erudition throughout Sung culture. It coincided with a period of growth and vitality in Ch'an's institutional life, reflected in the many large, populous monasteries of Northern Sung China and in the apparent rigor of their conformity to traditional monastic codes.[13] It also fostered a keen and prolific interest in the history of Buddhism. This last was most evident in the publication of numerous chronicles, hagiographical compendia, and so on, but it was also manifest in the careful attention paid to the hundreds of "old cases" *(ku-tse*—that is, the *kung-an)* drawn from the relatively new historical genre of "discourse records" *(yü-lu)* and made to comprise the even newer genre of *kung-an* anthologies. Perhaps most significantly, what I would call the conservative impulse in Ch'an generated a deep concern with continuity of lineage, i.e., with a sense of master-disciple descent by which contemporary Ch'an practitioners could assure themselves of access to, and continuing connection with, Buddhism's nourishing past.

All this was done, I would suggest, in the unspoken name of just those values which we conventionally associate with mārga. It was done for the purpose of ensuring coherence, tenor, and efficacious order in the spiritual lives of individuals and communities. Moreover, although none of the traditional schemes of Buddhist mārga (like those developed on foundations of Abhidharma, Yogācāra, T'ien-t'ai, etc.) was preserved intact in Sung Ch'an, new mārga strategies and techniques were created, most notably those based on *kung-an* meditation. These, as we will see, are no less forms of mārga for being unconventional, oblique, elusive, or less than obviously systematic.[14] They may, in fact, be essentially the old versions of mārga in new, creatively "vernacular" modes of expression—novel forms that reflect not obliviousness of the old Ch'an problematic of mārga, but only a tendency ceaselessly to renew it.

The conservative impulse in Ch'an, which I hope to show was notably strong during the Northern Sung, thus deserves more attention than it has been given either traditionally or of late. But that attention ought not to be restricted to a rehearsal of all the old Buddhist formulas of argument. The Sung expression of this little-known mode of Ch'an was as much a phenomenon of Sung cultural history as it was a reflex of themes internal to Buddhism. It occurred not only within the walls of Ch'an monasteries, nor only in the course of intimate conversations between Ch'an master and Ch'an student, nor only in the arcane pages of exclusively Buddhist literature. The Northern Sung was a period when Buddhism, true to the implications of Mahāyāna's distinctive acceptance of the secular world, and emboldened by its previous accomplishment of considerable feats of sinicization, could venture outside the monastery and take its public place in the larger world. The era's major monasteries were not forbidden cloisters but grand and open public institutions. The leading Ch'an figures of the day enjoyed eminence not only within clerical circles but also at court and among the secular elite generally. Both Buddhist images and Buddhist concepts and values abounded as never before in Sung art and literature. And much of the teaching of Buddhist monks was directed toward the laity rather than toward fellow monastics alone.[15]

As Ch'an monks during the Northern Sung pondered questions of Ch'an's continuity or discontinuity with the rest of Buddhism, and as they weighed the corollary questions of mārga and soteriology, they did so not only under the influence of earlier Ch'an and Buddhist reflection on these topics but also with attention to the concerns of the wider secular culture of which they were now an integral part. This proved to be a very consequential broadening of perspective. It meant that controversial issues like those sketched above could no longer be adjudicated according to exclusively contemplative or clerical criteria. Because Ch'an had chosen to speak to laymen as well as to monks, it had to speak to the problems that concerned laymen—problems of education, aesthetics, literary theory, public morality, politics, civil service examinations, bureaucracy, economics, even foreign relations. Having entered so wide an arena, Ch'an monks had to attend to the traditions of discourse that were customary there. Confucianism, for example, could no longer be kept at arm's length as mere *wai-hsüeh* (extrinsic, worldly learning); nor was it likely to be, as more Ch'an monks came to number among their closest friends and dearest students scholars and bureaucrats steeped in the revived and once again vigorous Confucian heritage. Thus we find Confucian terms and concepts occurring more and more frequently in Ch'an discourse and, by the same token, Ch'an discourse focused more often on traditional Confucian issues. In other words, the things that the literati took seriously Ch'an teachers also were required, and indeed inclined, to take seriously.

Of course, this does not mean that Ch'an simply sloughed off its Buddhist identity and capitulated to secular culture; rather, it brought to its lively engagement with that culture the uncompromising and often critical values of Buddhism. In the frequent conversation or correspondence between eminent monks and eminent statesmen, for example, the role of the Ch'an interlocutor was usually to remind the layman of the transience of the world in which he lived and of the insubstantiality of the goals for which he strove. Drawing on the resources of Buddhist psychology, the monk might alert the layman to the subtle ways in which the latter's passions and false discriminations could vitiate even his most well-intentioned efforts to fulfill his worldly responsibilities. In a more philosophical vein, he could draw attention to how even those things which might seem entirely objective and material are actually inextricable from one's own mind. Most important, he often urged his lay associate to consider that there must be some purpose or meaning to life beyond anything the world itself could offer. There is ample literary evidence that the Ch'an masters' teachings on such matters were effective and that many of the most prominent literati of the time were moved to serious reflection on Buddhist themes—not a few were, in one sense or another, actually converted to the Buddhist worldview.[16]

Nevertheless, the dialogue with the laity and with secular culture proceeded in both directions. Although Ch'an did not forfeit its character as a Buddhist tradition and continued to bring to bear on worldly matters the otherworldly or transcendental *(ch'u-shih-chien, lokottara)* perspective of Buddhism, the Ch'an teacher could no longer address questions of religious moment without at least tacitly considering their secular implications, their relevance to the experience of living men and women both in and out of the monastery, and their bearing on analogous issues raised in non-Buddhist intellectual and religious traditions. This inevitably affected (as, indeed, Buddhist principles of accommodation would allow it to affect) the answers Ch'an teachers could give to religious questions.

What I wish most to argue here is that questions of mārga and soteriology were prominent among the issues affected by Ch'an's participation in secular culture, and that the overriding consequence was the stimulation or support that participation gave to the conservative impulse in Ch'an. Ch'an's newfound worldly responsibilities and affinities served, I believe, to impede or abate its old centrifugal and radically anti-mārga tendencies. They strengthened, instead, its ties to its own larger heritage—to the codes of orderly religious and moral practice that made up the mārga portion of that heritage, and to a "broad church" vision of a Buddhism that was not restricted to small, elite groups of monastic illuminati but could accommodate persons of all capacities from all walks of life. They induced, one might say, a kind of Ch'an sobriety and moderation.

There is a term used in some traditions of Northern Sung Ch'an which I believe captures the character of this sober Ch'an conservatism better than any other, even though it was a focus of controversy in its own day and acquired over the centuries largely negative connotations. That term is "Wen-tzu Ch'an." Although this is often translated as "literary Ch'an," and so conveys the derogatory sense in which it was used by critics, I prefer the implicitly more affirmative translation, "lettered Ch'an." The latter is truer to the intention of those who employed, and perhaps coined, the term to distinguish their Ch'an, which encouraged the combination of spiritual discipline with literacy and learning, from the illiterate or anti-intellectual Ch'an that they despised as mere posturing.[17] "Wen-tzu Ch'an," therefore, was an inherently polemical term. Like the contemporary and similarly controversial phrase "Tao-hsüeh," it was used by some to disparage, by others to praise and inspire.[18]

During the Sung, the phrase "Wen-tzu Ch'an" had at least two orders of reference. First, it was a purely Buddhist shibboleth. In the immediate context of Ch'an's internal polemic, it stood in deliberate contrast to the older phrase *"pu-li wen-tzu."* For those who advocated "lettered Ch'an" (and I repeat that it was they who coined the term), it announced rather boldly, almost as if issuing a challenge, the decision to annul or at least seriously to qualify the conventional divorce of Ch'an from scriptural and doctrinal Buddhism. For the opponents of "lettered Ch'an," the same phrase had chiefly derogatory connotations and labeled an ersatz, merely "literary" Ch'an whose practitioners had allowed themselves to become entangled in the web of words.

But internal Buddhist polemic was not the only context in which the phrase "Wen-tzu Ch'an" had special significance. It also spoke to, and resonated with, certain dominant themes in the broader secular culture of the Northern Sung. In addition to its Buddhist associations, it had non-Buddhist implications that no Sung intellectual could have missed. Outside of Buddhism per se, but not at too great a distance therefrom, the Northern Sung witnessed a vigorous debate between two factions of the Confucian revival that was then in full spate. On the one hand, there were the advocates of "Tao-hsüeh" (study of the Way), those whom we in the modern West know best under the imperfect label, "Neo-Confucians." The Ch'eng brothers (especially Ch'eng I), their teachers (men like Chang Tsai and Chou Tun-i), their disciples (men like Hsieh Liang-tso and Yang Shih), and an appreciable but still relatively small number of their contemporaries were convinced that the Tao could be truly apprehended only directly, immediately, and introspectively. Only by concentrating on the innately available Tao—that is, only by attending to the fixed and universal moral principles *(li)* that were believed naturally to inhere in one's nature and mind as the very immanence of Tao—could one hope to achieve individual and communal realization of Heaven's Way. The goal was not just to study the literary and other artifacts created long ago by "the sages" of the past, but to become a sage oneself, here and now.

It is not surprising that these men, though they were all eminently learned and accomplished authors, should have been deeply suspicious of cumulative learning, and especially of literary pursuits. They believed that such undertakings were too likely to trivialize the intellectual life, to deflect from experiential "study" of the Way and from the all-important concentration on ethical endeavor, and to lead to mere polymathy and literary refinement for their own sakes. They also felt that literary pursuits could too easily become obsessive or self-serving preoccupations that would sap and waste one's moral and intellectual strength. Such fears, they believed, had already been borne out—for example, by the past and present literary corruption of the civil-service examination system, the consequences of which affected the whole nation. To be sure, the proponents of Tao-hsüeh made no Ch'an-like disavowal of all learning, nor were they inclined, after their unhappy experience with radical reform, to overhaul the examination system. Rather, they resorted to a retrenchment of the legitimate field of learning, which they strove to restrict to the classics and a few approved commentaries thereon. The other and vaster territories of traditional learning, together with literary creativity as something valuable in itself, they declared illegitimate.[19]

Ranged against the advocates of direct access to the Tao were the proponents of "Wen-hsüeh" (cultural or literary learning), a phrase quite different from "Tao-hsüeh" in connotation as well as denotation. These culturally more conservative literati were led by men like Su Shih and his disciples, who gloried in the abundance of culture afforded them by the Sung renaissance and who believed that access to the Tao is possible only through the diverse and cumulative mediation of culture. For them it was "only" by way of poetry, prose, calligraphy, painting, music, antiquarianism—together with appreciation and cultivation of the mysterious capacity for personal creativity and aesthetic sensibility from which such things flow—that the Tao might be perceived and realized. What they required was sustained and reverent attention to the diverse particularity of history and literary tradition as preserved in books and other cultural media, along with nurture of that intuitive creativity by which one might participate in the further growth of culture. Direct apprehension of the universal principles of the Tao, without the mediation of culture, was seen as a chimera.

Significantly, Wen-hsüeh advocates of such a cultural and especially literary path to realization of the Tao held that theirs was a responsible and realistic "gradual" approach. Advocates of Tao-hsüeh, they averred, were both irresponsible and mistaken in proposing a "sudden" or immediate apprehension of Tao. It is ironic that Su-shih, despite his generally favorable attitude toward Buddhism, could seize upon this alleged subitism of the harshly anti-Buddhist Tao-hsüeh partisans and use it as a cudgel against them, claiming that the "new learning" of Tao-hsüeh was to be avoided because, in its distrust and dismissal of culture and claim of direct access to the Tao, it was too much like Buddhism and Taoism![20]

We are, of course, tempted by the question of whether the Ch'an problematic of Wen-tzu Ch'an versus Ch'an as *pu-li wen-tzu* engendered or was engendered by the Confucian problematic of Wen-hsüeh versus Tao-hsüeh. Especially tempting is the prospect of arguing that the former was the case. However, as neither hypothesis is amenable to proof or disproof, we will simply note the indisputable fact that the two controversies influenced each other. They were carried out at the same time and obviously within earshot of each other, and there is a rhetorical similarity between them—an overlap of usage, rationale, and polemical strategy—that cannot be discounted as mere coincidence.[21] Thus, for every warning from a Ch'eng I that "literary endeavors" *(tso-wen)* can "harm the Tao" *(hai-tao)* if they consist only in "working away at chapter and verse *(chüan-wu chang-chü)* to delight the eyes and ears of others,"[22] one can cite an analogous warning from a Ch'an monk. Ta-hui, for example, said:

> Mental cultivation [lit., "mind craft"] is the root *(hsin-shu shih pen),* whereas literary composition and learning are the branches *(wen-chang hsüeh-wen shih mo);* yet contemporary scholars often discard the root to pursue the branch as they "search out passages and pick phrases," vying with each other in the study of flowery words and clever remarks.[23]

Just as Ta-hui often warned his lay students against wasting their minds in secular literary pursuits, so he frequently warned his fellow monks that they must "escape the dark caverns of vehicles and doctrines," cease "groping about in the vacuousness" of texts, and understand that words and letters are at best "like fingers pointing at the moon."[24] Apropos of Ch'an in particular, Ta-hui was quick to condemn the specious profundity of a certain kind of pretentiously discursive Ch'an, which he was distressed to believe was common in his day and in which he found true Ch'an practice replaced by mere rote intonation of deep-sounding Buddhist catchphrases. This he attacked as "mystagoguery" *(t'an-hsüan shuo-miao).*[25] But all this is relatively well known; what of the other side of each of these mutually analogous arguments?

It appears that the Ch'an monasteries of the Northern Sung, as well as the era's Confucian academies, harbored both "foxes" and "hedgehogs."[26] The "foxes" knew, and believed it necessary to know, "many things." They were concerned to exploit all the resources bequeathed to them by their respective traditions, despite their variety, and were loathe to reduce those traditions to single, unitary principles. The "hedgehogs," in contrast, knew, and felt it necessary to know, only "one great thing." Accordingly, they were little interested in, and often quite contemptuous of, anything other than that "one thing" which they held to be the key to all. It has been the "hedgehogs" of both traditions who have gotten the lion's share of attention throughout later history. Thus we know much more today about the singleminded monism of Tao-hsüeh[27] than we know about the ample pluralism of Wen-hsüeh, and more about the exclusivist, univocal Ch'an that rejects "words and phrases" than about the polyphonic, accommodating tradition known as "lettered Ch'an."[28] This has had the general effect of constricting our vision of Sung intellectual and religious history, and the particular effect of skewing our understanding of the relationship between Ch'an and mārga.

A Picture of Ambivalence: Fa-hsiu and the Place of Ch'an in the Religious and Secular Culture of Northern Sung China

Reproduced in Figure 1 is a hanging scroll dubiously attributed to the great Yüan dynasty painter Chao Meng-fu (1254–1322) and entitled *Hsi-yüan ya-chi t'u* (Elegant Gathering in the Western Garden). This is said to be Chao's pastiche—one of many done over the course of centuries by a variety of painters, both famous and anonymous—of an earlier work by the same title. The original, which seems not to have survived, was credited to the greatest of Northern Sung figure painters, Li Kung-lin (1049–1106), and was believed to have been done, as were most later renditions of the scene, in Li's characteristic "literati" *(wen-jen)* manner, a deliberately archaic and rather austere monochrome outline style known as *pai-miao* (lit., "plain sketch").[29] Scholars today doubt that Li Kung-lin painted the original version of this scene. Rather, they postulate an anonymous painter of the early Southern Sung as its inaugural creator, and assume that either that painter or his literary contemporaries found it useful to attribute the work to the great Northern Sung master, perhaps as an act of homage.

Whatever its prototype may actually have been, the purported Chao Meng-fu "copy," like the many later renditions of the same classic scene, has long been held to depict a gathering of sixteen eminent men of letters, artists, and statesmen of the Northern Sung. Their garden party is believed to have occurred in 1087, in Kaifeng, on the grounds of the estate of Prince Wang Shen (b. 1036, d. after 1089). Wang was a well-known painter in his own right, as well as a poet and patron related by marriage to the imperial family; he was son-in-law to Ying-tsung (r. 1063–1067), and thus also brother-in-law to Shen-tsung (r. 1067–1085) and an uncle of sorts to the young Che-tsung (r. 1085–1100).[30] According to a famous description of the scene questionably attributed to the artist and critic Mi Fu (1051–1107),[31] the guests were as follows: Shown in the lower foreground, seated at a table and absorbed in poetic composition and/or calligraphy, is the most distinguished member of the group, Su Shih (1037–1101).[32] At the same table are his host, Wang Shen, and two of his students, Ts'ai Chao[33] and Li Chih-i.[34] In the middle ground is Li Kung-lin himself, shown in the act of painting his famous illustration of T'ao Yüan-ming's *Kuei-ch'ü-lai tzu* (Homecoming). Among those clustered about Li, watching him, are Su Shih's brother Su Ch'e (1039–1112)[35] and the poet Huang T'ing-chien (1045–1105).[36] Above and behind them are two other groups. To the left is Mi Fu himself, the alleged author of the description we are now using, in the act of inscribing one of his beloved fantastic rocks, while the academician and official Wang Ch'in-ch'en[37] and an unnamed companion look on. To the right is the Taoist calligrapher Ch'en Ching-yüan,[38] portrayed playing a *p'i-p'a* while a student of Su Shih named Ch'in Kuan (1049–1100)[39] listens. Also present are a friend of Su Shih named Cheng Ching-lao[40] and two other Su followers, Ch'ao Pu-chih (1053–1110)[41] and Chang Lei (1054–1114),[42] all in the group around Li Kung-lin.[43] Elsewhere are two groupings of what may be ancient bronze vessels. These are unattended at the moment of the painting but had perhaps been assembled for the antiquarian delectation of Wang Shen's guests, most of whom, like many literati of the day, were probably collectors and connoisseurs of antiques.[44]

These distinguished personages and their manifold activities are all fascinating, but for our purposes it is most important to note another, relatively unobtrusive element in the painting. At some remove from the rest of the party—in the uppermost sector, and in the shaded seclusion of a thick bamboo grove separated from the main garden by a stream—sits an aged Buddhist monk reading a text with an attentive lay student. The description of the painting ascribed to Mi Fu identifies the layman as a minor poet and painter of the period named Liu Ching (1047–1100).[45] It also says that the subject of the teaching he is receiving from the old monk is "the theory of (or the essay on) nonarising" *(wu-sheng lun),* i.e., the teaching of emptiness.[46] It is the monk himself to whom I want to draw special attention. He is identified as the Ch'an master Fa-hsiu (1027–1090),[47] an eminent cleric nearing the end of his days and perhaps better known to the Chinese tradition by the honorific Yüan-t'ung Ch'an-shih, a title bestowed upon him in 1084 by an admiring Emperor Shen-tsung.[48]

Much of the interest that this painting has elicited from later Chinese commentators focuses on the traditional identification of the famous literati represented in it. It was thought to provide a rare and precious glimpse into the daily lives of some of the most famous figures of a famous age. However, the same interest has not extended to the one Buddhist monk included in the scene. To my knowledge, no traditional or modern scholar who has dealt with the painting has pursued the question of just who the Reverend Fa-hsiu was, why a Buddhist monk was included in the scene, or why this monk rather than another was deemed worthy company for the literary and artistic luminaries who fill the rest of the painting. It is not as though Buddhism was a negligible ingredient in Northern Sung culture, nor was Fa-hsiu a particularly inaccessible or obscure figure. Buddhism was never far from the center of the Northern Sung literary scene, and we know quite a bit about this particular cleric and the specific variety of Ch'an Buddhism he represented. We know, for example, that Fa-hsiu was well regarded in the highest secular and monastic circles both for his religious accomplishments as a Ch'an master and for his broad learning, cultivated tastes, and lambent wit. These facets of his fame are themselves of general significance, reminding us that Ch'an during the Northern Sung was hardly the rude, renegade, and anti-intellectual tradition of both earlier and recent Ch'an lore.

In more specific terms, we know that Fa-hsiu was a Ch'an monk in the sixth generation of the Yün-men lineage, a paramount house of Ch'an during the early Sung that was especially well known for its literary and ecumenical accomplishments.[49] His immediate predecessor in that line, the even better known T'ien-i I-huai (993–1064),[50] had been the student and chief successor of Hsüeh-tou Ch'ung-hsien (980–1052), who is—and was throughout the Sung—famous as the author of an influential early *kung-an* and poetry collection, the *Hsüeh-tou po-tse sung-ku.* This later became the core of the most famous of all *kung-an* anthologies, the *Pi-yen lu* (The Record of the Blue Grotto or, as it is most commonly known in the West, "The Blue Cliff Record"), compiled by the Lin-chi Ch'an monk Yüan-wu K'o-ch'in (1063–1135). Moreover, there is abundant independent evidence that Fa-hsiu was as famous outside the Saṃgha as he was within it. It can be demonstrated that he was well known—as teacher, friend, and colleague—to many of the other famous secular figures represented in the Western Garden painting. Thus the unobtrusive old monk, half hidden in a far corner of Wang Shen's garden, was not simply a stock type but a particular historical person as consequential in his own right as nearly all his companions in the painting were in theirs. He was an eminent cleric in what was then an especially influential lineage of Ch'an Buddhism, while at the same time he enjoyed the patronage and admiration of the leading figures in the secular culture of his day. The fact that he lived among both fellow monks and literati, together with the equally well-established fact of his eminence in both milieux, warrants our particular attention to whatever biographical and other information about him the tradition has preserved.

Born into the Hsin family of Lung-ch'eng, Ch'in-chou (mod. T'ienshui, Kansu), Fa-hsiu is said to have been conceived after his mother awoke from a dream in which she was visited by a wizened, bald old bonze who told her that he was from Mai-chi shan (Corn-rick Mountain).[51] The story has it that just prior to this auspicious dream an elderly monk, whose name had been forgotten but whose practice was said to be the daily chanting of the *Lotus Sūtra,* sought permission to take up residence, as a visiting itinerant monk, at the Ying-chien ssu, Maichi shan's chief monastery. The abbot of the place, a certain Master Lu, dismissed the old vagabond somewhat rudely, and as the monk left he said, "Someday soon I will place my bamboo pallet before these slopes, beneath the iron-bound range" (i.e., beneath this "Mt. Sumeru"). Later, Master Lu heard reports of the unusually premature birth of a baby boy nearby, and when he went to see him the infant (presumably the "old monk" redivivus) greeted the abbot with a smile. At the tender age of two the boy indicated a strong desire to follow Master Lu, who then adopted him into the monastery, thus fulfilling the old monk's prophecy.

Taking full ordination at age eighteen and finding himself possessed of exceptional natural abilities as well as an impressively stern and stately demeanor (Hui-hung describes it, appropriately enough, as the august bearing of a figure in a painting), Fa-hsiu first set his extraordinary talents on the course of Buddhist learning and exegetics. His acuity in analyzing scriptures and treatises—including works of Buddhist logic *(yin-ming),* Yogācāra *(Wei-shih)* texts, the *Diamond (Chin-kang) Sūtra,* the *Sūtra of Perfect Enlightenment (Yüan-chüeh),* and the *Flower Garland (Hua-yen) Sūtra*—soon earned him a reputation for erudition said to have reached as far as the capital. Nevertheless, it seems that the young prodigy was troubled early on by a problem that affected many Buddhists of those and other days: the problem of an alleged incompatibility between doctrinal or theoretical Buddhism—the so-called teachings *(chiao)*—and the practical or experiential Buddhism of Ch'an. We are told, for example, that at first Fa-hsiu was especially indebted to Tsung-mi's commentaries, particularly those on the *Hua-yen* and *Yüan-chüeh* scriptures, but that he grew dissatisfied with Tsung-mi's "studied Ch'an" *(hsüeh-ch'an).*[52] Also, although he had once had special respect for a certain Yüan Hua-yen (actually Lao Hua-yen, a.k.a. Huai-tung) of Peiching,[53] he is said to have grown disappointed in "Old Hua-yen's" criticism of exegetics *(fei-chiang).* His eventual judgment of both of these esteemed teachers of a former age was expressed as follows:

> If it be the case that doctrine *(chiao)* exhausts the Buddha's intent, then it is not fitting to criticize the doctrinal teachings as Master Yüan [i.e., Huai-tung] does. And if it be true that Ch'an contradicts the teachings, then one ought not to "study" Ch'an in the manner of Tsung-mi. But I do not believe that in what was transmitted to Mahākāśyapa there was anything apart from the Buddha's teachings.[54]

In one version of his biography it is reported that Fa-hsiu arrived at the same conclusion by noting an essential equivalence between Sudhana's pilgrimage, as a symbol of the path conceived in theoretical (Hua-yen) terms, and the travels from the West and the South, respectively, of Bodhidharma and Hui-neng, the latter two taken as symbolic of the path as it was charted in Ch'an. Why then, he asked himself, should he confine himself only to "the schools of nature and of characteristics"?[55]

In reaching this conclusion Fa-hsiu demonstrated a remarkable independence of mind. The conventional, doctrinaire options available in his day were basically two: either to emphasize the difference between Ch'an and doctrinal Buddhism, and then to choose one to the virtual exclusion of the other, or to espouse a reasonable and balanced, but perhaps also jejune, synthesis of both. Fa-hsiu, however, solved the problem of the relationship between experiential and theoretical Buddhism by determining that the very distinction between the two is invalid—that is, by insisting that what is written in the scriptures and treatises is just what is transmitted by the patriarchs, and vice versa. This judgment appears to have been a kind of personal spiritual breakthrough. It allowed Fa-hsiu, the biographies tell us, to give up "lecturing" or the career of a professional specialist in exegetics, without thereby abandoning the valued heritage of doctrine and scripture.

To mark this turning point in his spiritual and intellectual development, Fa-hsiu decided to set off on a kind of "Ch'an pilgrimage," in his case an extended journey to the South, during which he would test his newfound understanding. He is said to have announced to fellow students, with a bravado born of strong and confident commitment, and in the vigorous rhetoric typical of Ch'an, that he intended to "explore all the 'caves and caverns' [i.e., all the Ch'an monasteries or practice centers], to drag out the various sorts [of teachers residing therein], and to repay the Buddha's mercy by absolutely annihilating them." One of the Ch'an sites he visited early in his travels was the Hu-kuo Monastery in Sui-chou (mod. Sui-hsien, Hupei), where he came upon a stele that had been erected in memory of the late T'ang or Five Dynasties Ts'ao-tung Ch'an master, Ching-kuo.[56] Inscribed thereon was the following pair of recorded exchanges: "A monk once asked Pao-tz'u[57] about buddha-nature. Tz'u replied, 'Who lacks it?' Later, when another monk put this same question to Ching-kuo, he answered, 'Who has it?' and the questioning monk was thereby enlightened." Fa-hsiu was much amused by this and said, as he tried to catch his breath from laughing, "How could one dare to say that the buddha-nature is something one could 'have' or 'lack,' much less suggest that one could be enlightened by such statements!"

Eventually he arrived at the T'ieh-Fo Monastery in Wu-wei chün (mod. Wu-wei hsien, Anhui), where he presented himself to the renowned Ch'an master I-huai.[58] He is said to have found I-huai seated in formal posture and displaying a forbidding demeanor, but with tears streaming down his face and soaking his robes. Fa-hsiu, however, simply ignored this strange spectacle. I-huai then restrained his tears and asked, "What scripture is it, Reverend Sir, which you expound?" When Fa-hsiu replied that he specialized in the *Hua-yen ching,* I-huai asked him what the essential purport *(tsung)* of that text was. Fa-hsiu said that its cardinal meaning was mind *(hsin).* I-huai then asked if there were an essential purport to the doctrine of mind. To this Fa-hsiu could give no reply, and so I-huai said, "In even the smallest discrepancy yawns the distance separating *(hsüan-ke)* heaven from earth. Look to yourself and you will surely understand."

Thus did I-huai manage to transform a Hua-yen metaphysical abstraction—the doctrine of the mind as the ground on which the vast and the minute encompass each other—into an urgent Ch'an reminder of the necessity of close attention to the immediacies of one's own experience. At this, Fa-hsiu was taken aback and lost his composure. He trembled and made obeisance to I-huai, vowing to spend night and day learning the dharma from him. Fa-hsiu remained with I-huai for several years before achieving his own enlightenment. This is said to have occurred when the master posed to his students the "old case" in which Po-ch'ao asked Pao-tz'u,[59] "What is the time before the emotions arise?" and Pao-tz'u replied, "Separation" *(ke).*[60] I-huai then confirmed Fa-hsiu's attainment by announcing, "You are truly a vessel of the dharma; in the future my message will proceed with you."

Following his time with I-huai, Fa-hsiu spent approximately ten years wandering from temple to temple in the Anhui region. We are told that he led a very austere life during this period, and was impervious to the cold and hunger that were the lot of an itinerant monk. What did trouble him, however, and grievously so, were the sorry spiritual conditions in which he found the monasteries he visited, conditions in which "the Way of the patriarchs was not flourishing," and for which he harbored a strong sense of personal responsibility. From Anhui he went further south to Kiangsi and settled on Mt. Lu, residing for nearly twenty years at that mountain's Hsi-hsien Temple.[61] There his reputation as a strict and enlightened teacher grew steadily. It was on Mt. Lu that he met another teacher, Yün-chu Hsiao-shun (d. between 1064 and 1067), who served for a time as abbot of Hsi-hsien ssu. Hsiao-shun, like

Fa-hsiu's teacher I-huai, was a fifth-generation Yün-men master, but his particular line of descent was different from I-huai's. Fa-hsiu is said to have had several bouts of dharma combat with Hsiao-shun, provoked by the latter's criticism of I-huai's (and presumably also of Fa-hsiu's) particular style of Ch'an.[62] These encounters, in which Fa-hsiu did quite well, no doubt strengthened his reputation.

By the 1070's he must have been very well known indeed, for it was toward the end of that decade that Wang An-shih (1021–1086), then recently retired from his position as prime minister and newly appointed as lord of Shu (Shu Wang), invited Fa-hsiu to Kiangsu and offered him the abbacy of the Chiang-shan ssu (a.k.a. Chung-shan ssu), a position vacated by the recent death of a certain Master Yüan.[63] Fa-hsiu either did not accept that position or did not retain it long,[64] but he did remain in the Kiangsu region for several years, residing for a time at the nearby Ch'ung-fu Ch'an-yüan, a major Ch'an center of the day located in Ch'ang-lu (mod. Liu-ho). It was there that he acquired the nickname "Iron-Face Hsiu," which was meant, it seems, to suggest both the oft-noted severity of his personality and demeanor and the famed rigor of the style of Ch'an life which he exemplified and taught.[65]

It seems to have been during his years on Mt. Lu and in the Kiangsu region that Fa-hsiu's high repute among his fellow Ch'an monks was secured. He may at that time have come to the attention of the famous senior Yün-men monk Ch'i-sung (1007–1072).[66] Later, as the *Ta-hui P'u-chüeh Ch'an-shih tsung-men wu-k'u* (Ta-hui's Arsenal of the Ch'an School) records, the redoubtable Ta-hui would recount several anecdotes drawn from this middle period in Fa-hsiu's life, all stories that established Fa-hsiu as a true exemplar of Ch'an and thus testified to the lasting strength of his reputation among Ch'an monks of all lineages.[67]

The crowning phase of Fa-hsiu's public career began in 1084, when he was invited by Emperor Shen-tsung to come to the capital of Kaifeng and assume the office of inaugural *(k'ai-shan)* abbot of the newly established Fa-yün Monastery.[68] High-ranking court officers were deputed to witness the investiture, and they came bearing gifts of incense and robes. Although the emperor himself did not attend the ceremony, his symbolic presence was indicated by a rescript in his own hand which he had delivered by the Imperial Uncle Wang Shen, the very prince who hosted Li Kung-lin's "elegant gathering." The rescript Wang brought was probably the document that conferred upon Fa-hsiu the honorary title "Yüan-t'ung" (Perfectly Penetrating). Su Shih, though not present at the event, did refer to it two years later in the preface to an inscription he composed to mark the 1086 installation of the Fa-yün Monastery's great bell.[69]

Recipient of these highest of honors, Fa-hsiu quickly became a cynosure. As the biographies say, "literati *(shih-ta-fu)* visited him day and night with questions about the Tao," and he even preached at court. He is said to have met Ssu-ma Kuang (1019–1086), whose lack of appreciation for Buddhism he lamented, and as already noted, he also came to know and be admired by Su Shih. Su had apparently learned of Fa-hsiu earlier, either while he was still in exile in Huang-chou or as he was making his way from there to the capital. The two men seem to have corresponded with each other during the early 1080's, perhaps even before Fa-hsiu reached Kaifeng, and four short letters from the great poet to the venerable monk survive today.[70] No doubt the two men came to know each other even better after Su Shih returned to Kaifeng in 1086. Sometime after the monk's death in 1091, Su Shih made it known that he believed Fa-hsiu to have been, along with his dharma brother Hui-lin Tsung-pen (1020–1099),[71] one of two persons most responsible for the great efflorescence of Ch'an in the Sung capital.[72]

We have already seen that Fa-hsiu also knew Li Kung-lin and Huang T'ing-chien. In fact, he was apparently on quite familiar terms with both, as is indicated by several oft-repeated anecdotes. For example, he is said once to have teasingly reproved the great painter by telling him that his paintings of horses were so realistic as to engender concern that Li might be reborn as a horse (lit., "enter a horse's belly"). Fa-hsiu's remark seems to have been made in a half-humorous vein, yet the story goes that Li took the caution seriously and put aside his brush until Fa-hsiu encouraged him to take it up again, this time to paint images of Buddhist figures like Kuan-yin, Vimalakīrti, the arhats, and so on.[73] Likewise, Fa-hsiu is said to have chided Huang T'ing-chien about the sensual or voluptuous diction *(yen-yü)* of the latter's poetry, which he noted was so popular that men vied with one another to transmit and emulate it. When Huang laughed and asked if this would put him, too, "in the belly of a horse," Fa-hsiu responded that karmic retribution for using seductive words to excite the concupiscent minds of people throughout the world would not stop at mere equine rebirth. Huang, he said, should rather fear rebirth in hell itself.[74]

Fa-hsiu may have had a reputation for severity, but he seems also to have had an excellent sense of humor. Such bantering strictures against art and literature were no doubt made with tongue at least partly in cheek, although with an undertone of caution and serious reserve as well. In any case, that the impression Fa-hsiu made on Huang was serious and lasting is proved by several reverential references to him in Huang's surviving writings. Among these is an encomium *(tsan)* in which the poet confesses his grateful admiration of the eminent monk's renowned severity, taking it to be a manifestation of compassion especially well suited to the spiritually decadent times in which he believed they lived.[75]

As to Fa-hsiu's monastic following, the records indicate that he had no fewer than twenty-eight formal heirs.[76] One of the most famous was Fo-kuo Wei-po (d.u.), who succeeded him as a prominent resident and, later, abbot of the Fa-yün ssu.[77] Wei-po is best known as the author of the third of the great "transmission of the lamp" compendia, the *Chien-chung Ching-kuo hsü-teng-lu,* a text published in the summer of 1101 and accorded the signal honors of a preface composed by Emperor Hui-tsung (r. 1100–1125) and immediate inclusion in the canon. This thirty-fascicle Ch'an history is itself enough to establish Wei-po's credentials as a monk for whom Ch'an piety and scholarship were not incompatible. That he went so far as to hold that scriptural and doctrinal study were necessary complements to Ch'an was confirmed in 1104, when he published another scholarly work, a systematic catalogue of the Sung Buddhist canon entitled *Ta-tsang-ching kang-mu chih-yao lu.*[78] In the concluding section of this work, Wei-po pleaded for rapprochement between doctrinal Buddhism and Ch'an, asserting that practice of Ch'an without study of scripture and reflection on doctrine would result in a constricted and dangerously one-sided caricature of true Buddhism.

It is significant that Wei-po presented the complementary relationship between Ch'an and the four major doctrinal or scripturally based schools by means of an analogy drawn from the world of art, viz., the modeling of a figure of the Buddha in clay.[79] In the terms of this metaphor, Yogācāra Buddhism *(Tzu-en chiao)* is like the under-layer of clay applied to the skeletal framework of the Buddha figure to form its musculature; the Vinaya school *(Nan-shan chiao)* is like the external layer of fine plaster with which the clay of the statue is covered; T'ien-t'ai is like the set of five vital organs placed within the body of the statue;[80] Hua-yen *(Hsien-shou chiao)* is like the gloss of golden color applied to the plaster surface of the figure; and Ch'an *(Ch'an-men tsung)* is like the brilliant light emanating from the jewel-pupils of the figure's eyes. To be sure, this elaborate *p'an-chiao* (doctrinal classification) trope grants pride of place to Ch'an, implying that is a kind of quintessence of Buddhism. However, the point Wei-po says he is most concerned to make is that, just as a statue of the Buddha cannot be complete without all five of these stages in its fabrication, so Buddhism remains incomplete unless all five of its major component schools are given their due.

The principle of harmony between Ch'an and learned Buddhism, and the disposition to demonstrate that principle by means of artistic expression, is further exemplified in the only other of Wei-po's works to have survived, the *Wen-shu chih-nan t'u-tsan* (Illustrated Encomia [Recounting Sudhana's Journey to] the South as Directed by Mañjuśrī), a set of illustrated verses summarizing the final chapter of the *Hua-yen Sūtra.* This text, illustrations to the better editions of which are vaguely reminiscent of the style of Li Kung-lin's paintings, is a prime instance of the sort of combination of Ch'an, doctrinal Buddhism (Hua-yen), poetry, and pictorial art that Fa-hsiu's example could foster.[81]

There was also a significant connection between Fa-hsiu and the well-known Ch'ang-lu Tsung-tse (d.u.),[82] a Ch'an scholar-monk and one of the Sung era's leading advocates of the union of Ch'an and Pure Land.[83] Although this monk went on to study with Fa-hsiu's dharma brother Ch'ang-lu Ying-fu (d.u.), in whose lineage he is usually placed, it was Fa-hsiu who ordained him and served as his first teacher. Tsung-tse is especially famous in Ch'an history for having compiled in 1103 the earliest surviving Ch'an monastic code, the ten-fascicle *Ch'an-yüan ch'ing-kuei* (Pure Regulations for Ch'an Precincts).[84] This work of normative ecclesiological scholarship—together with the breadth of a Buddhism that could combine Pure Land, Ch'an, and even a strong advocacy of filial piety[85]—exemplifies an attitude toward Buddhist traditions harmonious with, and perhaps shaped by, the catholicity of Fa-hsiu's own piety.

The *Ch'an-yüan ch'ing-kuei,* at least in certain of its later editions, includes an early—perhaps the earliest surviving—manual of Ch'an meditation practice, a work that may well have been written by Tsung-tse himself. This brief handbook, the *Tso-ch'an i* (Liturgy of Seated Meditation), presents a fairly orthodox, even conservative picture of Ch'an meditation. The summary of Ch'an practice found therein is no radical departure from standard forms of Mahāyāna contemplative discipline, no transcendence of deliberate and meticulous effort, but a straightforward and sober digest of some of the most basic themes of traditional Chinese Mahāyāna meditation. Redolent even of other mainstream contemplative regimens like those of T'ien-t'ai and early "East Mountain" Ch'an, it resonates with the mārga-affirming implications of classical tathāgatagarbha doctrine. For certain later Ch'an or Zen figures, such as Dōgen (especially in his later years), this text represented a merely conventional Buddhism, a gradualist and instrumentalist understanding of meditation that was oblivious of the "understanding beyond words" that marks the true Zen of "sudden practice." But Dōgen's denigration of Tsung-tse's view of meditation may itself be seen as a variously motivated reversion to just that kind of radical, anti-mārga, and potentially antinomian Ch'an which Tsung-tse, Fa-hsiu, and so many other Northern Sung Ch'an monks were seeking to restrain and reform.[86]

Knowing, as we now do, at least the general lineaments of Fa-hsiu's life and teachings, let us return to the *Hsi-yüan ya-chi t'u* and resume our use of it as a visual allegory. What does the painting, taken together with the story of its eminent monk, suggest about the relationship between Ch'an Buddhism and the life of learning and letters during the Sung? Modern scholarly opinion, most thoroughly argued by art historian Ellen Johnston Laing, holds that the "Western Garden Gathering" is a fictitious event, that the original version of the painting was not painted by Li Kung-lin, and that the scene was probably first rendered (admittedly in Li's style) by an unknown artist of the early Southern Sung. Laing argues convincingly that the painting may well have been first conceived and executed in the early Southern Sung, as an exercise in nostalgic admiration for the "men of the Yüan-yu period (1086–1093)"—namely, for the party of conservative literati who dominated Chinese culture and politics in the era following Wang An-shih's experiments in reform. During the decades that immediately followed Yüan-yu, these men were condemned by the then-resurgent reform party, but their reputations were redeemed and they became heroes shortly after the 1126 fall of the North, which was then blamed on Wang's epigones, their enemies.

Although the painting may be only an imaginative and elegiac recreation *du temps perdu,* it is happily suggestive of certain aspects of Sung Ch'an that bear directly on our underlying theme. Note first that Fa-hsiu's presence is somewhat remote and aloof, even though he is a significant part of the composition, holding his own in the idyllic scene along with a distinguished and select company of far more famous cultural luminaries. One might even go so far as to say that, at least in the version of the scene attributed to Chao Meng-fu (Figure 1), Fa-hsiu does more than hold his own: he may actually be the culmination of the overall visual narrative of the painting. The eye of the viewer seems to be drawn first to the Su Shih cluster in the lower left part of the painting. From there it is led, along an ascending "S" curve, to the decreasingly congested Li Kung-lin and Mi Fu clusters, finally coming to rest on the tranquil pair of monk and attentive lay student. Apropos of this arrangement, one may again follow Ellen Johnston Laing who, in her article on this painting, quotes part of a colophon by the poet Tseng Chi (1084–1166), found on an unpublished and unnamed handscroll version of the scene: "At the end of the scroll an old Ch'an master and a scholar sit in silence opposite each other on rush mats amidst a bamboo grove, a stream, and rocks. Can this be without significance *(ch'i wu i yeh)*?"

Significance there must surely be, and it may lie precisely in the fact that Fa-hsiu's location in the scene places him in contrapuntal relationship to all the painting's other figures. It is as though we are meant to take special note of his difference from (particularly his apparent indifference to) the fascinating activities that preoccupy Wang Shen's other eminent guests.[87] There is a visible and marked contrast between the contemplative stillness embodied in the figure of the monk and the more active scenes of literary and artistic creativity that seem to lead the viewer's eye toward him. Is it too much to suggest an analogy to the larger

FIGURE 1. *Hsi-yüan ya-chi t'u* attributed to Chao Meng-fu; original in the collection of the National Palace Museum, Taipei, Taiwan, Republic of China (Catalogue no. YV.117)

FIGURE 2. Detail from an anonymous *Hsi-yüan ya-chi t'u,* now in the Freer Gallery of Art, Smithsonian Institution, Washington, D.C. (Catalogue no. 11.523), entitled "Personages in a garden;" sixteenth century. (Courtesy of the Freer Gallery of Art, Smithsonian Institution, Washington, D.C.)

Figure 3. Detail from an anonymous, purportedly Sung version of the *Hsi-yüan ya-chi t'u;* original in the collection of the National Palace Museum, Taipei, Taiwan, Republic of China (Catalogue no. SH.133.m)

FIGURE 4. Detail from *Hsi-yüan ya-ch'i t'u* attributed to Liu Sung-nien (ca. 1150–after 1225); original in the collection of the National Palace Museum, Taipei, Taiwan, Republic of China (Catalogue no. SH.109.e)

FIGURE 5. An anonymous, purportedly Ming version of the *Hsi-yüan ya-chi-t'u;* original in the collection of the National Palace Museum, Taipei, Taiwan, Republic of China (Catalogue no. MV.670)

FIGURE 6. *Hsi-yüan ya-ch'i t'u* attributed to Ch'iu Ying (1495–1552); original in the collection of the National Palace Museum, Taipei, Taiwan, Republic of China (Catalogue no. MV.441)

contrast between the contemplative spirituality of Buddhism and the profuse animation of secular literati culture? Could it not be that the placement of Fa-hsiu in the painting is actually the projection of a subtle and implicit caution, a reiteration of the qualification of cultural values that Buddhism has traditionally been concerned to assert? It seems not unreasonable to "read" Fa-hsiu's presence in the painting, in light of what we know about the monk himself, as a reminder of transcendental Buddhist values—as a caution against forgetting that even such great achievements in arts and letters as those that distinguished the Sung generally, and this group of Yüan-yu literati in particular, were in the end "empty," "transient," and "unarisen" *(wu-sheng)*. As the description of the painting attributed to Mi Fu says, just after its author has evoked the beautiful natural setting in which Fa-hsiu is seated, "There is in the world of men no joy of purity and serenity surpassing this. Alas, how difficult of achievement this is for those who are swept up in the pursuit of fame and profit and do not know enough to retreat from it."[88]

To support this interpretation, we can return to the realm of Ch'an discourse and cite first the most famous of the several anecdotes about Fa-hsiu retold approvingly by Ta-hui and later Ch'an figures:

> The Teacher [Ta-hui] said, "Once, upon the occasion of a snowfall, Ch'an Master Yüan-t'ung Hsiu observed that whenever it snows one can see that there are three kinds of monks. The best sort remain in the monks' hall in seated meditation. The middling sort grind ink and trim their brushes so they may write snow poems. The worst sort huddle about the brazier talking of food. In the *ting-wei* year [1127], when I [Ta-hui] was staying at Hu-ch'iu,[89] I saw all three kinds of monks, and I could not help but laugh to realize that the words of our predecessor were not empty."[90]

In this wry epigram we hear an echo of Fa-hsiu's half-jocular (but half-serious) remarks to Li Kung-lin and Huang T'ing-chien, cited above. Poetry, and by implication the other arts as well, can too easily be made into an ersatz religion, can too readily become the elegant but shallow diversion of those whom later Japanese Zen monks would call "shaven-headed laymen." Fa-hsiu is shown here, clearly, to be skeptical about the place of poetry in Ch'an.

The same point is made in another anecdote, this one offering actual examples of good and bad Ch'an usage rather than mere comment on them. Ta-hui tells us that Yün-chu Hsiao-shun (a.k.a. Shun Lao-fu)[91] once asked Fa-hsiu whether or not he had known T'ien-i I-huai. When Fa-hsiu replied that he had, Hsiao-shun asked for an example of I-huai's discourse. Fa-hsiu offered the following epigram: "One, two, three, four, five, six, seven. Before the lofty peaks I stand alone. I snatch the pearl from the black dragon's jaws. With a single word I expose Vimalakīrti." Hsiao-shun's response to this was terse but scathing. "Not good," he said, "what else have you got?" Fa-hsiu then related that once, when an old monk had come for an interview with I-huai, the master raised his wisk and asked, "Do you understand?" The old monk replied, "I don't understand." I-huai then said, "The earlobes, two pieces of skin; the teeth, all bone." Shun Lao found this anecdote much more to his liking and praised I-huai as a true spiritual guide *(chen shan-chih-shih)* whose latter remark should never be forgotten.[92]

Consider the contrast between these two examples of I-huai's Ch'an wordcraft offered by his student Fa-hsiu. The first is somewhat prolix, extravagantly figurative, even bombastic, marked by a self-consciously poetic or tropic quality. The second is extremely terse, deliberately flat and prosaic, actually rough and vernacular. Such contrast, and the explicit approval of the *entzauberte* mode of the latter example, seem to be yet another illustration of Fa-hsiu's (as well as Shun Lao's and Ta-hui's) distrust of poetic discourse or artful diction. They had their doubts about such elegant things because they saw them as too susceptible to use as mere counterfeits of true Ch'an experience. Of course, the style of expression they did favor, or something very much like it, was itself recognized as a literary value at the time. Many of the leading poets and critics of the Northern Sung expressly favored what was called an "even and bland" *(p'ing-tan)* style. This is a poetic diction that is sparse, direct, understated, and astringent—a style that was said sometimes to verge on the rough and vulgar. Mei Yao-ch'en (1002–1060) is perhaps the most famous exemplar of this style, but it was championed by others as well, like Ou-yang Hsiu and Su Shih.[93] Su Shih, in fact, once borrowed a similar term, *"tan-p'o"* (bland and tranquil), from the T'ang literatus and scourge of Buddhism, Han Yü, and used it to draw an analogy between the kind of poetry Su himself favored and the sort of insight and discourse he believed Ch'an required. Han Yü had once cited the "blandness and tranquility" of the Buddhists as proof of their lack of "heroic valor" *(hao-meng).* Su Shih turned that criticism into praise, affirming blandness and tranquility as positive virtues in both literature and religious life, and likening them to Buddhist notions of emptiness and quiescence. In a letter of farewell to a Ch'an poet-monk, he wrote (in Richard Lynn's translation):

> Your Eminence has studied the bitterness and illusory nature of things—
> Hundreds of reflections whose ashes have long become cold. . .
> So why ever try to contend with one's contemporaries
> To see whose writing will be most magnificent!
> A new poem should be like the most white of snows,

Its articulation at once so pure it's startling. . .
T'ui-chih [Han Yü] criticized cursive calligraphy thus. . . .
"I am rather astonished at the way the Buddhists
Regard the self as if it were a dried up hilltop well—
Submissively, they give voice to their blandness and placidity.
But who provides for the expression of heroism and valor?"
After careful consideration, I [Su Shih] don't think this is true.
Genuine skill is not just a matter of illusions and shadows.
If you want to make the language of your poetry marvelous *(miao),*
Don't ever reject emptiness *(k'ung)* and quietude *(ching).* . .
Since poetry and the dharma can do no harm to one another,
I must again ask your opinion about what I have said here.[94]

Fa-hsiu, of course, was not a literary critic. Nor do we know whether or not he wrote much poetry, although he surely wrote some.[95] Nevertheless, we do find in his recorded religious discourse both approval and several examples of a kind of religious "plain speech" that seems at least analogous to the "bland and even" style of so much Sung poetry. The image he deliberately projected later in his career was that of "the simple monk," the "dharma rube" or unsophisticated religious rustic whose spiritual life was wholesome and unadorned by the trappings of higher secular or sacred culture. Thus we are told that he once addressed his disciples from the lecture platform, saying,

> I am but a plain mountain monk, incapable of subtle discourse; I just respond to the moment. I can offer you food to eat and tea to drink,[96] but I have no "profound judgments of a master or patriarch" to render. This is how we Ch'an men are—artless. "If you try to walk on a balance beam, you will be stiff as iron" *(t'a-cho ch'eng-ch'ui ying szu t'ieh).*[97]

Of course, such cultivated "rusticity"—expressed, for example, in learned allusions to old texts that are no less subtle for being colloquial and folksy in their imagery—can actually be the most refined form of sophistication, and so it often was in both the sacred and the secular traditions of Northern Sung culture. One could even say of Fa-hsiu and many of his Ch'an contemporaries what was later said of his friend Huang T'ing-chien—that "he took the vulgar and made it elegant" *(i su wei ya).*[98]

Such claims of monkish simplicity, and such disavowals of the "profound judgments of masters and patriarchs," suggest that Fa-hsiu's distrust of secular arts and letters, seen as too susceptible to use as surrogates for genuine spirituality, was related to his equally serious distrust of purely religious learning if it, too, were severed from immediate experiences of the sort available in, say, meditation. The religious equivalent of "writing snow poems" was the composition of learned and abstruse phrasings of the dharma, the spinning of doctrine as a substitute for experience, and we have already seen something of Fa-hsiu's withering views of that. Even as a young man, when he weighed the quite learned Ch'an of a Tsung-mi and the radically quotidian Ch'an of a Huai-tung, he found neither alternative satisfying. Nevertheless, he was adamant in rejecting doctrinal reflection whenever it was divorced from Ch'an experience and Ch'an practice—a theme that reverberates throughout his latter life as well. Thus, in still another exchange with Hsiao-shun, again about Fa-hsiu's teacher I-huai, we encounter one of the earliest instances of a largely pejorative label that came traditionally to be given to the sort of inferior, discursive Ch'an which Fa-hsiu had rejected and which he criticized in the anecdotes recounted above. Hsiao-shun, Ta-hui tells us, was in the habit of criticizing I-huai for preaching what Hsiao-shun called "Kudzu Ch'an" *(k'o-teng Ch'an)*:[99]

> One day, Hsiao-shun heard that Ch'an Master T'ien-i Huai had died. He entered the dharma hall with palms joined in the gesture of reverence, and said, "How delightful that this old vine-pole has collapsed." Hsiu Yüan-t'ung was at that time serving as Rector *(Wei-na, Karmadāna)* in Hsiao-shun's congregation and was constantly being subjected to such abuse. He then said to his fellow monks, "I must reach some sort of understanding with this old fellow." That night, during the evening colloquy with the Master, he was again reviled as before. Fa-hsiu then stepped forth from the assembly and said, in a harsh voice, "How is it that you never manifest the middle way of the *Sūtra of Perfect Enlightenment*?"[100] Hsiao-shun replied, "I have kept you all standing here for too long; I bid you good-bye," and then he returned to the abbot's quarters. Fa-hsiu said, "This old fellow's 'whole body is an eye.'[101] Well may he revile Master Huai."[102]

Hsiao-shun's wont to taunt Fa-hsiu by criticizing his teacher's Ch'an style, and Hsiao-shun's specific retort to Fa-hsiu's angry response, may seem a bit less puzzling once it is understood that Hsiao-shun's phrasing is probably an allusion to a passage in the *Lin-chi lu* (Record of Lin-chi). The sixth discourse *(shang-t'ang)* in that work concludes when Lin-chi dismisses his audience with the phrase "I have kept you here too long; good-bye" (*chiu li chen-chung;* lit., "You've been standing a long time; take care of yourselves"). The intent of Hsiao-shun's allusion may have been to bring to Fa-hsiu's mind the message of that sixth discourse, in which Lin-chi claims, in accordance with a longstanding pedagogical principle of Buddhism, always to be able to fit his teaching precisely to the individual needs and circumstance of each of his students. Lin-chi says of himself,

> I always know exactly where each person is coming from *(tsung-shih i lai-ch'u)*. When a student presents himself just as he is, it is as if he had lost himself. And when he doesn't present himself just as he is, then he is as though bound without rope. Never make precipitous judgments. "Under-

> standing" and "not understanding" are both mistakes. I declare this openly. Let the world criticize me as it will.[103]

As an implicit justification for his criticism of I-huai, Hsiao-shun's use of this allusion suggests that he was intent on destroying any attachment Fa-hsiu might have had to the relatively discursive Ch'an style of his former teacher. The point is not that "Kudzu Ch'an" is mistaken and some other kind of Ch'an is correct. Remember that Hsiao-shun professes his "delight" at I-huai's death while making the gesture of respect with his hands, thus projecting a double meaning that Fa-hsiu seems at first to have missed. Rather, Hsiao-shun's point is that Fa-hsiu, having been bred to one particular sort of Ch'an, needed to be reminded that it had no absolute authority and could easily cease to be a vital discipline, becoming instead a mere habit. Moreover, Hsiao-shun was implying that Fa-hsiu should no more mind criticism of his teacher (and, by implication, of himself) than Lin-chi would have minded being criticized by the whole world.

The patterns of attitude and pronouncement seen in these anecdotes suggest that Fa-hsiu's placement in the *Elegant Gathering in the Western Garden* is symbolically appropriate—perhaps intentionally so. They corroborate the apparent significance of his pictured separation from, and evident indifference to, the activities depicted elsewhere in Wang Shen's garden. Fa-hsiu was clearly something of an alien amongst these painters, poets, calligraphers, musicians, antiquarians, and statesmen, just as he would have been amongst monks whose Buddhism consisted only of erudition and rehearsal of deep-sounding doctrinal formulae.

Yet there is more to Fa-hsiu's presence in the scene. That he is present at all is significant, as is the fact that a monk so renowned for his severity and his reservations about both "cultured" Ch'an and secular culture should so often have kept company with famous poets and artists. "Iron-Face Hsiu" may have been, as tradition holds, a very stern monk, but he was no fierce anchorite, no Buddhist St. Anthony of the Desert. Nor was he, like some Chinese Savonarola, an implacable and fanatical foe of all worldly culture. If Western analogies may be deemed useful in such characterizations, he was more like his near contemporary, the Cistercian monk Saint Bernard of Clairvaux (1090–1153). Bernard was an advocate of spiritual simplicity and a strong opponent of the debasement of ascetic piety into mere worldly aestheticism, but he was also a very learned man and a superb stylist in his own right. Although his most powerfully held conviction about literary learning and the monastic life was expressed in the epigram, "Christ is my grammar" *(Mea grammatica Christus est),* Bernard could also speak appreciatively of literature as "an ornament of the soul" *(scientia litterarum quae ornat animam).*[104]

I suspect that, *mutatis mutandis,* Fa-hsiu would have concurred in such views. If Fa-hsiu can be seen as representing, in both life and art, the Buddhist ideal of the *vita contemplativa,* then surely his association, in both the painting and history, with Su Shih, Huang T'ing-chien, and the like has some positive bearing on our general question of the relationship between Ch'an and higher Sung culture. It must tell us something about the compatibility of the two—about the degree to which cultural pursuits could legitimately be incorporated into the Buddhist religious life, and about the extent to which Buddhism could be, and was, incorporated into the secular culture of the Sung.

Again, an anecdote may shed light on the problem. Several versions of Fa-hsiu's biography tell us that when a certain monk once asked him to explain the principles of "achieving nirvāṇa without leaving saṃsāra and entering the Buddha's domain without leaving the realm of Māra," he replied, with the concision of metaphor typical of Ch'an, "the cow's milk is but an infusion of red earth" (i.e., barren clay).[105] It is difficult to be confident of one's interpretations of such enigmatic Ch'an remarks, particularly if they come to us bereft of commentary and cannot be identified as allusions to better known texts. Nevertheless, I would hazard that Fa-hsiu's point is roughly this: The world (i.e., saṃsāra or the realm of Māra) may seem base and sterile, like red clay, but just as it is from such seemingly barren material that cow's fodder grows, so one may distill from such lowly material the richest spiritual nourishment, the very "milk" of nirvāṇa and buddhahood. If this interpretation be correct, the epigram may well justify a monk's reserved and disciplined participation in the mundane pursuits of arts and letters. It may even serve as a warrant for his attendance at literary garden parties, particulary if, once there, he reminds the other guests of the ephemeral character of all such things.

Fa-hsiu's remark suggests that he did not hold Buddhism to be a spirituality that utterly shuns the world. Nor did he see it as requiring literal, fastidious, and complete avoidance of secular activities. For Fa-hsiu, what must be shunned is not the world itself but attachment to the world, and participation in worldly activities is to be avoided only to the extent that they entail abandonment or relaxation of religious discipline.

Such a view of the world of arts and letters is consonant with, and may actually derive from, Fa-hsiu's views on the religious equivalent of arts and letters—namely, the "studied Ch'an" or "Ch'an of words and letters" that had preoccupied him in his youth. Again note that he did not reject such learned Buddhism outright; rather, he incorporated it into the living discipline of Ch'an, recognizing that Ch'an presupposed all that was valuable in doctrine and scripture. Once this conclusion was reached, Buddhist learning and literature ceased to be the snare or tangle that it once seemed to be. What Fa-hsiu never ceased to reject, of course, were learning and letters pursued as mere surrogates for religious experience. But these he condemned no less than he condemned their opposite extreme—namely, the sort of "ignoramus Ch'an" that simply divorces itself from scripture and doctrine. If our severe and simple "mountain monk" could be both Ch'an master and master of Buddhist learning, it should not be surprising that he was also the abbot of a metropolitan monastery and a friend to renowned poets and painters. Nor is it incongruous that his most famous disciple, Wei-po, continued such affiliations while becoming both an eminent Ch'an teacher and a scholar-poet in his own right.

It would seem, therefore, that when we contemplate the old monk in the painting we have as much reason to focus on his presence in the scene as we have to note his distance from its foreground. Both the famous painting itself and the outline we have sketched of Fa-hsiu's life and teachings support the hypothesis that Ch'an Buddhism, for all its austerity, had reached in the Sung a kind of *détente* with the wider world of higher Chinese culture. This was not accomplished at the expense of Buddhism's autonomy and orthodoxy, nor did it result in a loss of the religion's traditional tension with the secular world, or in a relaxation of its essentially critical attitude toward all the world's constructs, sacred or profane. But it did allow Buddhism, precisely in its unflagging role as a critical tradition, to leave the cloister, so to speak, and take its place in the more public arena of civilized Chinese discourse.

This amounts, I believe, to a kind of fulfillment of the earlier promise of Chinese Buddhism, a culmination of its gradual process of sinicization, by which Buddhism wove itself into the fabric of Chinese civilization while simultaneouly altering the basic pattern of that fabric. The theoretical foundations of that change had been laid during the T'ang, in the creation of new schools of Chinese thought, such as Hua-yen. Its practical foundations were laid, also during the T'ang, especially with the creation of Ch'an Buddhism. But it was not until the Sung that Buddhism emerged from its own exclusively religious confines to become an integral part of the public order of concept, value, and action that China's intellectuals and men of letters then called *Wen* and *Tao,* "Culture and the Way."

The problem of how precisely to define and illustrate the role that Ch'an Buddhism played in this wider culture remains, but Fa-hsiu and the Western Garden painting suggest a beginning for that effort. The themes of ambivalence and ambiguity seem apposite to our consideration of both the monk and the painting. The Buddhist perspective, symbolized by both the historical and the pictorial Fa-hsiu, is ambivalent, in that accoutrements of both secular and sacred culture are treated as proper objects of some suspicion or caution for Buddhists, just as they always had been. Yet they are also recognized, more readily than ever before in China, as legitimate components of the Buddhist Way, provided they serve rather than replace the higher disciplines of religious experience. The perspective of Sung literati culture, represented best by the leaders of the Wen-hsüeh movement, is also ambivalent. On the one hand, the literati seemed favorably disposed to include Buddhism within the range of their culture's constitutive ideas and values. There was genuine and deep interest in Buddhism, not mere idle curiosity, on the part of many influential literati. On the other hand, the literati appeared to reserve Buddhism for use only *in extremis* or on the margins of cultural life, as a kind of hovering eschatological presence. They tended to place Buddhism mostly in the background of culture as a kind of *memento mori,* a constant reminder of such Buddhist "final things" as the transient insubstantiality of words and the transcendence of nirvāṇa.

Given the mutual ambivalence of both parties to this historical relationship, it is not surprising that the picture of the relationship presented to the modern scholar is, in its turn, inherently ambiguous. Contrary to long-held assumptions of its decline, we find Ch'an Buddhism during the Sung to be very much alive, actually flourishing as never before, and in the highest strata of society. We also find it (somewhat surprisingly perhaps) to be a tradition deeply rooted in literature, in the production and use of new genres of written religious discourse. Moreover, these new forms of Ch'an literature, which are what best distinguish Sung Ch'an from earlier phases of the tradition, are "classicist" in a sense that Chinese humanists or men of letters outside the Saṃgha could readily appreciate: they were texts employed in the common enterprise of *fu-ku,* the restoration and vital preservation of the sacred past. In matters of literary style, too, Ch'an and the secular belles lettres of the day often coincided and influenced each other.

On all these grounds, and more, the modern scholar could well build the argument that Ch'an became accepted as an important and integral component of Sung culture, and that Ch'an Buddhists cultivated a greater appreciation of both secular and sacred tradition by abandoning their isolation from the secular world and from the rest of Buddhism as well, and by participating more readily in public cultural life. Yet such a characterization of the relationship between Ch'an Buddhism and Sung literati culture does not tell the whole story. There remained considerable differences between the two, and despite their greater mutual involvement they did not entirely coalesce. Buddhism remained in appreciable degree aloof from the world, and Ch'an's participation in secular culture was still conducted with considerable reserve. Ch'an Buddhists were more literary in their religious orientations than they ever had been before, but they never ceased to worry about the still-acknowledged limitations of words and letters. Likewise, the secular literati of the day, pious Buddhists though they may have been in certain areas and periods of their lives, nonetheless confined their Buddhism to matters of relatively private religious and intellectual concern, remaining wholeheartedly Confucian, for example, in their civil and political lives. Nor can we ignore the steadily growing tradition of Tao-hsüeh, which was far less accommodating of Buddhism and which would eventually transform itself from an extremist minority movement into a dominant orthodoxy.

Such unsettled ambivalence and ambiguity, perhaps better understood as a continuing vital tension, was never finally overcome or relaxed. However, Fa-hsiu lived relatively early in the course of Buddhism's dialogue with secular literati culture. In succeeding generations other Ch'an Buddhists, like Hui-hung and Ta-hui, carried the dialogue further. Wen-tzu Ch'an, for example, would not come fully into its own, and the issues implicit in Fa-hsiu's life and teaching would not be made fully explicit, until the first several generations following his death. The inseparable questions of Ch'an's relation to literati culture and the role of literature and learning in Ch'an practice must be pursued into this later period if they are to be dealt with fully. To this our discussions of Fa-hsiu and the *Elegant Gathering in the Western Garden* are only a prelude.

Abbreviations and Conventions

CCC: Chih-cheng chuan (A Record of the Verifications of Insights), 1 *chüan.* By Hui-hung (1071–1128); date of completion uncertain. *HTC* 111:177–227.

CCHTL: Chien-chung Ching-kuo hsü-teng-lu (The Continued Lamp Record Published in the Chien-chung Ching-kuo Era), 30 *chüan.* By Fo-kuo Wei-po (d.u.); completed in 1101. *HTC* 136:1–414.

CLSPC: Ch'an-lin seng-pao chuan (Chronicles of the Ch'an Order), 30 *chüan.* By Hui-hung (1071–1128); completed in 1123. *HTC* 137:439–565.

CTCTL: Ching-te ch'uan-teng-lu (The Record of the Transmission of the Lamp Published in the Ching-te Era), 30 *chüan.* By Tao-yüan (d.u.); completed in 1004. *T* 51:196–467.

CTPTL: Chia-t'ai p'u-teng-lu (The Inclusive Lamp Record Published in the Chia-t'ai Era), 30 *chüan.* By Cheng-shou (1146–1208); completed in 1204. *HTC* 137:40–438.

CYL: Chih-yüeh lu (The Record of "Pointing at the Moon"), 32 *chüan.* By Ch'ü Ju-chi; completed in 1595. *HTC* 143:1–743.

ER: The Encyclopedia of Religion, 16 volumes. Mircea Eliade, Editor in Chief. New York: Macmillan and Free Press, 1987.

FHCL: Miao-fa lien-hua ching ho lun (The Lotus Sūtra Together with an Exposition Thereof), 7 *chüan.* By Chüeh-fan Hui-hung; date of composition unknown. *HTC* 47:701–835.

FTLTTT: Fo-tsu li-tai t'ung-tsai (A Comprehensive Registry of the Successive Ages of the Buddhas and the Patriarchs), 32 *chüan.* By Nien-ch'ang (1282–1323); completed in 1341. *T* 49:477–735.

FTTC: Fo-tsu t'ung-chi (A Chronicle of the Buddhas and the Patriarchs), 54 *chüan.* By Chih-p'an (1220–1275); completed in 1269. *T* 49:129–475.

HTC: Hsü tsang-ching (Tripiṭaka Supplement), 150 vols. Taipei: Hsin-wen-feng Ch'u-pan-she, 1977. Originally published as *Dainihon zokuzōkyō,* 750 vols. Kyoto: Zōkyō Shoin, 1905–1912. [Note: Citations of works in this series include the original *chüan* number of the particular work cited, but give the *HTC* volume and page numbers rather than those of the original Japanese edition.]

JAOS: Journal of the American Oriental Society

LCL: Lin-chien lu (Anecdotes from the "Groves" of Ch'an), 2 *chüan.* By Chüeh-fan Hui-hung; completed in 1107. *HTC* 148:585–647.

LCTC: Lin-chi tsung-chih (Lin-chi's Principal Message), 1 *chüan.* By Chüeh-fan Hui-hung; date of composition unknown. *HTC* 111:171–175.

LCYH: Leng-chai yeh-hua (Nocturnal Ruminations in the Chill Studio), 10 *chüan.* By Chüeh-fan Hui-hung; composed between 1111 and 1128. In *Pi-chi hsiao-shuo ta-kuan, cheng-pien* (Taipei: Hsin-hsing shu-chü, 1973) 2:893–909.

LYCHL: Leng-yen ching ho lun (The Śūraṃgama Sūtra Together with an Exposition Thereof), 10 *chüan.* By Chüeh-fan Hui-hung; completed in 1118. *HTC* 18:1–190.

LTHY: Lien-teng hui-yao (The Collated Essentials of the Consolidated Lamp [Records]), 31 *chüan.* By Wu-ming (d.u.); completed in 1183. *HTC* 136:415–950.

PEW: Philosophy East and West

SJCSY: Sung-jen chuan-chi tzu-liao so-yin (Index of Materials for the Biographies of Sung Figures), 6 vols. Revised and expanded edition. Edited by Wang Te-i et al. Taipei: Ting-wen Shu-chü, 1977. [Note: References to this work include both the volume and, following a colon, the page numbers.]

SKCSCP: Ssu-k'u ch'üan-shu chen-pen (Rare Works from the "Complete Collection of the Four Treasuries"), 13 series in 4,800 vols. Edited by Wang Yün-wu et al., 1934; rpt. Taipei: Shang-wu ch'u-pan-she, 1970–1982.

SMWTC: Shih-men Wen-tzu Ch'an (Stone Gate's [i.e., Hui-hung's] Lettered Ch'an), 30 *chüan.* Date of compilation unknown. A two-volume reprint of a 1921 typeset edition done at the T'ien-ning ssu in Changchow, Kiangsu, which was based in turn on a 1597 blockprint edition done at the Ching-shan ssu, Chekiang. Taipei: Hsin-wen-feng, 1973. [Note: Compare with the photolithic reprint of the same 1597 edition, found in *SPTK, ch'u-pien,* Lo no. 208.]

SPTK: Ssu-pu ts'ung-k'an (Collected Facsimiles of Works in the Four Categories). Three series *(pien),* each divided into four categories *(pu);* 465 titles, in 3,122 fascicles *(ts'e).* Shanghai: Commercial Press, 1919–1937. [Note: Works in this collection are cited by series *(ch'u, hsü, san)* and by serial number, as given in Karl Lo, *A Guide to the Ssu pu ts'ung k'an* (Lawrence, Kansas: The University of Kansas Libraries, 1965).]

SSCKL: Shih-shih chi-ku lüeh (An Outline of Historical Researches into the Śākya Family Lineage), 4 *chüan.* By Chüeh-an (b. 1286); completed in 1354. *T* 49:737–902.

SSCS: Sung-shih chi-shih (Annals of Sung Poetry), 100 *chüan* in 4 vols. Edited by Li E and Ma Yüeh-kuan. A critical and punctuated edition based on comparison of the original 1746 blockprint with other editions. Shanghai: Shang-hai ku-chieh ch'u-pan she, 1983.

T: Taishō shinshū daizōkyō (The Tripiṭaka Newly Compiled during the Taishō Era), 100 vols. Edited by Takakusu Junjirō, Watanabe Kaigyoku, and Ono Gemmyō. Tokyo: Daizō shuppansha, 1924–1932. [Note: Citations of works in this collection provide the original chüan number of the particular work cited when that is appropriate, followed by the *T* volume, page, and register numbers, sometimes with the line numbers as well.]

TCCL: T'ien-ch'u chin-lüan (Choice Morsels from the Imperial Kitchen), 3 *chüan.* By Chüeh-fan Hui-hung; date of compilation unknown. Photoreprint of a 1507 Kiangsu blockprint edition. Peking: Chung-hua shu-chü, 1958.

TMWK: Ta-hui P'u-chüeh Ch'an-shih tsung-men wu-k'u (Ch'an Master Ta-hui P'u-chüeh's Arsenal for the Ch'an Lineage), 1 *chüan.* Compiled by Tao-chien (d.u.); completed in 1186. *T* 47:943b–957c.

WTHY: Wu-teng hui-yüan (The Collated Essentials of the Five Lamps), 20 *chüan.* By P'u-chi (1179–1253); completed in 1252. Modern critical edition, punctuated and collated by Su Yüan-lei. Chung-kuo Fo-chiao tien-chi hsüan-k'an. Peking: Chung-hua shu-chü, 1984. [Note: Citations of this work provide the volume and pages numbers of the Peking edition, but also include the original chüan number so that references can be located in other editions, like *HTC* 138: 1–831.]

ZGDJT: Zengaku daijiten (The Encyclopedia of Zen Studies). New edition in one volume. Compiled by the Staff of the Zen Studies Encyclopedia Office, Komazawa University. Tokyo: Daishūkan Shoten, 1985.

Notes

1. I am particularly indebted to Bernard Faure and Lee Yearly—the respondents in the conference at which the first version of this paper was presented—for their acuity in posing these and other crucial questions. Thanks are also due to Paul Griffiths for his helpful comments on these issues. Note, too, the relevance of Anne Klein's chapter in this volume to the last of the questions mentioned, i.e., whether the path—which must be, in at least some sense, a kind of conditioning—can be said to generate or facilitate an attainment that is somehow unconditioned.

2. These two clauses are most familiar as the opening half of a four-part formula which goes on to assert that Ch'an is also "a direct pointing at the human mind by which buddhahood is achieved in the seeing of one's own nature" *(chih-chih jen-hsin/chien-hsing ch'eng-fo).* The locus classicus of the whole formula is a rather late text, Mu-an Shan-ch'ing's gloss on the term "singular transmission" *(tan-ch'uan)* in his *Tsu-t'ing shih-yüan* (Chrestomathy from the Patriarchs' Halls, *HTC* 113.132a), a work that was not compiled until 1108. However, the individual components of the formula, and the general claims they make, date back much earlier, perhaps to Bodhidharma himself. Even Yanagida Seizan, who has done so much to distinguish the legends of early Ch'an from its true history, accepts these traditional claims as definitive of classical Ch'an (see the concluding chapter, on "the fundamental essence" [*honshitsu*] of Zen, in his classic *Shoki Zenshū shisho no kenkyū* [Kyoto: Hōzōkan, 1967], 472). For an excellent discussion of Yanagida's and others' critical acceptance of traditional self-definitions of Ch'an, see the fifth chapter of Theodore Griffith Foulk's University of Michigan Ph.D. dissertation, *The "Ch'an School" and Its Place in the Buddhist Monastic Tradition* (Ann Arbor, Mich.: University Microfilms, 1987), 164–255. This view of the fundamental character of Ch'an has led to the widespread, but I think very dubious, view that Ch'an is essentially antinomian. Thus, for example, Ioan Petru Culianu, in the article on "Sacrilege" in the new *Encyclopedia of Religion,* defines antinomianism as "subversion of a religious or moral code" and goes on to say, "There are other religions in which antinomianism is fully accepted as the characteristic of a special school, such as Ch'an Buddhism in China or Zen Buddhism in Japan" (*ER* 12:557–558).

3. My thanks to Theodore Griffith Foulk for reminding me in private communication that even in the locus classicus of the *"pu-li wen-tzu. . ."* topos, i.e., in Mu-an's *Tsu-t'ing shih-yüan* (*HTC* 113.132a11–16), it is said that those Ch'anists who take the phrase literally, and thus understand Ch'an to be the actual abandonment of words and letters for a practice of "silent sitting" *(mo-tso),* are like "dumb sheep" *(ya-yang)* who display their doltish dependence on words and letters precisely by their literalist interpretation of the phrase "do not depend on words and letters."

4. See the remarks on this topic in the Introduction to this volume.

5. This text is traditionally attributed to Bodhidharma himself and, although some contemporary scholars are willing to accept that attribution, most are comfortable only with the more cautious view that it is a composite work formed during the period extending from the late sixth into the early eighth century. In any case, its crucial opening sections may date back to Bodhidharma and his immediate followers, and there are two important points about the text which are indisputable—that it is one of the earliest, if not the earliest, of all Ch'an texts, and that it has exerted great influence throughout Ch'an history. For an expert treatment of the text and its content, along with a precise and

complete English translation, see John R. McRae, *The Northern School and the Formation of Early Ch'an Buddhism,* Studies in East Asian Buddhism 3 (Honolulu: University of Hawaii Press, 1986), 101–117. See also Bernard Faure's more popularly oriented but expert and thoughtful French translation with commentary, *Le traité de Bodhidharma* (Paris: Le Mail, 1986). Note that in this early Ch'an text the "entrance of practice," which might be taken to counterbalance the "entrance of principle," is not so taken. Rather it is presented, in McRae's terms, as little more than "a didactic conceit, useful in the correct orientation of new students" (*Northern School,* p. 109). Note, too, Faure's observation that the tension between extremist and moderate Ch'an may be found in the earliest phases of Ch'an history (*Bodhidharma,* pp. 48–49).

6. On medieval Chinese uses of tathāgatagarbha doctrine for such purposes, see Robert M. Gimello's Columbia University Ph.D. dissertation, *Chih-yen and the Foundations of Hua-yen Buddhism* (Ann Arbor, Mich.: University Microfilms, 1976), 212–337. Note, too, Robert Buswell's argument that the apocryphal **Vajrasamādhi Sūtra* (*Chin-kang san-mei ching, T* 9.365c–374b) was composed precisely for the purpose of providing earliest Ch'an (i.e., the sort of Ch'an found in the *Erh-ju ssu-hsing*) with the kind of encouraging doctrinal support that was afforded by the Tathāgatagarbha Buddhism of works like the *Laṅkāvatārasūtra* and the *Ta-sheng ch'i-hsin lun;* see Robert E. Buswell, Jr., *The Formation of Ch'an Ideology in China and Korea: The Vajrasamādhi-Sūtra, a Buddhist Apocryphon* (Princeton, N.J.: Princeton University Press, 1989), esp. 74–122, 179–181.

7. This particular irenic gambit I have always found especially irritating and incoherent, as I have never been able to get past the contradiction obvious in any such juxtaposition of the terms "absolute" and "perspective."

8. The example par excellence of this polemic is found in the writings of Ta-hui Tsung-kao (1089–1163), a Lin-chi Ch'an monk whose life bridged the transition from Northern to Southern Sung. For thorough treatments of his championing of *k'an-hua* Ch'an, see Miriam Levering's 1978 Harvard Ph.D. dissertation, "Ch'an Enlightenment for Laymen: Ta-hui and the New Religious Culture of the Sung," and Robert E. Buswell, Jr., "The 'Short-cut' Approach of K'an-hua Meditation: The Evolution of a Practical Subitism in Chinese Ch'an Buddhism," in Peter N. Gregory, ed., *Sudden and Gradual: Approaches to Enlightenment in Chinese Thought,* Studies in East Asian Buddhism 5 (Honolulu: University of Hawaii Press, 1987), 321–377. Levering makes it clear that the targets of Ta-hui's strictures against "the Ch'an of silent illumination" *(mo-chiao Ch'an),* though long assumed to be the contemporary Ts'ao-tung master Hung-chih Cheng-chüeh (1091–1157) and his congeners, are really unknown ("Enlightenment for Laymen," pp. 261–274). The arguments against Ta-hui's position on such matters are best known in the form that the Japanese Sōtō master Dōgen Kigen (1200–1253) would later give them. Ignorant as we are about so much of Sung Ch'an, we cannot be sure that Dōgen's position had close antecedents in the China of Ta-hui's time, but it is certainly possible that it did.

9. Again see Buswell, "Short-cut," p. 348; and idem, "Ch'an Hermeneutics: A Korean View," in Donald S. Lopez, Jr., ed., *Buddhist Hermeneutics,* Studies in East Asian Buddhism 6 (Honolulu: University of Hawaii Press, 1988), 246–248.

10. This usage is apparently novel with the great Korean Ch'an patriarch Chinul (1158–1210), and I owe my acquaintance with it to Robert E. Buswell, Jr., *The Korean Approach to Zen: The Collected Works of Chinul* (Honolulu: University of Hawaii Press, 1983), 252–253, 260, and idem, "Chinul's Systematiza-

tion of Chinese Meditative Techniques in Korean Sŏn Buddhism," in Peter N. Gregory, ed., *Traditions of Meditation in Chinese Buddhism,* Studies in East Asian Buddhism 4 (Honolulu: University of Hawaii Press, 1986), 220–223.

11. See the various articles in Gregory, ed., *Sudden and Gradual.* Note that the curious combination "sudden realization and sudden cultivation" *(tun-wu tun-hsiu)* enjoys pride of place in the later Lin-chi tradition as the category into which *kung-an* practice is thought to fall. According to Tsung-mi, and later according to Chinul, the term "sudden cultivation" refers not to a practice that proceeds more quickly than gradual cultivation, nor even to one that is "all at once" rather than "by stages." Rather, it implies a practice in which the practitioner applies him or herself, perhaps repeatedly or for long periods of time, to a *single* meditative undertaking (like work on a *kung-an*) rather than to a progressive series of different undertakings. See Robert E. Buswell, Jr., "Chinul's Ambivalent Critique of Radical Subitism," in *Pojo Sasang* (Chinul's Thought), vol. 2 (Songgwang-sa: Pojo Sasang Yŏn'guwon, 1989). Of course, in other Zen traditions the same term can imply something quite different. One thinks, for example, of Dōgen, for whom "sudden practice" implied the identity of enlightenment with the bodily practice of *zazen.* On this see Carl Bielefeldt, *Dōgen's Manuals of Zen Meditation* (Berkeley: University of California Press, 1988), and note particularly his concluding discussion of what he calls the "recognition model" and the "enactment model" of meditation practice.

12. See Levering, "Enlightenment for Laymen," pp. 32–33.

13. See Foulk, *Monastic Tradition,* esp. pp. 62–99. Note particularly what he says about Dōgen's discovery of strict monastic orthodoxy in early Southern Sung "Ch'an" monasteries (i.e., monasteries over which Ch'an masters presided), a condition which no doubt prevailed during the Northern Sung as well, perhaps to an even greater degree.

14. For one intriguing suggestion as to how we might uncover the hidden cunning of *kung-an* practice as a "technique," the subtle "method" of its seeming "madness," see Chün-fang Yü, "Ta-hui Tsung-kao and *Kung-an Ch'an,*" *Journal of Chinese Philosophy* 6 (1979): 222–2, in which the author draws on the methods of phenomenological sociologists and enthnomethodologists to propose that *kung-an* are sophisticated dialogical contrivances designed to disconcert the practitioner and thus to separate him or her from the accustomed "commonsense world"—as, for example, one would be disconcerted if someone else were to reply to the innocuous question, "How are you?" by actually explaining how he or she is, or by asking what the question meant. For an analogous suggestion that *kung-an* practice and its connection with poetry exploit the subtle but still systematic resources of literature (metaphor, metonymy, and other tropes) to prompt estrangement from linguistically habituated attitudes, see Robert M. Gimello, "Poetry and the *Kung-an* in Ch'an Practice," *Ten Directions* 7 (Spring/Summer 1986): 9–10.

15. Here is not the place for the detailed argument that the point requires, but it must be noted that students of Sung Buddhism were operating under the handicap of a longstanding misconception, according to which Buddhism had already passed its "golden age" and was in a state of decline. In fact, Buddhism flourished during the Northern Sung, in both religious and worldly terms, and may well have exerted more influence on Chinese culture than ever before, even during its so-called heyday of the T'ang. For a brief discussion of the glimpses of Buddhism's institutional strength in the Northern Sung, as found in the travel diaries of visiting Japanese monks and in other contemporary sources, see Robert M. Gimello, "Imperial Patronage of Buddhism during the

Northern Sung," in *Proceedings of the First International Symposium on Church and State in China* (Taipei: Tamkang University Press, 1987), 71–85. Even the rise of Tao-hsüeh ("Neo-Confucianism"), its strong attack on Buddhism notwithstanding, bears this out. Although the anti-Buddhist strains of the Confucian revival are commonly cited in support of the claim that Buddhism was then declining, they actually testify, both in what they owe to Buddhism and in the frequent vehemence of their attack, to Buddhism's continuing strength. Moreover, the anti-Buddhist strains of this revival, though triumphant later, were in the minority during the Northern Sung itself. Every notice taken of an Ou-yang Hsiu's or a Ch'eng I's criticisms of Buddhism ought to be balanced against consideration of a Ch'ao Chiung's, a Yang I's, a Su Shih's, or a Huang T'ing-chien's admiration for it, especially as the latter was probably the more common, and in its own day the more influential, view. In this connection see Robert M. Gimello, "Li P'ing-shan, Hsing-hsiu, and the Place of Buddhism in Chin Culture," forthcoming.

16. No less a figure than Su Shih is only one of many possible examples. Consider what George C. Hatch, in his excellent biography of Su Shih, has to say about that great man's relationship to Buddhism, especially after his 1071 posting to the Hang-chou region. But like many other students of Sung life and letters who adhere to the old sinological tradition of disinterest in Buddhism, Hatch apparently finds it difficult to take Su Shih's Buddhism seriously. Indeed, in some of his phrasings Hatch seems to suggest that for Su Shih Buddhism was little more than an aesthetic reverie, an idle poetic and intellectual diversion. See Herbert Franke, ed., *Sung Biographies,* Münchener Ostasiatische Studien 16 (Wiesbaden: Franz Steiner Verlag, 1976) 3:900–968, esp. 939–953. For a more extensive treatment of Su Shih's interest in Buddhism, see Beata Grant's 1987 Stanford Ph.D. dissertation, "Buddhism and Taoism in the Poetry of Su Shih (1036–1101)."

17. The term "Wen-tzu Ch'an" is especially associated with the life and thought of the late Northern Sung Lin-chi Ch'an monk Hui-hung, who used it to characterize his own combination of Ch'an practice, Buddhist learning, and secular belles lettres. It may have been he who first coined the term. If this could be proved, it would mean that the conventional use of "Wen-tzu Ch'an" as a pejorative designating a merely literary imitation of true Ch'an—a use that seems to have first appeared shortly after Hui-hung's demise, in the teaching of Ta-hui—was actually a somewhat later use and a deliberate distortion of its original intent. For more on Hui-hung's possibly inaugural use of the term see Robert M. Gimello, "Ch'an Buddhism, Learning, and Letters during the Northern Sung: The Case of Chüeh-fan Hui-hung (1071–1128)," forthcoming.

18. For the use of the term "Tao-hsüeh" in a sarcastic and disparaging sense as well as in a sense implying praise, see James T. C. Liu, "How did a Neo-Confucian School Become the State Orthodoxy?" *PEW* 23 (1973): 491; and Conrad Schirokauer, "Neo-Confucianism under Attack," in John Winthrop Haeger, ed., *Crisis and Prosperity in Sung China* (Tucson: University of Arizona Press, 1975), 171.

19. On the conflicted attitudes of Tao-hsüeh scholars toward learning and the civil service examinations, see Liu, "Neo-Confucian School," p. 496.

20. I am drawing here especially on Peter Kees Bol's excellent Princeton Ph.D. dissertation, *Culture and the Way in Eleventh Century China* (Ann Arbor, Mich.: University Microfilms, 1982), a study of the thought of Su Shih and his foremost disciples. This, along with Bol's more recent but not yet published

research on the subject, is the best work available on Wen-hsüeh as a tradition of intellectual, and not only aesthetic, significance. See pp. 208–209 of the dissertation for Bol's summary of Su Shih's sudden-gradual distinction. Although Bol does not mention the possibility, it seems inconceivable that Su Shih was not here exploiting (and, of course, inverting) the old Ch'an distinction between the sudden and the gradual.

21. Such similarities have gone unnoticed, I believe, largely because too few of those who study the Sung Confucian revival also read the texts of Sung Buddhism (the latter being usually perceived as only the detritus of a supposedly "declining" tradition). Likewise, too few specialists in later Chinese Buddhism have been able to shake off the parochialism of their scholarly tradition so as to attend also to developments in the realms of *wai-hsüeh.* One can only hope for more exceptions to this sorry rule, more scholars of broad and interdisciplinary competence like, say, Araki Kengo.

22. See *Ho-nan Ch'eng-shih i-shu* 18, in *Erh-Ch'eng chi,* Li-hsüeh ts'ung-shu (Peking: Chung-hua Shu-chü, 1981), 1:239. I owe my acquaintance with this passage, and numerous Ch'eng I passages of similar import, to an as yet unpublished essay by Peter Bol entitled "Ch'eng Yi and the Cultural Tradition," part of which was presented to the Columbia University Seminar on Neo-Confucian Studies in February 1988.

23. From instructions to the otherwise unknown lay disciple Lo Chih-hsien found in the *Ta-hui P'u-chüeh Ch'an-shih yü-lu* 20 (*T* 47.898a6–8). See also the discussion in Levering, "Enlightenment for Laymen," pp. 82–102.

24. See Ta-hui's letter to a certain exegete *(chiang-chu)* named Tao-ming, in *Ta-hui yü-lu* 25 (*T* 47.916c23–917b6). Of course, Ta-hui is a figure of such subtlety and so many dimensions that he cannot be confined to any one category. His views on the relationship between learning and meditation are quite complex and resistant to easy definition. Thus, although he was severe in his castigation of overly discursive Ch'an, he was best known for his criticism of the Ch'an of silent illumination *(mo-chiao).*

25. See Ta-hui's reply to a letter from Li Lang-chung, in *Ta-hui yü-lu* 29 (*T* 47.935a22–b22). There he characterizes such mystagoguery as mere "flapping of the lips." See also Levering, "Enlightenment for Laymen," pp. 277–278.

26. For the classic statement of this shrewd metaphorical use of Archilocus' ancient aphorism, see Isaiah Berlin's "The Hedgehog and the Fox," originally published as a separate monograph (London: Weidenfeld and Nicholson, 1953) and reprinted in Henry Hardy and Aileen Kelly, eds., *Russian Thinkers,* "Isaiah Berlin: Selected Writings" (New York: The Viking Press, 1978), 22–81.

27. Chou Tun-i (1017–1073), a leading Tao-hsüeh "hedgehog," was once asked if sagehood were the sort of thing that could be "studied" or achieved through "learning" *(sheng k'o hsüeh hu).* His reply was in the affirmative, but it was also disingenuous. He knew that his anonymous questioner probably understood by *"hsüeh"* something highly literate and cumulative like "ample learning" *(po-hsüeh),* but he himself had in mind a drastic redefinition of the word *"hsüeh"* such that it meant something more like "spiritual cultivation" than "study." Thus, when the questioner probed further to ask if there were an "essential principle" *(yao)* to such "sagehood-through-*hsüeh,*" he replied that indeed there was, and that it consisted in "singleness" or "concentration on one thing" *(i),* viz., "the absence of desire" *(wu-yü).* This "singleness" is what I mean by Tao-hsüeh's "monism." It was "the one great thing" on which Chou Tun-i and other proponents of Tao-hsüeh believed they could rely, and on the basis of which they felt they could retrench the enterprise of letters and learning. See the opening passage of *Chin-ssu lu* 4; Wing-tsit Ch'an, trans., *Reflections*

on Things at Hand: The Neo-Confucian Anthology Compiled by Chu Hsi and Lü Tsu-ch'ien (New York: Columbia University Press, 1967), 123.

28. As far as modern Japanese and Western scholarship is concerned, the unsavory reputation of Wen-tzu Ch'an was confirmed by medieval and later Japanese judgments concerning the Gozan or "Five Mountains" Zen of Muromachi times. Gozan Bungaku and related art forms, which were cultivated by Zen monks in conscious emulation of Sung art and letters, were seen as factors in the corruption or weakening of medieval Zen. Such traditional judgments even now carry normative authority and exert considerable influence on contemporary assumptions of what Zen is or should be. Thus Philip Yampolsky, in an uncharacteristic expression of personal evaluation, was moved to write of Muromachi Zen that "it might not be an exaggeration to say that when Zen flourishes as a teaching it has little to do with the arts and that when the teaching is in decline its association with the arts increases." See Philip B. Yampolsky, trans., *The Zen Master Hakuin: Selected Writings* (New York: Columbia University Press, 1971), 9. One must not mistake artistic sensibility, however much it may exploit the imagery of Zen, for true Zen spirituality, but a general declaration that the two are mutually inimical flies in the face of universally available evidence for the often mutually enriching relationship between art and religion. For a thoughtful and learned discussion of this issue, particularly as it relates to the life of the great Muromachi Zen master Musō Soseki (1275–1351), see David Pollack, *The Fracture of Meaning: Japan's Synthesis of China from the Eighth through the Eighteenth Centuries* (Princeton, N.J.: Princeton University Press, 1986), 111–133; and idem, *Zen Poems of the Five Mountains,* American Academy of Religion Studies in Religion 37 (New York and Decatur: The Crossroad Publishing Co. and Scholars Press, 1985), which contains many well-translated examples of the sort of Chinese poetry, written by Japanese Zen monks, that comprises Gozan Bungaku.

29. Li Kung-lin (*tzu:* Po-shih, *hao:* Lung-mien), a major figure in the literati culture of his day, was particularly celebrated for his renderings of famous Buddhist subjects—e.g., scenes from the *Hua-yen ching* (misidentified by Basil Gray as Taoist scenes; see below), an oft-imitated portrait of Vimalakīrti, an evocation of Hui-yüan's *Lien-she* (Lotus Society), several paintings of arhats *(lo-han),* depictions of Pu-tai, icons of Śākyamuni and Kuan-yin, etc. But he was also esteemed for his illustrations of classical Confucian and literary texts—e.g., the *Hsiao-ching* (Classic of Filial Piety), T'ao Ch'ien's *Kuei-ch'ü-lai tz'u* (Homecoming), and the *Chiu Ko* (Nine Songs)—and for his paintings of Taoist immortals and horses. Although most celebrated as a figure painter, his landscapes were admired, too. As was common among literati painters of the period—and among poets and Ch'an teachers as well—Li was a careful student of the work of earlier masters and was given to working consciously in their styles. In his paintings of horses, for example, Li is said to have imitated Han Kan; as a landscape painter he is believed to have imitated Wang Wei; Wu Tao-tzu is said to have been his model for paintings of Buddhist figures; in his renderings of secular figures he is said to have followed Ku K'ai-chih; and the *Hsi-yüan ya-chi t'u* itself is said have been done in the style of another T'ang master, Li Ta-chao. For more on the theme of *fu-ku* (restoring the past) and neo-classicism in Chinese art and culture of the Sung and later periods, see Wen Fong, "Archaism as a 'Primitive Style,' " and Frederick W. Mote, "The Past in Chinese Cultural History," both in Christian F. Murck, ed., *Artists and Traditions: Uses of the Past in Chinese Culture* (Princeton, N.J.: Princeton University Press, 1976), 89–109 and 3–8, respectively. For general information concerning Li Kung-lin, see:

Richard Barnhart, *Li Kung-lin's Hsiao Ching t'u,* Princeton University Ph.D. diss. (Ann Arbor, Mich.: University Microfilms, 1967).

Idem, "Li Kung-lin's Use of Past Styles," in Murck, *Artists and Traditions,* 51–71.

Susan Bush, *Chinese Literati on Painting: Su Shih (1037–1101) to Tung Ch'i-ch'ang (1555–1636)* (Cambridge, Mass.: Harvard University Press, 1971), passim.

Susan Bush and Hsiao-yen Shih, *Early Chinese Texts on Painting* (Cambridge, Mass.: Harvard University Press, 1985), passim.

James Cahill, *An Index of Early Chinese Painters and Paintings: T'ang, Sung, Yüan* (Berkeley: University of California Press, 1980), 112–117.

Idem, "Li Kung-lin," in *Encyclopedia of World Art* (New York: McGraw-Hill, 1964) 9:247–251.

Ch'en Kao-hua, *Sung Liao Chin hua-chia shih-liao* (Peking: Wen-wu Ch'u-pan-she, 1984), 450–554.

Chou Wu, *Li Kung-lin,* Chung-kuo hua-chia ts'ung-shu (Shanghai: Shanghai Jen-min Mei-shu Ch'u-pan-she, 1959).

Idem, "Li Kung-lin," in *Li-tai hua-chia p'ing-chuan I: T'ang-ch'ien, T'ang, Wu-tai, Sung* (Hong Kong: Chung-hua Shu-chü, 1979), no consecutive paging.

Basil Gray, "A Great Taoist Painting," *Oriental Art,* n.s., 11 (Summer 1965): 85–94.

Robert E. Harrist, Jr., "A Scholar's Landscape: *Shang-chuang t'u* by Li Kung-lin," (Ph.D. diss., Princeton University, 1989).

Idem, "The Hermit of Lung-mien: A Biography of Li Kung-lin," forthcoming in a collection of essays on Li Kung-lin to be published by the Metropolitan Museum of Art.

Ellen Johnston Laing, "Real or Ideal: The Problem of the 'Elegant Gathering in the Western Garden' in Chinese Historical and Art Historical Records," *JAOS* 88 (1968): 419–435.

Idem, *Scholars and Sages: A Study in Chinese Figure Painting,* University of Michigan Ph.D. diss. (Ann Arbor, Mich.: University Microfilms, 1968).

Agnes E. Meyer, *Chinese Painting as Reflected in the Thought and Art of Li Lung-mien* (New York: Duffield and Co., 1923).

Hsiao-yen Shih, "Li Kung-lin," in Herbert Franke, ed., *Sung Biographies: Painters,* Münchener Ostasiatische Studien, Band 17 (Wiesbaden: Franz Steiner Verlag, 1976), 78–85.

Oswald Sirén, *Chinese Painting: Leading Masters and Principles* (1956; rpt. New York: Hacker Art Books, 1973) 2:39–61.

SJCSY 2:959–961.

Nicole Vandier-Nicolas, *Chinese Painting: An Expression of A Civilization,* Janet Seligman, trans. (New York: Rizzoli International, 1983), 119–127.

Arthur Waley, *An Introduction to the Study of Chinese Painting* (1923; rpt. New York: Grove Press, 1958), 196–200.

30. *Tzu:* Chin-ch'ing. See *SJCSY* 1:190–191. On Wang Shen the painter, see Shen Man-shih, "Wang Shen," in *Li-tai hua-chia p'ing-chuan I,* no consecutive paging.

31. Concerning Mi Fu (*tzu:* Yüan-chang), see *SJCSY* 1:541–544; also Nicole Vandier-Nicolas, *Art et sagesse en Chine: Mi Fou (1051–1107),* (Paris: Presses

Universitaires de France, 1963). The description of the painting is found in an undated supplement to the surviving portions of Mi Fu's collected works, the *Pao-chin ying-kuang chi,* and is reprinted in Ch'en Kao-hua, *Hua-chia shih-liao,* pp. 472–473. For an exhaustive discussion of its authenticity, and the authenticity of the painting itself, see Laing, "Real or Ideal."

32. *Hao:* Tung-p'o, *tzu:* Tzu-chan; *SJCSY* 5:4312–4324.

33. *Tzu:* T'ien-chi; *SJCSY* 5:3798–3799.

34. *Tzu:* Tuan-shu; *SJCSY* 2:947.

35. *Tzu:* Tzu-yu; *SJCSY* 5:4331–4333.

36. *Hao:* Shan-ku, *tzu:* Lu-chih; *SJCSY* 4:2903–2910.

37. *Tzu:* Chung-chih; *SJCSY* 1:350.

38. *Tzu:* T'ai-hsü; *SJCSY* 3:2623.

39. *Tzu:* Shao-yu; *SJCSY* 3:1872–1874.

40. An obscure figure known to us only as the recipient of four brief and uninformative extant letters from Su Shih. See K'ung Fan-li, ed., *Su Shih wen-chi,* Chung-kuo ku-tien wen-hsüeh chi-pen ts'ung-shu (Peking: Chung-hua shu-chü, 1986), 4:1674–1676. Cheng Ching-lao's obscurity no doubt has something to do with the fact that certain later descriptions of the scene do not find him there at all but suggest other identifications; see Laing, "Real or Ideal," pp. 421–422.

41. *Tzu:* Wu-chiu; *SJCSY* 3:1953–1954. Ch'ao Pu-chih was the scion of a distinguished literati family long known for its Buddhist piety and learning. His great grandfather's elder brother was Ch'ao Chiung (951–1034), the author of several important but neglected collections of Buddhist reflections, including the *Fa-tsang chin-sui lu* (*SKCSCP,* tenth series, vols. 1–4), which provide a valuable insight into the importance of Buddhist learning in early Northern Sung Wen-hsüeh.

42. *Tzu:* Wen-ch'ien; *SJCSY* 3:2232–2233.

43. Huang T'ing-chien, Ch'ao Pu-chih, Ch'in Kuan, and Chang Lei are known collectively as "the Four Scholars" and comprise the group of Su Shih's foremost acknowledged disciples. For a thorough study of this group, and the "literary learning" or "cultural learning" *(Wen-hsüeh)* tradition they represented during the late eleventh and the early twelfth centuries, see Bol, *Culture and the Way.* That they were recognized as a group and admired as such, not only in secular literary circles but also in the Wen-tzu Ch'an movement of Sung Buddhism, is indicated by a collective tribute to them penned by Hui-hung, the leader of the lettered Ch'an movement. See *SMWTC* 27:23a.

44. Although they are not the focus of attention at the moment depicted, the presence in the painting of a number of bronze vessels indicates, as one might have expected of a gathering of Sung literati, that antiquarian connoisseurship had its place—along with literary composition, calligraphy, painting, and music—among the day's edifying delights. Wang Ch'in-ch'en (see note 10) was especially well known as a collector of antiques, as was Li kung-lin himself. In other words, the full complement of Sung *wen-shih* avocations is represented in the "Western Garden" scene.

45. *Tzu:* Chü-chi; *SJCSY* 5:3862.

46. *Wu-sheng* (lit., "unborn") is the Chinese rendering of the concept first expressed in Sanskrit as *anutpāda* or *anutpattika,* as in the compound *anutpattika-dharma* (unarisen dharmas, *wu-sheng fa*). It refers to the ancient Buddhist doctrine that all things, being devoid of own-being or substantive self-nature, cannot be said ever to "come into existence" or "arise" as separate entities. It is not the Taoist "original nonbeing" *(pen-wu)* that some have taken it to be, but

rather the Buddhist "emptiness" *(śūnyatā, k'ung),* i.e., the intrinsic transience, indeterminacy, and consequent ineffability of things rather than their supposed derivation from some eternal meontic substratum.

47. The piece ascribed to Mi Fu, and several other literary sources describing this painting, refer to the monk by name, but in some later texts his name is forgotten or ignored and he is identified simply as "a certain monk," even though the names of all the other figures are carefully preserved. Not only his name but even the monk himself disappeared from certain later versions of the painting, e.g., the anonymous late Ming rendering owned by New York's Metropolitan Museum of Art and reproduced in Lin Yutang's *The Gay Genius,* following p. 16. Such neglect, I think, is a token of the declining interest in Buddhism that characterizes many later traditions of Chinese learning, and of their eventual ignorance of the place of Buddhism in Sung culture. In this connection we should note that Ellen Johnston Laing was worried by certain inconsistencies in the record regarding the monk's name. In those sources in which he is named, Fa-hsiu is not always referred to in precisely the same way. Sometimes he is called Yüan-t'ung Ta-shih; other times Yüan-t'ung Lao-shih; still other times simply Hsiu-lao, Hsiu Ch'an-shih, or Seng Yüan-t'ung. This should not be cause, as it was for Laing, to doubt the tradition that identifies the monk as Fa-hsiu, for the use of such variant epithets is quite common in later Chinese Buddhism. The one instance Laing cites of a truly different name (T'an-hsiu), found in a colophon on one anonymous version of the painting, is most likely an error. Moreover, in the biographies of Fa-hsiu and other contemporary sources there is ample evidence, some of which is presented below, that he was well known to many of the other figures depicted in the painting, including Li Kung-lin himself. This evidence renders the identification of the monk as Fa-hsiu no less certain than, say, the identification of the calligrapher-painter in the foreground of the painting as Su Shih.

48. In the summary of Fa-hsiu's career that follows, I rely especially on the biographies contained in two early works: first, the *CCHTL* (*HTC* 136.155a–158b), because it is the earliest (1101) and one of the most extensive, but also because it was written by Fa-hsiu's chief disciple Wei-po; and second, Hui-hung's *CLSPC* (*HTC* 137.543b–545b), which was written only thirty-three years after Fa-hsiu's death by someone who was not just a recorder of relevant events but a leading actor in the Wen-tzu Ch'an story we are concerned to tell. I have also compared Wei-po's and Hui-hung's accounts with those found in Hsiao-ying's 1155 *Yün-wo chi-t'an* (*HTC* 148.55b–56a), Wu-ming's 1183 *LTHY* (*HTC* 136.915a–916b), Tao-yung's 1197 *Ts'ung-lin shih-sheng* (*HTC* 148.55b–56a), P'u-chi's 1252 *WTHY* (2:1037–1039), Nien-ch'ang's 1341 *FTLTTT* (*T* 49.673c1–674a14), Chüeh-an's 1354 *SSCKL* (*T* 49.875b20–876a10), and Ch'ü Ju-chi's 1595 *CYL* (*HTC* 143.578a–579a). P'u-chi's work has become a favored source of information on the lives and teachings of the Ch'an monks whose biographies and selected sayings it contains, due to the care its compiler took in collating earlier sources. This work has been available since 1984 in a fine three-volume critical edition, punctuated and collated by Su Yüan-lei and published in Peking by Chung-hua Shu-chü in their Chung-kuo Fo-chiao tien-chi hsüan-kan series. I would recommend that henceforth this Peking edition be used at least together with, if not instead of, the *HTC* and other editions. It is this edition that I cite throughout the present chapter.

49. In early Sung, Yün-men was in close competition with Lin-chi for the status of most influential Ch'an lineage. Its importance has been traditionally overlooked since then, perhaps because it did not last long (Yün-men was even-

tually absorbed or supplanted by Lin-chi), but also perhaps because of bias against it, or ignorance of it, on the part of certain major chroniclers of Sung Buddhism. Tsan-ning (919–1001), for example, deliberately chose to exclude the very founder of the lineage from his *Sung kao-seng chuan;* see Ishii Shūdō, *Sōdai Zenshūshi no kenkyū* (Tokyo: Daitō shuppansha, 1987), 48, and Abe Chōichi, *Chūgoku Zenshūshi no kenkyū,* revised and expanded ed. (Tokyo: Kyūbun shuppansha, 1986), 467–488. Three major figures of the Northern Sung—Hui-hung (1071–1128), a member of the Huang-lung branch of Lin-chi but sympathetic to Yün-men, and Ch'i-sung (1007–1072) and Wei-po (fl. 1100), both of the Yün-men lineage itself—tried to rectify this situation in the several chronicles and biographical-anecdotal collections they wrote, but apparently their effect on the later tradition was limited, particularly in Japan, where the Yün-men never developed as a separate lineage. On Ch'i-sung's efforts to establish Yün-men, and on the influence of Yün-men monks during the early Northern Sung, see Huang Chi-chiang's University of Arizona dissertation, *Experiment in Syncretism: Ch'i-sung (1007–1072) and Eleventh-Century Chinese Buddhism* (Ann Arbor, Mich.: University Microfilms, 1986), esp. 115–140, 177–219. For more on the general subject of Ch'an in the Sung histories of Buddhism, see Jan Yün-hua, "Buddhist Historiography in Sung China," *Zeitschrift der Deutschen Morgenländischen Gesellschaft* 114 (1964): 360–381, and Helwig Schmidt-Glintzer, *Die Identität der Buddhistischen Schulen und die Kompilation buddhistischer Universalgeschichten in China: Ein Beitrag zur Geistesgeschichte der Sung-Zeit* (Wiesbaden: Franz Steiner Verlag, 1982).

50. The standard sources of hagiographical information on this monk, most of which include brief excerpts from his recorded sayings, are as follows: *CCHTL* 5 (*HTC* 136.88a–89a), *CLSPC* 11 (*HTC* 137.489a–b), *LTHY* 28 (*HTC* 136.908a–912a), *CTPTL* 2 (*HTC* 137.58a–59b), *FTLTTT* 18 (*T* 49.b16–c6), and *SSCKL* (*T* 49.870b18–27). Extensive quotations from three nonextant collections of his sayings comprise *chüan* 5 of Mu-an Shan-ch'ing's 1108 compilation, the *Tsu-t'ing shih-yüan* (Chrestomathy from the Patriarchs' Halls, *HTC* 113.126a–151a). In the early twelfth century, Sung Hui-tsung conferred upon him the posthumous title Chen-tsung Ta-shih.

51. This is the famous sheer-faced rock that juts dramatically out of low rolling hills about 30 miles southeast of T'ien-shui in Kansu. Since at least the early fifth century it has been a sacred Buddhist site, and its scores of natural and manmade caves contain great treasures of Buddhist sculpture and painting. It had long been regarded as a representation, or local counterpart, of the great axial mountain of Buddhist cosmology, Mt. Sumeru. Historical records indicate that, although it waxed and waned through history, during the Northern Sung it was the site of flourishing Buddhist institutions. See Michael Sullivan, et al. *The Cave Temples of Maichishan* (Berkeley and Los Angeles: University of California Press, 1969). For a novel treatment of Mai-chi shan as a Buddhist monastic center compared with monasteries of the Christian and other traditions, see Peter Levi, *The Frontiers of Paradise: A Study of Monks and Monasteries* (New York: Weidenfeld and Nicholson, 1988), 163–166.

52. I take *"hsüeh"* here as an adjective rather than a verb and thus understand *hsüeh-Ch'an* as having the pejorative connotation of "pedantic" or "bookish" Ch'an.

53. The question of this monk's identity is difficult and requires some extended discussion. The earliest of the Fa-hsiu biographies to mention him is that found in Hui-hung's *CLSPC,* and all others in which he later appears (e.g., *FTLTTT*) seem to derive from Hui-hung's reference. Most of these sources

leave his identity a mystery by calling him simply "Yüan Hua-yen," a name otherwise unattested except for an independent reference to him in another of Hui-hung's works, the *LCL* (*HTC* 148.586a–b). Another reference, in Chinul's *Chinsim chiksŏl,* seems to be simply a quotation of the opening lines of the *LCL* passage; see Buswell, *The Korean Approach to Zen,* pp. 175, 187–188. Whereas the references in the Fa-hsiu biographies identify Yüan as from Pei-ching, the *LCL* and Chinul references identify him as from Wei-fu, but these are just two Sung dynasty names for the district now known as Ta-ming in southeastern Hopei.

However, the matter does not end here. Apparently the issue of Yüan Hua-yen's identity was recognized as problematic early on, for apart from the indecisive texts already mentioned, there are several other sources that offer two conflicting identifications. One of the latest of the standard biographies of Fa-hsiu—the one in Chüeh-an's 1354 *SSCKL* (*T* 49.875b23–25)—offers the opinion that our Yüan Hua-yen is actually Fa-hsiu's elder dharma brother, a monk named Chung-yüan who died 1063. The *SSCKL* refers to the anti-exegetical monk in question as "Ch'an Master T'ien-po Yüan of Pei-ching" and adds the crucial comment that his style *(hao)* was Hua-yen. Now, there was a T'ien-po Yüan Ch'an-shih whose standard monastic name was Yüan-chung and whose honorary title was Wen-hui Ch'an-shih. He was a Yün-men monk who had been, like Fa-hsiu himself, a disciple of T'ien-i I-huai, having studied with him probably some years before Fa-hsiu did. He is a relatively well-known figure and information on his life, along with excerpts traditionally thought to be from his recorded sayings, is available in several of the standard sources: *CCHTL* 10 (*HTC* 136.160a–161b), *CTPTL* 3 (*HTC* 137.77b–78a), *WTHY* 16 (3:1041–1042), *FTTC* (*T* 49.473b25–28), *FTLTTT* (*T* 49.667c18–22), and *SSCKL* (*T* 49.872b3–c3).

All these sources note that Chung-yüan, like the presumptive Yüan Hua-yen, resided in the T'ien-po ssu in Pei-ching (a.k.a. Wei-fu, mod. Ta-ming). Given the fact that both the putative Yüan Hua-yen and the historical Chung-yüan were associated with the same city and temple, and considering Chung-yüan's close relationship with Fa-hsiu, it was not entirely unreasonable of Chüeh-an to assume, as he apparently did in his *SSCKL,* that the Yüan Hua-yen to whom earlier Fa-hsiu biographies and other texts had referred was actually Chung-yüan.

However, there is also good reason to doubt this identification. Chung-yüan and Fa-hsiu were near contemporaries, and Fa-hsiu would probably have come to know of his senior dharma brother only after he had himself become a disciple of I-huai. But the reference to Yüan Hua-yen in Fa-hsiu's biographies pertains to an earlier phase of Fa-hsiu's career, before he had become I-huai's disciple. Could Fa-hsiu have known of Chung-yüan that early, and would Chung-yüan's views have already become so well known as to have acquired the status in Fa-hsiu's mind of a model for one of the standard attitudes toward the relationship between Ch'an and doctrinal Buddhism? Neither seems likely. Also, Fa-hsiu's reference to Yüan Hua-yen contrasts him to Tsung-mi, but if Yüan Hua-yen is to be identified with Chung-yüan, one is faced with the troubling and dubious anachronism of a contrast between an eminent ninth-century figure and a not nearly so eminent figure of the eleventh century. Then, too, there is nothing in the recorded sayings of Chung-yüan, at least not in those we can judge to be authentic, to indicate that he was a particularly outspoken critic of learned or exegetical Buddhism. Finally, none of the biographies of Chung-yüan say that his *hao* was Hua-yen; this seems to have been pure surmise on Chüeh-an's part.

For all these reasons it seems improbable, despite the testimony of the *SSCKL,* that Chung-yüan could be our man. However, as early as the mid-twelfth century, an alternative identification had been adduced that must have been missed by Chüeh-an and those who accepted his suggestion. In 1155, a disciple of Ta-hui Tsung-kao named Hsiao-ying, in his *Yün-wo chi-t'an* (Anecdotes from the Lodge Reclining on Clouds; *HTC* 148.28a–b), identified our Yüan Hua-yen with a certain Huai-tung, also known as Lao Hua-yen. No independent biographical record of this monk is known, at least none in which he is so named, but he and his teachings are mentioned in Ta-hui's recorded sayings (*Ta-hui yü-lu* 26; *T* 47.923c8–12), and it was probably through Ta-hui that Hsiao-ying learned of him. In any case, Hsiao-ying tells us that Huai-tung, alias Lao Hua-yen, was also a resident of Pei-ching or Wei-fu (modern Ta-ming) and was also called T'ien-po after the local monastery of that name.

Most significantly, Huai-tung is best known as one who had repudiated an earlier attachment to learned Hua-yen in favor of an exclusive commitment to that "separate transmission outside the teachings," i.e. Ch'an. He is said thereafter to have advocated a very down-to-earth and quotidian Buddhism in which the dharma consisted not of labored and exclusively religious undertakings like study or exegetics but of quite ordinary activities like "walking, standing, sitting, lying down, eating, drinking, and conversing." This certainly seems to be the sort of teaching about which Fa-hsiu's biographies say he was so ambivalent. Moreover, Huai-tung is a much earlier figure than Chung-yüan. His exact dates are forgotten, but it is known that he flourished in the ninth century and that he was a minor disciple of classical Ch'an Master Hsing-hua Ts'un-chiang (830–838). The latter is well known as the foremost heir of none other than Lin-chi I-hsüan (d. 866), progenitor of the Lin-chi line.

Hsiao-ying argued that it is really this monk to whom Fa-hsiu's biographies and the other sources we have mentioned refer, and that it was Hui-hung's misreading or a misprint of "Yüan Hua-yen" for "Lao Hua-yen" which led him and then others, like Chüeh-an, into error. Although Hsiao-ying's identification of Huai-tung as the man in question cannot be independently verified, it does seem much more likely than the alternative identification of Chung-yüan, particularly in view of the fact that Huai-tung serves better—both chronologically and substantively—as a focus of contrast with Tsung-mi. Note, too, that this identification was accepted as correct in 1715 by the Ōbaku Zen scholar Kōhō Jitsuge (pronunciation uncertain) in his very useful *Zenrin kujitsu konmei shū* (Compendium of Confused Ch'an Names; *Kokuyaku Zenshū sōsho* 2:5 or *Zen-hsüeh ta-ch'eng* [Taipei: Chun-hua Fo-chiao wen-hua kuan, 1969], 5:23–24). Also, marginal collation notes in the *HTC* edition of the *LCL* (*HTC* 148.586a–b) mention that "another edition of the *LCL* reads 'Tung-lao' rather than 'Yüan-kung.' "

There is also a curious appendix to chüan 30 of the *CTCTL* (*T* 51.466b–467a) entitled "Address to the Assembly by Wei-fu Hua-yen Ch'ang-lao." This appendix appears only in certain editions of the *CTCTL,* not in all of them, and according to the *T* collation note, was added to Tao-yüan's 1004 compendium only in its 1601 Ming Tripiṭaka edition (but then, the *CTCTL* is a work known to have had a very complicated textual history, marred by repeated scribal and other errors; see Shiina Koyū and Suzuki Tetsuo, "Sō-Gen-han *Keitoku dentō roku* no shoshiteki kōsatsu," *Aichi Gakuin Zen Kenkyūjo Kiyō* [1973], 3:261–280). Some later scholars, following Hui-hung's and Chüeh-an's mistake, have attributed this longish passage to Chung-yüan, but it would seem to follow from what we have shown that it is really a document of ninth-century rather than eleventh-century Ch'an, and that it is most likely a remnant (perhaps the only one extant) of Huai-tung's recorded sayings. Later, of course—and again because of Hui-hung's original error—certain of Huai-tung's teachings were ascribed to Chung-yüan and even inserted into his biographies, thus further compounding the confusion.

Lest this long argument seem otiose, I would point out that the correct identification of the person in question is not only valuable in its own right, as the solution to a longstanding puzzle in Ch'an history; it also serves the underlying purposes of this study insofar as it reminds us that the extreme anti-exegetical Ch'an position that Fa-hsiu rejected was, in this instance, an inheritance from an earlier phase in Ch'an's history and not the opinion of a contemporary Sung figure. This is a further reminder of the evolution toward moderation and breadth which we argue Ch'an underwent during the transition from the late T'ang to the Sung.

54. This subtly worded remark seems susceptible to several slightly different interpretations. I take it to indicate first that Fa-hsiu held Ch'an and learned Buddhism to be compatible. He was certainly not choosing one to the exclusion of the other. However, I also take it to mean that he did not give the two equal recognition for, after acknowledging the compatibility between Ch'an and exegetical Buddhism, he implied that such compatibility warranted his confident and relatively singleminded commitment to Ch'an. Convinced that in accepting the transmission through Mahākāśyapa he would get just what is to be found in "the teachings" and not anything other or less than that, he did not need to treat Ch'an as something apart and different from the rest of Buddhism. By the same token, he could rely on Ch'an as in itself a genuine and sufficient transmission of the Buddha's truth. Having claimed the compatibility of Ch'an and exegetics, he could, as the text goes on to say, immediately thereafter put aside exegetics as a separate vocation and devote himself entirely to Ch'an, which he had now come to understand as subsuming exegetics.

55. *LTHY* (*HTC* 136.915a6–9). This use of the term "schools (or 'principles') of nature and characteristics" is a bit unusual. "School of nature" usually refers to the Hua-yen and associated traditions, whereas "school of characteristics" most commonly refers to allegedly lesser forms of elementary Mahāyāna Buddhism, like the *wei-shih* (representation-only) teaching of the Fa-hsiang school. Here such distinctions among various theoretically oriented traditions pale by comparison with the difference between all of them, on the one hand, and the practical or experiential orientation of Ch'an, on the other. Again, the point is not that Fa-hsiu rejected theoretical Buddhism, but that he chose to incorporate it into a Ch'an framework, just as Bodhidharma and Hui-neng had exemplified in their own lives the symbolic significance of Sudhana's mythic pilgrimage.

56. Also known as Shou-ch'eng Ch'an-shih (d.u.); see *WTHY* 13, 2:833. Shou-ch'eng was the founder of the Hu-kuo monastery where the stele was located.

57. Ch'an Master Hui-lang of the Pao-tz'u Yüan in Fu-chou (mod. Fukien) was a late T'ang or Five Dynasties Ch'an monk in the lineage of Hsüeh-feng I-ts'un (822–908). See *WTHY* 8, 2:463. He also appears in case forty-eight of the *Pi-yen lu*.

58. T'ien-i I-huai was, as noted above, a Yün-men Ch'an monk of the fourth generation after that line's founder, Yün-men Wen-yen (864–949). As a direct heir of Hsüeh-tou Ch'ung-hsien, he participated in the latter's temporary revival of Yün-men, which made that house preponderant during the mid-elev-

enth century and until the ascendancy of the Lin-chi line that would eventually absorb it. He was a very popular teacher; Fa-hsiu is but one of fifty-four of his disciples whose names have been preserved in Ch'an records (see *ZGDJT, Kei-fu* 10).

59. Po-ch'ao Chih-yüan was a little-known monk of the early Sung who belonged either to the lineage of Hsüeh-feng I-ts'un (822–908) or to that of I-ts'un's dharma brother, Kan-t'an Tzu-kuo. See *WTHY* 7, 2:386. Rcgarding Pao-tz'u, see note 57.

60. I have not been able to find this obscure exchange in any source other than Fa-hsiu's biographies, nor am I confident that I have translated Pao-tz'u's reply correctly. This is regrettable because the question may be that relatively rare thing, a Buddhist allusion to a Confucian classic. The opening lines of the *Chung-yung* (Doctrine of the Mean) speak of the state before the feelings or emotions are aroused. The word "separation" *(ke)* is the same term that appears in the phrase *"hsüan-ke"* (distant separation) which I-huai used earlier in the dialogue with Fa-hsiu quoted above.

61. An old monastery, first established during the Southern Ch'i (479–501), rebuilt during the T'ang, and given its name ("Sage's Roost") because a famous Ch'an layman named Li Po (772–831), a student of the Ma-tsu disciple Kuei-tsung Chih-ch'ang, once used it as a retreat. It was one of several Ch'an establishments on Mt. Lu during the Sung.

62. Yün-chu Hsiao-shun was, along with the famous Ch'i-sung, a disciple of Tung-shan Hsiao-ts'ung (d.u.). He thus traced his lineage back to the Yün-men founder, Yün-men Wen-yen (864–949), through Wen-yen's direct disciple Te-shan Yüan-mi (d.u). Fa-hsiu's teacher T'ien-i I-huai, in contrast, traced his and his teacher Hsüeh-tou Ch'ung-hsien's lineage back to Wen-yen through another of Wen-yen's direct disciples, Hsiang-lin Ch'eng-yüan (908–987). Criticism of the teaching of other Ch'an masters, carried out in the spirit of dharma combat, was not uncommon, even among different branches of the same Ch'an house. For standard versions of Hsiao-shun's biography and representative samples of his teaching, see *CCHTL* 5 (*HTC* 136.99); *LTHY* 28 (*HTC* 136.906); *CTPTL* 2 (*HTC* 137.60); and *WTHY* 15, 3:1003–1004. See below for more on Fa-hsiu's debates with Hsiao-shun concerning I-huai's Ch'an.

63. This may be Chiang-shan Tsan-yüan, a.k.a. Chüeh-hai Ch'an-shih, another Lin-chi monk who enjoyed the admiration and support of Wang An-shih. If so, however, there is a dating problem to be resolved because there are records indicating that this particular "Master Yüan" did not die until 1086. See *WTHY* 12, 2:730–731. Chung-shan or Chiang-shan was located just a few miles northeast of Sung-era Nanking and came to be called Chin-ling-shan in Ming, Ch'ing, and modern times (in the nineteenth century, it was the site of Yang Wen-hui's famous Buddhist printing center). During the Sung it was the site of several important Buddhist establishments and happened also to be Wang An-shih's residence for much of the time following his 1076 retirement, Wang having been throughout his life a very pious Buddhist layman. For an excellent treatment of Wang An-shih's life that is more sensitive than most to his Buddhist interests, see Jonathan Pease's 1986 Stanford Ph.D. dissertation, "From the Wellsweep to the Shallow Skiff: Life and Poetry of Wang An-shih (1021–1086)."

64. Hui-hung tells an anecdote (*CLSPC* 26 [*HTC* 137.544b]) according to which Fa-hsiu did not accept, or did not long retain, the office of abbot that was offered to him because, when Wang An-shih called on him shortly after his arrival at the monastery, Fa-hsiu was preoccupied with clerical duties and kept

the distinguished lord waiting. Wang was insulted and the result was Fa-hsiu's departure. No doubt this story endeared Fa-hsiu to Wang An-shih's critics, several of the most famous of whom later befriended the monk. It may have been this encounter that was recorded in another Li Kung-lin painting in which Fa-hsiu is said to have appeared, this one unfortunately lost. The anti-reform statesman Lu Tien (1042–1102, *SJCSY* 3:2648–2649; Franke, *Sung Biographies,* 2:687–691), in fascicle 11 of his collected writings entitled *T'ao-shan chi,* records that Li visited him in Kaifeng in 1089 and painted for him a work called *Wang Ch'ing-kung's Visit to Chung-shan,* in which the eminent monk was depicted standing beneath a pine tree. The Lu Tien passage is quoted in Ch'en Kao-hua, *Hua-chia shih-liao,* 475.

65. The story goes (*CLSPC* 26 [*HTC* 137.544b]) that a certain Ch'üan-chiao Ch'ang-lao, to whom I can find no other reference, once came to lecture to the monks of the Ch'ung-fu monastery but was greeted only by the ridicule of most of the audience, none of whom would rise to question him. Fa-hsiu, however, hastened to ask, "What is the self of Fa-hsiu?" Ch'üan-chiao laughed and said, "Iron-faced Hsiu doesn't even recognize himself." Fa-hsiu then said, "These clerics here are all deluded; I at least will acknowledge your fidelity to the dharma."

66. Among Ch'i-sung's preserved writings are three brief, undated letters addressed to a Yüan-t'ung Ch'an-shih, who was then residing on Mt. Lu (see *T'an-chin wen-chi* 10, *T* 52.702a). If the recipient of these letters had been our Fa-hsiu, then it is notable that the younger monk, who was 20 years junior to Ch'i-sung and thus only 45 at the time of Ch'i-sung's death, should have caught the favorable attention of one of the foremost Ch'an monks of the day. However, it is more likely that the Yüan-t'ung Ch'an-shih in question is actually Ch'i-sung's contemporary and dharma brother, Chu-na (1010–1071), who presided for a time over a Lu-shan temple named Yüan-t'ung and who was also, therefore, known as Yüan-t'ung Ch'an-shih. Chu-na and Ch'i-sung had both studied for a while with Tung-shan Hsiao-ts'ung (d. 1030). Concerning Chu-na, see *CCHTL* 5 (*HTC* 136.97b–98a); *CLSPC* 26 (*HTC* 137.542a–b); *WTHY* 16, 3:1020–1021; *FTLTTT* 19 (*T* 49.668b14–c2), and *SSCKL* 4 (*T* 864b19–c2).

67. *TMWK, T* 47.943c, 944c, 949c, 955a, 956a, and 957b. This work was compiled in 1186 by Ta-hui's disciple Mi-an Tao-ch'ien (d.u.). Unlike other collections of Ta-hui's remarks, the *Ch'an Arsenal* seems to have been designed especially for an audience of monks. Its purpose was apparently polemical and hortatory—to provide inspirational models of appropriate monastic conduct, thus highlighting just those particular styles of Ch'an, among the many available during his day, that Ta-hui found most worthy of emulation. Fa-hsiu, it seems, was one of Ta-hui's heroes.

68. This seems not to have been a major establishment—nothing on the order of, say, the Ta-hsiang-kuo ssu, the T'ai-p'ing Hsing-kuo ssu, or the K'ai-pao ssu which dominated the city. The only standard description of Northern Sung Kaifeng in which I have found any reference to the Fa-yün ssu is rather late and not very informative, viz., Li Lien's *Pien-ching i-chi chih* (Record of the Antiquities of Kaifeng), compiled in 1546 (*SKCSCP,* Series 10, vol. 96). Without citing his sources, Li Lien tells us (ibid., 10:15b) that there was a "Fa-yün ssu" located to the west of the Yün-chi bridge, outside the Nan-hsün Gate, and that it was razed by soldiers at the end of the Yüan (the Nan-hsün gate was the main southern gate of the city; I have not been able to locate the bridge on any map). Li also mentions (ibid., 10:25a) a "Fa-yün yüan" that had been erected

in 1010 by the northwestern wall of the city, at a bend of the Chin-sui river near the Kuo-tzu gate, and that was destroyed by the Chin armies in 1126, but it is probably with the former of these two establishments, the Fa-yün ssu, that Fa-hsiu was associated.

We also learn from the *FTLTTT* (*T* 49.687c28–688a2) that a Fa-yün ssu was "rebuilt" in 1082, somewhere on the southern outskirts of the city, at the behest of a grandee by the name of Chang Tun-li (fl. 1068–1102). Chang was very much like, and was indirectly related to, our noble host Wang Shen. Like Wang, he was a prominent painter and patron, and like Wang, he was married to one of Emperor Ying-tsung's daughters. It is not an unreasonable conjecture that the Fa-yün ssu had earlier been a kind of private chapel located on Chang's estate in the southern suburbs of the capital, and that he had reconstructed and expanded it to attractto the capital an eminent cleric like Fa-hsiu. For more on Chang Tun-li, see *SJCSY* 3:2410–2411; also Bush and Shih, *Early Chinese Texts,* 294.

69. *Su Shih wen-chi* 19, 2:561–562. This inscription makes effective use of references to the sound of a bell found in the *Shou-leng-yen ching* (Śūraṇgama Sūtra), with which Su Shih was clearly quite familiar. Su Shih apparently maintained some continuous connection with the Fa-yün temple; his collected writings include a short, undated composition commemorating the reconstruction of its bathhouse (*Su Shi wen-chi* 62, 5:1906–1907).

70. *Su Shih wen-chi* 61, 5:1885–1886. These are more like polite notes than letters, and they inform us of little other than the depth of Su Shih's commitment to Buddhism, born in part from his worldly disappointments, and of his great respect for Fa-hsiu. Internal evidence (e.g., reference to Su Shih's exile, etc.) indicates that the notes were written prior to Su's 1086 return to Kaifeng, perhaps during his slow progress back from the exile in Huang-chou, which had ended in the spring of 1084. During that period Su Shih visited several of the locales in which Fa-hsiu had recently been living, including Chung-shan, and this may be how he came to know of Fa-hsiu. However, in one of the missives Su Shih acknowledges that he owed his knowledge of Fa-hsiu to letters he had received from Huang T'ing-chien. From this we can deduce that Huang T'ing-chien had known Fa-hsiu either before the monk's 1084 arrival in the capital or immediately thereafter. Thus Huang may have introduced Fa-hsiu into the literati society of the capital. Both Huang and Su, of course, had close relations with other Ch'an monks as well, and Fa-hsiu, although he was revered by both, seems not to have been the chief Buddhist influence on either of the two great poets. For good, albeit brief, discussions of Su-shih's relationship to Buddhism, see Yoshikawa Kōjirō, "So Tō-pa no bungaku to Bukkyō," *Tsukamoto Hakushi shōju kinen: Bukkyōshi ronshū* (Kyoto: 1961), 939–950; Chikusa Masaaki, "So Shoku to Bukkyō," *Tōhō Gakuhō,* 36 (1964): 457–480; and Beata Grant, "Buddhism and Taoism in the Poetry of Su Shih" (Stanford Ph.D. diss., 1987). For a treatment of this topic as refracted by the lense of medieval Japanese Zen, see Asakura Hisashi, *Zenrin no bungaku* (Osaka: Seibundō, 1985), 457–499. I have not yet found comparable studies of Huang T'ing-chien's Buddhism, although this, too, is a topic that deserves extensive treatment in its own right.

71. Also known as Fa-k'ung and later as Yüan-chao Ch'an-shih, Tsung-pen was perhaps the most eminent of I-huai's many disciples. In 1082, after decades of prominence in Suchow and Hangchow, he was invited to the capital by Emperor Shen-tsung to preside over the Hui-lin Ch'an-yüan, an institution that was established in 1080 as one of the Ch'an components of the great Ta-hsiang-kuo temple complex and that quickly became one of the major centers of

Ch'an in Northern Sung Kaifeng. He eventually became chief abbot of the whole Ta-hsiang-kuo ssu compound, and served as host to Ŭich'on (1055–1101) when that royal Korean monk visited the Hsiang-kuo temple in 1085. See *CCHTL* 9 (*HTC* 136.142b–145b); *CLSPC* 14 (*HTC* 137.500a–502b); *LTHY* 28 (*HTC* 136.916a); *CTPTL* 3 (*HTC* 137.76a–77b); *FTTC* 27 (*T* 49.278c); *FTLTTT* 19 (*T* 49.677b–c); and *SSCKL* 4 (*T* 49.874c–875a, 876b).

72. Su Shih expressed this view in a letter inviting an otherwise unknown Ch'an monk named Ching-tz'u Fa-yung to come to the capital. He notes that at the time the invitation was extended, Fa-hsiu had already died and Tsung-pen had left the city. See *Su Shih wen-chi* 62, 5:1908.

73. The earliest version of this oft-told tale appears to be that found in Chüeh-fan Hui-hung's works—either the longer version found in his *LCYH* (8, 905b), which was composed between 1111 and 1128, or the shorter version found in his *CLSPC* (26; *HTC* 137.545a), which dates from 1123.

74. Not only does this exchange appear in Buddhist sources concerning Fa-hsiu (e.g., *CLSPC* 26 [*HTC* 137.545a]), it is also mentioned in Huang T'ing-chien's own writings. In his preface to a work entitled the *Hsiao-shan chi,* Huang confesses his dissolute youthful ways as a tippler and a composer of *Yüeh-fu,* and acknowledges his debt to Fa-hsiu as the only person ever to have called him properly to account for such behavior. He even specifies that the particular hell into which Fa-hsiu had said he was liable to be reborn was, appropriately enough, the "Hell of Slit Tongues." See *Yü-chang Huang hsien-sheng wen-chi* 16 (*SPTK* ed.), 163b; also *Sung-shih chi-shih* 92 (4/2223–4).

75. *Yü-chang Huang hsien-sheng wen-chi* 14, 137b–138a. In the same work one may also find two inscriptions *(ming)* written for the Fa-yün temple in which Fa-hsiu is mentioned; ibid. 13, 122b. For a brief discussion of Huang's relationship with Fa-hsiu (and one of the few pieces of modern scholarship that mentions the monk), see Chang Ping-ch'üan, *Huang Shan-ku te chiao-yu chi tso-p'in* (Hong Kong: Chung-wen Ta-hsüeh, 1978), 101–103. Of course, Huang T'ing-chien was well acquainted with a number of other Ch'an monks as well. For a discussion of the general question of Ch'an influence on Huang's poetry, see Richard John Lynn, "The Sudden and the Gradual in Chinese Poetry Criticism: An Examination of the Ch'an-Poetry Analogy," in Gregory, ed., *Sudden and Gradual,* pp. 381–427.

76. The most complete listing is in the lineage charts found in the *ZGDJT* (*Keifu* 10), which are based on an exhaustive survey of all the pertinent Ch'an histories. Note that Fa-hsiu's particular lineage of Yün-men Ch'an continues in the records for only three generations after him. This is probably due in part to the disruption caused by the Chin conquest of northern China. Note, too, that in addition to the forty-eight students listed as formal disciples, he had many other important students who went on to study with other teachers and were formally identified as their descendants—e.g., Fa-yün Shan-pen (1037–1109), who is listed as an heir of Hui-lin Tsung-pen. Nevertheless, Shan-pen's association with Fa-hsiu persisted, as we see in the fact that he was invited to serve as abbot of the Fa-yün ssu after Fa-hsiu's death.

77. See *CTPTL* 5 (*HTC* 137.100b–101a); *WTHY* 16, 3:1065–1066; *FTLTTT* 19 (*T* 49.678c–679a); and *SSCKL* 4 (*T* 49.880a–c). Eventually Wei-po left Kaifeng, perhaps to flee the Jurchen invaders, and he ended his days at the great T'ien-tung monastery, one of the largest Ch'an centers in the veritable forest of Ch'an temples located in the vicinity of Hangchow.

78. This thirteen-fascicle catalogue was apparently lost in China, but it was preserved in Japan. Sung printed editions of the work had been brought to

Japan in the fourteenth century and served as the basis of several later Japanese printings. One such, done in 1661, was the basis for the only modern edition of the work, viz., that found as item no. 37 in the second volume of the *Shōwa hōbō sōmokuroku* (*T* 99. 571–772). Wei-po tells us in his postface (ibid., 771a) that in the summer of 1103, while proceeding on a pilgrimage to Mt. T'ien-t'ai, he stopped at the Chih-che Ch'an Monastery near Chin-hua shan in Wu-chou (mod. Chin-hua hsien, Chekiang). There he found a copy of the Tripiṭaka that he decided to catalogue. The task kept him at Chih-che ssu through the winter, and the catalogue was not finished until the spring of 1104. The particular canon he used seems to have been a copy of the K'ai-pao edition, with some additions and some texts missing. According to Wei-po's numbering system, it contained 1,048 titles. See Ts'ai Yün-ch'en, *Erh-shih-wu-chung tsang-ching mu-lu tui-chao k'ao-shih* (Taipei: Hsin-wen-feng, 1983), 563–576. The last few pages of Wei-po's catalogue contain a brief summary of Ch'an history and a very interesting set of Ch'an justifications for such learned undertakings as the collection and study of scripture, both of which echo Fa-hsiu's arguments that Ch'an and doctrinal Buddhism cannot be divorced from each other.

79. *T* 99.771a14–20.

80. The Chinese practice of placing models of the five viscera in statues of the Buddha is well documented. Perhaps the best known example of this practice (significantly, a Sung example) is the famous sandalwood statue of Sākyamuni that the Japanese pilgrim-monk Chōnen (938–1016) brought back from China in 986 and had installed in the Seiryōji, a temple in the Saga district of Kyoto. This statue had been carved and sealed in 985, at the Kai-yüan ssu in Tai-chou. When the hollow cavity of the statue was opened nearly a thousand years later (in 1954), scholars found among the several fascinating articles contained therein a cloth replica of the five viscera which had been sewn by a group of Ta'i-chou nuns. See Gregory Henderson and Leon Hurvitz, "The Buddha of Seiryōji," *Artibus Asiae* 19 (1956): 5–55.

81. The most readily available edition of this text (but not the most interesting from an aesthetic point of view) is the one found in standard modern Japanese editions of the Tripiṭaka (*T* 45.793–806 and *HTC* 103.910–936). The work was first published around 1101. It was apparently lost in China by the early Yüan, but not before versions of it had been brought to Japan in the thirteenth or early fourteenth century. A Southern Sung Hangchow printing of the text, at least three copies of which survive in Japan, was the basis for several later Japanese editions, one of which was included in the *T* and *HTC*. See Jan Fontein, *The Pilgrimage of Sudhana: A Study of the Gaṇḍavyūha Illustrations in China, Japan, and Java* (Mouton: The Hague and Paris, 1967), 24–40; also Lokesh Chandra, *Sudhana's Way to Enlightenment*, Śata-piṭaka Series, No. 224 (New Delhi: Smt. Sharada Rani, 1975), 7–63. Neither Fontein nor any other scholar hazards an explicit comment as to whether or not Wei-po drew the illustrations of the text in addition to composing its encomia. The version in the *T* and *HTC*, however, includes as its final panel a portrait of Wei-po together with an encomium about him, and this, I should think, would count against the hypothesis that he was himself the artist. Perhaps the illustrations were done by his patron, the painter Chang Tun-li. The brief preface to Fo-kuo's work found in all extant editions was written by yet another Buddhist layman and literatus of the day, the former Prime Minister Chang Shang-ying (1043–1122), who was an associate of Huang T'ing-chien, Ta-hui, Yüan-wu K'o-ch'in, and several others whom we have had occasion to mention. As a particular friend of Hui-hung, Chang should be counted as an active participant in Wen-tzu Ch'an movement. See

Robert M. Gimello, "Chang Shang-ying: A Buddhist Apologist and Statesman of the Northern Sung," in Irene Bloom and Joshua Fogel, eds. *Varieties of Neo-Confucian Experience; A Festschrift for Wing-tsit Chan and Wm. Theodore de Bary,* forthcoming.

82. For biographical sketches of this monk, who is also known as Tz'u-chüeh Ch'an-shih, and for samples of his discourse, see *CCHTL* 18 (*HTC* 136.266a–267a), *CTPTL* 5 (*HTC* 137.101b–102a), *WTHY* 16, 3:1071–1072, Tsung-hsiao's (1151–1214) *Lo-pang wen-lei* 3 (*T* 47.193c), and P'u-tu's (1199–1290) *Lu-shan lien-tsung pao-chien* 4 (*T* 47.324c–325a). See also Yanagida Seizan's "Kaisetsu," in Kajitani Sōnin, et al., eds., *Shinjin-mei Shōdō-ka Jūgyū-zu Zazen-gi,* Zen no Goroku 16 (Tokyo: Chikuma Shobō, 1974), 231–233.

83. Tsung-tse figures prominently in the literature of Sung dynasty Pure Land Buddhism, and several of his shorter pieces on Pure Land themes have been perserved in important Sung and Yüan Pure Land compendia. See his *Kuan Wu-liang-shou Fo ching hsü* (Preface to the Amitāyurdhyāna Sūtra), his *Lien-hua sheng-hui lu-wen* (Charter for the Exalted Sodality of the Lotus Blossom), his *Ch'üan nien-Fo sung* (Verses Promoting Devotional Meditation on the Person of the Buddha Amtābha), and his *Hsi-fang ching-t'u sung* (Verses in Praise of the Pure Land of the West)—all in Tsung-hsiao's *Lo-pang wen-lei* (Assorted Texts on the Happy Land), *T* 47.167a–b, 177b–178b, 219b–220a.

84. For a brief summary of the contents of this work, see Martin Collcutt, *Five Mountains: The Rinzai Zen Monastic Institution in Medieval Japan* (Cambridge, Mass.: Harvard University Press, 1981), 141–142. The best critical and annotated edition of the text itself, together with a modern Japanese translation, is Kagamishima Genryū, et al., eds., *Yakuchū Zen'en-shingi* (Tokyo: Sōtōshū Shūmuchō, 1972).

85. Tsung-tse is said to have authored a collection of 120 pieces entitled *Writings in Promotion of Filial Piety (Ch'üan-hsiao wen).* This work does not survive in its entirety but is mentioned in other Sung and Yüan Pure Land anthologies, one of which quotes a very short excerpt from it. See Tsung-hsiao's (1151–1214) *Lo-pang i-k'ao* 2 (*T* 47.249a4–20) and Wang Jih-hsiu's (d. 1173) *Lung-shu tseng-kuang ching-t'u wen* (*T* 47.271a22–b4).

86. For this understanding of Tsung-tse's meditation manual, and its relationship to Dōgen's Zen, I am indebted especially to the work of Carl Bielefeldt. See his "Ch'ang-lu Tsung-tse's *Tso-ch'an i* and the 'Secret' of Zen Meditation," in Gregory, ed., *Traditions of Meditation,* pp. 129–161; and his groundbreaking monograph, *Dōgen's Manuals of Zen Meditation* (Berkeley: University of California Press, 1988), esp. 55–132. A critical annotated edition and modern Japanese translation of the *Tso-ch'an i* may be found in Kajitani, *Shinjin-mei,* pp. 145–164.

87. Again, I am grateful to Professor Ellen Johnston Laing for providing me with a photocopy of this colophon.

88. Ch'en Kao-hua, *Hua-chia shih-liao,* p. 473.

89. This is the mountain located a few miles northwest of the seat of Wu-hsien in Kiangsu. In 1126, Ta-hui had accompanied his teacher Yüan-wu K'o-ch'in on a flight south to escape the Chin invaders. For a time they stayed together at Chin-shan in southeastern Kiangsu, but in 1127, Ta-hui left Yüan-wu and traveled about 40 miles northwest to take up residence on Hu-ch'iu shan, where several monasteries were located. He stayed for about a year, residing at the Yün-yen ssu, a Ch'an institution that had been founded some decades earlier by Ch'i-sung. Beginning with the abbacy of Hu-ch'iu Shao-

lung (1077–1136), another disciple of Yüan-wu, the Yün-yen ssu became a flourishing center of the Yang-ch'i branch of Lin-chi Ch'an, one of the "ten-fields" *(shih-ch'a)* of the Southern Sung Ch'an ecclesiastical establishment and a major point of origin for several of the Rinzai lineages of Japan.

90. *TMWK, T* 47.956b9–12. This anecdote would later catch the attention of Japanese Zen monks during the Muromachi and subsequent periods. The development of Gozan literary culture at that time raised again the question of the relationship between Zen and poetry, and Musō Soseki (1275–1351), among others, found occasion to employ Fa-hsiu's and Ta-hui's quip as a warning against the danger of allowing literary pursuits to become distractions from true Zen practice (see Pollack, *Fracture of Meaning,* 129–130). Of course, Musō was himself an ardent and accomplished poet. Later still, Ikkyū (1394–1481) would compose two poems on the theme of this anecdote—poems 140 and 141 of the *Kyōunshū* (Crazy Cloud Anthology)—in which he would work an ironic Zen subversion of Fa-hsiu's original intent, suggesting that if Ta-hui had been truly compassionate he would not have ridiculed the monks who spoke of food but would have served them a supernal gourmet meal of the sort that Vimalakīrti had served his assembly of bodhisattvas. See Sonja Arntzen, *Ikkyū and the Crazy Cloud Anthology: A Zen Poet of Medieval Japan* (Tokyo: University of Tokyo Press, 1986), 116–117.

91. See note 60.

92. *TMWK, T* 47.949c11–17.

93. The best available treatment of this topic is in Jonathan Chaves, *Mei Yao-ch'en and the Development of Early Sung Poetry* (New York: Columbia University Press, 1976), esp. 114–132. Note Chaves' observation that "even and bland" style is associated with "rough diction" and need not imply only an etiolated or insipid quality. Note, too, the references Chaves has found to the "even and bland" as a style that "sticks in the mouth" and that is bitter and hard in taste, like olives. It was a label, he says, originally pejorative in connotation, which was later endowed with implications of praise and used to name positive literary values. All this is very reminiscent of Ch'an, and I suspect that further efforts to sort out the varieties of Sung Ch'an discourse according to the categories of Sung literary criticism would prove quite illuminating. The first of I-huai's two epigrams, the one that Shun Lao rejects, might profitably be compared, for example, to the diction of Hsi-k'un style poetry, to which the advocacy of *p'ing-tan* diction was a reaction (see ibid., pp. 64–68, 124, 131). Of course, this is simply the converse of the procedure followed by Yen Yü (ca. 1195 to ca. 1245) and others, who used Ch'an categories to classify and evaluate poetry (see Lynn, "Sudden and Gradual in Chinese Poetry Criticism," in Gregory, ed., *Sudden and Gradual*).

94. Lynn, "Sudden and Gradual in Chinese Poetry Criticism," in Gregory, ed., *Sudden and Gradual,* p. 385. The poem itself may be found, together with helpful annotation, in Wang Shui-chao, ed., *Su Shih hsüan-chi* (Shanghai: Shang-hai Ku-chieh Ch'u-p'an-she, 1984), 115–118. The monk to whom the poem was written was Tao-ch'ien, a.k.a. Ts'an-liao-tzu (1043 to ca. 1116). He was, like Fa-hsiu, a member of the Yün-men Ch'an lineage, having been a disciple of the little-known Ta-chüeh Huai-lien (1009–1090). A close friend of Su Shih, with whose career his became unfortunately entangled, Ts'an-liao-tzu was in his own day better known and respected as a poet than as a monk, and a collection of his works in twelve fascicles—the *Ts'an-liao-tzu shih*—survives today (*TPTK, san-pien: chi;* Lo no. 443). For more about Ts'an-liao-tzu see

FTTC (*T* 49. 210c–211a), *FTLTTT* (*T* 49.665c), *SSCKL* 4 (*T* 49.877c, 879a), and *SJCSY* 5:4458–4459; also Li E, *Sung-shih chi-shih* 91 (Shanghai Ku-chieh Ch'u-p'an-she ed., 1983), 4:2196–2199.

95. See, for example, the six brief verses which Wei-po included in fascicle 39 of the *CCHTL* (*HTC* 136.392b).

96. Note here (e.g., *WTHY* 16, 3:1038) the possible allusion to characteristic early Ch'an teachings about the identity of Ch'an and the ordinary activities of daily life, teachings like those of Huai-tung (a.k.a. Lao Hua-yen), for which Fa-hsiu is said to have harbored a markedly ambivalent admiration in his youth (see note 54).

97. *CCHTL* 10 (*HTC* 136.157b18–158a2). The last enigmatic statement in this passage (my translation of which is tentative and free) is taken from Hsüeh-tou Ch'ung-hsien's "note" or "capping phrase" *(cho-yü)* on one line in a famous *kung-an* about Chao-chou's paradoxical inability to explain the oft-quoted Ch'an saying, "The ultimate Tao is without difficulty." The note may now be found attached to this *kung-an* as it appears as case number 58 of the *Pi-yen lu.* A general theme of this case, and of Fa-hsiu's use of his forebear's phrasing, is the profound simplicity and spontaneity of Ch'an, qualities that are bound to be lost in any stiff or labored effort at profundity. But, of course, this itself is only the most artful sort of artlessness. In comparison with it, intentionally "profound" Ch'an, which is always an awkward and forced performance like "walking on a balance beam," is actually downright easy—better yet, facile. Fa-hsiu used this figure of speech more than once. We see another occurrence of it in another of the dialogues of Fa-hsiu recorded by his disciple Wei-po, *CCHTL* 10 (*HTC* 136.157b2).

98. This characterization of Huang's poetic talents is found in the writings of the Chin dynasty literatus and lay Buddhist, Li Ch'un-fu (*hao:* P'ing-shan, 1175–1234), who went on to say that Huang's poesy—in its odd combination of polished vulgarity, close attention to past models, and meticulous craftsmanship—is like the practice of Ch'an *(ts'an-ch'an).* See Ch'uan Hsüan-tsung, *Huang T'ing-chien ho Chiang-hsi shih-p'ai chüan,* Ku-tien wen-hsüeh yen-chiu tzu-liao hui-pien (Peking: Chung-hua Shu-chü, 1978), 1:181. For more on Li P'ing-shan's views of Ch'an and its relationship to literary culture, see Robert M. Gimello, "Hsing-hsiu, Li P'ing-shan," forthcoming.

99. *K'o-teng* refers to a creeping, vinelike plant the tendrils of which grow in dense tangles. In modern Chinese botanical usage it refers to the Kudzu plant proper, i.e., *Pueraria Thunbergiana,* and that is probably what it most commonly meant in earlier colloquial usage as well, although there is some indication that the same compound sometimes served as the designation for wisteria. In Ch'an usage, which seems to derive ultimately from a phrase in the *Laṅkāvatāra Sūtra* (*latā-vitāna-pada* = the *kleśas* as verbal superimpositions; see Paul Demiéville, trans., *Entretiens de Lin-tsi,* Documents Spirituels 6 [Paris: Fayard, 1972], 29), it was a synonym for "lettered" or "literary" *(wen-tzu)* Ch'an. Clearly, the term's primary use was as a pejorative, suggesting that "words and letters" are an impenetrable thicket in which one can too easily become entangled.

However, the word also has positive connotations in certain contexts, as when it is used to label the sort of beneficent verbal communication that links or intertwines master and disciple. Ta-hui himself often began letters to students by characterizing them as *k'o-teng* ("word-tendrils," perhaps). This is in part simply a routine and rhetorical nod to the typical Ch'an distrust of words, but it is not only that; it also suggests the spiritual benefit that may accrue to a teacher's use of discourse for compassionate, salvific purposes. Thus when Dōgen later used the term (J. *kattō*) as the title and theme of one chapter of the *Shōbōgenzō,* he stressed that the image of intertwining vines symbolizes Zen transmission as well as the tangle of verbalization. In this he claimed to be following the teachings of his Chinese master, T'ien-t'ung Ju-ching (1163–1228). *Kattō* as word-tangles, Dōgen says, can be cut only with other *kattō,* in the sense of links in the mind-to-mind transmission of Zen. For a graceful translation of Dōgen's "*Kattō*" chapter, see Kazuaki Tanahashi, ed., *Moon in a Dewdrop: Writings of Zen Master Dōgen* (San Francisco: North Point Press, 1985), 168–174. For a useful general summary of the various Ch'an uses of the term "*k'o-teng,*" based in part on the earlier work of great Tokugawa Zen scholar Mujaku Dōchū, see Yanagida Seizan, trans., *Rinzairoku,* Butten kōza 30 (Tokyo: Daizō shuppansha, 1972), 47.

100. The *Yüan-chüeh ching* (*T* 17.913–920) is an eighth-century Chinese apocryphon that combines themes from the Hua-yen and Tathāgatagarbha traditions. It attracted the special interest of the Hua-yen and Ch'an patriarch Tsung-mi (780–841), who wrote several influential commentaries on it, and it proved to be a major inspiration for many of his distinctive teachings, including his characteristic advocacy of the unification of Ch'an and doctrinal Buddhism. The text became quite influential during the late T'ang and the Sung, and seems to have been taken, along with the *Shou-leng-yen ching* (*Śūraṃgama Sūtra), as the expression of a kind of Buddhist gnosticism, i.e., a view that Buddhists have commonly called "the Śrenika heresy." Its central argument seems to be an assertion of utter difference between the realm of ordinary illusory experience and the immaculate and transcendent absolute that is thought to be embodied in the perfect and natural purity of the mind. Although frequently cited by Sung Ch'an teachers, its message was in fundamental respects contradictory to the Ch'an conviction that the absolute and the relative are mutually inextricable. Thus it was a controversial text and appears to have been condemned or questioned as often as it was praised. Exactly what aspect of the text's teaching Fa-hsiu had in mind when he used it to rebuke Hsiao-shun we simply cannot say. Perhaps it was intended to stand for a kind of inert or placid Ch'an, devoid of the sort of vital tension that Hsiao-shun's relentlessly critical attitude seeks to sustain. An unsatisfactory translation of the *Yüan-chüeh ching,* together with the comments of the Ming Buddhist Han-shan Te-ch'ing (1546–1623), is available; see Lu K'uan-yü (Charles Luk), trans., *Ch'an and Zen Teaching,* Series 3 (London: Rider & Co., 1962), 148–278.

101. This phrase, too, is an allusion. Hsüeh-tou Ch'ung-hsien, in the verse he composed to accompany the eighteenth of his "hundred old cases"—which verse is now found in the eighteenth case of the *Pi-yen lu*—uses the same trope. Yüan-wu K'o-ch'in would later use it again in his introduction to the eighty-ninth case of the same *kung-an* anthology. There are probably other early examples of its use to which Fa-hsiu might have been alluding, but I have not yet found them. I confess, too, that although the image of "a whole body being an eye" was probably meant to convey more than generic praise, its precise meaning eludes me.

102. *TMWK* (*T* 47.943c13–20).

103. *Chen-chou Lin-chi Hui-chao Ch'an-shih yü-lu* (*T* 47.497a2–8). For slightly variant translations of this passage, see Ruth Fuller Sasaki, et al., trans., *The Record of Lin-chi* (Kyoto: The Institute for Zen Studies, 1975), 5; and Demiéville, trans., *Entretiens de Lin-tsi,* pp. 39–40.

104. I take these quotations from a very erudite and wise book about literary learning and the Christian monastic life that even students of Ch'an Buddhist

monasticism would do well to read—Jean Leclerq, O.S.B., *The Love of Learning and the Desire for God: A Study in Monastic Culture,* trans. Catherine Misrahi (New York: Fordham University Press, 1961).

105. *CCHTL* 10 (*HTC* 136.157b3–4) and *WTHY* 3:1038, to cite just two of its occurrences.

Glossary

Ch'an 禪
Ch'an-chiao ho-i 禪教合一
Ch'an-lin seng-pao chuan 禪林僧寶傳
Ch'an-men tsung 禪門宗
Ch'an-yüan ch'ing-kuei 禪苑清規
Chang Lei 張耒
Chang Shang-ying 張商英
Chang Tsai 張載
Chang Tun-li 張敦禮
Ch'ang-lu 長蘆
Ch'ang-lu Tsung-tse 長蘆宗賾
Ch'ang-lu Ying-fu 長蘆應夫
Chao Meng-fu 趙孟頫
Ch'ao Chiung 晁迥
Ch'ao Pu-chih 晁補之
Che-tsung 哲宗
Chen-chou Lin-chi Hui-chao Ch'an-shih yü-lu 鎮州臨濟慧照禪師語錄
chen shan-chih-shih 眞善知識
Ch'en Ching-yüan 陳景元
Cheng Ching-lao 鄭靖老
Cheng-shou 正受
Ch'eng I 程頤
ch'i wu i yeh 豈無意邪
Ch'i-sung 契嵩
Chia-t'ai p'u-teng lu 嘉泰普燈錄
Chiang-shan ssu 蔣山寺
Chiang-shan Tsan-yüan 蔣山贊元
chiao 教
chiao-wai pieh-ch'uan 教外別傳
chieh-chiao hsi-Ch'an 藉教習禪
Chien-chung Ching-kuo hsü-teng lu 建中靖國續燈錄
chien-hsing ch'eng-fo 見性成佛
Chih-che Ch'an-ssu 智者禪寺
Chih-cheng chuan 智證傳
chih-chih jen-hsin 直指人心
Chih-p'an 志磐
Chih-yüeh lu 指月錄
Chin-ch'ing 晉卿
Chin-hua shan 金華山
Chin-kang 金剛
Chin-kang san-mei ching 金剛三昧經
Chin-ssu lu 近思錄
Chin-sui 金水
Ch'in Kuan 秦觀
Ch'in-chou 秦州
ching 靜
Ching-kuo 淨果
Ching-te ch'uan-teng lu 景德傳燈錄
Ching-tz'u Fa-yung 淨慈法涌
Chinsim chiksŏl 眞心直說
Chinul 知訥
Chiu-ko 九謌
chiu li chen-chung 久立珍重
cho-yü 著語
Chōnen 奝然
Chou Tun-i 周敦頤
Chu Hsi 朱熹
Chu-na 居訥
Ch'ü Ju-chi 瞿汝稷
ch'u-shih-chien 出世間
chuan-wu chang-chü 專務章句
Ch'üan-chiao Ch'ang-lao 全椒長老
Ch'üan-hsiao wen 勸孝文
Ch'üan nien-Fo sung 勸念佛頌
Chüeh-an 覺岸
Chüeh-fan Hui-hung 覺範慧洪
Chüeh-hai Ch'an-shih 覺海禪師
Chung-chih 仲至
Chung-shan ssu 鍾山寺
Chung-yüan 重元
Chung-yung 中庸
Ch'ung-fu Ch'an-yüan 崇福禪院
Dōgen Kigen 道元希玄
Erh-Ch'eng chi 二程集
Erh-ju ssu-hsing Lun 二入四行論
Fa-hsiang 法相
Fa-hsiu 法秀
Fa-k'ung 法空
Fa-tsang sui-chin lu 法藏碎金錄
Fa-yün Shan-pen 法雲善本
Fa-yün ssu 法雲寺
fei-chiang 非講
Fo-kuo Wei-po 佛國惟白
Fo-tsu li-tai t'ung-tsai 佛祖歷代通載

Fo-tsu t'ung-chi 佛祖統記
Fu-chou 福州
fu-ku 復古
Gozan 五山
Gozan Bungaku 五山文學
hai-tao 害道
Hakuin 白隱
Han Kan 韓幹
Han-shan Te-ch'ing 憨山德清
Han Yü 韓愈
hao-meng 豪孟
Ho-nan Ch'eng-shih i-shu 河南程氏遺書
honshitsu 本質
Hsi-fang ching-t'u sung 西方靜土頌
Hsi-hsien ssu 棲賢寺
Hsi-yüan ya-chi t'u 西園雅集圖
Hsiang-lin Ch'eng-yüan 香林澄遠
Hsiao-ching 孝經
Hsiao-shan chi 小山集
Hsiao-shun 曉舜
Hsiao-ying 曉瑩
Hsieh Liang-tso 謝良左
Hsien-shou chiao 賢首教
Hsin 辛
hsin 心
hsin-shu shih pen 心術是本
Hsing-hsiu 行秀
Hsing-hua Ts'un-chiang 興化存將
Hsiu Yüan-t'ung 秀圓通
hsüan-ke 懸隔
hsüeh 學
hsüeh-ch'an 學禪
Hsüeh-feng I-ts'un 雪峰義存
Hsüeh-tou Ch'ung-hsien 雪竇重顯
Hsüeh-tou po-tse sung-ku 雪竇百則頌古
Hu-ch'iu 虎丘
Hu-ch'iu Shao-lung 虎丘紹隆
Hu-kuo ssu 護國寺
hua-t'ou 話頭
Hua-yen 華嚴
Huai-tung 懷洞
Huang-chou 黃州
Huang-lung 黃龍
Huang T'ing-chien 黃庭堅
Hui-hung 慧洪
Hui-lang 慧朗
Hui-lin Ch'an-yüan 慧林禪院
Hui-lin Tsung-pen 慧林宗本
Hui-neng 慧能
Hui-tsung 徽宗
Hung-chih Cheng-chüeh 宏智正覺
huo-chü 活句
I-huai 義懷
Ikkyū 一休
i su wei ya 以素爲雅
I-ts'un 義存
Kaifeng 開封
K'ai-pao ssu 開寶寺
k'ai-shan 開山
K'ai-yüan ssu 開元寺
Kan-t'an Tzu-kuo 感譚資國
k'an-hua 看話
kattō 葛藤
ke 隔
ko-t'eng 葛藤
ko-t'eng Ch'an 葛藤禪
kōan 公案
Kōhō Jitsuge 格峰實外
k'ung 空
ku-tse 古則
Kuan Wu-liang-shou Fo ching hsü 觀無量壽佛經序
Kuan-yin 觀音
Kuei-ch'ü-lai tzu 歸去來辭
Kuei-tsung Chih-ch'ang 歸宗智常
kung-an 公案
Kuo-tzu men 國子門
Kyōunshū 狂雲集
Lao Hua-yen 老華嚴
Leng-chai yeh-hua 冷齋夜話
Leng-yen ching ho lun 楞嚴經合論
li 理
Li Chao-tao 李昭道
Li Chih-i 李之儀
Li Ch'un-fu 李純甫
Li E 厲鶚
Li Kung-lin 李公麟
Li Lang-chung 李郎中
Li Lien 李濂
Li P'ing-shan 李屏山
Li Po 李渤
li-ju 理入
Lien-hua sheng-hui lu-wen 蓮華勝會錄文
Lien-she 蓮社
Lien-teng hui-yao 聯燈會要
Lin-chi 臨濟
Lin-chi lu 臨濟錄
Lin-chi tsung-chih 臨濟宗旨
Lin-chien lu 林間錄
Liu Ching 劉涇
Liu-ho 六合
Lo Chih-hsien 羅知縣
lo-han 羅漢
Lo-pang i-k'ao 樂邦遺稿

Lo-pang wen-lei 樂邦文類
Lu 魯
Lu-chih 魯直
Lu-shan 廬山
Lu-shan lien-tsung pao-chien
廬山蓮宗寶鑑
Lu Tien 陸佃
Lung-ch'eng 隴城
Lung-mien 龍眠
Lung-shu tseng-kuang ching-t'u wen
龍舒增廣淨土文
Ma Tsu 馬祖
Ma Yüeh-kuan 馬曰琯
Mai-chi shan 麥積山
Mei Yao-ch'en 梅堯臣
Mi-an Tao-ch'ien 密菴道謙
Mi Fu 米市
miao 妙
Miao-fa lien-hua ching ho lun
妙法蓮華經合論
mo-chiao ch'an 默照禪
mo-tso 禪坐
Mu-an Shan-ch'ing 睦庵善卿
Musō Soseki 夢窓疎石
Nan-hsün men 南薰門
Nan-shan 南山
Nien-ch'ang 念常
Ou-yang Hsiu 歐陽修
pai-miao 白描
p'an-chiao 判教
Pao-chin ying-kuang chi 寶晉英光集
Pao-tz'u 報慈
Pao-tz'u yüan 報慈院
Pei-ching 北京
pen-wu 本無
Pi-yen lu 碧巖錄
p'i-p'a 琵琶
Pien-ching i-chi chih 汴京遺蹟志
P'ing-shan 屏山
p'ing-tan 平淡
Po-ch'ao Chih-yüan 白兆志圓
po-hsüeh 博學
Po-shih 伯時
pu-li wen-tzu 不立文字
P'u-chi 普濟
P'u-tu 普度
Rinzai 臨濟
Saga 嵯峨
satori 悟り
Seiryōji 清凉寺
Shan-ku 山谷
shang-t'ang 上堂
Shao-yu 少游
Shen-tsung 神宗
sheng k'o hsüeh hu 聖可學乎
shih-ch'a 十刹
Shih-men wen-tzu Ch'an 石門文字禪
Shih-shih chi-ku lüeh 釋氏稽古略
shih-ta-fu 士大夫
Shōbōgenzō 正眼法藏
Shou-ch'eng Ch'an-shih 守澄禪師
Shou-leng-yen ching 首楞嚴經
Shu Wang 舒王
Shun Lao-fu 舜老夫
Sōtō 曹洞
ssu-chü 死句
Ssu-ma Kuang 司馬光
Su Ch'e 蘇轍
Su Shih 蘇軾
Su Shih wen-chi 蘇軾文集
Sui-chou 隨州
Sung kao-seng chuan 宋高僧傳
Sung-shih chi-shih 宋詩紀事
Ta-chüeh Huai-lien 大覺懷璉
Ta-hsiang-kuo ssu 大相國寺
Ta-hui P'u-chüeh Ch'an-shih tsung-men wu-k'u
大慧普覺禪師宗門武庫
Ta-hui Tsung-kao 大慧宗杲
Ta-hui yü-lu 大慧語錄
Ta-ming 大名
Ta-tsang-ching kang-mu chih-yao lu
大藏經綱目指要錄
t'a-cho ch'eng-ch'ui ying szu t'ieh
踏著稱鎚硬似鐵
T'ai-chou 台州
T'ai-hsü 太虛
T'ai-p'ing Hsing-kuo ssu 太平興國寺
tan-ch'uan 單傳
tan-p'o 淡泊
T'an-chin wen-chi 鐔津文集
T'an-hsiu 曇秀
t'an-hsüan shuo-miao 談玄說妙
Tao-ch'ien 道謙
Tao-hsüeh 道學
Tao-yüan 道原
Tao-yung 道融
T'ao-shan chi 陶山集
T'ao Yüan-ming 陶淵明
Te-shan Yüan-mi 德山緣密
ting-wei 丁未
T'ieh-Fo ssu 鐵佛寺
T'ien-chi 、天啓
T'ien-ch'u chin-lüan 天厨禁臠
T'ien-i I-huai 天衣義懷
T'ien-ning ssu 天寧寺

T'ien-po ssu 天鉢寺
T'ien-po Yüan 天鉢元
T'ien-shui 天水
T'ien-t'ai 天台
T'ien-t'ung ssu 天童
Ts'ai Chao 蔡肇
tsan 讚
Tsan-ning 賛寧 贊寧
ts'an-ch'an 參禪
ts'an-chü 參句
ts'an-i 參義
Ts'an-liao-tzu 參寥子
Ts'an-liao-tzu shih 參寥子詩
Ts'ao-tung 曹洞
Tseng Chi 曾幾
Tso-ch'an i 坐禪儀
tso-wen 作文
Tsu-t'ing shih-yüan 祖庭事苑
tsung 宗
Tsung-hsiao 宗曉
Tsung-mi 宗密
Tsung-pen 宗本
tsung-shih i lai-ch'u 總識伊來處
Tsung-tse 宗賾
Ts'ung-lin sheng-shih 叢林盛事
Tuan-shu 端叔
T'ui-chih 退之
tun-wu tun-hsiu 頓悟頓修
Tung Ch'i-ch'ang 董其昌
Tung-lao 洞老
Tung-p'o 東坡
Tung-shan Hsiao-ts'ung 洞山曉聰
Tzu-chan 子瞻
Tzu-yu 子由
Tz'u-chüeh Ch'an-shih 慈覺禪師
Tz'u-en chiao 慈恩教
Ŭich'ŏn 義天
wai-hsüeh 外學
Wang An-shih 王安石
Wang Ch'in-ch'en 王欽臣
Wang-shen 王詵
Wang Wei 王維
Wei-fu 魏府
Wei-fu Hua-yen Ch'ang-lao
魏府華嚴長老
Wei-na 維那
Wei-po 惟白
Wei-shih 唯識
wen-chang hsüeh-wen shih mo
文章學問是末
Wen-ch'ien 文潛
Wen-hsüeh 文學
wen-jen 文人
Wen-shu chih-nan t'u-tsan
文殊指南圖讚
Wen-tzu Ch'an 文字禪
wu 悟
Wu-chou 婺州
Wu-ming 悟明
wu-sheng 無生
wu-sheng lun 無生論
Wu Tao-tzu 吳道子
Wu-teng hui-yüan 五燈會元
Wu-wei chün 無為郡
wu-yü 無欲
ya-yang 啞羊
Yang-ch'i 楊岐
Yang I 楊億
Yang Shih 楊時
Yang Wen-hui 楊文會
yao 要
Yen Yü 嚴羽
yen-yü 艷語
yin-ming 因明
Ying-chien ssu 應乾寺
Ying-tsung 英宗
Yü-chang Huang hsien-sheng wen-chi
豫章黃先生文集
yü-lu 語錄
Yüan 元
Yüan-chang 元章
Yüan-chao Ch'an-shih 圓照禪師
Yüan-chüeh ching 圓覺經
Yüan Hua-yen 元華嚴
Yüan-kung 元公
Yuan-t'ung Ch'an-shih 圓通禪師
Yüan-wu K'o-ch'in 圜悟克勤
Yüan-yu 元祐
Yün-chi ch'iao 雲驥橋
Yün-chu Hsiao-shun 雲居曉舜
Yün-men 雲門
Yun-men Wen-yen 雲門文偃
Yün-wo chi-t'an 雲臥紀譚
zazen 坐禪
Zen 禪
Zenrin kujitsu konmei shū
禪林口實混名集

Shortening the Path: Early Tendai Interpretations of the Realization of Buddhahood with This Very Body *(Sokushin Jōbutsu)*

Paul Groner

Introduction

One of the major characteristics of Japanese Buddhism has been a tendency to describe the ultimate goal of practice as being attainable either within a person's lifetime or soon after death. Discussions of how such attainments might be possible can be traced back to the early Heian period—as soon as Japanese monks such as Saichō (767–822) and Kūkai (774–835), the founders of the Tendai and Shingon schools, began developing their own views of the path.

A number of aspects of a shorter path to enlightenment could be enumerated, but three are particularly relevant to the discussion of the path in early Japanese Buddhism. First, Tendai and Shingon monks were relatively uninterested in the detailed presentations of rebirth and karma that had captured the attention of the Hossō (Ch. Fa-hsiang) monks that had dominated Nara-period (710–784) Buddhism. Although karma and rebirth are recurring themes both in popular literature concerning morality and in classical literature, they did not receive nearly as much attention from Tendai and Shingon monks interested in doctrinal issues. Second, although Japanese Buddhists were certainly attracted to celestial buddhas and bodhisattvas in their devotional worship and doctrinal discussions, they also brought the concept of buddhahood "down to earth," often insisting that it was attainable by ordinary people "with this very body" *(sokushin)*. Historical figures were called "bodhisattvas" *(bosatsu)*, sometimes during their lifetimes.[1] Monks advanced arguments which claimed that a person could manifest enlightenment even as he was beset by defilements. Third, discussions of the path were often based on two types of criterion: the enumeration of defilements to be eliminated and the manifestation of untainted wisdom. The two were often combined, but Japanese Buddhism gradually tended to place increasing emphasis on the problem of how the innately enlightened mind could be made manifest. At times, any semblance of balance between the two types was lost as scholars argued that the enlightened mind could be manifest even without eliminating defilements.

Early Japanese Tendai discussions of the concept of the realization of buddhahood with this very body *(sokushin jōbutsu)* offer an opportunity to investigate the arguments that led to these positions as Japanese thinkers both compared their positions with those found in Chinese T'ien-t'ai and defended them against Hossō criticisms.

This chapter consists of four major sections. In the first the historical background of the discussion is sketched, while the last three sections concern doctrinal issues. The second and third sections are based on issues raised in the Tendai scholar Annen's (841–889?) two-part definition of *sokushin jōbutsu* as realization of buddhahood while a worldling *(bonbu)* and within a single lifetime *(isshō jōbutsu).*[2] Arguments for the realization of buddhahood by worldlings typify efforts by Heian-period Tendai thinkers to explain how buddhahood might be made accessible to ordinary people during their current lifetimes, rather than remaining a goal solely for advanced practitioners. In arguing for the realization of buddhahood within a single lifetime, some Tendai thinkers gradually inflated their claims about the efficacy of their practices. In doing so, they discussed whether *sokushin jōbutsu* entailed full or partial realization of enlightenment, and whether a practitioner could leap past some stages or had to go through each stage in order.

The fourth section concerns Tendai efforts to reconcile differences between Chinese T'ien-t'ai and Esoteric Buddhist *(mikkyō)* claims about the efficacy of their practices. According to authoritative Esoteric scriptures, as well as Kūkai's Shingon school, Esoteric practices were superior to those from the exoteric tradition. However, such a position violated Saichō's dictum that the Perfect teaching and Esoteric Buddhism had the same purport. Tendai monks thus devoted considerable energy to discussing the relationship of the two traditions. In terms of the path, monks asked whether the two types of practices were simply alternate paths that led to the same goal or whether they were to be combined in a hierarchical fashion. Finally, in the conclusion, some of the factors that led Japanese monks to insist on realization of buddhahood with this very body are investigated and the practical import of these claims for Tendai monks is explored.

Historical Background

One year before his death, Saichō, the founder of the Japanese Tendai school, introduced a new term to Tendai discourse, "the realization of buddhahood with this very body" *(sokushin jōbutsu).*[3] Developing his argument in a line-by-line commentary on the *Lotus Sūtra* story of the realization of buddhahood by an eight-year-old Nāga girl, Saichō argued that sentient beings could quickly realize advanced stages on the path to buddhahood through the power of the *Lotus.*[4] Like several other terms adopted by Saichō, *sokushin jōbutsu* had rarely been used in China and was not particularly well defined. In addition, the absence of a developed set of commentarial positions on the story freed Saichō and his successors to develop their own views on the story and its implications for the path without constantly having to refer to Indian and Chinese views.

Saichō used the concept of *sokushin jōbutsu* primarily to bolster his claims for the superiority of Tendai practice and doctrine over those of the Hossō school. However, he died before he could develop his views in any detail, leaving a number of basic issues for his disciples to puzzle over. Among these were the practices that resulted in *sokushin jōbutsu,* the implications of emphasizing the physical aspects *(sokushin)* of realization, and whether the entire path could be traversed with only one lifetime of practice. Once Saichō had died the term could have simply been ignored, as were many other expressions introduced by Saichō, but several factors led to its becoming important in Tendai thought.

First, the term was intrinsically fascinating to Tendai monks. Realization with this very body suggested that buddhahood or high levels of the path were attainable in the immediate future. The second major factor that led Tendai monks to become interested in the term concerned events in the rival Shingon school. At approximately the same time that Saichō introduced *sokushin jōbutsu* to Tendai discourse, Kūkai, founder of the Shingon school, also became interested in the term, eventually writing an impressive tract on it entitled *Sokushin jōbutsugi* (*T* 2428).[5] As a result, *sokushin jōbutsu* came to have a central place in Japanese Esoteric doctrine and practice.

Kūkai's treatment of the term relied on different sources and doctrines than Saichō's discussion. In addition, Kūkai criticized Tendai doctrines in some of his other works, ranking Tendai below both the Shingon and the exoteric Kegon traditions. Tendai monks could not ignore Shingon teachings because the Shingon school's mastery of Esoteric Buddhism made it a major rival in recruiting able monks and procuring patronage from the Japanese nobility. As a result, Tendai monks were forced to refine their concept of *sokushin jōbutsu* in their own way, developing the implications of the story of the Nāga girl and incorporating some aspects of Esoteric Buddhism into their discussions. In the process, they raised a number of significant questions about the nature and length of the path to buddhahood.

A brief survey of some of the writings on *sokushin jōbutsu* by authors after Saichō will help orient the reader to some of the later development in the arguments. Approximately one or two decades after Saichō's death, Tendai leaders such as Gishin (781-833), Kōjō (779-858), Enchō (771-837), and Tokuen (b. 787) began compiling lists of questions concerning Tendai doctrine and practice and sending them to their Chinese counterparts. This literature, called the *Tōketsu* (Decisions from China [on Doctrinal Issues]), provides one of the major sources for this study.[6] It is particularly important because early Tendai monks expressed their interests in an open and uncomplicated manner. Many of their questions ask their Chinese counterparts for help in defining *sokushin jōbutsu* and the practices necessary for quick enlightenment. The answers by Chinese monks often demonstrate that they did not fully appreciate or sympathize with Japanese interests in a quicker and easier way to enlightenment.

Several years later, Ennin (794-864) played a particularly important role in the development of theories of *sokushin jōbutsu* after his return from China in 847. Although the term is mentioned only occasionally in his extant writing, several of Ennin's disciples—Anne (795-868), Rinshō (fl. late ninth century), and Annen (841-889?)—wrote on the subject. Texts entirely devoted to *sokushin jōbutsu* by Rinshō and Annen focused on exoteric sources for the teaching, particularly the story of the Nāga girl. Their writings include some of the most detailed discussions of the implications of the story of the Nāga girl for the path to enlightenment; but their analyses of the term are limited to theoretical considerations, often focusing on the reconciliation of seeming discrepancies between texts.

The term "*shiki*" (private record) in the title of the texts by Annen and Rinshō reflects the question-and-answer format of the text and suggests that they were probably used in debates. As a result, the texts should not be interpreted as describing a position with which all Tendai monks would have agreed. Although Shingon monks could treat Kūkai's *Sokushin jōbutsugi* as an authoritative text on *sokushin jōbutsu,* Tendai monks never had a single text that all could agree was the ultimate authority on the term. The Tendai school was divided into a number of factions that were usually based as much on personal and institutional alliances as on doctrinal positions. As a result, individual monks employed a variety of practices. Thus positions on issues such as the ease of realizing buddhahood might differ considerably within a faction. Even though monks often claimed to adopt the position of their teacher, they did not always actually do so, as the example of Ennin and Annen illustrates.[7]

Annen's interpretation of *sokushin jōbutsu* is further complicated by texts in which he interpreted it through Esoteric Buddhist thought and practice. Tendai interests in Esoteric Buddhism probably led monks to inflate claims for the efficacy of *sokushin jōbutsu,* arguing that it was much more effective than it had appeared to be in Saichō's brief discussion of it. Discussions of the practices that led to quick enlightenment appear often in Tendai texts on Esoteric Buddhism.

The views of Annen and his contemporaries can be contrasted with those of Hōjibō Shōshin (1136–1220 or 1131–1215), a Tendai monk who represented a conservative branch of Tendai interpretation. Shōshin, the author of authoritative commentaries on Chih-i's (538–597) writings, was not optimistic about the possibility of realizing buddhahood in a single lifetime. As a result, he was sharply critical of many of the theories concerning rapid realization of enlightenment. However, since these teachings had been maintained by highly respected Tendai scholars, Shōshin could not directly contradict them; instead, he had to explain away teachings such as *sokushin jōbutsu* as being theoretically possible but not especially practical.

In contrast, Tendai monks who stressed Esoteric Buddhist practices often felt that a high stage on the path to buddhahood, or buddhahood itself, could be attained. Thus the ninth-century Tendai Esoteric masters Ennin and Annen gave *sokushin jōbutsu* a more prominent place in their writings than did Shōshin. The diversity of Tendai monks' views on *sokushin jōbutsu* was not lost on their opponents. The Shingon monk Jippan (d. 1144) criticized Tendai teachings on the subject and concluded that the Kegon teaching on the realization of buddhahood within three lifetimes was superior because it was more consistent.[8] Some of the doctrinal arguments that led to the diversity of opinion among Tendai monks are discussed below.

The Ordinary Person and the Realization of Buddhahood

When Saichō argued that *sokushin jōbutsu* was a teaching that described some of those who had attained the stage of partial realization *(bunshō soku),* the fifth of the six degrees of identity, he noted that such an accomplishment was for skilled practitioners with advanced religious faculties. Indeed, he probably felt that relatively few individuals could hope to realize buddhahood during their current lifetimes, and that even those with advanced faculties might require three lifetimes. Saichō's attitude was in keeping with the Chinese patriarchs of the school who had not claimed very high spiritual attainments. For example, shortly before his death, Chih-i stated that he considered himself to be within the five ranks of disciples, a stage corresponding to the third of the six degrees of identity.[9] Even in later sources, such as the thirteenth-century history, the *Fo-tsu t'ung-chi* (Record of the Lineage of the Buddha and Patriarchs), Hui-wen (fl. first half of the sixth century) is said to have realized the first abode (equivalent to the fifth degree of identity) and Hui-ssu (515–577) to have entered the ten degrees of faith (equivalent to the fourth degree of identity).

Thus claims to have realized the fifth or sixth degrees of identity were rare in Chinese T'ien-t'ai.[10] Consequently, although Saichō had stressed the possibility of realizing buddhahood with one's current body, few of his Chinese predecessors or Japanese Tendai contemporaries seem to have hoped for such a realization during their own lifetime. However, within a few decades after Saichō's death, attempts were made to demonstrate that *sokushin jōbutsu* was relevant to greater numbers of people. If it could be shown to occur at the lower stages within the six degrees of identity, then it would become directly relevant to the practice of many ordinary monks.

One of the earliest efforts to apply *sokushin jōbutsu* to lower stages can be seen in Kōjō's questions to the Chinese T'ien-t'ai master Tsung-ying:

> Does the teaching of *sokushin jōbutsu* apply to those at the first abode [the fifth degree of identity] or does it also apply to those in [the fourth degree of] identity, resemblance *(sōji soku),* and onward? If we say that it applies to those of the first abode, then [the transition] from a lifespan and body determined by karmic cause *(bundan)* to a body and lifespan that are chosen *(hennyaku)* would certainly entail death and subsequent rebirth. How could this be called "the realization of buddhahood with this very body" *(sokushin jōbutsu)?* If the term *"sokushin jōbutsu"* applies to those from the stage of identity of resemblance onward, in which sūtras and śāstras is this teaching explained? If Hui-ssu and Chih-i preached this teaching, where are the relevant passages found?[11]

Tsung-ying replied that *sokushin jōbutsu* could be applied to the fourth of the six degrees of identity because "at the last state of mind within the identity of resemblance any obstacles to the first abode must be eliminated. . . . If ignorance is not eliminated at identity of resemblance, then how can one attain the first abode?" Although Tsung-ying's reply may seem to bring the stage at which *sokushin jōbutsu* can occur down only an instant, it nevertheless bridges the gap between the attainments open to the worldling *(bonbu)* with his defiled mind and those accessible to the sage *(shō)* who has begun to experience untainted wisdom, traversing the gulf between worldlings whose bodies and lifespans are karmically determined *(bundan)* and sages who can choose their bodies and lifespans. Thus his answer seems to allow for the possibility that worldlings who still have some of the coarser defilements might experience *sokushin jōbutsu.*

Once the gap between worldlings and sages had been crossed, subsequent Tendai monks extended *sokushin jōbutsu* to lower levels of the six degrees of identity. Tsung-ying's willingness to agree to Kōjō's suggestion may have been due to his interest in both T'ien-t'ai and Esoteric Buddhist teachings and practice. In several cases, he was more willing to accept Japanese suggestions for a freer interpretation of doctrine than some of the other T'ien-t'ai monks who answered the *Tōketsu.*[12]

Tsung-ying also advanced Kōjō's arguments by supplying several phrases from the *Lotus Sūtra,* the *Wu-liang-i ching* (Sūtra of Innumerable Meanings), and the writings of Chih-i and Hui-ssu which supported the argument that realization of high stages on the path could be completed within a single lifetime. These were all short passages that did not describe practices in any detail. For example, among the citations were "acquiesence to the unborn nature of phenomena with this body" from the *Wu-liang-i ching,* and "[A follower of] the Perfect teaching can leap *(chōtō)* to the tenth stage in a single lifetime with a body of flesh *(nikushin)*" from Chih-i's *Fa-hua hsüan-i* (Profound Meaning of the Lotus Sūtra).[13]

Tsung-ying also argued that both Hui-ssu and Chih-i had achieved the state of sages *(shō),* which meant attaining at least the fifth degree of identity. The troublesome passages in which Chih-i claimed to have reached only the third of the six degrees of identity on the path were dismissed as being due to Chih-i hiding his virtues out of modesty. According to Tsung-ying,

> Fa-tsang said that the virtuous practices of Hui-ssu and Chih-i are difficult to fathom. Did they realize virtual enlightenment *(tōgaku)* or supreme enlightenment *(myōkaku)?* Many of the learned monks in China believe that Hui-ssu must have been a sage on this earth. If this were not so, then how could he have abandoned the life that he had expediently assumed in China in order to become ruler of Japan and accomplish so much for Buddhism?[14]

By arguing that Hui-ssu, Chih-i, and others had actually attained high stages on the path, Tsung-ying suggested that the Japanese interest in rapid realization was justified.

If the stage at which a monk could realize *sokushin jōbutsu* were lowered, at least some of the time-consuming and difficult practices of the path could be eliminated. Kōjō suggested this when he asked about the significance of the Tendai teaching that each of the ten states of existence (or dharma realms) contains the other nine states. Thus a human being could be reborn in a state as miserable as a denizen of hell or attain a state as exalted as Buddha. To Kōjō, this teaching suggested the possibility of rapid realization of buddhahood. Kōjō also noted that the threefold truth of nonsubstantiality, provisional existence, and the middle is embodied in each of the realms, a teaching which implies that enlightenment must not be very distant.[15] Kōjō consequently asked whether a worldling who understood this teaching could enter the ranks of the buddhas with his current body, whether he would be able to master the *Lotus* meditation *(Hokke-zanmai),* and whether he could travel to different realms. Finally, he inquired whether "a person could naturally enter the ranks of the sages by simply knowing [the ultimate teaching] and not practicing religious austerities? If so, what stage would he realize?"

Tsung-ying warned against confusing the discussions of the practitioner's unchanging basic nature *(shōtoku)* which enabled him to realize enlightenment with discussions of religious practice. Although in principle *(ri)* "there is no difference between the gradual and sudden realization [of enlightenment]," when practice is considered, "the speed of realization depends on how hard a person strives. If you consider these factors, you will know whether a person will attain [his goal] in this lifetime or a future lifetime." Finally, Tsung-ying rejected Kōjō's suggestion that knowledge alone might be sufficient for the attainment of a higher stage on the path, saying, "[What you suggest] is like looking at a road but not traveling it. One cannot expect to finally arrive [at his destination]."[16]

Kōjō's question reflects the tension between defining the path as the manifestation of the innate nature of the mind (a theme brought out in such schemes as the six levels of identity) and defining it through the elimination of defilements (a theme emphasized in such lists as the fifty-two stages). Chinese T'ien-t'ai thinkers generally balanced these two schemes by equating the fifty-two stages with the six degrees of identity, whereas Kōjō's question clearly emphasized the manifestation of an enlightened mind over consideration of the defilements. As part of his effort to determine whether ordinary people could realize enlightenment, Kōjō asked whether buddhahood could be realized by someone who had not eliminated his defilements. In effect, he was asking whether major segments of the path might be eliminated or skipped by the practitioner, or whether a person could realize the mind of a buddha while he still had all or most of the defilements of a worldling.[17]

> Question: Can buddhahood be realized without cutting off the defilements, or not? If we say that the defilements must be cut off, then [we adopt the] same teachings as those who teach the three vehicles. If we say that a person realizes buddhahood while he still has defilements, then how can he realize buddhahood while he still has defilements which are [normally considered to be] obstacles [to enlightenment]? . . .
>
> Answer: In regard to your question . . . , the defilements are essentially identical to [the three truths of] nonsubstantiality, provisional existence, and the middle. If the defilements are eliminated, then the three truths are eliminated.[18]

Tsung-ying followed traditional Tendai lines when he continued by noting that the Buddha remains "within the great sea of defilements" in order to help sentient beings, but does not cling to either the concept of eliminating the defilements or the concept of not eliminating them: "He preaches both cutting off defilements and not cutting them off in accordance with the religious faculties of his audiences." Tsung-ying cautioned Kōjō that the bodhisattva who practiced in accordance with the Perfect teaching should not despise the Hīnayāna teaching that the defilements must be eliminated; belittling such a teaching would hinder his resolve to save all beings. Descriptions of the Buddha's relationship to the defilements did not necessarily apply to practitioners at earlier stages in their training, since they could lead to misunderstandings. Tsung-ying continued:

> If we discuss practice and realization *(shutoku),* then [we must note that] whether our vision of the principle is clear or obscured depends on the strength of our defilements. If our faculties are advanced and our defilements weak, then we can obtain realization in one lifetime. But if our faculties are dull and our obstacles heavy, then it will require at least two and perhaps many lifetimes to attain sagehood.[19]

Thus, although Tsung-ying was willing to agree with Kōjō that the term *"sokushin jōbutsu"* might be applied to monks late in the fourth degree of identity, he firmly argued that those in the early stages needed to practice assiduously and be concerned with the elimination of their defilements.

Several decades later, a number of Tendai monks were suggesting that *sokushin jōbutsu* might be applied to all six degrees of identity except the first, as the following passage from Ennin's disciple Rinshō suggests.

> Question: Is it the case that the teaching of the realization of buddhahood with this body applies only to the higher levels [of practitioners] and not to the remaining [lower] levels?
>
> Answer: According to one theory, the teaching applies to [the second degree,] verbal identity *(myōji soku)* and above, not just to the attainment of the first abode. . . .
>
> Question: Why does the doctrine [of *sokushin jōbutsu*] not apply to the [first level,] identity in principle *(ri soku)?*
>
> Answer: Identity in principle applies only to a person's innate *(shōtoku)* buddhahood. The issue of the realization of buddhahood is not relevant. Doctrines concerning the realization of buddhahood apply only to cases where practice results in realization.[20]

Rinshō's views were influenced by Esoteric teachings brought back from China by Ennin. On the basis of teachings and practices from a Chinese master of Esoteric Buddhism, Yüan-cheng, Ennin argued that the attainment of buddhahood could be classified into two major types:

(1) realization by worldlings *(bon'i jōbutsu),* and (2) realization by sages *(shōi jōbutsu).* In realization by worldlings, the practitioner had still not eliminated all defilements but had obtained the wisdom of a buddha. Such achievements were possible through the empowerment of and response to *(kaji)* the Buddha manifested through the three mysteries *(sanmitsu),* the basis of Japanese Esoteric practices.[21]

Because of such teachings, by the end of the ninth century buddhahood seemed to be much more accessible to Japanese Tendai monks than it had at the beginning of the century. A unique Japanese Tendai view of the path, based on a mixture of Tendai and Esoteric teachings, had begun to emerge.

The Realization of Supreme Enlightenment in a Single Lifetime

Saichō's discussion of realizing buddhahood within three lifetimes suggests that the term *"sokushin jōbutsu"* referred to partial realization of buddhahood within three lifetimes *(sanshō jōbutsu).* In part, this was because the transition between a life and body determined by karmic causes *(bundan shōji)* and a life determined by one's wishes *(hennyaku shōji)* seemed to require rebirth. However, Saichō's position seemed to contradict his use of the phrase "realization of buddhahood with this very body," since if death intervened between stages, buddhahood could hardly have been realized with the practitioner's current body *(genshin).* Moreover, waiting several lifetimes, although more promising than the Hossō school's timespan of three incalculable aeons, still placed buddhahood farther away than many Tendai monks wished. After Saichō's death, Tendai monks began to ask exactly how far a person can progress toward buddhahood with the religious practices of a single lifetime. Here, three aspects of this problem are discussed: (1) whether *sokushin jōbutsu* refers to realization within three lifetimes or during the practitioner's current lifetime; (2) whether partial or full realization can be gained within the practitioner's current lifetime; and (3) whether certain stages can be skipped.

Three Lifetimes versus the Current Lifetime

After Saichō's death, Tendai monks were more interested in how far one could progress in a single lifetime than in the realization of buddhahood within three lifetimes. Although brief discussions of the latter can be found in the texts by Rinshō and Annen, Tendai authors' main interest lay in determining whether the ultimate goal of buddhahood, or a stage close to it, could be realized within the practitioner's current lifetime.[22]

The trend toward deemphasizing the possibility of enlightenment in the next several lifetimes as an element of *sokushin jōbutsu* became evident soon after Saichō's death. In the *Min'yu benwakushō* (Essays Compassionately Explaining Delusions), Anne cited the *Kuan P'u-hsien p'u-sa hsing-fa ching* (Sūtra on the Meditation on the Bodhisattva Universal Virtue) passage that Saichō had quoted in order to support the view that followers of the *Lotus Sūtra* would realize buddhahood within three lifetimes. However, Anne quoted only the first part of the passage, which mentions realization in one lifetime. By omitting the last part of the passage, which says that realization might require two or three lifetimes, Anne clearly indicated that he was primarily interested in the realization of supreme enlightenment in this current lifetime.[23]

By Annen's time, the realization of enlightenment in a single lifetime had become an integral part of many presentations of *sokushin jōbutsu*, which Annen defined as having two major components: realization of buddhahood within a single lifetime *(isshō jōbutsu)*, and realization of buddhahood while a worldling *(bonbu)*.[24] The issue of realization within three lifetimes was not mentioned as an element of *sokushin jōbutsu*.

Partial versus Full Realization

Gishin (781–833), who accompanied Saichō to China and served as the second head *(zasu)* of the Tendai school, briefly discussed whether a person could become a buddha in a single lifetime in the *Tendai Hokkeshū gishū* (Collection of Tendai Lotus School Doctrines), as part of his treatment of the Perfect teaching:

> Question: According to this teaching, how much time is required to become a buddha?
> Answer: In a single lifetime, one can enter the abode *(jū)* in which the enlightened mind appears. . . .
> Question: Does "becoming a buddha in a single lifetime" *(isshō jōbutsu)* refer to partial realization *(bunshōka)* or to full realization *(kukyōka)*?
> Answer: [It refers to] partial realization, not full realization.
> Question: Should we not call such a person a bodhisattva rather than a buddha?
> Answer: If such a person is considered from above, he should be called a bodhisattva; but if he is considered from below, he is called a buddha.
> Question: According to the Perfect teaching, what is a fully realized buddha?
> Answer: The Tathāgata Birushana [Vairocana] in his self-oriented aspect.[25]

Gishin's position was close to that of Saichō; both equated *sokushin jōbutsu* with the partial realization of enlightenment, the fifth of the six degrees of identity *(roku soku)*.

Gishin's discussion clarified a number of important points. First, he noted that the term "realization of buddhahood" *(jōbutsu)* might not refer to the ultimate goal of the practitioner. Rather, when an ordinary person viewed an advanced practitioner, the ordinary person might consider the advanced practitioner to be a buddha, even though that practitioner had not yet realized the ultimate goal. Second, he argued that "the realization of buddhahood in a single lifetime" referred only to partial realization, not supreme realization. Like the Chinese T'ien-t'ai thinkers whom he cited in the *Tendai Hokkeshū gishū,* Gishin believed that the full realization of supreme enlightenment was an exalted state that could not be readily attained in a short period of time.

Enchō, Gishin's successor as head of the Tendai school, questioned whether the Nāga girl could really have made so much progress on the path to enlightenment in just one lifetime. In effect, he was asking whether *sokushin jōbutsu* was an ultimate teaching or merely an expedient one.

> Question: In an explanation of the stages of practice, there is a passage stating that a person can practice and attain the stages from the first degree [of the disciple *(shobon)*] to the first abode during a single lifetime. . . . Now my question is: If this is so, then are there any examples of people who have performed such a feat? If the Nāga girl is cited as an example, she must have attained this stage because of her practices during previous lifetimes. She therefore cannot be an example of what can be realized within a single lifetime. . . . If no example [of such an achievement exists,] then how can the teaching be valid?
>
> In addition, according to the [*Ta-sheng*] *ch'i-hsin lun* (The Awakening of Faith According to the Mahāyāna), "For the sake of weak-willed men, bodhisattvas sometimes demonstrate how to quickly attain Perfect enlightenment by leaping over stages. Other times, for the sake of those who are indolent, bodhisattvas state that men attain enlightenment at the end of countless aeons. Thus they can demonstrate innumerable expedient means and wondrous feats. But in reality all these bodhisattvas are the same, in that they are alike in their lineage, their capacity, their aspiration, and their realization; therefore there is no such thing as leaping over the stages, for all bodhisattvas must pass through the three terms of innumerable aeons [before they attain enlightenment.]" If rapid realization is merely an expedient teaching, then why do texts state that it is possible to practice for a single lifetime and realize [enlightenment] in that lifetime?[26]

In his question, Enchō asked about two vital issues. The first was whether it was possible to name anyone who had made remarkable practice in a single lifetime. The answer by the Chinese T'ien-t'ai monk Wei-chüan showed little appreciation of the urgency of Japanese concerns.[27] Enchō and others wanted concrete proof of the practicality of Tendai teachings through an example of someone who had made such rapid progress. The story of the Nāga girl was so remarkable that she was not a satisfactory model for practicing monks. Wei-chüan avoided answering the question by noting that when the buddha-nature of all existence is considered, expedient and ultimate are not to be distinguished.

The second issue was how to reconcile Tendai claims for the rapid realization of enlightenment with passages indicating that such claims were merely expedient teachings. In other words, how could statements that rapid realization was an expedient teaching devised to encourage "weak-willed men" be reconciled with Tendai claims that *sokushin jōbutsu* was the highest teaching? Wei-chüan answered by citing Hua-yen doctrines that "many aeons can be illuminated in a single instant." Such academic answers, although doctrinally correct, must have been frustrating for the practical Japanese monks, who wanted a straightforward answer about the amount of time buddhahood might require.[28]

A major component of the discussion over the efficacy of *sokushin jōbutsu* concerned how far the practitioner could progress in a lifetime of practice. Was it actually possible for an ordinary person to attain supreme enlightenment, the very highest stage, in a single lifetime? Or, as Saichō and Gishin seem to have indicated, was the goal of *sokushin jōbutsu* the attainment of partial realization?

In the *Min'yu benwakushō,* Anne compiled a number of scriptural citations supporting *sokushin jōbutsu,* many of which indicated that a stage higher than the first abode could be realized. Included were passages which suggested that the first, seventh, or tenth grounds, or even supreme enlightenment, could be attained.[29] Anne's search for other sources shows that Tendai monks did not always find the answer they wanted in the story of the Nāga girl. For example, although Annen stated that the Nāga girl had attained the fifth degree of the six identities (i.e., partial realization), he also argued that a practitioner could actually attain the sixth degree (ultimate identity or complete realization) through *sokushin jōbutsu.*[30]

Subsequent Tendai scholars generally agreed with Annen that the Nāga girl had achieved partial realization, even if they believed that *sokushin jōbutsu* could result in higher attainments.[31] During the fourteenth century, a slightly different approach was suggested, when monks such as Ninkū (1309–1388) maintained that if a person with the highest religious faculties could attain the first abode, he would advance to supreme enlightenment without further practice because of his superior faculties.[32]

Late in the twelfth century, Hōjibō Shōshin, the author of commentaries on Chih-i's three major works, discussed the problem of the rapid realization of buddhahood. By Shōshin's time, Japanese Tendai views on original enlightenment *(hongaku)* and on the rapid realization of enlightenment through Esoteric practices were well developed. Shōshin opposed these Japanese innovations and generally followed the views of Chih-i and Chan-jan (711–782). Because he was reacting against positions characteristic of Japanese Tendai, his criticism of certain aspects of rapid realization is more clearly stated than that of his Chinese predecessors. Shōshin presented his case in the *Hokke gengi shiki* (Personal Record on [Chih-i's] "Profound Meaning of the Lotus Sūtra"), his commentary on the *Fa-hua hsüan-i:*

> Question: Ignorance is difficult to eradicate and the Middle Way is difficult to realize. How can a person cut off so many [defilements] and suddenly attain the tenth ground in a single lifetime?
>
> Answer: . . . Rapid realization is for those with superior religious faculties. [However, even] the man with superior faculties must have previously practiced the various provisional teachings. Thus although we refer to sudden realization within the Perfect teaching, many aeons are required to go from the beginning to the end of the process.[33]

For Shōshin, the rapid attainment of the higher stages on the path was possible only when a person had practiced provisional teachings in earlier lifetimes, thereby maturing his religious faculties to a point from which he could make rapid progress in the Perfect teaching. Consequently, Shōshin saw the Nāga girl as someone who had practiced expedient teachings for aeons. Since she told Wisdom Accumulation Bodhisattva that she could attain buddhahood quickly through practicing the *Lotus Sūtra,* her claim of rapid realization must be accepted, but Shōshin argued that it applied only to her practice of the Perfect teaching in her current life, not to her previous practice of expedient teachings.[34]

Shōshin recognized that the realization of supreme enlightenment in a single lifetime could be justified by citing Tendai teachings and various sūtras, but argued that this possibility was theoretical only. When a search was conducted for examples of those who had realized supreme enlightenment in a single lifetime, although such legendary figures as the Nāga girl could be said to have done so, no examples of historical figures were to be found. Moreover, performing the many practices that benefited others—a major component of Mahāyāna paths—required long periods of time. Thus even if a person had directly received the Perfect teaching without first practicing the lower teachings, he would still need more than one lifetime of practice to complete the path.[35]

Skipping Stages versus Passing through Each One

A subsidiary question was whether a person who rapidly attained buddhahood could leap over *(chō)* some of the stages on the path and directly enter buddhahood or an advanced stage on the path, or whether he had to pass through each stage in the prescribed order. Sources from several texts played a role in this debate. According to a passage from the *Ta-jih ching (Mahāvairocanasūtra),* by reciting dhāraṇīs, "one could go through the stages in order *(shidai)* from the arising of the aspiration to enlightenment to the tenth ground."[36] Read literally, this passage seemed to support the position that one had to go through each stage but could do so rapidly. Moreover, since it came from one of the most authoritative Esoteric texts, it seemed to call into question the efficacy of Esoteric practices in promoting rapid realization. In contrast, excerpts from other texts indicated that the practitioner could leap over many stages and directly attain supreme enlightenment. For example, according to the *Lotus Sūtra,* "When this man preaches Dharma with joy, anyone who hears it for a moment shall straightaway achieve ultimate *anuttarasamyakasaṃbodhi* [enlightenment]."[37] In the *Fa-hua hsüan-i,* Chih-i mentioned the possibility of "leaping over" *(chōtō)* stages and going to the tenth stage in a single lifetime with a body of flesh *(nikushin).*[38]

Japanese Tendai teachers took a variety of positions on skipping stages. For example, Rinshō reflected Ennin's views when he claimed that "a person with the highest faculties does not pass through the earlier stages, leaping over them and entering the tenth stage."[39] Annen argued that the *Ta-jih ching* passage about going through the stages in the proper order should not be interpreted literally; rather, it referred to the stages presented in the Separate teaching in order to elucidate how Esoteric Buddhism allowed a person to leap over stages.[40]

Shōshin once again took a conservative position. Because he could not deny that Tendai texts mentioned leaping over stages, he argued that these passages had to be understood correctly. Although a practitioner might be able to leap past stages when practicing for his own benefit, his compassion and vows to strive to benefit others required that he not skip any stages.[41] Moreover, statements in texts about leaping over stages to buddhahood did not apply to actually skipping stages, but either to transcending the aeons which lesser teachings would have required or to making the transition from worldling to sage in one lifetime.[42] Shōshin's views are summarized in the following passage:

> Question: According to the sixth fascicle of the *Mo-ho chih-kuan* (Great Calm Abiding and Insight Meditation [by Chih-i]), in the Perfect teaching aspects of both leaping [over stages] and not leaping [can

be found].[43] Because [the practitioner] suddenly realizes supreme enlightenment, he leaps [over stages]. Because his compassion and vows are so profound, he does not leap [over stages]. Now when we speak of leaping *(chōtō)* in the passage [in the *Fa-hua hsüan-i*], how is it different?

Answer: In regard to realization of the ultimate goal, he does not leap. But in terms of the causal stages [leading to that ultimate goal], two types of leaping occur. First, when the practitioner quickly enters the ten grounds in a single lifetime, he leaps past many aeons [of practice]. Thus this can be called leaping. But this is not leaping over the grounds *(chii)*. . . . Thus according to the *Ta-jih ching,* "The practitioner can go through the stages in order *(shidai)* from the arising of the aspiration to enlightenment to the tenth ground. . . ."[44] Second, if a practitioner leaps to the tenth stage in an instant, this is only an expedient, like the Nāga girl realizing buddhahood with her current body *(sokushin jōbutsu).* Although it is called "leaping," it is not actually leaping [over stages].[45]

The difference between the positions held by Shōshin (who usually adopted a stance close to the traditional Chinese T'ien-t'ai view) and Annen is dramatic. Much of their disagreement arose because of differences in their evaluation of Esoteric Buddhism, the next subject considered.

The Application of Esoteric Practices to *Sokushin Jōbutsu*

The positions presented above have been based primarily on sources that approached *sokushin jōbutsu* from the perspective of the story of the Nāga girl in the *Lotus Sūtra* and Saichō's analysis of it in the *Hokke shūku* (Elegant Words of the Lotus Sūtra); little consideration is given to Esoteric teachings in most of these sources. For example, Esoteric teachings are barely mentioned in either Rinshō's *Tendai Hokkeshū sokushin jōbutsugi* (Doctrine of Realization of Buddhahood with This Very Body in the Tendai Lotus School) or Annen's *Sokushin jōbutsugi shiki* (Private Record concerning the Realization of Buddhahood with This Very Body), perhaps because both were written in response to debates that often focused on the *Lotus Sūtra.* Even though Rinshō criticized the Hossō school, he did not refer to Kūkai and the Shingon school in either positive or negative terms.[46] However, the rise of Shingon interpretations of *sokushin jōbutsu* played a major if often unspecified role in pushing thinkers such as Ennin and Annen to adopt more liberal interpretations of the term.

For example, during Ennin's lifetime Tendai monks interested in Esoteric Buddhism argued that full realization could be attained, whereas those who favored traditional T'ien-t'ai practices often argued for partial realization. The following passage relates part of a debate between Ennin and Tendai monks who followed the *Mo-ho chih-kuan* (and hence were known as *shikansō*) over the proper interpretation of a passage from I-hsing's commentary on the *Ta-jih ching* that mentioned "leaping *(chōshō)* to buddhahood *(Butsuji)*":[47]

> Now the advocates of the *Mo-ho chih-kuan* criticized this passage, saying, "The phrase 'leaping to the stage of buddhahood' *(Butsuji)* refers to entering the stage [i.e., the first abode] where the enlightened mind first arises in the Perfect teaching. No principle is indicated whereby the practitioner could realize the ultimate stage of buddhahood within a single lifetime."
>
> Ennin replied, "Since you already have the words 'the ten grounds are accomplished' *(manzoku),* which refer to the ten grounds of the Perfect teaching, when the text says buddhahood *(Butsuji),* it means the ultimate stage."[48]
>
> The advocates of the *Mo-ho chih-kuan* said, "Within the various teachings, we find references to entering the first abode within a single lifetime, but not to realizing the ultimate goal."[49]
>
> Ennin said, "According to the passage, 'the ten grounds are accomplished.' Our case is clear. When you argue that the various teachings do not have a passage [indicating that the ultimate goal can be attained in a single lifetime], you are one-sidedly claiming that only the first abode [can be realized in one lifetime], and not allowing for leaping *(chōshō)* to [the ultimate goal]. Followers of the Perfect teaching already have a doctrine that the practitioner can 'leap to the ten grounds in a single lifetime.'[50] Why don't you say so?"
>
> The advocates of the *Mo-ho chih-kuan* believed and yielded to Ennin.[51]

At the same time that they actively studied Esoteric teachings, Tendai monks had to defend the Tendai interpretation of *sokushin jōbutsu* against Shingon claims that exoteric Tendai was inferior to Esoteric Buddhism. The Tendai position was based on Saichō's argument that the Perfect teaching of the *Lotus Sūtra* and Esoteric Buddhism had the same purport *(enmitsu itchi).* For example, in the above passage, Ennin cited a sentence from the *Fa-hua hsüan-i,* indicating that the practitioner can "leap to the ten grounds in a single lifetime," to prove that exoteric Perfect teachings coincided with Esoteric doctrines on rapid realization. Thus Tendai monks had to respond to two sometimes conflicting demands. On the one hand, they had to defend and interpret the *Lotus Sūtra* story of the Nāga girl as a major source for *sokushin jōbutsu* (without Shingon criticisms of Tendai, the story might have quickly come to play a minor role as Esoteric doctrines became more central in Tendai thought). On the other hand, Tendai monks had to give Esoteric teachings a major role in *sokushin jōbutsu* and explain its relation to the story of the Nāga girl. Some of their attempts to combine Tendai and Esoteric teachings in interpreting *sokushin jōbutsu* are explored below.

Saichō did not specify exactly which practices were to be used to attain *sokushin jōbutsu.* In his discussions of the direct path *(jikidō)* to buddhahood, he did mention the use of ordinations with the Perfect precepts, the four types of Tendai meditation, and Esoteric practices based on the *Mahāvairocanasūtra.*[52] Although his discussion of *sokushin jōbutsu* in the *Hokke shūku* was based almost entirely on the *Lotus Sūtra,* without mention of Esoteric sources, his analysis of the Nāga girl's realization reflected his interest in Esoteric Buddhism. He compared her words to the Esoteric mystery of speech *(kumitsu)* and the transformation of her body to the mystery of the body *(shinmitsu).* In addition, Saichō's citation of a passage from the *Kuan P'u-hsien p'u-sa hsing-fa ching* (Sūtra concerning the Meditation of the Bodhisattva Universal Virtue) that identified Śākyamuni with Vairocana (Birushana) contributed to the impression that Esoteric Buddhism might be used to realize *sokushin jōbutsu.*[53]

Most of Saichō's immediate followers did not apply Esoteric practices to *sokushin jōbutsu.* Gishin did not mention them in his *Tendai Hokkeshū gishū,* nor was their role in *sokushin jōbutsu* mentioned in the questions that Enchō, Gishin, and Kōjō submitted to Chinese T'ien-t'ai monks. However, during this time, Kūkai had advanced Esoteric teachings concerning *sokushin jōbutsu.* A clear reference by a Tendai monk to the relationship between Esoteric Buddhism and *sokushin jōbutsu* appears for the first time in Tokuen's *Tōketsu.* Tokuen began by citing the traditional scriptural support for *sokushin jōbutsu*—namely, the story of the Nāga girl from the *Lotus Sūtra.* He then alluded to a passage from the apocryphal *Jen-wang ching* (Sūtra of the Benevolent King), "translated" by Amoghavajra, that mentions "realization of buddhahood with one's current body" *(genshin jōbutsu).*[54] Finally, he asked about Esoteric Buddhism:

> According to I-hsing's commentary on the *Mahāvairocanasūtra,* upon entering the gate of Esoteric Buddhism [Shingon], essentially there are three subjects: (1) the mystery of the body, (2) the mystery of speech, and (3) the mystery of thought. . . . By using these three expedients, a practitioner purifies his three types of activity *(sangō)* and [receives] the empowerment of and response *(kaji)* to the three Mysteries of the Tathāgata. Thus in this lifetime a person can complete the perfections of the [ten] grounds without going through aeons of practice and completing the various practices to vanquish the defilements. As is stated in the *Greater Perfection of Wisdom Sūtra (Ta-p'in ching),* "There are bodhisattvas who at the time of the aspiration to enlightenment attain the stage of nonretrogression [the eighth ground] and others who attain supreme enlightenment."[55]
>
> On the basis of the previously quoted passages [some monks of] the Shingon School say that through the empowerment and response from the mantra, the body is transformed into the golden one [of a buddha] without abandonment of the current body or acquisition of a [new and] separate body. But there are also [monks of the] Shingon school who reject this

> teaching and argue that the body which has arisen through ignorance [and its karmic results] must necessarily be abandoned and a new body without any taint *(muro)* must be obtained for supreme enlightenment [to be realized].
>
> If we speak of the realization of buddhahood with this body, then within our minds we should embody Birushana. When our bodies are identified with the three activities [or mysteries of the Buddha *(sanbyōdō)*], this [state] can be called "supreme enlightenment." However, we should not identify supreme enlightenment with a body which moves as if it were in a dream *(mukan no shin)*. If the Nāga girl did not abandon her body, then how could she have ascended to the Lotus throne?[56]

Tokuen's question contains the first clear reference to Esoteric sources in a Tendai discussion of *sokushin jōbutsu.* Although Esoteric practices eventually occupied a major place in such discussions, Tokuen maintained a skeptical attitude when he argued that supreme enlightenment must involve a profound mental transformation, not just the performance of Esoteric rituals in a dreamlike state.[57] Moreover, he questioned whether the Nāga girl was a good model for *sokushin jōbutsu,* since her transformation into a male and miraculous travel to a different land before attaining buddhahood suggested that she had indeed received a new body.

Tsung-ying's reply to Tokuen's question once again demonstrated that the Chinese T'ien-t'ai monks were interested in different issues than their Japanese counterparts. Tsung-ying did not even mention Esoteric Buddhism, but did note that the transformation of the Nāga girl was a change in sexual identity only, not a complete bodily change and not the beginning of a new life. Moreover, he did not seem to understand the importance of the practical issue of whether *sokushin jōbutsu* was a viable possibility for Japanese monks. After noting that only those with the most superior religious faculties could attain *sokushin jōbutsu,* he dismissed the urgency of the issue by stating that, once they were enlightened, the aeons that people with lesser religious faculties had spent practicing religious austerities would seem "like awakening from a dream of one hundred years and [realizing that it had been] only an instant."[58]

In 847, approximately a decade later, a major step was made toward introducing Esoteric sources into the discussion of *sokushin jōbutsu* when Anne listed twenty-five passages from the Buddhist canon that supported *sokushin jōbutsu* in his *Min'yu benwakushō.* Twenty of the twenty-five were from exoteric sources such as the *Hua-yen ching (Avataṃsakasūtra), Nieh-p'an ching* (Nirvāṇa Sūtra), and *Ying-lo ching* (Sūtra on the Garland of the Primordial Acts of the Bodhisattva). However, the other five were from Esoteric sources: one from the *Hsin-ti kuan ching* (Sūtra on the Discernment of the Mind-Ground), one from the *Ta-jih ching*

(Mahāvairocanasūtra), and three from the *P'u-t'i-hsin lun* (Treatise on the Enlightened Mind; *T* 1665), a text attributed to Nāgārjuna. Among the passages from the *P'u-t'i-hsin lun* was the following statement, which played a major role in Kūkai's *Sokushin jōbutsugi* because it provided the Esoteric Buddhist locus classicus for the term *"sokushin jōbutsu"*: "Only in the Mantra Vehicle is the realization of buddhahood with this very body found. Hence the method of samādhi is explained in it, but is missing in other teachings and not mentioned."[59]

Anne's citation of this passage was clearly the result of Tendai efforts to develop teachings that could compete with the Shingon school's use of Esoteric practices to realize *sokushin jōbutsu.* At the time Anne compiled the *Min'yu benwakushō,* at least some Tendai monks were probably relying on Kūkai's teachings as the basis of their practice of Esoteric Buddhism.[60] However, Anne's citation of the *P'u-t'i-hsin lun* may have seemed inappropriate to many Tendai monks because the passage implied that the exoteric teachings which had formed the basis of the Tendai interpretation of *sokushin jōbutsu* up to that time might be of lesser value than Esoteric practices. In addition, the passage seemed to deny the importance of the very exoteric sources that Anne had cited, and thus seemed to violate Saichō's position that the Perfect teaching and Esoteric Buddhism are identical in purport. Anne himself did not comment on the meaning of the passage and thereby ignored the difficulties of reconciling exoteric and Esoteric sources. However, he did note that "in Nāgārjuna's treatise the doctrine of *sokushin jōbutsu* is established as the ultimate teaching."[61]

When Ennin returned from China in 847, shortly after Anne had composed the *Min'yu benwakushō,* he began formulating a Tendai version of Esoteric Buddhism that could compete with Kūkai's Shingon school. In the process, he used terminology similar to that found in Saichō's discussion of *sokushin jōbutsu,* particularly in the classifications of exoteric and Esoteric Buddhism. Exoteric Buddhism described a path that required aeons, whereas Esoteric Buddhism led to the rapid realization of enlightenment.[62] In his discussions, Ennin referred to the superior speed of Esoteric practices by claiming that they led to "realization during one's current life" *(genshō shōtoku),* a goal identified with the three highest of the six degrees of identity.[63] The ultimate goal of buddhahood, however, could be attained through either exoteric or Esoteric practices; the difference lay both in the amount of time required and in the effectiveness of the practices themselves. Thus even though followers of exoteric practices might "perform aeons of practice, some attained [supreme enlightenment] and some did not."[64] Esoteric practices were both faster and more reliable.

Ennin countered Shingon criticisms that the *Lotus Sūtra* was an exoteric text by including it in the category of Esoteric Buddhism.

Although Ennin's view can be seen as a development of Saichō's dictum that the Perfect teaching and Esoteric Buddhism are identical in purport, the interpretation of the *Lotus Sūtra* as an Esoteric text is suggested by passages both in the *Lotus* itself and in the *Ta-chih-tu lun* (Commentary on the Greater Perfection of Wisdom Sūtra). The *Lotus Sūtra* refers to itself as "the secret essential of the buddhas" and "the secret treasure of the Thus-Come One." It warns that "it may not be distributed, then given at random to men."[65] Such views, though not identical to those found in Esoteric scriptures, were adopted by commentators on the *Lotus* such as Chih-i, but were ignored by others such as Tao-sheng (355–434) and Fa-yün (467–529). Later, I-hsing (673–727), author of the authoritative commentary on the *Ta-jih-ching,* used many of Chih-i's views on the Esoteric qualities of the *Lotus* in advancing his interpretation of Esoteric Buddhism. Thus Ennin's argument for the Esoteric nature of the *Lotus* had substantial precedents.[66]

Ennin claimed, however, that the *Lotus* and other one-vehicle sūtras were Esoteric only in principle *(yuiri himitsu),* not in terms of practice, because they did not mention the three mysteries *(sanmitsu).* In contrast, key Esoteric works such as the *Ta-jih ching* were Esoteric in both principle and practice *(riji gumitsu).*[67] This line of argument permitted Tendai monks to discuss the theoretical significance of the Nāga girl's story for *sokushin jōbutsu* while ignoring practical issues; those would be found in Esoteric scriptures. As a result, after Ennin discussions of *sokushin jōbutsu* based on the Nāga girl usually took the form of debate manuals rather than guides to practice.

Although Ennin brought a copy of the *P'u-t'i-hsin lun* back from China with him, he rarely if ever cited the text, perhaps because of its problematic implications for the harmony of Esoteric and Perfect teachings.[68] Yet because the *P'u-t'i-hsin lun* was a major source for Esoteric Buddhism, it could not be ignored for long. Enchin cited it occasionally; however, later in life he argued that it had not been written by Nāgārjuna but had been compiled by Amoghavajra. Enchin had probably noticed that several passages in the text were from I-hsing's commentary on the *Ta-jih ching,*[69] and although he still used the *P'u-t'i-hsin lun,* it did not play an essential part in his writings. In contrast, Enchin's contemporary, Annen, gave it a major role in his writings, arguing that it had been written by Nāgārjuna and that the passages from I-hsing's commentary had been inserted by a later monk.[70] After Annen, the *P'u-t'i-hsin lun* was generally recognized as an authoritative source for the Tendai Esoteric tradition.[71]

Many of the problems left undecided by earlier Tendai Esoteric thinkers were resolved in Annen's writings, which completed the systematization of the Tendai classification of doctrine and criticized some of Kūkai's teachings. His genius at systematic interpretation is reflected in his treatment of Esoteric Buddhism and *sokushin jōbutsu.* For example, Annen argued that "while the Nāga girl was in the ocean she heard the [*Lotus*] *Sūtra* from Mañjuśrī, received a prediction of her eventual buddhahood, and entered the first abode. She then went south and during the time 'she' went through the eight major events of a Buddha's life, 'she' practiced these [Esoteric] meditations."[72] Annen thus suggested that the practitioner of Perfect teachings would inevitably progress to Esoteric practices when he entered the first abode according to the Perfect teaching, if not before. The stages of the Perfect teaching above the first abode were therefore considered to be fictitious, with the actual stages being those of the Esoteric tradition.

In fact, Annen equated the stages from the first abode onward for the practitioner of the Perfect teaching with the stages from the worldling onward for the follower of the Esoteric teaching.[73] Hence someone considered a sage in the path according to the Perfect teaching might be a worldling according to the Esoteric path. Annen thus rejected Ennin's view that either exoteric or Esoteric practices could lead to supreme enlightenment; only Esoteric practices would result in the ultimate goal. Any cases of supreme enlightenment being realized by followers of exoteric teachings were explained as expedient measures taken to encourage those of lesser abilities.[74] Ennin had suggested one way of maintaining Saichō's dictum of the common purport of Perfect and Esoteric teachings while still giving Esoteric Buddhism the primary role in *sokushin jōbutsu;* in contrast, Annen clearly subordinated the role of the *Lotus Sūtra* in *sokushin jōbutsu.*

Several centuries later, Hōjibō Shōshin suggested an approach that restored the importance of traditional T'ien-t'ai meditations. In his interpretation of the troublesome passage on *sokushin jōbutsu* from the *P'u-t'i-hsin lun,* Shōshin wrote:

> Question: . . . If [the passage from *P'u-t'i-hsin lun*] is correct, then how could the doctrine [of *sokushin jōbutsu*] have been elucidated through the *Lotus Sūtra?*
>
> Answer: [Annen's] *Bodaishin gishō* (Explanations of the Doctrine of the Mind of Enlightenment) stated that although the [Esoteric] meditations were explained in the *Lotus Sūtra* and other texts, bodhisattvas to transmit the teaching were missing and it was not written down. Moreover, texts such as the *Lotus* are Esoteric *(himitsukyō),* as is explained in [Ennin's] *Soshitsujikyōsho* (Commentary on the *Susiddhikara* [Acts of Perfection] *Sūtra*). In addition, it is not the case that just one single type of practice results in *sokushin jōbutsu.* It is not written in any teaching that [only] Esoteric practices result in *sokushin jōbutsu.* The *Lotus* explains that through Perfect and Sudden meditation, the practitioner quickly realizes the body of a bud-

> dha. [The *P'u-t'i-hsin lun*] uses the word "missing" to indicate that the practices of the three mysteries are not present [in other texts], not to indicate that a teaching of *sokushin jōbutsu* is [completely] "missing."[75]

Despite Shōshin's efforts, the teaching of the realization of buddhahood with this very body sometimes came to be thought of only in terms of Esoteric Buddhism within the Tendai school. Many Tendai monks came to believe that Esoteric practices were superior to exoteric meditations such as those described in the *Mo-ho chih-kuan.* Although passages in exoteric works might refer to *sokushin jōbutsu,* it was believed that they had theoretical significance only and were of little use in practice. By the thirteenth century one of the topics in Tendai debate was, "Is the doctrine of *sokushin jōbutsu* limited to Esoteric teachings or does it also extend to exoteric teachings?"[76] The way the question was phrased implied that the Esoteric component was generally considered to be more important than the exoteric one.

Conclusion

The most striking characteristic of the early Tendai questions on *sokushin jōbutsu* that Japanese monks directed to their Chinese counterparts was the Japanese tendency to constantly inflate claims for the efficacy of practices and for the stages thereby attained. As time passed, Tendai monks suggested that *sokushin jōbutsu* applied to increasingly lower levels on the path, brought the practitioner to higher goals, and did so in shorter periods of times. Even when Tendai scholars received answers from their Chinese counterparts that were disappointing or missed the point, Japanese monks persisted in developing their views. Although later Tendai monks such as Hōjibō Shōshin criticized the more extreme claims for *sokushin jōbutsu,* arguments for either a shorter path or virtual elimination of stages came to dominate medieval Tendai thought. These trends, evident in Tendai by the second half of the ninth century, point toward the emergence of *hongaku* (innate enlightenment) thought and the views of the path that emerged in the Kamakura schools. To conclude this study, answers to two further questions are suggested: What factors led the Japanese to interpret the path in this manner, and what practical significance did these discussions of *sokushin jōbutsu* have for Tendai monks?

The Factors behind Tendai Insistence on a Shorter Path

Although no detailed answers to this complex issue can be advanced in this limited space, several important factors can be suggested. First, geographical isolation played a role. Tendai developed without much direct guidance from Chinese monks, who did not travel to Japan to insist on a balanced view of T'ien-t'ai doctrine and practice. In fact, Chinese T'ien-t'ai was moribund during much of the time when Japanese Tendai was developing. Although a few Japanese monks such as Ennin and Enchin spent long periods of study in China, they focused their attention on Esoteric Buddhism more than on Tendai. With no Chinese T'ien-t'ai monks in Japan, Japanese monks could ignore Chinese positions when they wished to do so and emphasize scriptural passages conducive to rapid realization.

Second, Esoteric Buddhism played a major role in Tendai discussions of *sokushin jōbutsu.* The physical side of buddhahood had played an important role in Chinese Esoteric Buddhism, even though it does not seem to have been emphasized in the literature to the extent that it eventually was in Japan. The physical side of Esoteric rituals, including special hand gestures (mudrā) and the physical performance of ritual actions, must have impressed Japanese monks. The physical emphasis in Esoteric Buddhism was even reflected after death. For example, when Shan-wu-wei (Śubhakarasiṃha), translator of the *Mahāvairocana-sūtra* and coauthor of the most authoritative commentary on that text, died, his body did not decay.[77] Thus both ritual performances and the legends surrounding one of the most important monks in the Japanese Tendai Esoteric lineage might have suggested to Tendai monks that realization of the highest truth should be accompanied by physical attainments.

Although the need to compete with the Shingon school was probably the most important factor in the development of Tendai Esoteric views of *sokushin jōbutsu,* it should not be overemphasized. Early Tendai monks devoted considerable effort to explaining *sokushin jōbutsu* in terms of the *Lotus Sūtra*'s story of the Nāga girl and studiously avoided mentioning Esoteric practices. However, Tendai efforts to compete with Shingon—and to develop interpretations of the *Lotus Sūtra* and a Tendai Esoteric tradition—lay behind many of the discussions of the term. With time, Tendai discussions of *sokushin jōbutsu* and the *Lotus* moved toward an accommodation with Esoteric Buddhist concerns, until the Esoteric perspective dominated exoteric discussions. When *sokushin jōbutsu* was discussed in exoteric terms, it was usually intended for use in the theoretical investigations of the path that occurred in the Tendai debate system. Inclusion of the term *"shiki"* (private record) in the titles of much of the literature on *sokushin jōbutsu* shows that it was intended for use by debating monks rather than as a guide for practice.[78] In contrast, the practical aspects of *sokushin jōbutsu* came to be dominated by the Esoteric Buddhist tradition.

A third set of factors that pushed Tendai monks toward shortening the path is found in the other traditions in Japan that permitted the realization of high spiritual states while still alive. Taoism was not established in Japan as an independent tradition, but Japanese monks and emissaries to China brought back Taoist longevity techniques and traditions about physical immortality. With the rise of Esoteric Buddhism during the early Heian period, Taoist immortality techniques influenced many intellectuals and Buddhist monks. Many of the this-worldly benefits of Taoist practices were similar to those promised in Esoteric Buddhist texts. Both Kūkai and Ennin were included in Ōe Masafusa's *Honchō shinsen den* (Biographies of Japanese Immortals).[79] Japanese emperors during the Heian period sometimes partook of alchemical potions, and immortals *(hsien)* were sometimes associated with buddhas. Kūkai was clearly aware of Taoism and wrote about it in his *Sangō shiiki* (Indications of the Goals of the Three Teachings) before he traveled to China.[80] Although Tendai and Shingon monks did not cite Taoist sources to support their views on *sokushin jōbutsu,* Taoist concerns with physical immortality might well have bolstered their interest in the physical dimensions of buddhahood.[81] In addition, the mummification practices that turned deceased practitioners into "buddhas in this very body" *(sokushin Butsu)* were affected by both Taoist teachings and Buddhist traditions surrounding *sokushin jōbutsu.*[82]

Shinto traditions that human beings might be installed as deities *(kami)* shortly after their death or, in the case of emperors, recognized as "kami that manifest themselves as men" *(arahitogami)* or as "present kami" *(akitsukami)* also may have contributed to setting the stage for *sokushin jōbutsu.* Notions such as these led Japanese monks to make exaggerated claims about the spiritual accomplishments of figures such as Gyōgi (670–749) and Shōtoku Taishi (574–622). However, neither Taoist nor Shinto traditions were mentioned in early Tendai discussions of *sokushin jōbutsu.* Tendai monks limited themselves to citing sources within their own tradition, just as they sometimes rigidly differentiated between discussions based on Esoteric and exoteric sources.

The Practical Significance of Discussions of Sokushin Jōbutsu

Although later sources included statements that a particular Tendai monk had realized a stage high on the path, contemporary sources for the lives of Tendai figures include few claims that *sokushin jōbutsu* or a particular stage on the path had been realized. Moreover, texts on *sokushin jōbutsu* by figures such as Anne, Rinshō, and Annen present both theoretical discussions of *sokushin jōbutsu* and a variety of scriptural evidence indicating the possibility of rapid realization, but few if any details about actual practices.[83] What practical role did discussions of *sokushin jōbutsu* play in the lives of Tendai monks?

The answer depends, of course, on which figure is investigated. For Saichō, *sokushin jōbutsu* was one of a series of ways to demonstrate the superiority of Tendai over Hossō teachings. For his disciples who composed the questions in the *Tōketsu* concerning *sokushin jōbutsu,* the topic played a vital role in their attempts to define a path to enlightenment and to determine the possibilities of rapid realization. However, with the establishment of an independent Tendai Esoteric tradition, discussions of *sokushin jōbutsu,* particularly those framed around the story of the Nāga girl, appeared increasingly in the context of debate manuals. In such cases attention was paid to reconciling contradictory doctrinal claims, not to laying out a scheme for practice. Actual practices were described in other genres, such as manuals for meditation or for Esoteric rituals, not in the debate manuals about *sokushin jōbutsu.*

Sokushin jōbutsu did have practical consequences for Japanese Buddhism, however. It laid the theoretical foundation for the many Tendai monks who used Esoteric practices to advance themselves on the path and to attract patrons. It also contributed to the rise of teachings on *hongaku* (innate enlightenment) and eventually to the formulations of the path found in the Kamakura schools.

Notes

1. Individuals usually were called *"bosatsu"* because of their efforts to help others rather than because they exhibited wisdom; see Yoshida Yasuo, *Nihon kodai no bosatsu to minshū* (Tokyo: Yoshikawa kōbunkan, 1988), 8-41. However, sometimes they were said to have reached specific stages on the path. Prince Shōtoku is said to have realized supreme enlightenment in Ssu-t'o's *Jōgū kōtaishi bosatsu den, Dainihon Bukkyō zensho* (Tokyo: Suzuki gakujutsu zaidan, 1970–1973; hereafter *BZ*), 71.122c8. *BZ* was first published in a different format in Tokyo by Bussho kankōkai, 1911–1922. Since I've used both sets, the edition is specified.

2. *Taizō kongō bodaishingi ryakumondōshō* 2, *T* 75.472a24–26.

3. For Saichō's views on *sokushin jōbutsu,* see Paul Groner, "The *Lotus Sūtra* and Saichō's Interpretation of the Realization of Buddhahood with This Very Body (sokushin jōbutsu)," in George and Willa Tanabe, eds., *The Lotus Sūtra in Japanese Culture* (Honolulu: University of Hawaii Press, 1989), 53–74. In writing this chapter, I benefited considerably from a seminal article by Fujita Kairyū ("Nihon Tendai ni okeru sokushin jōbutsu shisō," *Shūkyō kenkyū* new 11.3 [1933]: 459–480) as well as from a number of more recent articles by Ōkubo Ryōshun that are cited below. In addition, Ōkubo kindly supplied me with a copy of Rinshō's *Tendai Hokkeshū sokushin jōbutsugi.*

4. For the story of the Nāga girl, see *Miao-fa lien-hua ching* 4, *T* 9.35a18–c26; Leon Hurvitz, trans., *Scripture of the Lotus Blossom of the Fine Dharma* (New York: Columbia University Press, 1976), 198–201.

5. For a discussion of the difficulties in determining whether Saichō or Kūkai was the first to use the term *"sokushin jōbutsu,"* see Groner, "The *Lotus Sūtra* and Saichō's Interpretation," pp. 54–57. Sueki Fumihiko has suggested that the Hossō monk Tokuitsu (fl. early ninth century) may have played a key role in calling the importance of *sokushin jōbutsu* to the two men's attention through his criticism of the concept ("Nihon Bukkyō: Sokushin jōbutsu wo chūshin to

shite," *Higashi Ajia no Bukkyō,* Iwanami kōza Tōyō shisō 12 [Tokyo: Iwanami shoten, 1988], 201).

6. The sources for this article are discussed in more detail in Paul Groner, "Tendai Interpretations of the Realization of Buddhahood with This Very Body (sokushin jōbutsu) after the Death of Saichō: Sources and Preliminary Considerations," in David Chappell, ed., *Tendai Studies,* forthcoming. In that article, I suggest that Tendai *sokushin jōbutsu* literature played a variety of roles within Tendai thought, some of them only tangentially related to discussion of the path to enlightenment.

7. For a discussion of Annen's relationship with Ennin and the views of both on monastic discipline, which did differ significantly, see Paul Groner, "The *Fan-wang ching* and Monastic Discipline in Japanese Tendai," in Robert Buswell, ed., *Chinese Buddhist Apocrypha* (Honolulu: University of Hawaii Press, 1990); idem, "Annen, Tankei, Henjō and Monastic Discipline in the Tendai School: The Background of the *Futsū kōshaku," Japanese Journal of Religious Studies* 14.2–3 (1987): 131–132; and idem, *Saichō: The Establishment of the Japanese Tendai School,* Berkeley Buddhist Studies Series 7 (Berkeley: Center for South and Southeast Asian Studies, University of California, 1984), 298–302.

8. *Daikyō yōgishō* 6, *BZ* (Bussho kankōkai ed.) 42.434b15–435a17. The *Daikyō yōgishō* is a polemical defense of Shingon teachings against criticisms by monks from other schools, especially by the Tendai monks Enchin and Annen. Jippan, author of the *Daikyō yōgishō,* follows Kūkai's classification of doctrine by placing Kegon above Tendai teachings.

9. Ikeda Rosan, *Kokusei hyakuroku no kenkyū* (Tokyo: Daizō shuppansha, 1982), 390–391; *T'ien-t'ai Chih-che ta-shih pieh-chuan, T* 50.196b14. Chih-i suggests that he could have made more progress if he had devoted less time to his disciples. For a discussion of the six degrees of identity and their relation to *sokushin jōbutsu,* see Groner, "The *Lotus Sūtra* and Saichō's Interpretation," pp. 63–67.

10. *Fo-tsu t'ung-chi* 6, *T* 49.178c13–14, 180b30–31. Neal Donner has commented that Chih-i was generally uninterested in speculating about the speed with which a person could realize enlightenment, despite having had several "enlightenment experiences" himself (Donner, "Sudden and Gradual Intimately Conjoined: Chih-i's T'ien-t'ai View," in Peter Gregory, ed., *Sudden and Gradual: Approaches to Enlightenment in Chinese Thought* [Honolulu: University of Hawaii Press, 1987], 201–226). The attainments for Hui-wen and Hui-ssu were probably based on Chih-i's claim that he had realized the third degree of identity, with the teacher in each case having a higher degree of attainment than his disciple.

11. *Tōketsu, Nihon Daizōkyō* (Tokyo: Nihon daizōkyō hensankai, 1914–1922; hereafter *ND*) 46.422b12–16.

12. See Groner, *Saichō,* pp. 289–290, for Tsung-ying's discussion of the place of the *Ta-jih ching (Mahāvairocanasūtra)* in the Tendai system of the "five periods." Tsung ying is said to have mastered Sanskrit and to have taught Ennin the Sanskritic writing system *(siddhaṃ)* used in Esoteric ceremonies and the proper pronunciation of the *siddhaṃ* characters at the Hsi-ming Monastery in Ch'ang-an (Ono Katsutoshi, *Nittō guhō junrei kōki no kenkyū* [Tokyo: Suzuki gakujutsu zaidan, 1964–1969], 1:273–274). Tsung-ying may also have been influenced by Hua-yen teachings linking the realization of buddhahood with the completion of the degrees of faith *(shinman jōbutsu),* since his discussion is similar to this teaching. In fact, Annen explicitly identifies *shinman jōbutsu* with the Nāga girl in his *Bodaishin gishō* 1 (*T* 75.471b13–14).

Several of Kōjō's positions indicate that he was a willing advocate of doctrinal positions that allowed for a broad interpretation of the path and practice. He is one of the few Tendai monks who seriously considered the implications that Esoteric Buddhism had for monastic discipline. His most important text, the *Denjutsu isshinkai mon* (*T* 2379), includes passages indicating that he was familiar with some Ch'an teachings that might have led to his interest in a quicker path to enlightenment. For a discussion of Kōjō's views on the precepts, see Groner, *Saichō,* pp. 292–298.

13. *Wu-liang-i ching, T* 9.388c1. *Fa-hua hsüan-i* 2b, *Tendai Daishi zenshū* (Tokyo: Nihon Bussho kankōkai, 1970; hereafter *TZ*), *Hokke gengi* 2.138. The passage from the *Fa-hua hsüan-i* is discussed in more detail below because it eventually played a major role in Japanese Tendai discussions of rapid realization.

14. *Tōketsu, ND* 46.423a17–b3. The Hua-yen patriarch Fa-tsang (643–712) praises Hui-ssu and Chih-i in the *Wu-chiao chang, T* 45.481a25–26. Tsung-ying refers to the legend that Prince Shōtoku (574–622) of Japan was a reincarnation of Hui-ssu (515–577), a story that was actively spread by Japanese Tendai monks to aid them in their relations with their Chinese counterparts. Ennin dreamt that he was protected by Prince Shōtoku on his trip to China (Saeki Ariyoshi, *Jikaku Daishiden no kenkyū* [Tokyo: Yoshikawa kōbunkan, 1986], 240, 243–244); and Enchin mentioned the legend in his conversations with Chinese monks (Ono Katsutoshi, *Nittō guhō gyōreki no kenkyū* [Kyoto: Hōzōkan, 1982], 2:359, 365–366). The story was widely known among Chinese monks and referred to in the late Nara or early Heian period by Chien-chen's (J. Ganjin, 688–763) disciple Ssu-t'o (*Jōgū kōtaishi bosatsu den, BZ* [Suzuki ed.] 71.122). Even though Shōtoku was born three years before Hui-ssu died, this discrepancy does not seem to have bothered Japanese monks until the Kamakura period. Virtual enlightenment is the stage immediately preceding supreme enlightenment.

15. Later debate topics suggested that the three types of defilements were essentially identical and could be cut off with a single type of practice, namely, the three views realized in an instant *(sangan isshin)*. As a result, the path did not have to be defined by the defilements cut off. See Kouda Ryōsen, *Wayaku Tendaishū rongi nihyakudai* (Tokyo: Ryūbunkan, 1966), 101–105, 292–295.

16. *Tōketsu, ND* 46.423b8–424a7.

17. Kōjō probably based his question on a famous passage from Chih-i's writings: "The defilements are enlightenment *(bonnō soku bodai)*" (*Fa-hua hsüan-i* 9a, *T* 33.790b15). Kōjō may have been inspired in part by Chih-i's use of evil as the subject of some of his meditations. See Neal Donner, "Chih-i's Meditation on Evil," in David Chappell, ed., *Buddhist and Taoist Practice in Medieval Chinese Society* (Honolulu: University of Hawaii Press, 1987), 49–64; and Daniel Stevenson, "The Four Kinds of Samādhi in Early T'ien-t'ai Buddhism," in Peter Gregory, ed., *Traditions of Meditation in Chinese Buddhism* (Honolulu: University of Hawaii Press, 1986), 75–84. Related questions on the link between enlightenment and the defilements were asked by Enchō (*ND* 46.403a13–b7) and Tokuen (*ND* 46.417b7–418b8). Kōjō's interest in easier forms of practice is also reflected in his view of the precepts; see Groner, *Saichō,* pp. 292–298. Needless to say, if defilements are not used as the main criteria to define the path, a very different structure than that discussed in abhidharma texts is suggested.

18. *Tōketsu, ND* 46.424a8–b2.

19. Ibid. 46.424b4–16.

20. Rinshō, *Tendai Hokkeshū sokushin jōbutsugi* 11a–b. Annen's *Sokushin jōbutsugi shiki* (*Tendai sōsho* [Tokyo: Tendaishū daigaku shuppankai, 1922], 206–211)

includes a more extensive discussion on the relationship between the *roku soku* (six degrees of identity) and *sokushin jōbutsu.*

21. Ennin, *Soshitsujikarakyō ryakusho, T* 61.401b19–c5. For a discussion of Ennin's view of the realization by worldlings, see Chiba Shōkan, "Jikaku Daishi no sokushin jōbutsu ni tsuite," *Tendai gakuhō* 26 (1984): 166–168; Misaki Gisen ("Ennin no sekensō jōjū ni tsuite," *Tendai gakuhō* 26 [1984]: 50–55) has discussed some of the ramifications of the teaching for later Japanese culture.

22. Rinshō, *Tendai Hokkeshū sokushin jōbutsugi* 1b–2a; Annen, *Sokushin jōbutsugi shiki,* p. 186. Rinshō went beyond Saichō's position that even practitioners who had advanced faculties might require three lifetimes to realize buddhahood by arguing that even the dullest person who followed the Perfect teaching would realize buddhahood within three lifetimes. Enchin also noted that even the person with the dullest faculties within the Perfect teaching should be able to realize enlightenment within three lifetimes (*Kan Fugen bosatsu gyōhō kyō mongu gōki* 1, *BZ* [Bussho kankōkai ed.] 26.414a17–b16, 419a13–b3).

23. *Min'yu benwakushō,* in Eizan gakuin, ed., *Dengyō Daishi zenshū* (Tokyo: Sekai seiten kankōkai, 1975; hereafter *DZ*) 3.378–79; *Kuan P'u-hsien p'u-sa hsing-fa ching, T* 9.389c23–26; Bunnō Katō et al., *The Threefold Lotus Sūtra* (New York: Weatherhill, 1975), 348. Scholars are divided over whether Ennin allowed the term *"sokushin jōbutsu"* to refer to realization within three lifetimes. Asai Endō (*Jōko Nihon Tendai honmon shisōshi* [Kyoto: Heirakuji shoten, 1973], 366) claims that he did so. However, Ōkubo Ryōshun ("Ennin no sokushin jōbutsuron ni kansuru ichi ni no mondai," *Waseda Daigaku daigakuin bungaku kenkyūka kiyō, bessatsu* 10 [1983]: 46, note 3) has cited passages in Ennin's works that call Asai's interpretation into question.

24. *Taizō kongō bodaishingi ryakumondōshō* 2, *T* 75.472a24–26.

25. *BZ* (Suzuki ed.) 38.75a22–b3. For a discussion of the significance of the fifth of the six degrees of identity, see Groner, "The *Lotus Sūtra* and Saichō's Interpretation," pp. 64–67.

26. *Tōketsu, ND* 46.404b4–13. The translation of the *Ta-sheng ch'i-hsin lun* (*T* 32.581b3–8) with minor changes is from Yoshito Hakeda, *The Awakening of Faith* (New York: Columbia University Press, 1967), 87–88. Enchō's interest in the passage from the *Ta-sheng ch'i-hsin lun* may have arisen from Tokuitsu's use of it to criticize *sokushin jōbutsu* in the *Shingonshū miketsumon* (*T* 77.863c11).

27. All that is known of Wei-chüan is that he was a disciple of the eighth patriarch, Kuang-hsiu (770–844?), and that he probably participated in the revival of Buddhism after the Hui-ch'ang persecution (Ono, *Nittō guhō junrei kōki,* 1:388–389).

28. The interpretation of the story of the Nāga girl depended on whether it was considered to be an ultimate or provisional teaching, a difficult issue for Tendai monks. For a discussion, see Groner, "Tendai Interpretations."

29. *DZ* 3.371–383.

30. Annen, *Sokushin jōbutsugi shiki,* pp. 195–196, 204.

31. Ōkubo Ryōshun, "Shōshin no sokushin jōbutsuron," *Firosofia* 73 (1985): 145. In contrast, some Tōmitsu (Shingon) scholars argued that the Nāga girl had attained full enlightenment (ibid.).

32. Ninkū Jitsudō, *Dainichikyō gishaku sōketsushō, Tendaishū zensho* (Tokyo: Daiichi shobō, 1973), 10.275; Kouda Ryōsen, *Wayaku Tendaishū rongi hyakudai jizaibō* (Tokyo: Rinkōin, 1972), 525–527. Ninkū is famed as a scholar of both Pure Land (in the Seizan lineage of the Jōdoshū) and Tendai (in the Rozanji lineage). His *Dainichikyō gishaku sōketsushō,* important as one of the few Taimitsu (Tendai Esoteric) commentaries on the *Ta-jih ching,* draws on the teachings of

Ennin, Enchin, and Annen to advance the view that the first stage of the path is identical with the goal. See Ōkubo Ryōshun, "Ninkū no sokushin jōbutsuron," *Tendai gakuhō* 31 (1989): 134–138.

33. *Hokke gengi shiki* 3a, *TZ Hokke gengi* 2.140. Some Tōmitsu monks maintained similar positions on *sokushin jōbutsu* (Ōkubo, "Shōshin no sokushin jōbutsuron," p. 146).

34. *Hokke gengi shiki* 3a, *TZ Hokke gengi* 2.140.

35. *Hokke mongu shiki* 8b, *TZ Hokke mongu* 4.1999a1–19; *BZ* (Bussho kankōkai ed.) 22.681a. Shōshin's views on the rapid attainment of the higher stages of the path are discussed in Ōkubo Ryōshun, "Isshō nyūmyōkaku ni tsuite: Shōshin wo chūshin ni," *Tendai gakuhō* 26 (1984): 178–181; and idem, "Shōshin no sokushin jōbutsuron," pp. 145–158.

36. *Ta-jih ching (Mahāvairocanasūtra)* 1, *T* 18.1b3–4.

37. *Miao-fa lien-hua ching* 4, *T* 9.31a10–11; Hurvitz, trans., *Lotus,* p. 176. This passage is cited as support for the realization of supreme enlightenment in a single lifetime in such sources as the *Shūyō kashiwabara anryū* 3, *T* 74.489b8–9.

38. *Fa-hua hsüan-i* 2b, *TZ Hokke gengi* 2.138.

39. *Tendai Hokkeshū sokushin jōbutsugi* 9a. Esoteric Tendai had its own version of leaping past some stages *(hishō).*

40. *Bodaishin gishō* 4, *T* 75.524a5–6.

41. *Hokke mongu shiki* 8b, *TZ Hokke mongu* 4.1999a; *BZ* (Bussho kankōkai ed.) 22.679a. Shōshin's comment is reminiscent of Tokuitsu's criticism of *sokushin jōbutsu* in the *Shingonshū miketsumon* (*T* 77.863b8–c26).

42. *Hokke mongu shiki* 8b, *TZ Hokke mongu* 4.1999a–2000a; *BZ* (Bussho kankōkai ed.) 22.679a–b.

43. Chih-i, *Mo-ho chih-kuan* 6a, *TZ Maka shikan* 3.653–666.

44. *Ta-jih ching* 1, *T* 18.1b3–4.

45. *Hokke gengi shiki* 2b, *TZ Hokke gengi* 2.140. The question and answer are found in a long discussion of "leaping over" *(chōtō)* stages and going to the tenth stage in a single lifetime with a body of flesh *(nikushin).*

46. Annen also ignored Kūkai in his *Sokushin jōbutsugi shiki,* but mentioned Kūkai's teachings in works such as the *Bodaishin gishō.* However, even though Annen usually mentioned the author of the work he cited, when he quoted Kūkai's *Sokushin jōbutsugi* he did not mention Kūkai as the author (*T* 75.472a26–b2). Since some of the six versions of the *Ihon sokushin jōbutsugi* (*T* 77.384a–401b) attributed to Kūkai are very close to the *Himitsu sokushin jōbutsugi* (*Tendai sōsho, Annen senshū* 2.167–177) attributed to Annen, if their relationship were clarified, the role of Esoteric Buddhist teachings in early Tendai formulations of *sokushin jōbutsu* could be elucidated.

47. *Ta-jih-ching i-shih* 1, *Hsü-tsang-ching* (Taipei: Hsin-wen-feng ch'u-pan kuang-ssu, 1977; hereafter *HTC*) 36.521b14; *Ta-jih-ching su* 1, *HTC* 36.67b15.

48. *Ta-jih ching, T* 18.1b3–4. Although Ennin was pointing out the identity between *Butsuji* (buddha-ground) and the ten grounds, in other contexts the passage he cited also served as evidence for those who argued that a practitioner had to pass through all the stages in order *(shidai),* a process that might require a long period of time. I plan to consider the issue of whether the tenth land is identical to the buddha-ground in a forthcoming article on the physical aspects of *sokushin jōbutsu.*

49. The Tendai monks thus were following the position maintained by Saichō and Gishin.

50. *Fa-hua hsüan-i* 2b, *TZ Hokke gengi* 2.138.

51. Reported in both Enchin's *Dainichikyōsho shō* (*BZ* [Bussho kankōkai ed.]

26.678) and in a fuller form in Shōshin's *Hokke mongu shiki* 8b, *TZ Hokke mongu* 4.1998a. The translated text is a composite of these two sources compiled by Ōkubo Ryōshun, "Ennin no sokushin jōbutsuron," p. 44. The translation of *shikan no shosō* as "advocates of the *Mo-ho chih-kuan*" comes from the division of Tendai studies into an Esoteric course *(shanagō)* and an exoteric course *(shikangō)* based on exoteric sūtras and Chih-i's works, especially the *Mo-ho chih-kuan* (J. *Maka shikan).*

52. *Shugo kokkaishō, DZ* 2: 349.

53. The passage from the *Kuan P'u-hsien p'u-sa hsing-fa ching* (*T* 9.392c15–16) is cited in *Hokke shūku* (*DZ* 3.264, 266). For a discussion of the significance of this passage in Saichō's thought, see Groner, *Saichō,* pp. 260–262. Although Tendai monks maintained that Shaka-butsu (Śākyamuni) and Birushana-butsu (Vairocana) were identical, Shingon monks argued that Shaka was inferior to Birushana. The Tendai monk Tokuen included a question about this issue in his *Tōketsu* (*ND* 46.414b2–415b1). As a result, Shingon monks could argue that Esoteric texts were clearly superior to the *Lotus Sūtra* because they were preached by a superior form of the Buddha. Tendai monks could reply that Shaka and Birushana were identical and that the *Lotus* was essentially equal to the major Esoteric scriptures.

54. *Jen-wang ching* 2, *T* 8.841a20.

55. *Ta-jih-ching su, HTC* 36.58a9–15; *Ta-jih-ching i-shih, HTC* 36.512a9–15. Tokuen omitted several phrases within the passage without changing the meaning. The passage from the *Ta-p'in ching* (fasc. 2) cited by I-hsing is found at *T* 8.226a8–10.

56. *Tōketsu, ND* 46.416a5–17. Little is known of Tokuen's biography except that, like Ennin, he studied under Kōchi in Shimotsuke (Saeki, *Jikaku Daishiden,* pp. 348–353). He eventually became Saichō's student and was active in encouraging Tendai monks to study Esoteric Buddhism.

57. Tokuen's questioning of the identification of performing Esoteric ritual with buddhahood is reminiscent of the second of the three types of *sokushin jōbutsu* described in the *Himitsu sokushin jōbutsugi* (*Tendai sōsho, Annen senshū* 167) attributed to Annen—namely, the temporary realization of buddhahood during Esoteric rituals due to the Buddha's empowerment and response *(kaji sokushin jōbutsu).*

58. *Tōketsu, ND* 46.416b3–13.

59. *P'u-t'i-hsin lun, T* 32.572c13–14; cited in Kūkai's *Sokushin jōbutsugi, T* 77.381c11–13, and in Anne's *Min'yu benwakushō, DZ* 3.582. Although Saichō was aware of this text (*Hokke shūku, DZ* 3.78–79), he had not used it in his discussion of *sokushin jōbutsu.*

60. An example of this tendency is Enchō's 831 letter to Kūkai asking him to teach Tendai monks. See Groner, *Saichō,* p. 82, note 25.

61. *Min'yu benwakushō, DZ* 3.382.

62. Kiuchi Gyōō (*Tendai Mikkyō no keisei* [Tokyo: Keisuisha, 1984], 301) notes that the terminology Ennin used in his classification system was influenced by Saichō's discussion of *sokushin jōbutsu.*

63. Ōkubo, "Ennin no sokushin jōbutsuron," p. 41.

64. *Kongōchōkyōsho* 1, *T* 61.9c4–5. Ennin followed I-hsing in maintaining this position (*Ta-jih-ching su* 1, *T* 39.584a21–23).

65. *T* 9.10b8, 31b18–19, 39b18–19; Hurvitz, trans., *Lotus,* pp. 46, 178, 219. The *Ta-chih-tu lun* 4 and 100 classifies Buddhist teachings into categories and hints that the *Lotus Sūtra* is a secret teaching (*T* 25.84c16–85a6, 754b18–27).

66. These arguments are developed by Misaki Ryōshū, "Tendai ni okeru

'himitsu' to Taimitsu," *Mibu Taishun hakushi shōju kinen: Bukkyō no rekishi to shisō* (Tokyo: Daizō shuppansha, 1985), 448–454.

67. *Soshitsujikarakyō ryakusho* 1, *T* 61.393b14–26.

68. Ono, *Nittō guhō junrei kōki,* 4:570; Asai Endō, *Jōko Nihon Tendai,* p. 581.

69. *Sasa gimon* 1, *BZ* (Suzuki ed.) 38.217c3–5. Although Enchin does not directly refer to the passages from I-hsing's commentary in this passage, they are referred to in Annen's *Bodaishin gishō* 1, *T* 75.451b6–452a7.

70. *T* 75.451b6–452a7. Annen cited the *P'u-t'i-hsin lun* seventy-nine times in his *Bodaishin gishō* (*T* 2397), a text compiled just three years after Enchin had suggested that the *P'u-t'i-hsin lun* was by Amoghavajra. Moreover, the very structure of the *Bodaishin gishō* relies on the *P'u-t'i-hsin lun* (Kaneko Tesshō, "Annen oshō no enmitsugi ni tsuite," *Eizan gakuin kenkyū kiyō* 8 [1985]: 235). Disagreements between Enchin and Annen can be seen in a number of other sources (Groner, "Annen, Tankei, Henjō and Monastic Discipline," pp. 132–133).

71. Fukuda Gyōei (*Tendaigaku gaisetsu* [Tokyo: Bun'ichi shuppan kabushiki kaisha, 1954], 321) noted that the *P'u-t'i-hsin lun* is one of "the three sūtras and one śāstra" considered basic sources in the Taimitsu tradition. Fukuda also commented that whereas Shingon monks wrote a number of commentaries on the *P'u-t'i-hsin lun,* Tendai monks treated the text in a less direct manner, mentioning it in passing in texts such as the *Bodaishin gishō* (ibid., 344). The *Taishō shinshū daizōkyō sakuin* 40 (*jō*). 573b reveals that the citations of the *P'u-t'i-hsin lun* in Tendai works increase markedly from Annen onward.

72. *Bodaishin gishō* 1, *T* 75.471a10–12. In the next paragraph, Annen reiterates this position in response to the question, "In the *Lotus Sūtra,* the Nāga girl hears the [*Lotus*] *Sūtra* in the sea and realizes *sokushin jōbutsu* without using [Esoteric] meditations. Why is it necessary to use [Esoteric] meditations?"

73. *Bodaishin gishō* 2, *T* 75.481b12–15. In the third fascicle of the *Shingon kyōjigi* 3 (*T* 75.415a17–b22), Annen bases this approach on Chinese T'ien-t'ai arguments that the upper stages of the Hīnayāna, Pervasive, and Distinct teachings are all fictitious. For studies on Annen's view of the path, see Ōkubo Ryōshun, "Annen no gyōiron," *Indogaku Bukkyōgaku kenkyū* 33.1 (1984): 106–107; Kaneko Tesshō, "Annen oshō no Enmitsugi ni tsuite," *Eizan gakuin kenkyū kiyō* 8 (1985): 235–246; and Kiuchi Gyōō, *Tendai Mikkyō no keisei,* p. 369.

74. *Shingonshū kyōjigi* 3, *T* 75.415b23–c17.

75. *Hokke mongu shiki* 8b, *TZ Hokke mongu* 4.2000b12–19; *BZ* 22.680b11–681a1. The passage cited from Annen's *Bodaishin gishō* (fasc. 1 and 4) is found at *T* 75.471c3–4, 534a15–17. Shōshin makes the same point found in this passage again in the *Tendai Shingon nishū dōishō,* *T* 74.420c14–24. He follows it by noting that the three mysteries are appropriate for those with dull faculties during the latter period *(matsudai)* of the Dharma, but that Tendai meditations are more appropriate for those with better faculties (*T* 74.421a19–23). The term "missing" in the passage is from the sentence "*sokushin jōbutsu* . . . is missing in other teachings and not mentioned" (*P'u-t'i-hsin lun,* *T* 32.572c13–14).

76. Kouda Ryōsen, *Wayaku Tendaishū rongi hyakudai jizaibō* (Tokyo: Rinkōin, 1972), 209–214; idem, *Wayaku Tendaishū rongi nihyakudai* (Tokyo: Ryūbunkan, 1966), 494–497. Although debate texts generally focused on exoteric subjects, and could therefore be expected to be more sympathetic to the exoteric position on *sokushin jōbutsu,* the way this question is stated clearly revealed the Esoteric bias of most later discussions on the topic. In the modern survey of Tendai thought by Fukuda Gyōei, a study that generally reflects traditional Japanese Tendai views, *sokushin jōbutsu* is treated as a topic under Esoteric Buddhism.

Fukuda notes that although it is mentioned in exoteric texts, only in Esoteric treatments is the topic carried to its ultimate conclusion (*Tendaigaku gairon,* pp. 467–468). Despite the controversy associated with *sokushin jōbutsu* within the Tendai school, this teaching does not seem to have assumed the central position it had in Shingon thought. A survey of the indices of modern studies of Taimitsu, such as Misaki Ryōshū's *Taimitsu no kenkyū* (Tokyo: Sōbunsha, 1988) and Shimizutani Kyōjun's *Tendai mikkyō no seiritsu no kenkyū* (Tokyo: Bun'ichi kabushiki kaisha, 1972), reveals few entries for the topic.

77. *Hsü kao-seng-chuan* 2, *T* 50.716a7–17; Chou Yi-liang, "Tantrism in China," *Harvard Journal of Asiatic Studies* 8 (1945): 271–272. For Śubhakarasiṃha's place in the Japanese Tendai tradition, see Saichō's *Naishō Buppō sōjō kechimyakufu, DZ* 1.237–238.

78. For a discussion of the Tendai debate and examination system, see Paul Groner, "The Significance of Ryōgen's Revival of the Tendai Examination System," to be included in a forthcoming monograph on Ryōgen.

79. Inoue Mitsusada and Ōsone Shōsuke, *Ōjōden Hokke genki* (Tokyo: Iwanami shoten, 1974), 261–265. Approximately half of the biographies included in this collection, compiled around 1098, concern Buddhist figures. For a discussion of views of immortals during the Heian period with special reference to *sokushin jōbutsu,* see Matsuda Chikō, *Kodai Nihon Dōkyō juyōshi kenkyū* (Nara: Ningen seitaigaku danwakai, 1988), 297–312.

80. For a survey of Taoism in early Heian-period Japan, see Nakamura Shōhachi, "Nihon no Dōkyō," in Fukui Kojun et al., eds., *Dōkyō* (Tokyo: Hirakawa shuppan sha, 1983), 20–26.

81. Sueki Fumihiko, "Nihon Bukkyō: Sokushin jōbutsu," p. 197. For example, a passage in Ssu-t'o's *Jōgū kōtaishi bosatsu den* (*BZ* [Suzuki ed.] 71.122c8) noting that Shōtoku had abandoned his status as a lesser buddha *(shōbutsu)* to become a greater buddha *(daibutsu)* includes notes that equate *butsu* (buddha) with *sen* (immortal). Since Ssu-t'o was a disciple of Chien-chen, who brought the first T'ien-t'ai texts to Japan, Saichō was probably aware of this text. I plan to publish an article on the physical dimensions of *sokushin jōbutsu.*

82. For representative studies of *sokushin Butsu* that relate it to Shingon theories of *sokushin jōbutsu,* see Matsumoto Akira, *Miira-butsu no kenkyū* (Tokyo: Rokkō shuppan, 1985), and idem, *Kōbō daishi nyūjō setsuwa no kenkyū* (Tokyo: Rokkō shuppan, 1982). For a study of mummies in English, see Bernard Faure's forthcoming study on the subject.

83. Funaoka Makoto argues that doctrines such as *sokushin jōbutsu* were used primarily as theory. As evidence he notes the seeming contradiction between Kūkai's advocacy of *sokushin jōbutsu* and the Shingon traditions that Kūkai was deep in meditation awaiting Maitreya's arrival on earth (*Zenshū no seiritsu* [Tokyo: Yoshikawa kōbunkan, 1987], 138). Although Funaoka's position is useful in raising the issue of the practical import of such teachings, it is too extreme in denying any practical significance. *Sokushin jōbutsu* surely had practical significance at certain periods in Tendai history, especially for practitioners of Esoteric ritual.

Glossary

akitsugami 現神
Anne 安慧
Annen 安然
arahitogami 現人神
Asai Endō 浅井円道
Birushana 毘盧遮那
bonbu 凡夫
bon'i jōbutsu 凡位成仏
bosatsu 菩薩
bundan shōji 分段生死
bunshōka 分証果
bunshō soku 分証即
butsuji 仏地
Chan-jan 湛然
Chien-chen 鑑真
Chih-i 智顗
chii 地位
chō 超
chōshō 超証
chōtō 超登
Daikyō yōgishō 大経要義鈔
Dainichikyō gishaku sōketsushō 大日経義釈捜決抄
Dainichikyōsho shō 大日経疏抄
Enchin 円珍
Enchō 円澄
enmitsu itchi 円密一致
Ennin 円仁
Fa-hua hsüan-i 法華玄義
Fa-tsang 法蔵
Fo-tsu t'ung-chi 仏祖統記
Fujita Kairyū 藤田海龍
genshin jōbutsu 現身成仏
genshō shōtoku 現生證得
Gishin 義真
Gyōgi 行基
hennyaku shōji 変易生死
himitsukyō 秘密教
Himitsu sokushin jōbutsugi 秘密即身成仏義
hishō 被接
Hōjibō Shōshin 宝池房証真
Hokke gengi shiki 法華玄義私記
Hokke mongu shiki 法華文句私記
Hokke shūku 法華秀句
Hokke-zanmai 法華三昧
hongaku 本覚
Honchō shinsenden 本朝神仙伝
Hossō 法相
Hsi-ming 西明
Hsin-ti kuan ching 心地観経
Hua-yen ching 華厳経
Hui-ch'ang 会昌
Hui-ssu 慧思
Hui-wen 慧文
I-hsing 一行
Ihon sokushin jōbutsugi 異本即身成仏義
isshō jōbutsu 一生成仏
Jen-wang ching 仁王経
jikidō 直道
Jippan 実範
Jōgū kōtaishi bosatsuden 上宮皇太子菩薩伝
jū 住
kaji 加持
Kegon 華厳
Kōjō 光定
Kongōchōkyōsho 金剛頂経疏
Kuang-hsiu 広修
Kuan P'u-hsien p'u-sa hsing-fa ching 観普現菩薩行法経
Kūkai 空海
kukyōka 究竟果
kumitsu 口密
manzoku 満足
matsudai 末代
Miao-fa lien-hua ching 妙法蓮華経
Min'yu benwakushō 愍諭弁惑章
Mo-ho chih-kuan 摩訶止観
mukan no shin 夢感身
muro 無漏
myōji soku 名字即
myōkaku 妙覚
Nieh-p'an ching 涅槃経
nikushin 肉身
Ninkū 仁空
Ōe Masafusa 大江匡房
Ōkubo Ryōshun 大久保良峻
P'u-t'i-hsin lun 菩提心論
ri 理
riji gumitsu 理事具密
Rinshō 憐昭
ri soku 理即
roku soku 六即
Saichō 最澄
sanbyōdō 三平等
sangō 三業
sanmitsu 三密
sanshō jōbutsu 三生成仏
Sasa gimon 些々疑文
shanagō 遮那業

shidai 次第
shikangō 止観業
shikansō 止観僧
Shingon 真言
shinman jōbutsu 信滿成仏
shinmitsu 身密
shō 聖
shōi jōbutsu 聖位成仏
shōtoku 性得
Shōtoku Taishi 聖徳太子
Shugo kokkaishō 守護国界章
shutoku 修得
Shūyō kashiwabara anryū
宗要柏原案立
sōji soku 相似即
sokushin jōbutsu 即身成仏
Sokushin jōbutsugi 即身成仏義
Sokushin jōbutsugi shiki
即身成仏義私記
Soshitsujikarakyō ryakusho
蘇悉地羯羅経略疏
Soshitsujikyōsho 蘇悉地経疏
Ssu-t'o 思託
Sueki Fumihiko 末木文美士
Ta-jih ching 大日経
Ta-jih-ching i-shih 大日経義釈
Ta-jih-ching su 大日経疏
Ta-p'in ching 大品経
Ta-sheng ch'i-hsin lun 大乗起信論
Taizō kongō bodaishingi ryakumon-dōshō 胎蔵金剛菩提心義略問答抄
Tendai 天台
Tendai Hokkeshū gishū
天台法華宗義集
Tendai Hokkeshū sokushin jōbutsugi
天台法華宗即身成仏義
Tendai Shingon nishū doishō
天台真言二宗同異章
T'ien-t'ai 天台
T'ien-t'ai Chih-che ta-shih Pieh-ch'uan
天台智者大師別伝
tōgaku 等覚
Tōketsu 唐决
Tokuen 徳円
Tokuitsu 徳一
Tsung-ying 宗穎
Wei-chüan 維蠲
Wu-chiao chang 五教章
Wu-liang-i ching 無量義経
Ying-lo ching 瓔珞経
yuiri himitsu 唯理秘密
zasu 座主

No-Mind and Sudden Awakening: Thoughts on the Soteriology of a Kamakura Zen Text

CARL BIELEFELDT

Zen Soteriology

Zen Buddhism is famous for its no-nonsense approach to religious salvation. "We are," Zen likes to say of itself, "a special tradition apart from scripture that does not depend on the written word; we simply point directly at the person's mind, that he may see his own nature and become a buddha." The contrast between this self-definition and what we are used to in religion could hardly be starker, particularly when we consider what has been left out of it. There is no talk of God, of course, nor of a savior by whom we are redeemed; no mortal sin from which we are delivered, nor better land to which we shall repair. There is no holy writ to be revered nor divine revelation before which to bow; no church dogma to be believed nor church ritual to be performed. Instead, we are to abandon our rituals and dogmas, simply examine directly our own minds and see into our own natures. "Just turn the light around," says Zen, "and shine it back."

How are we to accomplish this revolutionary shining? Here Zen offers concrete, practical advice. We are to sit quietly in the exercise known as zazen (seated meditation), focusing our minds (perhaps on the enigmatic kōan stories of Zen tradition) until our conceptual thought processes have come to rest and we suddenly perceive things as they are "before" we have understood them. In this sudden perception, we discover the preconceptual level of consciousness that is the nature of our minds; in this discovery, or satori, we have become buddhas, freed forever from attachment to the false dualities of conceptual thought and done with the need for religion.

This is, to be sure, a crude model of Zen soteriology, but I think that something like this model (no doubt loosely derived from the sort of psychology cum metaphysics introduced to the West by the great Japanese

Zen scholar D. T. Suzuki) helps to account for some of the popularity of Zen in our day. It looks like a kind of "secular mysticism" for skeptical modern man: no dogma, no faith, no ritual; just a frankly utilitarian psychological technique for achieving an "altered state," a "peak experience" of raw reality that will radically and permanently transform our relation to ourselves and the world (presumably for the good). Perhaps so. Perhaps this is all there is to Zen Buddhism. But if we are to follow Zen's advice to question religious dogma, it may behoove us to ask about the status of Zen's own self-definitions; and if we are to represent skeptical modern (or perhaps "post-modern") man, we shall want to be suspicious not only of the epistemological claim that Zen Buddhism offers direct, preconceptual access to reality, but also of the historical notion that there is something called "Zen Buddhism" in the abstract—some single, definable religious entity that stands behind the various expressions, modern and premodern, of those who have called themselves Zen Buddhists. In particular, we may want to doubt whether our present model of Zen soteriology—or any given model—can adequately capture the range of what Zen Buddhists throughout history have wanted from their religion and how they have gone about getting it. This doubt arises not only from the historical range but also from the ambiguities of soteriology itself. Before I proceed to the historical case, I want to say a few words about these ambiguities.

Soteriological Models

The term "soteriology," drawn as it is from a branch of Christian theology, initially suggests the science of the salvific or healing function of the *sōtēr,* or savior, and in this sense seems a peculiarly inappropriate designation not only for our model of secular mysticism but for most (though perhaps not quite all) of what we find in the records of Zen. Yet, depending on how far we want to stretch the term from this initial theological context, it can reach to the very limits of religion itself and, at least by analogy, even beyond. Though these limits are by no means clear, and it would be naive to imagine that we can set neat stages in the stretching of "soteriology," it is helpful to distinguish narrower and broader senses of the term. The narrower senses tend to get fixed in one or both of two ways: (1) according to genre, by retaining the idea of a theological "science" and by limiting the extension of "soteriology" to explicit, more or less systematic accounts of religious goals and means; and (2) according to content, by accepting some version, more or less tightly defined, of the religious notion of salvation (though not necessarily of a savior) and by restricting "soteriology" to accounts of those religious goals, and their means, that are taken to be functionally or conceptually analogous to this notion. The former restriction yields a distinction between what we may call "theological" and "nontheological" religious expression. The latter restriction, when based on a loose definition of salvation as something like the final spiritual goal, gives a distinction between "ultimate" and "proximate" religious concerns; when derived from tighter criteria (such as notions of transcendence, liberation, transformation, and the like), it implies additional distinctions between forms of religion or religiosity that are "salvational" and "nonsalvational," "otherworldly" and "this-worldly," and so on.[1]

When thus restricted in these two ways to systematic, theological accounts of ultimate spiritual ends and their means, soteriology tends to be associated with the "great religions," and with the "great traditions" within those religions. When it is not thus restricted, there is a broader sense in which we can say that all religions have (or even are) soteriologies, insofar as all are cultural systems that have as a goal the justification of human experience (whether of individual or group) by bringing it into right relationship with a particular value structure. In this latter sense, "soteriology" intends little more than definitions of this relationship and the ways it is supposed to be achieved. Those "great" theological systems that define the relationship as individual salvation, seen as the transcendental solution to what is considered a radically problematic human condition, are in this sense simply subsets of the broader soteriological enterprise.

Buddhism is usually treated as such a "great" theological system, and discussion of its soteriology tends to assume the more restricted senses of the term, focusing on its systematic accounts of such transcendental ends as nirvāṇa or buddhahood, and on the renunciate's path of meditation and wisdom through which they are achieved. Yet as a historical phenomenon, the Buddhist religion is of course much more than this, and an adequate historical understanding even of its disparate theological systems can hardly do without some consideration of the broader soteriological interests within which they occur and with which they continually interact. Such an understanding must take into account not only what Buddhists should want and should do according to the norms of the "explicit," "official" soteriologies of the theologians, but also what Buddhists (including the theologians) have wanted and have done in the exercise of their "implicit," "de facto" soteriologies. Whether at explicit or implicit levels, it must acknowledge not only the "ultimate" soteriologies of final goals and means but also the many and varied "proximate" soteriologies of more immediate religious needs. Whether taken as ultimate or proximate, it must be willing to ask about the implicit soteriological purposes of the explicit soteriological systems themselves and be ready to recognize that both the production of such systems and the specific forms they take may well serve ends (whether individual or group) quite different from those defined by the systems themselves. Moreover, such an understanding must come to appreciate a wide range of soteriological genres—elite and popular, metaphysical and ethical, scientific and poetic, public and private, theoretical and practical, descriptive and prescriptive, and so on—each with its own ends and its own devices. And it must be sensitive to the complex conversation among these various kinds of soteriologies and to the ways they have talked to and against each other in particular historical, social, and intellectual settings, as they continually redefine what we call Buddhism.

One approach to understanding the major redefinitions of Buddhism that have recurred throughout its history is to see them as responses to crises or breakdowns in the soteriological conversation. Such crises can arise when, for whatever reasons, the perceived gap among the various soteriological models—and especially that between the dominant explicit and implicit models—no longer admits easy intercourse. At this point we can expect some attempt at reformation of the models—a reformation that typically tries simultaneously to lift the implicit and proximate to some "higher," more "orthodox" level of discourse and to lower the explicit and ultimate to some more accessible, more familiar stage of meaning. Something like this process was at work, I think, in the redefinitions of Buddhism that occurred in the early Kamakura (1185–1333), the period that saw the introduction of Zen to Japan.

The Kamakura Reform

According to the explicit soteriology of the regnant scholastic Mahāyāna systems imported to Japan from the T'ang, the ultimate goal of Buddhism was buddhahood—by official definition, a state transcending time and space, a state of omniscience, a state of substantial mastery over the forces of history and nature that gave one the paranormal powers through which a buddha was supposed to work for the spiritual benefit of all beings. This sublime state was not only the sufficient condition for liberation from the misery of rebirth in saṃsāra, it was also the necessary condition: in the standard versions of the Mahāyāna favored in Japan, there was no true liberation short of buddhahood.[2] The recognized means to this ultimate goal were appropriately daunting: they required a life of strictest renunciation and purest self-sacrifice, a life of perfect morality, profound meditation, and universal learning. Indeed, they demanded not just one such life but countless lives: by official sūtra count, it was to take no less than three great incalculable aeons to master the myriad practices and ascend the many stages of the bodhisattva's career.

In contrast to this imposing official religion, the implicit Mahāyāna soteriologies offered a range of considerably less exalted, more immediate goals. Generally speaking, I think it fair to say that most Buddhists of Japan, like most Buddhists elsewhere, whether monk or layman, probably looked to their religion less for final liberation from saṃsāra than for various kinds of consolation in saṃsāra—for the proximate resolution of particular personal problems, to be sure, but also for some broader, more comprehensive sense that these problems made sense; that in the big picture, their sufferings were not in vain; that in the long run, the ups and downs of their lives were headed more up than down. The means to such consolation were basically twofold: first of all, faith —faith in the compassionate power of the Buddha, the verity of the Buddhist teachings, and the purity of its institutions; and second, action —ethical action, to the extent possible, but more importantly, the ritual actions that were the most powerful forms of spiritual merit (donation of alms, recitation of sacred texts and formulae, participation in religious rites, and so on).

The gap between the explicit and implicit soteriologies was bridged by the notion that the means to consolation were also the first steps toward the official goal of liberation—steps that would eventually lead, through the laws of karma, to rebirth at higher spiritual levels, on which the distant ideal of buddhahood and the arduous path of the bodhisattva would one day become personally relevant. Yet for many Buddhists of the late Heian (794–1185) and Kamakura, this bridge no longer spanned the gap. On the near side, so to speak, the historical upheavals of the age, and the attendant prevalence and intensity of personal anxiety and pain, threw into doubt the hope that real consolation in saṃsāra could be found short of total liberation from it, raising the demand for more immediate access to the ultimate goal in this lifetime (or at least in the one to come). Meanwhile, on the other side of the gap, the possibility of actually achieving this goal in any lifetime looked increasingly remote. The validity of the sanctioned soteriological models was being undermined by two sorts of theological developments within the official systems themselves: one that gave exaggerated emphasis to the metaphysical interpretation of buddhahood and hence cast doubt on its status as real religious experience; and another that introduced the historical doctrine of the inevitable decline of the dharma and thus raised fears that no one in the present, final age could actually negotiate the bodhisattva path.[3] These theological doubts and fears were exacerbated by the increasing empirical evidence of the times that the established Japanese Buddhist institutions supposed to embody the official soteriology fell far short of the ideal.

To meet the new religious demand and to revalidate the Buddhist response, some of the Kamakura reformers looked back to China for culturally sanctioned but hitherto neglected soteriological strategies that might liberate them from the practical and theoretical difficulties of the old bodhisattva path. They found there two prime candidates in the flourishing traditions of Pure Land and Zen. Of these, perhaps the more radical, and surely the more popular, was that of the Pure Land. This movement took seriously the soteriological implications of the doctrine of the last, degenerate age. In effect (though of course it had ways to soften its break with tradition), it abandoned the remote, official ideal of buddhahood in favor of the more proximate goal of birth in the Western Paradise of the Buddha Amida—a goal already assured by Amida's vow to take into his land all who called on him in faith. Given this new goal, the movement could substitute for the difficult practices of the bodhisattva path the more accessible style of the implicit religion: faith in the saving vow of Amida, and ritual participation in the power of this vow through the recitation of his name. In the reformed soteriology, then, the same means by which one was consoled in this life—faith and ritual action—became the sufficient conditions for deliverance into the new final goal of the Pure Land.

In the Chinese Zen tradition, the Kamakura reformers discovered a soteriology that was in some ways structurally similar. While continuing to pay lip service to the traditional ideal of buddhahood, the Zen masters had brought the ideal down into the human sphere in two ways. First, they had "demythologized" the perfections of the Buddha, such that his omniscience tended to be seen simply as freedom from epistemological error and his supernormal powers over the world became his pure, spontaneous participation in the world, as enacted in the lifestyle of the Zen master himself. Second, they had taken advantage of the metaphysical definitions of buddhahood to emphasize that such a demythologized buddha was latent in the mind of every being and needed only to be recognized there. The single, simple practice of Zen meditation, in which one abandoned the erroneous thoughts that covered this latent buddha, was sufficient to uncover it and permit the Zen Buddhist to discover, in the new goal of satori, that his own mind already possessed the ultimate spiritual state.

We may notice here that, for all its reputation as a radical critique of religion, Zen Buddhism was theologically (and institutionally) more conservative than Pure Land: the end of its soteriology remained (in name, at least) the traditional goal of buddhahood; the way to this end remained (albeit in truncated form) meditation, one of the central spiritual practices of the standard bodhisattva path, and a practice traditionally left to the professional religious. This conservative quality made it easier for the Kamakura Zen Buddhist apologists to argue for the orthodoxy of their reform, but it also made it more difficult for them to bring that reform down to the implicit soteriologies of the mass of Japanese Buddhists. For all the theoretical proximity of the latent buddha-mind, to those without the actual experience of satori, it offered little consolation; for all the claimed spiritual power of Zen meditation, to those without the spiritual power to master the meditation—to those more comfortable with faith and ritual—Zen practice remained rather remote. In fact, many historical expressions of Zen have tended to remain rather remote and frankly elitist, but in spreading the religion in Kamakura Japan, the early Zen reformers did have ways of softening their definitions of both goal and practice to accommodate the values of the implicit soteriologies. Here I want to look at the ways such softening might be at work in one text of the period.

The *Zazen ron*

The *Shōichi kokushi kana hōgo* (Vernacular Dharma Words of the National Teacher Sacred Unity) is a work attributed to the important Kamakura figure Enni (or Ben'en, 1202–1280), one of the first and most successful exponents of Zen in Japan.[4] Like many of the early Japanese Zen converts, Enni began his career as a Tendai monk. After studying with a disciple of the famous Tendai and Zen teacher Yōsai (or Eisai), he traveled to the continent, where he was eventually certified in the understanding of his new faith by Wu-chun Shih-fan, a prominent master of the Yang-ch'i branch of Lin-chi who trained several of Japan's first Zen students. Soon after Enni's return to the islands in 1241, he was invited to the capital by the powerful Fujiwara minister Kujō Michiie and installed as the founding abbot of Michiie's grand new monastic complex, the Tōfukuji. From this exalted post he quickly became one of the most influential leaders of the nascent Japanese Zen movement, enjoying the patronage of both court and shōgunate, serving as the abbot of several important monasteries, and producing a goodly number of dharma descendants.[5]

Unfortunately, little of Enni's Zen teaching is preserved for us. We know that, like his forebear Yōsai and many of his Zen contemporaries, he retained broad interests in various forms of Buddhism and taught both the esoteric and exoteric systems popular in his day. Aside from a brief collection of his recorded sayings, his teachings on Zen are best known from the *Kana hōgo*. The provenance of this work, however, is quite problematic. The text is a brief tract, in the form of a catechism of twenty-four questions and answers preceded by a short introduction. It is traditionally said to have been written for Enni's patron, Michiie, and the vulgate version of the text ends with the complimentary close of an epistle and a colophon identifying it as Shōichi's private instructions to the minister. Nevertheless, not only this tradition but Enni's authorship itself are subject to considerable doubt.

Enni's *Kana hōgo* is perhaps more popularly known as the *Zazen ron* (Treatise on Seated Meditation), a title identical to that of a work attributed to Enni's contemporary Lan-ch'i Tao-lung (Rankei Dōryū, 1213–1278), the first Sung missionary to Japan. Tao-lung's text is of course written in Chinese, but one need not read far in it to recognize that it is a version of the Japanese work associated with Enni. It has been suggested that, when asked by Michiie for private instruction, the overworked abbot of Tōfukuji simply borrowed Tao-lung's text and put it into the vernacular.[6] But this suggestion is rather dubious. The association of Enni's text with Michiie seems to have been a late development and does not appear in the earliest extant version.[7] More importantly, whoever wrote the original text, and whether in Chinese or Japanese, it was probably not the Chinese master Tao-lung: the writing bears no resemblance to his other work, and the diction, scriptural sources, and religious themes of the *Zazen ron* all seem to stamp it as a work of Japanese authorship. I am reluctant at this point to hazard a guess about its provenance, but I do think the internal evidence of style and content allows us to accept the *Zazen ron* as a product of the early Kamakura; for my purposes here, this is enough.

By the early Kamakura, the Japanese had been Buddhists for some seven centuries, but they had not been Zen Buddhists. While Zen Buddhism had been enjoying a long and glorious history on the continent, the Japanese had continued to favor the older, more scholastic forms of Mahāyāna imported from the T'ang. Hence the first native converts to Zen were forced to contend with these established forms, and it is not surprising that, like the *Zazen ron,* much of the earliest Japanese Zen writing has a strongly apologetic character. As such, it tends to involve arguments for three general points: the orthodoxy of Zen, in terms acceptable to traditional Mahāyāna; the superiority of Zen over other forms of Mahāyāna; and the relevance of Zen to the religious needs of the community of Mahāyāna believers. Needless to say, such arguments are not necessarily mutually supportive: certain sorts of claims for the superiority of Zen, for example, can undermine the grounds for both orthodoxy and relevance; by the same token, overemphasis on orthodoxy may vitiate the case for superiority or rob the teaching of its appeal to those seeking new, more accessible forms of religion.

Of course, what one chooses to emphasize and how one goes about it depend to a large extent on the particular audiences and purposes of the argument. Thus, within the broad category of early Zen apologetic writing, we find quite disparate presentations of the religion. Yōsai's famous *Kōzen gokoku ron* (Promotion of Zen for Protection of the Country), for example, addressed as it was to the government and written to defend the faith against charges of antinomianism, emphasizes the institutional integrity and superior social benefits of Zen practice; Shōjō's *Zenshū kōmoku* (Outline of Zen Teaching), in contrast, composed in response to theological doubts among the author's colleagues in the

Kegon school, focuses on the legitimate place of Zen within the doctrinal structure of the Kegon orthodoxy.[8]

The *Zazen ron* is rather different from these more traditional, more learned essays. As its alternative title, *Kana hōgo,* indicates, it belongs to the popular new homiletic genre through which reformed versions of Buddhism (both Zen and others) were being spread throughout (at least the marginally literate levels of) late Heian and early Kamakura society. Given its intended audience, this genre eschewed the classical literary language of Chinese in favor of the contemporary vernacular; largely abandoned the traditional rhetorical device of argumentation through the marshaling of scriptural citation; and translated and reduced the complex technical vocabulary of scholastic Buddhism to a relatively few key religious notions. Due to both its audience and its purposes, the genre tended to put strong emphasis on the last of our apologetic points: the relevance and accessibility of the faith to everyman. Typically, as in the *Zazen ron,* it focused directly on the ultimate issue of individual salvation and offered more or less concrete advice on how to win salvation. Thus it was deeply concerned with soteriology. As we shall see in our text, not only this general concern but also the particular approaches taken to soteriology go hand in hand with the means and ends of the apologetic argument.

Sudden Awakening

Although the *Kana hōgo* is popularly called a "Treatise on Seated Zen," and although it opens by declaring this practice to be the very essence of Buddhism, the text as a whole is both more and less than an account of zazen—less, in that it does little to describe the actual techniques of seated meditation; more, in that it ranges well beyond this practice to offer an apologetic for a particular vision of Buddhism. This vision is very close to the sort of thing one finds in some of the literature of the early Zen movement of the T'ang, especially in the eighth-century texts associated with the so-called sudden teaching of the Southern school. Like that literature, it often seems to reduce Buddhism to a single, transformative insight into the ultimate truth.

When asked, for example, to explain how Zen can lead to buddhahood, the author of the *Kana hōgo* distinguishes between two kinds of practice: that of the traditional bodhisattva path, which is based on the accumulation of good karma and requires three great incalculable aeons; and that of the Zen way, which "points directly at the person's mind" *(jikishi ninshin)* and permits him simply to "see his nature and become a buddha" *(kenshō jōbutsu)* (7; 414).[9] Similarly, the author calls on us to abandon the quest for the paranormal spiritual powers developed on the path and simply "extinguish at once the three great incalculable aeons [of the bodhisattva path] and abruptly see our natures and become buddhas" (15; 416). Elsewhere, quoting "an ancient," he says, "When you suddenly recognize the Zen of the Tathāgata *(nyorai zen),* the six perfections and the myriad practices [of the bodhisattva path] are all complete within your body" (3; 412).[10] Dismissing the study of the Buddhist scripture, he remarks that "reading the true sūtra" consists of nothing but "awakening to the original mind and returning to the root source" (6; 413). Knowledge gained by studying the sūtras and śāstras is not "true knowledge," which lies only in "recognizing the inherent buddha-nature by turning the light around and shining it back *(ekō henshō)*" (16; 416). All the teachings of the sūtras are merely "a finger pointing at the moon"; all the words of the Zen patriarchs are simply "a tile [taken up] to knock on a gate": once the moon is seen and the gate opened, once we have "awakened to the one mind," the teachings are irrelevant (23; 419–420). The awakening to this mind itself suddenly dispells all the delusions and afflictions of saṃsāra; it is like the bright moon emerging from behind the clouds (18; 417), like a lamp taken into a dark cave (22; 419). There is no need for any spiritual verification beyond this awakening (2; 411).

As a kind of corollary to its emphasis on awakening, the *Zazen ron* repeats the classical Zen warnings against misguided attempts to overcome the afflictions *(bonnō,* Skt. *kleśa)* through meditation. This is the way of the Hīnayāna practitioners who, hating the afflicted state, try to "extinguish body and mind, becoming like dead trees, tiles and stones." This practice leads only to rebirth in the formless realm *(mushiki kai, ārūpyadhātu);* it is not "the true dharma" (12; 415). In a similar vein, the author rejects the notion that Zen practice is limited to seated meditation (19; 417) and criticizes those who "stop the thoughts of the three poisons *(sandoku)* [of desire, aversion, and delusion] only in zazen" and therefore "lack the authentic mind of the way *(dōjin)*" that "clarifies the root source of saṃsāra" (20; 418). In more general terms, he dismisses all efforts to seek buddhahood through religious endeavor: lesser types cling to the characteristics of things and seek the goal outside of themselves; higher types abandon these characteristics and turn within, trying to "rouse the mind to seek the mind"; both types fail to see that the afflictions are empty and the mind originally pure; their practices simply lead to more saṃsāra (22; 418–419).

As this last passage indicates, the rationale for the *Zazen ron*'s criticism of such spiritual practices is, not surprisingly, the ancient Mahāyāna notion of emptiness and the classical Zen teaching of the inherent buddha-mind *(busshin).* "Everything merely appears provisionally, like a dream, like an illusion" (11; 415); "when we awaken to the one mind, all things are empty, and not a single thing remains" (21; 418). "If we seek the source of the afflictions, they are like dreams, illusions, bubbles, or shadows" (22; 419); "when we open the gate of the great liberation *(dai gedatsu no mon)*, . . . there is no Buddha and no sentient being; from the beginning there is not a single thing" (23; 420). Since (as the usual Zen logic goes in these matters) "from the beginning the mind neither arises nor ceases, . . . saṃsāra is nirvāṇa"; since "the mind is originally pure, . . . the afflictions are enlightenment" (22; 418–419). In like fashion, since there are no real buddhas or sentient beings, they are equivalent (23; 419–420). To put this more ontologically,

> All beings have a self-nature *(jishō)*. This nature is intrinsically without arising or cessation; it constantly abides without change. Therefore, it is called the inherent self-nature. The buddhas of the three worlds [of past, present, and future] and all sentient beings have this same nature, which is the dharma body of the original ground *(honji hosshin)* (17; 417).

To put it more personally, "One's own mind is the Buddha" (2; 411). This buddha-mind is free from attributes and free from attachments *(musō mujaku)* (5; 413); it is immaculate, without concepts, with no thought of attainment (6; 413). It is, to use the standard metaphors, like the bright moon behind the clouds, like the clear mirror beneath the dust (18; 417). Because this mind is our "original lot" *(honbun)* (24; 421), we are buddhas from the beginning *(jiko honrai)* and not only as the fruit of the path (7; 414). It is only because this mind is covered by the clouds and dust of deluded thoughts *(mōnen)* that we fail to recognize it (18; 417); it is just because we believe that these thoughts are the "original mind" *(honshin)* that we wander in saṃsāra (17; 417). If we once awaken to the mind that is the source of these thoughts, we share in the supernatural clarity and power of buddhahood (18; 417).

Those familiar with the early Zen texts will recognize the standard moves of the sudden teaching, complete with the orthodox equivocation on the notion of buddhahood as ultimate truth and as realization of this truth, and the usual uncertainties on the question of whether we really need to eliminate deluded thoughts (as in 3; 412) or only (deludedly) think we do (21; 418). More interesting for our purposes here (and for Zen study more broadly) than these tricky bits of Zen soteriological strategy is the way in which the strategy is played out in the actual tactics of salvation. For these tactics, the opening questions posed by the sudden teaching become something like this: Assuming that being a "buddha from the beginning" is not quite the end of the matter, what is that end and how do we reach it? Assuming that the emptiness of deluded thoughts does not eliminate the need to eliminate (at least deluded thoughts about) them, how shall we proceed? In the apologetic context of our text, these questions take on a particular thrust: How is the Zen understanding of the ends and means of Buddhism related to other, more familiar versions of the religion—especially those Mahāyāna versions that also teach emptiness and posit an innate buddha-mind? And what are the implications of this understanding for those who choose to adopt the Zen religious life? Let us consider these two questions in order.

The Buddha-Mind School

The apologetic thrust and polemical concerns of the *Zazen ron* are already apparent in its opening section, which provides a brief introductory statement announcing the basic position of the text:

> The school of seated meditation *(zazen no shūmon)* is the way of the great liberation. All the various dharmas flow from this gate; all the myriad practices are mastered from this way. The mystic functions of wisdom and psychic powers are born from within it; the life of men and gods have opened forth from within it. Therefore, the buddhas have resided in this gate, and the bodhisattvas practice it and enter into this way. Even those of the Lesser Vehicle and non-Buddhists practice it, although they do not yet accord with the true path. All the exoteric and esoteric schools have their self-verification by attaining this way. Therefore, a patriarch has said, "All the wise men of the ten directions enter this school." (1; 411)[11]

Here we see a familiar style of Zen apologetic argumentation: Zen is the most orthodox form of Buddhism because it is the very essence of the religion, that "way of the great liberation" *(dai gedatsu no michi)* from which all else derives and toward which all else intends. All the Buddhist teachings and practices flow from Zen; all the Buddhist goals are achieved through Zen. Therefore, all religious seekers of whatever spiritual level—whether pagan or Buddhist, Hīnayāna or Mahāyāna, exoteric or esoteric—strive to practice this way; and all who would attain the great liberation of enlightenment must ultimately do so through this way.

If this opening statement reflects familiar Zen apologetic strategy, it also raises familiar questions about the implications of that strategy for understanding the relationship between Zen Buddhism and other forms of the religion. This question is immediately taken up in the first section of the catechism:

> Q: Why do you say that this Zen gate is the root of all the teachings?
> A: Zen is the buddha-mind. The discipline is its outer marks; the teaching is its explanation; the recitation of the [Buddha's] name is its expedient. These three samādhis have all come from the buddha-mind. Therefore, this school represents the root. (1; 411)

Zen is the "root" *(konpon)*—both the essence and source—of all Buddhism because it is the Buddha's own mind—that ultimate state of mind achieved by the Buddha, that enlightened set of mind from which he taught his religion, that fundamental quality of mind through which we are one with him. Here, of course, the *Zazen ron* is implicitly invoking the common Zen distinction between the buddha-mind *(busshin)* and buddha-teaching *(bukkyō)* schools—that is, between the tradition based on the actual experience of enlightenment, as transmitted from mind to mind by the Zen patriarchs, and the other Buddhist traditions that rely on the explanations of the experience in sūtra and śāstra.

To this distinction, the text seems to be coupling two other dichotomies regularly employed in Zen apologetics: (1) that between the ordinary, mundane religion of "marks" *(sō, lakṣana),* or phenomenal characteristics, and the noumenal Zen religion, which, being grounded only in emptiness, transcends all characteristics; and (2) that between religion based on "expedients" (*hōben, upāya,* in the sense both of the Buddha's accommodation to the spiritual level of the practitioner and of the practitioner's spiritual techniques appropriate to his or her level) and the Zen religion, based solely on the ultimate truth revealed to enlightenment and therefore beyond any need for such expedients. It is no accident that the styles of religious practice identified here with marks and expedients (i.e., discipline, *ritsu,* and recitation, *shōmyō,* respectively) were probably the two most powerful alternatives to Zen meditation in the new religious movements of the Kamakura—the former emphasized especially by the monastic reformers of the established Nara and Heian schools, the latter, as we have seen, by the swelling ranks of Amida devotees.

Taken by itself, the metaphysical claim that Zen represents the root buddha-mind, from which all Buddhism emerges, seems to leave open the question of how the Zen Buddhist is to view its relationship to the historical forms of the Buddhist religion. From one angle, this claim can be read to mean only that there is one spiritual truth (or state or practice)—here called "Zen"—that stands behind or runs through all forms of Buddhism, and that, insofar as they participate in (or express or aim toward) this truth, all forms are valid as the explanations, marks, and expedients through which the buddha-mind is made accessible to the world. This kind of reading is sometimes adopted by those in the tradition who emphasize the ultimate unity of the buddha-mind and buddha-teaching schools. It is a reading, however, that is not well suited to the advertisement of Zen as a compelling religious alternative, not only because it validates the spiritual utility of competing Buddhist forms, but also because it does not address the question of whether and in what way Zen actually takes some concrete, historical form beyond its merely metaphysical status as pure, transcendental essence. The author of the *Zazen ron* of course wants to promote such a form and hence must argue that Zen is not only the one truth that stands "behind" all forms of Buddhism but the supreme version of Buddhism that stands "above" all others and obviates or supersedes their practice. The argument takes two, probably not wholly compatible forms: one negative, which dismisses the ordinary goals and practices of the Buddhist path as being based on shallow understanding; the other positive, which locates Zen at the final stage of this path, as the culmination of all Buddhist religious endeavor.

Zen and the Path

We have already seen the negative form of this argument in the *Zazen ron*'s frequent attacks on traditional Buddhist accounts of the spiritual life. Here I shall consider just two examples, one theological, the other practical, that help show how the polemical positions of the apologetic impinge on soteriological issues. The first example concerns the common Buddhist expectation that the spiritual adept will possess (and be able to display) paranormal powers and supernatural qualities. According to the traditional theology, the buddhas, through aeons of cultivation on the path, were supposed to have perfected a wide range of such powers and qualities; but even less exalted types, insofar as they were masters of meditation, were held to be skilled in psychic travel, mental telepathy, and so on.[12] Thus it is not surprising that adherents of the early Zen school, which claimed to be the meditation school par excellence and to offer buddhahood to all, were embarrassed by such expectations and felt the need to counter them. The problem is directly addressed in our text:

> Q: Why is it that, although one who sees his nature and awakens to the way is immediately a buddha, he does not have the psychic powers *(jinzū)* and radiance *(kōmyō)* [of a buddha] or, unlike ordinary people, show the mystic functions *(myōyū)* [of a buddha]? (15; 416)

The answer comes in several forms. First it is held that the physical body, even of one who has seen his nature and become a buddha, because it is the karmic product of past delusion, does not display the powers and radiance. Behind this position one can imagine the common Mahāyāna distinction between the physical body of the Buddha (nirmāṇakāya) that appears in history and the spiritual body (saṃbhogakāya), known only to the advanced adept, that is the product and shows the signs of the Buddha's perfections. The text itself, however, does not invoke this distinction, and later on in section 15, it takes a rather different approach to the problem, declaring that the desire for paranormal powers is "the way of Māra and the pagan religions" *(tenma gedō)*. Even foxes, the author reminds us, have magical powers, but they are not particularly honored for that. In either case, whether it relegates them to a hidden world or limits them to the mundane world, the thrust is to dismiss the common understanding of the paranormal powers as irrelevant to the Zen religious program.

The real meaning of the powers, the text goes on to explain, is the "mastery of the six dusts and the deluded conceptions" *(rokujin mōsō)*—i.e., psychological freedom from attachment to the objects of sensory and intellectual experience. In like fashion, the "mystic functions" of the enlightened are identified with the sudden practice of one who, without requiring the three great incalculable aeons of aescetic practice, "abruptly sees his own nature and becomes a buddha"; and the supernatural "radiance," or aureola, supposed to emanate from the body of the Buddha is interpreted as the "light of wisdom" through which the Buddhist teacher saves beings from the "darkness of ignorance" (15; 416).

The *Zazen ron*'s redefinitions of the supernatural powers and qualities are quite typical of the way Zen apologetics likes to use the standard categories of Buddhist theology to its own ends; they are also quite suggestive of how this use at once closes and discloses the gap between ultimate and proximate soteriological concerns. On the one hand, the dismissal of the "literal" interpretation of the supernatural or superhuman character of buddhahood and its redefinition as an internal, epistemological state demystifies and humanizes the ultimate spiritual goal and thus reduces it to a level seemingly more accessible to actual experience. On the other hand, by dismissing the supernatural as irrelevant, this internalization and demythologization rob it of its power as a buffer between real and ideal. To the extent that the buddhas are within, there are no other powers "out there" to whom we can turn for solace and aid; we are left alone with ourselves. To the extent that buddhahood is directly within our reach, there is no safe distance from which we can gaze on the glories of the ultimate end to come, or across which we can imagine ourselves gradually progressing toward them; our proximate hopes and partial victories are in vain. In effect, our spiritual options have been reduced to indefinite suffering in saṃsāra or immediate ascent to supreme, perfect enlightenment.

The stark soteriological implications of the Zen apologetic are equally evident in our second example, the *Zazen ron*'s treatment of the traditional Buddhist practices of sūtra reading and recitation. In section 6, the interlocutor complains that the uncompromising Zen style of religion seems "difficult to believe in and difficult to practice" and asks whether one might not "seek the merits of reading the sūtras and reciting dhāraṇī, or keeping the precepts, or recollecting the Buddha and calling his name" (6; 413). The answer begins on a high note, by declaring that "the sūtras and dhāraṇī are not words: they are the original mind of all beings." This metaphysical interpretation is immediately followed by a rather different, more utilitarian reading: "They are speech, intended for those who have lost their original minds," taught simply in order to "bring about awakening to the original mind and put an end to birth and death in delusion" (ibid.).

Such a reading seems to hold out the hope that those who have lost their minds might yet make use of reading and recitation to regain them; and elsewhere the *Zazen ron* does somewhat grudgingly acknowledge the utility of scripture reading for those who, having not yet "awakened to the buddha-mind," must "rely on the finger" to "see the moon" (23; 419–420). But in our passage, the text immediately shifts back to its initial approach with the remark that "reading the true sūtra" consists simply of "awakening to the original mind" itself. It then goes on to dash any hope for the spiritual efficacy of reading or recitation: to use language to bring about realization is like saying "fire" to get warm or "breeze" to get cool, like trying to assuage one's hunger with the picture of a pastry or quench one's thirst with the word "water" (6; 413). Finally, the author moves his argument beyond the topic of language to a deeper religious issue: the problem here lies not merely in the futility of the particular practices of reading and recitation but in the more fundamental mistake of practicing the Buddhist dharmas with the intention of attaining something *(ushotoku).* This is "the great stupidity" of the ordinary man *(bonpu, pṛthagjana),* deluded by his belief in birth and death; in the "wisdom of the Great Vehicle," one "practices all dharmas with no thought of attainment" (ibid.).

If the rather rambling rhetoric of this passage reflects the venerable Zen tradition of a rough-and-ready approach to argumentation, its content reminds us of the tradition's readiness to play rough with the religious aspirations of proximate soteriology. The *Zazen ron*'s final warning in section 6 against the fundamental Buddhist practice of merit-making recalls the legendary opening statement of Zen in China, in which the First Patriarch, Bodhidharma, dismisses the pious deeds of the Liang Emperor Wu with the remark, "No merit whatsoever."[13] As in our passage, the patriarch goes on to contrast mundane notions of merit with "pure wisdom, perfect and profound." This wisdom, of course, is the *Zazen ron*'s perfect "wisdom of the Great Vehicle" *(daijō hannya)*—the knowledge that, as Bodhidharma says, "the substance is naturally empty and still." In the light of such wisdom, which sees through the causal structure of "birth and death," there is no confinement by that structure and hence no "thought of attaining" *(ushotoku no kokoro)* the spiritual fruits of karma within it. As Bodhidharma tells the emperor, "the primary sense of the holy truth" *(sheng ti ti-i i)* taught by the Buddha is that there is nothing particularly holy. Here again, if we are absolved of the obligation to perform the religious deeds that would make us holy, we are also deprived of the faith that such deeds will serve us in the short run or lead us in the long run to the goal. In this sense, at least, we can appreciate the interlocutor's lament that Zen is difficult to believe in and difficult to practice.

This difficulty of Zen is only intensified by some of the *Zazen ron*'s positive claims for the superiority of its religion—claims that seek to identify it with the highest levels of the spiritual path. For these purposes the apologetic must reaffirm the very notion of religious progress that we have just seen it dismiss, and in several places the *Zazen ron* does explicitly acknowledge the validity of such a notion. In section 7, for example, the author admits that "one who seeks buddhahood through accumulating the merits and good roots *(zenkon kudoku)* [of spiritual karma] may become a buddha after three great incalculable aeons," whereas one who "sees his nature" through Zen recognizes that he is a buddha from the beginning (7; 414). Here we seem to have two alternative forms of religion—one slow, the other quick—from which we are free to choose.

Elsewhere, however, the choice seems not so free. In section 14 we are told that "the three [ranks of the] wise and ten [stages of the] holy *(sangen jisshō)* [i.e, the *laukika* ranks of the *bhadra* and *lokottara* stages of the ārya that together constitute the bodhisattva path] are established for the sake of those of dull faculties *(donkon)*"; Zen, in contrast, is intended for those of such acute faculties *(rikon)* that they reach enlightenment at the very outset of the bodhisattva path, "when they first produce the thought *(hosshin, cittotpāda)* [of seeking enlightenment]" (14; 416).

Here we can see quite clearly how the apologetic is caught between two conflicting desiderata: by invoking the standard Buddhist hermeneutical categories of more and less spiritually advanced audiences and identifying itself with the former, it asserts its superior religious status at the expense of its relevance to those who count themselves among the latter. For the less spiritually advanced, it would seem, the old path, long and difficult as it is, remains the only choice. Indeed, however much we may celebrate the ease and speed with which the spiritually acute come to Zen practice, if we measure this practice against the stages of the traditional path followed by the dull, it is almost out of reach. When asked whether the bodhisattvas of the Great Vehicle have achieved Zen practice, the author of the *Zazen ron* responds that, until they have completed the tenth and final stage of their path, bodhisattvas still have not reached it; they only achieve it at the last moment of their careers, in the state of "virtual enlightenment" *(tōgaku)* from which they pass directly into buddhahood (13; 415).

The reason the bodhisattvas do not achieve Zen practice until the end of their careers is, we are told, that throughout their path they are still subject to the afflictions *(wakuchi no shō)*.[14] At first glance this may seem an odd way to explain the matter, since we have already been warned against making the Hīnayānist mistake of hating the afflictions and enjoined to understand them as empty and as enlightenment itself (13; 415, 418–419). This oddity is not peculiar to our text or to Zen: it is the sort of thing that comes easily to all Mahāyāna theologians, who can nimbly move back and forth across the distinction between ultimate and conventional levels of discourse. Though such moves are common throughout our text, at this point the author prefers a slightly different approach: to say that the bodhisattvas are subject to the afflictions, he explains, is simply to say that they have "aspirations to seek the dharma" *(guhō no nozomi)* and hence "do not accord with their original lot" (*honbun ni kanawa*[*zu*]) (13; 415).

In other words, the prime attitudinal failing that separates the religion of the traditional Buddhist path from Zen practice is its intentionality—the "thought of attainment" *(ushotoku no kokoro)* that is the key defect of merit-making. Zen practice begins where this failing stops, in the attitude that the *Zazen ron* calls "no-mind" *(mushin)*. Despite its seeming remoteness at the very end of the bodhisattva path, it is precisely this attitude of no-mind that the *Zazen ron* uses to span the gulf between real and ideal and bring the experience of awakening across from the other shore.

No-Mind

When asked how one is to use the mind *(yōjin)* in Zen spiritual practice, the author of the *Zazen ron* replies that the true use of the mind is no-mind and no-thought *(munen)* (5; 412–413). Since all things appear only provisionally, we should not consider *(shiryō)* them (11; 415); if we do not consider them—if we have "the ultimate [practice of] no-mind"—we put a stop to all false views and discriminations of thinking *(akuchi akuken shiryō funbetsu)* (9; 414). This way of no-thought, or no-mind, "does not consider any good or evil" (9; 414); hence it has no aspirations for merit *(kudoku)* (8; 414) or even for the buddhadharma itself (13; 415). It simply "sees all things without seeing them in the mind and hears all things without hearing them in the mind" (24; 421). This is by no means the Hīnayāna practice of stilling the mind (12; 415): indeed, it is beyond the stages of the bodhisattva path (13; 415) and eliminates the three aeons of the path (15; 416). One who "does not consider any good or evil" directly cuts off "the root source of saṃsāra"; he is "a buddha without beginning or end and is [practicing] Zen whether walking, standing, sitting or reclining" (19; 417).

The teaching of no-mind, or no-thought, is one of the most famous features of early Zen literature, especially that espousing the sudden doctrine. Like many of the central terms of this doctrine, "no-mind" and "no-thought" function at several levels, from concrete religious prescription to abstract metaphysical description. At the former level, they are associated with the common warnings about the evils of conceptual thought and with the standard injunctions to avoid "giving rise to thoughts" in regard to sense objects—injunctions no doubt reflected in the *Zazen ron*'s suggestive claim that, in no-mind, one "sees all things without seeing them in the mind." As I have pointed out elsewhere, this general psychological advice is sometimes linked in the early literature to a particular contemplative exercise in which one suspends consideration of good and evil and passively observes the arising and ceasing of one's thoughts until one has recovered, or uncovered, one's original mind. By the Kamakura, this exercise had been formalized as "the essential art of zazen" in the meditation instructions of the *Ch'an-yüan ch'ing-kuei* (Pure Rules of the Zen Gardens), the Sung Zen monastic code introduced to Japan around the turn of the thirteenth century.[15]

In this practical sense, then, "no-mind" could refer to a spiritual expedient for the psychological uncovering, and epistemological discovering, of the buddha-nature; as the *Ch'an-yüan ch'ing-kuei* says, once the waves of the mind are stilled, the pearl of enlightenment resting beneath will appear.[16] Even as it used the term in this sense, however, the tradition was acutely aware that the soteriological model resting beneath that use could threaten some of the claims of the sudden doctrine. Hence, at the upper end of the Zen theological spectrum, no-mind was simultaneously held to represent a metaphysical disclosing of the nature of the buddha-nature and a theoretical foreclosing of the expedience of spiritual expedients. At this higher level, the point of no-mind was not that one should avoid giving rise to thoughts *(pu ch'i nien)* but that thoughts do not arise *(nien pu ch'i)*. Everything that appears to the mind, as the *Zazen ron* says, does so only "provisionally" *(kari ni)* (11; 415); the mind itself—the inherent buddha-nature—is "intrinsically without arising and ceasing." We arise and cease in saṃsāra only to the extent that we believe our thoughts to be our original mind (17; 417). In this sense of no-mind, the only authentic Zen practice was the abandonment of such belief through the sudden recognition of the original mind.

Between the psychological and metaphysical senses of no-mind lay what we may loosely describe as an ethical sense of the term, which I am calling the "attitude" of no-mind—namely, the attitude of nonintentionality expressed in the early literature by the notions that Zen practice was "without action" *(wu-wei)*, "without artifice" *(wu-tso)*, and so on. Since the religious goal of buddhahood was inherent and not something to be achieved, the key to religious practice was, as the *Zazen ron* emphasizes, to give up merit-making and abandon aspirations for the dharma; since our distance from the goal is measured only by the persistence of our attempts to achieve it, one who abandons such attempts—one who, in the famous words of the Sixth Patriarch, "does not consider any good or evil"—immediately closes that distance. He is, as the *Zazen ron* says, "a buddha without beginning or end, [practicing] Zen whether walking, standing, sitting or reclining" (19; 417). To put the point a little differently, in the attitude of no-mind, Zen practice is its own reward—the direct, spontaneous expression of buddhahood in daily life.

As models for the religious life, these various traditional uses of no-mind are clearly in tension with one another: (1) the psychological use seems to imply a contemplative life aimed at cultivating the zazen exercise for control of the mind; (2) the metaphysical sense of no-mind tends to undermine such a religious style and, at least in theory, reduce spiritual practice to the single transformative experience of sudden awakening to the buddha-mind; and (3) the ethical use appears to dismiss the quest for such an experience and locate the goal of spiritual practice in the ongoing expression of the mind in action. From the broader perspective of intellectual history, the tension among these uses of no-mind may be viewed as a sudden-style analogue to such venerable Buddhist polarities as *śamatha* and *vipaśyanā, darśana* and *bhāvanā,* and to such enduring Chinese ethical dichotomies as knowledge and action, recovery and cultivation, and the like. But rather than pursue this broader perspective here, I want to ask how our text handles this tension in dealing with the troubled relationship between its twin themes of no-mind and sudden awakening.

Historically speaking, the Zen tradition was loath to abandon any of these three models of no-mind; hence the tension among them became a prime ideological factor in the development of variant interpretations of the tradition's sudden soteriology. By the thirteenth century, when the *Zazen ron* was written, these interpretations had already begun to crystalize in the two styles of teaching that would eventually dominate Japanese Zen: the so-called *kanna* (story viewing) Zen of the Rinzai school, based on the kōan teachings of the Sung figure Ta-hui (1089–1163); and the *mokushō* (silent illumination) Zen of the Sōtō, promulgated by Enni's famous Japanese contemporary, Dōgen (1200–1253). Ta-hui strongly rejected the notion that zazen was an end in itself and emphasized the need for the experience of awakening, brought about through concentration on the sayings of the Zen patriarchs; Dōgen criticized the utilitarian interpretation of zazen as means to an end and held that its practice was itself the enlightened activity of the patriarchs.[17]

Accustomed as we are to associating the Rinzai tradition with *kanna* Zen, the attribution of the *Zazen ron* to the Rinzai master Enni might lead us to expect it to offer a spiritual program designed to generate direct intuitive insight into the mind through kōan concentration. However, the *Zazen ron* makes no mention of the *kanna* technique and shows almost no awareness of the kōan stories so popular during the Sung, or of the considerable corpus of Zen transmission histories and recorded sayings already circulating in Japan. In fact, the *Zazen ron* seems blissfully ignorant of the contemporaneous disputes swirling around it over the interpretation of meditation and awakening. Yet to the extent that we can identify it with any position in these disputes, our text seems to fall closest to those that would emphasize the ethical attitude of no-mind.

Practice after Getting the Point

In his commentary to Dōgen's *Shōbō genzō* (Treasury of the Eye of the True Law), the Kamakura author Kyōgō criticizes Dōgen's rival Enni for teaching that zazen is a practice to be done only after one has "gotten the point" *(tokushi),* in contrast to Tao-lung, who is supposed to have made the opposite mistake.[18] Enni's follower Ichien has a similar charge against certain unnamed disciples of his master who say that zazen before one has "seen one's nature" *(kenshō)* is worthless.[19] Kyōgō, who probably felt some animosity toward Enni's more prosperous Rinzai movement, wanted to assert the superiority of Dōgen's Zen; Ichien, who has been called "a voice for pluralism," wanted to play down the distinction between Zen and Tendai meditation.[20] Whether or not their claims about Enni (or his followers) are historically accurate, we cannot say; but they do give us pause. Whether or not Enni actually wrote the *Zazen ron* I also cannot say; but I do see some interesting reflections of the claims in the text. Elsewhere I have written in passing that the remarks of Kyōgō and Ichien bear little relation to the *Zazen ron,* but I may have been wrong.[21]

The issue raised by these remarks can be put as follows: Is Zen meditation something to be done simply to gain a special insight, after which it is unnecessary? Or is it something else—something supposed to presuppose such insight, without which it is inauthentic? Clearly this issue is closely cognate to the dispute between *kanna* and *mokushō.* Though the *Zazen ron* does not enter into the dispute and, like many earlier Zen texts, can probably be read in either way, its treatment of no-mind seems to tip it heavily toward the latter style. Its penultimate dialogue is particularly interesting in this regard because it addresses the very issue raised by Kyōgyō and Ichien. The question here is, "After one has seen his nature, must he still use the mind [to practice]?" The answer, bits of which I have already cited for its emphasis on awakening, seems at first glance to be "no" and hence to be an assertion of the merely utilitarian view of Zen practice:

> All the teachings of the sūtras are like a finger pointing at the moon. . . . After one has awakened to the one mind, there is no use for any of them. All the words of the patriarchs are like a tile [taken up] to knock on a gate. . . . Once you have entered the gate, why pick up the tile? (23; 420)

Note, however, that the answer has sidestepped the question: the question had to do with the need for practice *(yōjin)* after awakening *(kenshō);* the answer concerns the role of the teachings in such practice. Before one has awakened, the text explains, "to the original meaning of the buddhas and patriarchs," one should study the Zen teaching of "seeing your nature and becoming a buddha"; after one has awakened, one will realize that "'seeing your nature' is nothing special *(kitoku)* and 'becoming a buddha' cannot be attained *(fukatoku)*" (ibid.).

The answer does emphasize the pivotal point of awakening, but it does not tell us on which side of that point we should put the cultivation of no-mind. I have no doubt that the author of the *Zazen ron* fully expected this cultivation to yield spiritual insights into Buddhism and therefore to serve as a means to an end; but this is not the prime justification he offers for it. On the contrary, we should remember that the key characteristic of no-mind is precisely its freedom from all aspiration for spiritual advancement: "Since [in the state of no-mind] we do not produce any views of cultivation, we do not aspire to become buddhas" (9; 414).

Where the text first takes up the notion of no-mind, it cites the *Diamond Sūtra*'s *(Vajracchedikā)* famous teaching that buddhas are free from "marks" *(lakṣaṇa)* and says, "The buddha-mind is without marks and without attachments *(musō mujaku)*. . . . Therefore, we should be without mind and without thought *(mushin munen)*" throughout all activities (5; 413).[22] This, I think, is the prime justification: we should practice no-mind because it puts into practice what is distinctive about our buddhahood. No-mind is not merely our practice but the very nature of our "original mind" (22; 419); it is not merely our mind but "the original teacher" *(honshi)* of all the buddhas of the three worlds. It is "the cardinal buddha" *(daiichi no butsu),* the realization of which is called the supreme perfect enlightenment of the buddhas (24; 422). It is probably this enlightened practice of no-mind that the author has in mind when he claims that Zen is itself the buddha-mind (1; 411) and reiterates that Zen cultivation represents "the ultimate of the buddha-mind" (4; 412). In the latter section, the concrete implications of this way of understanding Zen practice are expressed in dramatic terms:

> Even if you have not attained the way, when you sit in meditation for one period, you are a one-period buddha *(ichiji no butsu);* when you sit in meditation for one day, you are a one-day buddha; when you sit in meditation for one lifetime, you are a lifetime buddha. To have this kind of faith is to be one of great faculties, a great vessel of the dharma. (ibid.)

Sōtō exponents of the enlightened zazen of "just sitting" *(shikan taza)* would no doubt find little to quibble with here; advocates of *kanna* would surely smell the stench of silent illumination and ask what has happened to satori. The answer, I think, lies in the last line of this passage.

The fact that one can practice buddhahood without having "attained the way" *(tokudō)* reminds us that the *Zazen ron* has not abandoned the notion that its Zen practice leads somewhere, and that there is some difference between the practitioner who has attained the way and one who has not. Yet the soteriological thrust of our passage is not on this difference but on the simultaneity of practice and buddhahood; to focus on the difference and the spiritual attainments produced by the practice is to miss that thrust and put the horse before the cart. The cart here must go before the horse. The real awakening—the real turning point for the practitioner that frees him to put buddhahood into practice—must precede the practice, in some act of turning to it and taking it up. As soon as he turns to it and takes it up, he is a buddha, whether or not he has attained the way. If we call this turning point "getting the point," then Kyōgō's depiction of Enni's zazen could be applied to the *Zazen ron.*

Belief and Liberation

The difference between a style of Zen that teaches meditation practice only before awakening and one that speaks of it only after awakening can be seen in part as a reflection of the difference between psychological and metaphysical approaches to the interpretation of enlightenment. But in practical terms—in terms of the religious experience of the practitioner—that difference may also point to a distinction between two senses of the famous Zen call for a sudden "awakening" to, or sudden "seeing" of, the original nature. The former (the kind of seeing that occurs within, and comes as a result of, meditation practice) suggests a direct, intuitive apprehension of the higher state of mind that is supposed to be our original nature; the latter (the kind of seeing that precedes, and becomes the basis for, the practice) looks more like an act of intellectual assent to the doctrine of such a nature, and of emotional and volitional commitment to the religious course that is said to follow from that doctrine. The epistemological difference here is something like that between "knowing" and "knowing that." In soteriological terms, this difference can provide a distinction between the ultimate attainment of liberation through mystical identification with the buddha-mind and the more proximate goal of consolation in the certainty that there is such a mind.[23]

Traditional systems of Buddhist soteriology, of course, included analogous distinctions in their schemas of the path—distinctions, for example, between the initial "seeing" *(darśana)* of the truth, through which one eliminated the intellectual afflictions (usually counted as doubt and false views) and entered the transmundane path, and the final cessation of all cognitive and affective afflictions in complete enlightenment at the end of that path; or between the bodhisattva's preliminary knowledge of the metaphysical nature of all dharmas *(sarvajñatā),* which establishes him irreversibly on his religious course, and the full omniscience of buddhahood *(sarvākārajñatā).*[24]

It was no doubt in recollection of such distinctions that the famous T'ang scholar Tsung-mi (780–841) was able to divide the Zen spiritual experience into a first, sudden "awakening of understanding" *(chieh-wu)* of the buddha-nature, which launched one into authentic Zen practice, and a final "awakening of realization" *(cheng-wu)* of buddhahood, which was the culmination of such practice.[25] Tsung-mi's doctrine was directed against those within the Zen movement who wanted to draw antinomian conclusions from the sudden teaching; it sought to rationalize the teaching in terms of the path, to play down the soteriological significance of the initial understanding, and to emphasize the need to proceed to the final realization through a continued "gradual practice" *(chien-hsiu)* after the sudden awakening. In contrast, the message of the *Zazen ron,* directed as it is to those outside of Zen who seek alternatives to the hierarchies of the bodhisattva course, has little use for the notion of progressive stages in enlightenment but prefers to advertise the sufficiency of an initial awakening experience and to celebrate the freedom from spiritual need beyond.

The salvific power of the initial encounter with the buddha-mind teaching and the sense of liberation that follows from it are well expressed in sections 3 and 4 of the text. In the former, the questioner asks why we should abandon the spiritual merits of "the myriad practices and good works" of the traditional Buddhist path in favor of the sole dharma of "the one [buddha-]mind." The answer given is twofold: first, that this one practice fulfills all Buddhist practices; second, that, whatever practices we may do, in the end the only significant issue is "putting a stop to delusion and attaining the awakening" that is the necessary condition for buddhahood (3; 412). In the next section, the questioner pursues this second point. Surely Zen cannot guarantee such an awakening, "and, if it is not certain [that we will attain awakening], what good is there in cultivating [the buddha-mind teaching]?" The answer is that this teaching is itself "the way of inconceivable liberation" *(fushigi gedatsu no michi).* Hence, "if one but hears it, it forms the surpassing cause of bodhi *(bodai no shōin);* and, if one cultivates it, it is the ultimate of the buddha-mind *(busshin no shigoku).*" Simply to hear (and presumably to acknowledge) the good news of the buddha-mind is to be assured of the inconceivable liberation; simply to act on it is to be liberated. To seek awakening beyond this is to miss the point, since "the buddha-mind is basically without delusion and awakening" (4; 412).

Once we are assured of liberation, there is nothing to do but be liberated; once we have put the issue of awakening behind us, there is only the waking life before us. In other words, once we shift the turning point of the *Zazen ron*'s soteriology from the adept's achievement of mystical knowledge in meditation to the neophyte's experience of belief in the teaching, we also shift the religious role of its practice of no-mind from that of a concentration exercise designed to bring about the transcendental goal to that of a spiritual attitude or psychological habit that frees the believer from the demands of the path so that he may go about his business in the world. By allowing him to abandon all "considerations of good and evil," no-mind offers him an ongoing vehicle for liberation from nagging doubts about his spiritual state and the need to perfect it; by permitting him to "see all things without seeing them in the mind," it provides him with a moment-to-moment means for taking the world as it comes to him, in all its ambiguity. For no-mind, then, the karmic law of birth and death in saṃsāra holds no fear.

In the final, most poignant (and in some ways most religiously telling) passage of the *Zazen ron,* the questioner asks how the unenlightened man should use his mind *(yōjin)* to prepare himself for the end. The answer is that there is no end:

> When there is no thought and no mind, there is no birth and no death. . . . When we do not think that there is birth and death, when we are without mind and without thought, this is the same as the great nirvāṇa. . . . If we only cultivate no-mind and do not forget it, whether walking, sitting, standing or reclining, there is no special way to use the mind at the last. When we truly rest on the path of no-mind, [we go] like blossoms and leaves that scatter before the wind, like frost and snow melting in the morning sun.(24; 420–421)

If we have clearly come quite far from our initial model of Zen as a utilitarian approach to mystical experience, we have also come much closer to the values of the implicit soteriology of Kamakura Buddhism. While the orthodox ideal remains the ancient Zen call to the direct seeing of the buddha-nature, the operative goal is now the hearing of that call itself; while the official means to the ideal continues to invoke the traditional Zen practice of no-mind, the meaning of the means now lies not in its end but in itself.

By this reading, the *Zazen ron* is not far from the Pure Land. As in the contemporaneous Pure Land soteriology, the liberated state of buddhahood has come down to this world as the liberating fact of a buddha—not, to be sure, an external buddha who has vowed to free us from this land to another, but a buddha nonetheless, whose presence within promises to free us from our need to free ourselves. As in the Pure Land, this promise is activated by abandoning the old models of spiritual perfection in favor of faith in this buddha—not perhaps the *feducia* of the devotee's trust in that buddha's saving compassion, but at least the *fides* of the believer's assent to the saving fact. The promise is realized here, as in the Pure Land, through commitment to the ongoing expression of this faith in daily life—if not in the continuous celebration of the peerless power of this buddha's primal vow, then in the habitual reenactment of the markless wisdom of the inherent buddha-mind. The disagreement within Pure Land theology about whether such expression is to be found primarily in the inner life of piety or in the outward recitation of Amida's name has its analogue in the *Zazen ron*'s equivocation about whether its enactment of buddhahood is simply the internal habit of no-mind, "whether walking, standing, sitting or reclining," or whether it requires (or perhaps also is) the external ritual act of zazen—one period of which, we may recall, makes "a one-period buddha." Whichever is the case, in this style of Zen, as in the Pure Land, meditation is no longer an obstacle: one does not have to be good at it to be a buddha.

The Soteriology of Conversion

In the end, it will not do to overstate this "protestant" reading of the *Zazen ron*—a reading that represents, at most, a likely ideal type against which to test the more complex, more ambiguous mix of soteriological models found in this text. For example, the psychological distinction I have drawn between the mystical and intellectual experiences of the buddha-mind may not be easy to maintain in a teaching, like that of the *Zazen ron,* that tends to dismiss conceptual understanding as incapable of grasping religious truths; similarly, the soteriological distinction between ultimate and proximate stages in such experience cannot always be charted neatly in a text, like the *Zazen ron,* that wants to avoid the model of an articulated spiritual path. Nevertheless, as a heuristic device, the reading as a whole and some version of the distinctions on which it is based may help to make sense of the paradoxes of our text, to adjudicate the conflicting models of no-mind, and, more broadly, to take some of the mystery out of the sudden practice of Zen. At the very least, the notion of awakening as an act of faith points up the religious importance of that mystery and the extent to which it could—and in certain historical contexts probably did—serve as the main gateway (in the sense both of barrier and entrance) to Zen life.

The mystery of the sudden practice of Zen lies in its conflation of cause and effect. Whether the practice is reduced to the goal of awakening or whether the goal is embedded in the act of practice, the two must occur simultaneously. Theologically speaking, such a conflation is supposed to represent the culmination of the path, the crowning vision of the buddha himself, who sees no distinction between himself and the beings below him on the path. Because Zen claims to be the buddha-mind school, based solely on this vision, it must keep itself above any such distinction by collapsing the path and its goal and by asserting a transcendental plane of religion beyond the causal laws governing human spiritual works. Hence the key soteriological issue of the sudden practice becomes how one ascends to this higher plane and gains access to such religion. By definition, this cannot be done by climbing to it on the path but only by leaping to it from the path.

In existential terms, then, the path functions for the Zen Buddhist, perhaps no less than for the Pure Land believer, not as a road to freedom but as a symbol of bondage—as the law that binds him to cause and effect and thus chains him to the worldly plane. The power of the symbol grows, and the chains of the law bind ever more tightly, precisely to the degree that the would-be Zen Buddhist is a believing Buddhist whose faith is rooted in traditional scripture and whose religious life is grounded in the common assumptions and established practices of the path. For him, the leap to the higher perspective of Zen means abandoning his old faith, and the call to the sudden practice of Zen is a summons to a second "going forth" *(shukke)*—not from family life, this time, but from the familiar confines of Buddhist life.

The distance between the old law of the path and the new dispensation of Zen varies with the particular style of Zen teaching. In more conservative, more catholic styles that seek accommodation with the tradition, it may be merely the gap between alternative readings of what is taken to be a common spiritual system; in more radical, more protestant versions, it can become a yawning chasm—in effect, the gulf between saṃsāra and nirvāṇa itself, and hence the very stuff of Zen soteriology. Most Zen teachings probably fall somewhere between these extremes, but wherever they fall, Zen's distance from the path is most strongly felt and most explicitly expressed in those contexts in which the religion is addressing itself to the believing Buddhist and seeking to convert him to the faith. This was, of course, the context for many of the early Kamakura Zen teachings, as it had been for the T'ang originators of Zen.

By the late Heian and early Kamakura, when they first began to take Zen seriously as a religious alternative, Japanese Buddhists were quite familiar with the transcendental teaching of a supreme, sudden vehicle —a teaching they had long heard espoused by Kegon, Tendai, and Shingon scholars. What they lacked, and what seems to have most struck them about Zen (apart from the fact that it represented the preferred Buddhism of the Southern Sung elite), was (1) its claim to a religion based solely on the ultimate truth and perfect enlightenment of the buddha-mind itself, as transmitted outside scripture in the lineage of the patriarchs, and (2) its offer of a single, simple spiritual practice, beyond the techniques of the bodhisattva path, through which anyone could directly realize the buddha-mind and immediately accede to this lineage. Here was the ancient ideal of the final buddha-vehicle made flesh; and the sudden advent of men (not yet, so far as we know, women) claiming to be living buddhas and offering as much to everyman must have been a scandal to some learned doctors of the dharma.

Scandal or no, it certainly raised the question of just how these men understood their buddhahood and why they thought their practice immediately ensured it; dharma doctor or not, it raised both the eyebrows and the anxiety of those accustomed to looking at the final ideal from the safe distance of three incalculable aeons. Faced with such resistance, the early Zen apologists argued along two lines: one, as seen conspicuously in Dōgen's famous *kana hōgo* text, the *Bendō wa* (Talks on Pursuing the Way), that linked the Zen claims to the authority of the historical Buddha through the esoteric lineage of the patriarchs; the other, pursued by our *Zazen ron,* that grounded those claims in the ultimate import of the transhistorical buddha-mind. Though they differ in style, it is not surprising that both lines of argument end with a call for a leap of faith in the new dispensation, an abandonment of the old models of spiritual perfection, and a commitment to the life of buddhahood in the immediate world of everyday experience.

In one sense, the emphasis on these three elements—faith, and the abandonment and commitment that flow from it—can be seen as a reflex of the particular purposes of the apologetic genre itself: just as the goal of the genre was to turn the faith of its reader from the old religion and establish him in the new, so the goal of the new religion was to be found precisely in this turning. In this sense, the model of sudden awakening that I have proposed here might be styled a "soteriology of conversion," of a sort we could look for in Zen (and perhaps elsewhere) especially in those contexts of religious reformation where the new is pitted against the old. The original Mahāyāna soteriology itself arose in such a context, and there is another sense (not without its ironies) in which these same three elements in the new religion of Zen can be seen as a recapitulation or revalidation of the old model of the bodhisattva path, at least as it may have functioned at the implicit level.

In the religious structure of the *Zazen ron*'s call to a higher faith that abandons the old ideal in favor of renewed commitment to everyday experience, there seems to be what we might call a "poor man's parallel" to the bodhisattva's vow to relinquish the old goal of early nirvāṇa for the sake of indefinite service in saṃsāra. If the explicit consequences of this vow were supposed to demand three great incalculable aeons of heroic ascesis leading to buddhahood, the implicit result was the indefinite postponement of the demand for final transcendence and the rejustification of participation in the more proximate affairs of worldly life. At this implicit level, the *Zazen ron*'s critique of the bodhisattva path, despite (or precisely because of) its assertion of the radical immediacy of buddhahood, may amount to much the same result: whether the end of the path is too far away to see or too close at hand to miss, the way is open all the way to the horizon, and the wayfarer is free to linger along it where he will.

Notes

1. The tighter definition, in other words, would recognize soteriology only in the "ultimate" ends of those forms of religion that have some notion of "salvation" from the world; the looser definition would include as well the ultimate ends of forms that do not seek such salvation.

2. This was the soteriological dark side of the famous doctrine of the "one vehicle" taught in the popular *Lotus Sūtra (Saddharmapuṇḍarīka)*: if the doctrine proclaimed that everyone was really destined for the ultimate goal of buddhahood, it also revealed that no one really entered nirvāṇa except through buddhahood.

3. The former development, seen especially in the theology of the influential Tendai school, is now often referred to as the *hongaku,* or "original enlightenment," movement; the latter is, of course, the famous *mappō,* or "final dharma," doctrine that is widely (if perhaps somewhat too easily) used to explain the religious sensibilities of late Heian culture.

4. The text appears at *Zenmon hōgo shū* 2 (Tokyo: Kōyūkan, 1921), 411–422; I have published an English translation in *The Ten Directions* 9:1 (Spring/Summer 1988): 7–10.

5. For an English account of Enni's biography, see Martin Collcutt, *Five Mountains: The Rinzai Monastic Institution in Medieval Japan,* Harvard East Asian Monographs 85 (Cambridge, Mass.: Harvard University Press, 1981), 41–48.

6. On these grounds Enni's version has been dated between 1246, the year of Tao-lung's arrival, and 1252, when Michiie died; see Etō Sokuo, *Shōbō genzō josetsu: Bendō wa gikai* (Tokyo: Iwanami shoten, 1959), 156. The text of Tao-lung's *Zazen ron* can be found at *Kokuyaku zengaku taisei* 23 (Tokyo: Nishōdō shoten, 1930), 1–8; it has been translated into English by Thomas Cleary in *The Original Face: An Anthology of Rinzai Zen* (New York: Grove Press, 1978), 19–41.

7. A Muromachi manuscript discovered in the Hōsa bunko; see Sanae Kensei, "Hōsa bunko bon Shōichi kana hōgo no kenkyū (1): Honbun hen," *Zen bunka kenkyūjo kiyō* 6 (May 1974): 265–294.

8. For the *Zenshū kōmoku,* see Kamata Shigeo and Tanaka Hisao, eds., *Kamakura kyū bukkyō, Nihon shisō taikei* 15 (Tokyo: Iwanami shoten, 1971), 390–400.

9. Numerals in parentheses following citations refer to the pagination of the Japanese text in the *Zenmon hōgo shū* (see note 2 above); though the sections of the text are not numbered, for convenience of reference, I also supply the section number (always before the relevant page reference).

10. The quotation is from the *Cheng-tao ko* of the T'ang master Yung-chia; *Ching-te ch'uan-teng lu* 30, *T* 51.460a.

11. The words of the patriarch here are from the *Hsin-hsin ming,* attributed to the Third Patriarch of Zen, Seng-ts'an; *Ching-te ch'uan-teng lu* 30, *T* 51.457b.

12. So, for example, the five "supernatural knowledges" *(abhijña; jinzū),* held to be accessible to advanced yogis, whether Buddhist or pagan.

13. The conversation occurs at *Ching-te ch'uan-teng lu* 3, *T* 51.219a.

14. That is, the *kleśa-* and *jñeyāvaraṇa;* in the text's subsequent definition of the afflictions, only the former is mentioned.

15. See Kagamishima Genryū et al., *Yakuchū Zen'en shingi* (Tokyo: Sōtōshū shūmuchō, 1972), 279–284; for my discussion of this text and the contemplative practice of no-mind, see Carl Bielefeldt, "Ch'ang-lu Tsung-tse's *Tso-ch'an i* and the 'Secret' of Zen Meditation," in Peter Gregory, ed., *Traditions of Meditation in Chinese Buddhism,* Studies in East Asian Buddhism 4 (Honolulu: University of Hawaii Press, 1986), 129–161.

16. Kagamishima et al., *Yakuchū Zen'en shingi,* p. 283.

17. I have discussed these two styles of Zen in Carl Bielefeldt, *Dōgen's Manuals of Zen Meditation* (Berkeley: University of California Press, 1988).

18. *Shōbō genzō shō, Sōtō shū zensho, Shūgen* 1 (Tokyo: Kōmeisha, 1929), 348a.

19. Ichien, *Zōtan shū,* Yamada Shōzen and Miki Sumito, eds., Chūsei no bungaku 1:3 (Tokyo: Miyai shoten, 1973), 253, 255, 273.

20. Robert Morrell, *Sand and Pebbles (Shasekishū): The Tales of Mujū Ichien, A Voice for Pluralism in Kamakura Buddhism* (Albany: State University of New York Press, 1985).

21. Bielefeldt, *Dōgen's Manuals,* p. 76n.

22. The *Diamond Sūtra* passage cited here occurs in Kumārajīva's translation at *T* 8.750b.

23. It *can* provide such a distinction, but of course I do not mean to imply here that what I am calling the intuitive experience is necessarily supposed to be the ultimate soteriological goal.

24. The analogy here is to the soteriological distinction between proximate and ultimate stages of spiritual awakening, not to the epistemological characteristics of the awakening. The traditional schemas generally assumed that even the more proximate experiences here were the product of, and occurred within, yogic practice; to this extent, we might find a closer analogy in the common distinction between wisdom derived from hearing (or reading, *śrūtamayī*) and that derived from meditation *(bhāvanāmayī).*

25. See, for example, Tsung-mi's *Yüan-chüeh ching ta-shu ch'ao, ZZ* 1/14/3/280b. Tsung-mi's model has been well studied by Peter Gregory, in "Sudden Enlightenment Followed by Gradual Practice," in idem, ed., *Sudden and Gradual Approaches to Enlightenment in Chinese Thought,* Studies in East Asian Buddhism 5 (Honolulu: University of Hawaii Press, 1987), 279–320.

Glossary

akuchi akuken shiryō funbetsu 悪知悪見思量分別
bodai no shōin 菩提の勝因
bonnō 煩惱
bonpu 凡夫
bukkyō 佛教
busshin no shigoku 佛心の至極
Ch'an-yüan ch'ing-kuei 禅苑清規
Cheng-tao ko 證道歌
cheng-wu 證悟
chieh-wu 解悟
chien-hsiu 漸修
Ching-te ch'uan-teng lu 景德傳燈錄
dai gedatsu no mon 大解脱の門
daiichi no butsu 第一の佛
daijō hannya 大乘般若
Dōgen 道元
dōjin 道心

donkon 鈍根
ekō henshō 回光返照
Enni (Ben'en) 圓爾辯圓
fukatoku 不可得
fushigi gedatsu no michi 不思議解脱の道
guhō no nozomi 求法の望
hōben 方便
honbun 本分
hongaku 本覺
honji hosshin 本地法身
honshi 本師
honshin 本心
hosshin 發心
Hsin-hsin ming 信心銘
Ichien 一圓
ichiji no butsu 一時の佛
jikishi ninshin 直指人心
jiko honrai 自己本來
jinzū 神通
jishō 自性
kanna 看話
kari ni 假に
kenshō jōbutsu 見性成佛
kitoku 奇特
kōmyō 光明
konpon 根本
Kōzen gokoku ron 興禪護國論
kudoku 功德
Kujō Michiie 九條道家
Kyōgō 經豪
Lan-ch'i Tao-lung (Rankei Dōryū) 蘭溪道隆
mappō 末法
mokushō 默照
mōnen 妄念
munen 無念
mushiki kai 無色界
mushin 無心
musō mujaku 無想無著
myōyū 妙用
nien pu ch'i 念不起
nyorai zen 如來禪
pu ch'i nien 不起念
rikon 利根
ritsu 律
rokujin mōsō 六塵妄想
sandoku 三毒
sangen jisshō 三賢十聖
Seng-ts'an 僧璨
sheng-ti ti-i i 聖諦第一義
shikan taza 只管打坐
shiryō 思量
Shōbō genzō shō 正法眼藏抄
Shōichi kokushi kana hōgo 聖一國師假名法語
Shōjō 證定
shōmyō 稱名
shukke 出家
sō 相
Ta-hui 大慧
tenma gedō 天魔外道
Tōfukuji 東福寺
tōgaku 等覺
tokudō 得道
tokushi 得指
ushotoku 有所得
wakuchi no shō 惑智の障
Wu-chun Shih-fan 無準師範
wu-tso 無作
wu-wei 無爲
Yōsai (Eisai) 榮西
Yüan-chüeh ching ta-shu ch'ao 圓覺經大疏鈔
Yung-chia 永嘉
zazen no shūmon 坐禪の宗門
Zazen ron 坐禪論
zenkon kudoku 善根功德
Zenshū kōmoku 禪宗綱目
Zōtan shū 雜談集

Index

Abe, Masao, 25-26, 27, 28
Abhayākaragupta, 170, 172
Abhidharmadīpa, 72, 114, 130n.39
Abhidharmahṛdayaśāstra (Upaśānta), 70, 71, 76-77, 81, 102n.85
Abhidharma (Indian) tradition: achievement of nirvāṇa in, 84, 88-89, 309; and faith, 206; goal of mārga in, 66-68; history of texts in, 63-67, 74-75; and the ideal person, 10; mārga of, 14, 63-105 passim, 154, 203-204, 309; meaning of, 325; polarity between knowledge and concentration in, 65-66, 83-86; and possession *(prāpti),* 71, 73, 74, 86-90; scholasticism of, 148; structure of path in, 74-77; wholesome roots in, 14, 107-134 passim
Abhidharmakośabhāṣya (Vasubandhu), 72, 78, 82, 97n.36, 114, 118, 135, 151, 170
Abhidharmamahāvibhāṣā (Great Exegesis of Abhidharma), 108, 111, 115-118
**Abhidharmāmṛtaśāstra* (Ghoṣaka), 70
Abhidharmanyāyānusāra, 114
Abhidharmasamuccaya (Compendium of Abhidharma) (Asaṅga), 119-120, 121, 223-224n.40, 292
**Abhidharmavibhāṣāśāstra,* 97n.36
Ābhidharmikas, 155, 158
Abhisamayālaṃkāra (Maitreya). See *Ornament for Clear Realization*
Abhisamayālaṃkārālokā (Illumination of the "Ornament for Realization") (Haribhadra), 150, 166, 169, 171
Āgamas, 39, 112, 113, 114, 118
Ajita Kesakambali, 128n.19
akliṣṭa-ajñāna (undefiled ignorance), 135-136, 138-142
Akṣayamatinirdeśa (Teaching of Akṣayamati), 159
A-kya-yongs-'dzin. *See* dbYangs-can-dga'-ba'i-blo-gros
Amida, 480, 487
Amitābha, 23, 122
Amoghavajra, 456, 459
Ānanda, 334n.7
Andō Toshio, 344
Aṅgulimālīya (He Who Has a Necklace of Fingers), 131n.45
Aṅgulimālīyasūtra. See *Yang-chüeh-mo-lo ching*
Anne (795-868), 442, 449, 451, 457-458, 463
Annen (841-889?), 440, 442-443, 448, 449, 451, 453-454, 459-460, 463
An Shih-kao (n.d.), 313
antinomianism, 17, 25, 363, 375, 377, 412n.2
anuśaya (contaminants), 12
A-p'i-t'an chiu-shih-ba chieh ching (The Abhidharma Sūtra on the Ninety-eight Fetters or Contaminants), 98-99n.50
A-p'i-t'an p'i-p'o-sha lun (Abhidharmavibhāṣā), 128n.13
arhats: Abhidharma pseudo-etymologies for, 68; desirelessness of, 54, 57; ignorance of, 10, 135-145 passim; retrogression of, 89-90; *samucchinnakuśalamūla* compared to, 116; Tibetan translations of, 235, 259-260n.26
Aristotle, 181
Āryadeva, 179, 313
Āryāsaṅga, 164
Āryavimuktisena, 177
Asaṅga, 119-121, 160, 166, 174, 179, 187n.52, 232-233, 234, 292

āsrava (fluxes), 12, 66, 67–68, 98n.47
Aṣṭasāhasrikāprajñāpāramitāsūtra (Perfection of Wisdom in 8,000 Lines), 124, 158, 310
Asvabhāva, 162
Atīśa (982–1054), 21, 231, 232, 233, 234–235, 236, 266–267n.83
Aṭṭhakathā, 137
Aṭṭhakavagga: anti-*diṭṭhi* (view) polemic of, 17, 44–49, 361–362; anti-*diṭṭhi* (view) polemic of, addressed in commentaries, 49–57; "buddha" as "awakened" (adj.) in, 42; condemnation of desire in, 43, 44, 47, 48, 49–50, 54–58; continuity of path and goal in, 39–44; dhammas (truths) in, 45, 46, 47, 52; history of, 39; ideal persons in, 39–44, 46–47, 49, 53–54, 55; knowledge in, 42, 45–46, 47, 52–53; knowledge versus purification polarity in, 13; nibbāna in, 39, 40–41; and path as cultivation of social virtues, 147; personal responsibility for following path in, 43; purity *(suddhi)* and calmness *(santi)* in, 40, 46, 53–55; seclusion or separation *(viveka)* in, 40, 41, 45; security *(khema)* in, 40, 41
Autonomy School (*rang rgyud pa,* Svātantrika), 236
Avalokiteśvara, 154
Avataṃsakasūtra. See *Hua-yen ching; Hua-yen Sūtra; Flower Garland Sūtra*
avyākata (indeterminables), 170
Awakening of Faith in Mahāyāna, The (Ta-sheng ch'i-hsin lun), 23

Bateson, Gregory, 281, 282, 284
Bendō wa (Talks on Pursuing the Way) (Dōgen), 502
Bergson, Henri, 15
Bernard of Clairvaux (1090–1153), 405
Bhadanta, 104n.105
Bhadracaryāpraṇidhāna (Aspiration to the Deeds of Samantabhadra), 174
bhāvanā (cultivation), versus *darśana* (insight), 13, 494, 498
Bhāvaviveka, 169, 305n.57
bKra-shis-'khyil (Auspicious Circle), 232
bla-ma (Tibetan Buddhist guru), 198
Blo-bzang-rta-dbyangs (1867–1937), 256n.5, 289
bLo-bzang-rta-mgrin. *See* Blo-bzang-rta-dbyangs
Blunt, E. A. H., 155
Bodaishin gishō (Explanations of the Doctrine of the Mind of Enlightenment) (Annen), 460, 468n.46, 470n.70
Bodhicaryāvatāra (Guide to the Deeds of Enlightenment) (Śāntideva), 170, 177
Bodhicittavivaraṇa (Essay on the Mind of Enlightenment) (Nāgārjuna), 164
Bodhidharma, 14, 341, 352, 354, 356, 358, 361, 388, 412n.2, 412–413n.5, 490
Bodhipathapradīpa (Atīśa). See *Lamp for the Path to Enlightenment*
Bodhisattvacaryāvatāra (Śāntideva). See *Engaging in the Bodhisattva Deeds*
bodhisattva ground: first, 274, 277–285; seventh and eighth, 286, 292–294; sixth, 274, 285–292
bodhisattva path (in fifty-three stages), 9
Boethius, 18
Bonaventure, 18
Brahmaviśeṣacinīparipṛcchā, 315
Brief Expression of the Presentation of the Grounds and Paths of the Three Vehicles . . . (bLo-bzang-rta-dbyangs), 256n.5
bsTan-dar-lha-ram-pa, 242
Buddha: and ignorance, 136, 137, 138, 139, 489; liberating insight of, 201; as omniscient, 10, 135, 137, 140–141, 142, 149, 270, 480; paranormal powers of, 488–489; as physician, 4, 31n.2; salvation through grace of, 198–199; synopsis of teaching by, 14; and teaching on charity *(dānakathā),* 123; vision quest of, 197; words of, preserved in Theravāda tradition, 38–39. *See also* Śākyamuni Buddha
Buddhadāsa, 61n.38
buddhadhamma (truth, teachings of the Buddha), 37. *See also names of individual traditions and schools*
Buddhaghosa, 39, 49, 50, 112, 291
buddhahood with this very body *(sokushin jōbutsu),* 439–473 passim
buddha-mind, 486–488, 498–499, 502
Buddhism: antinomianism in, 17, 25; history of, 309–338 passim, 371–437 passim; paradox of desire in, 48–49, 55–58; rationalism in, 18; role of meditation in, 5–6, 19; scholasticism in, 18–20, 147–158 passim, 225, 483; soteriology as central to, 3–4, 477–478; spiritual pragmatism of, 3, 4; universalist dogma of liberation in, 107–108; warnings against reification of practice in, 24–25
Byang-chub-sems-dpa' Blo-gros 'byung-gnas-kyis zhus-pa'imdo (Sūtra of the Dialogue with Bodhisattva Blo-gros 'byung-gnas), 213–215

calming (of the mind): and calm abiding *(śamatha, zhi gnas),* 273, 274, 277–281, 287, 321; and mārga (path), 273–277
Candrakīrti, 161, 166, 175, 274, 285–288, 291, 293

caste system, 155, 186n.24
Catuḥśataka (Four Hundred) (Āryadeva), 179–180
Ch'an (Chinese) tradition: as anti-mārga/no-path tradition, 29, 253–255, 374–375; antinomianism in, 17, 25, 363, 377, 412n.2; antiritualism of, 355; encounter dialogue in, 335n.39, 339–369 passim; history of, 310–312, 324, 325–329; and ideal person as path, 12; mārga of, 14; master-student genealogy in, 11, 352–354, 359, 378; and personal standpoint *(tsung),* 311, 325–329; popularity of, 359; and secular culture, 29–30, 371–437 passim; as sudden teaching, 12, 15, 16, 17, 21, 374; sudden versus gradual paths in, 14, 362
Chang Lei (1054–1114), 385
Ch'ang-lu Tsung-tse. *See* Tsung-tse
Ch'ang-lu Ying-fu (d.u.), 393
Chang Shang-ying (1043–1122), 429–430n.81
Chang Tsai, 381
Chang Tun-li (fl. 1068–1102), 426–427n.68
Chan-jan (711–782), 452
Ch'an-lin seng-pao chuan (Chronicles of the Ch'an Order) (Hui-hung), 409
Ch'an-yüan ch'ing-kuei (Pure Regulations for Ch'an Precincts) (Tsung-tse), 393, 493
Ch'an-yüan chu-ch'uan-chi tu-hsü (Preface to the Collected Writings on the Source of Ch'an) (Tsung-mi), 329, 330
Ch'ao Chiung (951–1034), 419n.41
Chao Meng-fu (1254–1322), 384, 394
Ch'ao Pu-chih (1053–1110), 385
Ch'en Ching-yüan, 385
Ch'eng I, 367–368n.36, 381, 383
Cheng Ching-lao, 385
Ch'eng-kuan (738–839), 311, 316, 324, 329, 330
Cheng-shou (1146–1208), 409
Cheng-tao ko (Yung-chia), 503n.10
cheng-wu (enlightenment of full realization), 19, 498
Che-tsung (emperor, r. 1085–1100), 385
Chi (632–682), 316, 323
Chiang-shan ssu (a.k.a. Chung-shan ssu), 390
Chiang-shan Tsan-yüan (a.k.a. Chüeh-hai Ch'an-shih), 425n.63
Chiao-kuan kang-tsung (Outline of the Teachings and Meditation) (Chih-hsü), 322
Chia-t'ai p'u-teng-lu (The Inclusive Lamp Record Published in the Chia-t'ai Era) (Cheng-shou), 409
Chieh-shen-mi ching su (Commentary on the Saṃdhinirmocanasūtra) (Wŏnch'ŭk), 316
chieh-wu (initial enlightenment), 19, 498
Chien-chen, 466n.14, 471n.81
Chien-chung Ching-kuo hsü-teng-lu (The Continued Lamp Record Published in the Cheng-chung Ching-kuo Era) (Wei-po), 392, 409
chien-hsiu (gradual practice), 498
Chih-cheng chuan (A Record of the Verifications of Insights) (Hui-hung), 409
Chih Ch'ien, 132n.68
Chih-hsü (1599–1655), 322
Chih-i (538–597), 17, 314, 316, 317–318, 319, 321, 324, 332, 342–351, 352, 353, 361, 443–445, 452, 453, 459
Chih Lou-chia-ch'an (Lokakṣema?), 313
Chih-p'an (1220–1275), 410
Chih-tsang (458–522), 317
Chih-yen (602–668), 309, 311, 323–324
Chih-yüeh lu (The Record of "Pointing at the Moon") (Ch'ü Ju-chi), 409
Ching-hsin chieh-kuan fa (The Procedures for Purifying the Mind through Following the Precepts and Meditation) (Tao-hsüan), 322
Ching-hsiu Wen-t'eng. *See* Wen-t'eng
Ching-hua ch'uan-hsin-ti ch'an-men shih-tzu ch'eng-hsi t'u (Lineage Chart of the Masters and Students of Ch'an in the Transmission of the Mind Ground in China), 336n.43
Ching-kuo, 388
Ching-te ch'uan-teng lu (Records of the Transmission of the Lamp [Compiled during the] Ching-te [Period]) (Tao-yüan), 328–329, 342–343, 409
Ching-tz'u Fa-yung, 428n.72
Ch'ing-yüan Hsing-ssu, 352
Ch'in Kuan (1049–1100), 385
Chinul (1158–1210), 15, 413–414n.10, 414n.11
Ch'i-sung (1007–1072), 390, 420–421n.49, 425n.62, 430–431n.89
Chi-tsang (549–623), 316, 322, 334n.10
Chiu Ko (Nine Songs), 417–418n.29
Ch'iu Ying (1495–1552), 400
Chōnen (938–1016), 429n.80
Chou Tun-i (1017–1073), 381, 416n.27
Christian (Western) tradition: condemnation of Buddhism by, 25–27; rationalism versus faith in, 18; and revelation of God to humans, 18; scholasticism in, 18; within typology of Tibetan Buddhism, 239
Ch'üan-chiao Ch'ang-lao, 426n.65
Ch'uan-fa cheng-tsung lun (Treatise on the Transmission of the Dharma and the True Essence), 329

Ch'üan fa-pao chi (Annals of the Transmission of the Treasure of the Dharma), 328
Chuang-yen. *See* Seng-min
Ch'uan-hsin fa-yao (Essentials of the Transmission of the Dharma That Can Only Be Passed from Mind to Mind), 328, 357
Ch'üan nien-Fo sung (Verses Promoting Devotional Meditation on the Person of the Buddha Amitābha) (Tsung-tse), 430n.83
Chüeh-an (b. 1286), 411, 421–424n.53
Chüeh-fan Hui-hung, 410, 411, 428n.73
Chu Fo-nien (Dharmapriya), 132n.68
Chu Hsi (1130–1200), 27, 28, 367–368n.36
Ch'ü Ju-chi, 409
Chu-na (1010–1071), 426n.66
Chung-kuan lun (alt. *Cheng-kuan lun;* Treatise on the Middle [or Correct] View), 322
Chung lun (Treatise on the Middle), 322
Chung-yüan (d. 1063), 421–424n.53
Chung-yung (Doctrine of the Mean), 425n.60
Ch'u san-tsang chi chi, 334n.10
Compendium of Abhidharma (Asaṅga). See *Abhidharmasamuccaya*
Compendium of Ascertainments (rnam par gtan la dbab pa bsdu ba, Nirṇayasaṃgraha/Viniścayasaṃgrahaṇī) (Asaṅga), 160, 232–233, 234
Compilations of Indicative Verse (ched du brjod pa'i tshom, Udānavarga), 84, 259n.24
Confucianism, 25, 26–27, 311, 315, 316, 321, 325, 329, 330, 331–332, 363, 379, 383, 409
Confucius, 315
Consequence School (*thal 'gyur pa,* Prāsaṅgika), 236, 256n.5, 259n.26

Dainichikyō gishaku sōketsushō (Ninkū), 467–468n.32
Dalai Lama, Fifth. *See* Ngak-w̄ang-l̄o-sang-gya-tso
Dalai Lama, First. *See* Dge'dun grub
Dam-tshig bkod-pa'i rgyud (Tantra of the Array of Commitments), 216–217
Dante Alighieri, 189n.74
darśana (insight), versus *bhāvanā* (cultivation), 13, 494, 498
Dārṣṭāntikas, 78, 86
Dayal, Har, 147
dbYangs-can-dga'-ba'i-blo-gros (eighteenth century), 256n.5
death and dying: explanation in Highest Yoga Tantra, 263n.53; and mind of clear light, 244
defilements. See *kleśa*
Denjutsu isshinkai mon (Kōjō), 465–466n.12
Den-ma Lo-chö Rin-bo-chay, 237–238, 247, 248, 260–261n.27
Derrida, Jacques, 191n.108, 275, 298
Deussen, Paul, 203
Dewey, John, 25
Dge-ba-lha (Kalyāṇadeva), 170
Dge'dun grub (1391–1475; First Dalai Lama), 305n.57
Dge-lugs-pa (Tibetan) tradition: and conditioned versus unconditioned, 21, 269–308 passim; history of, 227–228; mārga (path) in, 150–152; role of defilements/afflictions in, 12, 150–158; scholasticism in, 18, 150; Shangs-pa teachings in, 193
Dharmacakrapravartanasūtra, 67
Dharmakīrti, 155, 172, 178, 256n.7
Dharmamitra, 169
Dharmaskandha, 96n.26
Dharmaśrī, 71, 102n.85
Diamond (Chin-kang) Sūtra (Vajracchedikā), 387, 496
Distinct Teaching of the One-vehicle, 309
Dkon-mchog-'jigs-med-dbang-po (1728–1791), 152, 153, 247, 248, 258–259n.21, 260–261n.27, 261n.28, 261–262n.33
doctrine, as focus of traditional religious studies, 4–5
Dōgen Kigen (1200–1253), 26, 34n.29, 326, 393, 413n.8, 414n.11, 432–433n.99, 494, 495, 502
Dohās (Saraha), 202
Douglas, Mary, 156, 157, 168
dPal-ldan-chos-rje. *See* Ngag-dbang-dpal-ldan
Dumont, Louis, 155, 156, 157

East Mountain Ch'an, 393
egotism, as altruism, 59n.11
eight great vehicles, 194
Eisai (Yōsai; 1141–1215), 312, 481, 482
Ekayāna, doctrine of, 141, 142
Ekottarāgama (Sequentially Numbered Collection), 113, 116, 119, 123
Eliade, Mircea, 198, 220n.17
emptiness, doctrine of, 176, 375, 484, 486
Enchin, 462
Enchō (771–837), 442, 450–451, 456
encounter dialogue: antecedents of, 341; definition of, 340–341; as part of Ch'an soteriology, 335n.39, 339–369 passim
Engaging in the Bodhisattva Deeds (Bodhisattvacaryāvatāra, Spyod 'jug) (Śāntideva), 277
Enni (Ben'en; 1202–1280), 263n.56, 481–482, 494, 495

Ennin (794–864), 442, 443, 447, 453, 454–455, 458–459, 460, 462, 463
Entrance to the Middle Way (Madhyamakāvatāra, Dby ma la 'jug pa) (Candrakīrti), 161, 175, 274, 281, 285–288
Erh-ju ssu-hsing lun (Treatise on the Two Entrances and the Four Practices), 375, 413n.6
Esoteric Buddhism. *See* Shingon Esoteric school
expedient means. *See* upāya

Fa-chieh kuan-men (Contemplation of the Dharmadhātu) (Tu Shun), 323, 324
Fa-hsiang (Hossō; Tz'u-en) school, 318, 331, 439, 441, 448, 454
Fa-hsiang tradition. *See* Yogācāra tradition
Fa-hsien (718–778), 324
Fa-hsiu (1027–1090), 355, 385–409 passim
Fa-hua hsüan-i (Profound Meaning of the Lotus Sūtra) (Chih-i), 445, 452, 453–454, 455
Fa-hua hsüan-lun (Profound Discussion of the Lotus Sūtra) (Chi-tsang), 316
Fa-hua i su (Commentary on the Meaning of the Lotus Sūtra), 314
Fa-ju (638–689), 367n.32
Fa-lang (507–581), 317
Fa-ts'ai, 326, 327
Fa-tsang (643–712), 35n.36, 309, 311, 316, 319–321, 323, 324, 334n.17, 445, 466n.14
Faure, Bernard, 15, 361
Fa-yün (467–529), 317, 459
Fa-yün Shan-pen (1037–1109), 428n.76
Fa-yün ssu, 390, 392
five paths, 8
five ranks (Ch. *wu-wei*, J. *goi*), 9
Five Stages (rim lnga, Pañcakrama) (Nāgārjuna), 263n.54
Flower Garland Sūtra. See *Hua-yen ching; Hua-yen Sūtra*
Foe Destroyer *(arhats),* 235, 259–260n.26
Fo-kuo Wei-po. *See* Wei-po
Fo-shuo Hai-i p'u-sa so-wen ching-in fa-men ching (The Buddha Speaks the Dharma Instruction Concerning Hai-i Bodhisattva's Question regarding the Seal of Purity), 124
Fo-tsu li-tai t'ung-tsai (A Comprehensive Registry of the Successive Ages of the Buddhas and the Patriarchs) (Nien-ch'ang), 410
Fo-tsu t'ung-chi (A Chronicle of the Buddhas and the Patriarchs) (Chih-p'an), 410, 443
Foucault, Michel, 159, 270, 298, 301n.17
four approaches *(catvāraḥ pratipannāḥ),* 8
four concentrations *(dhyāna, bsam gtan),* 273, 280
four cultivations of concentration *(samādhibhāvanā),* 83
four formless absorptions *(samāpatti, snyoms 'jug),* 273
four fruits *(catvāri phalāni),* 8, 76, 94n.18, 95n.24
Four Heavenly Kings (Caturmahārājikadeva), 114
four noble truths, 49, 67, 75–76, 83, 91, 135, 136, 140, 141, 151, 185n.21, 201, 213, 216, 236, 309, 365n.18
Four Scholars, 419n.43
four virtuous roots, 76
Fracture of Meaning, The (Pollack), 361
Freud, Sigmund, 182, 264n.57

Gaṇḍavyūhasūtra, 197
General Meaning of the Middle Way (Dbu ma'i spyi don) (Pan-chen Bsod-nams-grags-pa), 286
Ghoṣaka, 70, 80
Ghoṣavarman, 84–85, 103n.100
Gilkey, Langdon, 25–26, 27, 28
Gishin (781–833), 442, 449–450, 451, 456
Giving, virtue or perfection of *(dāna),* 14, 108, 123–126
gnosiology, 3, 22, 202, 433n.100
Gómez, Luis, 47
Good Explanation of the General Meaning, Clarifying the Difficult Points of [Tsong-kha-pa's] "Illumination of the Thought" (Rje-btsun Chos-kyi-rgyal-mtshan), 286
Gozan (Five Mountains) Zen, 417n.28
gradual cultivation, and concentration, 274. *See also* sudden and gradual teachings
Great Exposition of the Middle Way (Dbu ma chen mo) ('Jam-dbyangs-bzhad-pa), 286
Great Exposition of the Stages of the Path (Lam rim chen mo) (Tsong-kha-pa), 231, 234, 235, 261n.30, 262n.36, 285
Guide to the Bodhisattva's Way of Life (Śāntideva), 282
Gung-ru Chos-'byung, 232
Gyōgi (670–749), 463

Han Kan, 417–418n.29
Han-shan Te-ch'ing (1546–1623), 433n.100
Han Yü (768–824), 359, 402
Haribhadra, 150, 164, 166, 169, 171–172
Heart Sūtra, 154
Himitsu sokushin jōbutsugi (attrib. to Annen), 468n.46, 469n.57
Hīnayāna tradition: defilements as obstacles to enlightenment in, 447, 484, 492;

as fourth abode of the mind in Kūkai's hierarchy, 20; history of, 310, 314, 315, 318, 319–320, 331, 345; knowledge of paths of, 150; nirvāṇa in, 162
Hinduism, 25, 155, 157, 240
Hōjibō Shōshin (1136–1220 or 1131–1215), 443, 451–452, 453, 460–461
Hokke gengi Shiki (Personal Record on [Chih-i's] "Profound Meaning of the Lotus Sūtra") (Hōjibō Shōshin), 452
Hokke shūku (Elegant Words of the Lotus Sūtra) (Saichō), 454, 456
Homo Hierarchicus (Dumont), 155
Honchō shinsen den (Biographies of Japanese Immortals) (Ōe Masafusa), 463
Hossō (Ch. Fa-hsiang). *See* Fa-hsiang (Hossō; Tz'u-en) school
Ho-tse Shen-hui (684–758), 326
Ho-tse tradition, 326, 330
Hsiang-fa chüeh-i ching (Book of Resolving Doubts during the Semblance Dharma Age), 125
Hsiang-lin Ch'eng-yüan (908–987), 425n.62
Hsiao chih-kuan (Short Treatise on Calm Abiding and Insight Meditation) (Chih-i), 324, 332
Hsiao-ching (Classic of Filial Piety), 417–418n.29
Hsiao-shan chi (Huang T'ing-chien), 428n.74
Hsiao-shun (Yün-chu Hsiao-shun, a.k.a. Shun Lao-fu; d. between 1064 and 1067), 389–390, 401–402, 404–405, 431n.93
Hsiao-ying, 421–424n.53
Hsieh Liang-tso, 381
Hsi-hsien Temple, 389
Hsing-huang. *See* Fa-lang
Hsing-hua Ts'un-chiang (830–838), 421–424n.53
Hsin-hsin ming (Seng-ts'an), 504n.11
Hsin-ti kuan ching (Sūtra on the Discernment of the Mind-Ground), 457
Hsiu-hsin yao lun (Treatise on the Essentials of Cultivating the Mind) (Hung-jen), 362
Hsiu Yüan-t'ung, 404
Hsi-yüan ya-chi t'u (Elegant Gathering in the Western Garden) (attrib. to Chao Meng-fu), 384–386, 393–401, 405, 407, 409
Hsüan-tsang (d. 664), 97n.36, 100n.69, 108, 129n.30, 169, 311, 318–319, 321, 323
Hsüeh-feng I-ts'un (822–908), 352, 424n.57
Hsüeh-tou Ch'ung-hsien (980–1052), 386, 424–425n.58, 425n.62, 433n.101
Hsüeh-tou po-tse sung-ku (Hsüeh-tou Ch'ung-hsien), 386
Hsü kao-seng chuan (Continued Lives of Eminent Monks) (Tao-hsüan), 341
Huan (king, 146–167), 313
Huang T'ing-chien (1045–1105), 385, 391, 401, 403, 406, 427n.70, 428n.74
Hua-yen ching, 330, 389, 417–418n.29, 457. See also *Hua-yen Sūtra*
Hua-yen-ching k'an-ting chi (Record of Corrections of [Interpretations of] the Avataṃsaka) (Hui-yüan), 316
Hua-yen-ching su (Commentary on the Avataṃsaka) (Ch'eng-kuan), 316
Hua-yen-ching t'an-hsüan chi (Record of Investigations into the Mysteries of the Avataṃsakasūtra) (Fa-tsang), 316
Hua-yen i-sheng shih-hsüan men (Ten Profundities of the One-Vehicle of the Avataṃsaka) (Chih-yen), 323
Hua-yen sou-hsüan chi (Record of Seeking the Profound in Hua-yen) (Chih-yen), 323
Hua-yen (Flower Garland) Sūtra, 215, 315, 319, 320, 324, 387, 392. See also *Hua-yen ching*
Hua-yen tradition: and conditioned versus unconditioned, 23; as contrast to Ch'an tradition, 12; as gradual teaching, 15; history of, 310–312, 323–325, 407; and non-emptiness, 375; paradox between *chieh-wu* and *cheng-wu* in, 19; relationship to Ch'an, 392; scholasticism in, 18; stages in, 17–18, 20, 33–34n.28; teachings and personal standpoints conjoined *(tsung-chiao)* in, 311, 329–333; three-lifetime theory of, 128n.17. *See also* Kegon tradition
Hua-yen wu-chiao chang (Essays on the Five Teachings According to the Hua-yen Tradition) (Fa-tsang), 316, 319–321, 334n.17
Hua-yen wu-chiao chih-kuan (Tu Shun), 335n.28
Hua-yen yu-hsin fa-chieh chi (Fa-tsang), 335n.28
Hu-ch'iu Shao-lung (1077–1136), 430–431n.89
Hui-chi Shen-hsiu (n.d.), 324, 327, 328
Hui-hung (1071–1128), 387, 409, 415n.17, 420n.48, 420–421n.49
Hui-k'o, 341, 354, 356
Hui-kuan (n.d.), 314, 315, 317, 334n.10
Hui-lin Tsung-pen (1020–1099). *See* Tsung-pen
Hui-neng (638–713), 263n.56, 326, 327, 352, 354, 358, 388
Hui-ssu (515–577), 342, 343, 346, 347, 364n.9, 443–445, 466n.14

Hui-tsung (emperor, r. 1100–1125), 392
Hui-wen (fl. first half of sixth century), 443
Hui-yüan (n.d.), 311, 316, 324
Hui-yüan (338–416), 313–314, 417n.29
Hui-yüan (523–592), 316, 322, 334n.10
Hu-kuo Monastery, 388
Hung-chih Cheng-chüeh (1091–1157), 413n.8
Hung-chou school, 341, 343, 356–358
Hung-jen (600–674), 354, 362, 367n.32
Hurvitz, Leon, 347
Hwaŏm (Korean) tradition, 15

icchantika doctrine, 109, 112, 118–123
Ichien, 495
ignorance, of arhats, 10, 135–145 passim
Ihon sokushin jōbutsugi (attrib. to Kūkai), 468n.46
I-hsia lun (Treatise on the Barbarians and Chinese), 315
I-hsing (673–727), 455, 456, 459
I-hsüan (Lin-chi I-hsüan), 352
I-huai (T'ien-i I-huai; 993–1064), 386, 389–390, 401–402, 404–405, 425n.62
Ikkyū (1394–1481), 431n.90
Illumination of the Texts of Tantra, Presentation of the Grounds and Paths of the Four Great Secret Tantra Sets (Ngag-dbang-dpal-ldan), 256n.5
Illumination of the Thought, An Extensive Explanation of [Candrakīrti's] "Entrance to the Middle Way" (Dbu ma la 'jug pa'i rgya cher bshad pa dgongs pa rab gsal) (Tsong-kha-pa), 274, 285
illusory city, simile of, 161

Jaina tradition, 128n.17, 141, 142–143, 156
'Jam-dbyangs-bzhad-pa Ngag-dbang-brtson-grus (1648–1721), 150, 169–170, 179–180, 184n.9, 231–233, 234–235, 236–237, 258n.21, 274, 279, 286, 288, 289, 292, 294
'Jam-dbyangs Mkhyen-brtse'i dbang-po (1820–1892), 194
Jen-wang ching (Sūtra of the Benevolent King), 456
Jippan (d. 1144), 443
Jīvala, 84–85, 103n.100
**Jñānābhyudaya (ye-shes mngon-par 'byung-ba),* 203
Jñānaprasthāna, 68, 69, 80, 81, 96n.26
Jōdo Shinshū, 179
Jo-nang-pa (Tibetan) sect, 194
Jung, Carl, 245, 249, 264n.57

Ka-dam-pa Geshe Dol-pa-shes-rab-rgya-mtsho (1059–1131), 277
K'ai-shan. *See* Chih-tsang
Kamakura Zen Buddhism, 15, 16, 333, 475–505 passim
Kamalaśīla, 167
Kana hōgo (Enni). See *Zazen ron*
kanna (story viewing) Zen, 494, 495
Kant, Immanuel, 270, 279, 283, 284, 298, 303n.31, 304n.44
Kan-t'an Tzu-kuo, 425n.59
Kāśyapa, 352
Kathāvatthu, 137
Kay-drup, 243
Kegon (Japanese) tradition, 20, 501
Kensur Ngawang Lekden, 233, 235, 258n.20
Kermode, Frank, 192n.120
Khyung-po Rnal-'byor (d. ca. 1135), 193, 194–197, 198, 199–200, 201, 202
kleśa (defilements): abandonment of, 63–105 passim; character of, in Abhidharma texts, 68–74; in Dge-lugs-pa (Tibetan) tradition, 12, 150–158; distinguished from contaminants *(anuśaya),* 70–74; and elimination of wholesome roots, 117; and ignorance, 135, 136, 138, 139; and meditation, 484; as obstacles to mārga, 12–13, 182, 439–440, 446–448
kliṣṭasammoha (defiled delusion), 135, 136
Klong-chen Rab-'byams-pa, 194
knowledge: versus ignorance, 13; versus purification, 13–17
Kōhō Jitsuge, 421–424n.53
Kōjō (779–858), 442, 444–447, 456
Kong-sprul Blo-gros mtha'-yas (1813–1899/1900), 194
Kośa, commentary to, 135
Kosambisutta, 103n.100
Kōzen gokoku ron (Promotion of Zen for Protection of the Country) (Eisai), 482
Kṣemadatta, 80, 102n.85
Kṣitigarbha, 122
kuan ("view"), 321
Kuang-hsiu (770–844?), 467n.27
Kuang-tse. *See* Fa-yün
Kuan P'u-hsien p'u-sa hsing-fa ching (Sūtra on the Meditation on the Bodhisattva Universal Virtue), 449, 456
Kuan-ting, 342, 348, 349–350
Kuan Wu-liang-shou fo ching hsü (Preface to the Amitāyurdhyāna Sūtra) (Tsung-tse), 430n.83
Kuan Wu-liang-shou fo ching su (Commentary on the Sūtra on the Contemplation of the Buddha of Immeasurable Life) (Shan-tao), 323
Kuan-yin, 391
Kudzu Ch'an *(k'o-teng Ch'an),* 404–405

Kuei-ch'ü-lai tzu (Homecoming) (T'ao Yüan-ming), 385, 417–418n.29
Kuei-tsung Chih-ch'ang, 425n.61
Ku Huan (420–483), 315
Kūkai (774–835), 20, 439, 441, 454, 456, 458, 459, 463, 471n.83
Ku K'ai-chih, 417–418n.29
Kumarādza (1266–1343), 218n.3
Kumārajīva (344–413 or 350–409), 132n.68, 313–314, 315, 318, 366n.19
kung-an, 376, 378, 386
K'ung-mu chang (Essays on Articles within the Hua-yen ching) (Chih-yen), 324
ku-wen (ancient texts), 359
Kyai rdo mkhan po. *See* Ngag-dbang-mkhas-grub
Kyōgō, 495
Kyoto school, 27
Kyōunshū (Crazy Cloud Anthology) (Ikkyū), 431n.90
Kyunyŏ (923–973), 335n.30

Lacan, Jacques, 270, 279, 298, 301n.17, 303n.31
Laing, Ellen Johnston, 394, 420n.47
Lamotte, Étienne, 138, 148
Lamp for the Path to Enlightenment (byang chub lam gyi sgron ma, Bodhipathapradīpa) (Atīśa), 21, 231, 232, 234, 236
lam rim (stages of the path), 227, 228, 285
Lancaster, Lewis, 124
Laṅkāvatārasūtra (Descent to Śrī Laṅka), 121, 122, 159, 164, 189n.74, 413n.6, 432–433n.99
Lao Hua-yen (Yüan Hua-yen; Huai-tung), 387–388, 404, 421–424n.53, 432n.96
La Vallée Poussin, Louis de, 108
"leaping over" *(ch'ao-yüeh),* 15, 453–454, 468n.45
Legs bshad gser phreng (A Garland of Gold Eloquence) (Tsong-kha-pa), 150, 159, 171
Leng-chai yeh-hua (Nocturnal Ruminations in the Chill Studio) (Chüeh-fan Hui-hung), 410
Leng-yen ching ho lun (The Śūraṅgama Sūtra Together with an Exposition Thereof) (Chüeh-fan Hui-hung), 410
Li Chih-i, 385
Li Ch'un-fu (*hao:* P'ing-shan; 1175–1234), 432n.98
Lien-hua sheng-hui lu-wen (Charter for the Exalted Sodality of the Lotus Blossom) (Tsung-tse), 430n.83
Lien-teng hui-yao (The Collected Essentials of the Consolidated Lamp [Records]) (Wu-ming), 410
Li Kung-lin (1049–1106), 384, 385, 391, 392, 394, 401
Li Lang-chung, 416n.25
Li Lien, 426–427n.68
Lin-chien lu (Anecdotes from the "Groves" of Ch'an) (Chüeh-fan Hui-hung), 410
Lin-chi I-hsüan (d. 866), 404–405, 421–424n.53
Lin-chi (Chinese) tradition, 16, 21, 414n.11, 481
Lin-chi lu (Record of Lin-chi), 404
Lin-chi tsung-chih (Lin-chi's Principal Message) (Chüeh-fan Hui-hung), 410
Ling (emperor, 167–189), 313
Li Po (772–831), 425n.61
Li Ta-chao, 417–418n.29
Li T'ung-hsüan (635?–730?), 33n.28, 325
Liu Ching (1047–1100), 385
Liu Ch'iu (438–495), 334n.10
Liu miao-fa men, 365n.15
Liu miao-men (Six Wondrous Teachings) (Chih-i), 346
Liu Sung-nien (ca. 1150–after 1225), 398
Lo Chih-hsien, 416n.23
Lokakṣema, 132n.68. *See also* Chih Lou-chia-ch'an
Lo-pang i-k'ao (Tsung-hsiao), 430n.85
Lo-pang wen-lei (Assorted Texts on the Happy Land) (Tsung-hsiao), 430nn.82–83
Lotus Sūtra (Saddharmapuṇḍarīkasūtra), 141, 159, 161–162, 164, 313, 314, 315, 319, 387, 441, 445, 449, 452–456, 458–460, 462, 469n.53, 503n.2
Lu (Master Lu), 387
Lung-shu tseng-kuang ching-t'u wen (Wang Jih-hsiu), 430n.85
Lu-shan lien-tsung pao-chien (P'u-tu), 430n.82
Lu Tien (1042–1102), 425–426n.64
Lü (Vinaya) school, 311, 321, 322, 392
Lynn, Richard, 402

Madhyamakakārikā (Verses on the Middle Way), 313, 322
Madhyamakaśāstra, 175, 176
Madhyamakāvatāra (Candrakīrti). See *Entrance to the Middle Way*
Mādhyamika tradition, 56, 154, 166–167, 168, 174, 175, 269, 273, 313. *See also* Sanron tradition
Mahākāśyapa, 334n.7, 354, 424n.54
Mahāniddesa (commentary on *Aṭṭhakavagga*), 39, 49–54, 55, 57
Mahāprajñāpāramitāśāstra (Commentary on the Greater Perfection of Wisdom Sūtra). See *Ta-chih-tu lun*
Mahāprajñāpāramitāsūtra, 132n.66
Mahāsāṅghika school, 72, 116, 333n.1

Mahāsāṅghikavinaya, 126
Mahāvastu, 203
Mahāvibhāṣā, 69, 70, 71, 78–86, 88, 89, 96n.26, 122, 139, 144n.14, 362
Mahāvyutpatti, 155
Mahāyānasūtrālaṃkāra (Ornament of the Mahāyāna Sūtras) (Asaṅga), 120, 121, 162–163, 223–224n.40
Mahāyāna tradition: bipartite mārga in, 13; challenge to Theravāda tradition from, 55–56, 310; emptiness and nonemptiness in, 149, 153–154, 375, 484, 486; history of, 55–56, 310, 314, 315, 318, 331, 345, 502; and *icchantika* doctrine, 109, 112, 118–123; in Japan, 478, 482; and mārga (path), 148–149, 159, 203–204, 278, 343; nonabiding nirvāṇa of, 22; opinion of arhats, 116; and salvation through guru's grace, 198; and universal compassion, 21
Maitreya, 149, 197, 228, 259n.24, 334n.7, 471n.83
Maitreyanātha. *See* Maitreya
Makkhali Gosāla, 128n.19
Mañjuśrī, 166, 226, 334n.7, 460
mappō (final dharma), 503n.3
mārga (path): and anti-mārga traditions, 23–27; as central theme of Buddhism, 2, 6, 23–24, 27, 30–31, 147; and conditioned versus unconditioned, 21–23, 269–308 passim; definitions of, 2–3, 247–249; as descriptive versus prescriptive, 11, 19–20; direct types of, 15–17; goals of, 10–11, 170–182; and the ideal person, 10–12, 58–59n.6; as interminable, 15; of knowledge versus purification, 13–17; obstacles to, 12–13; organization of, 17–20; and ranking of rival doctrines, 20–21; schemes for, 6–9; and secular life (culture), 29–30, 371–437 passim; as sequence of stages, 11; sudden versus gradual, 15–17; as terminable versus interminable, 147–192 passim; and transcendence, 27–29. See also *kleśa;* no-path
Mar-pa Bka'-brgyud (Tibetan) school, 200
Mar-pa Chos-kyi-blo-gros, 200
matha' dpyod (decisive analyses), 227, 228–229
Ma-tsu Tao-i (709–788), 333, 340, 341, 343, 352, 354, 356–357, 358
Maudgalyāyana, 137
māyā, 203
Māyādhvakrama (The Sequence of the Path of Apparition) (Niguma), 194, 196, 202, 204–207; autocommentary on, 213–217; selections from, 207–213
meaning *(i* or *i-li),* 323–324
Meditations of a Tantric Abbot (Kensur Lekden), 233
Mei Yao-ch'en (1002–1060), 402
merit *(puṇya),* 14, 108, 116, 123–126
Mi-an Tao-ch'ien (d.u.), 426n.67
Miao-fa lien-hua ching ho lun (The Lotus Sūtra Together with an Exposition Thereof) (Chüeh-fan Hui-hung), 410
Miao-fa lien-hua ching hsüan-i (Profound Meaning of the Lotus Sūtra) (Chih-i), 316
Miao-li yüan-ch'eng kuan (Contemplation of the Wondrous Principle and the Perfectly Accomplished) (Hui-chi Shen-hsiu), 324, 335n.30
Michiie, Kujō, 481, 482
Mi Fu (1051–1107), 385, 394, 401
Mīmāṃsikas, 178
Min-yu benwakushō (Essays Compassionately Explaining Delusions) (Anne), 449, 451, 457, 458
Mipham, 272, 282, 296, 298
Mkhas-grub-rje Dge-legs-dpal-bzang-po (1385–1438), 184n.9, 192n.117
Mo-ho chih-kuan ([Treatise on] Great Calm Abiding and Insight Meditation) (Chih-i), 321–322, 342, 343, 345–346, 348, 365n.15, 453, 455, 461
mokushō (silent illumination) Zen, 494, 495
morality, and three trainings, 6–7
Mu'an Shan-ch'ing, 412n.2, 421n.50
Munimatālaṃkāra (Ornament of the Mind of the Sage) (Abhayākaragupta), 170, 172
Murti, T. R. V., 174
Musīla, 92n.1, 103n.100
Musō Soseki (1275–1351), 417n.28, 431n.90
mysterium tremendum, 240–244

Nāgārjuna, 22, 28, 56, 157, 164, 175, 176, 263n.54, 292, 313, 458, 459
Nan-yüeh Huai-jang, 333, 352, 357
Nārada, 92n.1, 103n.100
Nara (Japanese) schools *(Nanto rokushū),* 326, 439
Nāropā, 193, 195, 200
Neo-Confucianism, 25, 359–360, 363, 367–368n.36, 381, 414–415n.15
Ngag-dbang-dpal-ldan (b. 1797), 256n.5
Ngag-dbang-mkhas-grub (1779–1838), 245
Ngak-w̄ang-l̄o-sang-gya-tso (1617–1682; Fifth Dalai Lama), 251
Nien-ch'ang (1282–1323), 410
Niguma: as author of treatise on the path, 202–207, 218n.8; six doctrines of, 200–201; as teacher of Khyung-po Rnal-

'byor, 193, 194, 195–196, 198, 199, 200, 201, 202
Nikāyas, 114, 118, 203, 204
Ninkū (1309–1388), 451
Niraupamyastava (Hymn to the Peerless [Buddha]) (Nāgārjuna), 164
Nirṇayasaṃgraha/Viniścayasaṃgrahaṇī (Asaṅga). See *Compendium of Ascertainments*
nirvāṇa: as nonabiding, 22; relationship to mārga, 22; relationship to omniscience, 141–143
Nirvāṇa Sūtra (Nieh-p'an ching), 107, 108, 121, 123, 259n.24, 314, 315, 328
noble eightfold path *(ārya-aṣṭāṅga-mārga),* 7
no-mind *(mushin),* and sudden teaching, 17, 475–505 passim. *See also* sudden awakening
non-practice, condemnation of, 25
no-path, 253–255
no-self *(anātman),* 20, 310, 315
no-thought *(munen),* 492. *See also* no-mind
numerology, 20
Nyāyānusāra (Saṅgabhadra), 72, 78, 100n.69

Ōe Masafusa, 463
one vehicle versus three vehicles, 158–170
Opening the Eyes of the Fortunate (Kay-drup), 243
Ornament for Clear Realization (mngon rtogs rgyan, Abhisamayālaṃkāra) (Maitreya), 149, 150, 152, 158–159, 169, 175, 228, 229, 231
Ornament for the Great Vehicle Sūtras (Maitreya), 259n.24
Otto, Rudolph, 230, 240–244, 245
Ou-yang Hsiu, 367–368n.36, 402

Padmaprabha, 159
Pai-chang Huai-hai (720–841), 340
Pañcaviṃśatisāhasrikāprajñāpāramitāsūtra (The Perfection of Wisdom in 25,000 Stanzas), 149, 158, 175
Pan-chen Bsod-nams-grags-pa (1478–1554), 150, 161, 165, 184n.9, 274, 277, 278, 286, 288–290, 292, 293
P'ang Yün (d. 808), 31
Pao-lin chuan (Transmission from Pao-lin [ssu]), 343, 352, 356, 357
Pao-t'ang school (of Ch'an tradition), 25
Pao-tz'u, 388, 389
Pātañjala Yogasūtra, 141–142
Patañjali, 142
Path of Apparition (Niguma). See *Māyādhvakrama*
Path of Purification (Buddhaghosa), 291
P'ei Hsiu shih-i wen (P'ei Hsiu's Questions) (Tsung-mi), 330
perception, direct, 275–276, 279–281, 283, 285; yogic, 154, 281
Perfection of Wisdom sūtras, 149, 150, 160, 272, 309, 310, 313, 315
personal standpoint (Ch. *tsung,* J. *jibun no tachiba*), 311, 325–329
Pien-ching i-chi chih (Record of the Antiquities of Kaifeng) (Li Lien), 426–427n.68
Pieper, Joseph, 18
p'ing-tan (even and bland) style, 402–403
Pi-yen lu (The Record of the Blue Grotto) (Yüan-wu K'o-ch'in), 386, 433n.101
Platform Sūtra, 327, 352
Po-ch'ao Chih-yüan, 389, 425n.59
Poetics (Aristotle), 181
Pollack, David, 361
prajñā (insight), 7, 356
Prajñāpāramitāsūtra, 315
Prajñaptibhāṣya (Shih-she lun), 115, 129n.30
Prakaraṇapāda, 77, 78, 96n.26
Pramāṇavārttika (Dharmakīrti), 155, 172, 256n.7
Prāsaṅgika, 167, 273–275, 289–290. *See also* Mādhyamika tradition
Prasenajit (king), 113
Prasphuṭapadā (Clear Words) (Dharmamitra), 169
Precious Garland (Ratnāvalī, Rin ch'ei phreng ba) (Nāgārjuna), 175, 292
"Preface to the Sagely Teaching of the Tripiṭaka," 318
Presentation of Death, Intermediate State, and Rebirth (skye shi bar do'i rnam bzhag) (Ngag-dbang-mkhas-grub), 245
Presentation of the Grounds and Paths of Mantra . . . (dbYangs-can-dga'-ba'i-blo-gros), 256n.5
Presentation of the Grounds and the Paths (dKon-mchog-'jigs-med-dbang-po), 247, 260–261n.27, 261n.28, 261–262n.33
Pseudo-Dionysis, 18
Pubbaseliyas, and ignorance of the arhats, 137–138
P'u-chi (1179–1253), 411, 420n.48
Puggalapaññatti (Discourse on Human Types), 112, 119
Pūraṇa Kassapa, 128n.19
Pure Land Buddhism: achievement of nirvāṇa-like state in, 23; combined with Ch'an, 393; history of, 310–312, 321, 323; "other power" doctrine of, 23, 24; and paradox of desire, 57; and salvation through guru's grace, 199; and self-reliance, 3; and spirituality of faith, 22, 480, 499–500
purification: versus impurity, 13, 156–157; versus knowledge, 13–17
Purity and Danger (Douglas), 156

P'u-t'i-hsin lun (Treatise on the Enlightened Mind) (Nāgārjuna), 458, 459, 460–461, 470n.70
P'u-tu (1199–1290), 430n.82

quietism, 375, 377

Rab-'byams-pa (1308–1363), 193
raft, simile of, 5
rationalism, 18–19
Ratnagotravibhāga (Delineation of the Jewel Lineage), 119, 121, 123, 165, 179
Ratnāvalī (Nāgārjuna). See *Precious Garland*
Rdzogs-chen (Tibetan) tradition: and conditioned versus unconditioned, 21, 23, 269, 271–272, 296; and immediate cognition, 282; Shangs-pa teachings in, 193
Record of Lin-chi, 327
Red-mda'-ba (1349–1412), 281–282, 284, 286
Responding to Queries on the "Entrance" (Dbu ma la 'jug pa'i brgal lan) (Pan-chen Bsod-nams-grags-pa), 286
Rgyal-tshab-dar-ma-rin-chen (1364–1432), 166, 167, 176–179, 184n.9
Ricoeur, Paul, 157–158
Rinshō (fl. late ninth century), 442, 447, 448, 453, 454, 463
Rinzai (Japanese) lineages, 430–431n.89, 494
Rje-btsun Chos-kyi-rgyal-mtshan (1469–1546), 150, 160, 184n.9, 256n.5, 274, 286, 288–289
rnam-thars ("liberation"), 195
Rnying-ma (Old Translation, Tibetan) tradition (order), 21, 246, 251, 266n.81, 269–270, 296. *See also* Rdzogs-chen tradition
Ruegg, David Seyfort, 248

Ṣaḍbhuja-Jñānanātha, 193
Saddharmapuṇḍarīkasūtra. See *Lotus Sūtra*
Ṣaḍdharmopadeśa, 200
Saichō (767–822), 439, 440–442, 443–444, 448, 449, 451, 454–456, 458–459, 463, 469n.56
Śākyamuni Buddha: biography of, 353; death of, 225; final injunction of, 3, 325; and self-reliance for salvation, 3, 310, 325; Tibetan forms of teachings of, 228
sa lam (grounds and paths), 150–152, 227, 229
salt, simile of, 107
samādhi (concentration), 7
Samādhirāja (King of Samādhi), 172
samanvāgama, translations for, 129–130n.37
samāpatti (meditative techniques), 140
Saṃcayagāthā (Condensed Verses of the Perfection of Wisdom), 174
Saṃdhinirmocanasūtra (Sūtra Explaining the Profundities [of Doctrine]), 160, 169, 319
saṃyojana (fetters), 12
Saṃyuktābhidharmahṛdayaśāstra, 71, 78, 81, 97n.36, 102n.85
San-chieh-chiao (Three Stages Teaching) sect, 125, 311, 321
Saṅghabhadra, 72, 78, 81, 90, 98nn.46–47, 100nn.69–70, 102n.85, 102–103n.86
Saṅgītiparyāya, 76, 83–84
Sangō shiiki (Indications of the Goals of the Three Teachings) (Kūkai), 463
San-lun hsüan-i (Profound Meaning of the Three Treatises) (Chi-tsang), 316, 322, 334n.10
San-lun tradition, 311, 317, 322, 331
Sanron (Japanese) tradition, 20
San-sheng yüan-jung kuan-men (Contemplation of the Perfect Interfusion of the Three Sages) (Ch'eng-kuan), 324
Śāntideva, 170, 177, 202, 277, 282, 287
Saraha, 202
Śāriputra, 137, 141, 154, 159, 168
Śāriputrābhidharmaśāstra, 68, 109, 127n.5
Sarvāstivāda tradition: bipartite mārga in, 75; knowledge and concentration in, 76, 83–86, 90, 91; opinion of arhats, 116; and paths of vision and cultivation, 82–83, 89, 91; and removal of defilements, 13, 63–105 passim, 153; studied by Kumārajīva, 313
Śatakaśāstra (Treatise in One Hundred Verses), 314
satori, 480
Satyakaparivartta (Chapter on the True Ones), 165, 176
Sautrāntikas, 72–73
secular life (culture): and mārga (path), 29–30, 371–437 passim; and religion, 265n.74, 299
Seng-ch'ou (480–560), 351
Seng-ch'üan (n.d.), 317
Seng-min, 317
Seng-ts'an, 504n.11
Seng-yu, 98–99n.50
shamanism, 197–198, 206, 220n.17
Shangs-pa Bka'-brgyud (Tibetan) school: history of, 193–194, 199; and mārga (path), 202, 204–207; origin of tale of, 194–197
Shan-tao (613–681), 321, 323
Shan-wu-wei (Śubhakarasiṃha), 462
Shen-hsiu. *See* Hui-chi Shen-hsiu
Shen-hui. *See* Ho-tse Shen-hui

Shen-tsung (emperor, r. 1067–1085), 384, 385, 390, 427–428n.71
She-shan. *See* Seng-ch'üan
Shih-erh yin-yüan kuan-men (Contemplation of the Twelve Links of Dependent Origination) (Ch'eng-kuan), 324–325
Shih-men Wen-tzu Ch'an (Stone Gate's [i.e., Hui-hung's] Lettered Ch'an), 410–411
Shih-shih chi-ku lüeh (An Outline of Historical Researches into the Śākya Family Lineage) (Chüeh-an), 411
Shih-t'ou Hsi-ch'ien (700–790), 352
Shingon (Japanese) Esoteric school, 20, 207, 439, 440, 441, 442–443, 447–448, 454–461, 501
Shinran (1173–1262), 23, 34n.31, 61n.39
Shōbō genzō (Treasury of the Eye of the True Law) (Dōgen), 495
Shōichi, 481
Shōichi kokushi kana hōgo (Vernacular Dharma Words of the National Teacher Sacred Unity) (Enni). See *Zazen ron*
Shōjō, 482
Shōtoku Taishi (prince, 574–622), 463, 466n.14
Shou-ch'eng Ch'an-shih (d.u.), 424n.56
Shou-leng-yen ching (Śūraṅgama Sūtra), 427n.69, 433n.100
śīla (moral precepts), 6, 137
Six Doctrines of Nāropā, 200
Six Doctrines of Niguma (ni-gu chos-drug), 200–201
Smart, Ninian, 22, 226–227
Smith, Wilfred Cantwell, 253, 265n.74
Sokushin jōbutsugi (Kūkai), 441, 442, 458
Sokushin jōbutsugi shiki (Private Record Concerning the Realization of Buddhahood with This Very Body) (Annen), 454, 468n.46
Sŏn (Korean) tradition, 15, 16
Soshitsujikyōsho (Commentary on the *Susiddhikara* [Acts of Perfection] *Sūtra*) (Ennin), 460
soteriology (salvation): definitions of, 2–3, 225–226, 476–478; relationship to term *mārga,* 2–3
Sōtō Zen tradition, 23, 326, 494, 497
Sphuṭārtha (Clear Meaning), 150
Sphuṭārthāvyākhyā (Commentary to the *Kośa*) (Yaśomitra), 135
Sponberg, Alan, 362
śrāmaṇa groups, 362
Sri Lanka, 310
Śrīmālādevīsiṃhanāda (Lion's Roar of Śrīmālādevī), 162, 165, 174, 179
Ssu-fen lü (Vinaya) school. *See* Lü school
Ssu-ma Kuang (1019–1096), 391
Ssu-t'o, 466n.14, 471n.81
Stallybrass, Peter, 169
Stevenson, Daniel, 16–17, 349
Sthavira (Śrīlāta), 98n.45, 104n.107
Sthiramati, 162, 163, 187n.55
Subhūti, 158–159, 171
Su Ch'e (1039–1112), 385
sudden and gradual teachings: in Ch'an tradition, 12, 332, 376, 382–383; of Hui-kuan, 315
sudden awakening: and purity of mind, 263n.56; of Tao-sheng, 314; in Tibetan Buddhism, 255, 266n.81; as unconditioned, 270, 273–274, 275–277; in Zen Buddhism, 21, 393, 475–505 passim
Sudhana, 197, 388
Sukhasiddhi, 220n.16, 222n.26
Sukhāvatīvyūha-sūtra, 23
Sung kao-seng chuan (Lives of Eminent Monks [Compiled during the] Sung) (Tsan-ning), 341
Sung-shih chi-shih (Annals of Sung Poetry), 411
śūnyatā, versus mārga, 25, 27–28, 176, 363
Śūnyavādins, 176
Sūryasoma, 313
Su Shih (1037–1101), 382–383, 385, 390, 391, 394, 402, 406, 415n.16, 431–432n.94
Sūtra in Forty-two Sections, 366n.23
Sūtra of Perfect Enlightenment. See *Yüan-chüeh ching*
Sūtra on the Ten Grounds, 293
Sutta-nipāta, 39
Suzuki, D. T., 476
Suzuki Daisetsu, 327
Symbolism of Evil, The (Ricoeur), 157

Ta-chih-tu lun (Mahāprajñāpāramitāśāstra; Commentary on the Greater Perfection of Wisdom Sūtra), 313–314, 342, 344, 364n.9, 459
Ta-chüeh Huai-lien (1009–1090), 431–432n.94
Ta-chu Hui-hai (fl. ca. ninth century), 125–126
Ta-hsiang-kuo ssu, 427–428n.71
Ta-hui P'u-chüeh Ch'an-shih tsung-men wu-k'u (Ta-hui's Arsenal of the Ch'an School), 390, 411, 426n.67
Ta-hui Tsung-kao (1089–1163), 16, 359, 360, 377, 383, 390, 401, 402, 404, 409, 413n.8, 415n.17, 494
T'ai-tsung (emperor, r. 626–649), 318
Ta-jih ching (Mahāvairocanasūtra), 453–454, 455, 456, 457–458, 459, 462
Takasaki Jikidō, 121
Tamil Buddhism, 218–219n.9
T'an-luan (476–542), 321
Tao-an (312–385), 313

Tao-ch'ien (a.k.a. Ts'an-liao-tzu; 1043 to ca. 1116), 431–432n.94
Tao-chien (d.u.), 411
Tao-ch'o (562–645), 321
Tao-hsin, 341
Tao-hsüan (596–667), 321, 322, 341
Tao-hsüeh (study of the Way), 381–384, 409, 414–415n.15. *See also* Neo-Confucianism
Taoism, 311, 315, 316, 330, 331–332, 363, 383, 463
Tao-lung, Lan-ch'i (Rankei Dōruū; 1213–1278), 482, 495
Tao-ming, 416n.24
Tao-sheng (355–434), 314–315, 317, 459
Tao-yüan (d.u.), 409
T'ao Yüan-ming (a.k.a. T'ao Ch'ien), 385, 417n.29
Ta-pen ssu-chiao i (Doctrines of the Four Teachings) (Chih-i), 317, 321
Ta-p'in ching (Great Perfection of Wisdom Sūtra), 344, 456
Tārā (Tibetan diety), 226
Tarkajvālā (Blaze of Reasoning) (Bhāvaviveka), 169
Ta-sheng ch'i-hsin lun (Awakening of Faith in the Mahāyāna), 328, 413n.6, 450
Ta-sheng fa-yüan i-lin chang (Essays on the Mahāyāna Garden of Dharmas and Grove of Doctrines) (Chi), 316, 323
Ta-sheng i-chang (Essays on Mahāyāna Doctrines) (Hui-yüan), 123, 316, 322, 334n.10
Ta-sheng ta-i chang (Essay on the Great Meaning of Mahāyāna), 314
tathāgatagarbha (womb or embryo of buddhahood), 22
Tathāgatagarbha tradition: *icchantikas* in, 119, 122; innate and actualized enlightenment in, 23; and non-emptiness, 375; teachings that reveal the true mind in, 330
Ta-tsang-ching kang-mu chih-yao lu (Wei-po), 392
Tat tvam asi (You are that), 251–252
teachings *(chiao),* 311, 313–325
teachings and personal standpoints conjoined *(tsung-chiao),* 311, 329–333
ten abodes of the mind *(jūjūshin),* 20
ten *bhūmis,* 20, 153–154, 169–170, 185n.21
Tendai Hokkeshū gishū (Collection of Tendai Lotus School Doctrines) (Gishin), 449, 450, 456
Tendai Hokkeshū sokushin jōbutsugi (Doctrine of Realization of Buddhahood with This Very Body in the Tendai Lotus School) (Rinshō), 454
Tendai (Japanese) tradition: as eighth abode of the mind in Kūkai's hierarchy, 20; and *hongaku* (original enlightenment), 503n.3; shorter path to enlightenment in, 439–473 passim; sudden teaching in, 15–16, 501
ten (or six) perfections *(pāramitā),* 8–9
ten (or six) stages *(bhūmi)* of the bodhisattva's career, 8
ten special unions of method and wisdom, 307–308n.88
ten stages of realization, 20
ten virtues, 234
Te-shan Yüan-mi (d.u.), 425n.62
Thang-stong rgyal-po (fifteenth century), 193
theodicy, 2
Theravāda tradition: and evil, 112; history of, 38–39, 310; mārga of, 14, 55–58; omniscience of the Buddha/ignorance of the arhats, 137–138, 142; teachings (words) of the Buddha preserved in, 38–39, 55, 56, 57–58; and wholesome roots, 124. See also *Aṭṭhakavagga*
thirty-seven factors of awakening *(saptatriṃśad bodhipakṣikā dharmāh),* 8
Thomas Aquinas, 18
three clear intuitions *(vidyā),* 67
three knowledges, 149–150
three marks of existence *(trilakṣaṇa),* 7
Three Stages Teaching sect. *See* San-chieh-chiao sect
three trainings *(trīṇi śikṣāṇi),* 6–7
three vehicles versus one vehicle, 158–170
Tibetan Buddhism: history of, 225; and ideal person as path, 11–12; and Lamaism, 199, 222–223n.28; and liberating insight, 201–202; mārga (path) in, 15, 229, 230, 246–255; master-student genealogy in, 11; and mind of clear light, 229, 230, 244–246, 250, 251–252, 253–255; and salvation through guru's grace, 198–199, 206; and self-reliance for salvation, 226–227, 240; and shamanism, 197–198, 206; sources on, 227–229; typology of beings in, 13, 229, 231–240, 245–246, 253; and yogic perfection, 199–201, 206
T'ieh-Fo Monastery, 389
T'ien-ch'u chin-lüan (Choice Morsels from the Imperial Kitchen) (Chüeh-fan Hui-hung), 411
T'ien-i I-huai. *See* I-huai
T'ien-t'ai tradition: history of, 310–312, 314, 342, 349; meditation and wisdom in, 321–322; and non-emptiness, 375; relationship to Ch'an, 392, 393; role of defilements in, 12; sudden and gradual

teachings in, 16–17. *See also* Tendai tradition
T'ien-t'ung Ju-ching (1163–1228), 432–433n.99
Tilopā, 200–201
Ti-lun tradition, 317
Tōketsu (Decisions from China [on Doctrinal Issues]) (Tokuen), 442, 444, 456–457, 463, 469n.53
Tokuen (b. 787), 442, 456–457, 469n.53
Tokuitsu (fl. early ninth century), 464–465n.5
Treasury of Knowledge (Vasubandhu), 291, 292
Triśaraṇasaptati (Seventy Stanzas on the Triple Refuge) (Candrakīrti), 166
Ts'ai Chao, 385
Ts'an-liao-tzu. *See* Tao-ch'ien
Ts'an-liao-tzu shih, 431–432n.94
Tsan-ning (919–1001), 341, 420–421n.49
Ts'ao-tung Ch'an, 21
Tseng Chi (1084–1166), 394
Tshangs-pa kun-dga'i mdo (Sūtra of Brahma Ānanda), 217
Tso-ch'an i (Liturgy of Seated Meditation), 393
Tso-ch'an san-mei ching (Scripture of Seated Meditation and Samādhi) (Kumārajīva), 366n.19
Tsong-kha-pa (1357–1419), 150, 159, 160, 164–165, 167, 169, 171–176, 179–181, 183, 227–228, 231, 232, 234, 235, 249, 261n.30, 262n.36, 274, 277, 281, 283, 285–288, 290–291, 293, 298
Tsung-hsiao (1151–1214), 430nn.82–85
Tsung-mi (780–841), 16, 34n.30, 311, 326, 327, 329–333, 387–388, 404, 414n.11, 433n.100, 498
Tsung-pen (Hui-lin Tsung-pen; 1020–1099), 391, 427–428n.71, 428n.76
Tsung-tse (Ch'ang-lu Tsung-tse; d.u.), 393, 430n.83
Tsung-ying, 444–447, 457
Tsu-t'ang chi (Anthology of the Patriarchal Hall), 342–343, 351–353, 355, 357–358
Tsu-t'ing shih-yüan (Chrestomathy from the Patriarchs' Halls) (Mu'an Shan-ch'ing), 412n.2, 421n.50
Tui-ken ch'i-hsing fa (The Teaching on Generating Practice That Accords with Capacity), 125
Tung-shan Hsiao-ts'ung (d. 1030), 425n.62, 426n.66
Tu Shun (557–640), 311, 323, 324
"twofold frenzy," idea of *(loi de double frénésie),* 15
Tz'u-chüeh Ch'an-shih, 430n.82
Tzu-fang i-wang chi (Contemplation on Guarding against Forgetfulness) (Wen-ch'ao), 324
Tz'u-ti ch'an-men (Graduated Teaching of Meditation) (Chih-i), 342, 343, 344, 345, 346, 348

Udānavarga. See *Compilations of Indicative Verse*
Udraka Rāmaputra, 86
Ŭich'ŏn (1055–1101), 427–428n.71
Ŭisang (625–702), 309
uncommon absorption of cessation (**āsadhārananirodhasamāpatti, thun mong ma yin pa'i 'gog snyoms),* 274, 285–292
Upaniṣads, 362
**Upāsakaśīlasūtra.* See *Yu-p'o-sai chieh ching*
upāya (expedient means): in Ch'an, 344, 354, 355; definition of, 4; of perfecting mārga, 23; rejected in Zen Buddhism, 487

Vaccha, 170
Vaibhāṣika (Indian) tradition: bipartite mārga in, 13–14, 75; and omnisicence of the Buddha, 137, 142; role of defilements in, 12–13, 63–105 passim; scholasticism in, 18. *See also* Abhidharma tradition
Vajradhara (Buddha), 199
**Vajrasamādhi Sūtra (Chin-kang san-mei ching),* 413n.6
Vajrayāna (Indo-Tibetan) Buddhism: and mārga, 16, 194; and salvation through guru's grace, 198; and shamanism, 197; and yogic perfection, 200, 201
Vasubandhu (ca. 400), 72–73, 81, 114, 135–142, 151, 162, 170, 174, 291
Vasumitra, 102n.79
Vātsīputrīyas, 72
Vibhajyavādins, 70, 72, 73, 86
Vibhaṅga, 109
Vibhāṣā. See *Abhidharmamahāvibhāṣā*
Vijñānakāya, 75, 76
Vijñānavādins, 139
*Vilāsin (P'i-lo-hsien), 113–114, 119
Vimalakīrti, 391, 417–418n.29, 431n.90
Vimalakīrtinirdeśa (Teaching of Vimalakīrti), 168, 190n.91, 315
Vinaya school. *See* Lü school
vipaśyanā (discernment), 7
Visuddhimagga (Buddhaghosa), 17, 127n.4
Vyāsa, 142

Wang An-shih (1021–1086), 390, 394, 425n.63, 425–426n.64
Wang Ch'in-ch'en, 385, 419n.44
Wang Ch'ing-kung's Visit to Ching-shan (Li Kung-lin), 425–426n.64
Wang-chin huan-yüan kuan (Contemplation

of the Exhaustion of Defilements and the Return to Origin) (Fa-tsang), 324
Wang Jih-hsiu (d. 1173), 430n.85
Wang Shen (prince, b. 1036, d. after 1089), 384, 385, 390, 394, 405, 426–427n.68
Wang Wei, 417–418n.29
Warren, Henry Clark, 170
Weber, Max, 2
Wei-chüan, 451
Wei-po (Fo-kuo Wei-po; fl. 1100s), 392, 407, 420n.48, 420–421n.49
Wen (emperor, r. 581-604), 318
Wen-ch'ao (n.d.), 324
Wen-hsüeh (cultural or literary learning), 382–384
Wen-shu chih-nan t'u-tsan (Illustrated Encomia [Recounting Sudhana's Journey to] the South as Directed by Mañjuśrī) (Wei-po), 392
Wen-t'eng (Ching-hsiu Wen-t'eng), 351–352, 358
Wen-tzu Ch'an, 381–383, 409
White, Allon, 169
Whitehead, Alfred North, 25
wholesome roots *(kuśalamūla)*: definition of, 109–112; eradication of *(samucchinna-kuśalamūla)*, and *icchantika* doctrine, 109, 112, 118–123; eradication of *(samucchinnakuśalamūla)*, non-Vaibhāṣika, 112–114; eradication of *(samucchinnakuśalamūla)*, Vaibhāṣika, 114–118; as exclusionary doctrine, 262n.37; and merit *(puṇya)*, 108, 116, 123–126
Wogiwara Unrai, 119
Wŏnch'ŭk (Yüan-ts'e; 613–696), 169, 316
Writings in Promotion of Filial Piety (Ch'üan-hsiao wen) (Tsung-tse), 430n.85
Wu (emperor, r. 560–578), 318, 490
Wu (king), 14
Wu Chao (684–704), 125
Wu-chiao chang (Fa-tsang). See *Hua-yen wu-chiao chang*
Wu-chiao chih-kuan (Calm Abidings and Discernments of the Five Teachings) (Tu Shun), 324
Wu-chun Shih-fan, 481
Wu-liang-i-ching hsü (Introduction to the Sūtra of Innumerable Meanings) (Liu Ch'iu), 334n.10
Wu-liang-i ching (Sūtra of Innumerable Meanings), 445
Wu-ming (d.u.), 410
Wu-shih yao-wen-ta (Fifty Essential Questions and Answers) (Chih-yen), 324
Wu Tao-tzu, 417–418n.29
Wu-teng hui-yüan (The Collated Essentials of the Five Lamps) (P'u-chi), 411, 420n.48
Wu-Yüeh, 358
Wu-yün kuan (Contemplation of the Five Aggregates) (Ch'eng-kuan), 325

yāna controversy, 158–170
Yanagida Seizan, 341, 356
yāna movement, 310, 313
Yang-chüeh-mo-lo ching, 119, 131n.45
Yang Shih (1053–1135), 381
Yang Wen-hui, 425n.63
Yaśomitra (ca. 700), 135–136, 137, 138, 139, 140
Yen Yü (ca. 1195 to ca. 1245), 431n.93
Ye-shes gsal-ba'i rgyud phyu-ma (Subsequent Tantra Which Clarifies Pristine Cognition), 217
Ye-shes mngon-'byung (The Disclosure of Pristine Cognition), 216
Ying-chien ssu, 387
Ying-lo ching (Sūtra on the Garland of the Primordial Acts of the Bodhisattva), 457
Ying-tsung (emperor, r. 1063–1067), 384, 426–427n.68
Yoga, in Tibetan Buddhism, 199–201, 206
Yogācārabhūmiśāstra (Asaṅga), 17, 204
Yogācāra tradition: bipartite mārga in, 13; history of, 311, 323; *icchantika* in, 120; and mārga (path), 163, 166–167, 168, 203–204; relationship to Ch'an, 392; as sixth abode of the mind in Kūkai's hierarchy, 20
Yoga tradition (school), 141–142, 156
Yogic Autonomy Middle Way School (*rnal 'byor spyod pa dbu ma rang rgyud pa,* Yogācārasvātantrikamādhyamika), 256n.5
Yongs-'dzin-don-yod-dpal-ltan, 304n.50
Yōsai. *See* Eisai
Yüan (Master Yüan; d. 1086), 390, 425n.63
Yüan-cheng, 447
Yüan-chüeh ching (Sūtra of Consummate Enlightenment), 329, 330, 387, 404, 433n.100
Yüan-chüeh-ching tao-ch'ang hsiu-cheng i (Rituals for Practice and Realization at the Place of Practice According to the Sūtra of Consummate Enlightenment), 332
Yüan Hua-yen. *See* Lao Hua-yen
Yüan-jen lun (Essay on the Origins of Man) (Tsung-mi), 330, 331
Yüan-t'ung Ch'an-shih, 426n.66. *See* Fa-hsiu
Yüan-wu K'o-ch'in (1063–1135), 360, 386, 430–431n.89, 433n.101
Yüan-yu period (1086–1093), 394, 401
Yu-hsin fa-chieh chi (Record of the Mind's

Play amongst the Dharma-Realms) (Fa-tsang), 324
Yuktiṣaṣṭikā, 175
Yün-chu Hsiao-shun. *See* Hsiao-shun
Yung-chia, 503n.10
Yün-men lineage, 386, 420–421n.49, 424–425n.58, 428n.76
Yün-men Wen-yen (864–949), 424–425n.58, 425n.62
Yün-wo chi-t'an (Anecdotes from the Lodge Reclining on Clouds) (Hsiao-ying), 421–424n.53
Yu-p'o-sai chieh ching (Sūtra on the Lay Precepts), 126
zazen (seated meditation), 475, 483, 484, 494, 495
Zazen ron (Treatise on Seated Meditation) (Enni), 14, 362, 481–503 passim
Zen and Western Thought (Abe), 25
Zen Buddhism: as anti-mārga/no-path tradition, 29, 253–255; in China, 480; and doctrine, 6; mārga of, 14; as sudden teaching, 21, 393, 475–505 passim
Zenrin kujitsu konmei shū (Compendium of Confused Ch'an Names) (Kōhō Jitsuge), 421–424n.53
Zenshū kōmoku (Outline of Zen Teaching) (Shōjō), 482

Contributors

Carl Bielefeldt is an associate professor in the Department of Religious Studies at Stanford University. He is a specialist on early Japanese Zen whose major work to date is *Dōgen's Manuals of Zen Meditation,* which was corecipient of the 1990 Hiromi Arisawa Memorial Award from the Association of American University Presses with the Japan Foundation.

Grace Burford is an assistant professor in the Department of Theology at Georgetown University. Burford is a specialist on early Pāli literature and comparative religion. Her *Desire, Death, and Goodness: The Conflict of Ultimate Values in Theravāda Buddhism* has just appeared from Peter Lang Publishing. She is working on a book concerning women in Buddhism.

Robert E. Buswell, Jr. is a professor in the Department of East Asian Languages and Cultures at the University of California, Los Angeles. A specialist on Sino-Korean Buddhism and the East Asian Ch'an tradition, he is the author of *The Korean Approach to Zen: The Collected Works of Chinul* and *The Formation of Ch'an Ideology in China and Korea: The Vajrasamādhi-Sūtra, a Buddhist Aprocryphon,* and editor of *Chinese Buddhist Apocrypha.* His book on Buddhist monasticism in contemporary Korea is forthcoming.

Collett Cox is an associate professor in the Department of Asian Languages and Literatures at the University of Washington, Seattle. A specialist in Indian Buddhist Abhidharma, she has published several articles dealing with Abhidharma doctrinal controversies and is the author of *Disputed Dharmas: Early Buddhist Theories on Existence, An Annotated Translation of the Section on Factors Dissociated from Thought from Saṅghabhadra's Nyāyānusāra,* scheduled for publication in 1992 in the Studia Philologica Buddhica Monograph Series of the International Institute for Buddhist Studies.

Robert M. Gimello is a professor in the Department of East Asian Studies at the University of Arizona. A specialist in the early Hua-yen tradition, Gimello is the coeditor of *Studies in Ch'an and Hua-yen.* He has also published several influential articles on Buddhist interpretations of meditation and mystical experience. His most recent research focuses on Ch'an Buddhism during the Sung dynasty.

Paul Groner is an associate professor in the Department of Religious Studies at the University of Virginia. Groner is a specialist in the Japanese Tendai school whose major work to date is *Saichō: The Establishment of the Japanese Tendai School.* He has recently published a translation of Hirakawa Akira's *History of Indian Buddhism: From Śākyamuni to Early Mahāyāna.*

Jeffrey Hopkins is a professor in the Department of Religious Studies at the University of Virginia. A specialist in Tibetan scholasticism he is the author or translator of seventeen books on the Tibetan Buddhist tradition, the most prominent of which is his *Meditation on Emptiness.* He is completing a book on Tibetan contributions to the doctrine of mind-only.

Padmanabh S. Jaini is a professor in the Department of South and Southeast Asian Studies at the University of California, Berkeley. He is the author of numerous works dealing with Sanskrit Abhidharma literature, including *Abhidharmadīpa with Vibhāṣāprabhāvṛtti,* and has published extensively on the Pali apocryphal *Jātakas,* including an edition of the *Paññāsa-Jātaka* (two volumes), which he translated as *Apocryphal Birth-Stories* (also in two volumes). He is the premier Western specialist on the Jaina tradition, as is evidenced in his pioneering *The Jaina Path of Purification* and his most recent *Gender and Salvation: Jaina Debates on the Spiritual Liberation of Women.*

Matthew Kapstein is an assistant professor in the Department of Religion at Columbia University. A specialist in both Western philosophy and Indo-Tibetan Buddhism, Kapstein has coedited *Soundings in Tibetan Civilization* and cotranslated *The Nyingma School of Tibetan Buddhism: Its Fundamentals and History.* His current research focuses on the constructions of self and the construction of history in Buddhist and Western philosophical contexts.

Anne Klein is an associate professor in the Department of Religious Studies at Rice University. She is the author of *Knowledge and Liberation,* an epistemological study on the role of conceptual thought in Dge-lugs-pa theory and practice, and has recently published a sourcebook of Dge-lugs-pa materials on Sautrāntika, *Knowing, Naming and Negation.* Also the author of several articles on women and Buddhism, she is at work on a book juxtaposing feminist and Buddhist problematics of self. Her other ongoing research includes the translation and annotation of Dge-lugs-pa oral commentary on Tsong-kha-pa's *Dbu ma dgongs pa rab gsal (Clarification of* [*Candrakīrti's*] *"Entrance to the Middle Way"),* and Nying-ma oral commentary on Rdzogs-chen texts by Do-drup-chen III.

Donald S. Lopez, Jr., is a professor in the Department of Asian Languages and Cultures at the University of Michigan. His works on Indo-Tibetan Buddhism include *A Study of Svātantrika* and *The Heart Sūtra Explained.* He is also the editor of *Buddhist Hermeneutics* and coeditor of *The Christ and the Bodhisattva.*

John R. McRae is an assistant professor in the Department of Asian Studies at Cornell University. A specialist on early Ch'an, his major work to date is *The Northern School and the Formation of Early Ch'an Buddhism.* He is completing two manuscripts: a book on Ma-tsu Tao-i, which explores the transition from early to classical Ch'an; and an extensive study, with annotated translation, of the works of Shen-hui.

Yoshizu Yoshihide is a professor of Buddhist Studies at Komazawa University. A specialist on early Hua-yen Buddhism, his many publications include *Kegon-Zen,* a monumental study of the Chinese Hua-yen and Ch'an figure Tsung-mi, and a series of articles on Fa-tsang, which he is now expanding into a book.

HAWAII Production Notes

Composition and paging were done on the Quadex Composing System and typesetting on the Compugraphic 8400 by the design and production staff of University of Hawaii Press.

The text typeface is Baskerville and the display typeface is Compugraphic Palatino.

Offset presswork and binding were done by The Maple-Vail Book Manufacturing Group. Text paper is Glatfelter Offset Vellum, basis 45.